W9-CEW-475

IN Indiana

PEARSON

my World
GEOGRAPHY™

WESTERN HEMISPHERE

PEARSON

Boston, Massachusetts
Chandler, Arizona
Glenview, Illinois
Upper Saddle River, New Jersey

Acknowledgements appear on pages 629–632, which constitute an extension of this copyright page.

Taken from:
myWorld Geography, Western Hemisphere
by Gregory H. Chu, Susan Hardwick, Don Holtgrieve and Grant Wiggins
Copyright © 2011 by Pearson Education, Inc.
Published by Prentice Hall
Upper Saddle River, NJ 07458

Copyright © 2016 by Pearson Learning Solutions
All rights reserved.

This copyright covers material written expressly for this volume by the editor/s as well as the compilation itself. It does not cover the individual selections herein that first appeared elsewhere. Permission to reprint these has been obtained by Pearson Learning Solutions for this edition only. Further reproduction by any means, electronic or mechanical, including photocopying and recording, or by any information storage or retrieval system, must be arranged with the individual copyright holders noted.

All trademarks, service marks, registered trademarks, and registered service marks are the property of their respective owners and are used herein for identification purposes only.

Pearson Learning Solutions, 501 Boylston Street, Suite 900, Boston, MA 02116
A Pearson Education Company
www.pearsoned.com

Printed in the United States of America
6 7 8 9 10 V057 19 18 17 16 15

000200010271941195

MD

ISBN 10: 1323045295
ISBN 13: 9781323045299

Program Authors

Gregory H. Chu, a native of Hong Kong, is professor and chair of geography at the University of Wisconsin–La Crosse and editor of *FOCUS on Geography,* a journal published by the American Geographical Society. He earned his Ph.D. degree in geography from the University of Hawaii and has served as program director of Geography and Regional Science at the National Science Foundation, on the Editorial Board of *Cartographic Perspectives,* and on the Board of Directors of the North American Cartographic Information Society.

Susan Hardwick is a geography professor at the University of Oregon. She is an expert in the human geography of North America and is the past president of the National Council for Geographic Education. She is best known as the co-host of *The Power of Place,* an Annenberg geography series produced for public television. Professor Hardwick was awarded the Association of America's Gilbert Grosvenor Award in Geographic Education, the National Council for Geographic Education's Outstanding Mentor Award, and the statewide California Outstanding Professor Award when she taught at California State University, Chico, before moving to Oregon. She is the parent of four grown sons who all live on the west coast.

Don Holtgrieve received his Ph.D. degree in geography from the University of Oregon and was a professor of geography and environmental studies in the California State University system for 30 years. He now teaches geography and environmental planning at the University of Oregon. His attraction to geography was the interdisciplinary nature of the field and the opportunity to do research out-of-doors. Dr. Holtgrieve enjoys bringing his "real-world" experiences as a high school teacher, community planner, police officer, and consultant to government agencies into his writing and teaching.

Program Consultant

Grant Wiggins is the president of Authentic Education in Hopewell, New Jersey. He earned his Ed.D. degree from Harvard University and his B.A. from St. John's College in Annapolis, Maryland. Wiggins consults with schools, districts, and state education departments on a variety of reform matters, organizes conferences and workshops, and develops print materials and Web resources on curricular change. Over the past 20 years, Wiggins has worked on some of the most influential reform initiatives in the country, including Vermont's portfolio system and Ted Sizer's Coalition of Essential Schools. He is the coauthor, with Jay McTighe, of *Understanding by Design* and *The Understanding by Design Handbook,* the award-winning and highly successful materials on curriculum published by ASCD. He is also the author of *Educative Assessment* and *Assessing Student Performance*, both published by Jossey-Bass.

Academic Reviewers

Africa
Benjamin Ofori-Amoah
Department of Geography
Western Michigan University
Kalamazoo, Michigan

Australia and the Pacific
Christine Drake, Ph.D.
Department of Political Science
    and Geography
Old Dominion University
Norfolk, Virginia

Peter N. D. Pirie
Department of Geography
University of Hawaii at Manoa
Honolulu, Hawaii

East and Southeast Asia
Jessie P. H. Poon
Department of Geography
University of Buffalo
State University of New York
Buffalo, New York

Susan M. Walcott
Department of Geography
University of North Carolina
    at Greensboro
Greensboro, North Carolina

Europe
William H. Berentsen
Department of Geography
University of Connecticut
Storrs, Connecticut

Nancy Partner
Department of History
McGill University
Montreal, Quebec, Canada

Charles Rearick
Department of History
University of Massachusetts
Amherst, Massachusetts

Middle and South America
Connie Weil
Department of Geography
University of Minnesota
Minneapolis, Minnesota

North America
Mark Drayse
Department of Geography
California State University
Fullerton, California

South and Central Asia
Dr. Reuel R. Hanks
Department of Geography
Oklahoma State University
Stillwater, Oklahoma

Pradyumna P. Karan
Department of Geography
University of Kentucky
Lexington, Kentucky

Southwest Asia
Michael E. Bonine
School of Geography and
    Development
Department of Near Eastern
    Studies
University of Arizona
Tucson, Arizona

Shaul Cohen
Department of Geography
University of Oregon
Eugene, Oregon

Religion
Brent Isbell
Department of Religious Studies
University of Houston
Houston, Texas

Gordon Newby
Department of Middle Eastern
    and South Asian Studies
Emory University
Atlanta, Georgia

Robert Platzner, Ph.D.
Emeritus Professor
    of Humanities and
    Religious Studies
California State University
Sacramento, California

Master Teachers and Contributing Authors

George F. Sabato
Past President, California Council for
   the Social Studies
Placerville Union School District
Placerville, California

Michael Yell
President, National Council for
   the Social Studies
Hudson Middle School
Hudson, Wisconsin

Teacher Consultants

James F. Dowd IV
Pasadena, California

Susan M. Keane
Rochester Memorial School
Rochester, Massachusetts

Timothy T. Sprain
Lincoln Middle School
LaCrosse, Wisconsin

Marilyn Weiser
North Dakota Geographic
   Alliance Coordinator
Minot State Univesity
Minot, North Dakota

Reviewers

Carol Bacak-Egbo
Waterford Schools
Waterford, Michigan

John Brill
Bellevue School District
Bellevue, Washington

Helene Brown
Gwinnett County Public Schools
Lawrenceville, Georgia

Sherry Echols
Hartselle Junior High School
Hartselle, Alabama

Douglas Fillmore
Bloomington Junior High School
Bloomington, Illinois

Chad Hayes
Beadle Middle School
Omaha, Nebraska

Bill Huser
Prairie Catholic Middle School
Prairie du Chien, Wisconsin

Chuck Schierloh
Lima City Schools
Lima, Ohio

IN Indiana Reviewers

Scott Bauserman
Department Chair, Individuals
   and Societies
Westlane Middle School
Indianapolis, Indiana

Kyle Chezem
Teacher—7th Grade Social
   Studies
Kesling Middle School
LaPorte, Indiana

Cynthia Hamilton
Social Studies Department Chair
Thomas Jefferson Middle School
Valparaiso, Indiana

Welcome to my World Geography™!

We hope you enjoy learning more about your world and its people. One of the most difficult parts of studying world geography is that there are nearly 7 billion people in the world. It's very difficult to think about such a large number. To make it easier, the map on these pages shows the world divided into regions. Page numbers on the map indicate where in the book you can read about each region.

This map also shows how many people would live in each region if there were only 100 people in the entire world.

We hope you enjoy your exploration of your world.

The myWorld authors

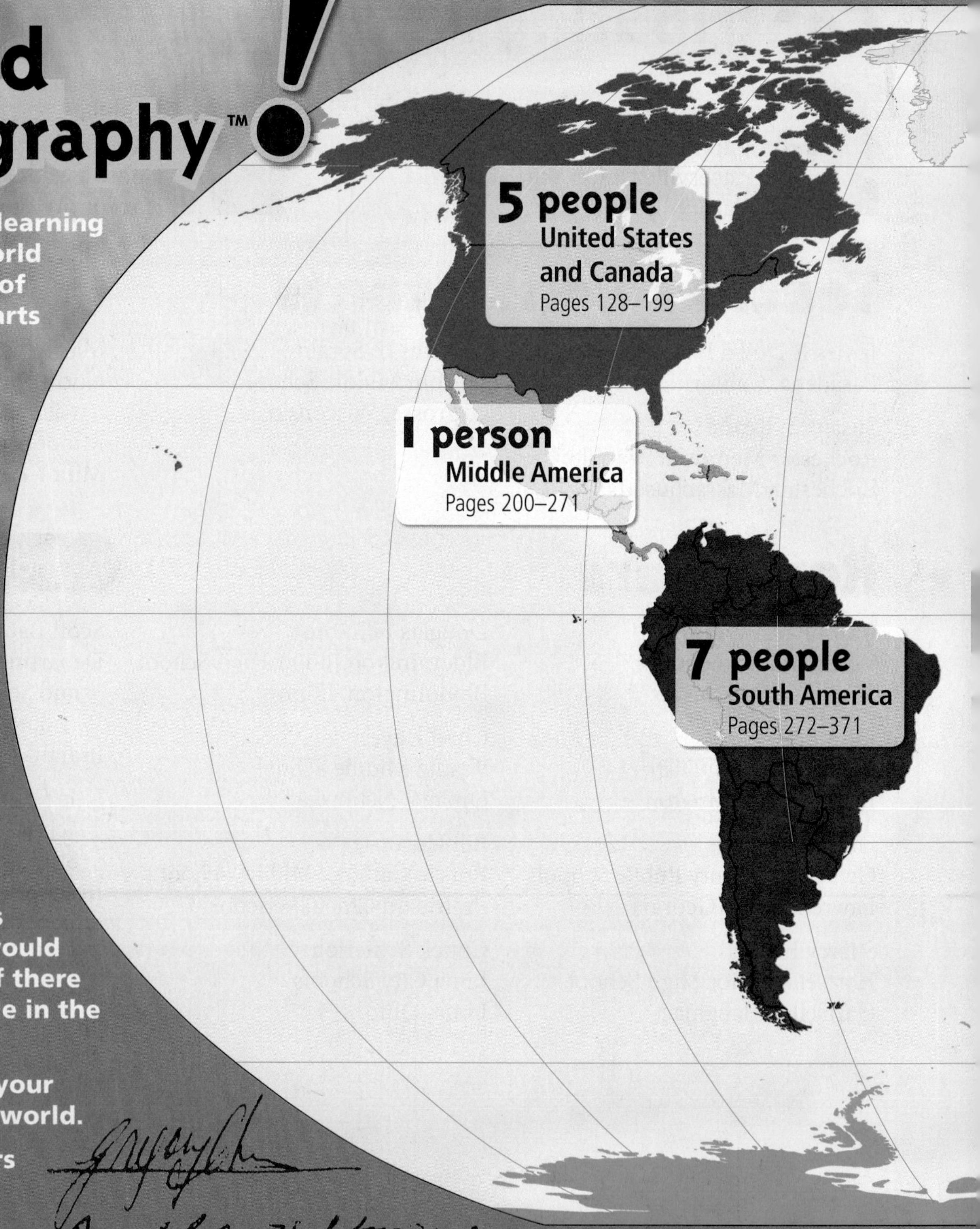

5 people
United States and Canada
Pages 128–199

1 person
Middle America
Pages 200–271

7 people
South America
Pages 272–371

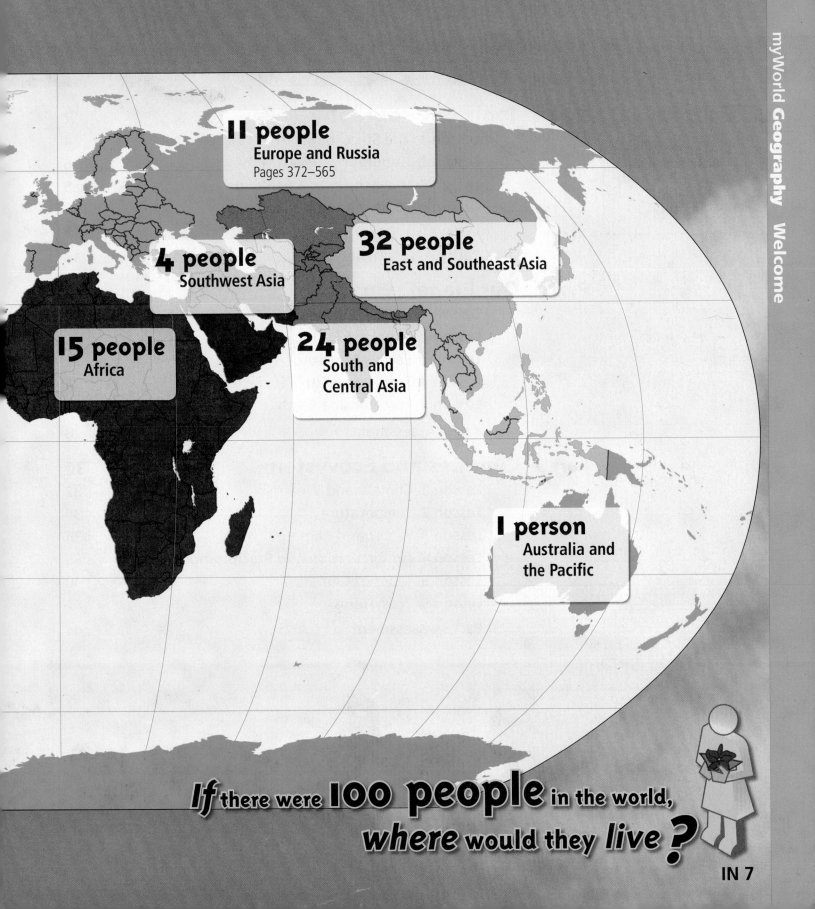

11 people
Europe and Russia
Pages 372–565

32 people
East and Southeast Asia

4 people
Southwest Asia

24 people
South and
Central Asia

15 people
Africa

1 person
Australia and
the Pacific

If there were **100 people** in the world,
where would they *live* **?**

IN 7

Contents

Core Concepts Handbook

IN Indiana

Academic Standards

6.3.2	6.3.6
6.3.3	6.3.8
6.3.5	

IN Indiana

Academic Standards

6.3.12	6.4.8
6.4.3	6.4.9
6.4.5	

IN Indiana

Academic Standards

6.1.16	6.2.5
6.1.18	6.2.6
6.1.19	6.2.7
6.2.1	6.3.11
6.2.4	

Unit 1 United States and Canada

IN Indiana

Academic Standards

6.1.4	6.3.3
6.1.11	6.3.4
6.1.13	6.3.5
6.1.16	6.3.6
6.1.20	6.3.7
6.1.21	6.3.8
6.1.22	6.3.9
6.1.23	6.3.10
6.2.1	6.3.12
6.2.6	6.4.1
6.2.7	6.4.2
6.3.1	6.4.4
6.3.2	6.4.6

Unit 2 Middle America

IN Indiana

Academic Standards

6.1.1	6.3.5
6.1.2	6.3.6
6.1.4	6.3.8
6.1.6	6.3.10
6.1.16	6.3.12
6.1.20	6.3.13
6.1.21	6.3.14
6.1.22	6.4.1
6.1.23	6.4.4
6.2.1	6.4.5
6.2.5	6.4.7
6.2.7	6.4.8
6.3.3	

myWorld Geography Contents

Unit 3 South America

IN Indiana

Academic Standards

6.1.1	6.3.2
6.1.4	6.3.4
6.1.6	6.3.7
6.1.18	6.3.8
6.1.20	6.3.9
6.1.21	6.3.12
6.1.22	6.3.13
6.1.23	6.4.2
6.2.5	6.4.5
6.2.7	6.4.6
6.3.1	

ɪɴ Indiana

Academic Standards

6.1.4	6.3.7
6.1.11	6.3.8
6.1.20	6.3.13
6.1.21	6.3.14
6.1.22	6.4.4
6.2.7	6.4.6
6.3.1	6.4.7
6.3.3	6.4.8
6.3.4	

Unit 4 Europe and Russia

IN Indiana

Academic Standards

6.1.1	6.1.20
6.1.2	6.1.21
6.1.3	6.1.23
6.1.4	6.2.1
6.1.5	6.2.2
6.1.6	6.4.1
6.1.7	6.4.2

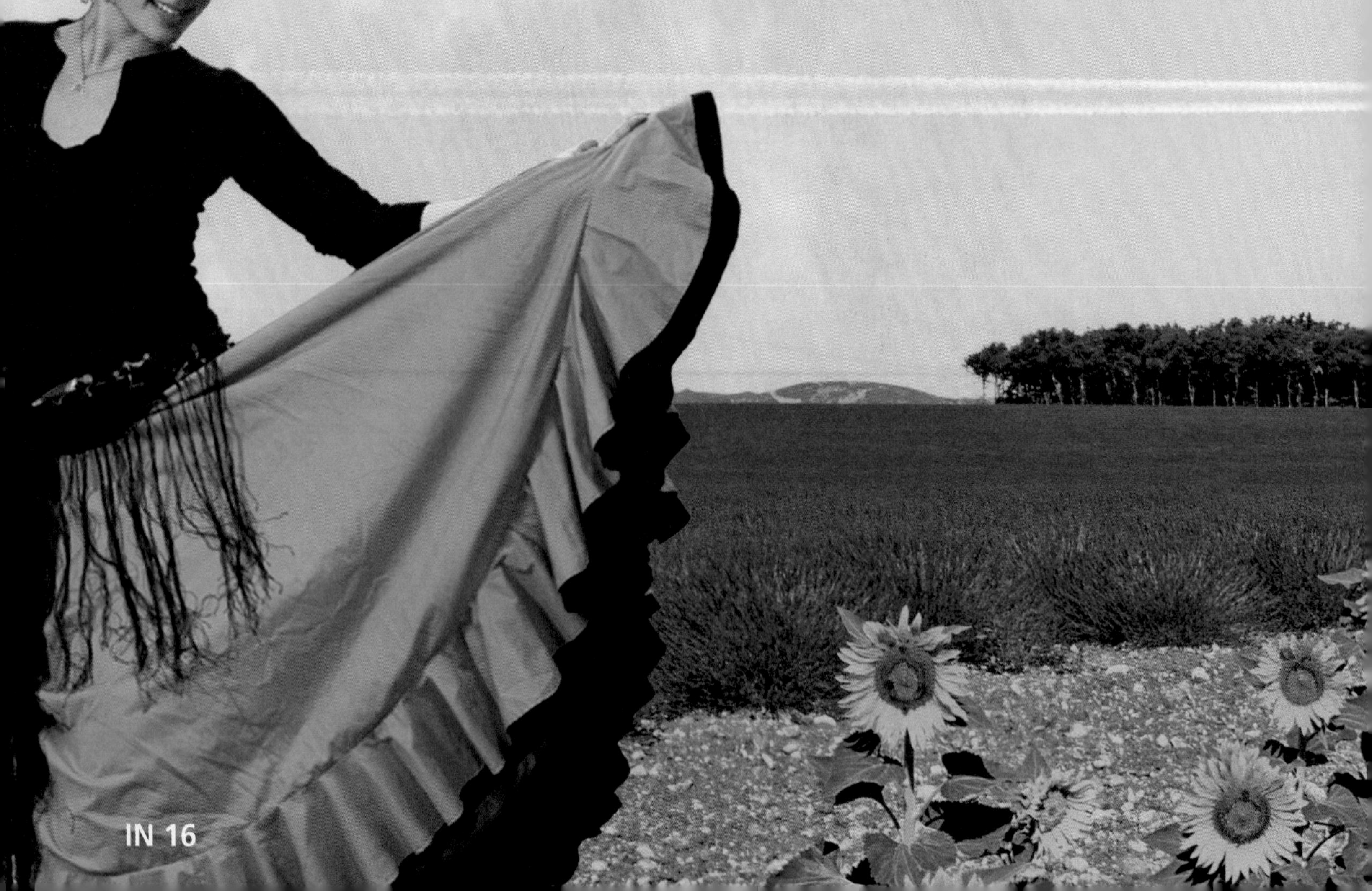

IN Indiana

Academic Standards

6.1.2	6.1.20
6.1.6	6.1.21
6.1.8	6.1.23
6.1.9	6.2.1
6.1.10	6.2.3
6.1.11	6.2.4
6.1.12	6.2.5
6.1.13	6.2.6
6.1.14	6.3.9
6.1.16	6.3.13

Unit 4 Europe and Russia (continued)

IN Indiana

Academic Standards

6.1.15	6.3.8
6.1.17	6.3.9
6.1.21	6.3.10
6.1.22	6.3.12
6.2.6	6.3.13
6.2.7	6.3.14
6.3.1	6.4.5
6.3.3	6.4.6
6.3.4	6.4.7
6.3.6	6.4.8

IN Indiana

Academic Standards

6.1.2	6.3.2
6.1.21	6.3.4
6.1.22	6.3.7
6.1.23	6.3.12
6.2.1	6.4.4
6.2.6	6.4.6
6.3.1	

Unit 4 Europe and Russia (continued)

IN Indiana

Academic Standards

6.1.4	6.2.7
6.1.15	6.3.1
6.1.16	6.3.3
6.1.17	6.3.5
6.1.18	6.3.8
6.1.21	6.3.12
6.1.22	6.4.4
6.1.23	6.4.6
6.2.1	6.4.7
6.2.5	

Connect to stories of real teens from around the world.

21st Century Learning

Learn new skills through interactive activities.

Closer Look

Photographs, maps, charts, illustrations, and text help you take a closer look at the world.

Case Studies

my worldgeography.com →

Go online to explore and investigate important global topics.

Primary Sources

my worldgeography.com →

Go online to compare viewpoints through eyewitness accounts and documents.

Charts, Graphs, and Diagrams

Diagrams and data help you visually access important information.

Charts, Graphs, and Diagrams (continued)

Maps

Interactive Maps help you actively learn and understand your world.

Maps (continued)

CONNECT

EXPERIE

Welcome to a new and exciting way to learn about world geography. The *myWorld Geography* program is a blend of technology, hands-on activities, and student books that will take you on a one-of-a-kind journey around the globe and through history. Get ready to connect, experience, and build an understanding of the world in a whole new way.

CONNECT

to Different Cultures and People

Develop a deeper understanding of your world by making personal connections to the people and places in *myWorld Geography*.

myStory videos introduce you to the stories, families, hopes, and challenges of 23 real teens from around the world.

my Story

Xiao
Age: 18
Home: Wutang village, China

Chapter 14

Regional Overview

East and
Southeas

East and Southeast Asia are region... mountains, vast plains, dense forest... crowded coastlines. These regions are... populated. The largest country in these... is China, which has more inhabitants tha... other country on Earth.

The Unit Ahead
- Chapter 21 China and Its Neighbors
- Chapter 22 Japan and the Koreas
- Chapter 23 Southeast Asia

Unit 8   East and Southeast Asia

my worldgeography.com

Plan your trip online by doing a Data Discovery Activity and watching the myStory Videos of the region's teens.

my Story

Xiao
Age: 18
Home: Wutang village, China
Chapter 14

my Story

Asuka
Age: 18
Home: Yokohama, Japan
Chapter 15

my Story

Ridwan
Age: 19
Home: Bukittinggi, Indonesia
Chapter 16

Rice fields in Bali, Indonesia

See for yourself at myWorldPearson.com/learnmore

CE UNDERSTAND

EXPERIENCE
the World in New Ways

Travel across regions and through time—without a passport. *myWorld Geography's* interactive approach using technology, student books, and classroom activities will make learning geography fun and exciting.

Take a virtual and interactive trip around the world with myWorldGeography.com.

UNDERSTAND
and "Own" Your Learning

myWorld Geography isn't just about reading content—it's about providing you with the tools so you really "get it."

Finding answers to the Essential Questions—found throughout the print, digital, and hands-on activities—helps you understand the key ideas of world geography.

China and Its Neighbors: Population Density

KEY

Population Density

Persons per sq. mile	Persons per sq. kilometer
500	195
300	115
150	60
25	10
1	1

Urban Areas
- More than 10,000,000
- 5,000,000–10,000,000
- Less than 5,000,000

0   400 mi
0   400 km
Lambert Conformal Conic Projection

Ulaanbaatar
Harbin
MONGOLIA
Changchun Jilin
Ürümqi
Shenyang
Kashgar
Beijing
Tianjin
Zibo
Yellow Sea
Xi'an
CHINA
Wuxi   Shang
Plateau of Tibet
Chengdu
Wuhan
East China Sea
Chongqing
Lhasa
Taipei
TAIWAN
TROPIC OF CANCER
Guangzhou   Shenzhen
Hong Kong
Bay of Bengal
South China Sea
Hainan

Name _____ Class _____ Date _____

? Essential Question

How can you measure success?

Preview Before you begin this chapter, think about the Essential Question. Understanding how the Essential Question connects to your life will help you understand the chapter you are about to read.

Connect to Your Life

1. Think of some ways to measure success in the categories shown in the chart below. List at least one way in each column. For example, under school you could list grades.

Measures of Personal Success

Family	Friends	School	Other (Sports, Arts, Chore

 **Peoples, Places and Cultures in Europe and the Americas**

Indiana Academic Standards for Sixth Grade Social Studies

Standard 1 History: Students explore the key historic movements, events and figures that contributed to the development of modern Europe and America from early civilizations through modern times by examining religious institutions, trade and cultural interactions, political institutions, and technological developments.

Historical Knowledge
Early and Classical Civilizations: 1900 B.C./B.C.E to 700 A.D./C.E.

6.1.1   Summarize the rise, decline, and cultural achievements of ancient civilizations in Europe and Mesoamerica.
Examples: Greek, Roman, Mayan, Inca, and Aztec civilizations

6.1.2   Describe and compare the beliefs, the spread and the influence of religions throughout Europe and Mesoamerica.
Examples: Judaism, Christianity, Islam and native practices in Mesoamerica and Europe

Medieval Period: 400 A.D./C.E. to 1500 A.D./C.E.

6.1.3   Explain the continuation and contributions of the Eastern Roman Empire after the fall of the Western Roman Empire.
Examples: Influence of the spread of Christianity in Russia and Eastern Europe

6.1.4   Identify and explain the development and organization of political, cultural, social and economic systems in Europe and the Americas.
Examples: Feudal system, manorial system, rise of kingdoms and empires, and religious institutions

6.1.5   Analyze the diverse points of view and interests of those involved in the Crusades and give examples of the changes brought about by the Crusades.
Examples: Increased contact between European and non-European peoples, impact on Jews and Muslims in Europe and the Middle East, changes in technology, and centralization of political and military power

6.1.6   Identify trade routes and discuss their impact on the rise of cultural centers and trade cities in Europe and Mesoamerica
Examples: Florence, Genoa, Venice, Naples, Tenochtitlan, Machu Pichu and Teotihuacan

6.1.7   Describe how the Black Death, along with economic, environmental and social factors led to the decline of medieval society

6.1.8   Compare the diverse perspectives, ideas, interests and people that brought about the Renaissance in Europe.
Examples: Ideas: the importance of the individual, scientific inquiry based on observation and experimentation, interest in Greek and Roman thought, and new approaches in the fine arts and literature; People: Leonardo da Vinci, Michelangelo, Nicholas Copernicus, William Shakespeare and Galileo Galilei

6.1.9   Analyze the interconnections of people, places and events in the economic, scientific and cultural exchanges of the European Renaissance that led to the Scientific Revolution, voyages of discovery and imperial conquest.

Early Modern Era: 1500 to 1800

6.1.10   Examine and explain the outcomes of European colonization on the Americas and the rest of the world.
Examples: The defeat of the Aztec and Incan empires by the Spanish, the rise of trading empires, Columbian exchange and slavery, Columbus' search for India

6.1.11   Compare and contrast Spanish, Portuguese, French, and British colonies in the Americas.

6.1.12   Describe the Reformations and their effects on European and American society.
Examples: Missionary activities, the rise of Calvinism and Lutheranism, Henry VIII's break with Parliament and the Catholic Church, the principle of separation of church and state, Papal reform, and the Council of Trent

6.1.13   Explain the origin and spread of scientific, political, and social ideals associated with the Age of Enlightenment/Age of Reason.
Examples: The American and French Revolutions and the spread of democratic ideals, the Scientific Revolution, and the influence on world religions resulting in the assimilation of religious groups

6.1.14   Describe the origins, developments and innovations of the Industrial Revolution and explain the impact these changes brought about.
Examples: Steam engine, factory system, urbanization, changing role of women and child labor

Modern Era: 1700 to the present

6.1.15   Describe the impact of industrialization and urbanization on the lives of individuals and on trade and cultural exchange between Europe and the Americas and the rest of the world.

6.1.16   Identify individuals, beliefs and events that represent various political ideologies during the nineteenth and twentieth centuries and explain their significance.
Examples: Liberalism, conservatism, nationalism, socialism, communism, fascism and popular sovereignty

6.1.17   Discuss the benefits and challenges related to the development of a highly technological society.
Examples: Atomic energy, computers and environmental change

6.1.18 Create and compare timelines that identify major people, events and developments in the history of individual civilizations and/or countries that comprise Europe and the Americas.

6.1.19 Define and use the terms decade, century, and millennium, and compare alternative ways that historical periods and eras are designated by identifying the organizing principles upon which each is based.

6.1.20 Analyze cause-and-effect relationships, keeping in mind multiple causations, including the importance of individuals, ideas, human interests, beliefs and chance in history.
Examples: The decline of Greek city-states, the destruction of the Aztecs, and state-sponsored genocide, including the Holocaust

6.1.21 Differentiate between fact and interpretation in historical accounts and explain the meaning of historical passages by identifying who was involved, what happened, where it happened, and relating them to outcomes that followed and gaps in the historical record.

6.1.22 Form research questions and use a variety of information resources to obtain, evaluate and present data on people, cultures and developments in Europe and the Americas.
Examples: Collect data and create maps, graphs or spreadsheets showing the impact of immigration patterns in Canada, the Chernobyl nuclear disaster on Russia and access to health care in the European Union (EU)

6.1.23 Identify issues related to an historical event in Europe or the Americas and give basic arguments for and against that issue utilizing the perspectives, interests and values of those involved.
Examples: The role of women in different time periods, decline of ancient civilizations, and attitudes toward human rights

Standard 2 Civics and Government: Students compare and contrast forms of government in different historical periods with contemporary political structures of Europe and the Americas and examine the rights and responsibilities of individuals in different political systems.

Foundations of Government

6.2.1 Compare and contrast major forms of governments in Europe and the Americas throughout history.
Examples: Greek democracies, Roman Republic, Aztec monarchy, parliamentary government, U.S. Republic, and totalitarianism

6.2.2 Explain how elements of Greek direct democracy and Roman representative democracy are present in modern systems of government.

6.2.3 Examine key ideas of Magna Carta (1215), the Petition of Right (1628), and the English Bill of Rights (1689) as documents to place limits on the English monarchy and how they have affected the shaping of other governments.

6.2.4 Define the term nation-state and describe the rise of nation-states headed by monarchs in Europe from 1500 to 1700.

Functions of Government

6.2.5   Discuss the impact of major forms of government in Europe and the Americas on civil and human rights.

6.2.6   Identify and describe the functions of international political organizations in the world today.
Examples: Examine the functions of the World Court, North Atlantic Treaty Organization (NATO) and the United Nations (UN).

Roles of Citizens

6.2.7   Define and compare citizenship and the citizen's role throughout history in Europe and the Americas.
Examples: Compare methods of voting; participation in voluntary organizations of civil society; and participation in the government in Great Britain, Russia, Brazil, Mexico and Canada.

Standard 3 Geography: Students identify the characteristics of climate regions in Europe and the Americas and describe major physical features, countries and cities of Europe and the Western Hemisphere.

The World in Spatial Terms

6.3.1   Demonstrate a broad understanding of the countries and capitals of Europe and the Americas.

6.3.2   Use latitude and longitude to locate the capital cities of Europe and the Americas and describe the uses of locational technology, such as Global Positioning Systems (GPS) to distinguish absolute and relative location and to describe Earth's surfaces.

Places and Regions

6.3.3   Describe and compare major physical characteristics of regions in Europe and the Americas.
Examples: Mountain ranges, rivers, deserts, etc.

6.3.4   Describe and compare major cultural characteristics of regions in Europe and the Western Hemisphere.
Examples: Language, religion, recreation, clothing, diet, music/dance, family structure, and traditions

Physical Systems

6.3.5   Give examples and describe the formation of important river deltas, mountains and bodies of water in Europe and the Americas.
Examples: Volga River, Canadian Rockies, Sierra Madre Mountains and Lochs in Scotland

6.3.6   Explain how ocean currents and winds influence climate differences on Europe and the Americas.

6.3.7   Locate and describe the climate regions of Europe and the Americas and explain how and why they differ.
Examples: Gulf Stream and North Atlantic Current

6.3.8   Identify major biomes of Europe and the Americas and explain how these are influenced by climate.
Examples: Rainforests, tundra, woodlands, and deserts

Human Systems

6.3.9   Identify current patterns of population distribution and growth in Europe and the Americas using a variety of geographic representations such as maps, charts, graphs, and satellite images and aerial photography. Evaluate different push and pull factors that trigger migrations
Examples: Rural and urban areas; immigration

6.3.10   Explain the ways cultural diffusion, invention, and innovation change culture.

6.3.11   Define the terms anthropology and archeology and explain how these fields contribute to our understanding of societies in the present and the past.

Environment and Society

6.3.12   Compare the distribution and evaluate the importance of natural resources such as natural gas, oil, forests, uranium, minerals, coal, seafood and water in Europe and the Americas.

6.3.13   Explain the impact of humans on the physical environment in Europe and the Americas.

6.3.14   Explain and give examples of how nature has impacted the physical environment and human populations in specific areas of Europe and the Americas.
Examples: Hurricanes, earthquakes, floods and drought

Standard 4 Economics: Students examine the influence of physical and cultural factors upon the economic systems of countries in Europe and the Americas.

6.4.1   Give examples of how trade related to key developments in the history of Europe and the Americas.
Examples: The growth of trading towns and cities in medieval Europe led to money economies, competition to expand world trade led to European voyages of trade and exploration, and Mayan trade in Mesoamerica led to colonization and the diffusion of art.

6.4.2   Analyze how countries of Europe and the Americas have been influenced by trade in different historical periods.
Examples: Increased production and consumption and lower prices

6.4.3   Explain why international trade requires a system for exchanging currency between various countries.

6.4.4   Describe how different economic systems (traditional, command, market and mixed) in Europe and the Americas answer the basic economic questions on what to produce, how to produce and for whom to produce.

6.4.5   Compare the standard of living of various countries of Europe and the Americas today using Gross Domestic Product (GDP) per capita as an indicator.

6.4.6   Analyze current economic issues in the countries of Europe or the Americas using a variety of information resources.
Examples: Use information sources such as digital newspapers, the Internet and podcasts to examine changes in energy prices and consumption, exchange rates and currency values.

6.4.7   Identify economic connections between the local community and the countries of Europe or the Americas and identify job skills needed to be successful in the workplace.

6.4.8   Identify ways that societies deal with helpful and harmful externalities (spillovers*) in Europe or the Americas.
Examples: Government support of public education and governments taxing or regulating pollution
  *   **externality (spillover):** the impact of an activity (positive or negative) on the well-being of a third party

6.4.9   Explain how saving and investing help increase productivity and economic growth and compare and contrast individual saving and investing options.
Examples: Savings accounts, certificates of deposit and stocks

Core Concepts Handbook

Part	Part	Part	Part	Part
1	**2**	**3**	**4**	**5**
Tools of Geography	**Our Planet, Earth**	**Climates and Ecosystems**	**Human– Environment Interaction**	**Economics and Geography**
Learn about the study of Earth.	Examine the forces that affect Earth.	Learn about how climate and weather affect the world and its lifeforms.	Explore the ways in which people use resources and affect the environment.	Study how people make economic decisions.
page 2	**page 16**	**page 30**	**page 46**	**page 56**

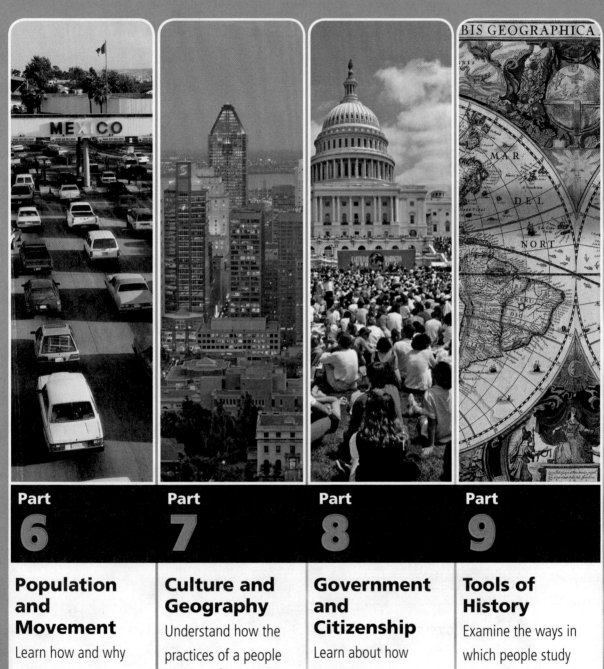

Part **6**	Part **7**	Part **8**	Part **9**
Population and Movement	**Culture and Geography**	**Government and Citizenship**	**Tools of History**
Learn how and why people live in certain places.	Understand how the practices of a people make up their culture, and how culture can change over time.	Learn about how people organize governments and what governments do.	Examine the ways in which people study history.
page 72	**page 84**	**page 102**	**page 116**

Tools of Geography

Several Maijuna people study a map.

A Peruvian toucan overlooks mountains and rain forest. The Maijuna live in a rain forest area.

Maijuna men use
a GPS device.

Jason
Young

Jason Maps in the Rainforest

Story by Miles Lemaire for myWorld

There were a number of things that took some getting used to for Jason Young when he first traveled to Peru. There was no electricity in the village where he was living, which meant that there was no place to charge his cell phone. The same was true for his computer, which he could not use much since there was no Internet connection.

He was alone in a foreign country, eating food that the hunters of the village provided for him. He ate toucan and piranha. "It is an entirely different world," Jason says. "The people there are living off the rainforest, so they go hunting and whatever they catch is what I eat."

Nothing about this place on the edge of the Amazon jungle felt like home to Jason. However, it was home to the people of the Maijuna (mai HU na) tribe and he was going to help them prove it.

According to Jason, the Maijuna "do not own the land where they live, and it is being threatened by things like logging. The Peruvian government wants to construct a road right through some of their traditional territory."

Fortunately, there is a way for the Maijuna to keep their land if they can prove their ownership of it. To do this, they need accurate maps of the area.

That is where Jason comes in. Jason studies geography, which deals with the human and nonhuman features of Earth. Using his geography skills, he has created maps to help the Maijuna prove their case. He used a GPS device, which uses satellites to locate places on Earth's surface.

Jason says, "I went down there and worked with them for four months over different field seasons. I worked with them to do what is called participatory mapping. It is where you have them draw what they believe is their territory on their traditional land. You use that to go out with a GPS unit and collect [data] points from each of the different spots. I actually took video interviews of them talking about the history of the spots that we went to."

Maijuna people took pictures of the spots, and Jason is working on putting them online in an interactive map. Eventually, users will be able to click on traditional sites to view videos or pictures.

"We are hoping to use that mostly as a teaching tool for safeguarding the Maijuna's traditions, as well as using it as a tool with which to speak to the government."

Jason's involvement with the Maijuna came to an end in 2009. Still, his bond with the Maijuna is so strong that he wants to revisit his new friends as often as he can. He feels that he has learned a lot from his experience.

"The level of poverty opened my eyes to how privileged I have been and how much potential I have to give back to the world," Jason says.

3

Geography: The Study of Earth

Key Ideas
- Geographers use directions to help locate points on Earth's surface.
- Geographers have drawn imaginary lines around Earth, dividing it into parts to help pinpoint locations.

Key Terms
- geography
- cardinal direction
- sphere
- latitude
- degree
- hemisphere
- longitude

→ **Visual Glossary**

Northwest · **North** · **Northeast**

West · **East**

Southwest · **South** · **Southeast**

Geography is the study of the human and nonhuman features of Earth, our home. Geographers try to answer two basic questions: Where are things located? Why are they there? To answer these questions, geographers study oceans, plant life, landforms, countries, and cities. Geographers also study how Earth and its people affect each other.

Directions

In order to study Earth, geographers need to measure it and locate points on its surface. One way to do this is with directions. Geographers use both cardinal and intermediate directions. The **cardinal directions** are north, east, south, and west. Intermediate directions lie between the cardinal directions. For example, northwest is halfway between north and west.

Latitude

Earth is an almost perfect **sphere** (sfeer), or round-shaped body. Geographers have drawn imaginary lines around Earth to help locate places on its surface. One of these is the Equator, a line drawn around Earth halfway between the North and South Poles. The Equator is also known as the 0-degree (0°) latitude line. **Latitude** is the distance north or south of the Equator. It is measured in degrees. **Degrees** are units that measure angles. Minutes (') measure smaller units. On this map, lines are drawn every 20° of latitude.

Lines of latitude form east-west circles around the globe. Lines of latitude are also called parallels, because they are parallel to one another. That means they never cross.

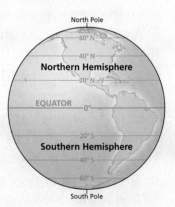

North Pole
60° N
40° N
Northern Hemisphere
20° N
EQUATOR
0°
20° S
Southern Hemisphere
40° S
60° S
South Pole

The Equator divides Earth in half. Each half of Earth is called a **hemisphere.** The half of Earth north of the Equator is known as the Northern Hemisphere. The half of Earth south of the Equator is the Southern Hemisphere.

Longitude

Geographers have also drawn imaginary north-south lines that run between the North Pole and the South Pole on Earth's surface. One of these lines is the Prime Meridian, which passes through Greenwich, England. The Prime Meridian and the other north-south lines measure **longitude,** or the distance in degrees east or west of the Prime Meridian. Lines of longitude are also called meridians.

The half of Earth east of the Prime Meridian is known as the Eastern Hemisphere. The half of Earth west of the Prime Meridian is the Western Hemisphere.

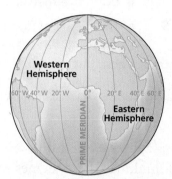

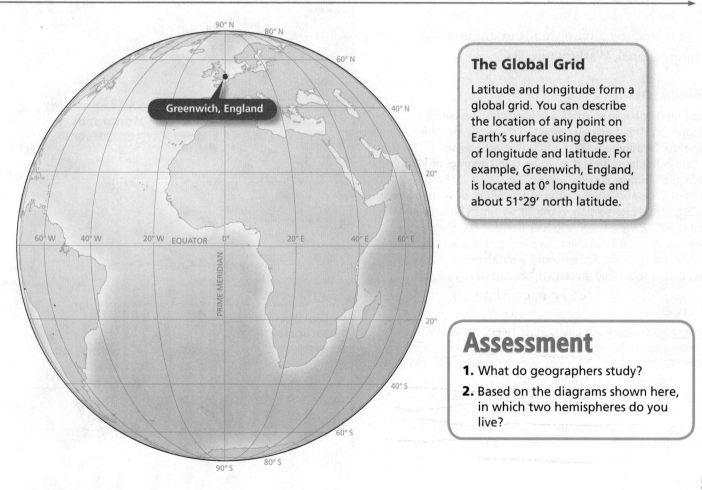

Greenwich, England

The Global Grid

Latitude and longitude form a global grid. You can describe the location of any point on Earth's surface using degrees of longitude and latitude. For example, Greenwich, England, is located at 0° longitude and about 51°29′ north latitude.

Assessment

1. What do geographers study?

2. Based on the diagrams shown here, in which two hemispheres do you live?

Geography's Five Themes

Key Ideas
- Using five themes can help you make sense of geography.
- The theme of location is used to describe where a place is found, while the other themes describe features of a place.

Key Terms • absolute location • relative location • place • region • movement • human-environment interaction

Visual Glossary

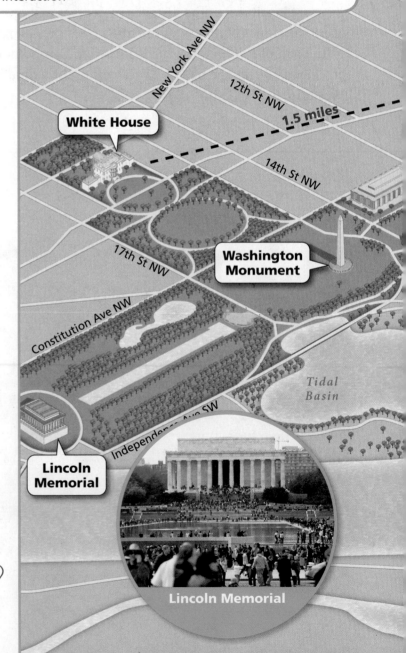

White House

Washington Monument

Lincoln Memorial

1st St NW

Ave NW

New York Ave NW

12th St NW

1.5 miles

14th St NW

17th St NW

Constitution Ave NW

Independence Ave SW

Tidal Basin

Lincoln Memorial

Geographers use five different themes, or ways of thinking. These themes are location, place, region, movement, and human-environment interaction. They can help answer the geographer's two basic questions: Where are things located? Why are they there? You can see how the five themes work by looking at the example of our nation's capital, Washington, D.C.

Location

Geographers begin to study a place by finding where it is, or its location. There are two ways to talk about location. **Absolute location** describes a place's exact position on Earth in terms of longitude and latitude. Using degrees of longitude and latitude, you can pinpoint any spot on Earth. For example, the absolute location of the center of Washington, D.C., is at the intersection of the 38°54' north latitude line and the 77°2' west longitude line. **Relative location,** or the location of a place relative to another place, is another way to describe location. For example, you can say that Washington, D.C, is about 200 miles southwest of New York City.

Place

Geographers also study place. **Place** refers to the mix of human and nonhuman features at a given location. For example, you might talk about how many people live in a place and the kinds of work they do. You might mention that a place is hilly or that it has a wet climate. As a place, Washington, D.C., is on the Potomac River. It has a humid climate with cool winters and hot summers. It is a major city and the center of government for the United States.

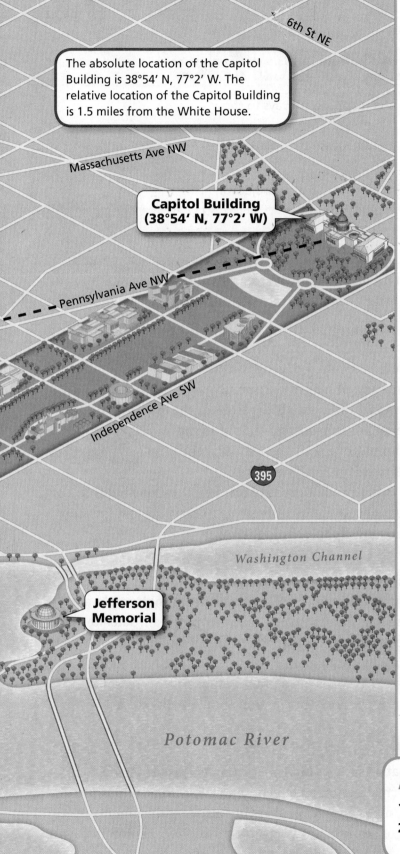

The absolute location of the Capitol Building is 38°54′ N, 77°2′ W. The relative location of the Capitol Building is 1.5 miles from the White House.

Capitol Building
(38°54′ N, 77°2′ W)

Jefferson
Memorial

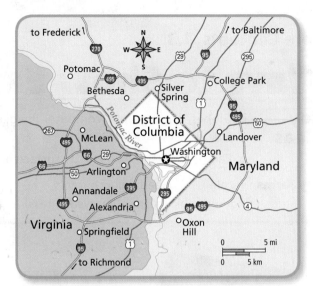

Region

Geographers use the theme of region to group places that have something in common. A **region** is an area with at least one unifying physical or human feature such as climate, landforms, population, or history. Washington, D.C., is part of a region called the Washington Metropolitan Area, which includes the city of Washington and its suburbs. This region shares a job market and a road and rail network. New technology, such as high-speed railroads, may give places new unifying features and connections. This can change the way people see regions.

Movement

The theme of **movement** explores how people, goods, and ideas get from one place to another. A daily movement of trucks and trains supplies the people of Washington with food, fuel, and other basic goods.

Human-Environment Interaction

The theme of **human-environment interaction** considers how people affect their environment, or their natural surroundings, and how their environment affects them. The movement of water from the Potomac River into Washington's water system is an example of human-environment interaction.

Assessment

1. What are the five themes of geography?
2. What is the difference between your hometown's location and your hometown as a place?

7

Ways to Show Earth's Surface

| **Key Ideas** | • Globes, photographs, computer images, and maps are all ways to show and view Earth's surface. |
| | • Each way of showing Earth's surface has advantages and disadvantages. |

Key Terms • scale • aerial photograph • satellite image • geographic information system (GIS) • distortion • projection

Visual Glossary

▲ An aerial photo taken in Antarctica (top) and a satellite image of Antarctica (above)

Geographers use a number of different models to represent Earth's surface. Each model has its own strengths and weaknesses.

Globes

A globe is a model of Earth with the same round shape as Earth itself. With a globe, geographers can show the continents and oceans of Earth much as they really are. The only difference is the **scale,** or the area a given space on the map corresponds to in the real world. For example, one inch on a globe might correspond to 600 miles on Earth's surface.

A globe would have to be hundreds of feet high to show the streets of your town. Such a globe would be impossible to carry around. Instead, people use flat maps to help them find their way.

Photographs

Geographers use photographs as well as maps. **Aerial photographs** are photographic images of Earth's surface taken from the air. **Satellite images** are pictures of Earth's surface taken from a satellite in orbit. They show Earth's surface in great detail. However, it can be hard to find specific features, such as roads, on a photograph. For this reason, maps are still the main way to show information about Earth's surface.

Geographic Information Systems

Geographic information systems (GIS) are computer-based systems that store and use information linked to geographic locations. GIS is useful not only to geographers and mapmakers but also to government agencies and businesses. It offers a way to connect information to places.

Map Projections

Flat maps and photos have one major problem. Earth is round. A map or photo is flat. Can you flatten an orange peel without stretching or tearing it? There will be sections that are stretched or bent out of shape.

Showing Earth on a flat surface always brings some **distortion,** or loss of accuracy in the size or position of objects on a map. Something is going to look too large, too small, or out of place.

To show a flat image of Earth's round surface, mapmakers have come up with different **projections,** or ways to map Earth on a flat surface. A few examples show how they differ.

▲ This projection shows the size and shape of Antarctica nearly correctly.

HOW TO SHOW OUR ROUND EARTH ON A FLAT MAP

The Equal-Area Projection

An equal-area map shows the correct size of landmasses. However, their shapes are distorted.

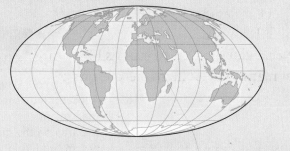

The Mercator Projection

The Mercator (mur KAYT ur) projection shows correct shapes and directions but not true distances or sizes. Mercator maps make areas near the poles look bigger than they are.

The Robinson Projection

The Robinson projection shows nearly the correct size and shape of most land areas. However, even a Robinson projection has distortions, especially in areas around the edges of the map.

Assessment

1. How are maps different from globes?
2. What are the strengths and weaknesses of each of the three projections in showing Antarctica?

Understanding Maps

Key Ideas	• Maps have parts that help you read them. • Though different maps show different things about a place, you can use the same tools to help understand them.

Key Terms • key   • locator map   • scale bar   • compass rose

→ **Visual Glossary**

Look at the maps on these two pages. One is a physical map of the state of Colorado. The other is a road map of Colorado. These maps cover the same area but show different kinds of information. Despite their differences, both maps have all of the basic parts that you should find on any map.

The map has a title that tells you the subject of the map.

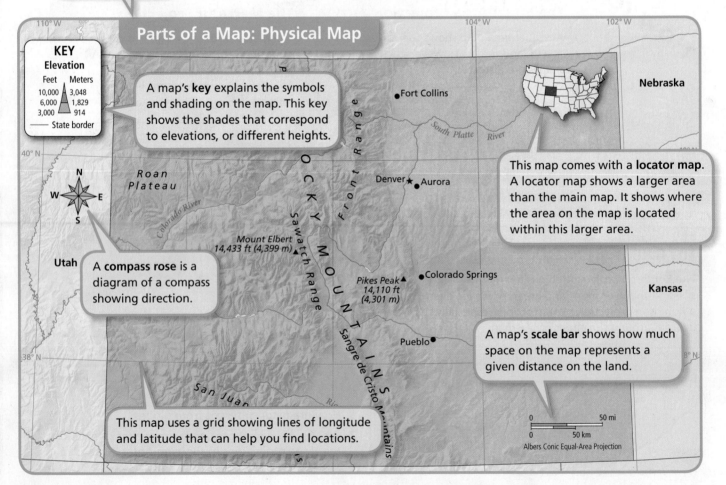

Parts of a Map: Physical Map

KEY
Elevation

Feet		Meters
10,000		3,048
6,000		1,829
3,000		914
— State border		

A map's **key** explains the symbols and shading on the map. This key shows the shades that correspond to elevations, or different heights.

This map comes with a **locator map**. A locator map shows a larger area than the main map. It shows where the area on the map is located within this larger area.

A **compass rose** is a diagram of a compass showing direction.

A map's **scale bar** shows how much space on the map represents a given distance on the land.

This map uses a grid showing lines of longitude and latitude that can help you find locations.

Mount Elbert
14,433 ft (4,399 m)

Pikes Peak
14,110 ft
(4,301 m)

0   50 mi
0   50 km
Albers Conic Equal-Area Projection

10

Reading a Map

Look at the map below. It is a highway map of the state of Colorado. This map looks different from the physical map of Colorado that you have just studied. However, it has the same parts that can help you read it. In fact, you can read most maps using the key, scale bar, and other map tools that you have learned about.

Find the key on this map. Using the key, can you find the route number of the Interstate highway that connects Denver and Colorado Springs, Colorado? Using the scale bar, estimate the number of miles between these two cities. Using the compass rose, find the direction that you would need to travel from Denver to Colorado Springs. Now you have learned to read a highway map!

Parts of a Map: Road Map

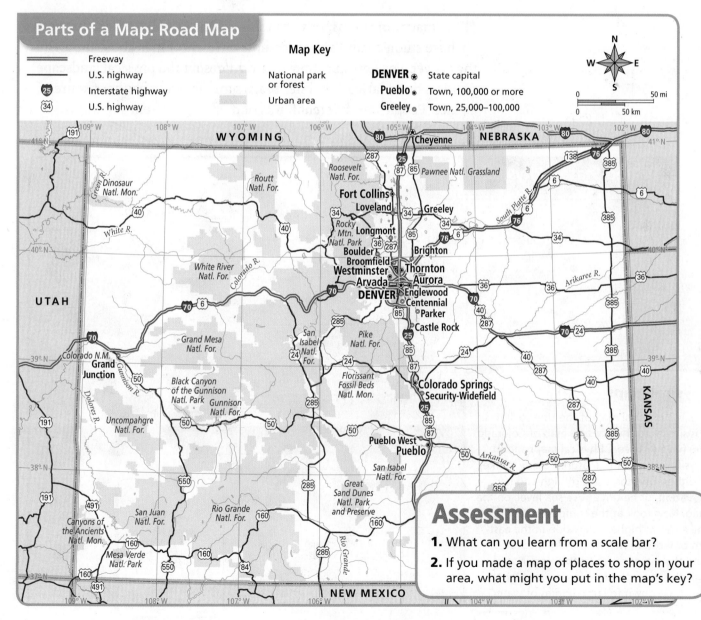

Map Key

Freeway	
U.S. highway	
25 Interstate highway	
34 U.S. highway	
National park or forest	
Urban area	

DENVER ⊛ State capital
Pueblo ⊙ Town, 100,000 or more
Greeley ○ Town, 25,000–100,000

Assessment

1. What can you learn from a scale bar?

2. If you made a map of places to shop in your area, what might you put in the map's key?

11

Types of Maps

Key Ideas
- Maps can show many different kinds of information.
- Political, physical, and special-purpose maps are the main types of maps.

Key Terms • physical map • elevation • political map • special-purpose map → **Visual Glossary**

The map projections, or ways to represent Earth's surface, that you have studied can be used to show different things about the area they cover. For example, they might represent the physical landscape, political boundaries, ecosystem zones, or almost any other feature of a place. People use different kinds of maps in different situations.

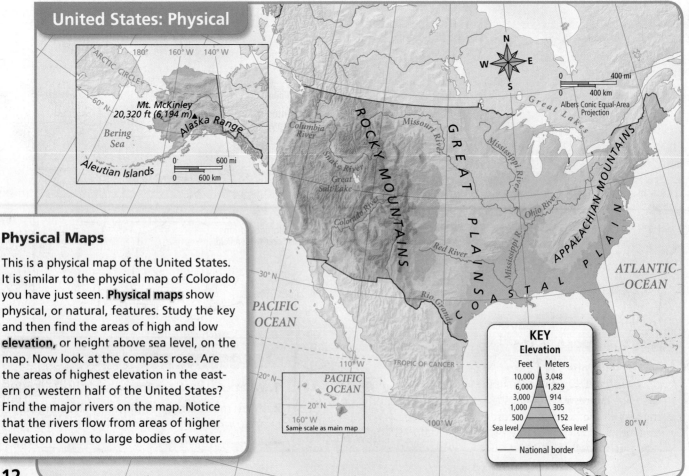

United States: Physical

Mt. McKinley 20,320 ft (6,194 m)

Alaska Range

Bering Sea

Aleutian Islands

ARCTIC CIRCLE

Columbia River

ROCKY MOUNTAINS

Snake River

Great Salt Lake

Colorado River

Missouri River

GREAT PLAINS

Mississippi River

Great Lakes

APPALACHIAN MOUNTAINS

COASTAL PLAIN

ATLANTIC OCEAN

Red River

Mississippi R.

Ohio River

Rio Grande

PACIFIC OCEAN

TROPIC OF CANCER

PACIFIC OCEAN

Same scale as main map

Albers Conic Equal-Area Projection

400 mi
400 km

KEY
Elevation

Feet		Meters
10,000		3,048
6,000		1,829
3,000		914
1,000		305
500		152
Sea level		Sea level

— National border

Physical Maps

This is a physical map of the United States. It is similar to the physical map of Colorado you have just seen. **Physical maps** show physical, or natural, features. Study the key and then find the areas of high and low **elevation,** or height above sea level, on the map. Now look at the compass rose. Are the areas of highest elevation in the eastern or western half of the United States? Find the major rivers on the map. Notice that the rivers flow from areas of higher elevation down to large bodies of water.

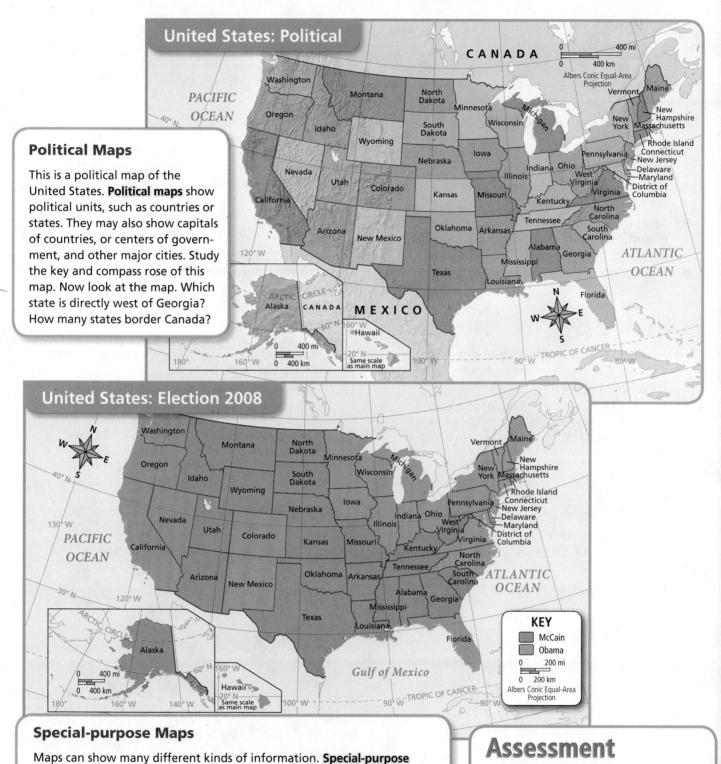

United States: Political

CANADA

Washington · Montana · North Dakota · Minnesota · Michigan · Vermont · Maine

PACIFIC OCEAN

Oregon · Idaho · Wyoming · South Dakota · Wisconsin · New York · New Hampshire · Massachusetts

Nevada · Utah · Colorado · Nebraska · Iowa · Illinois · Indiana · Ohio · Pennsylvania · Rhode Island · Connecticut · New Jersey · Delaware · Maryland · District of Columbia

California · Arizona · New Mexico · Kansas · Missouri · West Virginia · Virginia · Kentucky · North Carolina

Oklahoma · Arkansas · Tennessee · South Carolina · Alabama · Georgia · ATLANTIC OCEAN

Texas · Mississippi · Louisiana

Alaska · CANADA · MEXICO · Hawaii · Florida · TROPIC OF CANCER

0   400 mi
0   400 km
Albers Conic Equal-Area Projection

Political Maps

This is a political map of the United States. **Political maps** show political units, such as countries or states. They may also show capitals of countries, or centers of government, and other major cities. Study the key and compass rose of this map. Now look at the map. Which state is directly west of Georgia? How many states border Canada?

United States: Election 2008

Washington · Montana · North Dakota · Minnesota · Michigan · Vermont · Maine

Oregon · Idaho · Wyoming · South Dakota · Wisconsin · New York · New Hampshire · Massachusetts

Nevada · Utah · Colorado · Nebraska · Iowa · Illinois · Indiana · Ohio · Pennsylvania · Rhode Island · Connecticut · New Jersey · Delaware · Maryland · District of Columbia

PACIFIC OCEAN

California · Arizona · New Mexico · Kansas · Missouri · West Virginia · Virginia · Kentucky · North Carolina

Oklahoma · Arkansas · Tennessee · South Carolina · Alabama · Georgia · ATLANTIC OCEAN

Texas · Mississippi · Louisiana

Gulf of Mexico

Alaska · Hawaii · Florida · TROPIC OF CANCER

KEY
McCain
Obama

0   200 mi
0   200 km
Albers Conic Equal-Area Projection

Special-purpose Maps

Maps can show many different kinds of information. **Special-purpose maps** show the location or distribution of human or physical features. This map shows the results of the 2008 presidential election. A highway map is another kind of special-purpose map. Other special-purpose maps may show a region's weather patterns or other features. Study this map's key. Which presidential candidate won your home state in the 2008 election?

Assessment

1. What are the elements of a physical map?

2. What are the elements of a political map?

13

Tools of Geography

Part 1 Assessment

Key Terms and Ideas

1. **Compare and Contrast** What is the difference between **latitude** and **longitude**?

2. **Describe** What are some features of **place** and **region**?

3. **Analyze Cause and Effect** Why do map **projections** lead to **distortion**? Give a specific example.

4. **Discuss** What does the **scale bar** of a map show?

5. **Compare and Contrast** How do **aerial photographs** and **satellite images** show Earth's surface? What differences do you find between these types of images?

6. **Recall** What are the basic parts of a map, and what does each part show to readers?

7. **Categorize** What kind of map shows elevation?

8. **Summarize** What does a **political map** show?

Think Critically

9. **Problem Solving** Which kinds of maps could you use to choose a new city as your home? How would you use them?

10. **Decision Making** Which kinds of projections would best show the distance between your hometown and Washington, D.C., on a map of the United States? Explain.

11. **Synthesize** What can you learn from the latitude and longitude lines on a map?

12. **Categorize** Match each feature to the correct theme of geography: very flat landscape, four trains in and out of town every day, factory waste enters a local river, large Hispanic population across three states, and 42° S 147° E.

Identify

For each part of a map, write the letter from the map that shows its location.

13. title

14. compass rose

15. latitude line

16. longitude line

17. scale bar

18. key

19. What type of map is this?

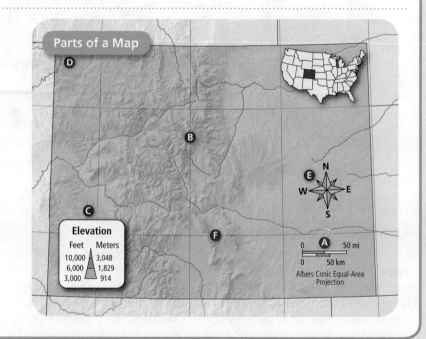

Parts of a Map

Elevation

Feet	Meters
10,000	3,048
6,000	1,829
3,000	914

0   50 mi
0   50 km

Albers Conic Equal-Area Projection

Journal Activity

Fill in the graphic organizers in your student journal.

Demonstrate Understanding Complete the Sum-It-Up activity in your journal to demonstrate your understanding of the Tools of Geography. After you complete the activity, discuss your map with a partner. Be sure to support your completed map with information from the lesson.

21st Century Learning

Evaluate Web Sites

Find three different web sites that generate maps. Compare the sites and rank each according to the following criteria:
- clarity and appearance of the maps
- option to create directions for drivers or walkers
- ability to locate addresses from incomplete information

Document-Based Questions

Success Tracker™
Online at myworldgeography.com

Use your knowledge of the tools of geography and Documents A and B to answer Questions 1–3.

Document A

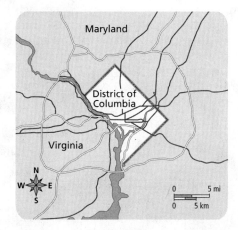

Document B

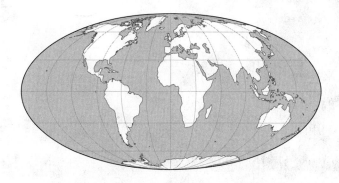

1. Which of the five themes of geography is best represented by this map?

   A location

   B place

   C region

   D human-environment interaction

2. What kind of projection does Document B show?

   A Mercator

   B equal-area

   C Robinson

   D global grid

3. **Writing Task** What are the advantages and disadvantages of the map shown in Document B? Explain your answer.

Core Concepts Part 2

Our Planet, Earth

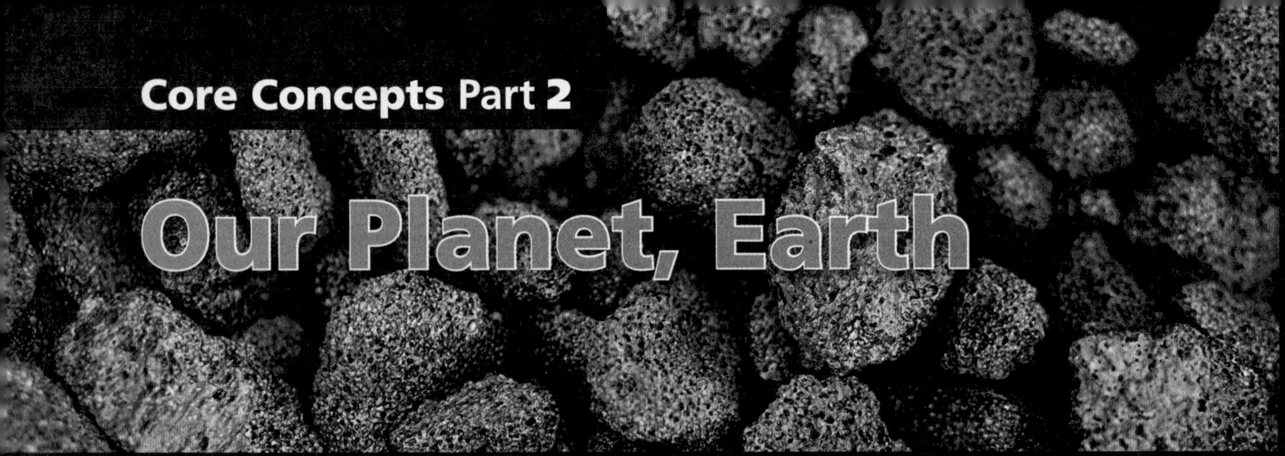

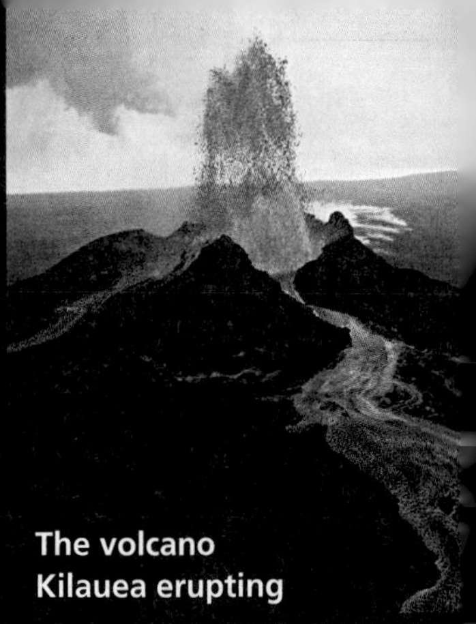

The volcano Kilauea erupting

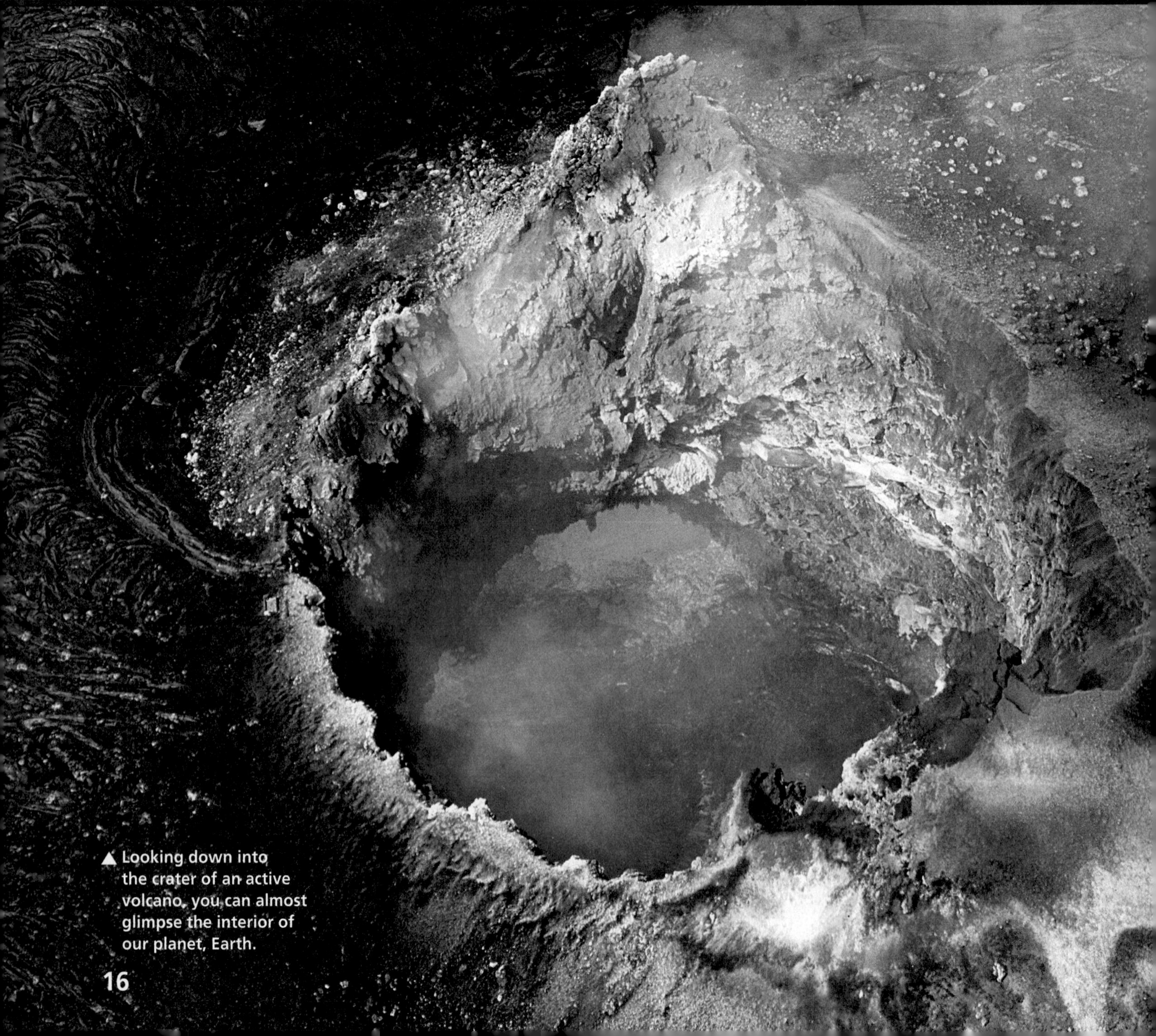

▲ Looking down into the crater of an active volcano, you can almost glimpse the interior of our planet, Earth.

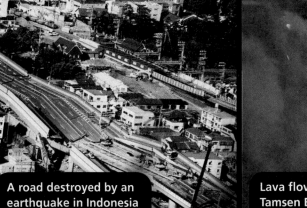

A road destroyed by an earthquake in Indonesia

Lava flowing into the sea (left)
Tamsen Burlak (right)

Tamsen Studies a Volcano

Story by Miles Lemaire for myWorld

As 21-year-old Tamsen Burlak watched the volcano Kilauea, in Hawaii, blow lava and ash into the sky she had only one thought: "This is pretty cool."

When she was a young girl, Tamsen didn't know much about what makes up our planet, Earth, only that she loved to collect rocks during nature hikes with her parents.

"I would always pick up rocks from everywhere that we went—anything that looked cool," she says. "It was probably around middle school or high school while I was looking at the rocks that I realized I wanted to know what they were called and how they formed. So I went out and bought a bunch of those field guides, geology dictionaries for rocks. That's when I found out the field name was geology." Tamsen knew what she wanted to study.

When she went to college, Tamsen studied geology, the field of science that deals with the structure of Earth. She concentrated on volcanoes and fault lines, places where earthquakes are likely to happen. Geologists like Tamsen investigate earthquake zones to find out how likely another earthquake is, and how destructive it will be. Earthquakes sometimes occur where volcanoes are erupting.

Tamsen was able to go to Hawaii to study. The islands that make up the state of Hawaii were formed by volcanoes. Lava flowed out of volcanoes, cooled, and formed new land over millions of years. Some of the islands still have active volcanoes. Tamsen visited Kilauea, where lava has been flowing since 1983.

"The active area I went to was part of a summer course I took on the big island of Hawaii. At that time Kilauea had just started erupting, so we were there for the first days of it," Tamsen said.

"It was really exciting," she added, but not always easy, "because of the volcanic gasses in the air. That sort of stuff can itch the throat and cause irritation, but I loved every second of it!"

Tamsen, who now has a degree in geology, says that she has been studying dormant, or inactive, volcanoes and earthquake zones for years. Her experience in Hawaii is something that she and her fellow geologists dream of.

"We'd all be really excited if there was an actual earthquake that we all got to study," says Tamsen, "but we just look at faults in the area, offsets, and the different rock types, and measure how much displacement has gone on and how big a threat we think it might be."

As Tamsen learned firsthand, studying the structure of Earth can be very exciting. Geologists face down erupting volcanoes in order to learn how to predict earthquakes and save lives. Understanding Earth may someday make that possible.

17

Earth in Space

Key Ideas
- Planet Earth moves around the sun.
- This movement causes places on Earth's surface to receive varying amounts of sunlight from one season to the next.

Key Terms
- orbit
- axis
- solstice
- revolution
- equinox

Visual Glossary

Earth, the sun, the planets, and the stars in the sky are all part of our galaxy, or cluster of stars. We call our galaxy the Milky Way because its stars look like a trail of spilled milk across a dark night sky. Our sun is one of its billions of stars.

Earth, the Sun, and the Seasons

Even though the sun is about 93 million miles (150 million km) away, it provides Earth with heat and light. To understand how far Earth is from the sun, consider that this distance is nearly 4,000 times the distance around Earth at the Equator.

Earth travels around the sun in an oval-shaped **orbit,** which is the path one object makes as it revolves around another. Earth takes 365 1/4 days, or one year, to make one **revolution,** or complete journey, around the sun.

Earth's **axis,** an imaginary line between the North and South Poles, is tilted relative to its orbit. Therefore, as Earth makes its revolution, the sun shines most directly on different places at different times. That is why seasons occur.

March Equinox

About March 21, the sun is directly overhead at noon on the Equator. At this point in Earth's orbit, its axis is tilted neither toward nor away from the sun. An **equinox** (EE kwih nahks) is a point at which, everywhere on Earth, days and nights are nearly equal in length. This is the spring equinox in the Northern Hemisphere and the fall equinox in the Southern Hemisphere.

June Solstice

About June 21, the North Pole is tilted closest to the sun. This brings the heat of summer to the Northern Hemisphere. This is the summer **solstice** in the Northern Hemisphere and the winter solstice in the Southern Hemisphere. A solstice (SOHL stis) is a point at which days are longest in one hemisphere and shortest in the other.

December Solstice

About December 21, the South Pole is tilted closest to the sun. The area north of the Arctic Circle is in constant darkness, while the area south of the Antarctic Circle has constant daylight. This is the winter solstice in the Northern Hemisphere and the summer solstice in the Southern Hemisphere. The lack of sunlight in the Northern Hemisphere brings the cold of winter.

September Equinox

About September 23, the sun is again directly overhead at noon on the Equator, and all of Earth has days and nights of equal length. This is the fall equinox in the Northern Hemisphere and the spring equinox in the Southern Hemisphere. Less-direct sunlight in the Northern Hemisphere brings the chill of fall.

Assessment

1. If it is summer in the Northern Hemisphere, what season is it in the Southern Hemisphere?

2. How can days be short and cold in one hemisphere when they are long and hot in another?

19

Time and Earth's Rotation

Key Ideas
- Earth's spinning movement causes day and night.
- This spinning also causes it to be different times in different places on Earth's surface.

Key Terms • rotation • time zone

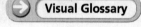
Visual Glossary

You have learned that Earth revolves around the sun in an oval-shaped orbit. Earth also moves in another way. This motion explains why day and night occur.

Rotation of Earth

As Earth revolves around the sun, it is also rotating, or spinning, in space. Earth rotates around its axis. Each complete turn, or **rotation,** takes about 24 hours. At any one time, it is night on the side of Earth facing away from the sun. As Earth rotates, that side of Earth turns to face the sun, and the sun appears to rise. The sun's light shines on that side of Earth. It is daytime. Then, as that side of Earth turns away from the sun, the sun appears to set. No sunlight reaches that side of Earth. It is nighttime.

Time Zones

Because Earth rotates toward the east, the day starts earlier in the east than it does farther west. Over short distances, the time difference is small. For example, the sun rises about four minutes earlier in Beaumont, Texas, than it does in Houston, 70 miles to the west. But if every town had its own local time, people would have a hard time keeping track. So governments have agreed to divide the world into standard **time zones,** or areas sharing the same time. Times in neighboring zones are one hour apart.

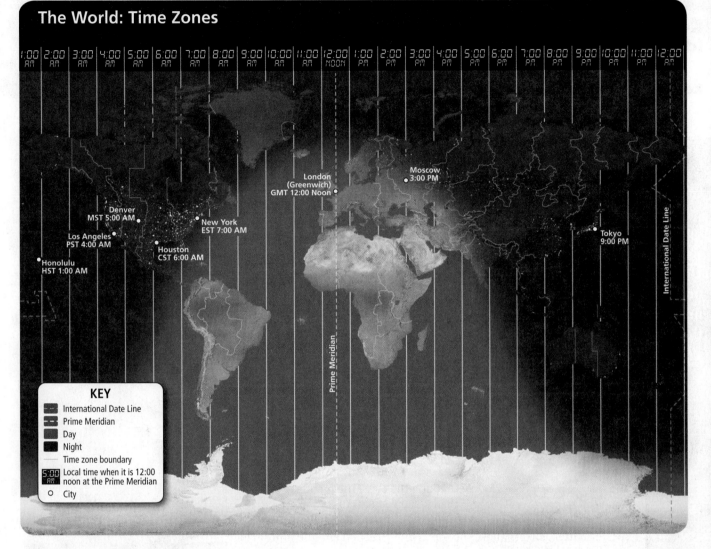

The World: Time Zones

| 1:00 AM | 2:00 AM | 3:00 AM | 4:00 AM | 5:00 AM | 6:00 AM | 7:00 AM | 8:00 AM | 9:00 AM | 10:00 AM | 11:00 AM | 12:00 NOON | 1:00 PM | 2:00 PM | 3:00 PM | 4:00 PM | 5:00 PM | 6:00 PM | 7:00 PM | 8:00 PM | 9:00 PM | 10:00 PM | 11:00 PM | 12:00 AM |

London (Greenwich) GMT 12:00 Noon

Moscow 3:00 PM

Denver MST 5:00 AM

New York EST 7:00 AM

Los Angeles PST 4:00 AM

Tokyo 9:00 PM

Houston CST 6:00 AM

Honolulu HST 1:00 AM

International Date Line

Prime Meridian

KEY
- International Date Line
- Prime Meridian
- Day
- Night
- Time zone boundary
- **5:00 AM** Local time when it is 12:00 noon at the Prime Meridian
- ○ City

The Prime Meridian

The Prime Meridian, in Greenwich, England, is at the center of one of these zones. The time in that zone is sometimes known as Greenwich Mean Time or Universal Time (UT). Other time zones are sometimes described in terms of how many hours they are behind or ahead of UT. (For example, Central Standard Time in the United States is UT – 6, or six hours behind UT.)

Assessment

1. What is the rotation of Earth?

2. If it is 8 P.M. in New York, what time is it in Los Angeles?

Earth's Structure

> **Key Ideas**
>
> - Earth is made up of different parts, above and below its surface.
>
> **Key Terms**
> - core
> - mantle
> - crust
> - atmosphere
> - landform
>
> 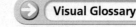 **Visual Glossary**

The diagram to the right reveals Earth's interior, or the parts beneath its surface. It also shows some of the parts above its surface. Understanding Earth's inner and outer structure will help you to understand the forces that shape the world we live in.

Earth's Core

A sphere of very hot metal at the center of Earth is called the **core**. Despite temperatures greater than 5,000°F (3,000°C), the inner core is solid because of the great pressure of the layers above it. The outer core is hot liquid metal.

Mantle

The **mantle** is a thick, rocky layer around the core. The mantle is also hot, with temperatures greater than 3,300°F (1,800°C). The mantle is solid, but its temperature makes it fluid, or able to flow. If you warm a stick of butter, you can move the top in one direction and the bottom in another. Even though the mantle is rock, its high temperature allows it to move something like a stick of warm butter.

Crust

The thin layer of rocks and minerals that surrounds the mantle is called the **crust**. The surface of the crust includes the land areas where people live as well as the ocean floor. The crust is thinnest beneath the ocean floor. It is thickest beneath high mountain ranges, such as the Himalayas, in Asia. In effect, it floats on top of the mantle. The great heat deep inside Earth and movements within the mantle help to shape Earth's crust.

Atmosphere

Above Earth's surface is the **atmosphere,** a thick layer of gases or air. It includes life-giving oxygen. Earth's atmosphere acts like a blanket. It holds in heat from the sun, which makes life possible.

Landforms

Only 25 percent of Earth's surface is land. There are many different **landforms,** or shapes and types of land. Two kinds of processes shape these landforms: processes beneath Earth's surface that push Earth's crust up, and processes on Earth's surface that wear it down.

Water

Water covers about 75 percent of Earth's surface. This water forms a layer above Earth's crust. The oceans hold about 97 percent of Earth's water. This water is salty. Most fresh water, or water without salt, is frozen in ice sheets around the North and South Poles. Only a tiny portion of Earth's water is unfrozen fresh water. People need this water for many things. Fresh water comes from lakes, rivers, and ground water, which are fed by rain and snow.

Assessment

1. What are Earth's three main layers?

2. What part of Earth's structure are oceans located on?

Forces on Earth's Surface

Key Ideas
- Forces such as wind, water, and ice shape Earth's surface.
- These forces produce a variety of different landforms.

Key Terms
- weathering
- valley
- erosion
- deposition
- plateau
- plain
- delta

⟶ **Visual Glossary**

An eroded landscape in the southwestern United States. ▼

Forces on Earth's surface wear down and reshape the land. Along with forces inside Earth, which you will read about later, forces on Earth's surface help create the landforms we see around us.

Wearing Away Earth's Surface

Weathering is a process that breaks rocks down into tiny pieces. There are two kinds of weathering: chemical weathering and mechanical weathering. In chemical weathering, rainwater or acids carried by rainwater dissolve rocks. In mechanical weathering, moving water, ice, or sometimes wind breaks rocks into little pieces. Mechanical weathering can happen after chemical weathering has weakened rocks.

Weathering helps create soil. Tiny pieces of rock combine with decayed animal and plant material to form soil. Soil and pieces of rock may undergo **erosion**, a process in which water, ice, or wind remove small pieces of rock. Soil is required to sustain plant and animal life, and for agriculture. Because of this, weathering is very important to human settlement patterns.

Shaping Landforms

Weathering and erosion have shaped many of Earth's landforms. These landforms include mountains and hills. Mountains are wide at the bottom and rise steeply to a narrow peak or ridge. Hills are lower than mountains and often have rounded tops. While forces within Earth create mountains, forces on Earth's surface wear them down. An area in which a certain type of landform is dominant is called a landform region.

The parts of mountains and hills that are left standing are the rocks that are hardest to wear away. Millions of years ago, the Appalachian Mountains in the eastern United States were as high as the Rocky Mountains of the western United States. Rain, snow, and wind wore the Appalachians down into much lower peaks.

Rebuilding Earth's Surface

When water, ice, and wind remove material, they deposit it farther downstream or downwind to create new landforms. **Deposition** is the process of depositing material eroded and carried by water, ice, or wind. Deposition creates landforms such as sandy beaches. **Plains,** or large areas of flat or gently rolling land, are often formed by the deposition of material carried downstream by rivers. Through deposition on the floor of the sea, rivers can create new land.

A **plateau** is a large, mostly flat area that rises above the surrounding land. At least one side of a plateau has a steep slope. At the top of this slope is usually a layer of rock that is hard to wear down.

Valleys are stretches of low land between mountains or hills. Rivers often form valleys where there are rocks that are easy to wear away.

This map shows the **delta** of the Nile River in Egypt. Deltas are flat plains built on the seabed where a river fans out and deposits material over many years.

Assessment

1. How is erosion different from weathering?
2. How do plains form from the tops of worn-down mountains?

25

Forces Inside Earth

Key Ideas	• Movements of hot, soft rock in Earth's mantle affect Earth's surface, forming volcanoes and pushing continents together or apart.

Key Terms	• plate tectonics	• plate	
	• magma	• fault	→ **Visual Glossary**

The volcano Kilauea in Hawaii spews molten rock. ▼

Forces deep inside Earth are constantly reshaping its surface. The theory of **plate tectonics** states that Earth's crust is made up of huge blocks called **plates**. Plates include continents or parts of continents, along with parts of the ocean floor. Earth's continental plates sit on streams of molten, nearly melted, rock called **magma**. Some scientists believe magma acts as a conveyor belt, moving the plates in different directions. Plates may move only an inch or two (a few centimeters) a year.

This movement slowly builds mountains. When two plates of crust push against each other, the pressure makes the crust bend to form steep mountains.

Earthquakes and Volcanoes

Earthquakes occur when plates slide against each other. They often occur at seams in Earth's crust called **faults**, often near the boundaries between plates. Earthquakes cause the ground to shake. Some earthquakes are too small for people to feel. But others can destroy buildings and cause great harm. For example, the 1906 San Francisco earthquake killed more than 3000 people.

The movement of continental plates creates great pressure inside Earth. Sometimes this pressure forces magma up through Earth's crust, forming volcanoes. Volcanoes spew magma from inside Earth. When magma erupts out of a volcano, it is called lava. Ash, rocks, and poisonous gasses also explode out of volcanoes during an eruption. Volcanic eruptions can be very dangerous for people. But volcanoes also serve an important purpose. When lava cools, new land forms. Undersea volcanoes even grow into islands after thousands of years of eruptions.

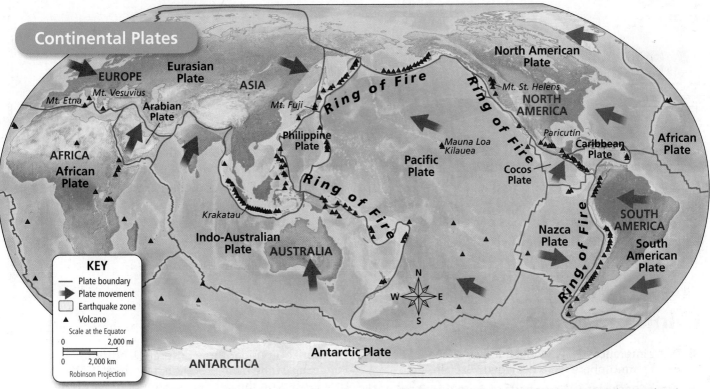

Continental Plates

KEY

- Plate boundary
- Plate movement
- Earthquake zone
- ▲ Volcano

Scale at the Equator

0   2,000 mi

0   2,000 km

Robinson Projection

The Plates of Earth's Crust The map above shows how Earth's plates fit together today. It also shows the directions in which plates are moving. As you can see on the map, earthquakes and volcanoes occur along plate edges.

Natural Hazards

Volcanoes and earthquakes are examples of natural disasters. They are also called natural hazards, meaning dangers. Other natural hazards include hurricanes, tornados, landslides, and floods.

These events threaten lives and property. But people can take steps to prepare for natural disasters, so that damage will not be as severe when they strike. For example, architects can design buildings that will not collapse when the ground shakes. Local governments can set routes for people to leave affected areas during a hurricane. Citizens can practice what to do during an earthquake, and keep emergency supplies at home.

Preparing for a Natural Hazard
Above: Damage caused by an earthquake
Right: Students hide under their desks for an earthquake drill

Assessment

1. How do forces inside Earth shape Earth's surface?

2. What are some ways people prepare for natural hazards?

27

Our Planet, Earth

Part 2 Assessment

Key Terms and Ideas

1. **Compare and Contrast** What is the difference between an **equinox** and a **solstice**?

2. **Analyze Cause and Effect** How does Earth's **orbit** influence climate on Earth?

3. **Describe** How is Earth's **axis** part of its **rotation**?

4. **Identify Main Ideas and Details** What is sunrise? In which part of the United States does sunrise occur earliest?

5. **Categorize** Which part of Earth's structure is the thinnest? Where is this part?

6. **Summarize** How do **weathering** and **erosion** shape Earth's surface?

7. **Sequence** Describe the process that causes movement of the continents.

Think Critically

8. **Draw Inferences** How would our lives change if Earth's atmosphere were damaged? Explain.

9. **Draw Conclusions** Which parts of Earth's orbit are best for warm-weather activities in the Northern Hemisphere? For cold-weather activities? Explain using the terms *equinox* and *solstice*.

10. **Ask Questions** To choose a safe location for a new town, what questions about Earth's structure and movement would you ask? Explain.

11. **Categorize** Consider three different landforms. For each, list the main process that formed it. Was that process on the interior or exterior of Earth? How are the different processes related?

Identify

Identify the time in each location if it is noon GMT.

12. **New York, New York**

13. **Houston, Texas**

14. **Denver, Colorado**

15. **Los Angeles, California**

16. **Anchorage, Alaska**

17. **Honolulu, Hawaii**

18. Compare the time of sunrise in New York, New York, with that in Houston, Texas. Which is earlier and which is later? Are these cities in the same time zone?

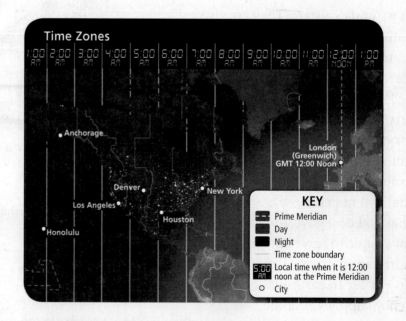

Journal Activity

Fill in the graphic organizer in your Student Journal.

Demonstrate Understanding Complete the Sum-It-Up activity in your journal to demonstrate your understanding of Our Planet, Earth. After you complete the activity, discuss your diagram with your class. Be sure to support your diagram with information from the lessons.

21st Century Learning

Make a Difference

Think about earthquake or volcano safety in your community or a community like yours in an earthquake or volcano danger area. Develop ideas to raise community awareness of the dangers and the ways people can avoid them. Share your ideas on a Web page, poster, or handout.

Document-Based Questions

Success Tracker™
Online at myworldgeography.com

Use your knowledge of our planet Earth and Documents A and B to answer Questions 1–3.

Document A

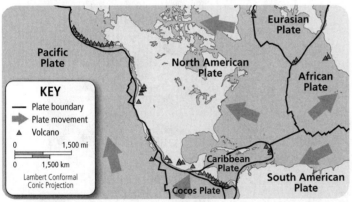

KEY
— Plate boundary
➡ Plate movement
▲ Volcano
0   1,500 mi
0   1,500 km
Lambert Conformal Conic Projection

Document B

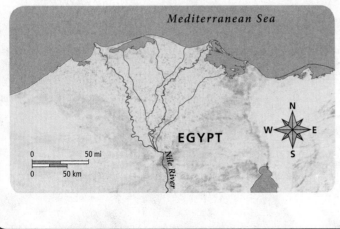

1. Why are there volcanoes where the North American Plate meets the Pacific Plate?

   A Erosion breaks down the land where plates meet.

   B Magma is forced through Earth's surface at plate boundaries.

   C Earth's rotation causes the sun to shine directly on this area.

   D Land in this area has been shaped by chemical weather.

2. How is the natural feature depicted on this map formed?

   A Tectonic plates push land upward.

   B A river flows into the ocean, depositing material on the seabed.

   C Wind and rain wear down mountains.

   D A river carves out a valley.

3. **Writing Task** Suppose a volcano forms on the ocean floor and grows thousands of feet upwards. Use that information and Document A to explain the many islands between Asia and Australia.

my worldgeography.com   Self-Test

29

Climates and Ecosystems

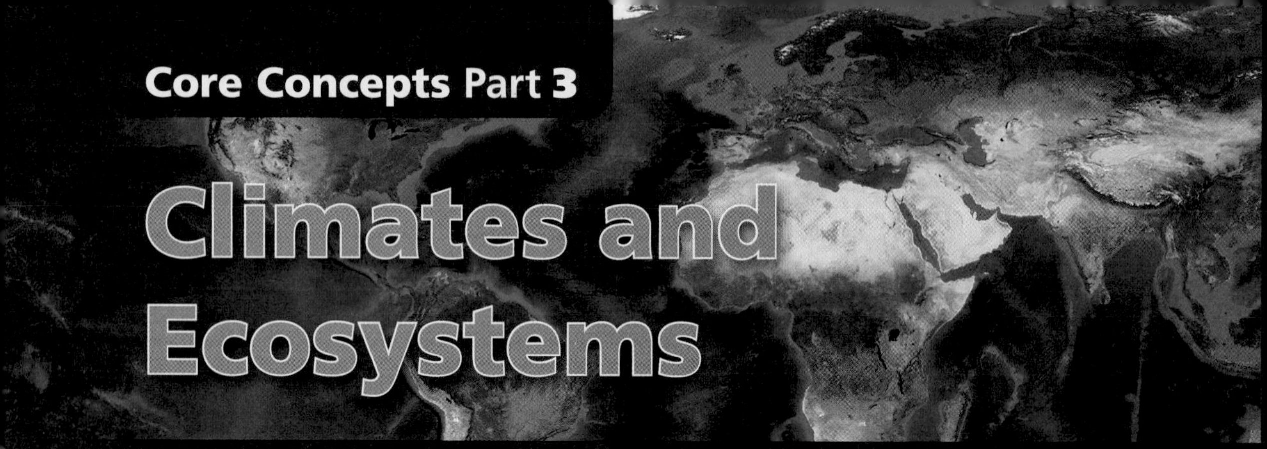

Hurricane Katrina spins toward New Orleans.

New Orleans residents trapped by floodwaters wave for help. ▲

Katrina caused severe destruction.

Airin McGhee

HURRICANE KATRINA STRIKES

Story by Miles Lemaire for myWorld Geography

Powerful tropical storms sweep across the southeastern United States and the Gulf Coast nearly every year. At first, teenager Airin McGhee thought that Hurricane Katrina would be just like any other storm. She was wrong. Instead, Katrina was so powerful that it flooded much of Airin's city, New Orleans, Louisiana.

When weather forecasters and government officials first started warning New Orleans residents about Hurricane Katrina in late August 2005, Airin was not worried. "Every year we would get the warning and up until that point it just never happened," she said. "Nobody expected Katrina to be like it was."

Fortunately, Airin and her mother and sister decided to leave New Orleans before the storm arrived. They drove through heavy traffic to Jackson, Mississippi, a city about 190 miles north of New Orleans. While they waited for the storm to pass, they feared the worst for their home, their city, and the friends and neighbors they had left behind.

Hurricane Katrina hit New Orleans on August 29. Its powerful winds ripped buildings apart and tore trees out of the ground. Worse, Katrina's winds and rain broke the levees, or raised flood barriers, that had protected much of the area. Millions of gallons of water poured through the broken levees into the city.

After Katrina ended, Airin's family tried to get news from friends in New Orleans. "I was really devastated for a while," Airin says, "because the cell phones were really bad and I just had all these thoughts of, 'Is this person okay? Is this person okay?' For weeks all … numbers had a busy signal and it was hard to get in touch with people."

When Airin's family was finally able to return to New Orleans, they saw the results of Katrina's destructive power in person. Years later, Airin's memories of what they saw are still strong. "We had six feet of water in our house," Airin said. "We lost everything. We lost my mom's car and my car, our entire house, including all the furniture and clothes … I pretty much lost everything."

It wasn't long before Airin's family was able to find another place to live, but they still feel the effects of the storm years later.

"I'll just never forget Katrina," Airin says. "It wiped away all my memories. I lost my high school diploma, all my pictures and things that you might take for granted. I collected things like my baby teeth and blanket. All those things are just gone."

When Airin thinks about how the storm affected her, she says, "It really taught me to value sentimental things. It changed how I do certain things, because now I want to capture every moment, and I find myself taking pictures of everything."

31

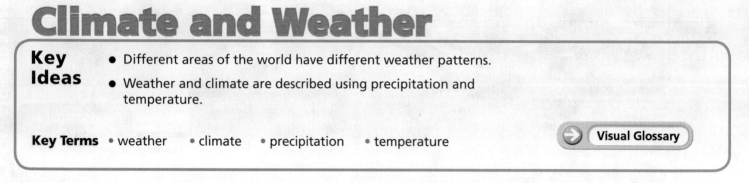
Climate and Weather

Key Ideas	• Different areas of the world have different weather patterns. • Weather and climate are described using precipitation and temperature.

Key Terms • weather • climate • precipitation • temperature

→ **Visual Glossary**

The climate of Iquitos (ee KEE tohs), Peru, is hot and wet year-round. ▼

You have learned about the powerful forces that shape Earth, including global movements, water, and sunlight. These forces also shape Earth's weather patterns. Weather patterns can vary widely from one region to another.

Weather or Climate?

Do you look outside before you choose your clothing in the morning? If so, you are checking the weather. **Weather** is the condition of the air and sky at a certain time. Or do you choose your clothing based on the normal weather for the time of year in the place where you live? If so, you dress according to your local climate. **Climate** is the average weather of a place over many years.

How you feel about today's weather may depend on your local climate. If you live in a place with a wet climate, you may be unhappy to see rainy weather, because your climate means that you get rain frequently. On the other hand, if you live in a dry climate where water is scarce, you might be very happy to see rainy weather.

Rain is a form of **precipitation,** which is water that falls to the ground as rain, snow, sleet, or hail. **Temperature** is a measure of how hot or cold the air is. Precipitation and temperature are the main ways to describe both daily weather and long-term climate.

Comparing Climates

One way to understand and compare climates is to use climate graphs. Climate graphs show the average climate for a place for each month of a year. A climate graph has a curved line that shows average temperatures. It has bars that show average monthly precipitation. The next page has two examples of climate graphs.

Chicago, Illinois

This is a climate graph of Chicago, Illinois, a city in the north central United States. It shows that Chicago has cold winters, hot summers, and moderate precipitation year-round. Notice that the line for temperature is much higher in July than it is in January. However, the heights of the bars for precipitation do not change much.

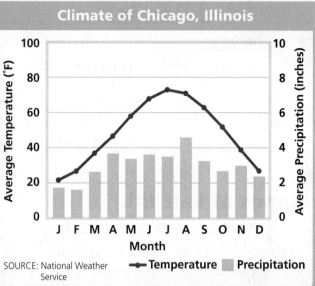

Climate of Chicago, Illinois

SOURCE: National Weather Service

—●— Temperature   ▇ Precipitation

Bangalore, India

In some parts of the world, precipitation changes greatly from season to season. This is a climate graph of Bangalore, India. It shows that most of Bangalore's rain falls during a rainy season that lasts from May to October. Almost no precipitation falls from January to March.

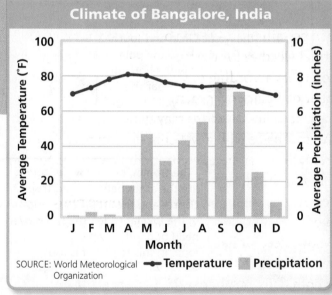

Climate of Bangalore, India

SOURCE: World Meteorological Organization

—●— Temperature   ▇ Precipitation

Assessment

1. How is climate different from weather?

2. How would you describe your region's climate?

Temperature

Key Ideas
- Differences in sunlight affect temperatures at different latitudes.
- Earth's temperature patterns change from season to season.

Key Terms
- polar zone
- high latitudes
- tropics
- low latitudes
- temperate zone
- middle latitudes
- altitude

⊘ **Visual Glossary**

Zones of Latitude

Energy from the sun heats Earth. Because of the tilt of Earth's axis, different areas of the planet receive different amounts of direct sunlight. As a result, some regions are warmer than others.

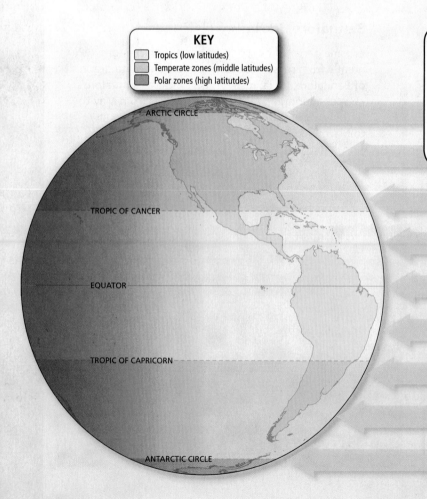

KEY
- ☐ Tropics (low latitudes)
- ☐ Temperate zones (middle latitudes)
- ☐ Polar zones (high latitutdes)

ARCTIC CIRCLE

TROPIC OF CANCER

EQUATOR

TROPIC OF CAPRICORN

ANTARCTIC CIRCLE

The **polar zones,** also known as the **high latitudes,** are the areas north of the Arctic Circle and south of the Antarctic Circle. In the polar zones, the sun is below the horizon for part of the year and near the horizon the rest of the year. Temperatures stay cool to bitterly cold.

The **tropics,** or the **low latitudes,** are the areas between the Tropic of Cancer and the Tropic of Capricorn. In the low latitudes, the sun is overhead or nearly overhead all year long. In this region, it is usually hot.

The **temperate zones,** or the **middle latitudes,** are the areas between the high and low latitudes. These areas lie between the Tropic of Cancer and the Arctic Circle in the Northern Hemisphere and between the Tropic of Capricorn and the Antarctic Circle in the Southern Hemisphere. They have a hot summer, a cold winter, and a moderate spring and fall.

Seasonal Changes in Temperature

Because of the tilt of Earth's axis, temperature patterns change from season to season. The maps below show the world's average monthly temperatures in January and July.

In January, it is winter in the Northern Hemisphere and summer in the Southern Hemisphere. In July, the seasons are reversed. Notice that temperatures are cooler year-round over western South America and other areas. The lower temperatures are due to the high altitude of these regions. **Altitude** is height above sea level. As altitude increases, temperature drops.

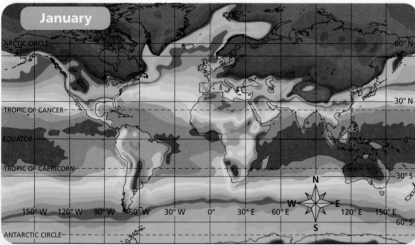

World: Average Monthly Temperature

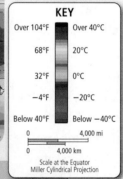

KEY

Over 104°F	Over 40°C
68°F	20°C
32°F	0°C
−4°F	−20°C
Below 40°F	Below −40°C

0   4,000 mi
0   4,000 km
Scale at the Equator
Miller Cylindrical Projection

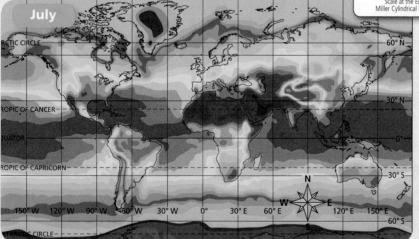

Assessment

1. Why are most of the tropics, or the low latitudes, warm all year?

2. How does the tilt of Earth's axis explain changes in temperature from one season to another in the temperate zones?

Water and Climate

> **Key Ideas**
> - Water affects climate and weather.
> - Water is always moving in the process called the water cycle.
>
> **Key Terms** • water cycle • evaporation
>
> → **Visual Glossary**

Like plants and animals, people need fresh water to live. All fresh water comes from precipitation. As you know, precipitation is water that falls from the sky in the form of rain, snow, sleet, or hail. Water also shapes climates.

Oceans and Climate

Oceans and other large bodies of water on Earth's surface help spread Earth's heat and shape climates. Global temperature differences and wind patterns create ocean currents, which act like large rivers within the oceans. These ocean currents move across great distances. They move warm water from the tropics toward the poles. They also move cool water from the poles toward the tropics. The water's temperature affects air temperature near it. Warm water warms the air; cool water chills it.

Bodies of water affect climate in other ways, too. Water takes longer to heat or cool than land. As air and land heat up in summer, water remains cooler. Wind blowing over the cool water helps cool land nearby. So in summer, areas near an ocean or lake will be cooler than inland

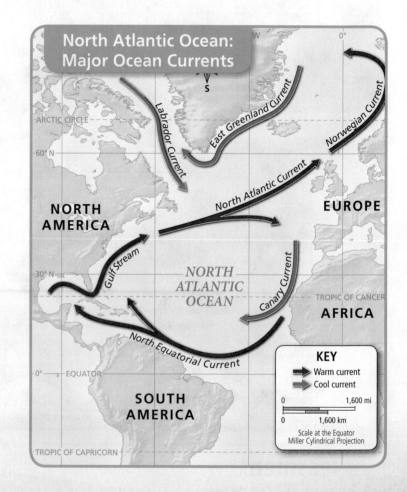

North Atlantic Ocean: Major Ocean Currents

KEY
→ Warm current
→ Cool current

0   1,600 mi
0   1,600 km
Scale at the Equator
Miller Cylindrical Projection

areas at the same latitude and altitude. In the winter, on the other hand, water remains warmer than land. So in winter, areas near oceans or lakes are warmer than inland areas.

For example, in the Atlantic Ocean, the Gulf Stream, a warm current, travels northeast from the tropics. The Gulf Stream and the North Atlantic Current carry warm water all the way to Western Europe. That warm water helps give Western Europe a much milder climate than other regions at the same latitude.

The Water Cycle

Earth's water is always moving in a process called the water cycle, shown in the illustration below. The **water cycle** is the movement of water from Earth's surface into the atmosphere and back. As water heats up, it moves from rivers, oceans, and lakes up into the air. As it cools, it falls to Earth's surface and flows back to rivers, oceans and lakes. The water cycle includes precipitation and evaporation. **Evaporation** is the process in which a liquid changes to a gas.

The Water Cycle

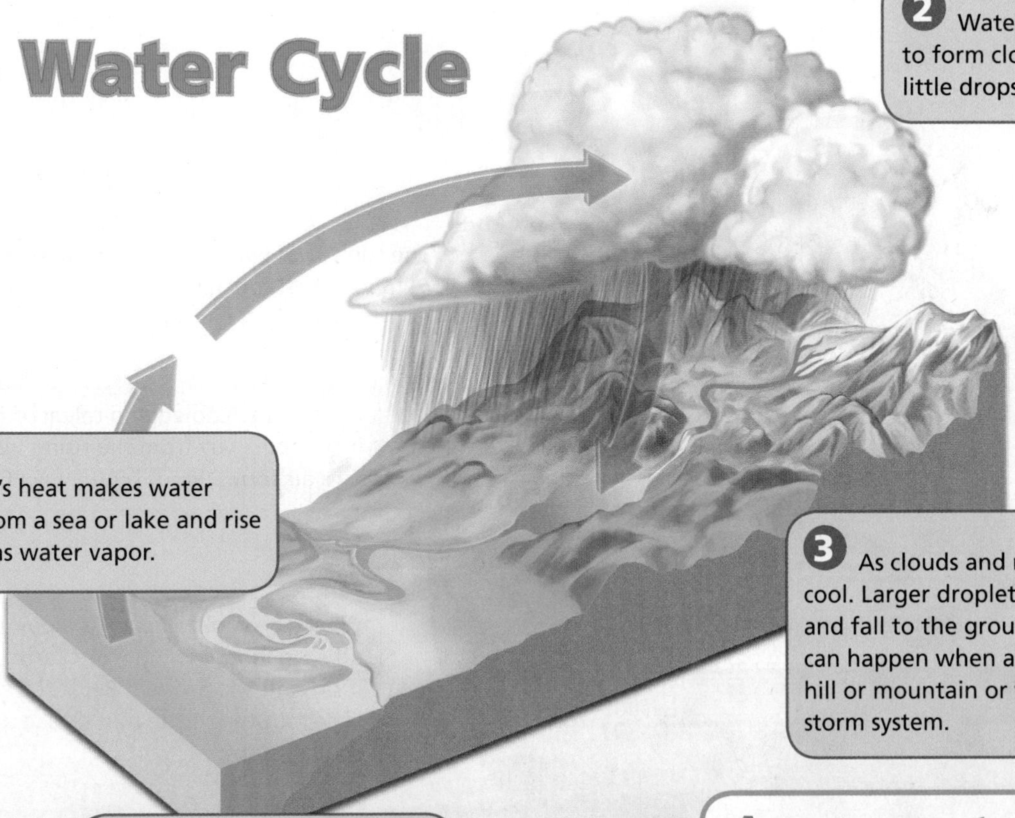

2 Water vapor condenses to form clouds made up of little drops of water.

1 The sun's heat makes water evaporate from a sea or lake and rise into the sky as water vapor.

3 As clouds and moist air rise, they cool. Larger droplets of water condense and fall to the ground as rain. This can happen when air moves up over a hill or mountain or when air rises in a storm system.

4 Water seeps into the ground or runs into streams. It then flows to a lake or ocean or evaporates.

Assessment

1. Why are coastal areas warmer than inland places in winter?

2. How does Earth's water move in the water cycle?

Air Circulation and Precipitation

> **Key Ideas**
> - Wind and air currents move heat and moisture between different parts of Earth.
> - Air movement leads to precipitation and intense storms.
>
> **Key Terms** • intertropical convergence zone • tropical cyclone • hurricane • tornado
>
> → **Visual Glossary**

Belts of rising and sinking air form a pattern around Earth. Air rises near the Equator, sinks at the edge of the tropics, rises in the temperate zones, and sinks over the poles. The **intertropical convergence zone,** or ITCZ, is the area of rising air near the Equator.

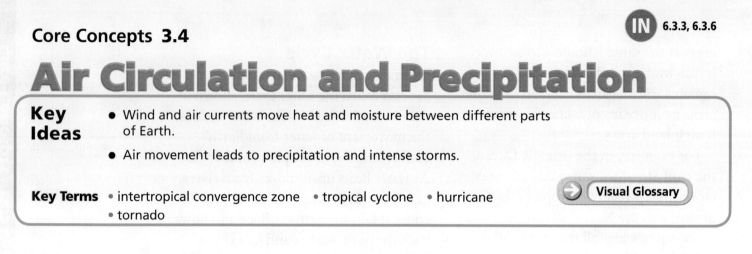

North Pole
60° N
30° N
Air cell
Rotation of Earth
Equator
Wind direction
30° S
60° S
South Pole

The sun's heat warms the air. Because warm air is lighter than cool air, warm air tends to rise.

Air that has cooled and released its moisture is pushed away from the rising warm air. This air forms winds high above Earth.

When the cool air reaches a point where air is no longer rising from Earth's surface, it sinks to the ground. Because cool air has little moisture, little rain falls in areas where cool air sinks.

As sinking air reaches the surface, it produces winds that blow along the surface and pick up moisture. These winds blow from areas of sinking air, or high pressure, to areas of rising air, or low pressure.

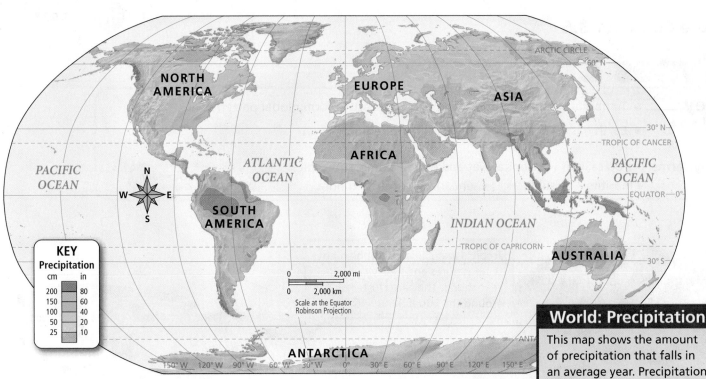

KEY
Precipitation

cm		in
200		80
150		60
100		40
50		20
25		10

0 ─────── 2,000 mi
0 ─────── 2,000 km
Scale at the Equator
Robinson Projection

World: Precipitation

This map shows the amount of precipitation that falls in an average year. Precipitation is heaviest near the Equator, where air usually rises. It is also heavy along coastlines, where moist air blows onshore and is forced to rise. Precipitation is lightest where cool air sinks near the poles and at the edges of the tropics, where deserts are normally found.

Raging Storms

Most storms occur when two air masses of different temperatures or moisture contents come together. Some storms bring small amounts of rain or snow, while others bring heavy wind and rain, causing great destruction.

A **tropical cyclone** is an intense rainstorm with strong winds that forms over oceans in the tropics. A **hurricane** is a cyclone that forms over the Atlantic Ocean. These storms can cause much damage. A **tornado** is a swirling funnel of wind that can reach 300 miles (500 km) per hour. Tornadoes can be more dangerous than hurricanes, but they affect smaller areas.

Most other storms are less dangerous. In winter, blizzards dump snow on parts of North America. Severe rainstorms and thunderstorms strike North America most often in spring and summer.

Assessment

1. Why is precipitation heaviest near the Equator?

2. How do physical processes such as air circulation and precipitation affect humans?

Tornadoes can cause severe damage.

39

Core Concepts 3.5

Types of Climate

Key Ideas
- Temperature, precipitation, and wind interact to form global patterns.
- Earth has a number of different climate regions.

Key Terms • tropical wet • tropical wet and dry • humid subtropical • maritime • subarctic • semiarid • arid • tundra

→ Visual Glossary

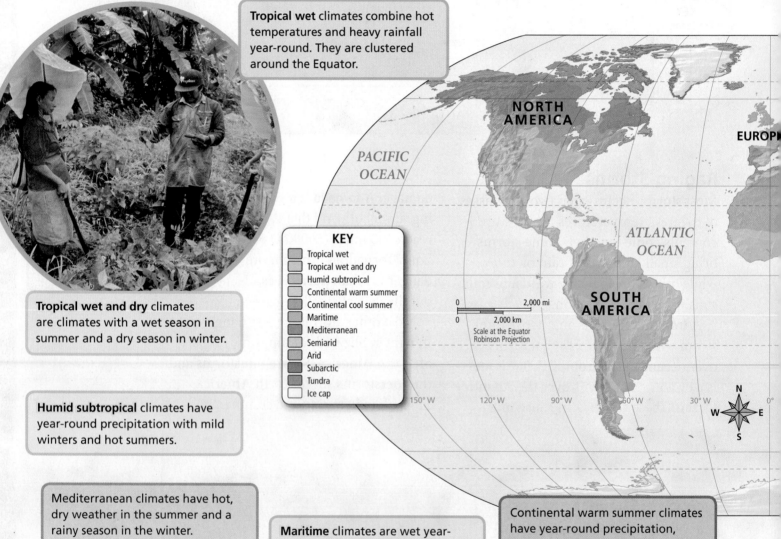

Tropical wet climates combine hot temperatures and heavy rainfall year-round. They are clustered around the Equator.

Tropical wet and dry climates are climates with a wet season in summer and a dry season in winter.

Humid subtropical climates have year-round precipitation with mild winters and hot summers.

Mediterranean climates have hot, dry weather in the summer and a rainy season in the winter.

Maritime climates are wet year-round, with mild winters and cool summers. They exist where moist winds blow onshore.

Continental warm summer climates have year-round precipitation, warm summers, and cold, snowy winters. Continental cool summer climates are similar, but they have generally lower temperatures.

KEY
- Tropical wet
- Tropical wet and dry
- Humid subtropical
- Continental warm summer
- Continental cool summer
- Maritime
- Mediterranean
- Semiarid
- Arid
- Subarctic
- Tundra
- Ice cap

NORTH AMERICA

PACIFIC OCEAN

ATLANTIC OCEAN

SOUTH AMERICA

EUROPE

0   2,000 mi
0   2,000 km
Scale at the Equator
Robinson Projection

150° W   120° W   90° W   60° W   30° W   0°

N W E S

You have already learned about the most important shapers of climate: temperature, precipitation, and wind. These factors form global patterns. For example, temperatures are warmest in and around the tropics and are coolest close to the poles. Precipitation is greatest near the Equator. These patterns of temperature and precipitation create world climate regions. Climate regions are areas that share a similar climate.

Subarctic climates have limited precipitation, cool summers, and very cold winters.

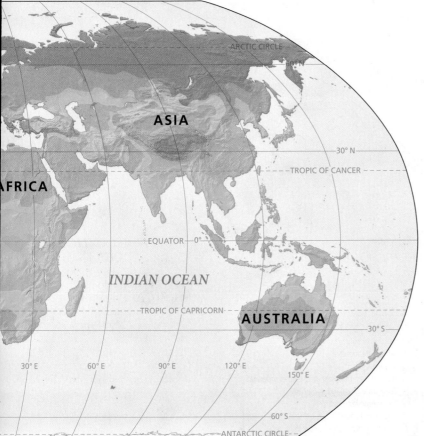

Semiarid, or dry, climates and arid, or very dry, desert climates occur where there is steadily sinking air.

Tundra climates have cool summers and bitterly cold, dry winters. Close to the poles, ice caps, or permanent sheets of ice covering land or sea, have bitter cold and dry climates year-round.

Assessment

1. In the winter, what kind of weather would you expect in a continental warm summer climate?

2. What factors explain the locations of Earth's tropical wet and tropical wet and dry climates?

Tropical or Subtropical Forest

Steady hot temperatures and moist air support the rich ecosystems known as tropical rain forests.

Temperate Forest

Moist temperate climates support thick forests of **deciduous trees,** or trees that lose their leaves in the fall. Some temperate forests include a mix of deciduous and evergreen trees.

Subarctic Forest

Coniferous trees are trees that produce cones to carry seeds. They also have needles. These features protect trees through the cold, dry winters of subarctic climates.

Tropical or Subtropical Grassland or Savanna

A **savanna** is a park-like landscape of grasslands with scattered trees that can survive dry spells. Savannas are found in tropical areas with dry seasons.

Temperate Grassland and Brush

Vast grasslands cover regions that get more rain than deserts but too little to support forests.

42

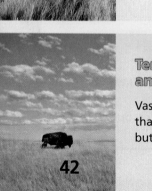

 **6.3.3, 6.3.8**

Ecosystems

Key Idea

- An ecosystem is a network of living things that depend on one another and their environment for survival.

Key Terms

- deciduous tree
- coniferous tree
- biome
- savanna
- ecosystem

→ **Visual Glossary**

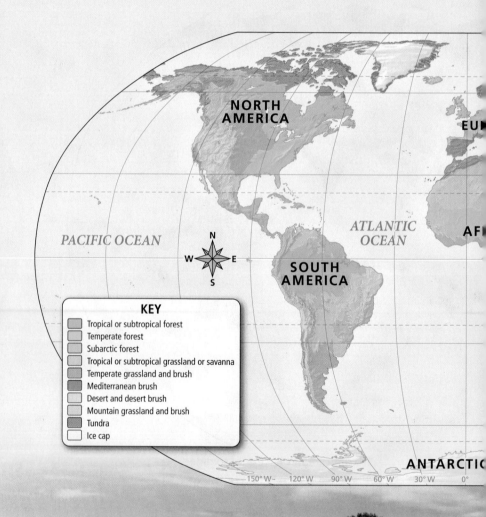

NORTH AMERICA

EU

PACIFIC OCEAN

N
W   E
S

ATLANTIC OCEAN

AF

SOUTH AMERICA

KEY
- Tropical or subtropical forest
- Temperate forest
- Subarctic forest
- Tropical or subtropical grassland or savanna
- Temperate grassland and brush
- Mediterranean brush
- Desert and desert brush
- Mountain grassland and brush
- Tundra
- Ice cap

ANTARCTIC

150° W   120° W   90° W   60° W   30° W   0°

The connections between living things and the environment form ecosystems. An **ecosystem** is a group of plants and animals that depend on each other and their environment for survival. A **biome** is similar to an ecosystem, but is a larger ecological community that is usually characterized by a dominant vegetation. This map shows Earth's major biomes.

Ecosystems and biomes can change over time due to physical processes or human activities. For example, a lack of rain in a temperate forest ecosystem might kill off many plants and animals.

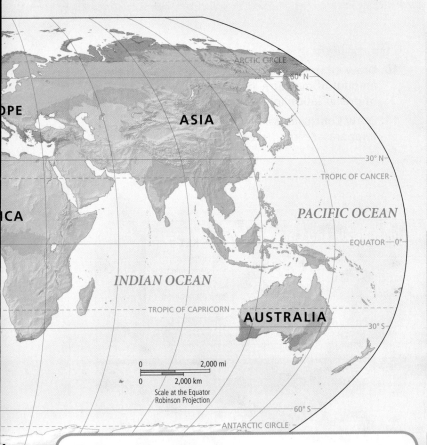

Mediterranean Brush

Shrubs and other low plants in Mediterranean climates have to hold water from winter rains to survive hot, dry summers.

Desert and Desert Brush

Dry semiarid areas and deserts with some rain support animals and low-lying desert plants. These plants need little water and can live in extreme temperatures. The driest desert areas have little or no plant life.

Mountain Grassland and Brush

In mountain grassland and brush regions, vegetation depends on elevation, since temperatures drop as altitude increases.

Tundra

The tundra is an area of cold climate and low-lying plants. Here, grasses grow and low shrubs bloom during brief, cool summers. Animals of the tundra are able to live with cold temperatures and scarce food.

Assessment

1. How do climate differences affect plant and animal life?
2. What features of the plants and animals in your own region let them live in your region's climate?

Ice Cap

Thick ice caps form around the poles, with their year-round climates of extreme cold. No plants can live on this ice.

43

Climates and Ecosystems

Part 3 Assessment

Key Terms and Ideas

1. **Summarize** What is a region's **weather**? What is a region's **climate**?

2. **Identify** What are the three most important factors of climate?

3. **Compare and Contrast** How do temperatures in the **low latitudes** differ from temperatures in the **middle latitudes**?

4. **Sequence** Rank these climates in terms of amount of precipitation, from most precipitation to least precipitation: **subarctic, arid, tropical wet.**

5. **Compare and Contrast** How are **deciduous trees** different from **coniferous trees**?

6. **Connect** What is the role of air temperature in the **water cycle**?

7. **Describe** How does the physical environment affect humans?

Think Critically

8. **Categorize** Explain in one sentence how today's weather is related to your region's climate.

9. **Predict** How would winter temperatures differ between two cities on the same continent at the same latitude, one on the coast and one inland?

10. **Draw Inferences** Use what you know about the amount of moisture in cool air to predict the level of precipitation in a tundra climate.

11. **Draw Conclusions** How does altitude affect temperature in different latitudes?

Identify

Answer the following questions based on the map.

12. What do the arrows on this map show?

13. In which zone of latitude is the West Wind Drift?

14. Is the North Atlantic Current warm or cool?

15. Is the California Current warm or cool?

16. Is the Brazil Current located in the Northern Hemisphere or the Southern Hemisphere?

17. Does the Benguela Current bring cool water to the polar zones or to the tropics?

18. What important parallel of latitude does the Kuroshio Current cross?

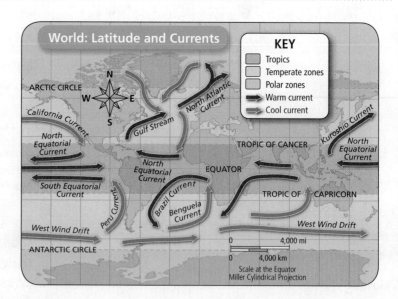

Journal Activity

Fill in the graphic organizer in your Student Journal.

Demonstrate Your Understanding Complete the Sum-It-Up activity in your journal to demonstrate your understanding of climates and ecosystems. After you complete the activity, discuss your predictions with a partner. Be sure to support your predictions with information from the lessons.

21st Century Learning

Give an Effective Presentation

Research and deliver an illustrated oral presentation on the features of one of the ecosystems described in Lesson 6. Be sure to address the following topics:
- Climate characteristics
- Effect of climate on animal and plant life
- Effect of climate on human life, including the economy

Document-Based Questions

Success Tracker™
Online at myworldgeography.com

Use your knowledge of climates and ecosystems and Documents A and B to answer Questions 1–3.

Document A

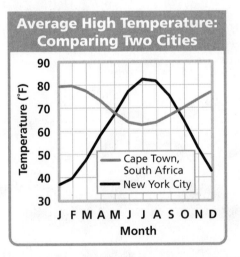

Average High Temperature: Comparing Two Cities

Document B

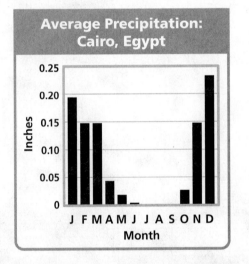

Average Precipitation: Cairo, Egypt

1. Examine Document A. Which of the following statements is true?

   A New York City and Cape Town are located in the same hemisphere.

   B New York City is in the Southern Hemisphere, while Cape Town is in the Northern Hemisphere.

   C New York City is in the Northern Hemisphere, while Cape Town is in the Southern Hemisphere.

   D none of the above

2. Examine Document B. Judging from the average precipitation Cairo receives, in which of the following climates is it most likely to be located?

   A tropical wet

   B maritime

   C arid

   D humid subtropical

3. **Writing Task** Using information from Document A as evidence, describe how a location's hemisphere affects its seasons.

my worldgeography.com Self-Test

45

Human–Environment Interaction

Young people support clean energy sources.

Oil leaks from an abandoned oil barrel in Alaska. ▲

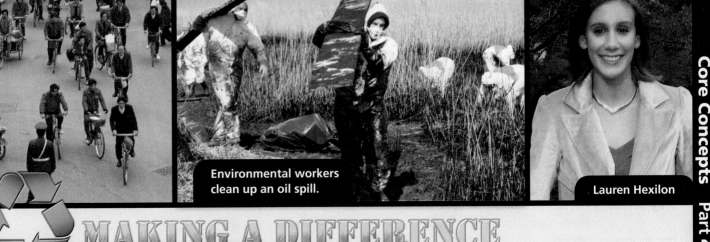

Environmental workers clean up an oil spill.

Lauren Hexilon

MAKING A DIFFERENCE

Story by Miles Lemaire for myWorld Geography

Lauren Hexilon wants to save the world.

Lauren has wanted to protect the environment for as long as she can remember. After she graduated from college recently, Lauren decided to go to work for the U.S. Environmental Protection Agency (EPA).

The EPA was an obvious choice for Lauren. After all, the organization's main focus is to protect human health and the environment. Today Lauren works with people who help protect public health and the environment in many ways. Some of their work deals with hazardous waste spills around the country. Hazardous waste includes chemicals, radioactive materials, and other waste dangerous to humans, wildlife, and the environment.

Cleaning up hazardous waste can be "a very long process," Lauren says. To dispose of waste safely, she explains, "you have to follow certain rules and procedures, so it takes a while to see a project from its beginning to its end."

Lauren doesn't clean up pollution and hazardous waste herself. Still, she helps protect the environment at her job each day. She spends much of her time working with young people to teach them about environmental issues. Raising public awareness is important, she says.

Right now Lauren is working with the University of North Texas on projects that help people understand threats to the environment. She is also helping to create an environmental video conference. This conference will connect young people from countries around the world. Lauren likes these projects because they teach people to protect the environment. Plus, she says, she gets to see the results of her work quickly.

But you don't have to work for the EPA to help prevent pollution and protect the environment. Lauren says that each of us makes choices every day that have an impact on the environment, whether we realize it or not. Take conserving energy, for example. "Flipping on a light switch, that's an environmental impact," says Lauren. "If you leave the light on, you're wasting electricity."

So what does Lauren think that young people should know about human interaction with the environment? Simply this: She would like each of us to think about how our actions affect the environment. Whenever possible, Lauren says, try to make good choices about your actions. For example, consider riding a bicycle or taking public transportation instead of driving in a car.

In fact, everyone can take small steps to improve the way they interact with the environment. We should think about "all the little things" we do each day, says Lauren. As she points out, "The little things add up."

47

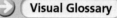

Environment and Resources

Key Ideas
- People depend on the environment for food, water, energy, and other natural resources.
- Some resources are replaced by Earth over time, but others are not.

Key Terms
- natural resource
- renewable resource
- nonrenewable resource
- fossil fuel

Visual Glossary

Humans depend on their natural environment to survive. We need the environment to provide energy, water, food, and other materials. In prehistoric times, people lived in areas where they could hunt, gather food, and find fresh water. Later, people settled where they found pasture for their livestock or fertile soils and sufficient water for farming. Today, rapid transportation and other technologies allow people to be less dependent on their immediate environment. However, people still need access to resources.

Natural Resources

Water is just one example of a **natural resource,** or a useful material found in the environment. People depend on many kinds of natural resources. These resources can be divided into two types: renewable and nonrenewable resources.

People use many natural resources in their daily lives. Above, a young woman in Chad uses soil to build a shelter. Below, German workers use metals to build an automobile.

Major Natural Resources			
Resource	Type	Formation	Major Uses
Soil	Renewable	Formed from rocks and organic material broken down by natural processes	Agriculture
Water	Renewable	Renewed through the water cycle	Drinking, agriculture, washing, transportation
Plants	Renewable	Usually grow from seeds; require water and sunlight	Food, lumber, clothing, paper
Animals	Renewable	Formed through natural reproduction; require water and food	Food, agricultural labor, transportation, clothing
Fossil fuels	Nonrenewable	Formed over millions of years from plant and animal material	Energy, plastics, chemicals
Minerals	Nonrenewable	Formed through a variety of natural geologic processes	Automobile parts, electronics, and many other human-made products

A **renewable resource** is a resource that Earth or people can replace. Examples of renewable resources include water, plants, and animals. All of these resources can be replaced over time if they are used wisely. For example, if you cut down a tree, another one can grow in its place. When dead plants decay, their nutrients increase soil fertility.

A **nonrenewable resource** is a resource that cannot be replaced in a relatively short period of time. Nonrenewable resources include nonliving things such as minerals, metal ores, and fossil fuels. **Fossil fuels** are nonrenewable resources formed over millions of years from the remains of plants and animals. Coal, natural gas, and petroleum are important fossil fuels. When nonrenewable resources such as fossil fuels are used up, they are gone.

Energy Resources

Sources of energy are important for human activity. Some sources, such as wind and sunlight, are renewable. Today, we mostly rely on nonrenewable energy resources such as coal and petroleum. Because these sources are nonrenewable, Earth will eventually run out of them.

Some countries have large supplies of petroleum and are able to export it, or sell it to other countries. Most countries, however, must buy petroleum and other energy resources from other countries.

Assessment

1. What do people need from the physical environment?
2. How are renewable and nonrenewable natural resources formed?

Land Use

Key Ideas	• People use land in different ways.
	• Land use can change over time.

Key Terms • colonization • industrialization • suburb  **Visual Glossary**

The ways people use land are affected by both the natural environment and culture. In many regions, land use has changed over time.

Reasons for Land Use

How people use land depends partly on the environment. For example, people living in temperate climates with fertile soil may use land mainly for farming. People in arctic areas may use land mainly for hunting. Even in similar environments, however, people may use land differently because they have different customs and ways of life.

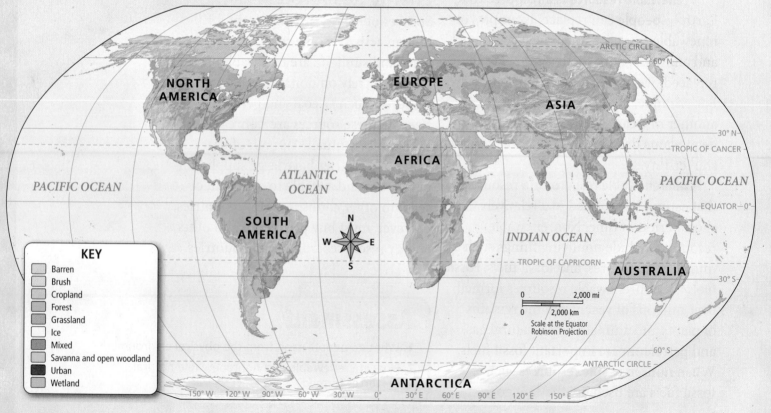

KEY

- Barren
- Brush
- Cropland
- Forest
- Grassland
- Ice
- Mixed
- Savanna and open woodland
- Urban
- Wetland

Changes in Land Use

Land use can change over time. For example, colonization has led to many changes in land use. **Colonization** is a movement of new settlers and their culture to an area. Settlers may change a region's landscape. For example, European colonists brought new crops and new ways of farming to the Americas, Africa, and Australia. These new ways led to dramatic changes in land use as Europeans cleared large areas of land for cropland and livestock pasture.

Since the 1800s, industrialization has changed landscapes in many countries. **Industrialization** is the development of machine-powered production and manufacturing. Large cities have grown around factories. Technology such as machines for clearing land and building roads has made it easier for people to change their environment. This environmental change has allowed the growth of suburbs. A **suburb** is a residential area on the edge of a city or large town.

In the United States and some other countries, most people live in cities or suburban areas. Although cities and suburbs cover a relatively small area, they are an important use of land. Land uses covering large areas include cropland, forests, and grassland.

Land use varies around the world. Above, Tokyo, Japan, is a large city with millions of residents. Below, these people from the Dominican Republic use land for agriculture.

A large portion of Rio de Janeiro, Brazil, is built on steep hills along the Atlantic Ocean. ▼

Assessment

1. How does land use vary from place to place and over time?

2. How have people adapted to and changed the environment?

People's Impact on the Environment

Key Ideas
- People affect the environment in many ways.
- People try to decrease the negative effects of using resources.

Key Terms • deforestation • biodiversity • pollution • spillover

→ (Visual Glossary)

All people need food, water, clothing, and shelter. To meet these needs, people have to use materials from their environment. As a result, people have impacts on the environment in their daily lives.

Extracting Resources

People extract, or remove, many kinds of natural resources from the environment. For example, to get wood for building houses, people cut down trees. Advances in technology have allowed people to extract some resources more easily. For example, to get petroleum for fuel, people drill deep wells, sometimes far into the ocean floor.

Extracting resources can harm ecosystems and the environment. For example, cutting down too many trees can cause deforestation. **Deforestation** is the loss of forest cover in a region. Animals that live in the forest may suffer as a result. Drilling oil wells and transporting oil can lead to oil spills, which harm the land and water. Deforestation and producing oil can also reduce biodiversity. **Biodiversity** is the variety of living things in a region or ecosystem.

A bird is covered in oil from an oil spill in Spain. Oil spills and other pollution can affect land, water, and animals. ▼

Other Impacts

People also affect the environment by growing food or producing other goods and services. For example, new technology has allowed farmers to plow more land for crops. But when land is cleared, soil is loosened and can erode, or wash away.

People's activities can also produce **pollution,** or waste that makes the air, soil, or water less clean. For example, many farmers use chemicals called fertilizers and pesticides to help plants grow and to kill pests. These chemicals can help farmers produce more food. They can also harm the environment by causing pollution.

Pollution is a **spillover,** which is an effect on someone or something not involved in an activity. For example, air pollution affects everyone who breathes the polluted air, even people who did not cause the pollution.

Finding the Best Solution

People try to increase the positive and decrease the negative effects of using resources. For example, using a resource might lead to economic growth but also create pollution that needs to be reduced. Working together, people, governments, and businesses can try to use resources wisely. In some cases, governments limit land use to preserve the environment.

▲ These wind turbines in Canada convert wind energy into electricity.

Advances in technology can also help protect resources and the environment. One way of protecting the environment is for people to use vehicles that burn less fuel, such as hybrid cars. Vehicles that burn less fuel create less air pollution. People can also use clean energy sources, such as solar power and wind power. They are considered clean energy sources because they do not pollute the air.

Assessment

1. How have new technologies affected people's ability to change the environment?

2. How might future uses of technology affect Earth?

Part 4 Assessment

Key Terms and Ideas

1. **Identify** List two **fossil fuels.**
2. **Recall** What is an example of a **natural resource**?
3. **Discuss** How might **colonization** affect a region?
4. **Paraphrase** In your own words, describe the causes and effects of **deforestation.**
5. **Sequence** Explain how **suburbs** develop.
6. **Summarize** How do people use natural resources?
7. **Cause and Effect** If a company pollutes a river, what is one possible **spillover**?

Think Critically

8. **Draw Inferences** Give two examples of ways technology has made people less dependent on the environment around them.
9. **Analyze Cause and Effect** Imagine that your state's supply of fossil fuels was suddenly cut in half. How might this affect daily life in your state?
10. **Solve Problems** Explain what the following statement means: *While trees are a renewable resource, it often takes human effort to make them renewable.*
11. **Synthesize** Imagine that a large factory is about to be constructed on the edge of a rain forest. How might this factory affect the region's biodiversity?

Identify

Answer the following questions based on the map.

12. India is a former British colony. Why do you think it was a valuable colony for Britain?
13. What natural resources are found in India?
14. What geographic features could also be natural resources?
15. How do you think land might be used in the Himalayas?
16. How do you think land might be used along the coast?
17. What environmental problems might use of India's natural resources cause?
18. How might altitude affect where people live in India?

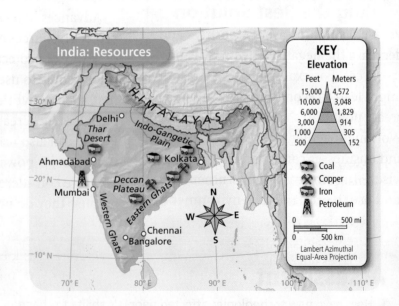

Journal Activity

Answer the questions in your Student Journal.

Demonstrate Your Understanding Complete the Sum-It-Up activity in your journal to demonstrate your understanding of human–environment interaction. After you complete the activity, discuss your answers in a small group. Be sure to support your answers with information from the lessons.

21st Century Learning

Search for Information on the Internet

Pollution can cause many harmful effects. Use online resources to research some of the effects of pollution and present your findings in a poster. When researching, remember the following:
- Use reputable Web sites, particularly those with addresses ending in *.gov* or *.edu*.
- Identify the site's author and check for bias.

Document-Based Questions

Success Tracker™
Online at myworldgeography.com

Use your knowledge of human–environment interaction and Documents A and B to answer Questions 1–3.

Document A

Pesticide Use in England and Wales, 1990–2005

SOURCE: The Environment Agency

Document B

1. **Examine** Document A. How has pesticide use changed in England and Wales in recent years?

   A It has increased.

   B It has decreased.

   C It has stopped completely.

   D It has not changed.

2. **Examine** Document B. Which of the following statements is true?

   A Major cities are spread out evenly across Massachusetts.

   B Most major cities are located far from Boston.

   C Most major cities are near Boston.

   D The location of Boston does not appear to have affected the locations of other cities.

3. **Writing Task** How might settlement and land use in Massachusetts be different if Boston were not its largest city? Explain your answer.

my worldgeography.com   Self-Test

Economics and Geography

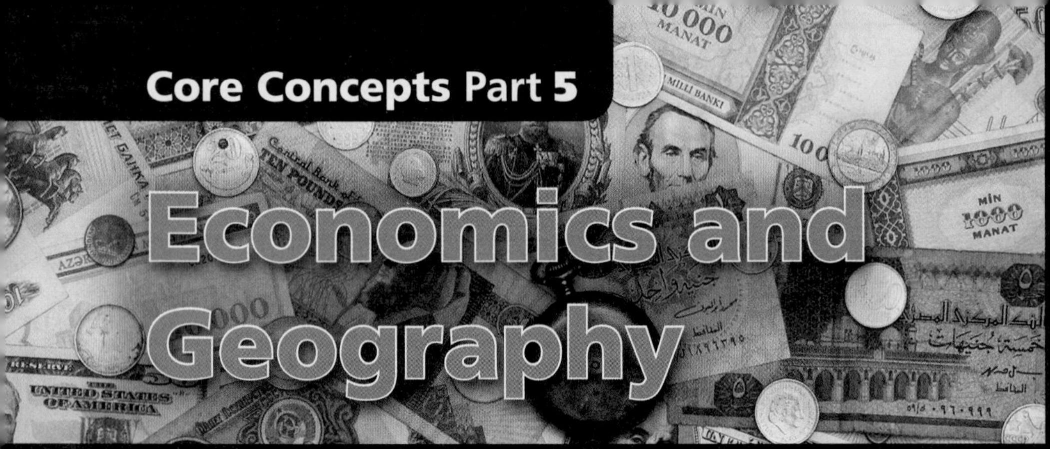

Surf shops are common in southern California.

Chris's childhood love of surfing helped inspire his first business.

56

Chris's business specializes in Web site design.

Chris Kerstner

An Extraordinary Entrepreneur

Story by Miles Lemaire for myWorld Geography

Chris Kerstner is still in his early twenties, but he has already created and successfully run four companies. In fact, Chris started his first business when he was still in middle school.

Chris is an entrepreneur, or a person who starts new businesses. "I surfed when I was a kid," Chris says, "so I'd repair surfboards for friends, and that kind of blossomed to the point where I was the main repair guy for all the local surf shops in Newport Beach [California]."

By the time he was old enough to drive, Chris had started a second business, this time on dry land: working on car stereos. This business grew quickly, Chris says. "It was like I had [an auto parts store] running out of my garage!"

Then, one night at a friend's party, Chris had an experience that led to his most successful company yet. "One of my friend's parents was talking to me about his small business and the Web designers that he had to deal with," Chris says. "He was telling me that they did great work but that they were never on time, and that he would pay anything for a Web designer who could get the work done on time. All I heard, as an entrepreneur, was 'I'll pay anything,' so immediately I turned around and said, 'Oh, yeah, I can do that. No problem!'"

The only problem was that Chris did not know anything about Web design. In fact, he did not even own a computer! But he did not let those obstacles stop him. Within a few weeks, Chris had taught himself how to design Web sites and had produced a Web site for his client.

It was this job that gave Chris the idea for his next company, which specializes in Web design and marketing. Chris created the company while attending business school at the University of Southern California. The company earned nearly $2 million during his first year of school alone. Today, Chris's business has offices in three countries. It has designed Web sites and marketing plans for many major companies.

Chris thinks that the business has been successful because of his belief in providing customers with fast, reliable service. That's the only way a company can survive in the fast-paced modern economy, he says.

So what advice would Chris give to someone else starting a business? Chris says that he loved his professors at business school, but that there was one thing he wished he had been taught in class: "Keep the customers happy. That's it! It's not complicated. … Just keep your customers happy, and that's it."

Economic Basics

Key Ideas
- People make choices about how to meet their wants and needs.
- Economies bring together people and businesses that make, sell, and buy goods and services.

Key Terms
- economics
- scarcity
- opportunity cost
- demand
- supply
- producer
- consumer
- incentive

→ **Visual Glossary**

Economics is the study of how people meet their wants and needs. People must answer three basic economic questions:

1. What goods and services should be produced?
2. How should goods and services be produced?
3. Who uses or consumes those goods and services?

The resources people use to make goods and services are called factors of production. The three main factors are land, labor, and capital. Geographers study where the factors of production are located.

Making Choices

There is no limit to the things that people want, but there are limits to what can be created. This difference between wants and reality creates **scarcity,** or having a limited quantity of resources to meet unlimited wants. Since people have limited money and time, they have to choose

Factors of Production

Entrepreneur
A person known as an entrepreneur combines resources to create new businesses.

Land, Labor, Capital
The three main factors of production are land and resources; human labor; and capital, or human-made goods like tools and buildings.

Goods and Services
Entrepreneurs use the factors of production to produce goods and services.

what they want most. Making a choice involves an **opportunity cost,** or the cost of what you have to give up.

Economics also involves demand and supply. **Demand** is the desire for a certain good or service. **Supply** is the amount of a good or service that is available for use. Demand and supply are connected to price. As the price of a product increases, people will buy less of it. That is, demand will decrease. If the price of the product decreases, demand will increase.

Supply functions in a similar way. If the price of a product increases, companies will make more of it. If the price of the product decreases, companies will make less of it. The price at which demand equals supply is the market price, or the market-clearing price.

Basic economic choices have influenced world events. For example, high demand for resources such as gold or oil has led to exploration and colonization.

Making Goods and Services

Economies bring together producers and consumers. **Producers** are people or businesses that make and sell products. **Consumers** are people or businesses that buy, or consume, products. Producers try to win consumers' business by offering better products for lower prices than other producers. If they sell more products, they

Supply and Demand of Apples

Price per Apple / Apples Sold

■ Supply   ■ Demand

usually increase production. But producers will not make more products if the sale price is less than the marginal cost. Marginal cost is the cost of making one more unit of the product. Therefore, the marginal cost for the producer sets a minimum price for the product.

Businesses make products because of economic incentives. An **incentive** is a factor that encourages people to act in a certain way. Money is an incentive. The desire to earn money gives most producers an incentive to make and sell products. The incentive to save money leads most consumers to look for lower prices.

Assessment

1. On the line graph on this page, what is the market-clearing price?

2. How might a change in the price of one good or service lead to changes in prices of other goods or services?

Economic Process

Key Ideas
- Producers and consumers exchange goods and services in a market.
- Competition is a key part of the economic process.
- Economic activity occurs at four levels.

Key Terms
- market
- competition
- profit
- inflation
- revenue
- recession
- specialization

▶ Visual Glossary

The economic process is complicated, but its basic idea is simple: Producers and consumers exchange goods and services in a market. A **market** is an organized way for producers and consumers to trade goods and services.

Exchanging Goods and Services

Throughout history, people have often engaged in barter, the trading of goods and services for other goods and services. Today, the means of exchange in a market is usually money. Modern governments issue money in the form of currency, or paper bills and metal coins. Different countries use different currencies. As a result, countries must establish the relative values of their currencies in order to trade. They must also establish a system for exchanging different currencies.

Businesses and the Economic Process

Businesses want to make a profit. **Profit** is the money a company has left after subtracting the costs of doing business. To make a profit, companies try to reduce expenses and increase revenue. **Revenue** is the money earned by selling goods and services. The price of resources affects revenue and profit. If resources become more expensive, the cost of making goods with them will also increase. Businesses' profits will drop.

Companies can increase profit and revenue through **specialization,** the act of concentrating on a limited number of goods or activities. Specialization allows people and companies to use resources more efficiently and to increase production and consumption.

Companies' profits are affected by **competition,** which is the struggle among producers for consumers' money. If one company raises the price of its products, another company may sell similar goods

Economists divide economic activity into four levels, as you can see in this table. ▼

Levels of Economic Activity	
Primary Industry	Collects resources from nature. Examples: farming, mining
Secondary Industry	Uses raw materials to create new products. Example: manufacturing
Tertiary Industry	Provides services to people and secondary industries. Examples: banking, restaurants
Quaternary Industry	Focuses on research and information. Example: education

Competition in the Market

Producers use resources to make different goods and services.

Buyers and sellers interact to trade goods and services in a market.

Competition between buyers and between sellers affects product price, quality, and marketing.

for a lower price to win more business. Companies use advertising to help increase demand for their products and to compete with other companies.

Nonprofit organizations are business-like institutions that do not seek to make a profit. Nonprofit organizations can include churches, museums, hospitals, and other bodies.

A healthy economy grows as companies produce and sell more goods and services. In a growing economy, prices may increase over time. This general increase in prices is called **inflation.**

Economies do not keep growing forever. Eventually, economic activity falls as production slows and consumers buy fewer goods and services. This lack of demand for goods and services can lead to increased unemployment. A decline in economic growth for six or more months in a row is known as a **recession.**

Assessment

1. Does a person always need money to obtain goods or services?

2. How does competition affect producers and consumers?

Economic Systems

Key Ideas
- Different societies have different types of economic systems.
- Most societies have economic systems with some element of government control.

Key Terms
- traditional economy
- market economy
- command economy
- mixed economy

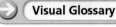
Visual Glossary

Every society has an economic system in which people make and distribute goods and services. There are four basic economic systems: traditional, market, command, and mixed. The roles of individuals, businesses, and government vary in each system. Economic goals, incentives, and government regulations can also vary.

Traditional Economies

A **traditional economy** is an economy in which people make economic decisions based on their customs and habits. They usually satisfy their needs and wants through hunting or farming, as their ancestors did. People in traditional economies usually do not want to change their basic way of life. Today, traditional economies are not common.

The Fulani people in Niger are livestock herders. ▶

Market Economies

A **market economy** is an economy in which individual consumers and producers make economic decisions. This type of economy is also called capitalism, or a free market. Market economies encourage entrepreneurs to establish new businesses by giving them economic freedom.

A consumer makes a purchase at a grocery store. ▶

Command Economies

A **command economy** is an economy in which the central government makes all economic decisions. This kind of system is also called a centrally planned economy. In a command economy, individual consumers and producers do not make basic economic decisions.

◀ In North Korea, government leaders make most economic decisions.

Mixed Economies

In reality, pure market or command economies do not exist. Most societies have mixed economies with varying levels of government control. A **mixed economy** is an economy that combines elements of traditional, market, and command economic systems. The diagram at left shows the circular flow of economic activity in a mixed economy.

Countries such as the United States and Australia have mixed economies that are close to pure market economies. In these countries, government makes some economic decisions. For example, government passes laws to protect consumers' rights. Government spending and taxation provide jobs and services and influence economic growth.

Countries such as North Korea and Cuba have mixed economies that are close to pure command economies. In these countries, government owns and controls most businesses.

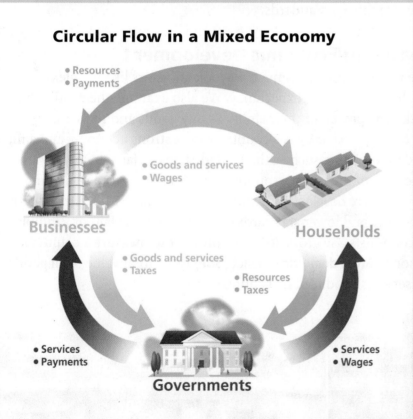

Circular Flow in a Mixed Economy

- Resources
- Payments

- Goods and services
- Wages

Businesses

Households

- Goods and services
- Taxes

- Resources
- Taxes

- Services
- Payments

- Services
- Wages

Governments

Assessment

1. What are the differences among traditional, command, and market economies?

2. What are some possible advantages of the free-market system used in the United States and other countries?

Economic Development

> **Key Ideas**
> - The level of a country's development has direct effects on the lives of its people.
> - There are many ways for a country to increase economic development.
>
> **Key Terms** • development • developed country • developing country • gross domestic product (GDP) • productivity • technology
>
> → **Visual Glossary**

Economists use the concept of development to talk about a country's economic well-being. **Development** is economic growth or an increase in living standards.

Measuring Economic Development

When we study development, we look at factors like people's education, literacy, and life expectancy. We also examine their individual purchasing power, or their ability to buy goods and services.

A **developed country** is a country with a strong economy and a high standard of living, such as the United States or Japan. Only about 20 percent of the world's countries are developed. The remaining 80 percent are **developing countries,** or countries with less-productive economies and lower standards of living, such as Haiti or Ethiopia.

Economists use gross domestic product to measure a country's economy. **Gross domestic product (GDP)** is the total value of all goods and services produced in a country in a year.

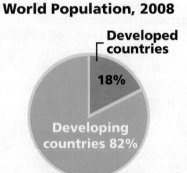

World Population, 2008

Developed countries 18%

Developing countries 82%

SOURCE: UN Population Division

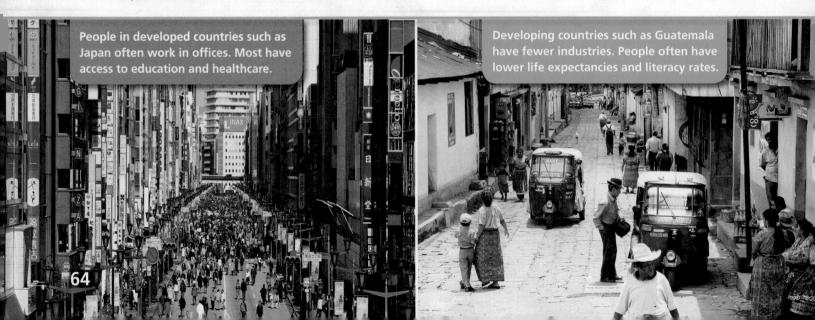

People in developed countries such as Japan often work in offices. Most have access to education and healthcare.

Developing countries such as Guatemala have fewer industries. People often have lower life expectancies and literacy rates.

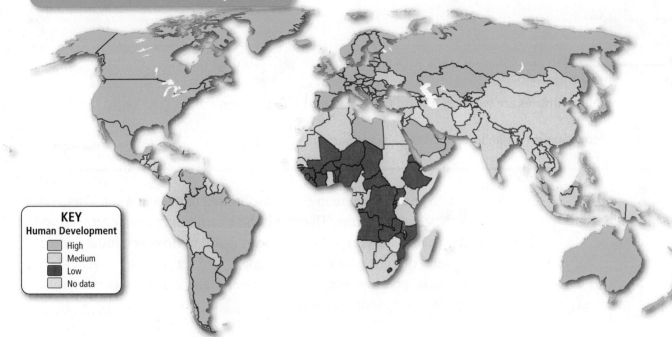

World: Human Development

KEY
Human Development
- High
- Medium
- Low
- No data

Increasing Development

A country can increase economic development in many ways. It can find more resources to use in creating products. It can invest in capital goods such as factories and equipment. It can improve education and training to increase human capital. Human capital is workers' skill and knowledge.

Highly skilled workers usually earn higher wages, or money paid for work. Wages are also affected by supply and demand. If there is a high demand for workers and a limited supply of applicants, companies must pay higher wages to attract workers.

A country can improve development by increasing **productivity,** or the amount of goods and services produced given the amount of resources used. A business that increases productivity can produce goods and services more efficiently. More productive workers often earn higher wages.

Improved technology can lead to economic growth. **Technology** is the practical application of knowledge to accomplish a task. Technological advances can create new products, such as computers. They can make it easier for people to communicate and do business. However, it can be difficult for poor countries to afford new technology.

Assessment

1. What factors do economists use to study development?

2. How might economic factors affect the use of technology in various places, cultures, and societies?

Trade

Key Ideas
- Individuals and countries trade with one another to get the things they need and want.
- Many countries are working toward the removal of trade barriers.

Key Terms • trade • export • import • tariff • trade barrier • free trade

→ **Visual Glossary**

In the past, most people grew or hunted their own food. They made their own clothing. They built their own homes. In short, people did nearly everything for themselves. Today, however, most people depend on others to supply the goods and services they need. Our world is interdependent. That is, people and countries depend on one another for goods and services.

Trade and Geography

To get the products we need and want, we engage in trade. **Trade** is the exchange of goods and services in a market. When individuals engage in trade, they do so because they gain from that trade. In other words, trade benefits both the buyer and the seller.

Geographic location can give a country or region advantages in trade. For example, a region that is close to an ocean can more easily ship goods overseas. On the other hand, a manufacturing plant located far away from a market will need to add transportation costs to its products, making them higher in price.

Container ships, such as the ones in this photo, carry most of the world's goods from one port to another. ▼

Types of Trade

All of the buying and selling that takes place within a country is known as domestic trade. Domestic trade involves producers and consumers located inside the same country.

Domestic producers and consumers can also engage in international trade, or trade with foreign producers and consumers. International trade involves exports and imports. **Exports** are goods and services produced within a country and sold outside the country's borders. **Imports** are goods and services sold in a country that are produced in other countries. International trade requires a system for exchanging types of currency.

Trade Barriers and Free Trade

If imported goods are cheaper than domestic goods, consumers will usually buy more of them. These lower prices can harm domestic producers by reducing their sales. Governments sometimes try to protect domestic producers through tariffs. A **tariff** is a tax on imports or exports. Tariffs are an example of trade barriers. A **trade barrier** is a government policy or restriction that limits international trade.

Today, many countries are working toward **free trade,** or the removal of trade barriers. Free trade gives consumers lower prices and more choices. However, domestic producers can suffer if consumers prefer cheaper imported goods.

United States and China: Trade

Goods exported from China to the United States
- Household goods, $58.4 billion
- Computers, $53.7 billion
- Clothing and shoes, $51.5 billion

Goods exported from the United States to China
- Computers, $8.6 billion
- Aircraft, $7.5 billion
- Machinery, $7.2 billion

Assessment

1. How might geography affect the locations of economic activities?

2. How might scarcity encourage international trade and make countries interdependent?

Money Management

Key Ideas
- People must manage money to have enough for their needs and wants.
- Many people save and invest money.

Key Terms • budget • saving • interest • credit • investing • stock • bond   → **Visual Glossary**

A man uses an automated teller machine (ATM) to access his bank account. ▼

Money is anything that is generally accepted as payment for goods and services. Money is a scarce resource that people must manage to have enough for their needs and wants. Because people's needs, wants, and incomes can change, it is important to plan ahead.

Budgeting, Saving, and Lending

A key tool in money management is a budget. A **budget** is a plan that shows income and expenses over a period of time. A budget's income should be equal to or greater than its expenses. A budget should also include money reserved for saving. **Saving** is the act of setting aside money for future use. Many people save by using banks. A bank is a business that keeps money, makes loans, and offers other financial services. Credit unions are nonprofit banks owned by their members.

How Banks Work

Deposit

Loan

BANK

Interest

Payments

Depositor

Borrower

Many people who save money in banks do so using checking or savings accounts. Banks may pay interest on money deposited in these accounts. **Interest** is the price paid for borrowing money. Interest is an incentive for people to save money. Banks also offer certificates of deposit (CDs), a type of savings account that pays a guaranteed interest rate, but requires that the saver keep the money in the bank for a certain length of time.

Banks use deposits to make loans to people and businesses around the world. These loans help people buy houses or make other large purchases. They help businesses get started or grow. As a result, banks are a big part of economic growth.

Loans are a form of credit. **Credit** is an arrangement in which a buyer can borrow to purchase something and pay for it over time, such as by using a credit card. Banks and other lending organizations charge borrowers interest on loans. As a result, it costs more for a borrower to purchase a good using credit than to pay cash for the good at the time of purchase.

Investing

Investing is the act of using money in the hope of making a future profit. Some people invest in stocks, bonds, or mutual funds. A **stock** is a share of ownership in a company. A **bond** is a certificate issued by a company or government promising to pay back borrowed money with interest. A mutual fund is a company that invests members' money in stocks, bonds, and other investments.

Investing options offer different levels of risk and return—the amount of money an investor might earn. In general, the safest investments offer the lowest rates of return. Compared to other investments, savings accounts offer lower interest rates and lower risks. Stocks are riskier but can earn a great deal of money for an investor if they increase in value. On the other hand, stocks can decline in value and become worth less than the stockholder paid. Bonds are less risky than stocks, but they usually offer a lower rate of return.

▲ Stockbrokers buy and sell stocks and bonds for investors at places such as the New York Stock Exchange.

Assessment

1. How do banks function?

2. Why do people invest money in stocks, bonds, and mutual funds?

Economics and Geography

Part 5 Assessment

Key Terms and Ideas

1. **Recall** What is the most common type of economy today?

2. **Define** What is a **tariff** and why do governments sometimes use them?

3. **Paraphrase** Explain the relationship among **revenue, profit,** and the costs of doing business.

4. **Sequence** How does increased **productivity** affect business owners, employees, **consumers,** and entire nations?

5. **Explain** What is **opportunity cost**?

6. **Identify Cause and Effect** What role does risk play in investment?

7. **Identify** What level of economic activity includes mining? What level includes medical care?

Think Critically

8. **Draw Conclusions** What problems or issues might a company face if it has a shortage of one or more factors of production?

9. **Decision Making** How do societies organize and make decisions about the production of goods and services?

10. **Draw Inferences** How do factors such as location, physical features, and distribution of natural resources influence the economic development of societies?

11. **Summarize** How do government policies affect free market economies such as the U.S. economy?

Identify

Answer the following questions based on the map.

12. What kind of trade is shown on this map?

13. What is a major U.S. export?

14. What is a major U.S. import?

15. What are three goods that the United States produces?

16. What are three goods that Mexico produces?

17. What possible area of competition is shown on this map?

18. The United States and Mexico participate in free trade. What U.S. industries might free trade help or hurt?

United States and Mexico: Trade

UNITED STATES

MEXICO

U.S. exports to Mexico:
Petroleum products
Plastics
Chemicals
Automobile parts
Electronics

Mexican exports to the United States:
Petroleum
Fruits and vegetables
Electronics
Computers
Automobiles

Journal Activity

Fill in the graphic organizer in your Student Journal.

Demonstrate Your Understanding Complete the Sum-It-Up activity in your journal to demonstrate your understanding of economics and geography. After you complete the activity, discuss your answers with the class. Be sure to support your answers with information from the lessons.

21st Century Learning

Search for Information on the Internet

China had a command economy for many years, but since the 1970s the government has reduced its control over the economy. Use the Internet to research China's changing economy. Create a timeline to share your findings. Use a variety of online sources, including
- encyclopedias
- national and international newspapers
- magazines and journals

Document-Based Questions

Success Tracker™
Online at myworldgeography.com

Use your knowledge of economics and geography and Documents A and B to answer Questions 1–3.

Document A

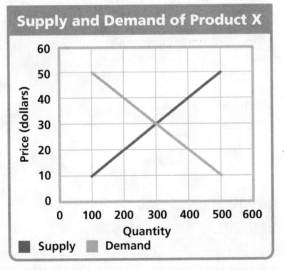

Supply and Demand of Product X

Document B

UN Human Development Index (HDI) Values, 2005	
Nation	HDI Value
Iceland	0.968
Samoa	0.785
Sierra Leone	0.336

SOURCE: *CIA World Factbook*

2. Examine Document B. The Human Development Index is a UN measure of levels of economic development and well-being in a country. Countries with higher HDI values have higher levels of development. Which of the following statements is true?

   A Samoa is less developed than Sierra Leone.

   B Samoa is more developed than Iceland.

   C Sierra Leone and Iceland are very different in terms of development level.

   D Sierra Leone is more developed than Iceland.

3. **Writing Task** A nation's rating in the UN Human Development Index is influenced by GDP per capita and people's education, literacy, and life expectancy. Why are these factors important to a country's development?

1. Examine Document A. Which of the following statements is true?

   A As the price of Product X increases, demand for it decreases.

   B As the price of Product X decreases, its supply increases.

   C As the price of Product X increases, demand for it increases.

   D As the price of Product X decreases, its supply does not change.

my worldgeography.com   Self-Test

Population and Movement

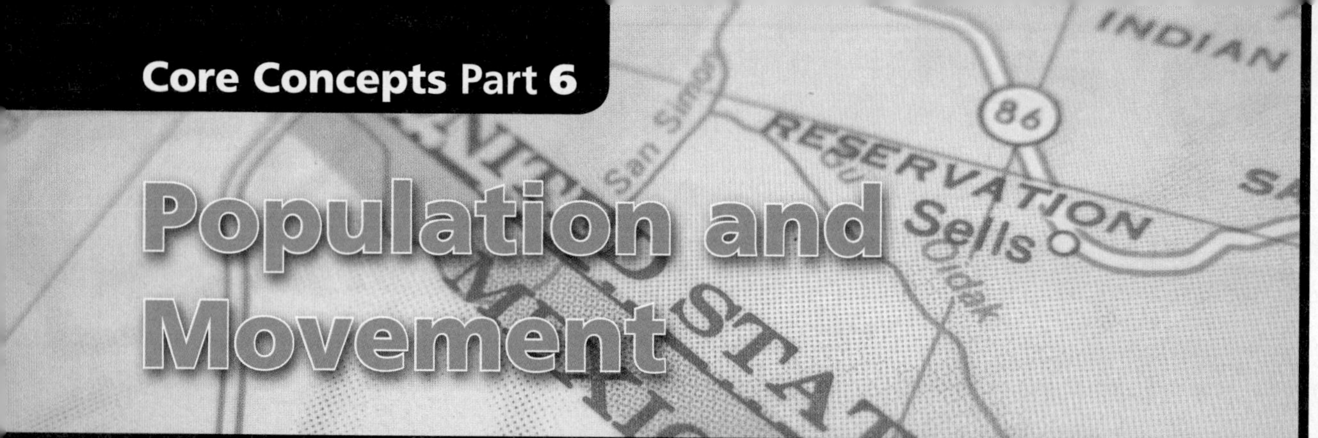
INDIAN
86
RESERVATION
Sells

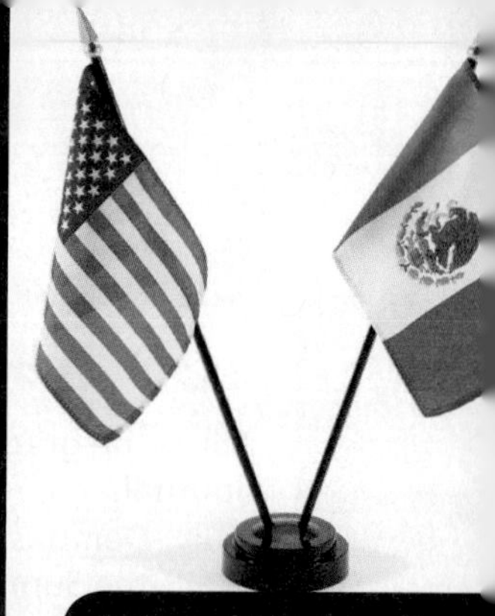

U.S. and Mexican flags

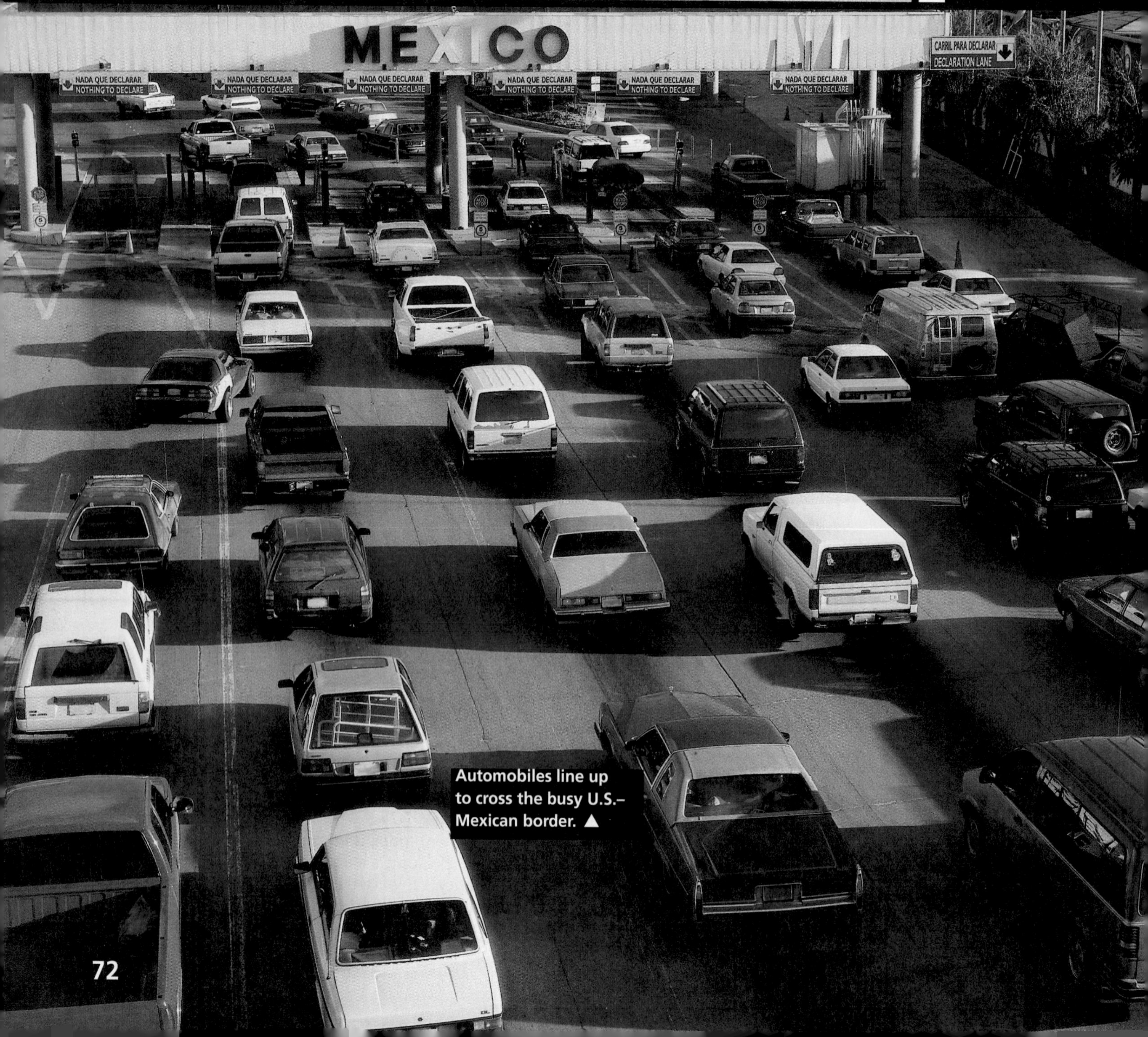
MEXICO
NADA QUE DECLARAR
NOTHING TO DECLARE
CARRIL PARA DECLARAR
DECLARATION LANE

Automobiles line up to cross the busy U.S.–Mexican border. ▲

U.S. students in a classroom

Ludwig Barragan

Searching for a New Home

Story by Miles Lemaire for myWorld Geography

Anyone who has ever moved to a new place knows that it can be hard to make friends and adjust to a new school. Moving to a different country can be even more challenging. You can ask Ludwig Barragan, who moved to the United States from Mexico a few years ago.

Like many other people, Ludwig and his mother decided to move in search of more opportunities and a better life. "My position in Mexico was fine economically," says Ludwig, "but I wanted to receive an education that I knew I wouldn't be able to get in Mexico. I love my country, yet the [school] system there was not what I wanted."

Ludwig and his mother moved to McAllen, Texas, a city on the U.S.–Mexican border. He looked forward to learning more about American culture and society.

Life in McAllen was an adjustment for Ludwig and his mother. "I would say that when you live so close to the border you live in a different world," Ludwig says. "You live in a place that is neither the U.S. nor Mexico."

Ludwig found that there were a number of different cultural groups in McAllen. "The number of immigrants [in] McAllen was huge," Ludwig says, "and there was a large community in my high school that spoke only Spanish. There was a second group there that were bilingual, and they were mainly people who were born in the U.S. but had parents that were from Mexico or spoke Spanish. It was hard to relate to them because … they didn't know the Mexican culture or values that I knew, yet they were not completely incorporated into the American culture."

At first, Ludwig felt that he didn't fit in. "I knew that I had to learn the language and the values even more. I tried to get in contact with the students that spoke mostly English. That's what I did and that's what helped me a lot."

Ludwig looked for ways that he could learn about the customs of his adopted country. He eventually joined the Junior Reserve Officers Training Corps (JROTC). The JROTC is a citizenship and military program supported by the U.S. armed forces. Ludwig says that the JROTC taught him much about life in the United States.

"My friends in Mexico made fun of me because here I was, a Mexican, carrying the U.S. flag with the JROTC," remembers Ludwig. "At first I said, 'Yeah, it's kind of weird,' but then later I realized that I don't have to feel bad about it. I chose this country because I love it and it doesn't mean that I love Mexico any less. I think … the beauty of immigration is that you can learn to love both cultures. I feel honored that I had a chance to carry the U.S. flag."

Population Growth

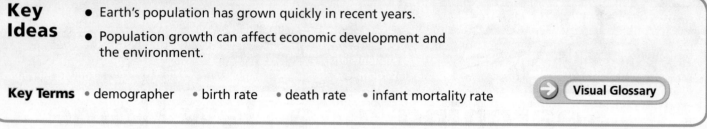

Key Ideas
- Earth's population has grown quickly in recent years.
- Population growth can affect economic development and the environment.

Key Terms • demographer • birth rate • death rate • infant mortality rate

→ **Visual Glossary**

Today, the world's population is around 7 billion. When people first began farming around 12,000 years ago, it was fewer than 10 million. Earth's population grew slowly, eventually reaching 1 billion by 1800. Since then, better food production and healthcare have caused a population boom.

Measuring Growth

Demographers are scientists who study human populations. They measure the rate at which a population is growing. To do this, demographers compare birth rates and death rates. The **birth rate** is the number of live births per 1,000 people in a year. The **death rate** is the number of deaths per 1,000 people in a year. When the birth rate is higher than the death rate, a population tends to grow. Population can also change when people move into or out of a region.

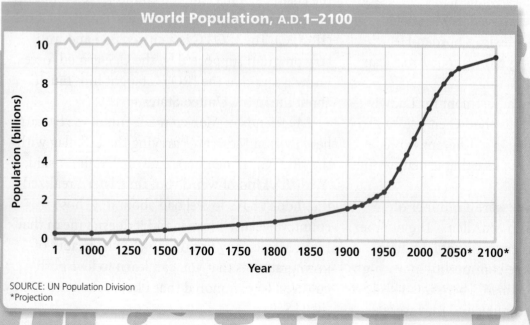

World Population, A.D. 1–2100

Population (billions) vs. Year

SOURCE: UN Population Division
*Projection

Causes and Effects of Population Growth

Improvements in hygiene, such as this water purifier in Uganda, can lead to population growth.

Causes of Growth

Until about two hundred years ago, the global birth rate was only slightly higher than the death rate. As a result, the population grew slowly. Then came the Industrial Revolution, which brought many changes.

Better medical care saved many lives. Improvements in food production increased the food supply and made food healthier. Living conditions improved. These and other changes led to a much lower death rate in most regions. By 1950, the world's population had begun to soar.

In Haiti, population growth has led to to overcrowding and poor living conditions. ▼

Effects of Growth

Population growth can have positive effects. For example, a growing population can produce and consume more goods and services. This can improve a country's standard of living. However, rapid population growth can also cause problems. The population can grow faster than the supply of food, water, medicine, and other resources.

The problems caused by rapid population growth are greatest in poor developing countries. A lack of clean food and water can lead to widespread starvation and disease. In these places, the **infant mortality rate**—the number of infant deaths per 1,000 births—is high.

The environment often suffers as well, as people use up resources to survive. Pollution is common. People cut down forests for firewood or clear land for farming. This can lead to desertification, or the spread of dry desert-like conditions. A lack of fertile soil makes it even harder to grow enough food.

Assessment

1. How are the birth rate and death rate used to measure population growth?
2. If the population of your town suddenly doubled, how might your daily life change?

Core Concepts 6.2

IN 6.3.9

Population Distribution

> **Key Ideas**
> - The distribution of a population can vary greatly within an area.
> - Population density has important effects on an area.
>
> **Key Terms** • population distribution • population density
>
> → Visual Glossary

A country's population is the total number of people living within its borders. That number can be large or small. Geographers study a country's population to learn more about life in that country.

Population Distribution

Population distribution is the spreading of people over an area of land. The world's population is distributed unevenly on Earth's surface. Some places have many people. Other places are almost empty. What factors lead people to live where they do?

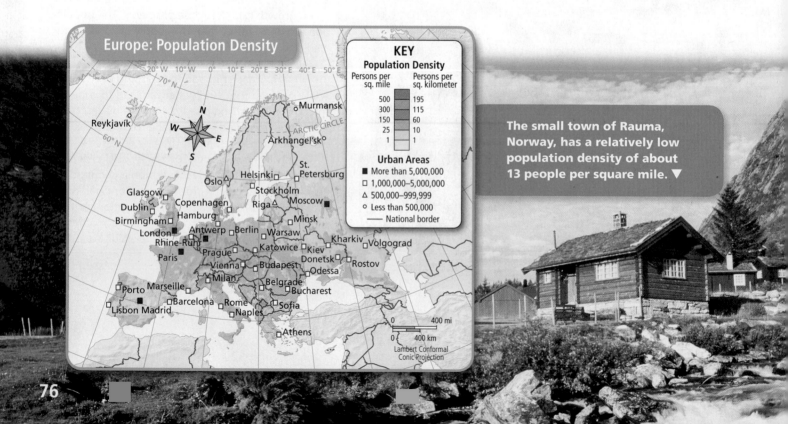

The small town of Rauma, Norway, has a relatively low population density of about 13 people per square mile. ▼

People try to live in places that meet their basic needs. Natural obstacles such as oceans, mountains, and extremely cold or hot weather limit the areas where people can live easily. Throughout human history, most people have lived in areas with fertile soil, fresh water, and mild climates. Regions with good soil and plenty of water became crowded. Places that were too cold or dry for farming never developed large populations.

After about 1800, improved transportation and new ways of making a living changed things. As factories and industries grew, the ability to farm became less important. Industrial centers and large cities could develop in regions that were less suited for farming. Today, population tends to be highest in areas that were centers of early farming, industry, or trade.

Population Density

Population density is the number of people per unit of land area. It is expressed as the number of people per square mile or square kilometer. Population density gives us a way to describe how thickly settled an area is. It also lets us compare places of different sizes and populations. The density figure for any country is an average. Population density can vary greatly from one part of a country to another.

Population density has some important effects on a region. The more people there are per square mile, the more crowded a place is. Cities with high population densities tend to have crowded roads and living conditions. These places require many resources to meet people's needs. Places with low population densities tend to have more undeveloped land.

London, in the United Kingdom, has a very high population density, about 13,000 people per square mile. ▼

Assessment

1. How are population distribution and population density different?
2. How might a rapid increase in a region's population density change the region?

Migration

| Key Ideas | • People move from one place to another for a number of reasons.
• People may move within a country or from one country to another. |

Key Terms • migration • emigrate • immigrate • push factor • pull factor

Visual Glossary

For thousands of years, people have migrated to new places. **Migration** is the movement of people from one place to another. Scientists believe that more than 50,000 years ago, a group of early humans migrated from Africa to Asia. Over many years, their descendants spread slowly across Asia and Europe. Some crossed from Asia to the Americas.

In the 1800s, many people migrated from Europe to the United States in search of a better life.

Forms of Migration

People often migrate within a country. In modern times, this internal migration has largely been movement to cities from the countryside. People generally migrate to cities to find jobs.

People also move from one country to another. When people leave their home country, they **emigrate,** which means to migrate out of a place. To enter a new country is to **immigrate,** or to migrate into a place. Moving to another country can lead to big changes in a person's life. For example, people moving to a new country may have to learn a new language and new customs. Mass migration can greatly change a region's culture and society. Migration can also affect a region's government, economy, and environment.

Reasons for Migration

People who migrate are often looking for a better life. They may move to escape poverty, a lack of jobs, or a harsh climate. In some countries, war or other conflict forces people to migrate. These reasons for migration are known as push factors. **Push factors** are causes of migration that push people to leave their home country.

Other reasons for migration are known as pull factors. **Pull factors** pull, or attract, people to new countries. One example of a pull factor is a supply of good jobs.

People generally migrate because they choose to do so. For example, millions of Europeans chose to migrate to the United States during the 1800s and early 1900s. Some of these people were Irish, fleeing a shortage of food. Others were Jews

These immigrants to the United States become U.S. citizens at a naturalization ceremony.

escaping persecution, or mistreatment. Millions more have come from Asia and Latin America since then.

History is also full of involuntary migrations. For the most part, these involved the forced movement of enslaved people. In the late 1400s European slave traders began buying and selling captured Africans. They shipped most of these enslaved people to the Americas. As many as 10 million enslaved Africans were forced to migrate to the Americas.

Assessment

1. Why did Europeans migrate to the United States in the 1800s and early 1900s?

2. Suppose your family migrated after a flood destroyed your home. Would the flood be considered a push factor or a pull factor? Explain.

Urbanization

Key Ideas

- Cities around the world have grown quickly over the last two hundred years.
- The growth of cities has created many challenges.

Key Terms • urban • rural • urbanization • slum • suburban sprawl

→ **Visual Glossary**

Panama City, Panama, had a population of 171,000 in 1950. By 2025, it is expected to grow to 2.4 million.

1950s

Panama City, Panama

Today

In many parts of the world, people are migrating to urban areas from rural areas. **Urban** areas are cities. **Rural** areas are settlements in the country. In China, for example, many new jobs have been created in cities in recent years. As a result, many rural Chinese workers have moved to cities in search of jobs. This process is known as urbanization. **Urbanization** is the movement of people from rural areas to urban areas.

The Shift from Rural to Urban

Over the last two hundred years or so, billions of people around the world have left rural agricultural areas to move to cities. In 2008, for the first time in history, more than half of the world's population lived in cities and towns.

In Europe and North America, urbanization began in the 1800s as modern industry developed. As a result, people moved to cities in search of jobs in factories and other businesses. Today, urbanization is happening most quickly in Asia and Africa. In those places, people move to cities in search of jobs, education, and better lives for their children.

Challenges of Urbanization

Rapid urbanization has created challenges for growing cities, especially those in poor countries. In some cases, cities simply have more people than they can handle. These cities cannot provide the housing, jobs, schools, hospitals, and other services that people need. One result is the spread of **slums,** or poor, overcrowded urban neighborhoods. Slums exist in cities around the world. Most people in slums live in run-down buildings or shacks. They are unable to meet their basic needs, such as enough food and clean water.

Urbanization can also create challenges in wealthy countries. Today, most large urban areas have a central core city. The core city has stores, office buildings, government buildings, and some housing. In wealthier countries, most people live in the suburbs surrounding the core city. As the population of a wealthy urban area grows, so does suburban sprawl. **Suburban sprawl** is the spread of suburbs away from the core city.

As suburbs spread, they replace farmland and other open spaces. New sewer lines, water lines, and roads must be built and maintained by the government. Because most people in suburbs use cars for transportation, suburban sprawl can increase pollution and energy use. Today, many towns and cities are working to limit sprawl.

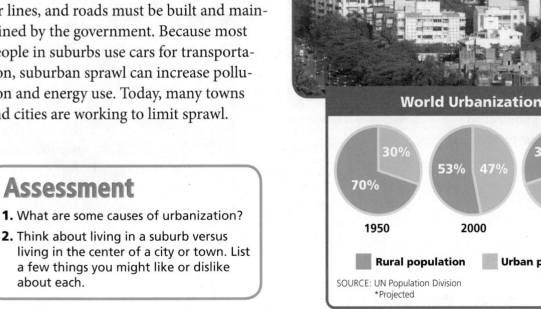

1950s

Mumbai, India, had a population of 2.9 million in 1950. By 2025, it is expected to grow to 26.4 million.

Mumbai, India

Today

World Urbanization

30%
70%
1950

53% 47%
2000

30%
70%
2050*

Rural population   Urban population

SOURCE: UN Population Division
*Projected

Assessment

1. What are some causes of urbanization?
2. Think about living in a suburb versus living in the center of a city or town. List a few things you might like or dislike about each.

Population and Movement

Part 6 Assessment

Key Terms and Ideas

1. **Identify** Define the terms **birth rate** and **death rate.**

2. **Summarize** Describe the process of **urbanization**.

3. **Recall** Name three negative effects of rapid population growth.

4. **Define** What is **migration**?

5. **Compare and Contrast** What is the difference between a **pull factor** and a **push factor**?

6. **Recall** What is **population density**?

7. **Explain** What factors affect **population distribution**?

Think Critically

8. **Draw Inferences** How do you think world population patterns might change in the future?

9. **Compare Viewpoints** What arguments could be made for living in an area that has a high population density or in one with a low population density? Explain your views.

10. **Synthesize** During the 1800s, millions of Europeans migrated to the United States. Identify at least one possible push factor and one possible pull factor behind this mass migration.

11. **Solve Problems** Imagine that you are a member of a city government that is trying to limit urban growth. What steps might you suggest?

Identify

Answer the following questions based on the map.

12. Describe London's population.

13. Which cities have populations between 500,000 and 1,000,000?

14. Which city is located at 0° longitude?

15. In general, where are the areas in the United Kingdom with the highest population density?

16. Describe Cardiff's population.

17. Which city is closest to 50° N latitude?

18. Which is the westernmost city shown on the map?

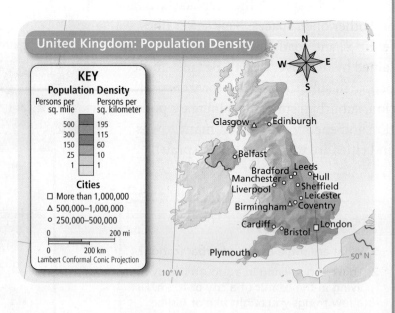

United Kingdom: Population Density

KEY
Population Density

Persons per sq. mile	Persons per sq. kilometer
500	195
300	115
150	60
25	10
1	1

Cities
□ More than 1,000,000
△ 500,000–1,000,000
○ 250,000–500,000

0   200 mi
0   200 km
Lambert Conformal Conic Projection

Journal Activity

Fill in the graphic organizer in your Student Journal.

Demonstrate Your Understanding Complete the Sum-It-Up activity in your journal to demonstrate your understanding of population and movement. After you complete the activity, discuss your predictions as a class. Be sure to support your predictions with information from the lessons.

21st Century Learning

Analyze Media Content

Find examples of recent articles about immigration to the United States. Then create a table to compare and contrast these articles. Ask yourself the following questions when reading:
- What is the main idea of each article?
- Does the author support every statement?
- Does the author show any bias?

Document-Based Questions

Success Tracker™
Online at myworldgeography.com

Use your knowledge of population and movement and Documents A and B to answer Questions 1–3.

Document A

Annual Birth & Death Rates in Selected Countries

Country	Birth Rate (per 1,000 people)	Death Rate (per 1,000 people)
Austria	8.7	9.9
Chad	41.6	16.4
Pakistan	28.4	7.9
Sri Lanka	16.6	6.1
United States	14.2	8.3

SOURCE: *CIA World Factbook*

Document B

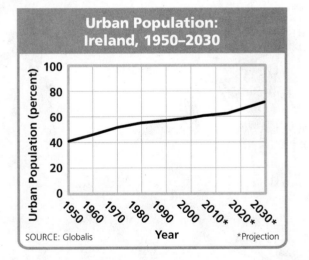

Urban Population: Ireland, 1950–2030

SOURCE: Globalis   Year   *Projection

1. Examine Document A. How does population growth in the United States most likely compare with that in Pakistan and Chad?

   A It is much faster.

   B It is much slower.

   C It is much faster than growth in Pakistan but slower than growth in Chad.

   D It is much faster than growth in Chad but slower than growth in Pakistan.

2. Examine Document B. What might be one cause for Ireland's changing rate of urbanization?

   A more dependence on agriculture

   B a higher death rate

   C growth in industry

   D housing shortages

3. **Writing Task** How do you think a graph showing urban population in Asia since 1950 might compare to Document B? Explain your answer.

my worldgeography.com   Self-Test

Culture and Geography

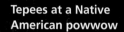

Tepees at a Native American powwow

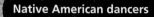

Native American dancers

84

Joanna Baca (at right) dances at a powwow.

Joanna Baca

EXPLORING CULTURE THROUGH DANCE

Story by Miles Lemaire for myWorld Geography

When Joanna Baca and her family moved to Las Vegas, Nevada, from the Native American Navajo reservation in Shiprock, New Mexico, she looked for things that reminded her of home—and her Navajo culture.

"Most of our family stayed back home," Joanna says. "After we first moved here [Las Vegas], we didn't think there was anyone out here that was Native American, and it actually took us a while to find someone we knew."

In an effort to make their new city feel like home, Joanna and her family looked for community organizations that promoted Native American culture. Joanna eventually discovered the Las Vegas Indian Center. Among other things, this organization helps Native American high school students apply to and get accepted at colleges.

"[The Center helps] Native American kids find out what colleges are good for them," Joanna says. "They teach us that college is possible for Native American kids, not just for the kids that live on the reservation, but for kids who live in the city, too."

The more time Joanna spent with the organization, the closer she felt to her Navajo culture. She decided that she wanted to get involved in more aspects of Native American culture, especially traditional forms of dance.

Joanna had grown up going to powwows with her family. A powwow is a gathering where Native American people dance, sing, and honor Native American cultures. "I'd just see all the dancers there and how beautiful they were," Joanna remembers. She decided that she wanted to learn more about Native American dance. "I did ballet, jazz, and hip-hop before, and I thought they were fun," she says, "but I wanted to do something cultural, because dancing is a big part of my culture."

It has been several years since Joanna first started studying and performing Native American dances. She loves how these traditional forms of dance help her connect to her culture. But she also thinks dance is a wonderful way for non-Native American people to learn more about native culture.

"We go to events where they have dancers from all over the world, and they'll have a bit of everyone's culture in this one little get-together," Joanna says. "So we shared food, we were part of the dancing there, and a lot of people were like, 'Oh that's nice, I've never seen that type of dance before, what kind is that?' We'd tell them that it's Navajo, or native and … it got them very interested. Some of those people would come to the show again just to see our part of the performance and to see what it was all about."

85

What Is Culture?

| **Key Ideas** | • Every culture has a distinctive set of cultural traits. |
| | • Earth has thousands of different cultures. |

Key Terms • culture • cultural trait • norm • culture region • cultural landscape

→ **Visual Glossary**

All people have the same basic needs and wants, such as food, clothing, and shelter. But different cultures respond to those needs and wants in different ways. **Culture** is the beliefs, customs, practices, and behaviors of a particular nation or group of people.

Where Culture Comes From

The features that make up a culture are known as cultural traits. A **cultural trait** is an idea or way of doing things that is common in a certain culture. Cultural traits include language, laws, religion, values, food, clothing, and many other customs. Children learn cultural traits from their parents and other adults. People also learn cultural traits from the mass media and from organizations such as schools, social clubs, and religious groups. Common cultural traits are called norms. A **norm** is a behavior that is considered normal in a particular society.

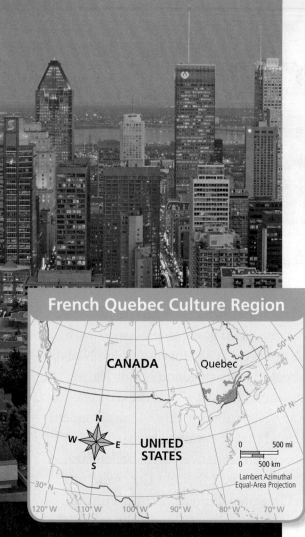

French Quebec Culture Region

CANADA   Quebec

UNITED STATES

0 500 mi
0 500 km

Lambert Azimuthal
Equal-Area Projection

120°W 110°W 100°W 90°W 80°W 70°W

50°N 40°N 30°N

Culture Regions

A **culture region** is an area in which a single culture or cultural trait is dominant. In Canada, French Canadian culture dominates much of the province of Quebec. The people of Quebec who have this culture identify themselves as French Canadian or Québécois (kay bek WAH).

Cultural Landscapes

Human activities create **cultural landscapes,** or geographic areas that have been shaped by people.

◄ Bolivia

Left, Egypt; below, Ukraine

Some cultural traits remain constant over many years. But culture can change over time as people adopt new cultural traits. For example, the way Americans dress today is very different from the way Americans dressed 100 years ago.

The environment can also affect culture. For example, the environment of a region influences how people live and how they earn their living. Humans can also shape their environment by creating cultural landscapes. The cultural landscape of a place reflects how its people meet their basic needs for food, clothing, and shelter. These landscapes differ from one culture to another.

Culture and Geography

Earth has thousands of different cultures and culture regions. In a specific culture region, people share cultural traits such as religion or language.

Culture regions are often different from political units. Occasionally, a culture region may cover an entire country. In Japan, for example, nearly everyone speaks the same language, eats the same food, and follows the same customs. A country may also include more than one culture region. For example, the French Canadian culture region of Quebec is one of several culture regions in Canada.

Culture regions can also extend beyond political boundaries. For example, many of the people who live in Southwest Asia and northern Africa are Arab Muslims. That is, they practice the religion of Islam. They also share other cultural traits, such as the Arabic language, foods, and other ways of life. This region of Arab Muslim culture covers several countries.

Clothing

Styles of clothing vary in different cultures.

A Spanish-born Swedish woman practices flamenco, a traditional Spanish dance. ▶

▲ A Saudi Arabian woman

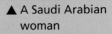

Weddings in Japan (above) and Indonesia (left)

Assessment

1. Does every country form a single culture region? Explain.

2. What are some elements of the cultural landscape in the area where your school is located?

Food

People in different cultures eat different types of food.

◀ A man in Saudi Arabia sells vegetables.

Women in Ukraine selling potatoes and other produce

Families and Societies

Key Ideas

- The most basic unit of any society is the family.
- Family structures vary in different cultures, but every society has organized relationships among groups of people.

Key Terms • society • family • nuclear family • extended family • social structure • social class

Visual Glossary

Culture, society, and family are all related. A **society** is a group of humans with a shared culture who have organized themselves to meet their basic needs. Societies can be large or small. A group of a few dozen hunter-gatherers is a society. So is a country of more than a billion people, such as India or China.

Nuclear and extended families are two kinds of family unit.

Nuclear Family

Kinds of Families

The most basic unit of any society is the family. A **family** is two or more people who are closely related by birth, marriage, or adoption. Traditionally, one person heads a family. A man has been the head of the family in many societies throughout history. Today, however, men and women often share this responsibility.

Family structures vary in different cultures. Two common family units are the nuclear family and the extended family. A **nuclear family** is a family that consists of parents and their children. An **extended family** is a family that includes parents, children, and other family members, such as grandparents, aunts, uncles, and cousins. Extended families are more common in developing countries. In some places, extended families work together on farms. In other places, relatives work separately but live together in order to share resources.

Extended Family

Kinds of Societies

Every society has a social structure. A **social structure** is a pattern of organized relationships among groups of people within a society. People interact with one another, with groups, and with institutions. For example, you have ties to friends and family members. You probably attend a school. You may also take part in a sports team or some other group. Adults have ties to coworkers and to economic institutions such as businesses and banks. Families may also have ties to religious institutions, such as a church, a synagogue, or a mosque.

Societies vary around the world and can change over time. All societies have some common institutions. These include government, religious, economic, and educational institutions.

Societies also have differences. One basic difference has to do with a society's economy. Some societies rely mainly on farming. Others depend on industry.

Industrial societies often organize members according to their social class. A **social class** is a group of people living in similar economic conditions. In modern societies, the main groupings are upper class, middle class, and lower (or working) class. The size of the world's middle class has increased greatly in recent years.

Assessment

1. What aspects of culture do all societies share?
2. What aspects of culture differ among societies?

Social Structure

This girl's social structure includes her relationships with people, groups, and institutions.

89

Indo-European

Speakers 2.722 billion
Main languages English, German, Swedish, Afrikaans (South Africa), French, Spanish, Portuguese, Italian, Russian, Polish, Farsi (Iran), Hindi (northern India), Bengali (Bangladesh, India), Greek

Sino-Tibetan

Speakers 1.259 billion
Main languages Mandarin Chinese (northern China), Cantonese (southeastern China), Min Nan Chinese (Taiwan), Tibetan (Tibet), Burmese (Myanmar)

Niger-Congo

Speakers 382 million
Main languages Ibo and Yoruba (Nigeria), Xhosa (South Africa), Twi (Ghana), Swahili (Kenya, Tanzania, Uganda)

Afro-Asiatic

Speakers 359 million
Main languages Arabic (Southwest Asia, North Africa), Hebrew (Israel), Hausa (West Africa)

Austronesian

Speakers 354 million
Main languages Malay (Malaysia), Javanese (Indonesia), Tagalog (Philippines), Maori (New Zealand)

Dravidian

Speakers 223 million
Main languages Telugu (India), Tamil (India, Sri Lanka)

Language

Key Ideas

- Language provides the basis for culture.
- Language can unify people or keep them apart.

Key Term

- language

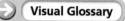 **Visual Glossary**

Cultures could not exist without language. **Language** is a set of spoken sounds, written symbols, or hand gestures that make it possible for people to communicate.

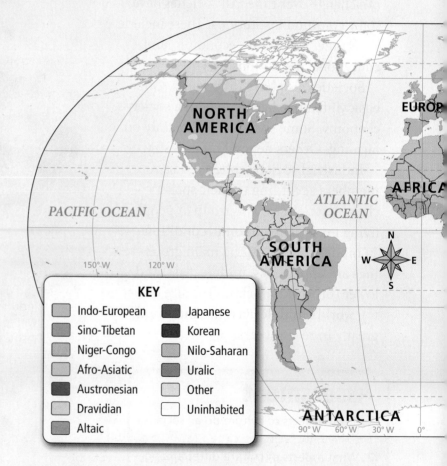

KEY

- Indo-European
- Sino-Tibetan
- Niger-Congo
- Afro-Asiatic
- Austronesian
- Dravidian
- Altaic
- Japanese
- Korean
- Nilo-Saharan
- Uralic
- Other
- Uninhabited

Without language, people would not be able to share information or ideas. They could not pass on cultural traits to their children.

Languages often vary from one culture to another. Within a country, differences in language can keep cultures apart and make it harder to unify the country. Language differences can also keep countries apart by preventing communication.

People who speak different languages sometimes turn to a third language in order to communicate with each other. In modern times, English has often served as the world's common language.

The map below shows the locations of the world's major language groups. Languages in each of these groups share a common ancestor. This ancestor was a language spoken so long ago that it gradually changed to become several related languages.

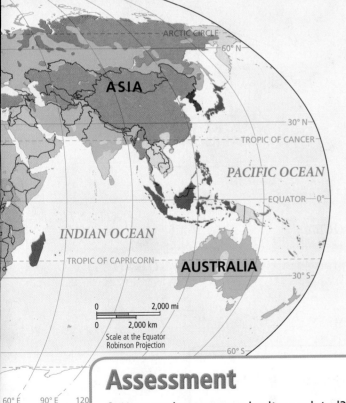

Altaic

Speakers 140 million
Main languages Turkish, Kazakh (Kazakhstan), Bashkir (Russia), Tatar (Russia), Uighur (China), Mongolian (Mongolia)

Japanese

Speakers 123 million
Spoken mainly in Japan.

Korean

Speakers 66 million
Spoken mainly in North Korea and South Korea.

Nilo-Saharan

Speakers 38 million
Main languages Luo (Kenya), Maasai (Tanzania), Kanuri (Niger)

Uralic

Speakers 21 million
Main languages Hungarian, Finnish, Estonian, Sami (Norway, Sweden, Finland), Samoyed (Russia)

Other

Speakers 394 million
These include Native American languages (North and South America), Paleosiberian languages (eastern Russia), Aboriginal languages (Australia), and languages spoken in Southeast Asia.

Assessment

1. How are language and culture related?

2. Which continent has the greatest number of language groups? Why might this be so?

Core Concepts 7.4

Religion

Key Ideas	• Religious beliefs play an important role in shaping cultures. • The world has many different religions.

Key Terms • religion • ethics 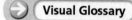 **Visual Glossary**

Judaism

Judaism is based on a belief in one God, whose spiritual and ethical teachings are recorded in the Hebrew Bible. It began in the Middle East around 2000 B.C. By A.D. 100, Jews lived in Europe, Southwest Asia, and North Africa. The Jewish state of Israel was established in 1948. There are about 14 million Jews.

Christianity

Christianity is based on the teachings of Jesus, who Christians believe was the son of God. The Christian Bible is their sacred text. Christianity began in Southwest Asia around A.D. 30 and spread to Europe and Africa. It later spread to the rest of the world. There are about 2.07 billion Christians.

Islam

Islam is based on the Quran, a sacred text. The Quran contains what Muslims believe is the word of God as revealed to Muhammad beginning in A.D. 610. Islam spread quickly across Southwest Asia and North Africa, then to the rest of the world. There are about 1.25 billion Muslims.

An important part of every culture is religion. **Religion** is a system of worship and belief, including belief about the nature of a god or gods. Religion can help people answer questions about the meaning of life. It can also guide people in matters of **ethics**, or standards of acceptable behavior. Religious beliefs and values help shape cultures.

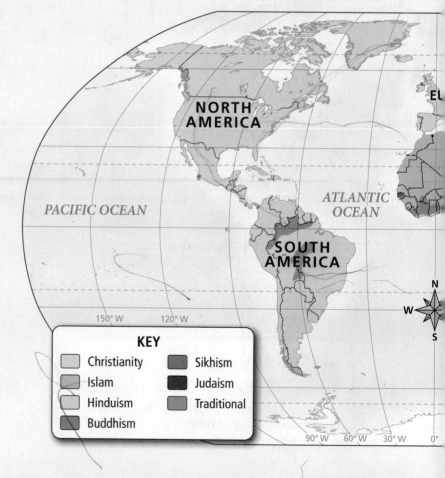

KEY
- Christianity
- Islam
- Hinduism
- Buddhism
- Sikhism
- Judaism
- Traditional

The world has many religions. Jews, Christians, and Muslims believe in one God. Members of other religions may believe in several gods.

All religions have prayers and rituals. Followers also observe religious holidays. For example, Jews celebrate the world's creation on Rosh Hashanah and their escape from slavery in Egypt on Passover. On Yom Kippur, Jews seek forgiveness for their wrongdoings. Christians celebrate Jesus' birth on Christmas and his return to life on Easter. For Muslims, the holy month of Ramadan is a time to avoid food during daytime, to pray, and to read the Quran.

The world's major religions began in Asia. Hinduism, Buddhism, and Sikhism first developed in India. Judaism, Christianity, and Islam began in Southwest Asia before spreading throughout the world.

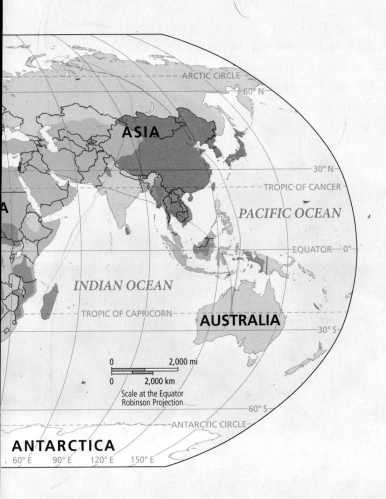

Hinduism

Hinduism evolved gradually over thousands of years in South Asia. It has several sacred texts. Hindus believe that everyone in the universe is part of a continuing cycle of birth, death, and rebirth. There are about 837 million Hindus.

Buddhism

Buddhism is based on the teachings of Siddhartha Gautama, known as the Buddha, who was born in India about 563 B.C. The Buddha's teachings include the search for enlightenment, or a true understanding of the nature of reality. There are about 373 million Buddhists.

Sikhism

Sikhism is based on the writings of several gurus, or prophets. Guru Nanak founded Sikhism about A.D. 1500 in South Asia. Sikhism's teachings include the cycle of rebirth and the search for enlightenment. There are about 24 million Sikhs.

Traditional Religions

Traditional religions include thousands of distinct religions. These religions tend to be passed down by word of mouth instead of through sacred texts. Each has its own set of beliefs. Examples include many African religions.

Assessment

1. How does religion help shape a culture?

2. What does the map tell you about the major religion where you live?

A print of a fish by Japanese artist Katsushika Taito, 1848

The Arts

Key Ideas
- Art is an important part of culture.
- Works of art can reveal much about society.

Key Terms
- universal theme
- visual arts
- architecture
- architect
- music
- literature

Visual Glossary

Visual Arts

Art forms meant to be seen, such as painting, sculpture, and photography, are known as the **visual arts.** The visual arts can express emotions and spiritual ideas. They can also show us what life is like in other cultures and how people lived in the past. For example, a painting created in Italy in 1600 can show us how Italian people lived during this period.

The arts are an important aspect of culture. Works of art can reflect a society by dealing with topics or issues that are important to that society. Art can even shape society. For example, books that describe poverty or environmental problems can help win public support for solving those problems. Art can also deal with universal themes. A **universal theme** is a subject or idea that relates to the entire world. For example, the paintings of Pablo Picasso, the songs of the Beatles, and the written works of William Shakespeare deal with the universal themes of love, death, peace, and war.

Architecture

Architecture is the design and construction of buildings. A person who designs buildings is an **architect**. Architecture can show us what a society values and how it uses its resources. For example, are a society's most impressive buildings its religious buildings or its government buildings? Architectural works can be important cultural symbols.

This art museum in Bilbao, Spain, was designed by architect Frank Gehry.

Music

Music is an art form that uses sound, usually produced by instruments or voices. Music varies widely in different societies and cultures. It also changes over time as our tastes change. What one person considers beautiful music might be unpleasant noise to someone from a different place or time period. As a result, music can tell us about a society's tastes.

A Peruvian man plays a flute near the Inca ruins at Machu Picchu, Peru.

Literature

Literature is written work such as fiction, poetry, or drama. Literature can tell us what ideas a society considers important. By describing harmful things in society, literature can push for change.

A performance of Shakespeare's
A Midsummer Night's Dream

Assessment

1. What are two ways in which the arts are related to society?
2. What might a painting of a main street in your area tell a stranger about your society?

95

Cultural Diffusion and Change

Key Ideas
- Cultures change over time.
- Cultural traits can spread from one culture to another.

Key Terms • cultural hearth   • cultural diffusion   • diversity   → Visual Glossary

Chinese people in France celebrate the Chinese New Year.

All cultures change over time. That is, their cultural traits change. In general, for a new cultural trait to be adopted by a culture, it must offer some benefit or improvement over an existing trait.

How Cultural Traits Spread

A **cultural hearth** is a place where cultural traits develop. Traits from cultural hearths spread to surrounding cultures and regions. Customs and ideas can spread in many ways, including settlement, trade, migration, and communication. **Cultural diffusion** is the spread of cultural traits from one culture to another.

In the 1500s, Spanish explorers and settlers brought horses to the Americas. Many native peoples saw the advantages of using horses for moving quickly and for hunting. Horses soon became part of some Native American cultures.

Cultural traits can also spread through trade. Traders can move among different cultures. As they travel, they carry with them elements of their own culture, such as food or religious beliefs. Traders expose people to these new traits. If people find that an unfamiliar religion or other cultural trait improves their lives, they may make it a part of their own daily lives. For example, hundreds of years ago, Muslim traders helped spread Islam from Arabia to other cultures in Asia and Africa.

In a similar way, migrants spread cultural traits. Migrants bring cultural traditions with them to their new homelands. Over time, many migrants, or immigrants, have come to the United States. Immigrants have brought with them foods, languages, music, ideas, and other cultural traits. Some of these new ways of doing things have become part of American culture.

Technology and Culture

Technology also helps spread culture. The Internet, for example, has made instant communication common. Today, Americans can find out instantly what people in places such as Peru, India, or Japan are wearing, eating, or creating. If we like some of these traits, we may borrow them and make them a part of our culture.

Rapid transportation technologies, such as airplanes, make it easier for people to move all over the world. As they travel, people may bring new cultural traits to different regions.

Cultural change has both benefits and drawbacks. If customs change too quickly, people may feel that their culture is threatened. Some people worry that rapid communication is creating a new global culture that threatens diversity. **Diversity** is cultural variety. These people fear that the things that make people and cultures unique and interesting might disappear. They worry that we might end up with only a single worldwide culture.

Assessment

1. Why do cultures change?
2. What cultural traits have you borrowed in the last few years?

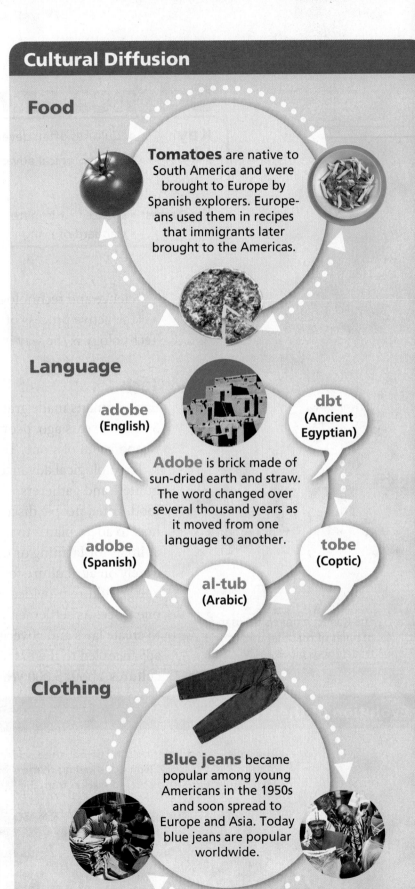

Cultural Diffusion

Food

Tomatoes are native to South America and were brought to Europe by Spanish explorers. Europeans used them in recipes that immigrants later brought to the Americas.

Language

adobe (English)

dbt (Ancient Egyptian)

Adobe is brick made of sun-dried earth and straw. The word changed over several thousand years as it moved from one language to another.

adobe (Spanish)

tobe (Coptic)

al-tub (Arabic)

Clothing

Blue jeans became popular among young Americans in the 1950s and soon spread to Europe and Asia. Today blue jeans are popular worldwide.

97

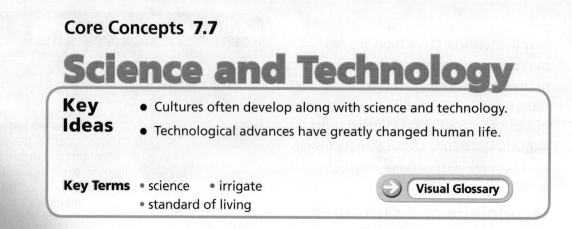

Core Concepts 7.7

Science and Technology

Key Ideas
- Cultures often develop along with science and technology.
- Technological advances have greatly changed human life.

Key Terms
- science
- irrigate
- standard of living

⊙ Visual Glossary

The Roman empire's thousands of miles of roads let armies and trade goods move easily.

Science and technology are important parts of culture. **Science** is the active process of acquiring knowledge of the natural world. Technology is the way in which people use tools and machines.

Technology and Progress

Early humans made gradual advances in technology. About 3 million years ago, people first learned how to make tools and weapons out of stone. They later discovered how to control fire.

Technological advances changed cultures. Early humans were hunters and gatherers who traveled from place to place to find food. Later, people discovered how to grow crops. They learned how to adapt plants to make them more useful. They tamed wild animals for farming or used them as food. Over time, people began to rely on agriculture for most of their food.

Agriculture provided a steady food supply and let people settle in one place. As settlements grew and turned into cities, people began to create laws and governments. They developed writing. These advances led to the first civilizations, or societies with complex cultures, about 5,000 years ago.

Evolution of the Wheel

The wheel transformed culture. Below, the Sumerian Standard of Ur, about 2600 B.C., showing chariots pulled by donkeys; at right, a covered wagon from the 1800s

Early civilizations developed new technologies that allowed people to grow more crops. People invented tools such as the plow to help increase food production. They built canals and ditches to **irrigate,** or supply water to, crops. Cultures that lacked writing developed more slowly. Over time, agriculture and civilization spread across the world.

Modern Technology

Beginning around 1800, people developed new technologies that used power-driven machinery. This was the Industrial Revolution. It led to the growth of cities, science, and many new businesses. Eventually, people developed even more advanced technologies such as automobiles, airplanes, computers, and space travel.

All of these advances in science and technology have greatly changed people's lives and raised their standard of living. **Standard of living** is the level of comfort enjoyed by a person or a society. Modern technology also helps to connect people, products, and ideas.

Political decisions and belief systems can affect the use of technology. For example, the Chinese government has limited Chinese citizens' use of the Internet. This is an attempt to control discussion of government policies and other issues. Many religions have used technology as part of their practices. For example, religious groups have used the printing press to print the Hebrew Bible, the Christian Bible, the Quran, and other holy writings. Today, some religious organizations use radio, television, and the Internet to broadcast their beliefs.

Technology and Culture

Technological Advances	Effects on Culture
Control of fire	Allowed humans to cook food, have light, protect themselves from animals
Irrigation	Increased food production; allowed people to do jobs other than farming; led to growth of cities
Wheel	Led to improved transportation in the form of carts and carriages; eventually led to trains, cars, and other vehicles
Printing press	Allowed the mass production of books; spread knowledge and ideas, increasing the number of educated people
Steam engine	Steam-powered machines performed work once done by hand; people moved to cities to find work in factories.
Refrigeration	Kept food fresh and safe longer; allowed food to be shipped over long distances from farms to cities

Assessment

1. What are science and technology?

2. How do you think technology might change culture in the future?

Over time, wheels led to better forms of transportation. At left, a French bicycle poster from 1925; below, a car from the 1950s

CYCLES ONYX

LES BICYCLETTES ONYX SONT LIVRÉES AVEC CERTIFICAT DE GARANTIE

Etablissements GUERRIER
SAINT-ETIENNE

99

Culture and Geography

Part 7 Assessment

Key Terms and Ideas

1. **Define** What is **culture**?
2. **Recall** What is **religion**?
3. **Summarize** Does migration cause **cultural diffusion**? Explain why or why not.
4. **Connect** Are all **cultural traits** also **norms**? Explain.

5. **Draw Conclusions** How can **language** both unify and divide cultures?
6. **Compare and Contrast** What is the difference between a **nuclear family** and an **extended family**?
7. **Explain** Explain the relationship between technology and a **standard of living**.

Think Critically

8. **Draw Inferences** As technology makes it easier for people to travel to different countries, how might world culture regions change?
9. **Make Decisions** What other aspects of culture might link people in a country who speak different languages?

10. **Identify Evidence** Give two examples of ways in which today's cultures are influenced by past cultures.
11. **Draw Conclusions** How do you think ethics guide a country's laws?

Identify

Answer the following questions based on the map.

12. What does this map show?
13. What is the most widely spoken dialect in China?
14. What do the two purple and pink colors represent on the map?
15. What does the color orange represent on the map?
16. Across from which island do Chinese speakers of the Min dialect live?
17. Which dialect is spoken just to the north of the largest area of the Min dialect?
18. Not including the areas shown on the map as "other dialects or languages," in what part of China are most non-Mandarin dialects spoken?

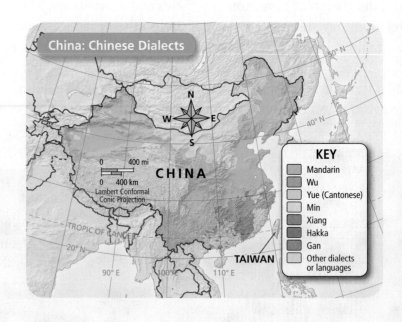

China: Chinese Dialects

KEY
Mandarin
Wu
Yue (Cantonese)
Min
Xiang
Hakka
Gan
Other dialects or languages

Journal Activity

Fill in the graphic organizer in your Student Journal.

Demonstrate Your Understanding Complete the Sum-It-Up activity in your journal to demonstrate your understanding of culture and geography. After you complete the activity, discuss your drawing with a partner. Be sure to support your answers to the questions with information from the lessons.

21st Century Learning

Work in Teams

Working with your partners, choose a country that is not familiar to anyone in your group. Then research and create an illustrated informational brochure about the country's culture. Be sure to
- provide examples of the country's art
- identify and describe the country's major religions and languages

Document-Based Questions

Success Tracker™
Online at myworldgeography.com

Use your knowledge of culture and geography and Documents A and B to answer Questions 1–3.

Document A

Main Language Spoken in U.S. Homes, 1980–2000

Percentage / Year

SOURCE: U.S. Census Bureau

■ English   ■ Other

Document B

" What a society [judges] important is [preserved] in its art."

—Harry Broudy

1. Examine Document A. Which of the following statements is probably true?

   A Migration to and cultural diffusion to the United States are likely decreasing.

   B Migration to and cultural diffusion to the United States are likely increasing.

   C Migration and cultural diffusion are unrelated to the changes shown in the graph.

   D Migration and cultural diffusion are no longer taking place in the United States.

2. Read Document B. Which of the following statements might Harry Broudy agree with?

   A Art does not reveal clues about past societies.

   B Art does not show the artist's beliefs.

   C Paintings reflect culture better than music does.

   D Looking at art is a good way to learn more about a society.

3. **Writing Task** Think of a favorite piece of art, such as a painting, a song, or a book. Then write one paragraph about what that piece of art reveals about your culture and beliefs.

my worldgeography.com   Self-Test

Government and Citizenship

Supporters hold campaign signs.

A group of congressional interns

Voters in the 2008 presidential election

Anne Marie Sutherland

Serving Her Country

Story by Miles Lemaire for myWorld Geography

Anne Marie Sutherland has been trying to get people to vote since before she was old enough to join them at the polls.

Anne Marie is the daughter of a high school government teacher. She became interested in politics as a child. Her first experience with a political campaign was the U.S. presidential election in 1996, when she was just nine years old. "[M]y friends and I made some signs and walked up and down the street with them before the election," Anne Marie says. "We started talking to people, and we stayed up all night to see who would win."

As Anne Marie grew older, her interest in the political process increased. In 2000 and 2004, she worked as a volunteer on George W. Bush's presidential campaigns. In the 2008 presidential primaries, she helped manage candidate Mitt Romney's campaign in Atlanta, Georgia.

"We did lots of grassroots work," Anne Marie says about her work with the Romney campaign. "We were talking to different folks, getting signs out, working on some strategies for the area."

When Romney failed to win the Republican nomination for president, Anne Marie worked for 2008 Republican nominee John McCain. She looks back on her work with the Romney and McCain campaigns as a great learning experience. Most of all, she loved discussing political issues with people.

"What I took away from that opportunity was working directly with voters," Anne Marie says. "That's not something that you get to do for very long in politics [before] you move up and start taking on larger roles."

Anne Marie soon began taking on larger roles herself, winning an internship with U.S. Senator Saxby Chambliss. As part of her internship, Anne Marie helped other young people achieve their own goals. As she explains, "Every year a senator appoints a certain number of graduating [high school] seniors to the United States military academies. ... so I put most of my energy into working on that process.

"I love doing that," she says, "because what I'm able to do is [to help] prepare our future military leaders at such a young age. ... [S]ometimes when I'm working with them, I honestly think, 'This young student could really be our future president, or could be leading us in a major war, or could be the leader of any one of the branches of the military.' You never know."

Now 22 years old, Anne Marie is about to graduate from college with a degree in political science. She isn't content with helping other people achieve their dreams. "Maybe there is a campaign of my own in the future," she says. "I'd do anything I can to serve my country."

103

Foundations of Government

Key Ideas
- Governments are created to keep order in a society and provide for the people's common needs.
- A government's powers are either limited or unlimited.

Key Terms • government • constitution • limited government • unlimited government • tyranny

Visual Glossary

Hammurabi's Code is a set of laws created in ancient Babylon—now Iraq—around 1760 B.C. The code was carved onto a large stone slab, below. The photo at the bottom of the page shows the ruins of ancient Babylon. ▼

A **government** is a group of people who have the power to make and enforce laws for a country or area. The basic purpose of government is to keep order, to provide services, and to protect the common good, or the well-being of the people. Governments make and enforce laws to keep order. Protecting the common good can include building roads and schools or defending the country from attack. Governments also collect taxes, or required payments, from people and businesses. Governments use these taxes to pay for the goods and services they provide. The purpose of government has not changed much throughout history.

Origins of Government

Long before modern governments existed, people lived together in groups. These groups often had leaders who kept order and made decisions for the group. This was a simple form of government.

More complex governments first appeared in Southwest Asia more than 5,000 years ago. By that time, groups of people had begun to settle down. Villages grew into cities. People found that they needed an organized way to resolve problems and oversee tasks such as repairing irrigation canals and distributing food. They formed governments to manage those tasks.

Powers of Government

Today, most governments have a constitution. A **constitution** is a system of basic rules and principles by which a government is organized. A constitution also identifies the powers a government has. A government's powers are either limited or unlimited.

Limited Government

People gather in front of the U.S. Capitol.

Today, most constitutions call for limited government. **Limited government** is a government structure in which government actions are limited by law. Limited governments work to protect the common good and provide for people's needs.

In the United States, government actions are limited in order to protect people's individual freedoms. Generally, people in a limited government may gather freely to express their opinions and work to change government policies.

Unlimited Government

Chinese police arrest a protester.

Unlimited government is a government structure in which there are no effective limits on government actions. In an unlimited government such as China, a ruler or a small ruling group has the power to make all decisions for a country or society. This much power can lead to **tyranny,** which is the unjust use of power.

Unlimited governments often do not protect citizens' basic rights. They may censor, or restrict, citizens' access to the Internet and other forms of communication technology.

Assessment

1. How do constitutions limit the powers of government?

2. How do limited and unlimited governments differ?

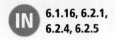

Political Systems

> **Key Ideas**
> - Types of states have varied throughout history.
> - There are many different kinds of government.
>
> **Key Terms** • state • city-state • empire • democracy • nation-state • monarchy • authoritarian • communism • totalitarianism

→ **Visual Glossary**

A **state** is a region that shares a common government. The first real states—called city-states—developed in Southwest Asia more than 5,000 years ago. A **city-state** is an independent state consisting of a city and its surrounding territory. Later, some military leaders conquered large areas and ruled them as empires. An **empire** is a state containing several countries. Geographic features such as rivers and mountains sometimes helped governments control territory by protecting against invasion.

A man votes in Kenya's 2007 presidential election.

Democracy

Examples Direct democracy: ancient Athens; representative democracy: United States

- **Democracy** is a form of government in which citizens hold political power; citizens are the ultimate source of government power and authority.

- In a direct democracy, citizens come together to pass laws and select leaders.

- In a representative democracy, citizens elect representatives to make government decisions.

- The powers of a democratic government are usually limited.

Queen Elizabeth II of the United Kingdom

Nation-States

Today, most states are nation-states. A **nation-state** is a state that is independent of other states. The United States is an example of a nation-state. We often use the general words *nation* or *country* to refer to nation-states.

All nation-states have some common features. For example, nation-states have specific territory with clearly defined borders. Nation-states have governments, laws, and authority over citizens. Most are divided into smaller states or provinces that contain cities and towns.

Forms of Government

Each state has a government, but there are many different kinds of government. Throughout history, most states were autocracies (ruled by a single person) or oligarchies (ruled by a small group of people). Today, however, many states have some form of democracy in which citizens hold political power.

A large statue of former leader Kim Il-Sung stands above people in communist North Korea.

Monarchy

Examples Absolute monarchy: Saudi Arabia; Constitutional monarchy: United Kingdom

- A **monarchy** is a form of government in which the state is ruled by a monarch.
- A monarch is usually a king or queen.
- Power is inherited by family members.
- Absolute monarchs have unlimited power.
- Monarchs in constitutional monarchies are limited by law and share power with other branches of government.
- The powers of a monarchy can be limited or unlimited.

Authoritarian Government

Examples Nazi Germany, Cuba, North Korea

- An **authoritarian** government is one in which all power is held by a single person or a small group.
- One common form of authoritarian government is **communism,** a political and economic system in which government owns all property and makes all economic decisions.
- Another form of authoritarian government is **totalitarianism**, a system in which a strong central ruler attempts to control all aspects of people's lives through force or coercion.
- The powers of an authoritarian government are unlimited.

Assessment

1. What are states, city-states, and nation-states?
2. Which form of government relies most on its citizens? Explain your answer.

107

Political Structures

Key Ideas	• Political structures help governments operate in an organized way.
	• The U.S. government follows basic democratic principles.

Key Terms • unitary system • federal system

Visual Glossary

Central Government

Central governments are responsible for national affairs.

U.S. Capitol

Regional Government

Regional governments include state or provincial governments.

Texas State Capitol

Local Government

Local governments include county, city, and town governments.

Trumbull, Connecticut, town hall

Countries distribute power between the central government and smaller units of government. We can learn more about how a government functions by examining its structure and principles.

Systems of Government

Governments can distribute power in three basic ways: the unitary system, the federal system, and the confederal system. In a **unitary system,** a central government makes all laws for the entire country. In a **federal system,** power is divided among central, regional, and local governments. In a confederal system, a group of independent states join together and give limited powers to a common government. Most countries have a unitary system. The United States and some other countries have a federal system. The confederal system is rare.

Principles of Government

Every government has basic principles that affect the way it serves its people. Authoritarian governments may seek to control all aspects of society, even people's actions and beliefs. For example, some authoritarian governments limit citizens' use of communications technology such as the Internet. Most democratic governments act to protect individual rights and the common good.

In the United States, government follows basic democratic principles. For example, government follows the rule of law. That is, government powers are defined by laws that limit its actions. Also, government decides issues by majority rule. A law cannot pass unless the majority—most—representatives vote for it. At the same time, the majority may not take away the basic rights and freedoms of minority groups or individuals. In other words, government must balance majority rule with minority rights.

Branches of Government

Under the U.S. Constitution, power is divided among the three branches of government: the legislative, executive, and judicial branches. This division is called separation of powers. The Constitution also establishes a system of checks and balances that limits each branch's power. Each branch has some power to change or cancel the actions of the other branches.

Legislative Branch

The legislative branch establishes laws. In a representative democracy like the United States, citizens elect legislative representatives to make decisions for them. The legislative branch also imposes taxes, or required payments. Taxes are used to pay for government services and public goods such as roads, parks, fire departments, and national defense. Public goods are owned by everyone in the country.

U.S. Congress

Executive Branch

The executive branch carries out, or enforces, the laws. It also provides for the country's defense, conducts foreign policy, and manages day-to-day affairs. The United States and some other countries have a presidential system with an elected president as the head of the executive branch. Other democracies, such as the United Kingdom, have a parliamentary system. In this system, the parliament, or legislative branch, chooses a prime minister as chief executive.

U.S. President Barack Obama

Judicial Branch

The judicial branch makes decisions about disputes. It does this through courts of law. These courts can range from local criminal courts to the highest court in the land. In the United States that court is called the Supreme Court. Among other things, the Supreme Court interprets the law. That is, it judges how a law should be applied and whether the law violates the Constitution.

U.S. Supreme Court

Assessment

1. What are the three branches of government?

2. What are three key democratic principles?

Conflict and Cooperation

Key Ideas
- Governments and international organizations cooperate for many reasons, including avoiding war and improving trade.
- Conflict can have serious effects on countries.

Key Terms • sovereignty • foreign policy • treaty • diplomacy

(→ **Visual Glossary**)

Every nation-state, or country, has clearly defined territory and sovereignty over that territory. **Sovereignty** is supreme authority, or power. Every country also has a central government. The central government takes care of matters that affect the whole country. This includes dealing with other countries' governments. Interactions between governments can take the form of conflict or cooperation.

Conflict

Most countries have a **foreign policy,** a set of goals describing how a country's government plans to interact with other countries' governments. A country's foreign policy reflects its values and intentions. Geographic factors such as location, physical features, and distribution of natural resources can influence foreign policy.

A country's foreign policy can lead to conflict with other countries. Wars and fighting begin for many reasons. Some wars begin as conflicts over control of land or resources. Others result from religious disagreements, political revolutions, or conflict between ethnic groups. Wars can lead to widespread death and destruction.

Food being distributed in Angola. ▼

Public Health Organizations

International Red Cross and Red Crescent Movement Provides medical aid, food, and other relief services to victims of war or natural disasters

World Health Organization Fights disease, especially among the world's poor, by providing health information, medical training, and medicine

Cooperation

Many people view the world as a global community in which people should cooperate to avoid conflict and help others. This cooperation may take the form of a **treaty,** a formal agreement between two or more countries.

The United Nations (UN) is the largest international organization that works for peace. Nearly every country in the world belongs to the UN. Governments send representatives to the UN to engage in diplomacy. **Diplomacy** is managing communication and relationships between countries. The UN Declaration of Human Rights lists the rights that all people should have, including life, liberty, and security. The UN works to protect these rights around the world.

The International Court of Justice, also known as the World Court, is the highest court of the United Nations. Any nation may bring a dispute to the World Court, but both parties have to agree to follow the court's ruling, which limits its power.

Governments also cooperate for reasons other than avoiding conflict. For example, governments often work with one another to improve their countries' economies through trade. International trade can provide new goods and markets. Trade agreements involving multiple countries have become common in recent years.

This water pump in South Africa was funded by the World Bank.

Economic Organizations

World Bank Provides loans for projects aimed at promoting economic development

International Monetary Fund (IMF) Seeks to prevent and resolve economic crises by offering advice, information, technical training, and loans

Humanitarian Organizations

United Nations (UN) Seeks to encourage international cooperation and achieve world peace but sometimes faces criticism

CARE International Seeks to end world poverty through development and self-help

◀ UN peacekeeping troops in Bosnia

Assessment

1. What are some of the functions of international organizations?

2. How do governments resolve conflict and cooperate?

Citizenship

> **Key Ideas**
> - Citizens have basic rights, but those rights come with responsibilities.
> - Rights and responsibilities can vary widely in different countries.
>
> **Key Terms** • citizen • civic life • civic participation • political party • interest group
>
> → **Visual Glossary**

The United States is a representative democracy. In a democracy, all political power comes from citizens. A **citizen** is a legal member of a country. In the United States, most people become citizens by being born on U.S. territory. Immigrants to the United States can become citizens through a legal process known as naturalization.

Rights and Responsibilities

Citizens' rights and responsibilities can come from a number of sources. These sources include constitutions, cultural traditions, and religious laws.

Americans' basic rights are protected by the Bill of Rights, a part of the U.S. Constitution. The Bill of Rights and other laws protect rights such as freedom of speech and freedom of religion. If the government violates these rights, citizens can fight the injustice in court. For the most part, these rights are also guaranteed to noncitizens.

Immigrants to the United States become citizens at a naturalization ceremony. ▼

Americans also have responsibilities. For example, we have the right to speak freely, but we also have the responsibility to allow others to say things we may not agree with. Our responsibilities include a duty to participate in government and **civic life,** or activities having to do with one's society and community. Voting is both a right and a responsibility for U.S. citizens.

Rights and responsibilities can vary widely in different countries and societies. Although most democratic governments protect basic human rights, nondemocratic governments often do not. Citizens who live in autocracies or oligarchies usually cannot take part in government or express their views openly.

Citizenship Worldwide

Ideas about rights and responsibilities can change over time. Many countries have become democracies over the past 200 years. These democracies now protect basic human rights such as freedom of expression and freedom from unfair imprisonment. Some of these countries did not protect these rights in the past or did not protect these rights for all people.

Today, international trade, transportation, and communication have linked the world's people. As a result, some people think that we should consider ourselves to be citizens of a global community. They believe that we are responsible for supporting human rights and equality for all people around the world.

Civic Participation

Voting is one type of **civic participation**, or taking part in government. Here are some others:

- Keeping informed about local, state, and national issues
- Contacting an elected representative, such as a state legislator or member of Congress
- Voicing opinions at town meetings
- Taking part in public gatherings, protests, or demonstrations
- Signing a petition, a formal request for government to do something
- Running for public office
- Getting involved in a political party—a group that supports candidates for public offices
- Joining an interest group—a group that seeks to influence public policy on certain issues

Assessment

1. What is the main source of American citizens' basic rights?
2. How do the roles and responsibilities of citizens vary between democratic and nondemocratic countries?

113

Part 8 Assessment

Key Terms and Ideas

1. **Recall** There are two types of democracy: direct and representative. Which kind of **democracy** is the United States?

2. **Identify** Describe the powers of an **unlimited government.**

3. **Connect** Why did **governments** first develop thousands of years ago?

4. **Describe** How does the U.S. government balance legislative, executive, and judicial power?

5. **Compare and Contrast** How are the **unitary system** and the **federal system** similar and different?

6. **Paraphrase** Explain **diplomacy** in your own words.

7. **Identify** Name two ways American **citizens** can participate in the political process.

Think Critically

8. **Draw Inferences** Consider that you can freely read about your government's actions and policies on the Internet. How might Internet access differ in a country with an authoritarian government?

9. **Make Decisions** Do you think that people who live in a democracy should be required to fulfill their civic responsibilities?

10. **Synthesize** Imagine that a country shares its borders with three others. How do you think its geography might relate to its foreign policy?

11. **Draw Conclusions** Who do you think is more likely to speak out against the government: a citizen in a limited government or a citizen in an unlimited government? Explain.

Identify

Answer the following questions based on the map.

12. Which country is the westernmost member of the European Union?

13. Which EU members border Latvia?

14. List the EU members with territory located to the north of 60° N latitude and to the east of 0° longitude.

15. Which EU members border Slovenia?

16. How many members made up the European Union in 2009?

17. What sea do Spain and Greece border?

18. How would you describe EU membership?

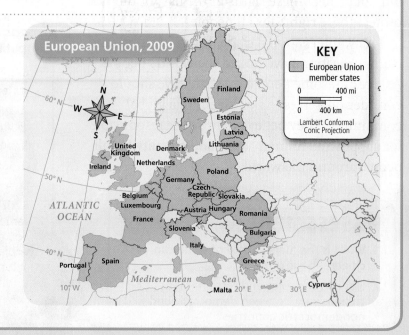

Journal Activity

Fill in the graphic organizer in your Student Journal.

Demonstrate Your Understanding Complete the Sum-It-Up activity in your journal to demonstrate your understanding of government and citizenship. After you complete the activity, discuss your If-Then statements with a small group. Be sure to support your statements with information from the lessons.

21st Century Learning

Analyze Media Content

Authoritarian governments usually allow little media freedom. Find political news articles from authoritarian and democratic countries. Then compare and contrast them in a short essay. Remember to
- include excerpts from a variety of articles
- discuss how the government might influence what is published

Document-Based Questions

Success Tracker™
Online at myworldgeography.com

Use your knowledge of government and citizenship and Documents A and B to answer Questions 1–3.

Document A

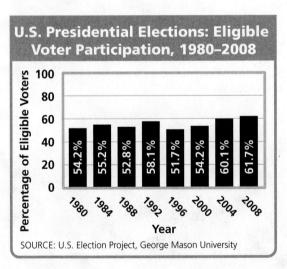

U.S. Presidential Elections: Eligible Voter Participation, 1980–2008

Year	Percentage
1980	54.2%
1984	55.2%
1988	52.8%
1992	58.1%
1996	51.7%
2000	54.2%
2004	60.1%
2008	61.7%

SOURCE: U.S. Election Project, George Mason University

1. Examine Document A. How has eligible voter participation changed in the time period shown?

A It has declined steadily.

B It has increased steadily.

C It has declined since 1996.

D It has increased since 1996.

Document B

" The accumulation of all powers, legislative, executive, and judiciary, in the same hands, whether of one, a few, or many … may justly be pronounced the very definition of tyranny."

—James Madison, *The Federalist,* No. 48

2. Read Document B. Which of the following statements would James Madison agree with?

A Separate branches of government are unnecessary.

B Unlimited government is not a form of tyranny.

C Separate branches of government are essential.

D A unitary system of government is ideal.

3. **Writing Task** Do you agree or disagree with James Madison? Write a short essay in which you respond to Madison's quotation. Be sure to explain your position clearly, supporting it with information from the lessons.

myworldgeography.com Self-Test

115

Tools of History

Inca ruins in Peru

An archaeologist sketches a dig in Lima, Peru.

Archaeologists at a dig

Brian McCray

Digging for Clues

Story by Miles Lemaire for myWorld Geography

Brian McCray likes to dig in the dirt. But Brian isn't just playing around. He's an archaeologist who has traveled around the world to dig up objects from the past and learn more about the people who made them.

Carrying out an archaeological dig isn't as simple as picking a location, grabbing a shovel, and starting to dig, Brian says. He spends weeks or months researching the history of the dig's location before a shovel goes into the ground. Brian will study maps, look at photographs, and read written descriptions of the area. He wants to know as much as possible about the site before he begins to explore it.

Once an archaeological dig begins, archaeologists like Brian carefully examine all the objects found at the site. Then they record and save the objects for future research. Keeping good records is very important. All archaeological sites are drawn and mapped carefully, with detailed information about where each object was found. It can take months or years to fully examine all of the artifacts, or objects made by people, found at an archaeological site.

"The things that are deeper in the ground are, in most cases, older than the things closer to the surface," says Brian. "We keep track of every layer of soil and what we find there."

Brian's research has allowed him to travel throughout the Americas. He has studied sites in the northern United States, the Caribbean, and western South America. Brian has worked with the Digital Archaeological Archive of Contemporary Slavery. This research has helped historians learn more about the lives of enslaved Africans in North America and the Caribbean. But his most interesting discovery was in the Andes Mountains in South America. In the Andes, Brian studied something that researchers still don't fully understand.

"It was actually what appears to be a swimming pool," Brian says. "It was constructed by the Incas at the very end of the Incan Empire." That was almost 500 years ago.

What was the "pool" used for? "Who knows?" Brian says. "It was a big sunken court with really amazing cut-stone masonry and five or six canals bringing water down into it from up the hill ... It's way too cold up there for anyone to want to swim all that often."

But although Brian and his fellow archaeologists don't yet know why the Incas built this pool, you can be sure that they'll keep digging to find out the answer. Who knows? Maybe Brian will be the one to finally uncover the truth.

Measuring Time

Key Ideas
- Throughout history, societies and cultures have organized time in different ways.
- People have used a number of different calendars to measure time.

Key Terms • historian • timeline • chronology • period • prehistory

→ **Visual Glossary**

It can be hard to describe the concept of time. But **historians**—people who study events in the past—know that organizing time is important if we want to understand past events.

Using a Timeline

Historians use timelines as a tool. A **timeline** is a line marked off with a series of events and dates. Historians use timelines to put events in a **chronology,** a list of events in the order in which they occurred.

A timeline can cover a day, a year, a decade (ten years), a century (one hundred years), a millennium (one thousand years), or any other period in history. A **period** is a length of time singled out because of a specific event or development that happened during that time. A period is also known as an era or an epoch. Historians use periods and eras to organize and describe human activities.

Historians mark timelines in intervals based on the events they want to cover. The timeline below is broken into millenia, because it shows events that happened many years apart. Another timeline, comparing events that occurred in the same century, might be marked in decades.

The timeline on this page shows watershed events—important points in history. Below, a Sumerian writing tablet. ▼

3200 B.C. Sumerians develop the earliest known form of writing.

A.D. 1945 World War II ends.

| 3000 B.C. | 2000 B.C. | 1000 B.C. | A.D. 1 | A.D. 1000 | A.D. 2000 |

1766 B.C. China's Shang dynasty begins.

A.D. 250 Maya Classic period begins in Mexico and Central America.

A.D. 1492 Christopher Columbus sails to the Americas.

Organizing Time

The past is often split into two parts, prehistory and history. **Prehistory** is the time before humans invented writing. *History* refers to written history, which began about 5,200 years ago.

We can also organize history by beginning with a key event from the past. Today much of the world uses the believed birthdate of Jesus as a key event. Years before that event are labeled B.C., for "before Christ," or B.C.E., for "before common era." Years after Jesus's birth are labeled A.D., meaning *anno Domini,* Latin for "in the year of our Lord." These years are also known as C.E., for "common era."

The Jewish calendar counts the years since the creation of the world, according to Jewish tradition. The Islamic calendar is dated from the year that the prophet Muhammad moved to the city of Medina.

Throughout history, societies have used different calendars. Maya and Aztec priests made calendars for farming and religious purposes. Today much of the world uses the Gregorian calendar, which has a 365- or 366-day year. It is based on the movement of Earth around the sun. The Jewish year, based on both sun and moon, varies from 353 to 385 days to adjust to the solar year. The Islamic year, however, is based on the cycles of the moon and lasts about 354 days.

Calendar Systems

Calendars are based on the movements of Earth, the moon, the stars, or a combination. Throughout history, people have used different methods to create calendars. The objects shown here were all different ways of measuring the passage of time.

Astrolabe This astrolabe was used by Muslim astronomers to calculate the positions of the sun, moon, planets, and stars. ▶

◀ **Aztec Calendar Stone** The Aztecs had two calendars: a 365-day agricultural calendar and a 260-day religious calendar.

Roman Calendar Early Roman calendars were based on the movements of the moon and had 10 months and 304 days. Later, the calendar had 12 months and 355 days. ▶

Assessment

1. How do people organize time?
2. If you created a timeline of everything you did yesterday, what would you choose to be the first event? What would be the last event? How would you decide which events are important enough to include on the timeline?

119

Historical Sources

Key Ideas
- Historical sources can provide important information.
- Historians must evaluate the accuracy and reliability of sources.

Key Terms • primary source • artifact • secondary source • bias

Visual Glossary

Historians try to accurately understand and describe the past. To understand past events, historians study historical sources.

Primary and Secondary Sources

A **primary source** is information that comes directly from a person who experienced an event. It consists of what the person writes, says, or creates about the event. Primary sources include letters, diaries, speeches, and photographs. Artifacts are also primary sources. An **artifact** is an object made by a human being, such as a tool or a weapon. We use primary sources to understand events from the points of view of people who lived at the time in which they happened.

Books, articles, movies, and other sources that describe or make sense of the past are secondary sources. A **secondary source** is information about an event that does not come from a person who experienced that event.

This U.S. poster created during World War II is an example of a primary source. ▼

We Can Do It!

WAR PRODUCTION CO-ORDINATING COMMITTEE

Letters written by soldiers are primary sources.

Primary Sources

66 Yesterday, December 7, 1941—a date which will live in infamy—the United States of America was suddenly and deliberately attacked by naval and air forces of the empire of Japan . . . No matter how long it may take us to overcome this premeditated [planned] invasion, the American people in their righteous might will win through to absolute victory. 99

—President Franklin D. Roosevelt, December 8, 1941

Evaluating Historical Sources

Historical sources do not always give a true account of events. Even primary sources can be wrong or misleading. An author's personal opinions may have influenced what he or she recorded. Sometimes the author may not remember the event accurately. A historian must decide what, if anything, to trust in a primary source.

A historian must also be cautious when using secondary sources. Not all secondary sources are equally reliable. For example, the Internet includes millions of well-researched articles, books, and other reliable secondary sources. However, any Internet search will also find many inaccurate Web sites.

Historians and students of history—like you—must evaluate a source to determine its reliability. When you examine primary and secondary sources, ask yourself questions like these:

- Who created the source material? A witness to an event may be more trustworthy than someone looking back at the event from a later time. However, a scholar or publication with a good reputation is also a reliable source. For example, a college professor who specializes in Chinese history would be a reliable source on China.
- Is the information fact or opinion? A fact is something that can be proved true or false. An opinion is a personal belief. Opinions are valuable not as a source of facts but as a clue to the author's judgments or feelings.
- Does the material seem to have a bias? A **bias** is an unfair preference for or dislike of something. Biased material often leaves out facts that do not support the author's point of view.

The painting and article below are secondary sources. ▼

Secondary Sources

66 Japanese planes attacked the U.S. naval base at Pearl Harbor, Hawaii, on December 7, 1941.... This disaster caused the American public to support an immediate American entry into the war. 99

—*History of Our World*, Prentice Hall, 2008

Assessment

1. What is a primary source?
2. Which online source will likely be more accurate, an encyclopedia or a personal journal such as a blog? Explain.

121

Archaeology and Other Sources

Key Idea
- Archaeology and other historical sources offer clues to what life was like in the distant past.

Key Terms
- archaeology
- oral tradition
- anthropology

→ **Visual Glossary**

Machu Picchu, Peru, is an Incan city abandoned in the 1500s and largely forgotten until the 1800s.

Archaeologists Louis and Mary Leakey found many fossil remains of human ancestors in Africa's Olduvai Gorge.

The Temple of Inscriptions in Palenque, Mexico, contains the tomb of the Maya ruler Pakal, who died in A.D. 683. ▼

Over time, much of the ancient world has disappeared. Large cities have collapsed into ruins. Buildings are buried under layers of soil and sand or covered by thick forests. The artifacts that show what life was like in ancient times are often buried or hidden. The science of archaeology aims to uncover this hidden history. **Archaeology** is the scientific study of ancient cultures through the examination of artifacts and other evidence.

Archaeologists and Anthropologists

Archaeologists are part treasure hunters and part detectives. They explore the places where people once lived and worked, searching for artifacts such as tools, weapons, and pottery. Archaeologists study the objects they find to learn more about the past.

Artifacts can help us identify the resources available to ancient people. They can help us understand how these people used technology and how they adapted to their environment.

Anthropology also helps historians understand the past. **Anthropology** is the study of humankind in all aspects, especially development and culture. Anthropologists seek to understand the origins of humans and the ways humans developed physically. This field often involves studying fossils—bones and other remains that have been preserved in rock.

Anthropologists also try to determine how human cultures formed and grew. Clues to the past can come from a culture's oral traditions. **Oral tradition** is a community's cultural and historical background, passed down in spoken stories and songs.

New Zealand's Maori people have passed down many aspects of their culture through oral tradition. ▼

Thousands of clay statues were buried in the tomb of China's first Qin emperor in 210 B.C.

Assessment

1. What do archaeologists do?

2. How do archaeology and anthropology help us understand the past?

123

Core Concepts 9.4

Historical Maps

Key Ideas
- Historical maps offer visual representations of historical information.
- Historical maps show information about places at certain times.

Key Term • historical map

Visual Glossary

When you read about a historical event like an important battle, it can be hard to get a clear picture of what really happened. You may have to understand how landforms like rivers and hills affected the battle. Or perhaps the location of a nearby town, railroad, or road influenced the fighting. Sometimes the best way to learn about a historical event or period is by examining a historical map.

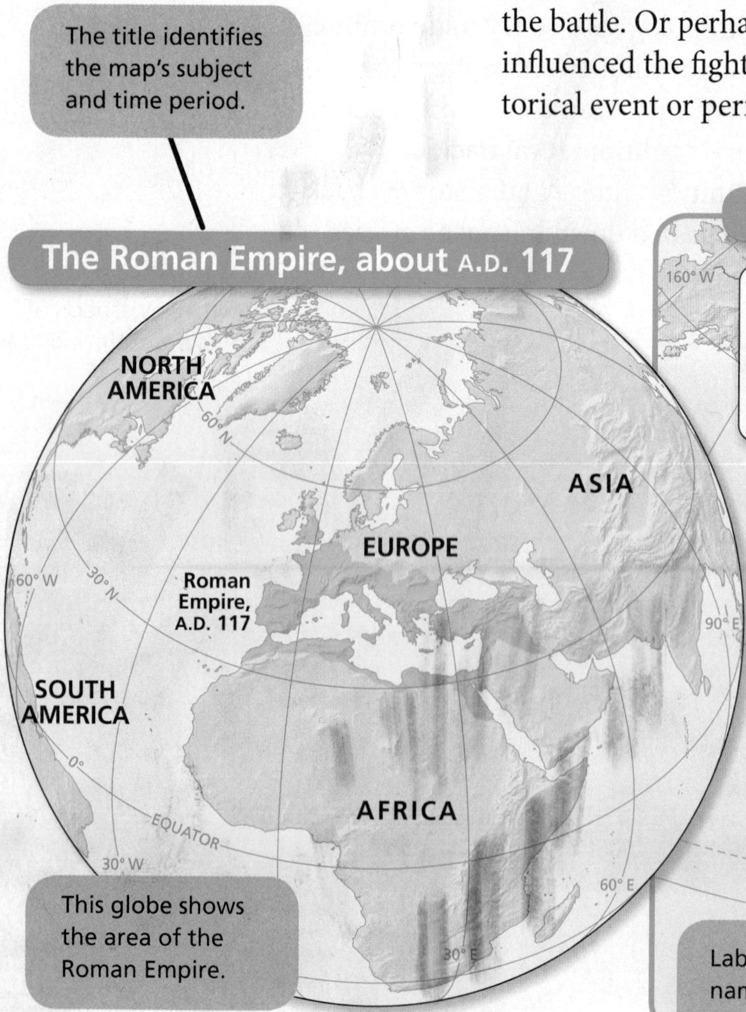

The title identifies the map's subject and time period.
The Roman Empire, about A.D. 117
NORTH AMERICA
ASIA
EUROPE
Roman Empire, A.D. 117
SOUTH AMERICA
AFRICA
60° N
30° N
60° W
90° E
0°
EQUATOR
30° W
30° E
60° E
This globe shows the area of the Roman Empire.

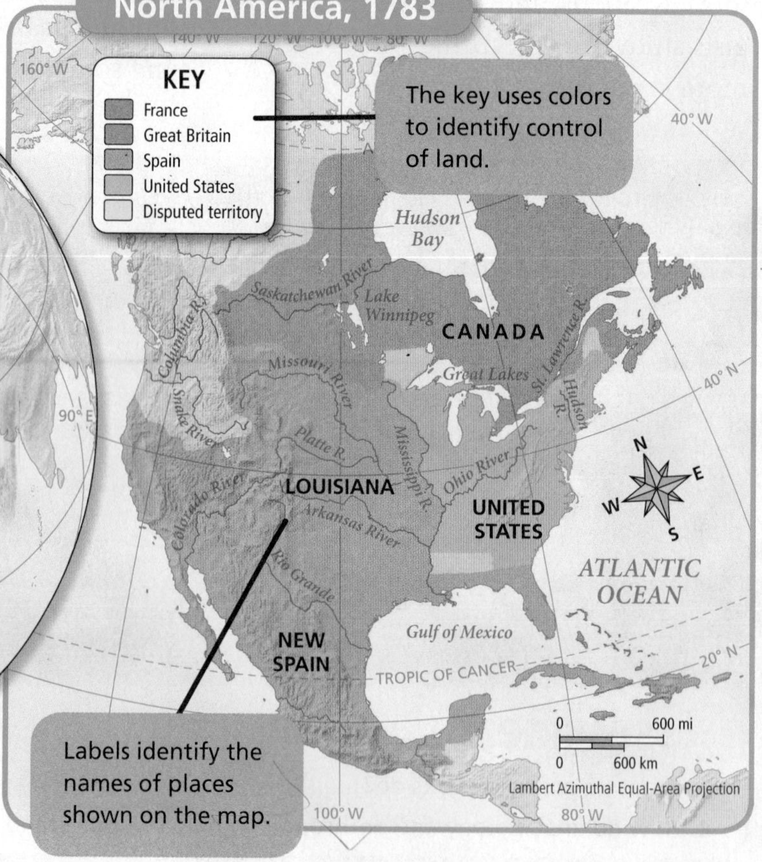

North America, 1783
KEY
France
Great Britain
Spain
United States
Disputed territory
The key uses colors to identify control of land.
Hudson Bay
Saskatchewan River
Lake Winnipeg
CANADA
Columbia R.
Missouri River
Great Lakes
St. Lawrence R.
Hudson R.
Snake River
Platte R.
Mississippi R.
Ohio River
LOUISIANA
Colorado River
Arkansas River
UNITED STATES
Rio Grande
ATLANTIC OCEAN
Gulf of Mexico
NEW SPAIN
TROPIC OF CANCER
N
E
S
W
0 600 mi
0 600 km
Lambert Azimuthal Equal-Area Projection
160° W
140° W
120° W
100° W
80° W
40° W
40° N
20° N
Labels identify the names of places shown on the map.

A **historical map** is a special-purpose map that provides information about a place at a certain time in history. Historical maps can show information such as migration, trade patterns, or other facts.

Historical maps have similar features. Most have a title and a key. Most use colors and symbols to show resources, movement, locations of people, or other features. Use the following four steps to become familiar with historical maps.

1. Read the title. Note the date, the time span, or other information about the subject of the map. If the map includes a locator map, examine it to see what region is shown.

2. Study the map quickly to get a general idea of what it shows. Read any place names and other labels. Note any landforms.

3. Examine the map's key. Pick out the first symbol or other entry, read what it stands for, and find an example on the map. Repeat this process for the remaining key entries until you understand them all.

4. Study the map more thoroughly. Make sure you have a clear understanding of the picture the map presents. If you need help, reread the related section of your textbook or examine the map again.

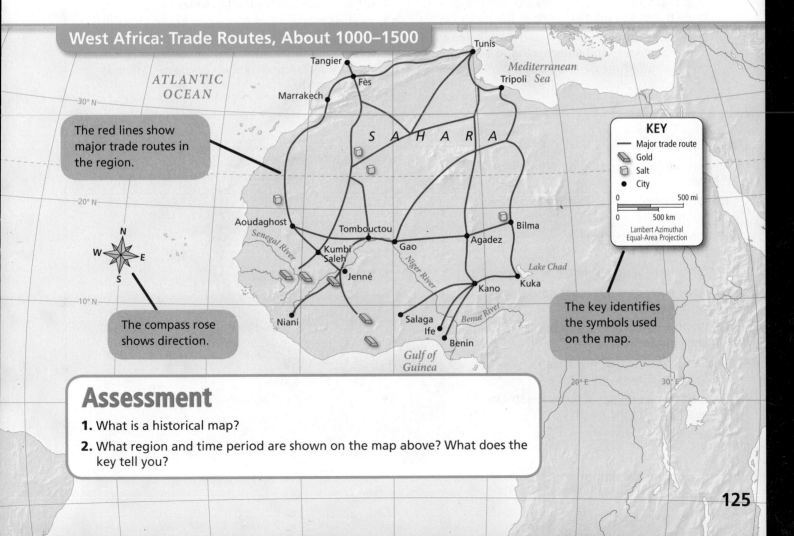

West Africa: Trade Routes, About 1000–1500

The red lines show major trade routes in the region.

The compass rose shows direction.

The key identifies the symbols used on the map.

KEY
— Major trade route
🔷 Gold
▱ Salt
● City

0   500 mi
0   500 km
Lambert Azimuthal
Equal-Area Projection

Assessment

1. What is a historical map?

2. What region and time period are shown on the map above? What does the key tell you?

Part 9 Assessment

Key Terms and Ideas

1. **Summarize** What is **archaeology**?

2. **Identify** When a person who did not experience an event describes the event, is the description a **primary source** or a **secondary source**?

3. **Compare and Contrast** Explain the difference between history and **prehistory.**

4. **Identify Cause and Effect** What do archaeologists do with **artifacts**?

5. **Synthesize** How do **timelines** show historical events or periods?

6. **Identify** What do **historical maps** show?

7. **Recall** What three questions should you ask when evaluating a source?

Think Critically

8. **Make Decisions** Imagine that you are creating a map that will show ancient trade routes. Name three things you might include in the map's key.

9. **Draw Conclusions** How do you think the work of archaeologists and anthropologists can help present and future generations?

10. **Draw Inferences** Why do you think so many different calendars still exist today?

11. **Analyze Primary and Secondary Sources** Imagine that you are writing a biographical profile of a famous political leader. Give examples of reliable primary and secondary sources you might use in your research.

Identify

Answer the following questions based on the map.

12. What area of the United States is shown on the map?

13. What do the light yellow dots represent?

14. What time period is shown on the map?

15. What color dots represent hurricanes with the highest wind speeds?

16. What large body of water borders Texas and Louisiana?

17. List two states that have been struck by category 4 hurricanes.

18. How many category 5 hurricane strikes are shown on the map?

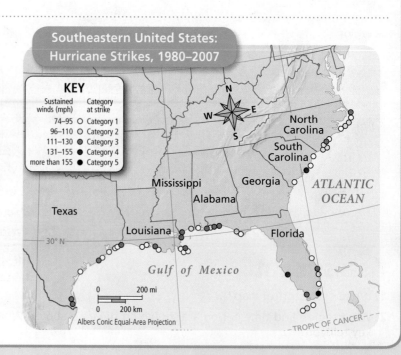

Southeastern United States:
Hurricane Strikes, 1980–2007

KEY

Sustained winds (mph)	Category at strike
74–95	○ Category 1
96–110	○ Category 2
111–130	◔ Category 3
131–155	◕ Category 4
more than 155	● Category 5

North Carolina

South Carolina

Mississippi   Georgia   ATLANTIC OCEAN

Alabama

Texas

30° N

Louisiana   Florida

Gulf of Mexico

0   200 mi
0   200 km
Albers Conic Equal-Area Projection

TROPIC OF CANCER

Journal Activity

Fill in the graphic organizer in your Student Journal.

Demonstrate Your Understanding Complete the Sum-It-Up activity in your journal to demonstrate your understanding of the tools of history. After you complete the activity, discuss your plan for using historical resources with a small group. Be sure to support your plan with information from the lessons.

Develop Cultural Awareness

Oral tradition remains an important part of many cultures. Research a song or story still passed on by oral tradition today, either in your own culture or in another. Then share the song or story with the class. Be sure to address the following topics:

- Origins of the song or story
- Cultural significance of the song or story

Document-Based Questions

Success Tracker™
Online at myworldgeography.com

Use your knowledge of the tools of history and Documents A and B to answer Questions 1–3.

Document A

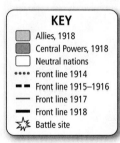

KEY
- Allies, 1918
- Central Powers, 1918
- Neutral nations
- •••• Front line 1914
- ▪ ▪ Front line 1915–1916
- — Front line 1917
- ▬ Front line 1918
- ✶ Battle site

1. Document A is a key to a historical map showing Europe during World War I. What information does this map not give you?

A location of front line in 1917

B locations of battles

C members of the Central Powers in 1918

D outcome of World War I

Document B

" [Alexander] was only twenty years old when he succeeded to the crown, and he found the kingdom torn into pieces by dangerous [groups of people]."

— Plutarch, *Life of Alexander,* about A.D. 100

2. Document B is an excerpt about the ancient Greek leader Alexander the Great, written by a historian about 400 years after Alexander's death. Which of the following best describes this excerpt?

A primary source

B secondary source

C artifact

D prehistoric

3. Writing Task Using information from Documents A and B and your knowledge of the tools of history, describe how historians use sources to understand and explain historical events.

my worldgeography.com Self-Test

The United States and Canada

The United States and Canada occupy the North American continent. This region has fertile plains, rugged mountains, and large metropolitan areas. The two countries share a common border and similar climates, including temperate and arctic regions.

What time is it there?

Washington, D.C.	Ottawa, Ontario
9 A.M. Monday	9 A.M. Monday

ARCTIC OCEAN

ARCTIC CIRCLE

60° N

CANADA

PACIFIC OCEAN

Ottawa

ATLANTIC OCEAN

UNITED STATES

Washington, D.C.

30° N   30° W

KEY
— National border
⊘ Capital city
Orthographic Projection

TROPIC OF CANCER

Gulf of Mexico

120° W   90° W   60° W

The Unit Ahead

➡ **Chapter 1** The United States

➡ **Chapter 2** Canada

my worldgeography.com

Plan your trip online by doing a Data Discovery Activity and watching the myStory Videos of the region's teens.

my Story

Vy
Age: 18
Home: Texas,
United States

Chapter 1

my Story

Alyssa
Age: 19
Home: Ottawa,
Canada

Chapter 2

Niagara Falls

Regional Overview
Physical Geography

Canadian Cordillera

Rocky Mountains

Great Plains

Canadian Shield

Great Lakes

PACIFIC
OCEAN

The Rocky Mountains and
Canadian Cordillera are part
of the same mountain range.

Gulf of
Mexico

The Canadian Shield, with its thousands of lakes and bays, covers more than half of Canada.

Appalachian Mountains

ATLANTIC OCEAN

The Appalachian Mountains are the oldest mountain range in North America.

The Great Plains are found in the central areas of both countries and sustain farming.

Regional Flyover

Suppose you fly in an airplane across the continent of North America. If you began on the west coast of the United States, you would fly over the coastal mountain ranges, the Sierra Nevada ranges, then the Rocky Mountains. These mountain ranges extend along the entire Pacific coast of both the United States and Canada. They are part of the Canadian Cordillera, or "parallel mountain ranges."

As you traveled eastward, the Great Plains would appear, spreading across the interior of the United States and Canada. To their north, the Canadian Shield stretches to beyond the Arctic Circle. There in Canada's Arctic Region, many islands are permanently covered by snow and ice.

If you continued flying east you would cross the Mississippi River, which flows from the northern United States to the Gulf of Mexico. Soon you would arrive on the east coast of the United States. You would have flown more than 2,500 miles and covered an entire continent.

→ **In-Flight Movie**

Take flight over North America and explore the region from the air.

my worldgeography.com

In-Flight Movie

Regional Overview
Human Geography

Where People Live

During the 1900s, large numbers of people living in the United States and Canada moved from rural areas to cities. Many were attracted to urban areas by the prospect of increased job opportunities and higher pay.

Urban Population, 1900

KEY
Urban Population, 1900

3,500,000
300,000
30,000

1900 U.S. Census
1901 Canadian Census

Immigrants arriving at
Ellis Island, New York

Urban Population, 2000

KEY
Urban Population, 2000

22,000,000
3,500,000
43,000

2000 U.S. Census
2001 Canadian Census

Modern-day Toronto

Lambert Azimuthal
Equal-Area Projection

 **my World IN NUMBERS**

Between 1910 and 2007, many people emigrated to the United States and Canada. As you can see from the graphs, the places of origin of the people who moved to the United States changed over time.

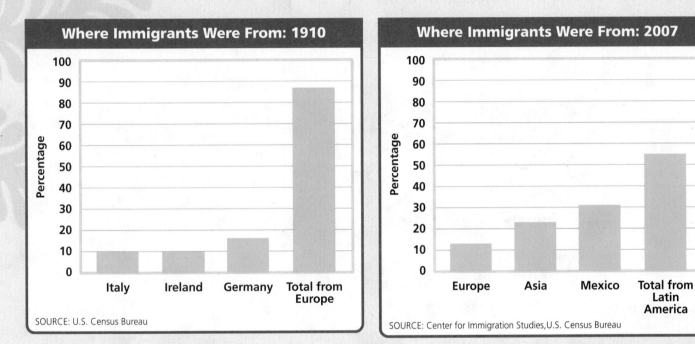

Where Immigrants Were From: 1910

Percentage (y-axis: 0 to 100)

Italy | Ireland | Germany | Total from Europe

SOURCE: U.S. Census Bureau

Where Immigrants Were From: 2007

Percentage (y-axis: 0 to 100)

Europe | Asia | Mexico | Total from Latin America

SOURCE: Center for Immigration Studies, U.S. Census Bureau

Put It Together

1. What physical features are common to both the United States and Canada?

2. What physical feature might keep northern Canada from being more settled?

3. Compare the places of origin of immigrants who settled in the United States in 1910 and 2007.

Size Comparison

Including Alaska and Hawaii, the United States is two percent smaller than Canada.

my worldgeography.com   Data Discovery

➜ **Data Discovery**

Find your own data to make a regional data table.

133

Chapter 1

The United States

Essential Question

How can you measure success?

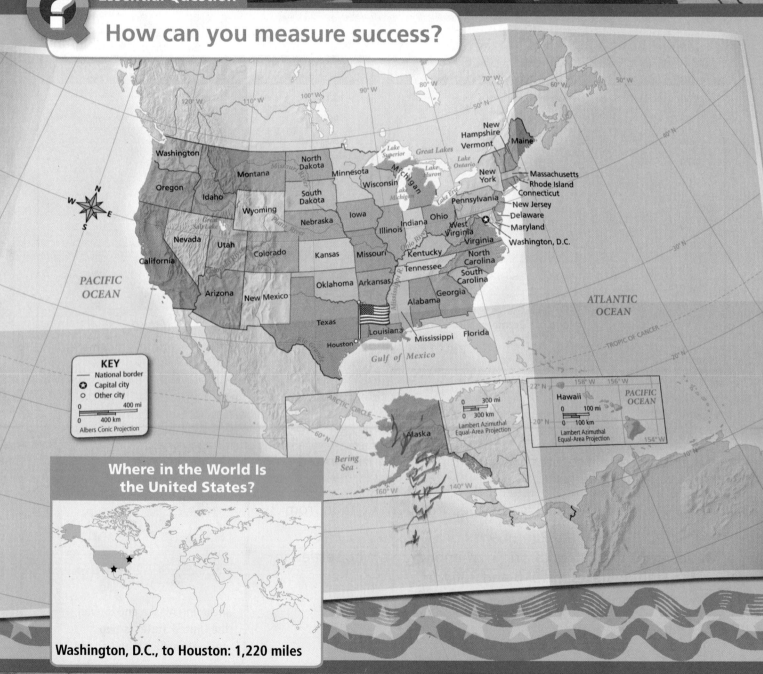

KEY
— National border
✪ Capital city
○ Other city

0   400 mi
0   400 km
Albers Conic Projection

Where in the World Is the United States?

Washington, D.C., to Houston: 1,220 miles

my Story

Finding Opportunity

Explore the Essential Question

- at my worldgeography.com
- using the **myWorld Chapter Activity**
- with the **Student Journal**

In this section, you'll read about Vy, a young Vietnamese-American college student. What does Vy's life tell you about the opportunities immigrants have found in the United States?

Story by Jake Johnson for myWorld Geography Online

Vy is an all-American teenager. She was born in Houston, Texas, and has never faced the kind of hardships her parents and grand-parents endured. Vy's parents and grandparents were born in Vietnam. They were forced to flee their native land after the fall of Saigon during the Vietnam War. Her father was only 13 when he arrived in the United States. He couldn't speak a word of English. At 18, Vy cannot speak Vietnamese.

Despite Vy's ancestry, Vietnam is a foreign and faraway place to her. She is entirely at home in the United States. Vy is one of 36,000 students who attend the University of Houston—the second-most ethnically diverse national university in the country. As a freshman, she is trying to balance academics with a job at her father's business, DI Central, a computer-related data company. She currently assists the marketing department by compiling information about customers and contacting those customers to conduct satisfaction surveys. She has yet to declare a major but thinks she might follow in her father's footsteps by focusing on business.

my worldgeography.com On Assignment

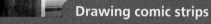

With friends, and heading home from school

Drawing comic strips

Quick to acknowledge her parents' tremendous sacrifices, Vy's greatest fear is letting them down. She feels she has been given luxuries her parents never had and should be even more successful than they've been.

Vy has her own car and her own cellphone, but she admits nothing is more important than the freedoms found in America. "I think so many people here take for granted that they can do what they want and say what they want. That's a choice not everyone gets to make in other countries," she says.

Such freedom has allowed Vy great independence. At the same time, she refuses to bury her family's roots and seems driven by her heritage. She has left behind her interest in high school sports to focus on college. Her textbooks and laptop now consume afternoons once spent at the mall. "My day starts at my dad's office at 9 A.M. and most

Vy and her sister, Ly, walk the dog.

Growing up, sports were important to Vy.

The family reconnects at dinner.

Vy working at her dad's office.

nights I don't get home until 7 or 8. I don't really have the free time that I used to." When she does have time to herself, she draws comic strips to express her feelings and plays ping-pong with her dad—a fierce opponent who, she jokes, takes the game too seriously.

Vy still lives at home. She shares a very close relationship with her two older sisters and younger brother. She credits her mother with maintaining a strong cultural bond. Her mother prepares traditional Vietnamese meals, with beef and fish dishes, and she insists the family eat together.

Three years ago, Vy took her first trip to Vietnam. Her family spent a month touring the country. The experience was bittersweet. "The cities were so dirty and so crowded, and the people seemed to have so little," says Vy. "I almost felt guilty that I had so much."

Although she still finds it impossible to imagine what her parents endured, it's a trip she says she will always treasure. Visiting Vietnam allowed Vy a unique opportunity to learn more about the land her parents call home, but she is quick to confess, "I just couldn't wait to get home and have a cheeseburger."

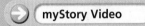 myStory Video

Join Vy on her trip to the city.

Meet the Journalist

Name Jake Johnson
Favorite Moment Dinner with the family

A visit to Vietnam

Chapter Atlas

 Indiana

6.3.1 Understand the countries and capitals of Europe and the Americas.

6.3.3 Describe and compare major physical characteristics of regions in Europe and the Americas.

6.3.6 Explain how ocean currents and winds influence climate differences on Europe and the Americas.

6.3.7 Locate and describe the climate regions of Europe and the Americas and explain how and why they differ.

6.3.9 Identify current patterns of population distribution and growth in Europe and the Americas and evaluate factors that trigger migrations.

Key Terms • climate • temperate • migration • metropolitan area • population density

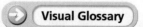 **Visual Glossary**

Reading Skill: Label an Outline Map Take notes using the outline map in your journal.

Plains in western Wyoming with the Rocky Mountains in the distance.

◀ A young rancher ▶

Physical Features

The United States is located in the northern hemisphere. The country has 50 states, and 48 of these states are located in the middle of North America. These 48 states are sometimes called the "Lower 48" or the "continental United States." The area stretches between the Atlantic and the Pacific Oceans. The remaining two states are Alaska and Hawaii. Alaska is in the far north on either side of the Arctic Circle. Hawaii is in the Pacific Ocean. While the United States is very large, it is about half the size of Russia.

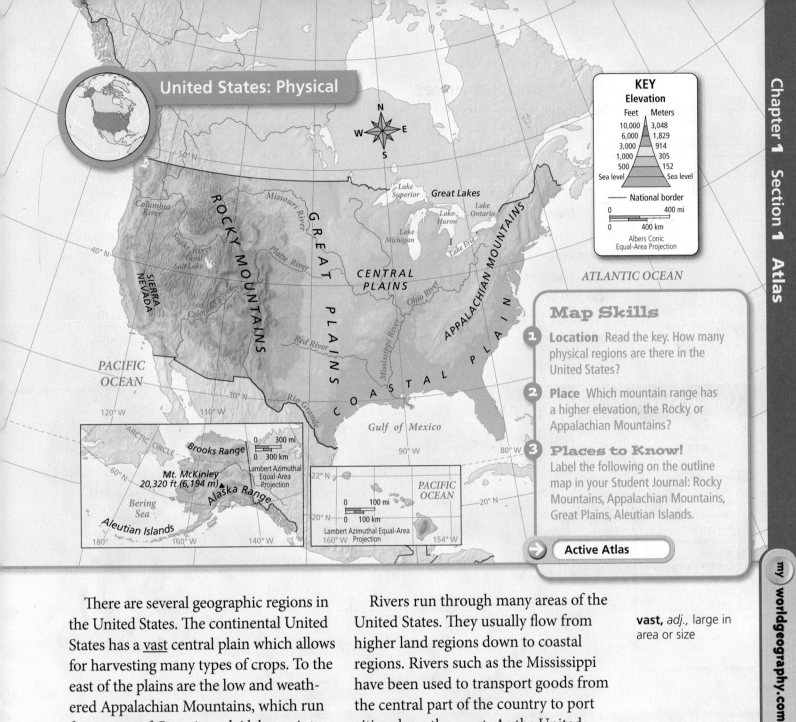

United States: Physical

KEY
Elevation

Feet	Meters
10,000	3,048
6,000	1,829
3,000	914
1,000	305
500	152
Sea level	Sea level

National border

0   400 mi
0   400 km
Albers Conic
Equal-Area Projection

ATLANTIC OCEAN

PACIFIC OCEAN

ROCKY MOUNTAINS

SIERRA NEVADA

Columbia River

Missouri River

Snake River

Great Salt Lake

Platte River

Colorado River

Red River

Rio Grande

GREAT PLAINS

CENTRAL PLAINS

Lake Superior

Great Lakes

Lake Michigan

Lake Huron

Lake Ontario

Lake Erie

Ohio River

Mississippi River

APPALACHIAN MOUNTAINS

COASTAL PLAIN

Gulf of Mexico

50° N

40° N

30° N

120° W

110° W

90° W

80° W

ARCTIC CIRCLE

Brooks Range

Mt. McKinley
20,320 ft (6,194 m)

Alaska Range

Bering Sea

Aleutian Islands

0   300 mi
0   300 km
Lambert Azimuthal Equal-Area Projection

60° N

180°

160° W

140° W

22° N

20° N

PACIFIC OCEAN

0   100 mi
0   100 km
Lambert Azimuthal Equal-Area Projection

160° W

154° W

Map Skills

1 **Location** Read the key. How many physical regions are there in the United States?

2 **Place** Which mountain range has a higher elevation, the Rocky or Appalachian Mountains?

3 **Places to Know!** Label the following on the outline map in your Student Journal: Rocky Mountains, Appalachian Mountains, Great Plains, Aleutian Islands.

Active Atlas

There are several geographic regions in the United States. The continental United States has a <u>vast</u> central plain which allows for harvesting many types of crops. To the east of the plains are the low and weathered Appalachian Mountains, which run from parts of Georgia and Alabama into Maine. Farther east is the Atlantic Ocean. To the west are the high and rugged Rocky Mountains, which run north from New Mexico, through Canada, and into Alaska. In the far West, there are the Sierra Nevada Mountains and the Pacific Coast. Hawaii, located in the middle of the Pacific Ocean, has several active volcanoes.

Rivers run through many areas of the United States. They usually flow from higher land regions down to coastal regions. Rivers such as the Mississippi have been used to transport goods from the central part of the country to port cities along the coast. As the United States grew, people settled towns along these transportation routes. Towns near rivers often grew into major cities, like Cincinnati, Ohio, Albany, New York, and New Orleans, Louisiana.

Reading Check Which two states are not included in the Lower 48?

vast, *adj.,* large in area or size

my **worldgeography.com** Active Atlas

Climate and Resources

The average temperature and precipitation over a long period of time creates a region's **climate**. Cool winters and warm summers make most of the United States **temperate**, or moderate. Extremely cold or extremely hot temperatures are rare. Northern states have a colder climate, and southern states have a warmer climate. Most climate areas in the United States are mild.

Weather in the United States is also impacted by wind patterns. Most wind travels across the country from west to east. In the winter, cold winds from the north and northwest bring chilling temperatures to the Midwest and East. As the seasons change from summer to early fall, air from the South Atlantic Ocean and the Gulf of Mexico travels north. Warm air from this area sometimes brings severe tropical storms with very high winds called hurricanes.

While hurricanes only affect some regions, the most common natural disaster in the United States is flooding. Floods

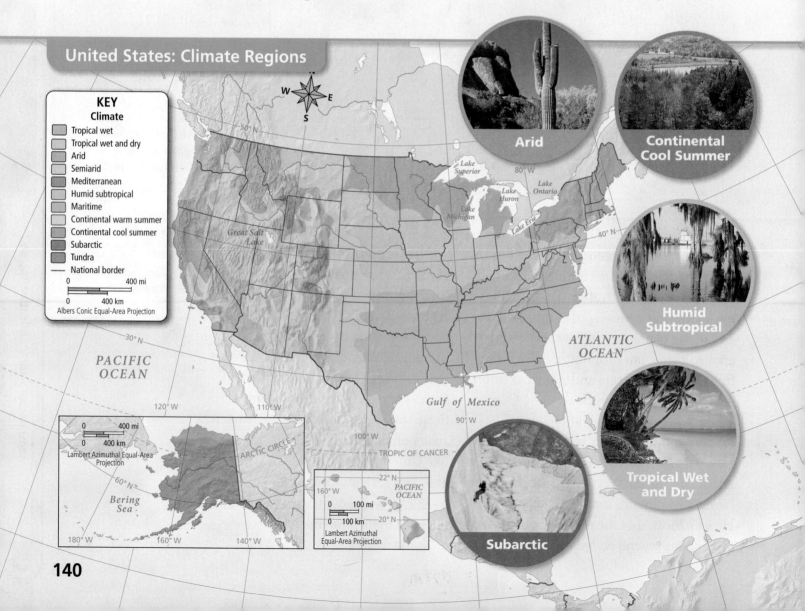

United States: Climate Regions

KEY
Climate
- Tropical wet
- Tropical wet and dry
- Arid
- Semiarid
- Mediterranean
- Humid subtropical
- Maritime
- Continental warm summer
- Continental cool summer
- Subarctic
- Tundra
- — National border

0   400 mi
0   400 km
Albers Conic Equal-Area Projection

Arid

Continental Cool Summer

Humid Subtropical

Tropical Wet and Dry

Subarctic

PACIFIC OCEAN

ATLANTIC OCEAN

Gulf of Mexico

Great Salt Lake

Lake Superior
Lake Michigan
Lake Huron
Lake Ontario
Lake Erie

50° N
40° N
30° N
80° W
120° W
110° W
100° W
90° W

TROPIC OF CANCER

0   400 mi
0   400 km
Lambert Azimuthal Equal-Area Projection

ARCTIC CIRCLE

60° N

Bering Sea

180° W   160° W   140° W

22° N
20° N
160° W
PACIFIC OCEAN
0   100 mi
0   100 km
Lambert Azimuthal Equal-Area Projection

140

occur when rainfall brings more water than rivers or drainage systems can carry.

In spite of weather conditions in many areas that can sometimes be difficult, people have found that natural resources make living in these areas of the United States worthwhile. Water, wood, and metals support businesses such as farming, fishing, and building.

Farmers harvest crops in the Great Plains and prairies in the middle of the country. This region produces some of the most widely grown crops in the world, including corn and soybeans.

Producing energy has also been very important to the success of the United States. Texas produces oil, Wyoming mines coal, and Alaska has natural gas. These resources and energy have been used to produce goods such as clothing and cars throughout the country's history. Having more resources meant industries could produce more goods. This has helped the United States economy grow.

Reading Check What is the most common natural disaster in the United States?

myWorld Activity
A Panel of Regions

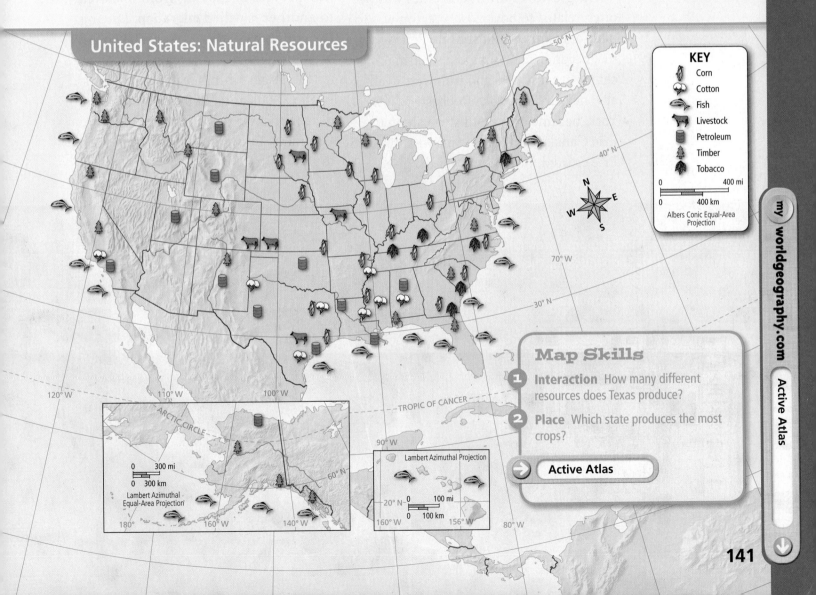

United States: Natural Resources

KEY

- Corn
- Cotton
- Fish
- Livestock
- Petroleum
- Timber
- Tobacco

0   400 mi
0   400 km
Albers Conic Equal-Area Projection

ARCTIC CIRCLE
0 300 mi
0 300 km
Lambert Azimuthal Equal-Area Projection

Lambert Azimuthal Projection
0 100 mi
0 100 km

TROPIC OF CANCER

Map Skills

1 Interaction How many different resources does Texas produce?

2 Place Which state produces the most crops?

Active Atlas

myworldgeography.com

Active Atlas

Migration and Settlement

The physical features of the United States have an important influence on where people settle and build communities. The first European settlements in North America were located along the Atlantic Ocean and the Gulf of Mexico. Fishing, logging, and farming were important to the economy and the livelihood of the people who lived close to these resources in the Northeast. Large plantation farms in the South grew cotton, tobacco, and sugar.

The growth of towns and cities was often related to how close a region was to natural resources. Pittsburgh, Pennsylvania, became important as a steel-making center because coal and iron were available nearby. Cities like Rochester, New York, became important stops along the Erie Canal. Man-made waterways like the Erie created travel routes for the goods farmers produced in the Midwest to markets for those goods in New York City.

As the United States grew, people sold more of the goods they produced to people in other cities and other countries. To transport these goods, railroads and river passages connected river towns with newer railroad towns. As people built railroads, towns and cities sprang up along their routes. Chicago is one example.

From the nation's beginnings, many people from all over the world immigrated, or moved to the United States. The process of moving from one area to another is called **migration**. During the country's early years, enslaved Africans brought to America by force made up the largest number of immigrants. In the 1800s and 1900s, people from different parts of Europe, including Germany, Italy, and Ireland, migrated to the United States.

West
Manufacturing and shipping brought many people to San Francisco. The Asian community is more than 30 percent of the city's population.

Midwest
As the United States expanded west, Chicago became an urban center because it was a center of railroad transportation.

United States: Regions

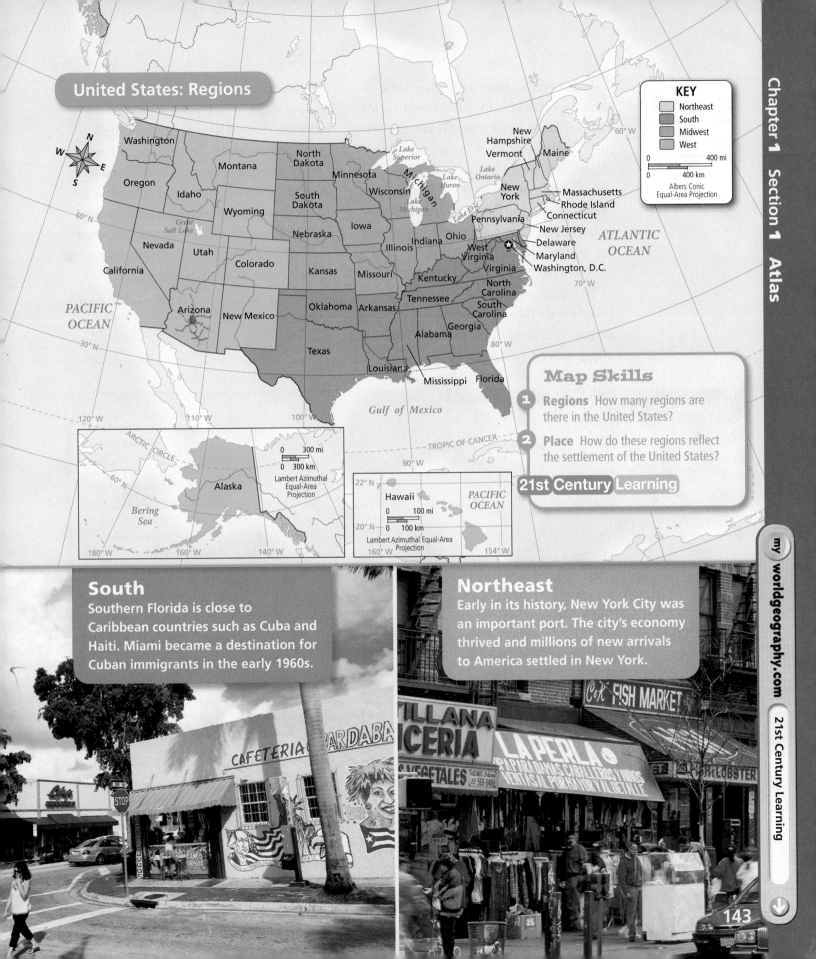

KEY

	Northeast
	South
	Midwest
	West

0   400 mi
0   400 km

Albers Conic
Equal-Area Projection

Washington
Oregon
Idaho
Montana
North Dakota
Minnesota
Wisconsin
Michigan
New Hampshire
Vermont
Maine
New York
Massachusetts
Rhode Island
Connecticut
Pennsylvania
New Jersey
Delaware
Maryland
Washington, D.C.
West Virginia
Virginia
Kentucky
North Carolina
South Carolina
Georgia
Alabama
Tennessee
Mississippi
Florida
Louisiana
Texas
Oklahoma
Arkansas
Missouri
Kansas
Nebraska
Iowa
Illinois
Indiana
Ohio
Colorado
Utah
Nevada
California
Arizona
New Mexico
Wyoming
South Dakota

Lake Superior
Lake Huron
Lake Michigan
Lake Erie
Lake Ontario

Great Salt Lake

ATLANTIC OCEAN

PACIFIC OCEAN

Gulf of Mexico

TROPIC OF CANCER

60° W
70° W
80° W
90° W
100° W
110° W
120° W
60° N
40° N
30° N

ARCTIC CIRCLE

Alaska

Bering Sea

60° N
180° W
160° W
140° W

0   300 mi
0   300 km

Lambert Azimuthal Equal-Area Projection

Hawaii

PACIFIC OCEAN

22° N
20° N
160° W
154° W

0   100 mi
0   100 km

Lambert Azimuthal Equal-Area Projection

Map Skills

1 **Regions** How many regions are there in the United States?

2 **Place** How do these regions reflect the settlement of the United States?

21st Century Learning

South

Southern Florida is close to Caribbean countries such as Cuba and Haiti. Miami became a destination for Cuban immigrants in the early 1960s.

Northeast

Early in its history, New York City was an important port. The city's economy thrived and millions of new arrivals to America settled in New York.

Today, many American cities such as New York, Miami, Florida, Los Angeles, California, and Houston, Texas, are growing rapidly because of immigration from other countries. Most newcomers move to look for jobs which are found in urban areas. Also, there is considerable internal migration, or people moving within the United States. In recent years, people have moved to cities from rural areas.

Today, approximately 304 million people live in the United States. Nearly 80 percent of those people live in urban areas.

These areas are either single cities or several cities which are geographically close together. These areas are called **metropolitan areas**. The number of people who live in one area are an area's **population density**. Generally, population densities are lowest in western states such as Wyoming and Montana. Some rural areas have experienced a population loss as more and more people move to cities to find jobs.

Reading Check What is one reason people live near rivers and other waterways?

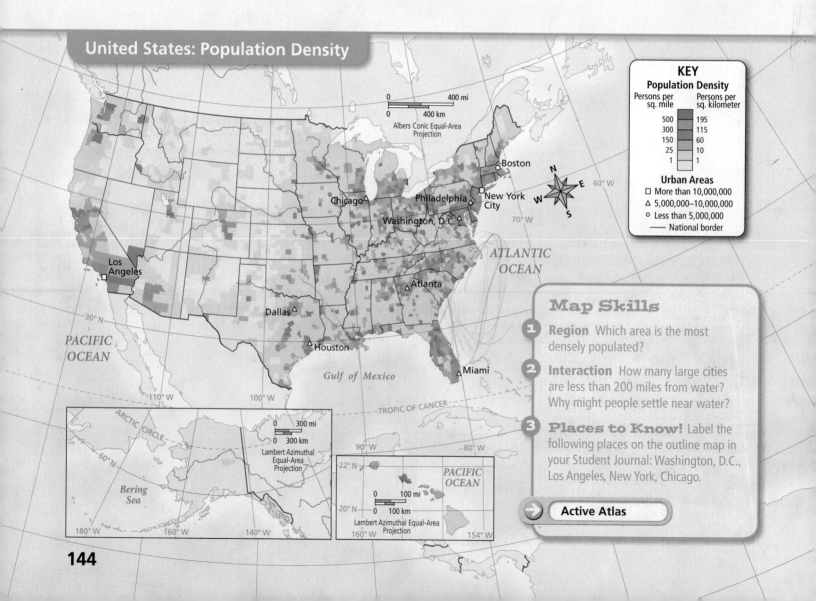

United States: Population Density

KEY
Population Density

Persons per sq. mile	Persons per sq. kilometer
500	195
300	115
150	60
25	10
1	1

Urban Areas
□ More than 10,000,000
△ 5,000,000–10,000,000
○ Less than 5,000,000
— National border

0   400 mi
0   400 km
Albers Conic Equal-Area Projection

0   300 mi
0   300 km
Lambert Azimuthal Equal-Area Projection

0   100 mi
0   100 km
Lambert Azimuthal Equal-Area Projection

Map Skills

1 Region Which area is the most densely populated?

2 Interaction How many large cities are less than 200 miles from water? Why might people settle near water?

3 Places to Know! Label the following places on the outline map in your Student Journal: Washington, D.C., Los Angeles, New York, Chicago.

→ **Active Atlas**

Environmental Impact

The growth and expansion of the United States had a negative effect on our environment. In the 1800s and early 1900s, industries in the United States used many raw materials such as iron, coal, and oil. Mining and burning coal created air pollution. Dumping coal and other industrial waste polluted water throughout the country. As the population of towns and cities increased, wildlife and fish populations decreased. By the 1960s, however, more and more people began to see how human activity affected the environment.

Today, citizen groups, companies, and the government are looking for ways to <u>minimize</u> the impact our large population has on the environment. Paper manufacturers have developed ways to manage forests to make sure trees will be available for future generations. Scientists are developing ways to produce energy that use fewer natural resources, while industries have developed products that use less energy.

▲ People drive electric vehicles to use less oil products.

minimize, *v.,* to reduce in size or degree

As a result of this work, the environment has improved but problems caused by pollution still exist. National, state, and local laws require pollution cleanup by companies and regulate resource use.

Reading Check How have people tried to minimize their impact on the environment?

Section 1 Assessment

Essential Question

How can you measure success?

Key Terms

1. Use the following terms to describe the United States: temperate, migration, metropolitan areas, population density, migration.

Key Ideas

2. Describe how the United States is able to produce agricultural products sold throughout the world.

3. What part have natural resources played in the growth of the United States economy?

4. Do most people in the United States live in rural areas or in the cities?

Think Critically

5. **Compare Viewpoints** What are the benefits of migration into the United States? What are the challenges?

6. **Draw Inferences** What are two reasons people would be more inclined to drive electric or hybrid cars?

7. How have natural resources created financial wealth for the United States? Go to your Student Journal to record your answers.

myworldgeography.com Active Atlas

History of the United States

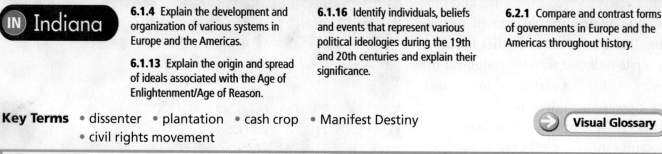

IN Indiana

6.1.4 Explain the development and organization of various systems in Europe and the Americas.

6.1.13 Explain the origin and spread of ideals associated with the Age of Enlightenment/Age of Reason.

6.1.16 Identify individuals, beliefs and events that represent various political ideologies during the 19th and 20th centuries and explain their significance.

6.2.1 Compare and contrast forms of governments in Europe and the Americas throughout history.

Visual Glossary

Key Terms • dissenter • plantation • cash crop • Manifest Destiny • civil rights movement

Reading Skill: Sequence Take notes using the graphic organizer in your journal.

A modern Native American ceremony ▼

Native American societies lived in North America for thousands of years until Europeans began settling the continent in the 1500s. Thirteen of the English colonies separated from Great Britain during the American Revolutionary War. Leaders of the thirteen former colonies established a new form of government and created the United States.

Early History of the United States

European explorers first arrived in North America in the 1400s, looking for faster ways to reach valuable goods in the East. Native Americans' lives changed dramatically when large numbers of Europeans, and European diseases, came into their lands.

Native American Groups of the East and Midwest Native American societies varied depending on the natural resources available to them. People living in the Eastern woodlands hunted, grew crops, and fished the Atlantic. They used logs and bark to build houses. The Plains Indians lived in semi-permanent villages, growing crops and hunting buffalo on the grasslands. Those who lived farther west were nomadic. When Spanish explorers brought horses to North America, these native groups used the horses to follow herds of buffalo.

Native American Groups of the West
The harsh, dry lands in present day Nevada could not support agriculture. Native Americans there lived in small, scattered groups. Southwest Native Americans grew corn and lived in large villages or towns built out of stone or adobe. Along the west coast, Native Americans depended on the resources of the Pacific Ocean and coastal forests.

First European Settlements In the 1500s, European countries began competing to establish colonies in North America. English kings hoped that North American colonies would provide wealth. Religious **dissenters,** or people whose beliefs differed from the official religion in their country, also settled colonies.

The first English settlement in North America was Jamestown, Virginia, in 1607, followed by the Massachusetts Plymouth Colony in 1620. By 1733, the 13 original English colonies that later became the United States had been settled.

The English Colonies In New England, rocky soil and a cold climate limited agriculture, although forests and oceans allowed shipbuilding, fishing, and trade.

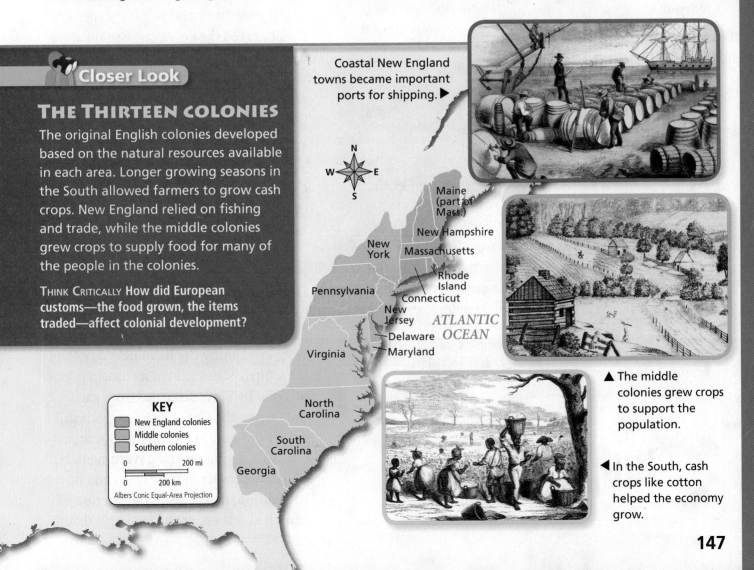

Closer Look

THE THIRTEEN COLONIES

The original English colonies developed based on the natural resources available in each area. Longer growing seasons in the South allowed farmers to grow cash crops. New England relied on fishing and trade, while the middle colonies grew crops to supply food for many of the people in the colonies.

THINK CRITICALLY How did European customs—the food grown, the items traded—affect colonial development?

Coastal New England towns became important ports for shipping. ▶

Maine (part of Mass.)
New Hampshire
New York
Massachusetts
Rhode Island
Pennsylvania
Connecticut
New Jersey ATLANTIC
Delaware OCEAN
Maryland
Virginia
North Carolina
South Carolina
Georgia

KEY
New England colonies
Middle colonies
Southern colonies
0   200 mi
0   200 km
Albers Conic Equal-Area Projection

▲ The middle colonies grew crops to support the population.

◀ In the South, cash crops like cotton helped the economy grow.

147

established, *v.,* enacted, caused to be recognized

The middle colonies had rich soils, a longer growing season, and large river systems for transporting crops.

The southern colonies had a warmer climate to support agriculture on very large farms called **plantations.** Plantations grew **cash crops,** or crops grown mainly for sale to other colonies or countries.

Reading Check Why did England establish colonies in North America?

Preserving Democracy: The Separation of Powers

Leaders in a democracy are elected. The Constitution established a system of government where no single person or group can gain too much power. The three branches of government check, or limit, the power of the other branches.

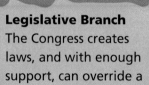

Executive Branch
The President sets policy, vetoes, and carries out laws created by the legislative branch.

Legislative Branch
The Congress creates laws, and with enough support, can override a President's veto.

Judicial Branch
The Supreme Court interprets the Constitution and laws created by Congress.

A New Country

For about 150 years, the colonies grew and developed their own local political, cultural, and economic systems.

Government in the Colonies Each colony had its own legislature and governor. The governor was expected to keep in contact with the British Parliament, but because of the distance between the colonies and England, the colonies learned over time to govern themselves.

From 1754 to 1763, Britain fought and won a war in North America against France and gained new territories. To rule the territory and pay war expenses, Britain taxed the colonists. Britain also established new rules in North America to govern the larger territory. These rules and taxes angered the colonists.

American Revolution and Beyond In 1774, each colony sent representatives to a colonial meeting called the Continental Congress in Philadelphia. The Congress drew ideas from the Enlightenment, a movement to understand the world by observing nature and using reason. Colonists used Enlightenment ideas in the Declaration of Independence to argue that the British government was not protecting their natural rights to freedom.

After winning the Revolutionary War, the United States gained its independence in 1783. In 1787, delegates from each state wrote the Constitution, which still guides our nation today. This document created a strong central government, but also gave powers to state government. In addition, it established separation of church and state, or the principle that the country would not support one religion for the people to follow.

Reading Check Why did the colonists protest against England?

Expansion and Growth

Over the next 50 years, Americans created new states, often leading to conflict with Native Americans. While the nation expanded geographically, its economy also expanded, changing the culture of the country.

Westward Expansion After the Revolutionary War, Americans headed westward to find land and wealth. In 1803, the United States bought the Louisiana Territory from France, doubling the country's size. **Manifest Destiny,** the idea that the country should expand across the continent, swept the nation.

As Americans moved westward, they encountered the many Native American groups who already lived there. The government signed land treaties with Native Americans, but these treaties were later broken, and the government forced Native Americans to live on plots of land called reservations.

Internal Divisions As territories became states, conflicts between people in the North and the South grew worse. The South's plantation-based economy relied heavily on enslaved labor. Southerners wanted the new states to allow slavery, while Northerners opposed slavery in those states. Some politicians supported the idea of popular sovereignty, which meant allowing people in each new territory to decide whether they would allow slavery. Leaders hoped that this idea

principle, *n.,* a rule or standard

myWorld Activity
Living Timeline

Map Skills

1 **Place** Which five countries did the United States acquire land from?

2 **Regions** What effect did these countries have on today's culture?

➔ **Active Atlas**

Manifest Destiny

OREGON COUNTRY
(Agreement with Britain, 1846)

Ceded by Britain, Convention of 1818

Albers Conic Equal-Area Projection

Disputed with Great Britain until 1842

Great Lakes

Missouri River

MEXICAN CESSION
(Treaty of Guadalupe Hidalgo, 1848)

LOUISIANA PURCHASE
(Purchased from France, 1803)

THE UNITED STATES
(1783)

ORIGINAL 13 STATES

Ohio River

Colorado River

GADSDEN PURCHASE
(Purchased from Mexico, 1853)

Arkansas River

Red River

TEXAS ANNEXATION
(Annexed by Congress, 1845)

Mississippi River

PACIFIC OCEAN

Rio Grande

Annexed, 1810

Annexed, 1812

FLORIDA
(Ceded by Spain, 1819)

ATLANTIC OCEAN

Gulf of Mexico

TROPIC OF CANCER

ARCTIC CIRCLE

Bering Sea

ALASKA
(Purchased from Russia, 1867)

Lambert Azimuthal Equal-Area Projection

HAWAII
(1898)

Lambert Azimuthal Equal-Area Projection

0   400 mi
0   400 km

0   300 mi
0   300 km

0   100 mi
0   100 km

United States Influence Grows

Since the 1800s, the United States has become more involved in world events. Leaders have tried to gain resources, expand the United States economy, and influence world events in order to protect these interests.

→ Timeline

1898 The Spanish American War established Cuba's independence from Spain and brought Guam and Puerto Rico within the influence of the United States.

1919 President Wilson promoted United States security through membership in the League of Nations. Congress voted against joining the League, but the United States later joined the United Nations.

1948 World War II destroyed much of Europe. With the Marshall Plan, the United States helped deliver food and rebuild affected countries.

would help resolve the conflict between Northerners and Southerners, but that did not happen. In 1861, several Southern states declared independence, which sparked the Civil War, one of the world's bloodiest wars. When the war ended, the nation started to rebuild.

The Industrial Revolution New types of machines developed during the Industrial Revolution made farming easier and meant fewer people needed to work the land. Factories turned out goods rapidly and cheaply. Man-made waterways called canals, steamboats, and railroads moved goods faster than ever before. As a result, the American economy expanded, and people moved in large numbers from farms to the growing cities where much of the manufacturing was located.

Reading Check What was Manifest Destiny?

A Developing Power

Throughout the 1900s, the United States economy, and its population, continued to expand. Immigrants poured in from other countries. They also had an important influence on American culture.

The Role of Immigration From the nation's beginning, immigrants have moved to the United States. Between the American Revolution and the Civil War, most immigrants came from Ireland or Germany. In the early 1900s, large numbers of Italians, Polish, and Hungarian immigrants, as well as Jewish people from throughout Europe, came to America. Immigrants worked in factories, built railroads, opened businesses, and populated cities. Immigrants came to America for different reasons, but finding new opportunities was a common theme.

66 America lives in the heart of every man who wishes to find a region where he will be free to work out his destiny as he chooses. 99

—President Woodrow Wilson

The Great Depression and World War II Beginning in 1929, the Great Depression caused the American economy to suffer. Banks closed, and people lost jobs and homes. In response, President Franklin D. Roosevelt created the New Deal, which aimed to create jobs for the unemployed and proposed new rules for banks and businesses. Roosevelt's policies greatly expanded the federal government.

In 1939, World War II began in Europe and the Pacific. The United States tried to remain neutral. However, Japan bombed American naval bases in 1941, and the United States entered the war. The United States and its allies won the war in 1945. Many industries expanded to make goods needed for warfare. Though life had been difficult during the war, World War II helped expand the economy.

Expanding Prosperity After World War II the United States was a world superpower, or a country with dominant military, economic, political, and cultural influence. The economy expanded, and the middle class grew larger. People wanted to buy more goods and services, and the economy grew to provide them.

Not all Americans benefited, however. African Americans struggled for equality with white Americans. In the 1960s, a movement for equality began, called the **civil rights movement**. Protesters challenged racial discrimination, sometimes losing their lives in the process. Congress passed new laws in the 1960s that gave African Americans equal rights. The civil rights movement had a huge influence on other groups, including women, Native Americans, and immigrants.

Reading Check What was the civil rights movement?

IN Indiana CONNECTIONS

Almost **400,000** men and women from Indiana served in the U.S. military during World War II.

Section 2 Assessment

Key Terms

1. Use the following key terms to explain important events in the country's history: dissenter, plantation, cash crop, Manifest Destiny, civil rights movement.

Key Ideas

2. How did Native American culture reflect the resources available to these groups?

3. How did Europeans change the physical landscape of North America?

4. What effect did immigration have on the United States economy?

Think Critically

5. **Synthesize** What is the relationship between natural resources and the economy?

6. **Draw Conclusions** What are some reasons African Americans could not exercise many of their civil rights before the 1960s?

Essential Question

How can you measure success?

7. What are the advantages and disadvantages to a country acquiring more land? Go to your Student Journal to record your answers.

The United States Expands

 **Indiana**   **6.1.22** Form research questions and use resources to present data on people, cultures and developments in Europe and the Americas.   **6.1.23** Identify issues related to an event in Europe or the Americas and give arguments for and against that issue.

Key Terms • adapt • annex • vital

Europeans came to North America looking for opportunity. They looked for land to farm, and sometimes they looked for wealth. When Europeans arrived in North America, they brought their culture. The Native Americans they met had their own diverse cultures. As more Europeans traveled west, they often cooperated with Native Americans. But as expansion continued, the differences between both groups led to conflict.

Native Americans Before European Contact

For centuries, Native American groups lived throughout North America. Each group **adapted,** or changed its lifestyle, to the resources in its environment.

In the woods of the northeast, Native Americans hunted animals like deer, fished in rivers, and grew corn, beans, and squash. On the

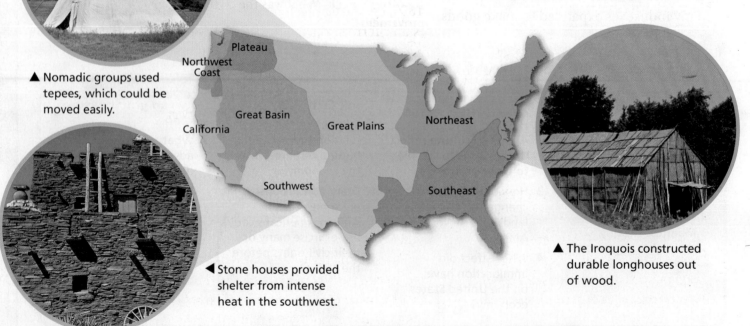

▲ Nomadic groups used tepees, which could be moved easily.

Plateau
Northwest Coast
Great Basin
California
Great Plains
Northeast
Southwest
Southeast

◀ Stone houses provided shelter from intense heat in the southwest.

▲ The Iroquois constructed durable longhouses out of wood.

◀ This painting captured the idea that Americans were destined to move west. A mythic figure guides settlers, lighting the dark wilderness as they travel.

Great Plains, Native Americans hunted buffalo and used the animals for food, clothing, and housing. In the dry Southwest, Native Americans used the little water available to grow corn.

When Europeans arrived in North America, they learned from Native American groups. Native Americans sometimes gave food to the new arrivals, helping them survive the early years of their colonies. They taught the settlers how to grow local crops, such as corn and squash. They traded furs with settlers. Increasingly, however, relations between the two groups were marked by conflict as they fought for control of the land.

Reading Check How did settlers benefit from contact with Native Americans?

The United States Expands

At first, the United States only occupied the area east of the Mississippi River. In 1803, the government purchased the Louisiana Territory from France. This vast area strected from the Mississippi to what now includes Montana and Wyoming.

In the 1800s, many Americans believed in "manifest destiny." In this view, it was the destiny of Americans to move west. By the 1840s, thousands of people were moving to places like Oregon, where they found rich farmland. In 1846, Britain gave up its claim to present-day Oregon and Washington.

During this time, the desire to expand led to conflict. In 1845, the United States **annexed**—or took control of—Texas. Just a few years before, Texas had won inde-

LOOKING WEST

From the country's beginning, the United States saw opportunity in the land west of the thirteen original colonies. Affordable land and the prospect of gold led thousands of settlers to move west. The process often forced others from land they once occupied.

EVENT Georgia settlers found gold in 1829. This and the search for land led Americans to demand that native groups move west.

RESULT In 1830, Congress passed the Indian Removal Act, which forced thousands of Native Americans to move west. Cherokees traveled to Oklahoma on what became known as the Trail of Tears (right).

EVENT The Mexican government, which owned Texas, offered land grants to American settlers.

RESULT Americans who settled in Texas refused to follow land grant guidelines, which, among other guidelines, required settlers to follow the Mexican constitution and become Roman Catholic. After losing a battle at the Alamo (left), Texas won independence and later joined the United States.

EVENT Many territories in the west held important minerals such as copper, iron, and coal. California, Alaska, and Colorado had gold. The discovery of gold in California (right) led to the California Gold Rush in the late 1840s.

RESULT With the Gold Rush in California, San Francisco was settled and quickly grew into a center of economic activity.

pendence from Mexico. The annexation strained relations between the United States and Mexico and war erupted. When the United States emerged the winner, Mexico gave up almost all the land it held in what is now the United States. The remainder was purchased in 1853.

Another purchase was made a little more than thirteen years later, when the United States bought Alaska from Russia. In 1898, the government annexed Hawaii.

Reading Check Which two areas were annexed?

Effects of Expansion

Expanding into new territories changed the lives of the new settlers and native people. It also helped the United States succeed economically.

Impact on Native Americans Native Americans sometimes cooperated with the new settlers, giving horses or guidance to those traveling west. Sometimes there was conflict.

As more settlers moved west, Native Americans found it difficult to maintain their way of life. Some Native Americans moved to new areas. Others grew angry as settlers broke agreements that had limited where the settlers could live. These Native Americans decided to fight, hoping to drive away settlers, and keep their land. Native Americans lost these wars.

Resources and Economic Expansion
Obtaining new lands helped the United States grow economically. New Orleans, Louisiana, became an important American port city. Farmers in the Ohio and Mississippi River valleys sent their crops downriver to New Orleans where the crops were then sent east or abroad. The forests of Washington state were used to build homes, factories, and ships. These resources all helped fuel the growing American economy.

Newly acquired lands provided another **vital,** or important, resource—space. The American population kept growing, not only as families had children but also as immigrants arrived from other countries. These new arrivals, who often had escaped conflict or poverty in their home countries, tried to build new lives in the United States and its territories.

Reading Check How did resources help the United States economy grow?

Assessment

1. Why did Native Americans in different areas follow different lifestyles?

2. What was the idea of "manifest destiny"? What was its result?

3. What led to conflict with some Native American groups as the nation expanded?

4. How did Europeans and Native Americans differ in how they used the available resources?

5. What do you think was the most important effect of expansion, finding more resources or the opportunity to settle in new areas? Explain your answer.

The United States Today

IN Indiana

6.3.4 Describe and compare major cultural characteristics of regions in Europe and the Western Hemisphere.

6.3.10 Explain the ways cultural diffusion, invention, and innovation change culture.

6.4.2 Analyze how countries of Europe and the Americas have been influenced by trade in different historical periods.

6.4.4 Describe how different economic systems in Europe and the Americas answer the basic economic questions.

6.4.6 Analyze current economic issues in the countries of Europe or the Americas using a variety of resources.

Key Terms • market economy • export • import • economic region • diplomacy

Visual Glossary

Reading Skill: Analyze Cause and Effect Take notes using the outline map in your journal.

Vy working at her father's office. ▼

Throughout its history, the United States has played an important part in events around the world. Today, the United States economy still has a global effect. Advances in technology have added to the country's growth. The United States carries a high volume of the world's Internet messages. As a result, American culture, including music and other forms of entertainment, spreads more easily between American citizens and people around the world.

The United States Economy

The United States has a **market economy,** where individuals and businesses make the majority of buying and selling decisions. American companies are leaders in medical science, agriculture, entertainment, and banking.

Influence on the World Economy Americans continually buy products from and sell products to many countries. Farm products are our most important **export,** a good that is shipped to different areas of the world. Clothing, cars, and household goods are generally **imports,** or goods brought to the United States. Many of the products we use are imported from China, India, and Japan, where the cost of making things is lower than in the United States. Oil is imported from Mexico, South America, and Middle East countries like Saudi Arabia. Oil is so important that its price affects all the countries of the world.

Canada and Mexico are America's largest trading partners. Our special relationship with these neighboring countries is governed by North American Free Trade Agreement (NAFTA). NAFTA is one

my Story **📷 Photo**

Closer Look

THE UNITED STATES ECONOMY

The United States economy has changed greatly in the last century. Fifty years ago, most Americans worked in farming and manufacturing, such as building cars or making clothes. Today, the economy is primarily based on services like medical research, computers and technology, education, and retail store sales. Slightly more than eight percent of Americans work in manufacturing.

THINK CRITICALLY How does technology like the combine pictured below affect the number of people who work in agriculture?

Nearly ten percent of the United States population works in transportation.

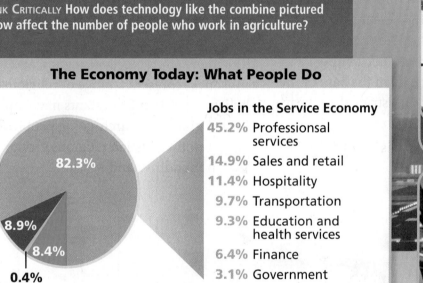

The Economy Today: What People Do

82.3%

8.9%

8.4%

0.4%

Jobs in the Service Economy

45.2% Professionsal services

14.9% Sales and retail

11.4% Hospitality

9.7% Transportation

9.3% Education and health services

6.4% Finance

3.1% Government

■ Service   ■ Manufacturing

■ Agriculture   ■ Other

SOURCE: U.S. Bureau of Labor Statistics, 2007

Scientific research is a service.

Finance in New York

Although less than one percent of Americans work in agriculture, it remains an important part of the economy.

...oys many people.

of many agreements among countries to increase trade for less cost.

The Economy at Home Throughout the United States, there are many **economic regions**, or places where people do particular kinds of work. One example of an economic region is near the Great Lakes, where the auto manufacturing industry was first established. Other economic regions include the Midwest, where agriculture is important, and the Pacific Northwest, where forestry has been a major part of the economy. In southern California, entertainment and computer products form the base of the economy. Service industries affect nearly every part of the country.

Reading Check What is NAFTA?

American Culture

Culture is a pattern of activities, language, and habits common to a group of people. Culture is expressed in many ways, including the religion we practice, the foods we prefer, the music we like, and how we dress. The United States is a land of many kinds of people. Over nearly three centuries, people from other places have contributed to American culture.

Origins of Culture People new to the United States often bring aspects of their culture from their home country. The many churches, synagogues, and mosques represent a range of religious beliefs. Christian Protestants make up the largest group of church-going people. The largest non-Christian religious groups are Jewish, Buddhist, and Muslim.

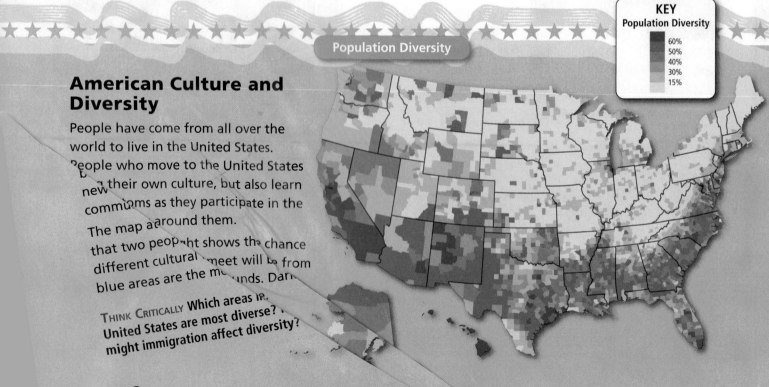

Population Diversity

KEY
Population Diversity
60%
50%
40%
30%
15%

American Culture and Diversity

People have come from all over the world to live in the United States. People who move to the United States b___ their own culture, but also learn new commi_ms as they participate in the The map a_round them.

that two peop_ht shows th_ chance different cultural _meet will b_ from blue areas are the m___nds. Dar___

THINK CRITICALLY Which areas in___ United States are most diverse? ___ might immigration affect diversity?

The many foods we eat are another aspect of culture. The many different kinds of restaurants <u>illustrate</u> the diversity of culture in the United States. Popular music and sports also have cultural and geographic roots.

While many cultures have influenced people in the United States, American culture has spread around the globe. It is difficult to go anywhere in the world without seeing the effect of American fast food restaurants, pop music, and television. The Internet has made American culture even more accessible.

Immigration Today Because the United States offers economic and cultural freedom for everyone, it is no surprise that millions of people would like to relocate to the United States. Most of the population increase in the last ten years has been the result of immigration. After finding a place to live in the United States, most immigrants want to stay and become citizens. It is possible to be a citizen of the county where one is born and also a citizen of the United States. American citizenship allows someone to practice free speech, go to school, and to vote during elections. While these rights may seem common, they are sometimes not guaranteed in other countries.

Groups of immigrants from the same country often choose to live in the same community or neighborhood. You can find diverse communities in almost all large cities, such as Washington, D.C., Los Angeles, New York, and Chicago. Immigrant groups in these cities add to the workforce of the existing economy.

Illustrate, *v.,* to show by example

myWorld Activity
Classmate quiz

→ Culture Close-up

SCHOOL BUS

State and federal leaders address the effects of immigration and look for fair ways to allow some immigrants into the country. They hope to ensure that new residents will have a chance to work and contribute to the American economy.

Reading Check What is one way American culture spreads throughout the world?

promote, *v.,* to support or encourage

Soldiers deliver food as part of the USAID program. ▼

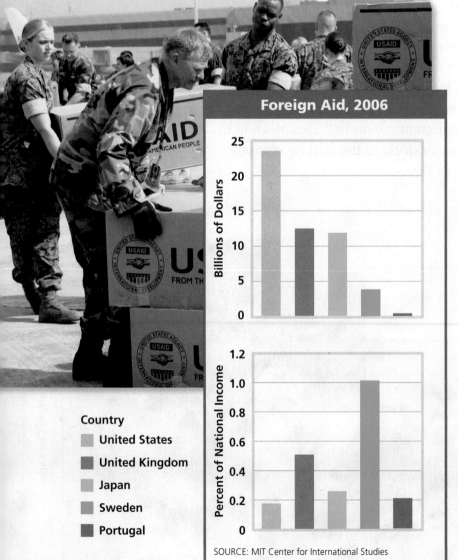

Foreign Aid, 2006

Billions of Dollars

Percent of National Income

Country
- United States
- United Kingdom
- Japan
- Sweden
- Portugal

SOURCE: MIT Center for International Studies

The United States as World Leader

The size of the American economy and the military allows the country to pursue its interests in many parts of the world.

Foreign Policy The United States, like most other countries, tries to <u>promote</u> and protect its interests and the concerns of its allies. Interests such as how countries will trade goods are often negotiated, or discussed, by government and business leaders. The process of making decisions through discussion is called **diplomacy.** Diplomacy can also be used to address conflicts among groups of people. While diplomacy is usually the first way the United States addresses conflict among people, diplomacy does not always work.

On September 11, 2001, terrorists, or people who use violence against innocent people to harm their enemies, attacked the United States. The terrorists took control of four passenger airplanes. One crashed into the Pentagon in the greater Washington D.C. area, one crashed in Pennsylvania, and two hit the World Trade Center towers in New York City.

The attacks focused the American military on removing the Taliban in Afghanistan from power. The United States led this effort, and soon after its success, President George W. Bush argued that both

Chart Skills

How much more aid does the United States offer than the United Kingdon?

Data Discovery

Afghanistan and Iraq posed a threat to the United States. In Iraq, President Bush argued that Saddam Hussein had weapons of mass destruction. The military removed Hussein from power quickly, but conflict between groups in Iraq led to continued fighting for several years.

Economic and Social Intervention While the United States pursues military interests, it also works to meet the needs of people through aid programs. Organizations like the United States Agency for International Development (USAID) and the Peace Corps support a wide variety of efforts to provide food and teach people the skills they need to survive.

The United States government works with several countries to stop conflicts in north and central Africa. Private organizations, such as the Bill and Melinda Gates Foundation, provide healthcare.

The United States continues to use its economic, political, and military resources to discourage conflict. President Barack Obama described the balance between using force and diplomacy in his inaugural address.

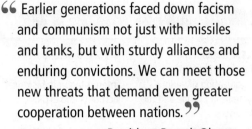

66 Earlier generations faced down facism and communism not just with missiles and tanks, but with sturdy alliances and enduring convictions. We can meet those new threats that demand even greater cooperation between nations. 99

—President Barack Obama

Reading Check What is diplomacy?

◀ Former Secretary of State Hillary Clinton and former British Prime Minister Gordon Brown

Section **3** Assessment

Key Terms

1. Use the following terms to describe the role of the United States in the world today: market economy, export, import, economic region, diplomacy.

Key Ideas

2. What is a market economy?

3. How do trade agreements like NAFTA increase trade?

4. What are some recent examples of the United States influencing world events through its foreign policy?

Think Critically

5. **Draw Conclusions** How does immigration affect the United States economy and culture?

6. **Draw Inferences** How is it in the interest of the United States to offer economic and social aid to foreign countries?

? Essential Question

How can you measure success?

7. Are there disadvantages to government involvement in events that take place around the world? Go to your Student Journal to record your answer.

myworldgeography.com   Data Discovery

American Democracy

IN Indiana

6.1.4 Explain the development and organization of various systems in Europe and the Americas.

6.1.21 Differentiate between fact and interpretation in historical accounts and explain historical passages.

6.1.23 Identify issues related to an event in Europe or the Americas and give arguments for and against that issue.

Writings like the Declaration of Independence and the Gettysburg Address have played an important role in shaping American democracy. Jefferson's list of complaints about the British king not only justified the patriots' war for independence but also paved the way to a civil government. In honoring those lost in the Civil War's bloodiest battle, Lincoln declared his vision for a united, democratic America. By analyzing these excerpts, you will better understand some of the key ideas of American democracy.

▲ The Declaration of Independence outlined principles for a new form of government.

Stop at each circled letter on the right to think about the text. Then answer the question with the same letter on the left.

A Summarize According to Jefferson, who has rights and who can take them away?

B Paraphrase In your own words, rephrase Jefferson's argument about the purpose of government.

C Analyze Cause and Effect Given the context of war, what do you think Jefferson was trying to bring about by saying it was proper to abolish a government?

endowed, *v.,* given; provided
unalienable, *adj.,* not to be taken away
deriving, *v.,* getting from a source
consent, *n.,* agreement

Declaration of Independence

❝ We hold these truths to be self-evident, that all men are created equal, that they are <u>endowed</u> by their Creator with certain

A <u>unalienable</u> Rights, that among these are Life, Liberty and the pursuit of Happiness. That to secure these rights, Governments are

B instituted among Men, <u>deriving</u> their just powers from the <u>consent</u> of the governed, that whenever any Form of Government becomes destructive of these Ends, it is the Right of the People to alter or to

C abolish it, and to institute new Government… ❞

—Thomas Jefferson
Declaration of Independence, July 4, 1776

Thomas Jefferson

Stop at each circled letter on the right to think about the text. Then answer the question with the same letter on the left.

D **Connect** What document is Lincoln quoting?

E **Summarize** Put into your own words what Lincoln is saying is different and special about the United States.

F **Draw Inferences** Lincoln refers to "people," not Northerners or Southerners. Based on this word choice, how do you think he wants Americans to treat each other after the war?

conceived, *v.,* formed

dedicate, *v.,* to set apart for a purpose

in vain, *adj.,* for no reason

perish, *v.,* to die; be destroyed

The Gettysburg Address

❝ Four score and seven years ago our fathers brought forth on this continent, a new nation, <u>conceived</u> in Liberty, and <u>dedicated</u> to the proposition that all men are **D** created equal.

Now we are engaged in a great civil war, testing whether that nation, or any nation so conceived **E** and so dedicated, can long endure …

[W]e here highly resolve that these dead shall not have died <u>in vain</u>—that this nation, under God, shall have a new birth of freedom—and that government **F** of the people, by the people, for the people, shall not <u>perish</u> from the earth. ❞

—Abraham Lincoln, Gettysburg Address, Nov. 19, 1863

Abraham **Lincoln**

Listening to the Gettysburg Address ▼

Analyze the Documents

1. **Draw Inferences** Why do you think Lincoln quotes the Declaration of Independence in his speech at Gettysburg?

2. **Writing Task** Go back to the two documents and find textual evidence, words, or phrases, that supports the following statement: *A strong religious tradition and a commitment to civil government are two important trends in the history of American democracy.*

Chapter Assessment

Key Terms and Ideas

1. **Summarize** How did having land lead to population growth in the United States?

2. **Analyze Cause and Effect** How did the Industrial Revolution affect the environment?

3. **Recall** What is the idea behind **Manifest Destiny**?

4. **Sequence** How did the availability of **cash crops** lead to developing **plantations**?

5. **Explain** How does **diplomacy** encourage cooperation among countries?

6. **Compare and Contrast** What is the relationship between **metropolitan areas** and **population density**?

7. **Describe** What do trade agreements do to encourage economic growth?

Think Critically

8. **Analyze Primary and Secondary Sources** What does President Obama's statement in Section 3 tell you about United States foreign policy?

9. **Compare and Contrast** What are the cultural similarities and differences between the four regions of the United States?

10. **Draw Inferences** How has settlement in the original 13 colonies affected today's population?

11. **Core Concepts: Economic Systems** How has the free market created economic growth?

Places to Know

For each place, write the letter from the map that shows its location.

12. Rocky Mountains

13. Chicago

14. Great Plains

15. Washington, D.C.

16. Aleutian Islands

17. Appalachian Mountains

18. Los Angeles

19. **Estimate** Using the scale, estimate the distance between Washington, D.C., and Chicago.

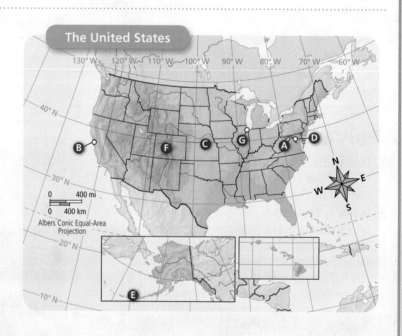

The United States

Essential Question

myWorld Chapter Activity

Follow your teacher's instructions to create a script for a documentary about how immigration has shaped the United States. Research major immigrant groups using the chapter activity cards and myWorld Geography online. Describe reasons people migrated, including when and where they settled, and the effect each group had on the United States.

21st Century Learning

Search for Information on the Internet

Using reliable sources online, research a civil rights leader. Using at least two resources, find and record the following information:
- Name
- Hometown
- Contribution(s) to the civil rights movement

For each source, write a sentence explaining why your source is reliable.

Success Tracker™
Online at myworldgeography.com

Document-Based Questions

Use your knowledge of the United States and Documents A and B to answer Questions 1–3.

Document A

" In the new law[s] which will be necessary for you to make, I desire you would remember the ladies. We will not hold ourselves bound by any laws in which we have no voice or representation."
—Abigail Adams to John Adams, March, 1776

" We know better than to repeal our masculine systems. [But] we are obliged to go fair and softly, and, in practice, you know we are the subjects."
—John Adams to Abigail Adams, April, 1776

Document B

" It is essential that measures be enacted aimed at unemployment relief. The first is the enrollment of workers by the federal government for public employment. The second is grants to States for relief work. The third extends to a broad public works labor-creating program."

—Franklin D. Roosevelt, March 21, 1933

1. Which statement best describes the effects of the American Revolution on women, according to Document A?

   A Women had fewer political rights.

   B Women were expected to take on new responsibilities in the government.

   C Women were encouraged to fight during the Revolutionary War.

   D John Adams and the other Founding Fathers were unwilling to allow women to vote.

2. Based on Document B, what was the most likely criticism of Roosevelt's New Deal?

   A The New Deal did not create jobs.

   B His program caused the economy to suffer.

   C The New Deal greatly expanded the federal government.

   D Roosevelt's program led us into World War II.

3. **Writing Task** Why did Roosevelt think that creating jobs was important for the economy? Explain your answer.

my worldgeography.com Self-Test

165

Chapter 2

Canada

Essential Question

Is conflict unavoidable?

KEY
— National border
— Provincial or territorial border
⊛ National capital
★ Provincial or territorial capital

0   400 mi
0   400 km
Lambert Azimuthal
Equal-Area Projection

ARCTIC OCEAN

Baffin
Bay

Nunavut

Iqaluit

Labrador
Sea

Yukon

★ Whitehorse

Northwest
Territories

★ Yellowknife

Newfoundland and Labrador

PACIFIC
OCEAN

Hudson
Bay

★ St. John's

British
Columbia

Alberta

★ Edmonton

Saskatchewan

Manitoba

Quebec

New
Brunswick

Prince
Edward
Island

★ Charlottetown

★ Fredericton

★ Quebec

★ Halifax

Nova
Scotia

Regina ★

Winnipeg ★

Ontario

St. Lawrence
River

Great Lakes

★ Victoria

Ottawa ⊛

Toronto ★

ATLANTIC
OCEAN

Where in the World Is Canada?

Washington, D.C., to Ottawa: 460 miles

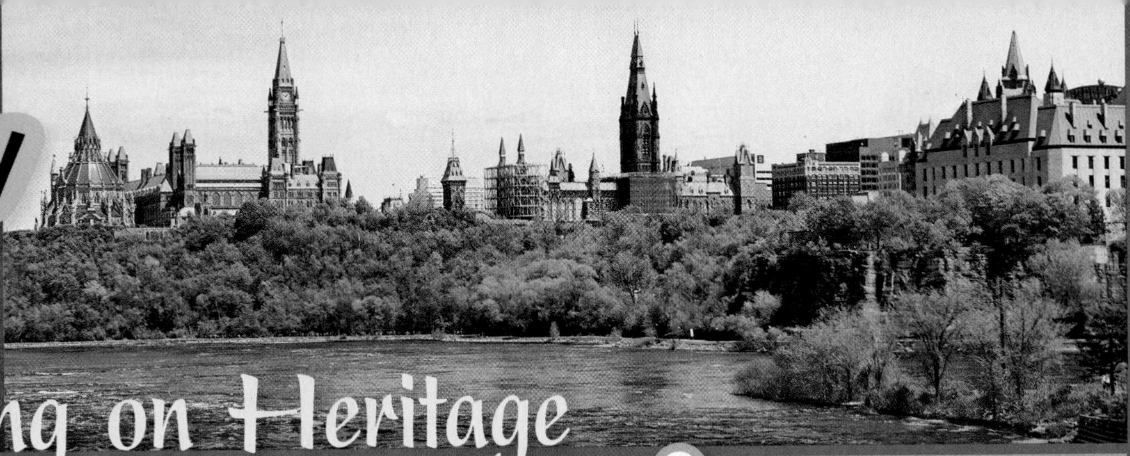

my Story

Drawing on Heritage

Explore the Essential Question

- at my worldgeography.com
- using the **myWorld Chapter Activity**
- with the **Student Journal**

In this section you'll read about Alyssa, a Canadian from the province of Ontario. What does Alyssa's story tell you about life in Canada?

Story by Jake Johnson for myWorld Geography Online

During the Spring in Ottawa, Canada, the ice melts, the grass begins to grow, and the city's waterways flow freely. Most Canadians begin to enjoy the beautiful outdoors of the nation's capital. But 20-year-old Alyssa heads north in the spring to visit her extended family in the snowy city of Iqaluit, Nunavut. In the 1950s some of Alyssa's family, including her mother Martha, were relocated from Inukjuak, in northern Quebec, to Grise Fiord, near the Arctic Circle. It is Canada's northernmost community, earning it the Inuit name of *Aujuittuq,* meaning "place that never thaws."

Canada's indigenous populations are diverse, and Alyssa is a prime example of that diversity. Her mother's family is Inuk Inuit, and her father is Cree. The Inuk Inuit people are often labeled "Eskimos." Alyssa considers the term "Eskimo" not only incorrect, but disrespectful. "Eskimo," interestingly, is a Cree word, which means "eaters of raw meat." Alyssa explains, "There is an indigenous population in Canada, and within that population there are three different groups. There are Métis, First Nations, and Inuit. Specifically, I am Inuit. The Inuit are native to Canada's northern regions.

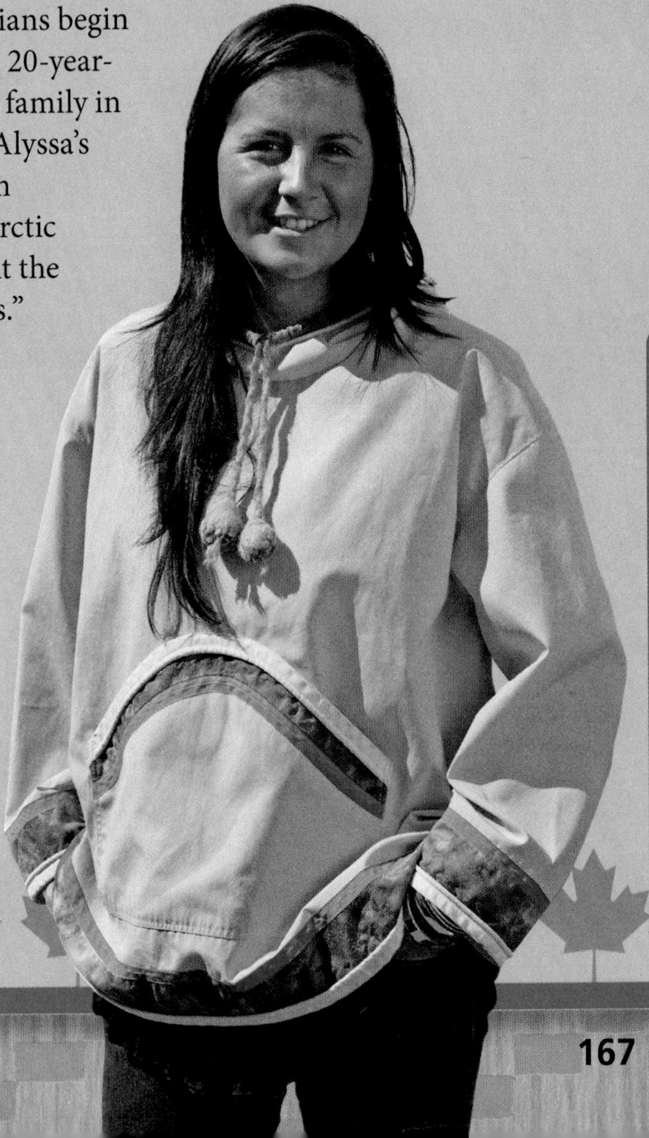

Alyssa and her aunt in an igloo at Iqaluit

Alyssa participates in a "Culture Circle" with younger Inuit children.

Working at Inuit Tapiriit Kanatami

Alyssa and her coworkers enjoy a lunch of traditional Inuit foods.

The First Nations are indigenous tribes that receive governmental support, and Métis are people who have mixed backgrounds of indigenous and French or Scottish heritage. It is a bit complex, eh?"

A few days later, back in Ottawa, Alyssa jumps into her work at the Inuit Tapiriit Kanatami (ITK), which means "The Inuit Brotherhood of Canada." "ITK is a national organization for Inuit, and it works on environmental, health and socio-economic issues for Inuit," says Alyssa.

On one particular day, several of Alyssa's coworkers gather in the break room. Alyssa has brought caribou, narwhal, and arctic char fish from Iqaluit. Coworkers have planned a "Country Food" luncheon. "We don't have the opportunity to do this all the time, since we live in southern Canada. So this is really nice," beams Alyssa. Her dishes are a big hit. There is plenty of bannock (Inuit fried bread), and a prized delicacy, raw narwhal skin.

Recently, Alyssa has seen a wide range of weather. In the north the weather was below freezing. Ottawa has been sunny and mild. But this morning brings powerful wind gusts and rain showers. Alyssa heads

Bannock, Inuit fried bread

Dried arctic char fish

Alyssa plays soccer.

Alyssa and her mother, Martha

to the University of Ottawa, where she is a political science major, with a minor in aboriginal studies. "I learn a lot about my traditions at school, so it helps me do my work at ITK." Today she wears a cool-weather parka. Alyssa proudly points out that her mother made the parka, complete with fox fur trim. She hurries to get out of the rain and to her next appointment.

Children await Alyssa's visit at the Ottawa Inuit Child Care Centre. Alyssa joins the children in daily rituals. Traditional songs, dancing, and language lessons bring a smile to Alyssa's face as she practices the customs of her heritage. The time goes quickly, but before she goes she joins in a friendly game of "throat singing." Women sing harsh melodic tones back and forth until one of them loses the rhythm. Alyssa loses the match, and almost loses her voice.

At the end of the workday Alyssa heads to her family's home in the countryside in Almonte, Ontario. After soccer practice with her local women's team, Alyssa goes to her parents' house where she shares video of her Iqaluit trip with her mother, Martha. Martha's face lights up at the glow of her family's campfire. "I am going up there in a few days, I can't wait," says Martha. They spend some precious minutes together and smile, united by the sights of their icy homeland. For this young Inuit woman there is a lot to smile about.

Meet the Journalist

Name Jake Johnson
Favorite Moment "When Alyssa shared with her mother the video of her trip to the north, you could see a love for their distant family and their heritage."

→ **myStory Video**

Join Alyssa in Canada.

Alyssa in the parka her mother made

my worldgeography.com

myStory Video

Chapter Atlas

IN Indiana

6.3.1 Understand the countries and capitals of Europe and the Americas.

6.3.2 Use latitude and longitude to locate the capital cities of Europe and the Americas and describe the uses of locational technology.

6.3.5 Give examples and describe the formation of river deltas, mountains and bodies of water in Europe and the Americas.

6.3.8 Identify major biomes of Europe and the Americas and explain how these are influenced by climate.

6.3.12 Compare the distribution and evaluate the importance of natural resources in Europe and the Americas.

Key Terms • precipitation • tundra • permafrost • mixing zone

→ **Visual Glossary**

🌐 **Reading Skill: Label an Outline Map** Take notes using the outline map in your journal.

A view of downtown Vancouver

Physical Features

Canada is located immediately north of the United States. These two bordering nations have much in common. Overall, many Americans and Canadians enjoy a high standard of living. Both countries are physically large. After Russia, Canada is the second-largest country in the world in total land area.

While many people in Canada live near the United States border, Canada's geography offers many other places for people to live and work. There are several major regions in Canada. Each region is defined by its geography and its climate. The

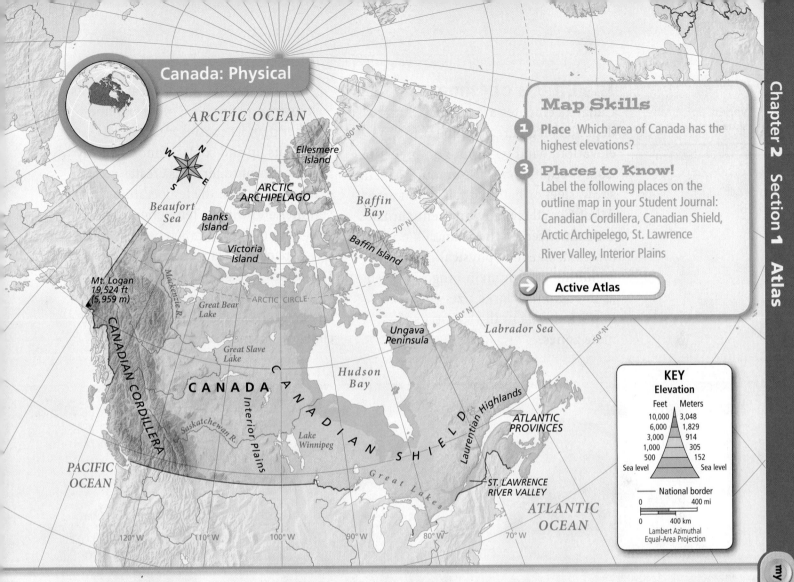

Canada: Physical

ARCTIC OCEAN

Ellesmere Island

ARCTIC ARCHIPELAGO

Beaufort Sea

Banks Island

Baffin Bay

Victoria Island

Baffin Island

Mt. Logan 19,524 ft (5,959 m)

Mackenzie R.

Great Bear Lake

ARCTIC CIRCLE

CANADIAN CORDILLERA

Great Slave Lake

CANADA

Ungava Peninsula

Labrador Sea

Hudson Bay

C A N A D I A N   S H I E L D

Interior Plains

Saskatchewan R.

Lake Winnipeg

Laurentian Highlands

ATLANTIC PROVINCES

PACIFIC OCEAN

Great Lakes

ST. LAWRENCE RIVER VALLEY

ATLANTIC OCEAN

Map Skills

1 **Place** Which area of Canada has the highest elevations?

3 **Places to Know!**
Label the following places on the outline map in your Student Journal: Canadian Cordillera, Canadian Shield, Arctic Archipelego, St. Lawrence River Valley, Interior Plains

Active Atlas

KEY
Elevation

Feet	Meters
10,000	3,048
6,000	1,829
3,000	914
1,000	305
500	152
Sea level	Sea level

National border

0   400 mi
0   400 km

Lambert Azimuthal Equal-Area Projection

Arctic region includes a chain of islands in Canada's far north called the Arctic Archipelago. Most of this region is within the Arctic Circle. Below the Arctic is the Canadian Shield, a massive, rocky area dotted with thousands of lakes. The Canadian Shield extends from Hudson Bay to the Canadian Cordillera. To the east are the Atlantic Provinces, which include the northern parts of the Appalachian Mountains. West of the Atlantic Provinces is the St. Lawrence River Valley, the most populous region in Canada. Farther west are the Interior Plains, which are part of the same geographic formation as the Great Plains in the United States. Finally, the Canadian Cordillera, the northern section of the Rocky Mountains, and the Pacific coast are in Canada's west.

Most citizens live in the southern and coastal areas of Canada. Regions like the St. Lawrence River Valley, the Atlantic Provinces, and the Southwest coast of Canada have moderate climates. In addition, these areas have <u>fertile</u> soils for farming, and other resources that help support large populations.

Reading Check What is the Canadian Shield?

fertile, *adj,* nutrient rich, well-suited for growing plants

The Effects of Climate

varied, *adj,* diverse; showing variety

Canada's climates are <u>varied</u>. Climate depends on an area's temperature, elevation, wind patterns, and precipitation. **Precipitation** is the amount of rain, snow, sleet or hail that falls in an area. All of Canada's many different climates are influenced by the country's northern location. Canada's physical geography—including its mountain ranges, as well as the country's large size—plays an important role in the country's climate zones.

The large size of Canada means that its vast interior plains have more extreme weather than its coastal areas, because land heats up and cools off more quickly than bodies of water. This creates greater extremes between the temperatures in the summer and winter. Temperatures on the coast do not vary as much because those areas are close to large bodies of water.

The part of Canada located closest to the United States has less-varied climates. It has small areas of semiarid and maritime climates, but most of the area has a conti-

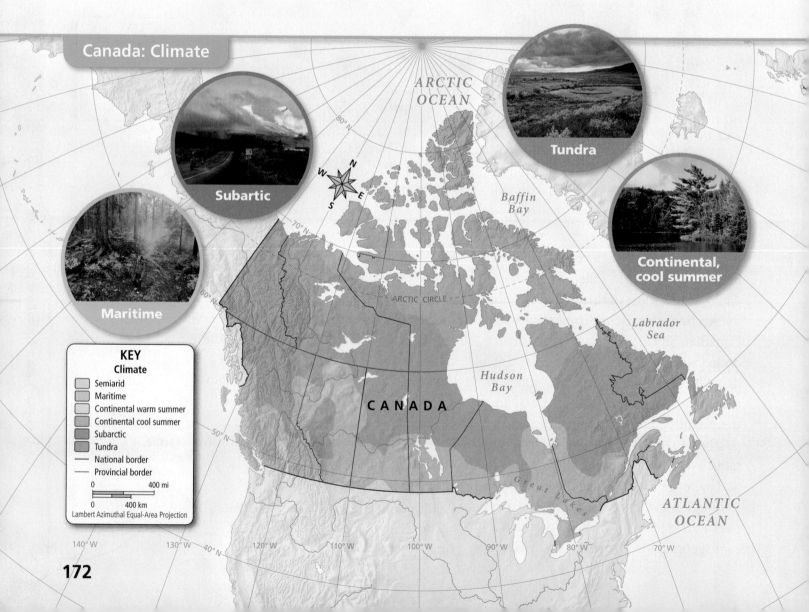

Canada: Climate

ARCTIC OCEAN

Subartic

Tundra

Maritime

Continental, cool summer

80° N

70° N

60° N

50° N

40° N

ARCTIC CIRCLE

Baffin Bay

Labrador Sea

Hudson Bay

CANADA

Great Lakes

ATLANTIC OCEAN

KEY
Climate

Semiarid
Maritime
Continental warm summer
Continental cool summer
Subarctic
Tundra
National border
Provincial border

0   400 mi
0   400 km
Lambert Azimuthal Equal-Area Projection

140° W   130° W   120° W   110° W   100° W   90° W   80° W   70° W

nental cool summer climate. Summers are often hot and humid, while winters are very cold. In the maritime climate region on Canada's Pacific coast, more rain than snow falls each year and temperatures are more moderate. Northern Canada has subarctic and **tundra** climates with long, cold winters. The tundra is an area with limited vegetation, such as moss and shrubs. In this area, freezing temperatures last through the winter and summer. In the warmest weeks of the year, the temperature is rarely higher than 50 degrees Fahrenheit. In the subarctic zone, summers are generally short, cool, and rainy. Summer temperatures only reach the mid 60s to low 70s Fahrenheit.

Climate has had an important effect on where people decide to live. Outside of Canada's large cities, the country only averages about two people per square mile. This sparse population distribution is directly due to the challenges of Canada's physical geography, especially its harsh northern climates.

Reading Check What causes extreme temperature changes in the interior plains?

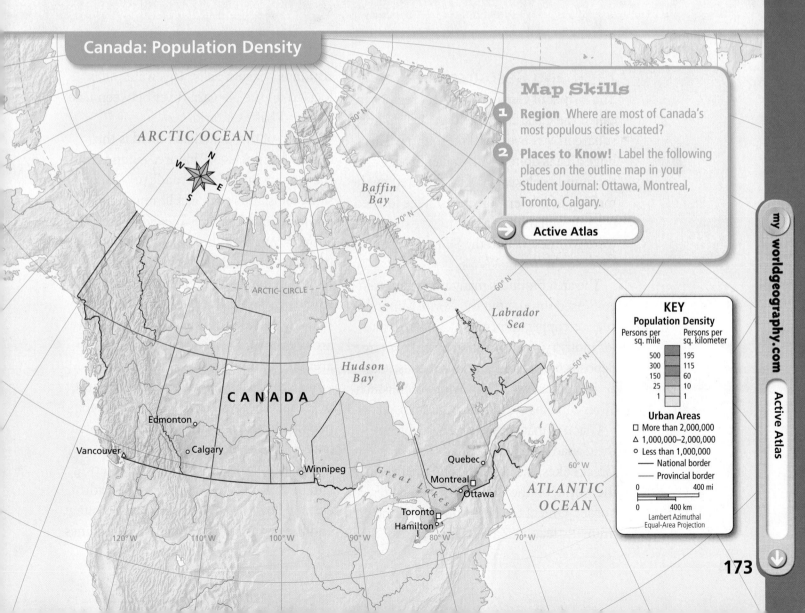

Canada: Population Density

Map Skills

1 **Region** Where are most of Canada's most populous cities located?

2 **Places to Know!** Label the following places on the outline map in your Student Journal: Ottawa, Montreal, Toronto, Calgary.

➔ **Active Atlas**

KEY
Population Density

Persons per sq. mile	Persons per sq. kilometer
500	195
300	115
150	60
25	10
1	1

Urban Areas
□ More than 2,000,000
△ 1,000,000–2,000,000
○ Less than 1,000,000
— National border
— Provincial border

0   400 mi
0   400 km

Lambert Azimuthal Equal-Area Projection

ARCTIC OCEAN

Baffin Bay

ARCTIC CIRCLE

Labrador Sea

Hudson Bay

CANADA

Edmonton
Vancouver
Calgary
Winnipeg
Great Lakes
Quebec
Montreal
Ottawa
Toronto
Hamilton

ATLANTIC OCEAN

173

The Continental Railroad

The St. Lawrence Seaway

Land and Resources

The largest of Canada's physical regions is called the Canadian Shield. Its 2.8 million square miles cover half the country. This huge area is dotted with ancient rocks and thousands of lakes and bays, created by the melting of glaciers, or sheets of ice formed by compacted snow. The Shield extends from Minnesota and the St. Lawrence River to the Arctic Circle.

The area produces many important minerals used throughout the world. Minerals such as copper, iron, and nickel, are vital for industry. The Canadian Shield has large deposits of lead and precious metals, such as gold and silver. The province of Saskatchewan contains very large uranium reserves.

Glaciers that spread southward from the Canadian Shield created the five Great Lakes, the largest group of lakes in the world, on the Canada-United States border. One of the best-known and most dramatic features in the Great Lakes region is Niagara Falls. This waterfall is located on the Niagara River between Lake Erie and Lake Ontario.

North of the Canadian Shield is the Arctic Archipelago. This area extends into the Arctic Circle and is made up of thousands of islands such as Ellesmere and Baffin islands, that are covered by ice and snow throughout the year. While the area thaws temporarily in the summer, most of the soil remains permanently frozen. This soil that never thaws is called **permafrost.**

On both sides of the St. Lawrence River are the the St. Lawrence Lowland. The area surrounding the St. Lawrence and Great Lakes is often called the heartland of Canada because a majority of Canada's people, industries, cities, and fertile farmland is located here.

Canada has many other lakes, rivers, and bays. Rivers are used to create hydroelectric power. Dams hold the river water, and then channel it through large turbines that produce electricity. The longest and most important river in Canada is the St. Lawrence River. This river, along with a series of canals and locks, connects the Great Lakes to the Atlantic Ocean, providing an important transportation route from Canada's interior to the sea.

South of the St. Lawrence Lowlands is the Appalachian region. Here, low, rounded mountains and a rugged coastline separate the Atlantic Provinces from the rest of Canada. The Appalachians extend from Newfoundland in the north

to the state of Georgia in the southern United States. The economy in the Atlantic Provinces is similar to the northern New England states. It is based on fishing, forestry, agriculture, and tourism.

While there is fishing along both the Atlantic and Pacific coasts of Canada, one of the best-known fishing areas in the world is an area called the Grand Banks. The area is located off the Atlantic coasts of Newfoundland and Labrador. Warm waters from the Gulf Stream and cold waters from the Labrador Current meet in

myWorld Activity
Resource Attraction

Canada: Natural Resources

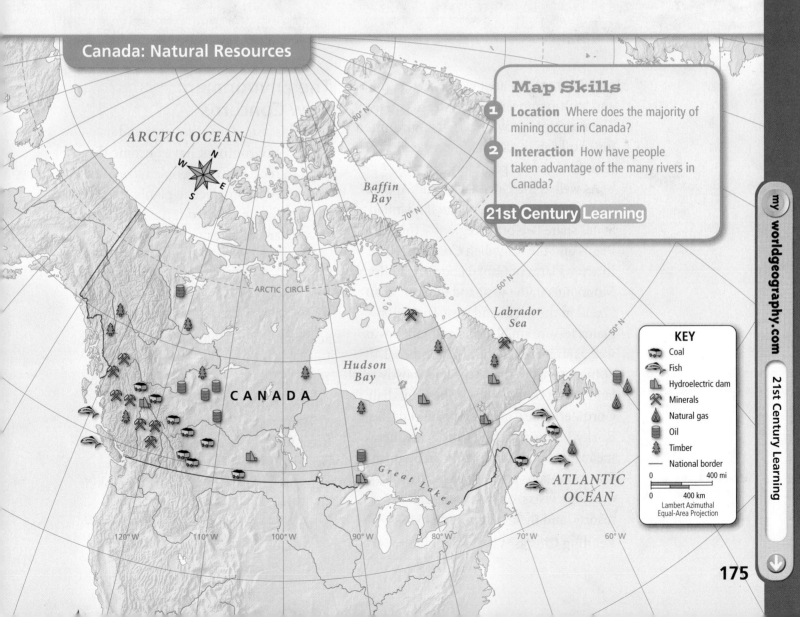

Map Skills

1 **Location** Where does the majority of mining occur in Canada?

2 **Interaction** How have people taken advantage of the many rivers in Canada?

21st Century Learning

KEY

🚗 Coal
🐟 Fish
⛏ Hydroelectric dam
⚒ Minerals
🛢 Natural gas
🛢 Oil
🌲 Timber
—— National border

0   400 mi
0   400 km
Lambert Azimuthal
Equal-Area Projection

A Changing Economy

Earlier in its history, Canada depended heavily on its natural resources, like cod fishing. Today, the economy is more diverse, and Canada's government regulates cod fishing to protect its natural resources.

Cod fishing in Newfoundland, 1950s

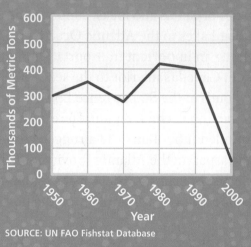

Cod Catch in Canada

Thousands of Metric Tons (y-axis: 0, 100, 200, 300, 400, 500, 600)

Year (x-axis: 1950, 1960, 1970, 1980, 1990, 2000)

SOURCE: UN FAO Fishstat Database

---

a **mixing zone,** an area where waters mix and stir up nutrients from the ocean floor. The nutrients provide a rich environment for plankton in the mixing zone. Fish then feed on the plankton.

As well as the Great Lakes and Appalacian Mountains, Canada and the United States share two other regions—the Great Plains and the Canadian Cordillera. The Interior Plains of Canada border the Rocky Mountains in the west and the Canadian Shield in the north and east. The grassy plains feature small farms and ranches as well as sources of natural gas and coal.

In contrast to the fertile and mostly level land in the Great Plains is the Canadian Cordillera, the Canadian portion of the Rocky Mountains. The word "cordillera" means "chain of mountains" in Spanish. The mountains are famous for their <u>dramatic</u> vistas, or views, popular ski resorts, and their rich mining history.

Reading Check What is a mixing zone?

dramatic, *adj.,* interesting, exciting, or impressive

The Environment: New Concerns

Canada's abundant resources and its natural environment have become threatened in recent years. People have over-developed hydroelectric plants, extracted too many minerals from the land, and have clear-cut forests.

Cleaning up air pollution in Canada requires efforts by both the United States and Canada. The Canada–United States Air Quality Agreement helped reduce acid rain in the 1990s. More recently, the Border Air Quality Strategy, passed in 2003, has helped reduce smog near the border between the two countries.

There is also concern about using fossil fuels for heating, transportation, and electricity. Using these resources increases the amount of carbon dioxide and other gases released into the atmosphere. These gases trap heat and contribute to global warming.

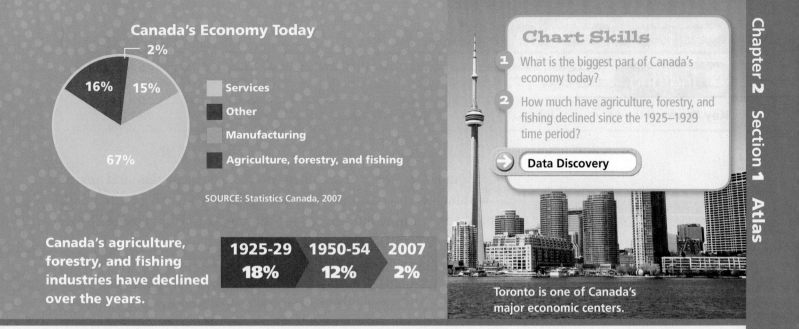

Canada's Economy Today

2%
16%
15%
67%

- Services
- Other
- Manufacturing
- Agriculture, forestry, and fishing

SOURCE: Statistics Canada, 2007

Canada's agriculture, forestry, and fishing industries have declined over the years.

1925-29	1950-54	2007
18%	12%	2%

Chart Skills

1. What is the biggest part of Canada's economy today?

2. How much have agriculture, forestry, and fishing declined since the 1925–1929 time period?

→ Data Discovery

Toronto is one of Canada's major economic centers.

Canada crafted its own Climate Change Plan in 1997. This legislation provides guidelines to help reduce global warming. Despite these efforts, however, the Arctic ice cap continues to melt, and other environmental challenges caused by global climate change continue.

The Arctic region is especially vulnerable to climate change because of its fragile environment. Damage to Arctic land and water takes years to heal. Pollution from oil and gas spills is also a dangerous threat to plants and animals in this sensitive region. As urban growth, air and water pollution, and the overextraction of its natural resources continue, Canada will face many challenges to both its environmental and its economic future.

Reading Check What has Canada done to reduce pollution and improve air quality?

Section 1 Assessment

Key Terms

1. Use these terms to describe the climate in Canada: precipitation, tundra, permafrost, mixing zone.

Key Ideas

2. Identify and describe Canada's largest landform.

3. Why are the Grand Banks ideal for fishing?

4. How has Canada's economic development been similar to that of the United States?

Think Critically

5. **Draw Conclusions** How does Canada's climate affect where people live?

6. **Analyze Cause and Effect** In what ways has economic development affected Canada's natural environment?

Essential Question

? **Is conflict unavoidable?**

7. What agreements reflect cooperation between the United States and Canada? What environmental issues do they involve? Go to your Student Journal to record your answers.

my worldgeography.com | Data Discovery

Canada's Icy North

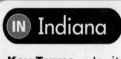

6.1.22 Form research questions and use resources to present data on people, cultures and developments in Europe and the Americas.

Key Terms • Inuit • igloos • Northwest Passage

Canada's far north accounts for two fifths of Canada's land area and much of its coastline. This vast region has a harsh environment, however. For nine months of the year, the far north is covered by ice and snow. January temperatures average –22 degrees Fahrenheit. In the summer thaw, temperatures only reach 59 degrees Fahrenheit. Although the environment is a difficult place to live, Canadians and native people have made use of the available resources.

Inuit Survival Strategies

Some three or four thousand years ago, a native people called the **Inuit** settled in the Arctic regions of North America. Few plants survive in the region, so the Inuit depended on hunting. They lived nomadically, traveling often. In summer, they rode dogsleds to hunt caribou. In winter, they ventured into the icy waters, where they harpooned seals and even whales. They also fished and hunted walruses.

Hunting provided clothing, transportation, and food. Clothing made from caribou fur shielded them from the bitter winter winds. Living in a treeless landscape, the Inuit could not make wooden houses. In summer, they made temporary shelters from animal skins. In winter, they built homes called **igloos** from blocks of snow.

Reading Check How did the Inuit make use of their environment to live?

◄ Inuit hunter dressed in fur

European Exploration

After the voyage of Christopher Columbus, European explorers sailed west to try to find a sea route to Asia. Some headed south and ended up finding a passage around southern South America. Others sailed north, looking for a water route to Asia called the **Northwest Passage.** Explorers believed that this route would carry them north of what is now Canada to the Pacific Ocean.

Many expeditions set out to find this elusive, or difficult-to-find, passage. None succeeded. The long winters and ice-clogged waters north of Canada made passage difficult, and many explorers died in the effort. Not until the early 1900s did an expedition cross from the Atlantic Ocean to the Pacific Ocean along this route.

The search for the Northwest Passage had unexpected results. Europeans made contact with the Inuit and other native peoples. They began hunting whales in the northern seas, as whale oil was a useful product. Some set up trading posts along the shores of Hudson Bay. There, they traded goods such as cooking pots, blankets, gunpowder, and bullets for beaver furs and deerskins.

Reading Check What were the explorers who searched for the Northwest Passage seeking?

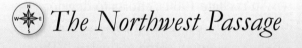

The Northwest Passage

Many Europeans attempted to sail across the icy, arctic waters of northern Canada to find an easy passage to Asia. Unfortunately, finding a short route to Asia proved to be very difficult.

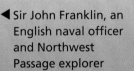

◄ Sir John Franklin, an English naval officer and Northwest Passage explorer

◄ Sir John Franklin commanded the HMS *Erebus* and the HMS *Terror* on his failed expedition.

The Polar Environment

The polar region is unique. The melting sea ice, or ice pack, near the north pole indicates a changing climate. There are different explanations for these changes, but it is clear that the northern region provides a window into the changes affecting all of Earth.

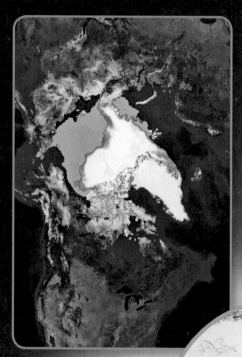

The satellite image on the left shows a shrinking polar ice pack. The green area shows the average ice coverage from 1979 to 2007. Orange shows minimum ice coverage in 2005, then a record low. The white area shows the minimum ice in 2007, almost 25 percent less than in 2005. Many scientists believe that as ice melts, Earth will absorb more sunlight and become warmer. The temperature changes could affect climates around the world.

▲ Climate change threatens to melt the ice pack that is home to polar bears.

▲ Charged particles from the sun enter Earth's magnetic field to produce the Northern Lights.

The North in Canada Today

The north remains an important part of Canada today, and potential mineral wealth makes it even more important. But the land and the people face challenges.

Resources of the North Canada's far north is rich in resources. It has anywhere from one third to one half of Canada's total oil reserves. Large amounts of natural gas lie under the Beaufort Sea. Diamonds are being mined in Nunavut. The government of Canada believes that even more mineral riches lie in this region. Recently, the prime minister announced a major effort to explore the area.

In the late 1900s, efforts to develop these resources slowed because native peoples claimed some of the land. Those claims have been largely settled, and exploration is now underway.

A new challenge has emerged, however. Canada has claimed the waters of the Northwest Passage through the Arctic Archipelago, giving it the right to any minerals found on the ocean floor. Other nations say that these waters are international. Disputes over ownership could hamper Canada's ability to use these resources.

Fragile Environment The far north is not only a difficult environment in which to live. It is also a fragile one—small changes can upset the balance of nature.

In recent decades, many scientists say, overall temperatures on Earth have been rising. They point out that the ice in the waters north of Canada has been melting.

Inuit Life Today

Category	Inuit	Canadians
Median income	$13,699	$22,120
Unemployment rate (males)	23%	5%
Life expectancy	66.9 years	79.5 years

Source: *Inuit Tapirit Kanatami, Inuit in Canada: A Statistical Profile*

▲ Inuit boys in Cape Dorset, near Baffin Island

This melting does have some benefits. Ships move more easily through the waters. Also, scientists can now more easily search for minerals in these waters and extract them when they are found.

Melting ice poses problems, though. Animals that depend on long-established climate patterns will have to adapt or perish. Changes to animal populations affect Inuit people who still depend on hunting.

The Inuit Today Contact with Europeans changed the Inuits' lives in many ways. They adopted European goods, using rifles instead of harpoons or bows and arrows to hunt. Today, fewer Inuit follow the traditional nomadic lifestyle. Some continue to practice traditional arts and crafts, however.

Living in the harsh north poses problems. The Inuit lag behind Canadians as a whole in many measures of economics and health. One good sign is that the Inuit population is growing. Also, the establishment of Nunavut in 1999 gave the Inuit greater control over their own land and resources.

Reading Check What international dispute could limit Canada's ability to exploit resources?

Assessment

1. Why did the Inuit have to live nomadic lives?

2. Why was the search for the Northwest Passage important even though early voyages failed?

3. Why is the environment of the far north so fragile?

4. How might the Inuit benefit if the natural resources of the far north are developed?

5. Why do you think more Inuit have adopted modern customs and fewer Inuit follow traditional customs? Explain your answer.

History of Canada

 **Indiana**

6.1.4 Explain the development and organization of various systems in Europe and the Americas.

6.1.11 Compare and contrast various colonies in the Americas.

6.1.20 Analyze cause-and-effect relationships in history.

Visual Glossary

Key Terms • compromise • First Nations • New France • province • dominion

Reading Skill: Sequence Take notes using the graphic organizer in your journal.

An Iroquois man performing a ceremony in front of an Iroquois longhouse ▼

The history of Canada is unique. While native peoples have lived in Canada for thousands of years, Canada has absorbed many different kinds of people throughout its history. There has been tension among these groups of people, but Canada has usually resolved these conflicts peacefully through **compromise,** or establishing common ideas that people agree to follow.

Canada's Early History

Many thousands of years ago, people migrated across a land bridge from Asia to North America. By the 1500s, distinct groups of Native Americans lived throughout the land that is now Canada. Each group had its own culture, shaped by the geography and natural resources available to it.

Native Canadian Groups Native groups who lived south of the Arctic region in Canada are known as the **First Nations.** They shared similar lifestyles, using the available resources to build houses and make clothing, although groups developed distinct political systems, economies, and religious beliefs.

The Algonquins were skilled hunters who lived in present-day Quebec. Their birch-bark canoes and dog sleds helped them hunt large areas. The Iroquois lived in what is now southern Canada, in large farming villages. They grew corn in the milder climate, trading it for Algonquian forest products.

To the west, Plains dwellers structured their lives around hunting buffalo. Farther west, the mild climate and resources of the Pacific Coast, including salmon, whales, and forests, maintained populations such as the Yale and Yekooche people.

The Inuit people lived and continue to live in the Arctic region of the far north, and are not part of the First Nations. Inuits migrated year-round, in search of animals to hunt in their harsh climate.

Contact With Europeans Europeans first arrived off the coast of eastern Canada in the late 1400s, seeking a route from Europe to Asia, called the Northwest Passage. Although they did not find this route, they did find fish and animal furs. European fishermen stayed along the coasts, drying their catches and returning each year to Europe. European pursuit of furs had far-reaching effects for the First Nations people and for Canadian history.

As European traders made their way inland, they traded wool cloth and metal goods for Native American furs. Trading posts sprang up throughout southeastern Canada. A complex relationship developed between Europeans and Native Americans, as each sought to control the profitable fur trade. However, like the European colonists who were settling other areas, these traders carried many diseases and many native people died even as the fur trade grew in strength.

Reading Check What does the term *First Nations* describe?

France and Britain Struggle for Control

For more than 200 years France and Britain struggled to claim territory, control the fur trade, and secure Native American allies.

New France In 1534, Jacques Cartier arrived in eastern Canada and claimed it for France, giving it the name **New France.** Although French traders established a profitable fur trade in New France, it took many years for them to settle in colonies. In 1608 Samuel de Champlain established a colony at present-day Quebec City. Over the next hundred years, the French settled the region near the St. Lawrence River. For 200 years, the fur trade supported New France's economy.

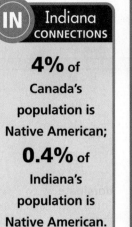

IN Indiana CONNECTIONS

4% of Canada's population is Native American; **0.4%** of Indiana's population is Native American.

Trading Post in central Canada ▼

British Canada British fur traders also operated trading posts outside of New France. They learned that the best land for furs was north of New France, around Hudson Bay. In 1670 the British king granted this territory to the Hudson Bay Company.

As the French and British settled their territories, conflicts grew. Each wanted to <u>dominate</u> the fur trade. Each had native people as allies, who increasingly fought each other for influence with the Europeans. These struggles were most intense during the Seven Years' War, fought from 1756 to 1763. This war, which began in Europe and spread to America, resulted in victory for Britain. Canada became British.

Reading Check What was the Seven Years' War?

dominate, *v.,* to control, to manage all aspects

Roots of a Nation

Canada was now a colony of Britain, yet it had a history of French culture, language, and government. Also, most French Canadians were Roman Catholic, while most new British settlers in Canada were Protestant. This diversity presented Canadians with challenges as the colony became a country.

The Quebec Act When Britain took control of Canada, it wanted the colony to be British. Yet, to avoid rebellion, it knew that it had to recognize the rights of French Canadians. With the Quebec Act of 1774, Britain allowed religious freedom and French laws. The act also extended Quebec's boundaries. American colonists saw this territory as theirs, and strongly opposed the Quebec Act.

Closer Look *Conflict and Compromise*

The Battle of Quebec, 1759

Britain and France fought to control early Canada. Britain won control of the area. Immediately, leaders in Canada had to balance the interests of the French and British citizens. Later, Canada won independence from Britain through negotiation and compromise, and without a revolutionary war.

THINK CRITICALLY What factors might have led Britain to negotiate with British- and French-Canadian citizens?

1756–1763
Seven Years' War
Fighting between France and Britain during the Seven Years' War made Canada part of the British empire.

1774
The Quebec Act
The Quebec Act was Parliament's first attempt at balancing the interests of both British and French citizens.

It is hereby declared, That His Majesty's Subjects professing the Religion of the Church of Rome, of, and in the said Province of Quebec, may enjoy the free Exercise of the Religion of the Church of Rome; and that the Clergy of the said Church may enjoy their accustomed Dues and Rights.

myWorld Activity
Culture Clash

A Canadian Identity Develops The Quebec Act helped drive a wedge between Canada the other British colonies in America. After the United States won independence from Britain in 1783, Americans who had remained loyal to Britain poured into Canada. To avoid conflict between the French and the new British citizens, Britain divided the colony into Upper and Lower Canada in 1791. Both colonies would remain under British rule, but Lower Canada would retain French customs, language, and religion.

During this time, the United States felt Britain should withdraw from areas bordering the United States and Canada, such as the area that is now northern Maine.

In 1812, the United States declared war on Britain, and quickly invaded Canada.

Nearly three years later, neither Britain nor the United States won. Americans saw the war as a great victory. Canadians viewed the victory as theirs. The conflict united Canadians against a common enemy—the United States.

While Canadians felt some unity as a result of the War of 1812, hard times fell on the Canadian people. Food shortages and disease plagued Lower Canada. Groups formed to oppose British rule, and several rebellions broke out. As a result, the British granted some control to the Canadian people. The 1840 Act of Union reunited Upper and Lower Canada into one **province,** or a territory that is under the control of a larger country. Britain still maintained control over all of Canada.

Reading Check What were Upper and Lower Canada?

1840
Act of Union
The Act created the Province of Canada, established a system of elected leaders, and led to a bicultural government of French and British Canadians.

The Arrival of Lord Sydenham, who oversaw the union of Upper and Lower Canada.

Canadians celebrate the passing of the British North American Act on July 1 every year.

1867
British North America Act
The act created the Dominion of Canada. While still part of Britain, Canada was effectively united and independent.

Canada Grows

Over the next 100 years, Canada experimented with different forms of government, working out its relationship with Britain. The country expanded and <u>prospered</u>, with the help of immigrants.

prospered, *v.,* was successful

The Dominion of Canada In the 1800s, Britain feared American westward expansion. To strengthen its position, Britain passed the 1867 British North America Act, creating a new confederation called the Dominion of Canada. A **dominion** is a territory that governs itself but is still tied to its colonizing country. The Dominion of Canada included all of the provinces of British Canada except Prince Edward Island and Newfoundland. Britain would still control Canada's foreign affairs, but the country would govern itself. Like the United States, the Dominion of Canada divided its powers between national and provincial, or state, governments.

In the late 1800s, Canada had expanded its territory. By 1905, the nation had five new provinces, stretching to the Pacific coast. The First Nations people who lived in the west resisted this expansion. The Canadian government feared wars with native people similar to those in the United States. It worked to solve conflict through treaties, which resulted in many native groups being forced to move to reservations.

The Role of Immigration In the early 1900s, Canada's economy grew by leaps and bounds. New technology and better agricultural methods increased exports of Canada's main crop, wheat. The growing economy was also fueled by a growth in population, especially from immigrants, who created a strong labor force.

In the early 1900s, the Canadian government encouraged immigration to Canada, especially of farmers. From 1901 to 1911, Canada's population grew by about 34 percent. In 1901, immigrants made up 12 percent of the population. By 1911, they made up 22 percent of the population. Most of these immigrants were British, American, or Jews from Russia. Immigration continued steadily throughout the 1900s, adding to Canada's diversity.

Reading Check What was the Dominion of Canada?

British, Russian, and American immigrants in the early 1900s ▼

Independent Canada

In the years after the Dominion of Canada was created, Britain had less to do with governing the country. Canada began establishing itself as a world leader.

World War I Canada was still part of the British Empire when World War I began. When Great Britain entered the war in 1914, this meant Canada joined the fight as well. The war demanded many human and natural resources from Canada. The country began to collect an income tax to pay for services, which made the country less dependent on Britain. In 1918, Canada created an air force separate from Britain's. By the end of the war, Canada proved that it was ready to act as an independent nation. In 1931, Britain recognized Canada's ability to act independently of the British Empire. Canada, however, remain linked to Great Britain. Canada's courts were still tied to Britain, and the country's constitution was officially an act of Parliament.

Canada's Challenges Canada faced its first major challenge as an independent country with the Great Depression of the 1930s. As in the United States and across the world, prices for exports fell, there were widespread crop failures, and unemployment rose. New political parties formed to demand that the government do more to help people.

As in the United States, joining World War II helped lift Canada out of the Depression. Canada's economy grew rapidly to support the war. Industries and agriculture expanded, new jobs were created, and businesses developed new technologies. The economy, once dependent on agriculture, became much more diversified. This began a period of growth that carried Canada into the next century.

Reading Check What was an important effect of World War I?

▲ A poster recruits Canadians for World War I.

Section 2 Assessment

? **Essential Question**
Is conflict unavoidable?

Key Terms

1. Who are the First Nations?

2. What compromise did Britain make when it took control of Canada?

3. What is the difference between a province and a dominion?

Key Ideas

4. Identify the relationship between natural resources and European settlement.

5. How did New France shape Canadian culture?

6. Describe the interdependence established between Canada and Britain in 1867.

Think Critically

7. **Summarize** What role did conflict play in Canada's early history?

8. **Analyze Cause and Effect** How did Canada's participation in World War II affect its economy?

9. How did Canada gain its independence from Britain? Go to your Student Journal to record your answer.

Defining Canada

IN Indiana

6.1.21 Differentiate between fact and interpretation in historical accounts and explain historical passages.

6.1.23 Identify issues related to an event in Europe or the Americas and give arguments for and against that issue.

Canada is a multicultural nation. Diversity can cause conflict, however. Some in Quebec have demanded special status within Canada's constitution to protect their rights and unique culture. In response, the Quebec government formed a commission to explore how to maintain Quebec's identity and accommodate diversity. Meanwhile, Canada attempts to accommodate many cultures in addition to French Canadians. All these groups wrestle with the issue of defining Canada's identity.

▲ People gather to oppose Quebec's separation.

Supporting greater independence for Quebec ▼

Stop at each circled letter on the right to think about the text. Then answer the question with the same letter on the left.

Ⓐ Compare Viewpoints How does the writer say Quebeckers and Canadians outside Quebec see matters differently?

Ⓑ Summarize According to the writer, how has the national government harmed Quebec?

Ⓒ Analyze Cause and Effect How do some Quebeckers feel as a result of what they claim is Canada's failure to recognize Quebec's authority?

Quebeckers, *n.,* French-speaking people of Quebec

autonomy, *n.,* power to act independently

Quebec: A Special Case

❝ Quebeckers have accepted the fact they were a nation within a nation. But Canadians have refused to recognize the existence of a Quebec Ⓐ people or nation within Canada. . . .

 Most Quebeckers . . . would have preferred to find a way to have Quebec's specific needs taken into account within the federal system. Canada, however, fails to adequately protect the French language outside Quebec, and refuses to fully recognize the Quebec government's Ⓑ authority and autonomy in matters of language and culture within Ⓒ Quebec's territory. ❞

—Michel Seymour, "Quebec and Canada at the Crossroads," 1998

188

Stop at each circled letter on the right to think about the text. Then answer the question with the same letter on the left.

D Summarize What fear do Quebeckers have?

E Analyze Causes and Effects What effect do French-speaking immigrants have on Quebec's French-speaking population?

F Draw Inferences Why do you think the author believes it is important to maintain a French-speaking population in Quebec?

succumb, *v.,* give in

don, *v.,* put on

scenario, *n.,* possible outcome

verges on, *v.,* nears

Accommodation within Quebec

66 French-speaking Québec must not <u>succumb</u> to fear, the temptation to withdraw and reject, nor <u>don</u> the victim's mantle. In other words, it must reject this <u>scenario</u> of **D** inevitable disappearance. . . . The proportion of Quebeckers of French-Canadian origin is declining, from 80% of Québec's population in 1901 to 77% in 1991. . . . Québec will have to rely increasingly on immigration. However, [due to] the contribution of **E** French-speaking immigrants, . . . the proportion of Quebeckers whose mother tongue is French now <u>verges on</u> **F** 80%. . . . 99

—Gérard Bouchard and Charles Taylor, *Building the Future: A Time of Reconciliation*

▲ André Boisclair, a former leader of the Parti Québécois

The Chateau Frontenac, Quebec City ▼

Analyze the Documents

1. **Comparing Viewpoints** How is the perspective of Seymour similar to that of Bouchard and Taylor?
2. **Writing Task** Take the role of Canada's prime minister. Write a speech that explains how you see Canada's relations with the province of Quebec.

Canada Today

IN Indiana

6.2.6 Describe the functions of international political organizations in the world today.

6.2.7 Define and compare citizenship and the citizen's role throughout history in Europe and the Americas.

6.3.4 Describe and compare major cultural characteristics of regions in Europe and the Western Hemisphere.

6.3.10 Explain the ways cultural diffusion, invention, and innovation change culture.

6.4.1 Give examples of how trade related to key developments in the history of Europe and the Americas.

Visual Glossary

Key Terms • cultural mosaic • constitutional monarchy • plural society

Reading Skill: Compare and Contrast Take notes using the graphic organizer in your journal.

Queen Elizabeth visits Canada.

Although Canada and the United States have a great deal in common, the history, politics, and cultures of these two countries are distinct. As discussed in the previous chapter, the United States fought against Great Britain to win independence. Canada, on the other hand, broke away from Great Britain slowly, through political means.

Governing Canada

Today's Canadian cultural and political landscape is the result of many years of competition and compromise among the native peoples of Canada, the Europeans settlers, and the home countries of those settlers, namely France and Great Britain. While the United States is viewed as a melting pot, Canada is known as a **cultural mosaic**. Here, people from different areas retain their cultural identity. Canada is also bilingual and multicultural, with both French and English as national languages.

Historical Ties to Britain One of the major differences between Canada and the United States is Canada's long and enduring relationship with the United Kingdom. The British Queen, Elizabeth II is the Canadian head of state. As you have read, the British government first created Canada when it passed the British North America Act. More than a century later, in 1982, Canada created its own constitution. It needed to address issues that were unique to Canada such as language rights for French-speaking Quebec, financial support for regional economies, and government protection of Canada's transportation and other industries. This constitution was called the Charter of Rights and Freedoms. It serves the same function as the American Bill of Rights and it reflects Canada's slow separation from Britain.

Canada's government system is a **constitutional monarchy,** where the power of the king or queen is limited by the constitution. Canada's government is made up of three branches: the executive, <u>legislative</u>, and judicial. Canada also uses a federal system to balance power between the federal government in Canada's capital city, Ottawa, and the governments in each of its provinces and territories.

Heads of State Canada's executive branch of government is made up of the governor general, who represents the British monarch (currently Queen Elizabeth II of England), the prime minister, and the cabinet. The prime minister is in charge of determining government policies and steering legislation in Canada, while the Queen's role is mostly ceremonial. Since 1952, the governor general position has alternated between an English Canadian and a French Canadian. By custom, the person appointed to this position is bilingual.

The prime minister and the cabinet are elected members of the House of

legislative, *adj.,* referring to the law-making branch of Canadian government

Canada's Government

Canada is a federation—several provinces and territories are linked by a single, larger government. Canada's head of government is the prime minister, who runs the executive branch. The governor general gives the sovereign's approval to parliament bills and other actions.

Legislative

Parliament

House of Commons   Senate

Parliament creates and passes bills. The leader of the majority party becomes prime minister.

Executive

Sovereign

Prime Minister   Governor General

Britain's king or queen, the sovereign, and the governor general have limited duties.

Judicial

Judiciary

Supreme Court   Federal Court

The judicial branch applies and interprets the laws of Canada's constitution.

Commons. The leader of the majority party in the House of Commons becomes prime minister. In this system there are no divisions between the executive and the legislative branches of government in Canada as there are in the United States.

The structure of Canada's government is designed to benefit its citizens. Beginning with Prime Minister Pierre Trudeau in the early 1970s, the government has continued to create programs to balance the needs of both French and English-speaking Canadians. Since then people have focused more on celebrating Canada's multiethnic, multilingual, and multicultural population.

myWorld Activity
Trade Partner Search

Reading Check What is a constitutional monarchy?

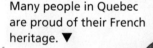

Many people in Quebec are proud of their French heritage. ▼

Canada's Role in the World

Canada has a growing and dynamic economy based on natural resources, well-developed services, and technology. Canada's high-end internet system and well-educated workforce are particularly important to the country's economy. Canada is currently second in the world in terms of total Internet users (despite its relatively small population), and it ranks first in the percentage of college and university graduates in its total population.

There are other reasons Canada has emerged as a world leader in economic development and trade. Along with its highly skilled population, Canada has a literacy rate of 99 percent, one of the highest in the world. Unemployment is low. Canada has developed a high quality of life, healthcare for every citizen, policies for cleaning up the environment, and a modern transportation system.

Trade Canada's trade network has been affected by political agreements with its nearest neighbor and most important trading partner, the United States. Passage of the North American Free Trade Agreement (NAFTA) in 1994, for example, eliminated all trade barriers between Canada, the United States, and Mexico. NAFTA legislation has resulted in more than one billion dollars of goods crossing the Canadian–U.S. border each day! NAFTA, as well as Canada's active participation in the World Trade Organization (WTO) has increased trade. More goods and services flow out of

Canada (exports) and more goods and services flow into Canada (imports).

Much of this international trade consists of exporting Canada's natural resources to other countries. Profits made by exporting natural resources make up one third of Canada's economic activity.

Peacekeeper Canada is known throughout the world as a peacekeeping nation. Many Canadian soldiers, sailors, and aviators today work to stop wars from developing by serving the United Nations as peacekeepers. Peacekeepers go into other countries to help guard borders and protect people—not to fight battles. Canadian soldiers have provided support for United States troops in Afghanistan and Iraq. Some peacekeepers are not in the military, but help with negotiations between groups or provide other services in conflict areas.

The United Nations (UN) was founded after World War II by fifty different countries, including Canada. Although more than seventy countries have participated in peacekeeping missions for the UN, Canada is among the leading countries in providing support to United Nations missions over the years. In addition, despite its small population, Canada is the fourth-largest contributor to the high cost of maintaining the peacekeeping efforts of the UN.

Reading Check Why is Canada known as a peacekeeping nation?

Canada as Peacekeeper

After World War II, countries looked for ways to prevent widespread war. One idea was to send troops to contain and prevent fighting. In 1956 Canada put this idea into practice. Egypt had gained control of the Suez Canal, which connects the Mediterranean and Red Sea. Britain and France wanted to control the canal, which threatened war with Egypt. Canada's Lester Pearson proposed sending United Nations troops to limit fighting and find a peaceful resolution.

Canada has participated in nearly every United Nations peacekeeping mission since 1956.

Canada has sent troops and other officials to prevent conflict in places such as Haiti, Bosnia, the Dominican Republic and Somalia.

A Canadian peacekeeper stops to speak with a woman in Port-au-Prince, Haiti. ▶

193

French
French Canadians have maintained a distinct culture in Quebec.

→ Culture Close-up

First Peoples
First Nations people include many diverse native groups in Canada.

Chinatown
Chinese Canadians have strong communities in cities like Toronto.

Caribbean Festival
Caribbean peoples have made Canada their home more recently.

The Cultural Mosaic

As discussed earlier in this chapter, Canada's population is a mix of indigenous people, descendants of early colonizers from England and France, and immigrants from other countries. Although English and French are Canada's two official languages, Canada is a **plural society.** This means that its distinctive cultural, ethnic, and racial groups are encouraged to maintain their own identities and cultures. Canada adopted the policy of multiculturalism in the 1970s. Multiculturalism encourages Canadians to maintain the cultures and traditions of their parents and grandparents.

Canada has a long history of immigration. In the 1800s, jobs to construct railroads and the availabilty of land created opportunities for citizens. Canada's population became more diverse after the 1960s when Canada changed its immigration laws.

This increase in the racial diversity of Canada's immigrant groups has continued in recent years. In 2004, nearly half of all Canadian immigrants came from Asia and Pacific Rim countries. The presence of more people born in Asia, Latin America, and Africa has risen dramatically as economic, environmental, and political problems in the world continue.

Today, the most diverse cities in Canada are Toronto, Montreal, and Vancouver. Toronto, Canada's largest city, is one of the world's most cosmopolitan and ethnically diverse metropolitan areas. More than half of all schoolchildren in Toronto speak a language other than English at home.

Along with the descendants of earlier European settlers, this city is now home to immigrants from Asia, Africa, the Caribbean, and Latin America. Other, smaller cities also attract new immigrants.

Immigrants account for 70 percent of all labor force growth in Canada, a proportion that experts <u>project</u> will grow to 100 percent in the next ten years.

Maintaining a distinctive Canadian identity remains one of Canada's biggest challenges. American movies, television programs, and pop music flow easily into Canada and dominate its media. Efforts to curb the Americanization of Canadian culture include a law that requires that Canadian TV and radio programs contain a certain percentage of "Canadian content." There has also been an explosion of Canadian fine arts, films, television, and popular music during the past thirty years that help carry on an identity and values that are uniquely Canadian.

As Canada moves forward, its geography and the diversity of its people continue to be important to its future. Managing regional economic differences, maintaining independent foreign policies, protecting culture, and balancing trade and political relationships with the United States remain important.

Reading Check **What is a plural society? How has immigration affected Canada?**

project, *v.,* to calculate a thing that will occur

ᵐʸ Story **📷 Photo** Alyssa visits a culture circle at the Ottawa Inuit Child Care Center.

Section 3 Assessment

Key Terms

1. Use the following terms to describe Canada's culture: cultural mosaic, plural society.

Key Ideas

2. What position does the British monarch play in Canada's government?

3. Why is international trade important to Canada's economy?

4. What accounts for the uniqueness of Canada's cultural diversity?

Think Critically

5. **Compare and Contrast** How is Canada's government different from that of the United States?

6. **Draw Inferences** How has the government tried to balance the needs of French- and English-speaking Canadians?

Essential Question

Is conflict unavoidable?

7. Why is Canada known as a peacekeeping nation? Go to your Student Journal to record your answer.

Chapter Assessment

Key Terms and Ideas

1. **Compare and Contrast** How are a **cultural mosaic** and a **plural society** different from each other? How are they similar?

2. **Sequence** What were the major events in Canada's transition from a British colony to an independent nation?

3. **Explain** How does climate affect population distribution in Canada?

4. **Compare and Contrast** How are the **First Nations** and the Inuit different from each other?

5. **Explain** In what ways was the Quebec Act a **compromise**?

6. **Describe** During its years as a **dominion,** what was Canada's relationship with Britain?

7. **Summarize** How do natural resources contribute to Canada's economy?

Think Critically

8. **Determine Relevance** How does geography explain why it is important for Canada and the United States to address environmental issues jointly?

9. **Draw Conclusions** What were some of the lasting effects of the fur trade?

10. **Analyze Information** What geographical factors might explain why most of Canada is sparsely populated?

11. **Core Concepts: Trade** What is trade? How does Canada's economy reflect the importance of international trade?

Places to Know

For each place, write the letter from the map that shows its location.

Identify the following:

12. **Arctic Archipelago**

13. **St. Lawrence River**

14. **Canadian Shield**

15. **Ottawa**

16. **Calgary**

17. **Interior Plains**

18. **Estimate** Using the scale, estimate the distance between Ottawa and Calgary.

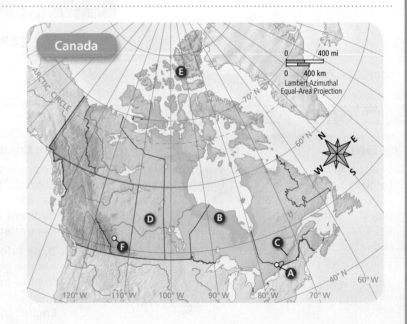

my worldgeography.com Self-Test

Essential Question

Chapter Transfer Activity

Follow your teacher's instructions to form groups and role-play a family moving to Canada. Review information about Canada's geographic regions and rank them by desirability. Choose an area for settlement and present your choice to the class. Compare your choice to the choices of your classmates. Then compare your choice to that of actual settlers.

21st Century Learning

Develop Cultural Awareness

Choose one of Canada's provincial flags. Do research to discover the significance of the symbols it displays. Present your findings to the class.

Document-Based Questions

Success Tracker™
Online at myworldgeography.com

Use your knowledge of Canada and Documents A and B to answer Questions 1–3.

Document A

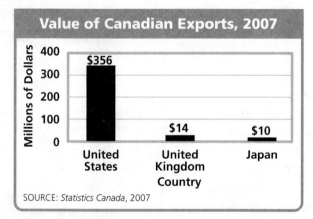

Value of Canadian Exports, 2007

Millions of Dollars

- United States: $356
- United Kingdom: $14
- Japan: $10

Country

SOURCE: *Statistics Canada*, 2007

Document B

" Construction of dams in Manitoba for the generation of electricity resulted in the decline of fishing and a significant drop in beaver and muskrat populations. Responding on behalf of his people, a First Nations chief commented, "Hydro is breaking our hearts."

—John Miswagon, Pimicikamak Chief

1. Which of the following best explains why the highest percentage of Canadian trade occurs with a single country?

   A Canada and the United States share a common language.

   B There is a high demand for Canadian products in the United States.

   C Canada and the United States share the same continent.

   D Canada and the United States have reciprocal trade agreements.

2. Which of the following best explains Miswagon's statement?

   A His people are grieving over the destruction of wildlife.

   B His people do not believe that increased generation of electricity is necessary.

   C His people are unhappy because they will not share in the profits.

   D The dams threaten his people's sustainable way of life.

3. **Writing Task** Should a nation be concerned about the environmental impact of its development? Explain your answer.

Road Trip:

Explore the Interstate Highway System

Your Mission You and your classmates will propose one new north–south interstate and one new east–west interstate. To gather information for your proposal, divide into four task-force teams: history, mapping, statistics, and planning.

Before the Information Superhighway, there was the Interstate Highway System. After World War II, American prosperity boomed. Everyone wanted a new car. People drove their cars to their new homes in the suburbs. In the summer, families went on driving vacations. Gradually, cars grew larger and could travel hundreds of miles on a single tank of gas. Yet, there were almost no wide, smooth roads between major cities.

Construction of the Interstate Highway System (IHS) began in 1956. The system initially called for 41,000 miles of new roads as well as uniform construction standards. By having regulations calling for uniformity on these new roads, the government could ensure greater safety for drivers. It is because of these regulations that signs along the interstate look the same anywhere in the United States.

The IHS helped make America a nation of drivers.

STEP 1

Identify Roles and Responsibilities.

Each task force must understand how its efforts will contribute to the report that is presented by the planning team. The history task force will explore the early years of the IHS and why it continues to be important today. The mapping task force will study the existing IHS and try to find regions under-served by highways. The statistics task force will research who uses the IHS and explain what these data mean. The planning task force will synthesize these data to propose new roads for the IHS.

STEP 2

Determine Your Goals.

Eack task force should focus on its specific goal. The goal of the history team is to consider how the IHS has evolved over time and what its future needs might be. The mapping task force's goal is to consider how America's changing needs affect the roadway system. The statistics task force should look for data on the IHS. The focus of the planning team is to coordinate the findings of all teams and to assemble this information in a proposal for new roads.

STEP 3

Regroup and Communicate.

Each task force member should individually research the group's topic. Some teams may choose to research together. Share ideas and respond to good points by including them in your report. Reach conclusions as a group and acknowledge the efforts of your teammates when you give your report. Keep in mind that your reports are requesting that the government spend millions of dollars but that the project will benefit the entire nation.

Middle America

Middle America is the "middle" region of the Americas, so-called because it forms a land bridge between North and South America. Caribbean island nations, including Cuba, also belong to the region. Mexico is the region's largest country. Middle America is prone to natural disasters such as hurricanes, earthquakes, and volcanic eruptions.

What time is it there?

Washington, D.C.	Mexico City, Mexico
9 A.M. Monday	8 A.M. Monday

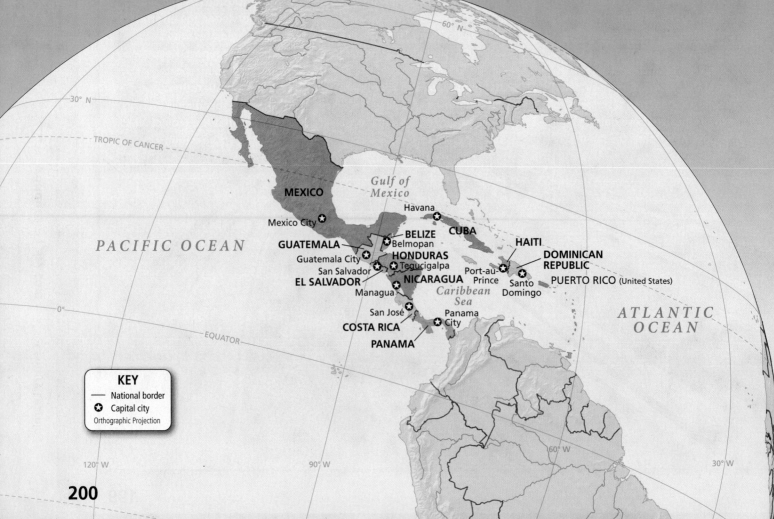

KEY
— National border
⊕ Capital city
Orthographic Projection

The Unit Ahead

my worldgeography.com

Plan your trip online by doing a Data Discovery Activity and watching the myStory Videos of the region's teens.

my Story

Carolina
Age: 16
Home: Tamaulipas, Mexico

Chapter 3

my Story

Luis
Age: 17
Home: Limón, Dominican Republic

Chapter 4

The Maya ruins of Tulum, south of Cancun on the Yucatán Peninsula

Regional Overview
Physical Geography

The Sierra Madre ranges lie near both of Mexico's coasts.

Baja California

Gulf of California

Sierra Madre Occidental

Mexican Plateau

Sierra Madre Oriental

Gulf of Mexico

Yucatán Peninsula

Greater

Caribbean

PACIFIC OCEAN

Southern Mexico's rain forest supports diverse animal and plant life.

Active volcanoes dot the west coast of Nicaragua.

Cuba is the largest island in the Caribbean Sea. It belongs to a group of islands called the Greater Antilles.

ATLANTIC OCEAN

Antilles

Sea

Lesser Antilles

Regional Flyover

Suppose you are flying in an airplane across Middle America. If you begin in the north and fly southeast, you would fly over the Sierra Madre Occidental mountain range in Mexico. Mexico's central plateau and the second range of the Sierra Madres are both to the east. As you continue flying south, you would see the lush vegetation of lower Mexico's rain forests.

East of Mexico is the Caribbean Sea and its many islands. Cuba, Jamaica, Puerto Rico, and Hispaniola, which includes both Haiti and the Dominican Republic, are part of the Greater Antilles. The Virgin Islands, Antigua, and other smaller islands make up the Lesser Antilles.

Your flight turns southwest over Central America. Soon you notice an isthmus, or a narrow land bridge between two larger land masses. The isthmus includes Costa Rica and Panama, the southernmost country of Middle America, where your flight ends.

➔ **In-Flight Movie**

Take flight over Middle America and explore the region from the air.

my worldgeography.com In-Flight Movie

203

Regional Geography
Human Geography

Middle America's Economy

People who live in Middle America have a variety of jobs. In countries such as Haiti, the majority of people farm for a living. In Mexico, many people work in factories that manufacture goods for export, or for sale in other countries. In Central America and the Caribbean, many people work in the region's thriving tourism industry.

Despite the variety of economic activities, many people in this region are poor. Natural disasters, such as hurricanes, continually cause economic setbacks. Some people emigrate, or move to other countries. Many immigrants who find work in the United States send money to family members back home.

Factory worker in Mexico

Farming in Haiti

Eco-tourism in Costa Rica

The Panama Canal

KEY

1,073 Number of documented emigrants to the United States, 2007

0   300 mi
0   300 km
Lambert Azimuthal Equal-Area Projection

Gulf of Mexico

148,640

738

29,104

−31

40   25

415

30,405 28,024

3   347   38

19,375

1,073

66   23

428   928

17,908   7,646

567   689

21,127   3,716

Caribbean Sea

55

93   751

6,829

2,540   1,916

ATLANTIC OCEAN

PACIFIC OCEAN

40

my World
IN NUMBERS

	Mexico	Honduras	Costa Rica	Haiti
Literacy rate (15 years of age or older)	91.0%	80.0%	94.9%	52.9%
Income earned by wealthiest 10% of population	37.1%	42.2%	37.4%	47.70%
Urban population**	75.0%	46.0%	61.0%	37.0%
People employed in agriculture	15.1%	39.2%	14.0%	66.0%

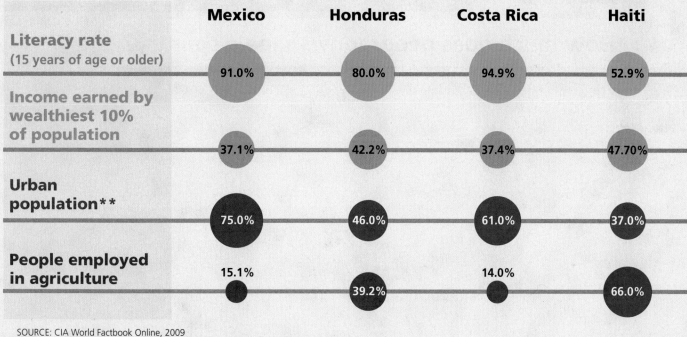

SOURCE: CIA World Factbook Online, 2009
** SOURCE: Population Division of the United Nations Secretariat, 2003

Put It Together

1. What are two of Mexico's main physical features?

2. What type of natural disasters frequently occur in Middle America?

3. Compare Mexico and Haiti. What is the relationship between the percentage of urban population and the percentage of people employed in agriculture?

→ **Data Discovery**

Find your own data to make a regional data table.

Size Comparison

The United States is about twice as big as Middle America.

Chapter 3

Mexico

? Essential Question

How much does geography shape a country?

KEY
— National border
⊛ Capital city
○ Other city

0   300 mi
0   300 km
Lambert Conformal Conic Projection

Tijuana

Ciudad Juárez

110° W   100° W

90° W

80° W

30° N

Rio Grande

Gulf of California

Gulf of Mexico

Monterrey

Torreón

San Nicolas
de Guadalupe

TROPIC OF CANCER

Zapopan   León

Guadalajara

Nezahualcóyotl

Caribbean Sea

20° N

Toluca   Mexico City
Puebla

PACIFIC OCEAN

Where in the World Is Mexico?

Washington, D.C., to San Nicolas de Guadalupe:
1,610 miles

Carolina and
her burro

my Story

A Long Way from Home

Explore the Essential Question

- at my worldgeography.com
- using the myWorld Chapter Activity
- with the Student Journal

In this section you'll read about Carolina, a young woman from Mexico's state of Tamaulipas. What does Carolina's story tell you about life in Mexico?

Story by Monica Maristain for myWorld Geography Online

During the week, Carolina rises early every day, as breakfast is served promptly at 6:30 A.M. Carolina attends Technical High School #1 in Solis, Mexico. She shares a room in a boarding house with three other girls. It hasn't been easy. Carolina's family could not pay for her to attend the school, but through hard work she was able get a scholarship that made it possible. Carolina will be the first in her family to finish her high school and preparatory school studies. "I have seen how my sisters who did not study live, and I do not want that type of life for myself," she says.

After school Carolina works in the school's computer lab until 6 P.M. and then attends a study session until 8 P.M. After dinner at 8 P.M., there is time to spend with her three roommates, or finish up any homework that still needs to be done. "We are supposed to be in bed by 10 P.M.," Carolina laughs, "but often we are still awake when they come by at 11 P.M. to check on us and turn off the lights."

Carolina knows if she wants to go to a university and get a degree she has to get good grades in school and get another scholarship. Carolina hopes to study medicine or communications in college. "Among my family and in my community there aren't too many professionals," Carolina

my worldgeography.com On Assignment

With friends at school

Eating at home

admits. "That is what I wish for the most. . . to get my diploma and to have a better future."

Each weekend Carolina travels by bus for three hours back to her home town. Along the way, she talks about how very different her life is at home. "San Nicolas de Guadalupe is a farming community full of hayfields and animals and plenty of dirt and dust," she says.

Fortunately, there are many other things that Carolina loves about her home. "The people there are very friendly," Carolina says. "When we have celebrations, everyone helps with the preparation of food and other things that need to be done."

Carolina, like most of the people in her home town, is one of the Mazahua, an indigenous group. Carolina can speak her native language in addition to Spanish, but many young people cannot. "I have cousins and if I speak to them in Mazahua, they sit there thinking, 'What did she say?' They say

Back home in San Nicholas de Guadalupe, Carolina visits a market to get ingredients for dinner. On the right, a clay table and roller are used in making tortillas.

Carolina's family in San Nicholas de Guadalupe

Carolina on her way to the cyber cafe

that they should not speak Mazahua, because they will not be accepted at school or because speaking Mazahua is something bad." Carolina is very concerned that if her people's native language is lost it will not be long before her entire culture vanishes. "So much is already being lost. Only the older women still dress in the traditional way."

It is already dark by the time Carolina steps off the bus in San Nicolas de Guadalupe and there is little left to do but have dinner and head off to bed for some much-deserved rest.

Carolina's weekends at home are spent doing household chores or helping in the fields, but usually she finds some time for fun. One of her favorite activities is riding her bike. She also likes to do traditional Mazahua crafts such as embroidery and knitting. Then, of course, there are Mazahua festivals. "I like to dance," Carolina says. "The cumbia (a dance from Colombia) and the quebradita, which is a Mexican version of the cumbia—at my house we dance to everything!"

As the music plays in the background and the sun sets on another weekend in San Nicolas de Guadalupe, Carolina finally gets a chance to sit back and enjoy the moment. Tomorrow morning as she boards the bus back to school, she won't be leaving this all behind. . .she'll be taking it with her into the future.

Meet the Journalist

Name David House
Favorite Moment Spending time with Carolina's warm, welcoming family

→ **myStory Online**

Join Carolina as she shows you more about her life in San Nicolas de Guadalupe.

my worldgeography.com (myStory Video)

IN Indiana

6.3.3 Describe and compare major physical characteristics of regions in Europe and the Americas.

6.3.6 Explain how ocean currents and winds influence climate differences on Europe and the Americas.

6.3.8 Identify major biomes of Europe and the Americas and explain how these are influenced by climate.

6.3.12 Compare the distribution and evaluate the importance of natural resources in Europe and the Americas.

6.3.13 Explain the impact of humans on the physical environment in Europe and the Americas.

→ **Visual Glossary**

Key Terms • sinkhole • altitude • hydroelectric power • irrigate

🌐 **Reading Skill: Label an Outline Map** Take notes using the outline map in your journal.

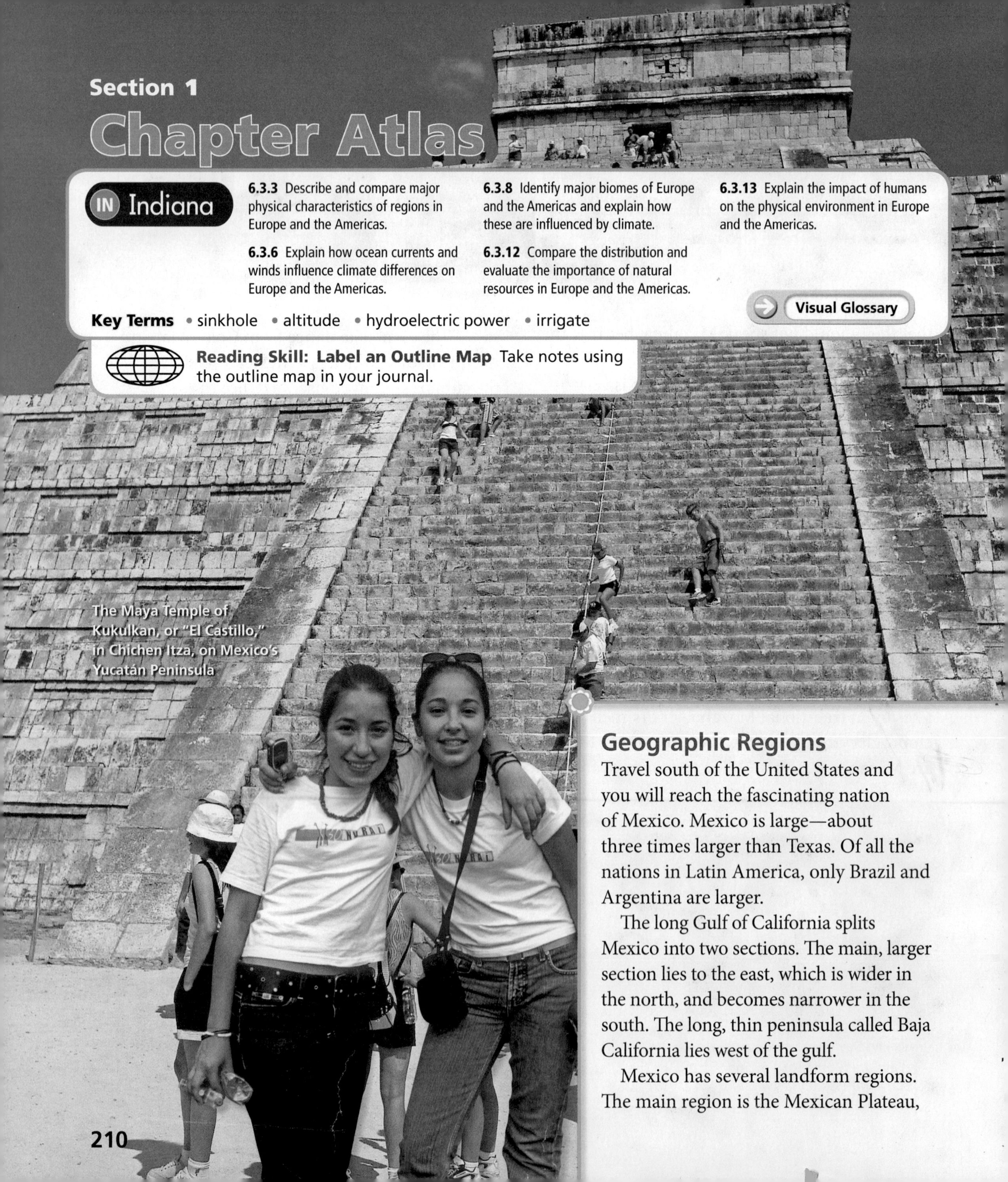

The Maya Temple of Kukulkan, or "El Castillo," in Chichen Itza, on Mexico's Yucatán Peninsula

Geographic Regions

Travel south of the United States and you will reach the fascinating nation of Mexico. Mexico is large—about three times larger than Texas. Of all the nations in Latin America, only Brazil and Argentina are larger.

The long Gulf of California splits Mexico into two sections. The main, larger section lies to the east, which is wider in the north, and becomes narrower in the south. The long, thin peninsula called Baja California lies west of the gulf.

Mexico has several landform regions. The main region is the Mexican Plateau,

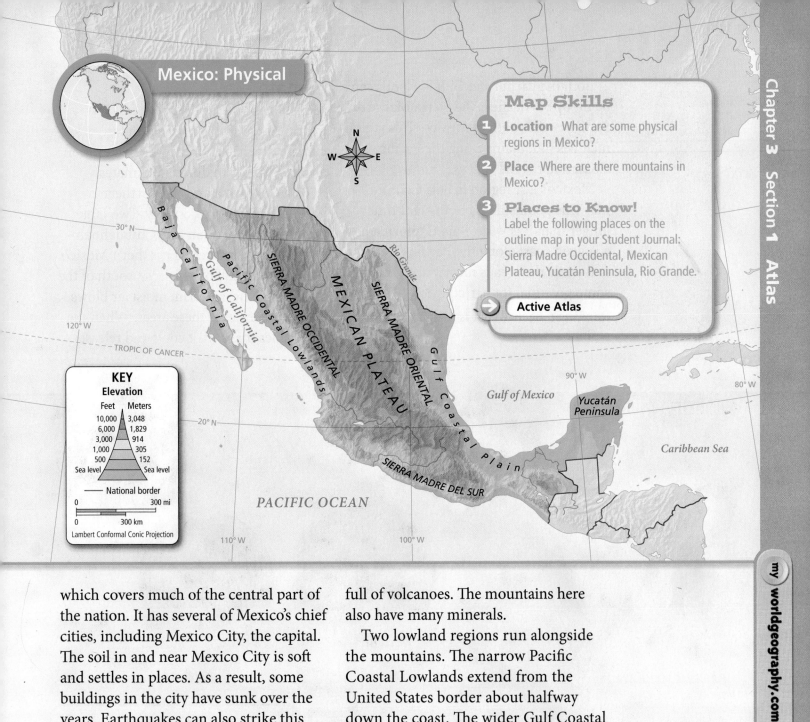

Mexico: Physical

Map Skills

1 **Location** What are some physical regions in Mexico?

2 **Place** Where are there mountains in Mexico?

3 **Places to Know!** Label the following places on the outline map in your Student Journal: Sierra Madre Occidental, Mexican Plateau, Yucatán Peninsula, Rio Grande.

Active Atlas

KEY
Elevation

Feet	Meters
10,000	3,048
6,000	1,829
3,000	914
1,000	305
500	152
Sea level	Sea level

—— National border

| 0 | 300 mi |
| 0 | 300 km |

Lambert Conformal Conic Projection

which covers much of the central part of the nation. It has several of Mexico's chief cities, including Mexico City, the capital. The soil in and near Mexico City is soft and settles in places. As a result, some buildings in the city have sunk over the years. Earthquakes can also strike this area and cause great damage.

Flanking the Mexican Plateau are two long mountain chains. Forming the western flank are the Sierra Madre Occidental. East of the plateau rise the Sierra Madre Oriental, which are rich in minerals. These two chains meet at the south of the Mexican Plateau in a region full of volcanoes. The mountains here also have many minerals.

Two lowland regions run alongside the mountains. The narrow Pacific Coastal Lowlands extend from the United States border about halfway down the coast. The wider Gulf Coastal Plain stretches from the border to the Yucatán Peninsula, which juts north into the Gulf of Mexico. The Yucatán is covered by a shell of limestone with many caves underground. Sometimes the roofs of these caves <u>collapse</u>, forming depressions, or sunken areas called **sinkholes.**

collapse, v., to crumble or fall

Both the Pacific and Gulf lowlands can be hit by hurricanes. The Sierra Madre del Sur cover the south of Mexico. This region includes mountains along the Pacific Coast and rugged valleys.

Mexico's last region is Baja California. This peninsula is about eight times longer than it is wide. Baja California has a rugged coast along the Pacific Ocean, and while the area is mostly arid, there is some potential for agriculture.

Reading Check What is Mexico's main region?

Climate

Mexico has several climate areas. The nation's large size is one reason for climate diversity. Differences in elevation also contribute to different climates.

Baja California and the northern parts of Mexico are very dry. Two large deserts—the Sonoran and Chihuahuan deserts—cover much of northern Mexico.

More than half of Mexico is south of the Tropic of Cancer. Warm, moist air blows off the oceans over these areas. When the air reaches the land, it cools and releases

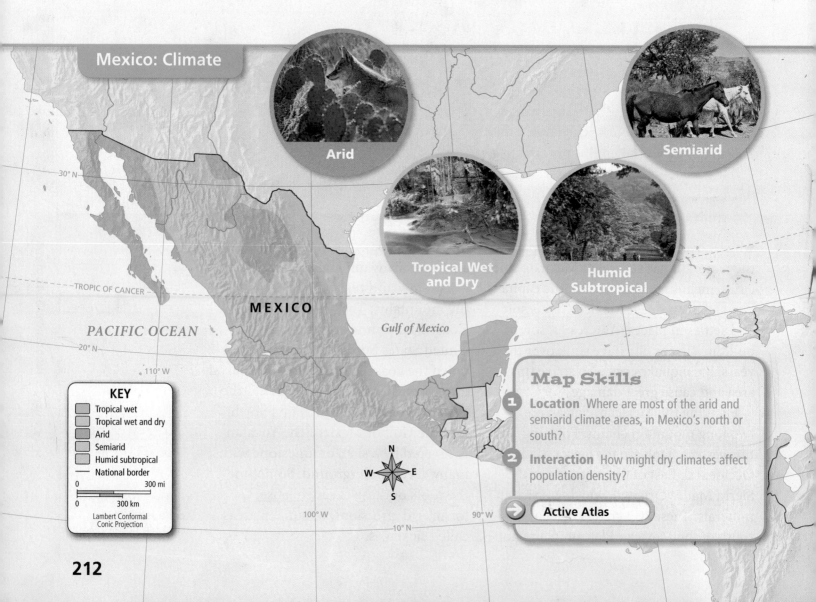

Mexico: Climate

Arid

Semiarid

Tropical Wet and Dry

Humid Subtropical

30° N

TROPIC OF CANCER

20° N

110° W

MEXICO

PACIFIC OCEAN

Gulf of Mexico

KEY
- Tropical wet
- Tropical wet and dry
- Arid
- Semiarid
- Humid subtropical
- — National border

0   300 mi
0   300 km

Lambert Conformal Conic Projection

N
W   E
S

100° W   90° W

10° N

Map Skills

1 **Location** Where are most of the arid and semiarid climate areas, in Mexico's north or south?

2 **Interaction** How might dry climates affect population density?

➤ **Active Atlas**

water. As a result, the southern part of Mexico receives more rain than the north. People can grow crops in the southern Mexican Plateau. Thick rain forests grow in the Yucatán and southern Mexico.

In the late summer and early fall, hurricanes can hit the tropics. Communities along the coast can be badly damaged by the high winds and heavy rains brought by these powerful storms.

Temperatures in the tropics do not vary much during the year. Farther north, temperature changes are more dramatic.

Climate in Mexico also varies by **altitude,** or height above sea level. The higher you go, the cooler the temperatures are. Even in the tropics, cities on mile-high plateaus have moderate temperatures. If you climb higher, you reach colder land. The tops of mountains are covered with snow.

Mexico's climate patterns have affected where people live. It is very difficult to grow crops in the hot, dry northern areas. As a result, few people live in northern Mexico. The cooler temperatures and heavier rainfall of the southern part of the Mexican Plateau make a better climate for growing food. For this reason, the areas around Mexico City in the south have long been the population centers. The thick rain forests farther south make traveling there difficult. Also, heavy rains wash away the soil, making farming difficult. For these reasons, the rain forest region has relatively few people.

Reading Check What are two reasons that Mexico has many different climate areas?

Closer Look

Ecosystems of Mexico

Mexico's ecosystems host unique animal and plant life. The Sonoran Desert in northwest Mexico is very dry with little vegetation. The Gulf and Pacific coastal lowlands are dry in the north, but support agriculture in the south. Rainforests host dense vegetation and diverse wildlife.

Think Critically How do ecosystems change from north to south?

The pronghorn antelope and the yucca plant are found in the Sonoran Desert. ▶

KEY
- Desert
- Rain forest
- Coastal lowland
- Other

▲ The tarantula is found in the rain forest and lives between 6 and 11 years.

Mexico's gulf coastal lowlands have lagoons and swampy areas.

my worldgeography.com Active Atlas

Land Resources

The mountains and plateaus of Mexico contain many important resources. Mexico produces more silver than any other nation in the world. Copper and iron are other major metal products. Mexico also mines gold, zinc, and lead.

Mexico's most important natural resource is petroleum. Mexico is one of the top producers of oil in the world. The oil is drilled from wells under the Gulf of Mexico, along the Gulf coast, and in high elevations in the south. The nation has large unused reserves of oil as well. Some of these deposits are difficult to tap,

however. Mexico needs to invest more in developing these areas so that it can continue to produce oil.

Mexico also has natural gas in some of the areas that produce oil. Mexico has yet to fully use this resource. About one sixth of the nation's electricity comes from **hydroelectric power,** or power generated by water running through channels in dams. These dams have been built along fast-running rivers on the edges of the central plateau and in high southern elevations.

Much of Mexico's energy industry is along the Gulf coast, where the oil is

myWorld Activity
Mexico's Resources

Mexico: Economic Activity

N W E S

30° N

Gulf of Mexico

MEXICO

TROPIC OF CANCER

20° N

PACIFIC OCEAN

Map Skills

1 **Region** What region produces most of Mexico's mined resources?

2 **Location** Where are Mexico's oil reserves?

21st Century Learning

KEY

Corn
Oil
Natural gas
Mines
Hydroelectric power
Industrial area

0   300 mi
0   300 km
Lambert Conformal Conic Projection

110° W   100° W   90° W

located. Refineries near Veracruz and in northeastern Mexico turn the oil into various products. In the past, manufacturing plants were clustered in Mexico City. The government has tried to reduce crowding there by encouraging more manufacturing in the north.

Because of mountains, poor soils, and dry climates, only about one fifth of Mexico's land can be used for farming. Less than that is actually farmed. Major crops include corn, wheat, beans, sugar cane, and many fruits and vegetables. Coffee is an important export crop. The waters off the Baja California peninsula support a large fishing industry. Northern Mexico has many cattle ranches.

For several centuries, relatively few people owned large amounts of land in Mexico. The majority of people worked the land for these privileged few. In the 1900s, the government passed laws to break up these large estates and give land to the poor. Now, though, many families have such small holdings that they can only grow enough to feed their families.

Reading Check What is Mexico's most important resource, and where is it found?

A worker turns a valve wheel at a Pemex refinery, Mexico's national oil company. ▼

Oil Production in Mexico

Mexico produces more oil than many countries in the world. While selling oil to other countries has brought money to Mexico, this money has made the country dependent on the amount of oil other countries buy.

2007 Oil Production per Day

United States
8,457,000

Mexico
3,501,000

Iraq*
2,096,500

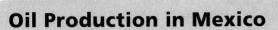 **1 million barrels**

*In 2002, the last year before the Iraq War, production was 2,500,000 barrels per day.

SOURCE: *CIA World Factbook*, U.S. Energy Information Administration

Chart Skills

How does Mexico's oil production compare to the United States and Iraq?

21st Century Learning

Environmental Impact

Mexico had about six times more people in the early 2000s than it did in the early 1900s. Health improvements were important factors in this population growth. The rate of growth has slowed in recent years, but Mexico's population is still growing faster than that of the United States.

About three quarters of the people now live in cities, far more than in the past. Mexico City is by far the largest city, with nearly one sixth of all Mexicans living in and around the city. In fact, it is one of the largest cities in the world.

Many cities along the border of Mexico and the United States have grown very rapidly in recent years. Many of the new arrivals live in quickly built, <u>inadequate</u> housing. These cities are plagued by over-crowding, and a lack of water and sewer systems.

Pollution from the spread of industry and the growth of these cities has become a major problem in northern Mexico. Air pollution is also a serious problem in

inadequate, *adj.,* not sufficient or suitable

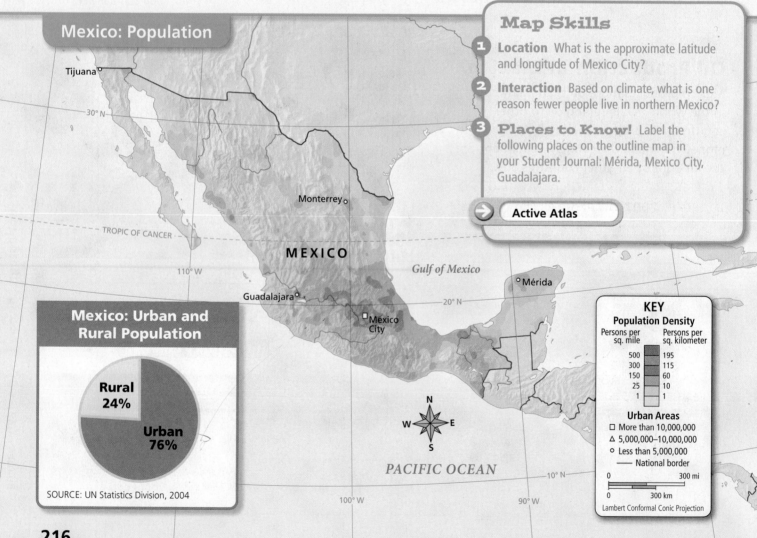

Mexico: Population

Map Skills

1 Location What is the approximate latitude and longitude of Mexico City?

2 Interaction Based on climate, what is one reason fewer people live in northern Mexico?

3 Places to Know! Label the following places on the outline map in your Student Journal: Mérida, Mexico City, Guadalajara.

Active Atlas

Mexico: Urban and Rural Population

Rural 24%

Urban 76%

SOURCE: UN Statistics Division, 2004

KEY
Population Density

Persons per sq. mile	Persons per sq. kilometer
500	195
300	115
150	60
25	10
1	1

Urban Areas
□ More than 10,000,000
△ 5,000,000–10,000,000
○ Less than 5,000,000
— National border

0   300 mi
0   300 km
Lambert Conformal Conic Projection

Mexico City, where clouds of unhealthy air can hang above the city for days.

The growth of Mexico's population has led to increased demand on the land. Farmers need to **irrigate,** or bring water to the land, in drier areas. Over time, though, salt builds up in the soil of irrigated fields. That salt ruins the fertility of the soil. Overgrazing by cattle is another concern. Because of irrigation and overgrazing, some of Mexico's fragile land is becoming desert.

Another environmental issue is deforestation in the south, where poor farmers cut down and burn trees to open new land for farming. Because the heavy rains there wash nutrients out of the soil, the land can produce crops for only a few years. Farmers then move on, cutting down trees in a new area. Some of the southern forests have valuable woods. Harvesting of these trees also contributes to the rapid destruction of Mexico's forests.

Reading Check How has rapid population growth affected northern Mexico?

Mexico City is located in a valley, and it is difficult for polluted air to escape the city. Population contributes to the amount of pollution, which leads to sickness.

19.4 million people
4 million cars
20 million lost workdays annually

Source: UN Data; SMA; Third World Cities

Section 1 Assessment

Key Terms

1. Use the following terms to describe Mexico: sinkhole, altitude, hydroelectric power, irrigate.

Key Ideas

2. What natural disasters can strike Mexico?

3. What are Mexico's mineral resources?

4. How has Mexico's population changed in recent decades?

Think Critically

5. **Identify Evidence** Why does northern Mexico have relatively few people?

6. **Synthesize** How do environmental challenges in northern and southern Mexico differ?

Essential Question

How much does geography shape a country?

7. What is one reason much of Mexico's population growth has occurred in and around Mexico City? Go to your Student Journal to record your answer.

Rise and Fall of the Aztecs

(IN) Indiana

6.1.1 Summarize the rise, decline, and cultural achievements of ancient civilizations in Europe and Mesoamerica.

6.1.4 Explain the development and organization of various systems in Europe and the Americas.

6.1.20 Analyze cause-and-effect relationships in history.

6.1.22 Form research questions and use resources to present data on people, cultures and developments in Europe and the Americas.

6.2.1 Compare and contrast forms of governments in Europe and the Americas throughout history.

Key Terms • peninsular • criollo • mestizo • Nahuatl

In what is today Mexico, the Aztecs built a large empire. Although they did not control the region for very long, their population grew quickly. Soon they controlled many native groups in the area, and their capital, Tenochtitlán, became a center of culture and trade. The Aztec empire was so large that its culture spread widely. As a result, the Aztecs left lasting effects on Mexico.

Becoming Powerful

The Aztecs settled in the Valley of Mexico—where Mexico City now is—in 1325. Clearly, though, the Aztecs built on the foundations of earlier peoples—and expanded those traditions.

Following earlier practices, they built terraces on the steep valley walls. These step-like patches of land held water, allowing farmers to grow crops on hillsides. The Aztecs also built irrigation ditches to bring water to their fields. The most impressive Aztec achievement, though, was the way they grew crops within Lake Texcoco. The Aztecs built islands by layering mud on top of woven branches. Then they used these islands to grow crops to feed a growing population. Because Tenochtitlan was located close to territory controlled by other groups, the Aztecs were able to create trade routes to those cultures and trade goods and surplus crops with them. As their empire spread, Aztec culture also spread to these groups.

The Aztecs were ruled by a monarch, but their military leaders led them to conquer other peoples. Their rule could be harsh, as they turned some of the conquered peoples into slaves. They killed some slaves as sacrifices to their gods, believing that doing so would ensure the gods' protection.

Reading Check How did the Aztecs turn a lake into fields for farming?

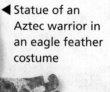

◀ Statue of an Aztec warrior in an eagle feather costume

The Spanish Arrive

When Hernán Cortés landed in Mexico, he had only 500 soldiers with him. The soldiers faced an empire with an army of thousands. Nevertheless, Cortés and his soldiers defeated the Aztec empire.

Several factors contributed to the Spaniards' success. The Spanish were armed with muskets and cannons, which were far more powerful than the clubs and blades used by Aztecs. The Spanish also had horses that allowed the army to move quickly. The Aztecs had no horses.

The Spanish also benefited because many native peoples who had been conquered by the Aztecs joined the Spanish to fight the Aztecs. These peoples had long resented harsh Aztec rule.

Finally, the Spanish unknowingly brought European diseases to Mexico. Native Americans had never been exposed to illnesses like measles and smallpox. Without defenses against these diseases, hundreds of thousands of native people died.

Reading Check Why did other native peoples join the Spanish in fighting the Aztecs?

A City on a Lake

Mexico City was built on top of the Aztec capital of Tenochtitlán. The Aztecs built the city on an island in the middle of Lake Texcoco. Aztec construction efforts slowly filled in the lake. Over the years, some modern buildings built on this waterlogged soil have begun to sink into the ground.

The Plaza de las Tres Culturas, or "Plaza of the Three Cultures," is a mix of Aztec, Spanish colonial, and modern buildings. ▼

The map below shows modern Mexico City with the outline of the former Lake Texcoco. ▼

Ecatepec de Morelos

Plaza of Three Cultures

MEXICO CITY

Nezahualcóyotl

KEY
- ○ City today
- ═ Major roads today
- ─ Minor roads today
- ▨ Lake Texcoco, 1521
- △ Plaza of Three Cultures

219

Garden on a Lake

Chinampas allowed the Aztecs to grow enough food to feed their ever-expanding population. In the shallow parts of Lake Texcoco, builders drove posts into the bottom of the lake. Between these posts, layers of woven branches and mud created a base to grow crops. Willow trees were planted so the roots would anchor the beds to the lake below.

It took about eight days of digging mud and weaving strips of wood to build a chinampa. ▼

Original canals and chinampas still exist today.

Effect of Spanish Rule

Spanish rule changed society in Mexico. When the Spanish took control of Tenochtitlán, they built new buildings and renamed it Mexico City. Cortés and his soldiers were given vast estates, where they forced Native Americans to farm. Native peoples were also put to work in gold and silver mines. Spanish landowners often treated them harshly. They had few rights.

The Roman Catholic Church played an important role in changing Mexico. Missionaries converted native people to Christianity, which helped establish Spanish customs.

Colonial Mexico developed a new social order. At the top of society were the **peninsulares,** people who came to Mexico from Spain. Although they made up the smallest number of the population, the peninsulares held the most important government jobs. Next highest were the **criollos,** people of Spanish descent who were born in Mexico. Criollos were prohibited from having the highest government posts. Criollos eventually resented the fact that their opportunities were limited by the peninsulares. The next class of people were **mestizos,** or people with mixed Spanish and native backgrounds. Some mestizos paid the government so they could be called criollos. At the bottom of the social ladder were native peoples. The greatest number of people in colonial society were native.

Reading Check What position did native peoples hold in Spanish colonial society?

Reminders

The Aztec heritage lives on in many ways in modern Mexico. When the government built a giant outdoor stadium in the 1960s, it proudly named the new structure after the Native American empire. Aztec Stadium still stands in Mexico City after hosting the 1968 Summer Olympic Games and countless other events.

The **Nahuatl** language of the Aztecs lives on in Mexico today. Many words for foods common to Mexico were absorbed into Spanish from Nahuatl. Examples are *avocado, chili, chocolate,* and *tomato.* Such animal names as coyote and ocelot are also Nahuatl words.

Some remains of Aztec life can be seen in Mexico's landscape. The huge open plaza called the Zócalo in the center of Mexico City was the site of a giant plaza in Aztec times. Still, since the Spanish built Mexico City on top of Tenochtitlán, Aztec remains are hidden. Getting at these buildings might mean damaging important buildings from Spanish colonial times.

Sometimes, though, researchers uncover new information that can change the way we look at the past. Recently, an Aztec pyramid was discovered in Mexico City. Scientists think the structure might be as much as 800 years old. If it is in fact that old, this discovery may prove that the Aztecs settled in the Valley of Mexico earlier than historians had thought.

Reading Check Why are Aztec buildings in Mexico City hidden?

▲ A modern market where chilis, avocados, and tomatoes are sold.

▲ The Mexican flag shows an image from an Aztec myth. The myth told the Aztecs to settle where they saw an eagle on a cactus eating a snake. The Aztecs saw this eagle on an island in Lake Texcoco.

Assessment

1. Why did the Aztecs sacrifice some of the people they conquered to their gods?

2. What factors helped the Spanish conquer the Aztec Empire?

3. What was the difference between peninsulares and criollos?

4. How have parts of Aztec culture continued in Mexico today?

5. What are the similarities between the Aztecs and Spanish in how each group treated the people they conquered?

History of Mexico

IN Indiana

6.1.4 Explain the development and organization of various systems in Europe and the Americas.

6.1.6 Identify trade routes and discuss their impact on the rise of cultural centers and cities in Europe and Mesoamerica.

6.1.20 Analyze cause-and-effect relationships in history.

Visual Glossary

Key Terms • maize • astronomy • aqueduct • conquistador • Mexican Revolution

Reading Skill: Analyze Cause and Effect Take notes using the graphic organizer in your journal.

Pendant depicting a Maya ruler, from A.D. 600–1521 ▼

Early civilizations in Mexico were able to take great advantage of the resources available to them. These societies developed complex farming techniques. Spanish conquerors arrived in the 1500s, bringing disease that killed many native people. Many native Mexicans were forced into slavery and poverty. The struggles of these early years continued into the 1900s.

Early Mexico

The first people to live in what is now Mexico settled in the area thousands of years ago. They survived by hunting animals and gathering plants. About 7,000 years ago, native peoples first began growing a wild grass called **maize,** or corn. This step marked the beginning of agriculture in the Americas.

Over time, native peoples added other crops, including beans, squash, and chili peppers. As they produced more food, their population grew and they formed larger communities.

Olmec Rule Around 1500 B.C., the Olmec civilization arose along Mexico's Gulf coast. The Olmecs developed a complex political system, a religion, and a system of hieroglyphics, in which symbols stand for words. The Olmecs also developed a calendar.

The Olmecs traded with nearby peoples. Through this trade, the Olmecs influenced Native American cultures that came later.

Maya Civilization The Maya lived in what are now southern Mexico, Guatemala, and Belize. They built several dozen cities with thousands of people. These cities had pyramid-shaped temples of stone decorated with sculptures.

The Maya excelled at **astronomy,** the study of the stars and planets. They used their learning to construct several calendar systems that worked together to guide their farmers and to plan religious ceremonies.

Maya civilization declined around A.D. 900. Still, Maya cities continued in the Yucatán Peninsula. Thousands of Maya still live in Mexico today.

Sometime after A.D. 200, the city of Teotihuacan was built near current-day Mexico City. It contained huge monuments, such as pyramids and temples. The city's residents traded with and influenced the cultures of other people in the region. Historians don't know why Teotihuacan was abandoned around A.D. 700.

Emergence of the Aztecs In the 1400s, a new power, the Aztecs, arose in Mexico.

The Aztecs settled in the Valley of Mexico in the 1300s. They built their capital, Tenochtitlán, on an island in the middle of a lake. With 150,000 people, the city was the largest ever built by Native Americans.

The Aztecs grew corn, squash, beans, and other foods and were excellent engineers. They built **aqueducts,** or channels that carried water, to their capital, and canals to make transportation easier.

The Aztecs also had a strong army. After A.D. 1500, they had conquered and controlled 5 million people or more.

Reading Check What was remarkable about Tenochtitlán?

Ancient Civilizations of Mexico

Ancient Mexico was home to some of the most complex civilizations in the Western Hemisphere. The Olmecs, Maya, and Aztecs existed at different times in Mexico's history, although each had effects long after the decline of their civilizations.

Timeline

▲ **Olmecs B.C. 1500** Olmec art influenced later cultures in ancient Mexico.

Maya A.D. 300–900 Maya weaving techniques still survive today. ▶

▲ **Aztecs A.D. 1200–1521** Montezuma II ruled over the Aztec empire, which influences Mexican culture today.

my **worldgeography**.com Timeline

Struggle for
POWER

Diego Rivera became a well-known artist from Mexico in the early 1900s. His art outlining Mexico's history appears in the National Palace in Mexico City. The paintings begin with the Aztecs, whose empire was reaching its height of power when the Spanish arrived. Seeking gold, the Spanish soon overpowered the Aztecs.

▲ Tenochtitlán, the Aztec capital, was one of the largest cities in the world, with advanced engineering and a complex economy.

Spanish Rule to Independence

In the late 1400s, explorers from Spain sailed to the Americas and began building colonies. The Spanish heard stories of a people—the Aztecs—who had large cities and vast amounts of silver and gold. The Spanish set out to find these people, leading to an encounter that changed the history of Mexico.

convert, *v.,* to cause someone to adopt a different religion

myWorld Activity
To Dig or Not to Dig

Arrival of Cortés In 1519, Spanish conquistador Hernan Cortés landed in Mexico. A **conquistador** is a soldier-explorer. The Aztecs greatly outnumbered Cortés and his 500 soldiers. Yet in just two years, Cortés defeated the Aztec Empire. Tens of thousands of Aztecs and their subjects died in the fighting.

Cortés destroyed Tenochtitlán and built Mexico City in its place.

Culture Change Under the Spanish, the lives of native peoples changed. Settlers from Spain and their descendants held the highest place in society. Native peoples had few rights. Priests came to Mexico to <u>convert</u> Native Americans to the Roman Catholic religion. The church became an important part of life in the new colony. Churches were built in the centers of towns and cities, and church officials became leaders in the colony.

Spain Struggles By the 1700s, Spain's empire had weakened. Spain's rulers decided to change the political and economic system to improve conditions in Mexico. They made new laws that led to increased trade. As Mexico's economy revived, Spain raised taxes and sent new officials to rule Mexico.

While Spain tried to improve Mexico,

▲ After almost two years of fighting, the Spanish conquered the Aztecs. Soon after, the Aztecs were forced to become laborers.

▲ Spanish missionaries worked to convert native people to Christianity.

new ideas swept across Europe and the Americas. A movement called the Enlightenment questioned the rule of kings, and proposed that people had basic rights—rights that many in Mexico did not enjoy. People in North America acted on these ideas and declared independence from Great Britain. Their founding of the United States stood as an example to Spain's colonies.

Separating from Spain Early in the 1800s, the French emperor Napoleon Bonaparte invaded Spain. He named his brother Spain's new king. The French put a new person in control, who briefly ruled Mexico. In 1810, Mexicans launched a revolt that ended in 1821 with Mexico winning independence from Spain.

Reading Check How long did it take for Mexico to win independence?

Challenges for the Republic

While Mexicans had won independence, they faced new challenges. For many decades, their leaders struggled to solve the nation's problems.

Troubled Beginnings After the United States won independence, its new government struggled. In a few years, though, Americans wrote a new constitution that brought stability. The same did not happen in Mexico. The Mexican people did write a constitution, but different leaders competed for power. For the first few decades of Mexico's existence as a nation, they could not create a stable government.

In the middle 1800s, Benito Juárez became the leader of Mexico. He promised to make many changes that would help the nation's poor. Juárez

225

Struggle for
POWER
continued

Colonial divisions between privileged Spanish and poor Native Americans caused tension. After independence, leaders like Porfirio Díaz made reforms, but problems remained. Widespread poverty led to revolution in 1910. By 1917, Mexico had its current constitution, which laid the groundwork for a more stable society.

THINK CRITICALLY How have gold, land, and oil created conflict in Mexico?

▲ Porfirio Díaz, upper left, encouraged economic growth using natural resources, like oil. Businesses prospered, but few shared in the wealth.

estate, *n.,* a large piece of land or property

promised to break up the large <u>estates</u> that the wealthy held and give some of this land to poor farmers.

Some Mexicans resented the changes Juárez made because they would lose wealth and power. They sought help from France. The French government sent an army that defeated Juárez. Then, France put an Austrian noble named Maximilian in control of Mexico. He tried to bring peace to the nation, but Juárez's supporters fought on. After several more years of fighting, Maximilian was overthrown. Back in power, Juárez was unable to make all the reforms he wanted.

Mexico under Díaz From the 1870s to 1911, Mexico's leader was Porfirio Díaz. At first, he tried to put in place many of the reforms of Juárez. He also tried to build Mexico's economy by inviting

foreign companies to build railroads and do other projects. Only a small number of Mexicans benefited, though. The great majority of people still lived in poverty. They worked long hours and had few rights and little food.

Mexican Revolution Unrest spread. Finally, in 1910, a candidate for president that Díaz supported lost the election to an opponent. Díaz had the opponent arrested and declared his man the winner. This action, along with Mexico's history of widespread poverty, sparked the **Mexican Revolution,** a period of armed rebellion in which Mexican people fought for political and social reform.

Constitution of 1917 The fighting eased in 1917, when a new constitution was declared. The new constitution made the government responsible for improving

▲ *Tierra y Libertad* means "Land and Liberty," which referred to the idea that more people should be able to own land.

▲ The final panel shows foreign investors and the promise of Mexico's natural resources.

Mexicans' lives. It declared the goal of giving land to poor farmers and more rights to workers.

Venustiano Carranza became president of Mexico but did not make many of the constitutional changes he promised. In a few years, leaders joined to overthrow him. In the next few decades, Mexico's leaders made some reforms, but the poor continued to suffer.

Reading Check What caused the Mexican Revolution in 1910?

Section 2 Assessment

Key Terms

1. How did the Maya use their knowledge of astronomy?

2. What is a conquistador?

Key Ideas

3. What important role did the Olmecs play among Mexico's native peoples?

4. How did the development of Mexico's government differ from that of the United States?

5. What changes did the Constitution of 1917 promise to Mexico's people?

Think Critically

6. Synthesize What role did the Roman Catholic Church play in colonial Mexico?

7. Draw Inferences What details support the idea that the Mexican Revolution was not a complete success?

Essential Question

How much does geography shape a country?

8. How did Mexico's geography and the struggle for resources affect the history of Mexico? Go to your Student Journal to record your answer.

The Mexican Revolution

IN Indiana

6.1.21 Differentiate between fact and interpretation in historical accounts and explain historical passages.

6.1.23 Identify issues related to an event in Europe or the Americas and give arguments for and against that issue.

Costumes for the anniversary of the revolution ▼

By 1910, a dictator named Porfirio Díaz had ruled Mexico for more than 30 years. Under Díaz, a small group of rich landowners controlled most of Mexico's land and wealth. Meanwhile, the majority of Mexicans were very poor. In 1911, Mexicans began a revolution. Soon, the revolutionaries broke into several groups. The leader of one group, General Emiliano Zapata, promised to take dramatic steps to help Mexico's poor. Fighting continued until 1920. Eventually a new constitution was written that promised reforms to help the poor.

Stop at each circled letter on the right to think about the text. Then answer the question with the same letter on the left.

A **Identify Main Idea and Details** What economic problems does the plan address?

B **Draw Inferences** Why did leaders of the revolution believe that owning land would improve conditions for Mexico's people?

C **Compare Viewpoints** How do you think the Mexican poor and the landowners would react to this part of the plan?

monopolized, *adj.,* held exclusively by a few

expropriated, *v.,* seized; taken

proprietors, *n.,* owners

Goals for a Second Revolution

[B]ecause lands, timber, and **A** water are <u>monopolized</u> in a few hands, for this cause there will be <u>expropriated</u> . . . part of those monopolies from the powerful <u>proprietors</u> of them . . . in order that the pueblos and citizens of Mexico may **B** obtain . . . fields for sowing and laboring, and Mexicans' lack of **C** prosperity and well-being may improve in all and for all. "

— Emiliano Zapata, 1911, "The Plan of Ayala," in *Zapata and the Mexican Revolution,* by John Warwick Jr.

Emiliano **Zapata**

228

Stop at each circled letter on the right to think about the text. Then answer the question with the same letter on the left.

D Summarize Why do the farm laborers have little freedom to leave?

E Compare and Contrast How does the life of peons in the 1920's compare to life before the Mexican Revolution?

F Analyze Cause and Effect What is the effect of this system on Mexican farm laborers?

peons, *n.,* workers of the hacienda

bondage, *n.,* slavery

haciendado, *n.,* owners of a hacienda, a large farm or ranch

meager, *adj.,* of small quantity

abject, *adj.,* reduced to the lowest level

George M. McBride on Land Ownership in Mexico, 1923

❝ The <u>peons</u> upon a Mexican hacienda are theoretically free. . . . As a matter of fact, however, many of them are held upon

D the estate in <u>bondage.</u> . . . By a system of advance payments, which the peons are totally unable to refund, the <u>haciendados</u> are able to keep them permanently under financial obligations and hence to oblige them to remain upon the estates to

E which they belonged. . . So <u>meager</u> is the compensation received by the peon that

F he is kept in the most <u>abject</u> poverty. ❞

—George M. McBride,
The Land Systems of Mexico, 1923

Modern-day farmer
working the land ▼

Analyze the Documents

1. **Draw Conclusions** How does the situation described in the second document compare to the economic complaint in the Plan of Ayala?
2. **Writing Task** Write a newspaper article from a 1920s viewpoint stating whether you think the Mexican Revolution was a success and explaining why or why not.

Mexico Today

IN Indiana

6.2.7 Define and compare citizenship and the citizen's role throughout history in Europe and the Americas.

6.3.10 Explain the ways cultural diffusion, invention, and innovation change culture.

6.4.1 Give examples of how trade related to key developments in the history of Europe and the Americas.

6.4.7 Identify economic connections between the community and the countries of Europe or the Americas

and identify job skills needed to be successful in the workplace.

6.4.8 Identify how societies deal with externalities in Europe or the Americas.

Key Terms • Institutional Revolutionary Party (PRI) • National Action Party (PAN)
• free market • remittance

Visual Glossary

Reading Skill: Identify Main Ideas and Details Take notes using the graphic organizer in your journal.

Voters participate in a recent election. ▼

The history of Mexico includes many struggles between rich and poor, as well as between native peoples and people of Spanish descent. Today, there are fewer struggles and Mexico's government is far more stable. The country's rich culture draws on the history of its diverse people. Mexico's economy continues to grow with increased manufacturing and trade. But the country still faces many social and economic challenges.

Governing Mexico

Mexico, like the United States, is a federal republic. A federal government shares power with state governments. Mexico has 31 states and a federal district. Since Mexico is a republic, its people elect their leaders. Those leaders then propose and enact laws.

Structure of Government Mexico's government has other similarities to the government of the United States. Mexico has a constitution. The Constitution of 1917 defines the structure of government, and states that all Mexico's people enjoy certain basic rights.

Mexico's national government is divided into three branches. The legislative branch creates laws. The executive branch, led by the president, carries out the laws. The judicial branch interprets the laws and decides whether actions of the other branches follow the constitution.

Mexico has a system of checks and balances between branches of government. The president has traditionally had more power than other branches, although Mexico's congress has gained more power recently.

Political Parties For many decades, a single political party <u>dominated</u> Mexico's government. That party is the **Institutional Revolutionary Party,** called the PRI after its name in Spanish. In 1929, the PRI gained control of Mexico's government. Every six years, the president would name another PRI member to succeed him, and that person would easily win the election.

In the late 1900s, many Mexicans voiced frustration over this one-party rule. They wanted to see more open elections, in the hopes that this change would produce better government. In 1999, President Ernesto Zedillo created some reforms. As a result, the 2000 presidential election was more fair than any earlier Mexican election. Candidate Vicente Fox, of the **National Action Party** (PAN), won the election.

Fair elections continued in later years. The PAN and other parties also gained more seats in Mexico's congress and in state governments. In 2006, Mexico's people elected another PAN leader, Felipe Calderón, president.

dominate, *v.,* to control, or rule over

Citizens' Rights All Mexican people 18 or older have the right to vote in elections. Mexico's constitution actually requires people to vote in elections, although the law is not enforced.

Reading Check How did government in Mexico change in the 2000 election?

Mexican Politics, Then and Now

From 1929 to 2000, the Institutional Revolutionary Party (PRI) ruled Mexican politics. Presidents were often corrupt and made sure the person they picked won each election. In 2000, Vicente Fox became the first president who was not a member of the PRI.

Plutarco Calles made a "political machine" to ensure PRI victory.

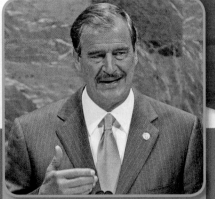

Vicente Fox broke the 71-year rule of the PRI.

Felipe Calderón, of the PAN, won a close election in 2006.

People and Culture

With about 116 million people, Mexico is second in population only to Brazil among all Latin American countries. It has the largest Spanish-speaking population in the world—nearly three times more than Spain itself.

Cultures Blend Like many nations in the Americas, Mexico has a culture that blends, or mixes, traditions. Mexico's culture combines Spanish and Native American influences. In fact, about three out of five Mexicans have mixed Spanish and Native American ancestry. About one in three people is Native American. Most speak Spanish as well as their native language. Native Americans live mainly in southern Mexico. Many are Maya who live in the Yucatán Peninsula. Many members of another group, the Zapotecs, live in the Southern Highlands.

Mexicans honor mixed heritage on October 12. On this day—the Día de la Raza, or "Race Day"—Mexicans celebrate the contributions that all peoples have made to Mexican culture.

Mexico's art reflects its many cultures. Talented Mexican artists, following Native American tradition, have painted murals. These large-scale paintings are mounted on building walls and celebrate Mexico's history. Famous muralists include Diego Rivera and David Alfar Siqueiros. Another well-known Mexican artist, Frida Kahlo, painted self-portraits. José Clemente Orozco sculpted plaster.

Blending Cultures

From mariachi bands to celebrating the Day of the Dead, Mexico has a rich cultural history.

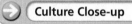

Culture Close-up

Día de la Raza, Columbus Day in some countries, is a celebration of the many cultures in Mexico.

During Day of the Dead celebrations, marigolds decorate graves in honor of ancestors.

Religion The religious practices of Mexico's people also show the mixing of different cultures. About three quarters of the people practice the Roman Catholic faith. A growing number, though, belong to Protestant churches. This is especially true among poor people living in cities. Some Mexicans blended Christian and traditional Native American beliefs, which is shown by celebrating the Day of the Dead.

Education Mexico's leaders have been working hard to improve education. The government has invested more in education by building schools, hiring teachers, and providing books and supplies. Today, about 91 percent of Mexicans over 15 can read and write. This is a sharp improvement since 1970.

Furthering their education will prepare Mexican children for the modern workplace. Increasingly, students in Mexico study English, which reflects continued economic ties between the United States and Mexico.

Still, education lags in rural areas, where some schools do not offer all grades. Many rural Mexicans move to cities to access better schools for their children. Students such as Carolina travel long distances to the schools they attend.

The government has tried to improve education for Native American children by providing textbooks and instruction in their native languages and in Spanish.

Reading Check What share of Mexico's population can read and write?

People prepare hand-made goods for the Day of the Dead celebrations, including candy and paper flags, called papel picado (above).

Spanish mariachi bands play quick-tempo music in restaurants, festivals, weddings, and other gatherings throughout Mexico.

Mexico's Economy

dynamic, *adj.*, active, or showing progress

Mexico has built a <u>dynamic</u> and growing economy. The nation now has one of the top economies in Latin America and one of the most productive economies in the world. For decades, Mexico depended on oil production to earn money while a large section of the population farmed. Now it has a more diverse economy.

Mexico's Economy at a Glance For most of the 1900s, Mexico's government tightly controlled the economy. The government owned some important enterprises, including the national oil company. It also put strict limits on other industries. As a result, economic growth lagged. In the late 1900s, leaders adopted **free market** ideas, which means the government took away complex rules and let new companies compete. The result was more economic growth and more jobs.

Mexico has also built closer economic ties to the United States. In the 1990s, Mexico, the United States, and Canada signed NAFTA, the North American Free Trade Agreement. The three countries promised to take away rules that blocked trade between each other. For the most part, this meant taxes on goods that the countries traded with each other would be lower, so that goods could move between countries at a lower cost. As a result, trade with the United States has led to a growing Mexican economy, more manufacturing jobs, and increased pay for Mexican workers.

Mexico's Workers Approximately four out of six Mexican workers work in service industries. These industries include finance, communications, and healthcare. Tourism is an important service industry in Mexico too. Many people come from other countries to enjoy its beautiful resorts and the fascinating remains of its Native American cities. Another important service industry for Mexico is entertainment. Its television workers produce telenovelas, which tell complex stories with many characters. These long-running series delight not only Mexicans but people in other countries as well.

About one quarter of Mexican workers labor in factories. They process foods and make chemicals, iron and steel, clothing, cars, and electronic goods. Some of the factories they work in are owned by foreign companies.

Mexico's Gulf coast supports an active tourism industry. ▼

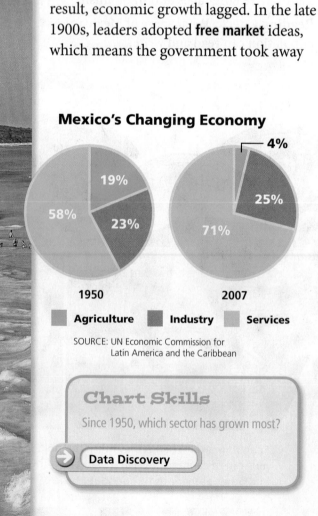

Mexico's Changing Economy

19%
58%
23%
1950

4%
25%
71%
2007

■ Agriculture ■ Industry ■ Services

SOURCE: UN Economic Commission for Latin America and the Caribbean

Chart Skills

Since 1950, which sector has grown most?

➔ Data Discovery

Only four percent of Mexican people work on a farm. Some farmers grow cash crops such as coffee and fruits. Others tend the large herds of cattle that roam huge ranches in the north of Mexico. Many farmers, though, are among the nation's poorest people.

Some of Mexico's poor cannot find jobs in Mexico. They travel north to the United States to work. They send part of their earnings back home to support their families. These payments, called **remittances,** are an important part of Mexico's economy. They help many poor families survive.

Mexico has a large share of young people in its population. They will be entering the workforce soon. The economy has to grow rapidly to provide enough jobs for all these new workers. If not, Mexicans will continue to leave the country looking for a place to work.

Reading Check Why do some workers leave Mexico for the United States?

myWorld Activity
Help Wanted: Mexico

Map Skills

Region Where do most remittances go, to the north, to the south, or to central Mexico?

Active Atlas

The Remittance System in Mexico

A remittance is money earned in one country that is sent back to support families and others in a person's home country. The map below shows which Mexican states receive the most remittance money.

KEY
Total Remittances to Mexico by State
Millions of dollars, 2006

- More than 1,500
- 851–1,500
- 501–850
- 251–500
- 25–250

▲ Higher wages in the United States create opportunity.

my worldgeography.com Data Discovery

235

The Impact of Trade

In the 1990s, Mexico entered into the North American Free Trade agreement. While this agreement has led to more manufacturing jobs and increased trade, Mexico's economy is very dependent on the United States.

THINK CRITICALLY How does the amount of goods the United States buys affect Mexico's exports?

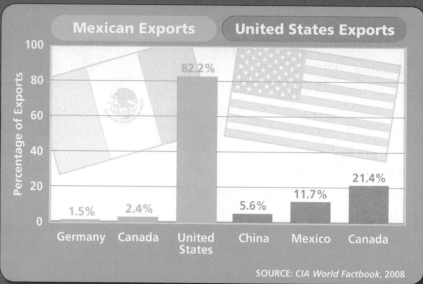

Mexican Exports | **United States Exports**

Percentage of Exports

82.2%

21.4%

11.7%

5.6%

1.5% 2.4%

Germany Canada United States China Mexico Canada

SOURCE: *CIA World Factbook*, 2008

Oil provided a base for Mexico's modern economy. Changing oil prices, however, made the economy unstable.

Many agricultural products, including coffee, fruits, and vegetables are shipped to the United States. Manufacturing goods, such as shoes and automobiles, has helped Mexico find other sources of income. This is known as diversifying an economy.

CAFE

MEXICO EXPORTA T.I.E.V.

$100 CORREOS R. DAVIDSON

ZAPATOS

MEXICO EXPORTA T.I.E.V.

$60 CORREOS R. DAVIDSON

Trade

Trade has become very important to Mexico's economy. Earnings from selling oil and oil products help finance the government. Manufactured goods and some crops are also major exports. Trade has brought many benefits—but also some problems.

Increased trade has allowed Mexico's economy to grow. Mexico belongs to the World Trade Organization (WTO), where it works with other countries to lower trade barriers. It has free trade agreements with more than forty other nations. Mexico's leaders hope to expand NAFTA to include more nations from Latin America in a zone called the Free Trade Area of the Americas (FTAA).

Providing Jobs Growing trade has led to more jobs in Mexico. However, Mexican workers earn less than those in the United States and Canada. Many manufacturers placed factories in Mexico to take advantage of lower wages.

Mexican workers make more than factory workers in China and other growing economies. Some Mexicans worry that more manufacturing jobs in China will lead to job loss in Mexico.

The Downside of Trade Dependence on trade has caused some problems, too. Some American companies have sold corn and apples in Mexico at lower prices than what Mexican farmers can afford to charge. As a result, Mexican farmers sell less.

Also, Mexico's great dependence on the United States means its economic success is closely linked to the United States economy. When the economy of the United States is doing well, Mexico benefits. When the United States economy slows down, Mexico also suffers. As a result, Mexico saw very slow economic growth in 2008. Since 2011, however, the gross domestic product of both Mexico and the United States has increased.

Reading Check What is NAFTA, and how has it affected Mexico's economy?

IN Indiana **CONNECTIONS**

Indiana's exports total **$34.2** billion annually.

$4 billion of Indiana's exports go to Mexico.

Section 3 Assessment

Essential Question

Key Terms

1. How did the Institutional Revolutionary Party stay in power for so long?

2. How are remittances important to Mexico?

Key Ideas

3. How does Mexico's Constitution of 1917 affect the government?

4. How has the government tried to improve education for Native Americans in Mexico?

5. What steps did Mexico's government take to change the economy starting in the 1990s?

Think Critically

6. **Identify Evidence** What are two examples of ways that Mexico reveals its blended culture?

7. **Draw Conclusions** What do the names of Mexico's political parties suggest about the goals of each party?

How much does geography shape a country?

8. How has Mexico benefited from having abundant deposits of oil? Go to your Student Journal to record your answer.

Chapter Assessment

Key Terms and Ideas

1. **Recall** In what part of Mexico do **sinkholes** form?
2. **Explain** How does **irrigation** damage farmland?
3. **Compare and Contrast** What are the environmental differences between northern Mexico and southern Mexico?
4. **Sequence** Name the three major native Mexican civilizations in chronological order. Give the name of the **conquistador** who brought about the end of the native empires.
5. **Describe** What was life like for the natives during Spanish rule?
6. **Synthesize** What is the difference between the war for independence in 1810 and the **Mexican Revolution** that occurred in 1910?
7. **Explain** Why do some Mexicans go to the United States in order to send **remittances** to their families?
8. **Discuss** What recent changes have occurred in the Mexican economy, and have they resulted in economic improvement?

Think Critically

9. **Identify Evidence** Of which resources are Mexicans making good use and which resources do they need to develop further?
10. **Make Inferences** What were the problems caused by the PRI party holding power in Mexico for more than 70 years?
11. **Predict** What would happen to the Mexican economy if tourism dropped dramatically?
12. **Core Concepts: People's Impact on the Environment** What environmental problems will Mexico face during the next 10 years?

Places to Know

For each place, write the letter from the map that shows its location.

13. **Yucatán Peninsula**
14. **Sierra Madre Occidental**
15. **Mexico City**
16. **Mexican Plateau**
17. **Rio Grande River**
18. **Mérida**
19. Using the scale, estimate the distance between Mexico City and Mérida.

Mexico: Cities and Features

30° N

N
W E
S

TROPIC OF CANCER

20° N

0   300 mi
0   300 km
Lambert Conformal Conic Projection

110° W   100° W   90° W

my worldgeography.com Self-Test

Essential Question

myWorld Chapter Activity

Judging Mexico's Leaders Assess the achievements of Mexico's leaders, including Montezuma, Cortés, Maximilian, Juarez, Zapata, and Calderón. Judge whether or not the leaders met their goals for Mexico and analyze the effects of the leaders' success or failure on Mexican history.

21st Century Learning

Analyze Media Content

Find three articles online about the presidential race in 2006, between Felipe Calderón and Andrés Manuel López Obrador. Analyze the articles. Is there evidence of bias, or a favoring of one view over another? Does the article suggest the election results were fair? Do supporters of Obrador or Calderón feel the results were fair? Explain your answer.

Document-Based Questions

Success Tracker™
Online at myworldgeography.com

Use your knowledge of Mexico and Documents A and B to answer Questions 1–3.

Document A

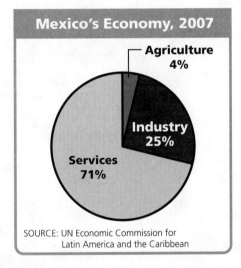

Mexico's Economy, 2007

Agriculture 4%

Industry 25%

Services 71%

SOURCE: UN Economic Commission for Latin America and the Caribbean

Document B

" The mountains here are rugged and difficult, so that they can hardly be crossed, even on foot. Twice I have sent people to conquer them, but they have never been able to do anything against these Indians, who are well armed and entrenched in their mountains."

—Hernando Cortés to Charles V, 1526

1. What kind of work do most Mexican people do for a living?

   A Most people work in agriculture.

   B More than half of the people work in either agriculture or industry.

   C Most people work in the service areas of the economy.

   D More people choose to work in industry than in the service areas of the economy.

2. What was the advantage the Aztecs had that Cortés described to Charles V?

   A The Aztecs were familiar with the territory.

   B Aztec weapons were superior to Spanish weapons.

   C The Aztecs built camps in the mountains.

   D The Spanish were outnumbered.

3. **Writing Task** What does the description Cortés gives of Mexico's landscape suggest about the availability of farmland?

Chapter 4

Central America and the Caribbean

? Essential Question

Is it better to be independent or interdependent?

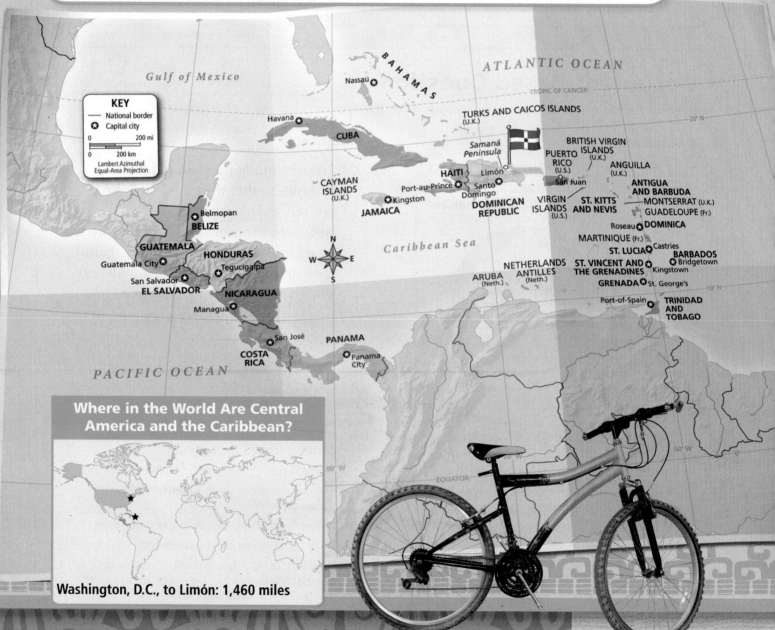

KEY
— National border
⊙ Capital city

0   200 mi
0   200 km
Lambert Azimuthal
Equal-Area Projection

Gulf of Mexico

ATLANTIC OCEAN

BAHAMAS

Nassau ⊙

TROPIC OF CANCER

20° N

Havana ⊙

CUBA

TURKS AND CAICOS ISLANDS
(U.K.)

Samaná
Peninsula

PUERTO
RICO
(U.S.)

BRITISH VIRGIN
ISLANDS
(U.K.)

ANGUILLA
(U.K.)

CAYMAN
ISLANDS
(U.K.)

HAITI

Limón

San Juan

ANTIGUA
AND BARBUDA

Port-au-Prince

Santo
Domingo

⊙ Kingston

JAMAICA

DOMINICAN
REPUBLIC

VIRGIN
ISLANDS
(U.S.)

ST. KITTS
AND NEVIS

MONTSERRAT (U.K.)

GUADELOUPE (Fr.)

Belmopan

BELIZE

Roseau ⊙ DOMINICA

MARTINIQUE (Fr.)

Caribbean Sea

GUATEMALA

HONDURAS

ST. LUCIA ⊙ Castries

BARBADOS
⊙ Bridgetown

Guatemala City ⊙

Tegucigalpa

N

NETHERLANDS
ANTILLES
(Neth.)

ST. VINCENT AND
THE GRENADINES

Kingstown

San Salvador ⊙

W   E

GRENADA ⊙ St. George's

EL SALVADOR

NICARAGUA

S

ARUBA
(Neth.)

Port-of-Spain ⊙

TRINIDAD
AND
TOBAGO

Managua ⊙

10° N

San José ⊙

PANAMA

COSTA
RICA

⊙ Panama
City

PACIFIC OCEAN

60° W

Where in the World Are Central America and the Caribbean?

80° W

EQUATOR

Washington, D.C., to Limón: 1,460 miles

my Story

Working for the Future

? Explore the Essential Question

- at my worldgeography.com
- using the my World Chapter Activity
- with the **Student Journal**

In this section, you'll read about Luis, an ambitious teenager living in a rural community in the Dominican Republic. What does Luis's story tell you about life in the Dominican Republic?

Story by César Namnúm for myWorld Geography Online

Luis's day usually begins with some chores around his house, a quick breakfast, and a bike ride to work. Luis lives in the rural town of Limón in the Dominican Republic. Limón is located on the Samaná Peninsula a few hours north of the Dominican Republic's capital city, Santo Domingo. The peninsula, shown in the photo at the top of this page, has white sandy beaches and lush tropical forests. It is home to a number of beautiful waterfalls. Perhaps the most spectacular waterfall in the region is Salto de Limón, which drops 150 feet into a deep pool of water. "A lot of tourists come to this area," Luis says, "and nearly all of them want to see the falls."

Luis knows about tourists: he works as a tour guide leading visitors to Salto de Limón. The tourists usually ride horses on the journey, while Luis walks on foot to guide them.

my worldgeography.com On Assignment

Salto de Limón drops 150 feet into a deep pool of water.

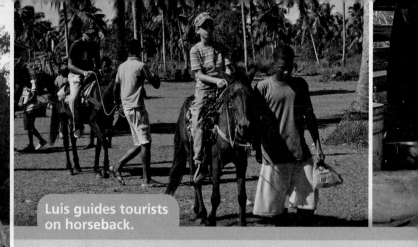

Luis guides tourists on horseback.

Walking with tourists to a waterfall may sound like a simple job, but it is not. Visitors to the falls must climb up a steep trail for more than an hour to reach Salto de Limón. It can be a dangerous hike during the rainy season, when the trail is wet and slippery. But Luis has made this trip more than 200 times, and he knows the way well. When he was a child, he and his friends came here to swim and hunt for fresh fruit. Now Luis is almost 17 years old, and he enjoys taking tourists to this special place.

The natural beauty of the Samaná Peninsula makes it very popular with tourists. As a result, the government and the region's people are working to protect the waterfalls and the surrounding area. A local group of tourism-based businesses helps encourage the protection of natural resources and the environment.

In Limón, Luis lives with his grandmother, Doña Graciela, and a few brothers and cousins. "My mother has been in Puerto Rico for

Luis's cousins

Luis lives with his grandmother.

Luis enjoys a meal with his family.

Attending school is very important to Luis.

eight years and my uncle lives in New York," he says. "My grandmother raised me."

Luis thinks of himself as an ordinary teenager. He begins a typical day by doing housework and shopping for groceries. "After my chores I like to go bike-riding," Luis says with a smile. He usually rides the mile or so to work, where he meets tourists ready to travel to Salto de Limón.

When Luis returns from leading a tour group to the falls, he is hot, tired, and often covered with mud. Then he gets ready to go to school in the afternoon. Not all Dominican children his age attend school, but Luis thinks it is important. "I want to finish my studies and get my worker's permit so I can work in the city," he says. Getting a work permit would lead to many opportunities for Luis. He wants to earn enough money to provide for his family, and he would love to be able to visit his mother in Puerto Rico.

Because it is not always tourist season in Limón, Luis also does chiripeos, or side jobs around town. Sometimes he works at construction sites. At harvest time, he helps the owner of a small organic coffee plantation pick and dry coffee beans. And, he adds, "Sometimes I go with my cousin to help with his grandmother's conuco." A conuco is a small plantation where families grow crops for their own use. Luis helps take care of the crops. Sometimes there are crops left over to sell, and Luis is able to make extra money.

No matter where you find Luis, one thing is clear: he is an extremely hardworking young man with a very bright future.

→ **myStory Video**

Join Luis as he shows you more about his life in the Dominican Republic.

Meet the Journalist

Name César Namnúm
Favorite Moment Seeing Luis's energy and determination

Chapter Atlas

 Indiana

6.3.5 Give examples and describe the formation of river deltas, mountains and bodies of water in Europe and the Americas.

6.3.6 Explain how ocean currents and winds influence climate differences on Europe and the Americas.

6.3.8 Identify major biomes of Europe and the Americas and explain how these are influenced by climate.

6.3.13 Explain the impact of humans on the physical environment in Europe and the Americas.

6.3.14 Explain how nature has impacted the physical environment and human populations in areas of Europe and the Americas.

→ **Visual Glossary**

Key Terms • isthmus • hurricane • biodiversity • tourism • deforestation

🌐 **Reading Skill: Label an Outline Map** Take notes using the outline map in your journal.

▼ San Pedro Volcano, Lake Atitlán, Guatemala

Two Maya girls from Guatemala share a laugh.

Physical Features

Central America connects North America and South America and separates the Atlantic Ocean from the Pacific Ocean. It includes Belize, Guatemala, El Salvador, Honduras, Nicaragua, Costa Rica, and Panama. Some geographers also include the southern portion of Mexico. Central America is an **isthmus,** or a strip of land with water on both sides that connects two larger bodies of land. The isthmus is divided by the Panama Canal, a human-made trade route between the Atlantic and the Pacific.

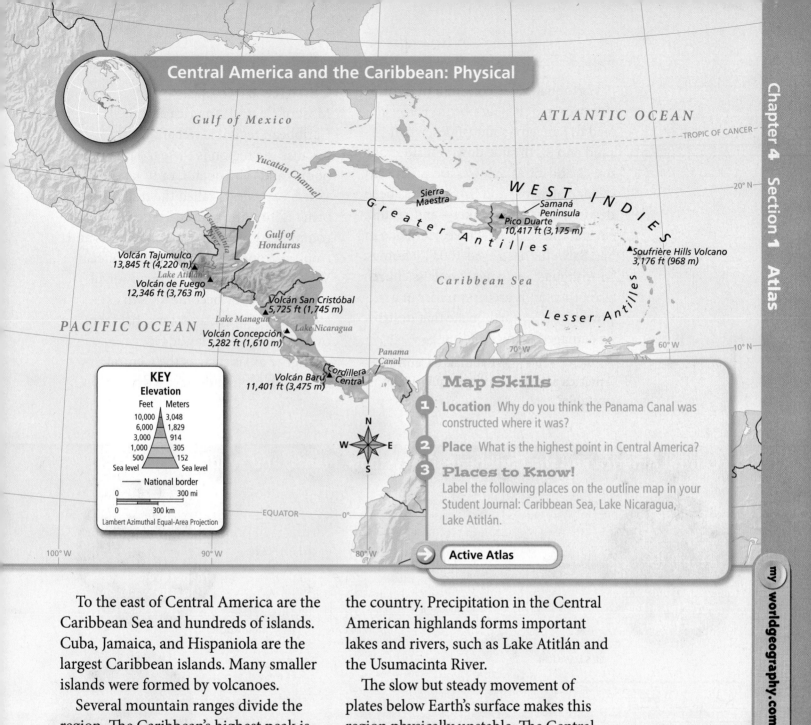

Central America and the Caribbean: Physical

Gulf of Mexico

ATLANTIC OCEAN

TROPIC OF CANCER

20° N

Yucatán Channel

Sierra
Maestra

WEST INDIES

Samaná
Peninsula

▲ Pico Duarte
10,417 ft (3,175 m)

Greater Antilles

▲ Soufrière Hills Volcano
3,176 ft (968 m)

Gulf of
Honduras

Caribbean Sea

Volcán Tajumulco
13,845 ft (4,220 m) ▲

Lake Atitlán ▲
Volcán de Fuego
12,346 ft (3,763 m)

Volcán San Cristóbal
5,725 ft (1,745 m) ▲

Lesser Antilles

10° N

PACIFIC OCEAN

Lake Managua

Lake Nicaragua

70° W

60° W

Volcán Concepción
5,282 ft (1,610 m) ▲

Panama
Canal

Volcán Barú ▲
11,401 ft (3,475 m)

Cordillera
Central

Map Skills

1 **Location** Why do you think the Panama Canal was constructed where it was?

2 **Place** What is the highest point in Central America?

3 **Places to Know!**
Label the following places on the outline map in your Student Journal: Caribbean Sea, Lake Nicaragua, Lake Atitlán.

KEY
Elevation

Feet	Meters
10,000	3,048
6,000	1,829
3,000	914
1,000	305
500	152
Sea level	Sea level

— National border

0 ___ 300 mi
0 ___ 300 km
Lambert Azimuthal Equal-Area Projection

EQUATOR

0°

100° W   90° W   80° W

Active Atlas

To the east of Central America are the Caribbean Sea and hundreds of islands. Cuba, Jamaica, and Hispaniola are the largest Caribbean islands. Many smaller islands were formed by volcanoes.

Several mountain ranges divide the region. The Caribbean's highest peak is Pico Duarte in the Dominican Republic. Mexico's Sierra Madre mountains extend south into Guatemala, El Salvador, and Honduras. Some of the mountains of the Sierra Madre are high enough to be covered with snow in winter. In Panama, the Cordillera Central mountain range divides the western and eastern parts of the country. Precipitation in the Central American highlands forms important lakes and rivers, such as Lake Atitlán and the Usumacinta River.

The slow but steady movement of plates below Earth's surface makes this region physically unstable. The Central America and the Caribbean region has more than eighty active volcanoes. Volcán de Fuego in Guatemala is perhaps the most active. The Soufrière Hills Volcano in Montserrat had a <u>major</u> eruption in 1997. Today much of Montserrat is closed to people and more than half of its population has moved away.

major, *adj.,* of great importance

my worldgeography.com   Active Atlas

Earthquakes are common in Central America and the Caribbean. They can lead to dangerous mudslides, when mud and earth slide down hillsides onto towns and cities in lower areas. The city of San Salvador in El Salvador has been destroyed by earthquakes—and rebuilt—several times. In 2001 an earthquake in San Salvador destroyed 100,000 homes. In Antigua, Guatemala, roofless churches and other ruins are a reminder of a powerful 1773 earthquake that destroyed or damaged many buildings.

Reading Check What makes Central America and the Caribbean physically unstable?

Climate and Life

Most of Central America and the Caribbean region is wet and warm because the region is close to large water bodies and the Equator, or 0° latitude. Warm east winds called the trade winds bring rain to the region. These year-round rains provide water for forests and tropical crops like bananas and coffee. When the trade winds form powerful rainstorms, they become known as **hurricanes,** or intense storms that form over the tropical Atlantic Ocean.

Higher areas such as the Central American highlands have a dry season

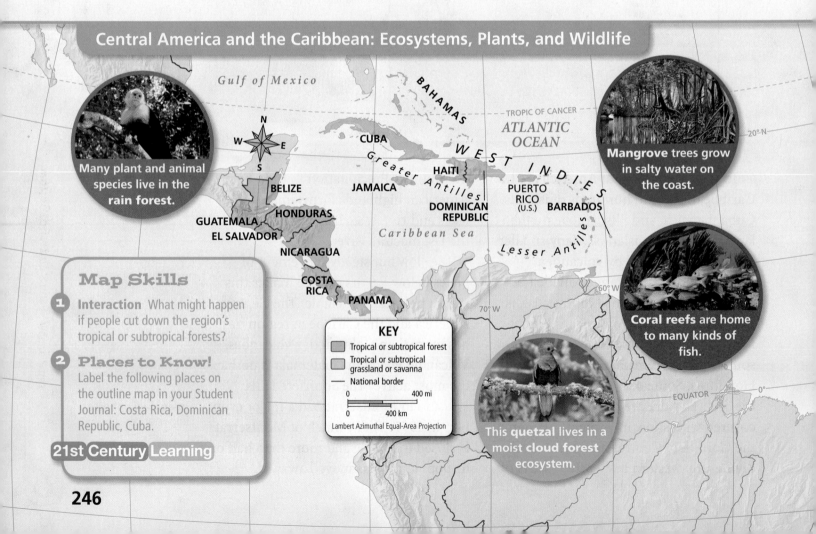

Central America and the Caribbean: Ecosystems, Plants, and Wildlife

Gulf of Mexico

BAHAMAS

TROPIC OF CANCER

ATLANTIC OCEAN

CUBA

WEST INDIES

20°N

Mangrove trees grow in salty water on the coast.

Greater Antilles

HAITI

JAMAICA

PUERTO RICO (U.S.)

BARBADOS

Many plant and animal species live in the **rain forest.**

BELIZE

DOMINICAN REPUBLIC

HONDURAS

GUATEMALA

EL SALVADOR

Caribbean Sea

Lesser Antilles

NICARAGUA

60°W

COSTA RICA

PANAMA

70°W

Coral reefs are home to many kinds of fish.

Map Skills

1. **Interaction** What might happen if people cut down the region's tropical or subtropical forests?

2. **Places to Know!** Label the following places on the outline map in your Student Journal: Costa Rica, Dominican Republic, Cuba.

21st Century Learning

KEY
- ▨ Tropical or subtropical forest
- ▨ Tropical or subtropical grassland or savanna
- — National border

0 ——— 400 mi
0 ——— 400 km
Lambert Azimuthal Equal-Area Projection

This **quetzal** lives in a moist **cloud forest** ecosystem.

EQUATOR

0°

246

and a rainy season. The area's mountains block the trade winds, leading to less rain in the winter months. The lack of rain between December and April can lead to water shortages. As a result, these areas cannot support tropical forests. They are, however, suitable for cattle ranching.

The Central American highlands have a relatively <u>dense</u> population. Most people in Central America live in the highlands because of the dry, cool highland climate. This climate allows people to grow a variety of crops.

Caribbean countries have generally lower elevations. Their climates are similar to the lower areas of Central America.

Due to the region's warm, wet weather, tropical and subtropical ecosystems cover Central America and the Caribbean. Tropical rain forests cover most areas that have not been cleared of trees. Tropical grasslands have formed in regions where people have cut down rain forests. Some countries, such as Costa Rica, have a rare ecosystem called cloud forest. Cloud forests are higher and cooler than lowland forests, with moist clouds that are near the ground. They support diverse wildlife.

Most Caribbean islands are surrounded by an underwater ecosystem known as coral reef. Reefs are largely made up of tiny organisms—coral—that produce a substance similar to limestone as they grow. Over time, coral reefs become large underwater islands that are home to a wide variety of tropical fish and other marine life. This variety of living things is called **biodiversity.**

Reading Check What is an underwater ecosystem common in the Caribbean Sea?

Hurricane Havoc

The region's unique ecosystems, warm days and nights, and beautiful beaches attract visitors from many parts of the world. However, the region's powerful hurricanes can cause great damage and keep visitors away.

Residents of Caribbean islands and coastal countries like Honduras face an average of eight hurricanes a year. Hurricanes usually occur in summer and early fall. These storms can bring several inches of rain an hour, as well as powerful 150-mile-per-hour winds that can harm many people and destroy entire towns.

myWorldActivity
Location Equation

dense, *adj.,* crowded

Hurricanes can cause serious damage in the region.

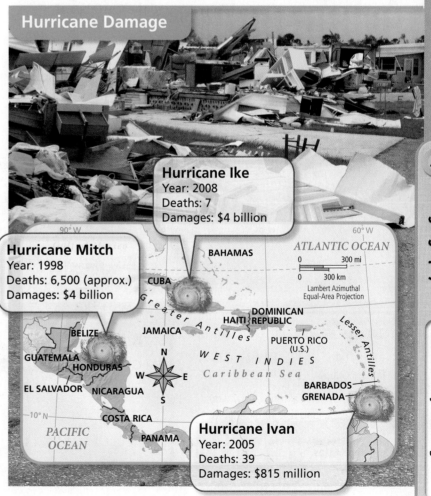

Hurricane Damage

Hurricane Ike
Year: 2008
Deaths: 7
Damages: $4 billion

Hurricane Mitch
Year: 1998
Deaths: 6,500 (approx.)
Damages: $4 billion

BAHAMAS

CUBA

ATLANTIC OCEAN

0   300 mi
0   300 km
Lambert Azimuthal
Equal-Area Projection

Greater Antilles

HAITI DOMINICAN REPUBLIC

BELIZE JAMAICA

GUATEMALA

HONDURAS

EL SALVADOR NICARAGUA

PUERTO RICO (U.S.)

Lesser Antilles

W E S T   I N D I E S

Caribbean Sea

COSTA RICA

PACIFIC OCEAN

PANAMA

BARBADOS
GRENADA

Hurricane Ivan
Year: 2005
Deaths: 39
Damages: $815 million

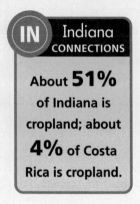

IN Indiana
CONNECTIONS

About **51%** of Indiana is cropland; about **4%** of Costa Rica is cropland.

Recently, hurricanes have become stronger and more frequent. Some scientists believe that this change is due to higher air and sea temperatures, also known as climate change, or global warming.

Hurricanes threaten people's safety and cause widespread destruction. Strong hurricanes, such as Hurricane Ike (2008) and Hurricane Mitch (1998), have damaged the region's roads, farms, schools, and businesses. Countries often depend on help from foreign countries and international aid groups like the International Red Cross and Red Crescent Movement to rebuild after hurricanes.

Reading Check How do hurricanes affect Central America and the Caribbean?

Land Use

Despite environmental dangers like hurricanes and earthquakes, the region's people still find ways to live off the land. But the countries in Central America and the Caribbean are small compared to countries in North or South America. Due to their relatively small sizes, these countries have few natural resources.

Common Land Uses Most Central Americans in rural areas are farmers. Those in urban areas work in commerce and manufacturing. Mining is a land use in some countries. In Jamaica, bauxite is mined for making aluminum. The region produces some petroleum, but most countries must import oil.

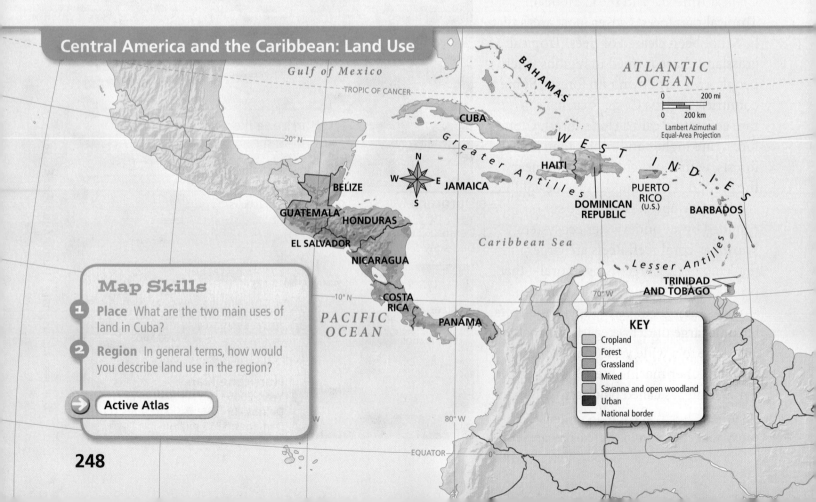

Central America and the Caribbean: Land Use

Map Skills

1 **Place** What are the two main uses of land in Cuba?

2 **Region** In general terms, how would you describe land use in the region?

Active Atlas

KEY
Cropland
Forest
Grassland
Mixed
Savanna and open woodland
Urban
— National border

Warm temperatures and fertile soil make large-scale agriculture possible in the lowlands of Central America and the Caribbean. Plantations, or large commercial farms, grow cash crops such as sugar or coffee. Cash crops are usually sold to other countries rather than sold locally. In fact, much of the food eaten in the region is imported from other countries.

When farmers do have small plots of land to grow their own crops, they keep what they need for their families and sell the surplus, or what is left over, at local markets. In places where it is too dry to grow many crops, ranchers raise livestock, particularly cattle. Cattle ranching, however, employs relatively few workers. It can also cause environmental problems, such as erosion, which is the removal of soil by wind or water.

Tourism Tourism is one of the most important land uses in Central America and the Caribbean. **Tourism** is the business of providing food, places to stay, and other services to visitors from other places. It is the fastest-growing part of the Caribbean economy.

The Bahamas and Jamaica have two of the region's largest tourist-based economies. Tourists spend money while they shop and see sights. They go scuba diving on coral reefs and hiking in rain forests. Cruise ships and resorts employ many local workers. However, these jobs usually pay local workers very little. Foreign companies and investors make most of the profit earned from tourism.

Reading Check Name three ways that the region's people live off the land.

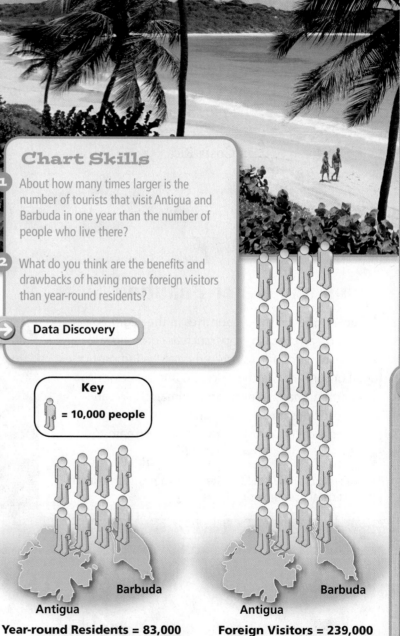

The region's beaches and other natural features attract many tourists, who often outnumber the year-round population.

Chart Skills

1 About how many times larger is the number of tourists that visit Antigua and Barbuda in one year than the number of people who live there?

2 What do you think are the benefits and drawbacks of having more foreign visitors than year-round residents?

➡ **Data Discovery**

Key

👤 = 10,000 people

Barbuda

Antigua

Year-round Residents = 83,000

Barbuda

Antigua

Foreign Visitors = 239,000

Antigua and Barbuda
Tourist versus Year-round Population, 2005

SOURCE: UN Population Division and UN World Tourism Organization

my worldgeography.com   Data Discovery

Environments in Danger

While people depend on the land for food and energy, they sometimes harm the very environments they need to survive. Some people question whether tourism is the best way to use land. The presence of many tourists increases the population density, which can make life more difficult for local people. Water shortages are common, particularly in busy tourist areas like Jamaica or during the dry season of popular tourist regions in Costa Rica.

Pollution Large-scale farming can have environmental consequences. Most small countries in the region grow cash crops such as sugar or coffee to export to other countries. Pesticides and chemicals used to grow large amounts of a single crop can pollute the water supply. Water pollution can kill plants and animals, harming ecosystems such as coral reefs. This decreases biodiversity, one of the region's main tourist attractions.

Pollution also contaminates commercial fishing areas, killing fish. This is a

Closer Look

Crops and Water Pollution

The economies of small countries in the region often depend on a few cash crops, such as corn and sugar cane. Many large farms use chemicals called pesticides to kill organisms that harm crops. But pesticides can also harm humans, plants, and animals. Rain can wash pesticides into streams and rivers. This water pollution—called runoff—travels downstream to oceans, killing coral reefs and fish.

THINK CRITICALLY **How could pollution from pesticide runoff affect coastal economies?**

A sugar plantation in Barbados

Farmers apply pesticides to protect crops.

When it rains, pesticides wash off crops and flow into rivers.

Rivers carry pesticides through many different habitats.

Toxic waters drain into the ocean.

Pesticides can kill marine life and harm ecosystems.

major concern for countries that engage in commercial fishing for export, such as Belize and Honduras.

Deforestation Before large numbers of people occupied the region, tropical forest covered most of the land. Centuries later, ranching, farming, and the need for timber led to **deforestation,** or the clearing of large numbers of trees. When there are no tree roots, soil erodes and cannot absorb moisture. Without moisture, land becomes useless for farming.

Haiti has lost the greatest percentage of its forests of any country in this region. As a result of deforestation and its effects on soil, Haiti has trouble producing enough food to feed its people.

Loss of habitat has also caused a decline in wildlife diversity. Many valuable medicinal plants have been lost. Some Native American groups, such

as the Miskito people in Honduras and Nicaragua, live in the rain forests along the Caribbean coast. For them, deforestation means losing their homes.

Reading Check What are the effects of deforestation?

When rain forests are destroyed, animals like the jaguar lose their homes and face extinction. ▶

Section 1 Assessment

Key Terms

1. What makes Panama an ideal place for building a canal?

2. How do tourists and tourism affect Central America and the Caribbean?

Key Ideas

3. Describe the effects of a hurricane on a country's land, structures, and people.

4. What is the relationship among climate, biodiversity, and tourism in Central America and the Caribbean?

5. How can large-scale farming harm the environment?

Think Critically

6. Ask Questions Referring to the graph that compares the number of year-round residents with foreign tourists, write a question for the Antigua and Barbuda minister of tourism.

7. Draw Conclusions Based on what you have learned about ecosystems and economic activities, what do you think might happen if one of the region's ecosystems was destroyed?

Essential Question

Is it better to be independent or interdependent?

8. How might the frequency of natural disasters affect a country's ability to be independent? Go to your Student Journal to record your answer.

History of Central America and the Caribbean

IN Indiana

6.1.1 Summarize the rise, decline, and cultural achievements of ancient civilizations in Europe and Mesoamerica.

6.1.2 Describe and compare the beliefs, the spread and the influence of religions throughout Europe and Mesoamerica.

6.1.4 Explain the development and organization of various systems in Europe and the Americas.

6.1.20 Analyze cause-and-effect relationships in history.

Key Terms • Maya • colony • encomienda • hacienda • independence • dictatorship

Visual Glossary

Reading Skill: Analyze Cause and Effect Take notes using the graphic organizer in your journal.

◄ The steps of a Maya temple climb toward the sky, where the Maya believed the gods lived.

Early civilizations in Central America and the Caribbean grew in the centuries before Europeans arrived. But when Spanish explorers began to seek gold in the 1500s, the conflict and colonization that followed changed the region forever.

Early Civilizations

Around 1000 B.C., Native Americans known as the **Maya** began settling in what is now Guatemala. Over time, the Maya culture developed into a great civilization and a center of trade.

Maya Civilization The Maya developed a highly accurate calendar and a system of writing that used symbols. They were skilled at mathematics, architecture, astronomy, weaving, and sculpture. Maya farmers grew maize, or corn, and other crops, often using irrigation.

The Maya were organized into city-states, each with its own ruler. Maya cities often fought each other for land and power, but trade helped unite Maya civilization. Each city had large pyramid-shaped temples. These temples

◄ Archaeologists and linguists have spent many years learning the complicated system of Mayan writing.

were the sites of religious celebrations to honor the many Maya gods. Maya priests studied the stars and planets. Cities also had outdoor courts where Mayas played a special ball game.

Maya civilization began to decline around A.D. 900. Historians believe that this decline was caused by a combination of factors, including war, crop failures, and environmental problems.

Early Caribbean Peoples The Caribbean islands were home to two main groups of people now known as the Arawak and the Carib. They grew a variety of plants for food, gathered fruits, and harvested shellfish from the sea. Caribbean peoples used canoes for traveling among the islands. These islands were divided into villages and ruled by chiefs.

Reading Check Summarize the region's early civilizations.

Colonization and Slavery

In 1492, Christopher Columbus sailed across the Atlantic Ocean from Europe, arriving in the Bahamas. The Spanish explorers who followed him to the region established colonies and mined natural resources. In the process, they killed or enslaved millions of Native Americans.

Spanish Colonization Early Spanish explorers were in search of gold and other riches. They also wanted to convert the native people to Christianity. By the early 1500s, the Spanish had conquered the entire region and formed a colony in what is now Panama. A **colony** is a group of people living in a new territory with

ties to a distant state. The Spanish called this colony the Kingdom of Guatemala.

Leaders called viceroys ruled the Spanish colonies. The government <u>established</u> the encomienda (en koh mee EN dah) system. **Encomienda** was a legal system to control Native Americans in the Spanish colonies. Under encomienda, Spanish officials could tax Native Americans or force them to work. In return, Spaniards were required to teach them Christianity. But encomienda soon turned into a system of slavery without religious teaching. As a Spanish priest wrote,

establish, v., to set up

> 66 [Spaniards] had as little concern for their souls as for their bodies, all the millions that have perished having gone to their deaths with no knowledge of God. 99
> —Bartolome de las Casas, 1542

Spaniards used violence to force Native Americans to work (top). Enslaved Africans later replaced Native Americans as laborers (bottom). ▼

Culture Close-up

import, *v.,* to ship in from another country

Spanish landowners created **haciendas,** or huge farms and ranches. Many native people had died from disease or abuse, so the Spanish <u>imported</u> enslaved Africans to work the land.

Slavery in the Caribbean By the 1600s, other European countries had formed Caribbean colonies. They grew cash crops, especially sugar cane, which required huge amounts of land and labor. As did the Spanish in Central America, these sugar planters imported enslaved Africans to do the work. Sugar, slaves, rum, tobacco, and molasses formed a triangular system of trade connecting the Caribbean, Europe, and Africa. This system of trade made the Europeans who ruled the colonies very wealthy.

Reading Check What was the encomienda system in the Spanish colonies?

myWorld Activity
Corners of History

Ending Foreign Control

For more than 200 years, European countries controlled the region. Unrest exploded in the 1800s.

Rebellion in Haiti In the late 1700s, the people of Saint-Domingue revolted against their French rulers. An enslaved man named Toussaint L'Ouverture (too SAN loo vehr TOOR) led the rebellion. In 1804, after years of fighting, the people declared their **independence,** or the right to rule themselves. They renamed the country Haiti.

Spanish Rule Ends In 1821, the Kingdom of Guatemala declared independence from Spain. Two years later, most of Central America formed the United Provinces of Central America. For years, the United Provinces struggled over political differences. By 1840, this state had broken into independent republics.

Before Independence

- Colonies are ruled by monarchies.
- Rulers live far away in Europe but tax people in the colonies.
- Colonial leaders called viceroys control large areas of land.
- Most native people and some enslaved Africans work the land that belongs to the viceroys.
- Almost everything grown or made in the colonies is exported to European markets.

Toussaint L'Ouverture was an inspiration to other colonists who wanted to break free from Europe. ▶

After Independence

- Independent constitutional republics are established.
- Former viceroys or landowners often become presidents of the new countries.
- Many poor landless people work for relatively few landowners.
- Republics are dependent on foreign markets to sell their goods.
- Exported goods benefit the landowners, making them richer.
- Landowners support dictators who keep matters the same.

Depending on Outsiders After independence, many countries looked to foreign investors to help build their economies. Over time, the region's economies came to depend on other countries, especially the United States.

In the Caribbean, U.S. investors rebuilt and took control of industries such as sugar, coffee, and bananas. They also took over land and built enormous plantations. The United States government gained control of land in Panama and built the Panama Canal, an important trade link between the Atlantic and Pacific Oceans.

Dictatorship and Democracy While American economic influence grew, democracy did not. Throughout the 1900s, **dictatorships,** or governments controlled by a single leader, became common. Dictators like Fulgencio Batista of Cuba limited political freedom. However, Batista was able to develop Cuba's economy. As the Cuban economy grew, U.S. investors profited. Then Fidel Castro led a communist revolution in Cuba, taking power in 1959. When Castro took U.S.-owned property, the United States ended relations with Cuba.

By the late 1900s, people in the region had grown tired of being controlled by dictators and other countries. Conflict broke out in many places. In Guatemala, a deadly civil war lasted nearly forty years. In Nicaragua in the 1970s, rebels took power from a dictatorship; in turn, a new dictatorship took power from the rebels. By the 1980s and 1990s, the last Caribbean colonies had finally gained their independence. Now they needed to make democracy work.

Reading Check What happened when Castro took power from Batista in Cuba?

Fidel Castro led a communist revolution to take power in Cuba. ▶

Section 2 Assessment

Essential Question

Is it better to be independent or interdependent?

Key Terms

1. How did the encomienda system make Spain wealthy?

2. What makes a government a dictatorship?

Key Ideas

3. How did the Maya, the Carib, and the Arawak feed themselves?

4. Why did the Spanish begin to import enslaved Africans?

5. Why did newly independent nations look to foreign investors?

Think Critically

6. **Draw Conclusions** What do you think motivated Americans to invest in Central America and the Caribbean?

7. **Synthesize** What aspects of colonialism might have helped lead to dictatorships?

8. Were the Spanish colonists independent or interdependent? Go to your Student Journal to record your answer.

The Maya

IN Indiana

6.1.1 Summarize the rise, decline, and cultural achievements of ancient civilizations in Europe and Mesoamerica.

6.1.21 Differentiate between fact and interpretation in historical accounts and explain historical passages.

Maya civilization reached its height around A.D. 250. Religion was an important element of Maya civilization. Maya city-states included great pyramid-shaped temples where the Maya worshiped their gods. The Temple of the Inscriptions, in what is now Palenque, Mexico, was built as the tomb of a Maya ruler. The *Popol Vuh* is a written description of the Maya religion and gods. This book was written in the 1500s, after the Spanish conquered the region. It explains the Maya belief that the gods made people from corn, the most important Maya crop.

▲ A Maya sculpture

Examine the photograph on the right. Then answer the questions below.

A **Identify Details** Describe the appearance of this temple.

B **Analyze Primary Sources** Why would this temple have been hard to build?

C **Infer** What does this temple suggest about the power of Maya rulers?

Temple of the Inscriptions, Palenque ▶

A Maya Temple

Read the text on the right. Stop at each circled letter. Then answer the question with the same letter on the left.

D **Identify Main Ideas and Details** According to this account, who discovered corn?

E **Infer** Who are the gods in this passage? How do you know?

F **Draw Conclusions** Why might the Maya have believed that the first people were made from corn?

gruel, *n.,* thin, watery cereal

gourd, *n.,* dried, hollow shell of a squash

Popol Vuh

66 We will now return to the story of man's creation. . . . The corn used to create the first men was found in the place called Paxil and K'ayala'. Yak the wildcat, Utiw the coyote, K'el the parrot and Joj the crow, were the creatures who **D** discovered this food. . . .

Then our Makers Tepew and **E** Q'uk'umatz began discussing the creation of our first mother and father. Their flesh was made of white and yellow corn. . . . Then Grandmother Ixmukane ground the white and yellow ears of corn to make enough gruel to fill nine gourds to provide strength, muscle and power to the four new men.

The names of the first four men were, in order, B'alam Ki'tze', B'alam Aq'ab', Majukutaj **F** and Iq' B'alam. Only a miracle could have made the first fathers out of . . . corn. 99

—*Popol Vuh: A Sacred Book of the Maya,* retold by Victor Montejo, translated by David Unger

A Maya codex, or folding book ▼

Analyze the Documents

1. **Draw Conclusions** How might the powers of rulers and the importance of religion have been linked in Maya life?
2. **Writing Task** How do Maya city-states, religion, and artifacts show evidence of an advanced civilization? Write a paragraph explaining your ideas.

257

Central America and the Caribbean Today

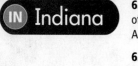

IN Indiana

6.2.1 Compare and contrast forms of governments in Europe and the Americas throughout history.

6.2.5 Discuss the impact of major forms of government in Europe and the Americas on civil and human rights.

6.2.7 Define and compare citizenship and the citizen's role throughout history in Europe and the Americas.

6.3.10 Explain the ways cultural diffusion, invention, and innovation change culture.

6.4.7 Identify economic connections between the community and the countries of Europe or the Americas and identify job skills needed to be successful in the workplace.

Key Terms • carnival • Santeria • diaspora • microcredit • ecotourism

→ **Visual Glossary**

Reading Skill: Summarize Take notes using the graphic organizer in your journal.

▼ A Maya weaver from Guatemala

A history of colonialism and slavery influences many aspects of life in Central America and the Caribbean. Although the countries in the region share a cultural heritage, their societies blend a variety of traditions and influences. Today, these nations reflect the complexity of culture and life in the region.

Woven Cultures

The region's West African, Native American, French, Danish, British, and Spanish cultures weave together to form a diverse society. Most people in the Caribbean are of African descent and many people in the region speak Spanish, but there is great diversity in religion, ethnicity, language, and other aspects of culture.

Religion in the Caribbean Today, 90 percent of the people in the Caribbean are Roman Catholic. Still, the Caribbean's cultural celebrations, such as Carnival, mix African, Native American, and European religious traditions. **Carnival** is a religious festival in late winter primarily observed by Roman Catholics. In the Caribbean, Carnival includes large parades with bright costumes, music, and dancing that show the influence of West African culture. Most Caribbean countries celebrate Carnival.

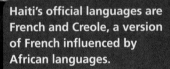

Closer Look

One Region, Many Faces

Most people in Central America and the Caribbean have been influenced by a number of different cultures. The religions people practice, the art they make, and the languages they speak show how the region's people have created new cultures from many traditions.

THINK CRITICALLY **How do different cultures affect the region?**

▲ Caribbean music is known for its percussion, a tradition strongly influenced by West African music.

Haiti's official languages are French and Creole, a version of French influenced by African languages.

Native American languages are common in Guatemala. This boy speaks the Mayan language Achi.

This girl from Puerto Rico speaks Spanish and English, but she has Native American ancestors.

Like most other people from the Dominican Republic, Luis speaks Spanish.

→ Language Lesson

In Cuba, a popular religion called **Santeria** combines Catholic and West African beliefs. For example, the Santeria god Changó is a spirit from an ancient African religion. In Haiti, voodoo also includes elements of Catholic and West African beliefs. In Jamaica, Rastafarianism combines Christianity with the belief that the former emperor of Ethiopia descended from Israel's King Solomon and was divine. Trinidad has a growing number of believers in Hinduism and Islam. Recently, some Central American and Caribbean people have joined Protestant churches.

Indigenous Traditions Mestizos, or people of Spanish and indigenous background, are the largest ethnic group in Central America. In Guatemala, however, the Maya are the largest ethnic group. Most Guatemalans speak a form of Maya as their first language, although they learn Spanish in school. Many Mayas mix traditional religious rituals with European ones, such as combining the names of Catholic saints with stories about Maya gods. Most Maya women wear traditional, multicolored woven fabrics.

my worldgeography.com Language Lesson

Going Global Many people in Central America and the Caribbean face widespread poverty. As a result, some people have migrated to North America or Europe in search of work. This spread of people from one place to many others is called a **diaspora**. After finding jobs, many immigrants send money, or remittances, to support their families.

Wherever people go, they bring their food, music, and beliefs. This leads to cultural diffusion, or the spread of cultural traits. Regional foods such as burritos and Cuban sandwiches are now popular in North America, Europe, and parts of Asia. Caribbean music has also traveled far from its roots. Salsa from Puerto Rico, merengue from the Dominican Republic, and reggae from Jamaica can be heard in many parts of the world.

Reading Check In what ways is Caribbean culture a blend of other cultures?

Government and Change

Central American and Caribbean people live in a region of change. People migrate to other countries and then return. Hurricanes can destroy crops and homes. Even governments can change quickly.

Democracy in the Region Most governments in Central America are presidential democracies in which a president is the head of government. In the Caribbean, many countries are democracies with parliamentary systems. In a parliamentary system, a prime minister is chosen from the parliament, or the legislative body of government. Most countries in the region select leaders in democratic elections. Often, citizens are legally required to vote.

Costa Rica has the region's most stable democracy. Costa Ricans have been electing their rulers since 1899. However, most of the region's democracies are less stable. Governments in poorer countries may change if voters are unhappy that leaders have failed to improve living conditions.

In fact, the lack of social services such as healthcare and education can lead to widespread anger and violence. Military takeovers and political violence are common. In Guatemala, civil war made

Central America and Caribbean Literacy and Life Expectancy

Country	Literacy	Life Expectancy
Costa Rica	95%	77 years
Dominican Republic	87%	73 years
Guatemala	69%	70 years
Haiti	53%	61 years

SOURCE: *CIA World Factbook*

Haiti is one of the poorest nations in the world. Anger over poverty has led to violence.

Chart Skills

The Dominican Republic and Haiti share the same island. Why might there be such a great difference in their literacy and life expectancy rates?

Data Discovery

democracy almost impossible until a 1996 peace agreement. In Haiti, 20,000 U.S. troops occupied the country to end a violent uprising in 1994. Since 2004, thousands of United Nations troops have helped keep peace in Haiti.

Dictatorship in Cuba Although most countries have removed their dictators, Cuba has not. Fidel Castro was the dictator of Cuba from 1959 to 2008, when he designated his brother Raúl to replace him. Cuba is a socialist republic with a command economy. The Communist Party is the only official political party.

Cubans cannot choose their leader, but they do vote for representatives to the National Assembly. These elections are unfair, however, since most races have only a single candidate. While Cuba <u>restricts</u> political and economic free-dom, the government offers some social services that neighboring countries lack. For example, college and healthcare are practically free for Cubans.

Calls for Change Movements to improve the lives of people in the Caribbean and Central America continue. Throughout the region, there is a call to improve education and healthcare. In some places, voters have elected leaders who believe that government must help the poor and have more control over the economy. In other countries, such as the Dominican Republic, voters have turned to conservative leaders with the hope that they will be tough on crime and encourage foreign investments.

Reading Check What makes it difficult to achieve a stable democracy?

Freeing Up the Economy

One of the region's major economic goals is to increase capital investment, or investment in factories and technology. Capital investment can lead to economic growth. Government leaders often encourage foreign companies to build factories and other facilities in their countries. Countries also seek to improve human capital through education and training for workers.

Free-Trade Agreements One way the region's countries work to improve their economies is through free-trade agreements. Free trade is a system in which goods and services are traded between countries without government restrictions such as tariffs. Members of a free-trade association work to increase the amount of goods traded and to reduce taxes on products made in one member country and sold in another.

restrict, *v.,* to limit or prevent

Costa Rica has a stable government, a stable economy, and a relatively high standard of living.

my worldgeography.com Data Discovery

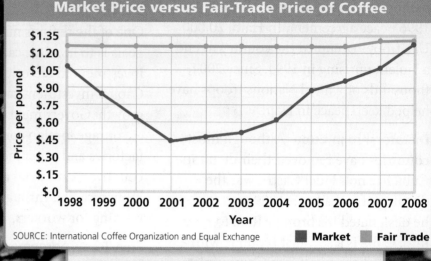

Market Price versus Fair-Trade Price of Coffee

SOURCE: International Coffee Organization and Equal Exchange

■ **Market**　■ **Fair Trade**

Chart Skills

Fair trade can help guarantee stable prices and wages, while market prices can go up and down quickly. How does the market price for coffee compare to the fair-trade price?

→ **Data Discovery**

myWorldActivity
Is Free Fair?

One example of a free-trade association is the Caribbean Community (Caricom). Another is the Central America-Dominican Republic-United States Free Trade Association (CAFTA-DR), which also includes the United States.

Benefits and Drawbacks There are benefits and drawbacks to international free-trade agreements. Low taxes can encourage foreign businesses to build factories, creating jobs. CAFTA-DR has helped increase manufacturing in the region. However, some people worry that free trade helps wealthy countries more than poor countries. For these people, fair trade offers more benefits. Supporters of fair trade believe in paying workers fair wages and protecting the environment. They are often willing to pay more for goods that have been produced fairly.

Reforming Farms Free trade also affects farming. Farmers produce large amounts of food for free markets, and they often use a great deal of pesticides and fertilizer. This can harm the environment. In addition, most farmers do not own the crops they raise and thus cannot profit from international trade.

A few countries, such as Guatemala, have passed land-reform laws. These laws take some land from powerful landowners and divide it among poor farmers. Poor farmers can sometimes get small loans, called **microcredit,** to start their own farms. Some farmers form cooperatives, or groups of people who share the profits of their business. Many coffee and cacao growers now belong to cooperatives.

Reading Check How are people trying to improve the region's economy?

Ecotourism

Large luxury tourist resorts can cause environmental problems by using large amounts of resources, such as clean water. Still, tourism is an important part of the region's economy. One growing type of tourism is **ecotourism,** or tourism that focuses on the environment and seeks to minimize environmental impact. Ecotourism often involves exploring nature on foot or horseback. Tourists may sleep in simple huts or cabins. They may eat local food and require fewer imported goods to meet their needs.

Some people worry that ecotourism will change native cultures or harm natural habitats. But the Kuna Yala Reserve in Panama provides a successful example of ecotourism. In this case, the indigenous people themselves plan and manage an ecotourism program.

66 [The Kuna Yala recognize] the importance of their natural surroundings and the need to protect their culture … [They know] how to manage the growth of tourism. 99

—a Costa Rican travel agent

luxury, *n.,* pleasure or comfort

Reading Check What are the benefits of ecotourism?

Story 📷 **Photo**

Luis's job as a tour guide depends on ecotourism.

Section 3 Assessment

Key Terms

1. What are some effects of the Caribbean diaspora?

2. How has ecotourism affected Central America and the Caribbean?

Key Ideas

3. Describe the cultures in Central America and the Caribbean.

4. What causes democratic governments in the region to change frequently?

5. How might land reform, microcredit, and cooperatives affect the economy?

Think Critically

6. **Compare and Contrast** How are the governments of Cuba and Costa Rica different?

7. **Compare Viewpoints** How might a small farmer's and an American factory owner's viewpoints on CAFTA-DR differ?

Essential Question

Is it better to be independent or interdependent?

8. In what ways are the economies of Central America and the Caribbean independent and interdependent? Go to your Student Journal to record your answer.

Cuba: Revolution to Today

IN Indiana

6.1.16 Identify individuals, beliefs and events that represent various political ideologies during the 19th and 20th centuries and explain their significance.

6.1.23 Identify issues related to an event in Europe or the Americas and give arguments for and against that issue.

6.2.5 Discuss the impact of major forms of government in Europe and the Americas on civil and human rights.

6.4.4 Describe how different economic systems in Europe and the Americas answer the basic economic questions.

6.4.5 Compare the standard of living of various countries of Europe and the Americas today using GDP as an indicator.

Key Terms • ally • literacy • rationing • embargo

Cuba has been a communist country for more than 50 years. Communism has had mixed results. Although Cubans have good access to healthcare and education, the government limits citizens' rights. The government also keeps strict control of the economy. Cubans cannot freely elect their leaders or criticize the government. Today, however, Cuba is slowly changing as the government allows more economic freedom. Will political freedom follow?

Historical Overview

Spain ruled Cuba for nearly 400 years. Then, in 1898, the United States defeated Spain in the Spanish–American War and took control of Cuba. In 1902 Cuba gained its independence.

The United States kept a strong influence in Cuba after independence. The U.S. government supervised Cuba's economy and its foreign relations. American investors and businesses developed sugar plantations and other industries. By the 1950s, Cuba was one of the

Fidel Castro, below right, took control of Cuba in 1959. ▼

2007
Año 49 de la
REVOLUCIÓN

Levels of Freedom, 2008

KEY
Freedom, 2008
- Free
- Freedom limited
- Not free

Map Skills

This map shows levels of political rights and civil liberties such as religious freedom. How does freedom vary around the world?

wealthiest countries in Central America. But a small group of people—including many Americans—controlled much of the wealth. Most Cubans were very poor.

In 1952 Fulgencio [fool HEN see oh] Batista took power as a dictator. Under his rule, gambling and criminal activities flourished. Batista became increasingly unpopular with the Cuban people.

In 1959 Batista was overthrown in a revolution led by Fidel Castro. Castro said that he wanted to reform Cuba and improve conditions for the Cuban people. His ideas inspired many others in Central America. Before long, however, Castro formed a communist dictatorship that limited Cubans' political liberties. Many people fled Cuba for the United States. Cuba became an ally of the Soviet Union. An **ally** is a political or military partner.

Reading Check What kind of government did Fidel Castro form?

Communism in Cuba

Castro created a communist society in Cuba. Under communism, there are no social classes and no private property. Government owns all property and makes all economic decisions.

The Cuban government took control of farms and businesses. The government made all decisions about what products to produce, what prices to charge, and what wages to pay workers.

Castro wanted all Cubans to enjoy a decent standard of living. He wanted to erase the gap between wealthy and poor people. The government set up a system that provided social benefits to all people. All Cubans got free healthcare and free education. As a result, health conditions and literacy improved. **Literacy** is the ability to read and write.

Reading Check How did the Cuban government influence the economy?

Comparing Cuba and the United States

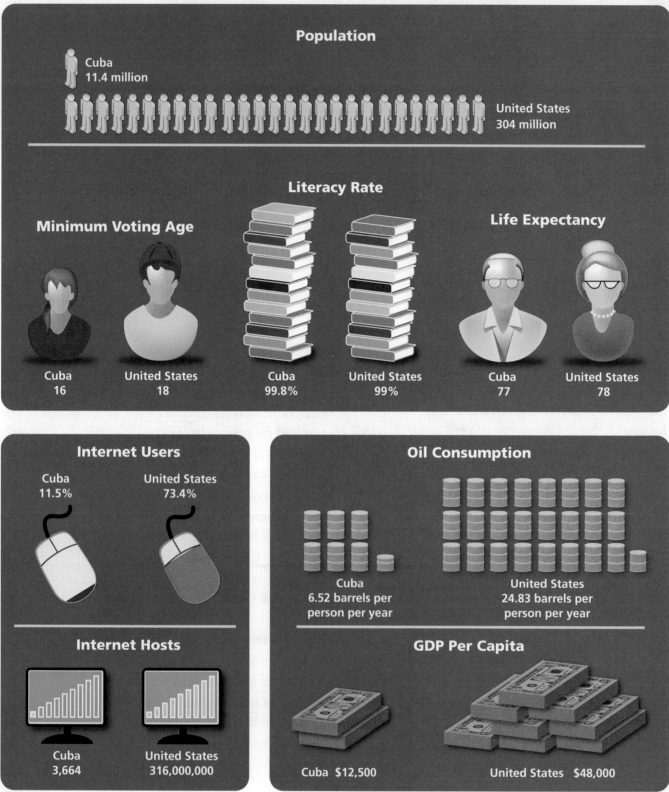

Population

Cuba
11.4 million

United States
304 million

Minimum Voting Age

Cuba
16

United States
18

Literacy Rate

Cuba
99.8%

United States
99%

Life Expectancy

Cuba
77

United States
78

Internet Users

Cuba
11.5%

United States
73.4%

Internet Hosts

Cuba
3,664

United States
316,000,000

Oil Consumption

Cuba
6.52 barrels per
person per year

United States
24.83 barrels per
person per year

GDP Per Capita

Cuba $12,500

United States $48,000

SOURCE: *CIA World Factbook*

Dream versus Reality

In reality, Castro's communist ideal did not work. Cuba's economy did poorly. The country did not produce enough goods to supply its people. As a result, the government had to set up a rationing system. **Rationing** is the controlled distribution of scarce resources and goods, such as food.

Cuba relied on economic aid from other communist countries, especially the Soviet Union. But those countries had problems too. In 1991 the Soviet Union fell apart. After that, Cuba had even more trouble providing for its people.

As conditions got worse, more Cubans became discontented. Some tried to leave the island. Others began to speak out against the government. But the government cracked down, putting its critics in prison. Many countries criticized Cuba for its lack of rights and freedom.

Reading Check Why did Cuba's economy suffer?

Cuba's Future

In 2008 Fidel Castro's brother, Raúl, became president. Raúl Castro introduced a number of small economic and political reforms. For example, the government removed restrictions against the use of cellphones. It also sought to improve food production by allowing farmers to use some state-owned land.

Better relations with the United States might lead Cuba to become more democratic. For years, the United States has enforced an embargo against Cuba. An **embargo** is the prohibition of trade with a certain country. But in 2009, U.S. President Barack Obama announced that the U.S. government would loosen restrictions on American travel to Cuba. He also signaled U.S. willingness to trade with Cuba if Cuba moves toward democracy and the protection of human rights.

Reading Check What big change occurred in Cuba in 2008?

Because of the U.S. embargo on trade with Cuba, many cars in Cuba date from the 1950s. ▼

Assessment

1. How did Cuba become a communist country?

2. What impact has communism had on Cuba?

3. How does the Cuban government restrict Cubans' actions?

4. How did Cuba change in 2008?

5. Compare and contrast life in Cuba and the United States.

Chapter Assessment

Key Terms and Ideas

1. **Summarize** What are the different natural disasters that commonly affect Central America and the Caribbean?

2. **Explain** What are the geographic factors of Central America and the Caribbean that make the region well suited for **tourism**?

3. **Describe** Describe how the **Maya** civilization rose and what it accomplished.

4. **Cause and Effect** Why did the Spanish set up the **encomienda** system and what were the results of that system?

5. **Compare and Contrast** How was life in Central America and the Caribbean similar before and after **independence**?

6. **Recall** What are the main roots of Caribbean and Central American culture?

7. **Define** What does DR-CAFTA stand for and what does it allow?

Think Critically

8. **Draw Inferences** What does land ownership have to do with poverty in Central America and the Caribbean today?

9. **Sequence** Put the following terms in chronological order and explain your reasons: dictatorships, colonization, slavery, encomienda, independence.

10. **Draw Conclusions** Why might the leader of a Central American or Caribbean country find it hard to have a stable government?

11. **Core Concepts: Human-Environment Interaction** What are the benefits and drawbacks of large-scale agriculture in Central American and Caribbean countries?

Places to Know

For each place, write the letter from the map that shows its location.

12. **Caribbean Sea**
13. **Lake Atitlán**
14. **Cuba**
15. **Costa Rica**
16. **Lake Nicaragua**
17. **Dominican Republic**
18. **Estimate** Using the scale, estimate the distance between Costa Rica and the Dominican Republic.

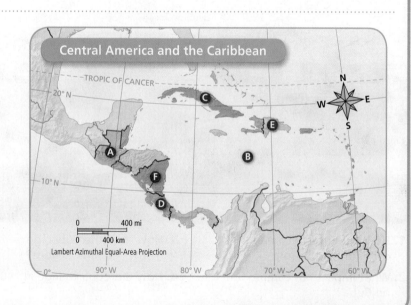

Central America and the Caribbean

Essential Question

Chapter Transfer Activity

Venturing in Nicaragua Follow your teacher's instructions to find out more about the different environments, businesses, natural hazards, and opportunities in Nicaragua. Then prepare a plan for a particular kind of tourism business that you will use to seek government or private investment funds.

21st Century Learning

Develop Cultural Awareness

Choose two cultures different from your own that are a part of your community. Then use the Internet or other sources to learn more about these cultures. Write a reflection about how what you learned might change the way you relate to someone of that culture. You might consider researching the following cultural aspects:
- food
- religious practices
- clothing
- gender roles

Document-Based Questions

Success Tracker™
Online at myworldgeography.com

Use your knowledge of Central America and the Caribbean and Documents A and B to answer Questions 1–3.

Document A

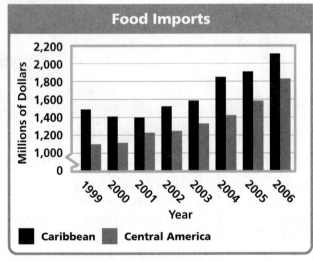

Food Imports

Millions of Dollars

Year: 1999, 2000, 2001, 2002, 2003, 2004, 2005, 2006

■ Caribbean   ■ Central America

SOURCE: U.S. Department of Agriculture Economic Research Service and U.S. Trade Internet System

Document B

" You will be engaged in subsistence agriculture in which you will be doing your own small farming … We need to ensure that our people can feel secured in obtaining not only high quality nutritious food, but it should also be at affordable prices as well … [Right now] we are importing almost everything that we eat."

—St. Kitts and Nevis Prime Minister Denzil L. Douglas, 2008

1. Which of the following best explains the change shown in Document A?

   A The Caribbean is suffering from a drought.

   B Factory workers are taking jobs on farms.

   C Free-trade laws have made it easier for food to be imported.

   D Foreign food is of better quality than Caribbean or Central American food.

2. What slogan would best fit Prime Minister Douglas' new plan for food production?

   A Food Through Trade

   B Back to the Land

   C Worldwide Vegetables

   D Industry Rules

3. **Writing Task** Write a radio announcement persuading people in St. Kitts and Nevis to grow their own vegetables.

Young and Unemployed in Middle America

Your Mission Study the graphs showing education, literacy, and foreign investment in Belize, Guatemala, and Mexico. Use what you learn to propose a jobs program that helps young people find work in those countries.

In Middle America, the job market is generally weak. Finding a job is even more difficult for young people in this region. They want to work, but they may lack training or transportation. The job market also suffers when business development is slow. Finding a solution to high unemployment rates requires learning more about the factors and circumstances that have led to this situation.

Being young and unemployed in Middle America is part of the problem, but your ideas can be part of the solution.

STEP 1

Identify the Problem.

Employment is desirable not simply because it generates income. Having a job means working toward a goal, learning new skills or information, and improving one's quality of life. Belize, Guatemala, and Mexico are very different nations. They also share certain characteristics. Before you can propose an employment solution, you have to learn more about why people there are unemployed.

STEP 2

Analyze the Data.

As you analyze the graphs, recall what you read in this unit about the geography, history, and current situation in Middle America. How might factors such as education affect unemployment? Do additional research to fill in the gaps in your analysis. You might also find that newspaper articles and photographs provide helpful information about job markets in faraway countries.

STEP 3

Propose a Solution.

Working in groups, prepare a presentation based on one of the graphs provided on the next page. Explain the data in the graph and show how it relates to unemployment in all three subject nations. Integrate what you have learned into your group's final presentation on the proposed government jobs program. Your solution should be flexible enough to work in each nation, given its unique circumstances.

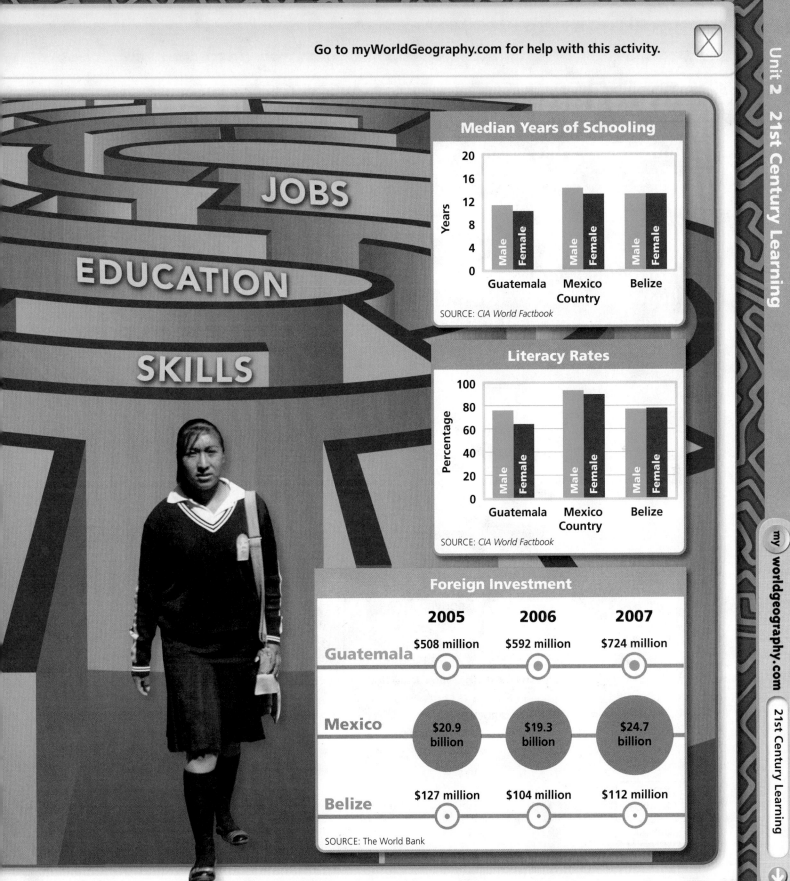

JOBS

EDUCATION

SKILLS

Median Years of Schooling

Years

20
16
12
8
4
0

Male Female | Male Female | Male Female
Guatemala | Mexico | Belize

Country

SOURCE: *CIA World Factbook*

Literacy Rates

Percentage

100
80
60
40
20
0

Male Female | Male Female | Male Female
Guatemala | Mexico | Belize

Country

SOURCE: *CIA World Factbook*

Foreign Investment

	2005	2006	2007
Guatemala	$508 million	$592 million	$724 million
Mexico	$20.9 billion	$19.3 billion	$24.7 billion
Belize	$127 million	$104 million	$112 million

SOURCE: The World Bank

South America

South America has an amazing variety of climates and landforms, including huge mountains, deserts, and rain forests. Around 371 million people live in South America. The largest country in South America is Brazil. Brazil includes most of the Amazon rain forest, a huge forest that stretches from the Andes Mountains in the west to the Atlantic Ocean in the east.

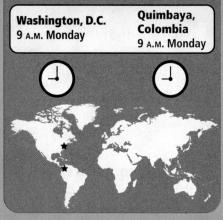

What time is it there?

Washington, D.C.	Quimbaya, Colombia
9 A.M. Monday	9 A.M. Monday

30° N

Caribbean Sea

TROPIC OF CANCER

GALÁPAGOS ISLANDS (Ecuador)

★ Caracas

Bogotá ★

VENEZUELA

ECUADOR

COLOMBIA

Georgetown ★

Quito ★

GUYANA

Paramaribo ★

EQUATOR

0°

Cayenne ★ **FRENCH GUIANA** (France)

SURINAME

PERU

Lima ★

PACIFIC OCEAN

La Paz ★

BRAZIL

BOLIVIA

★ Sucre

TROPIC OF CAPRICORN

★ Brasília

PARAGUAY

CHILE

★ Asunción

Santiago ★ **ARGENTINA**

30° S

URUGUAY

ATLANTIC OCEAN

Buenos Aires ★

★ Montevideo

KEY

— National border

★ Capital city

Orthographic Projection

90° W   60° W   30° W   0°

my **worldgeography.com**

Plan your trip online by doing a Data Discovery Activity and watching the myStory Videos of the region's teens.

my **Story**

Daniella

Age: 15

Home: Armenia, Colombia

Chapter 5

my **Story**

Omar

Age: 14

Home: Potosí, Bolivia

Chapter 6

my **Story**

Vinicius

Age: 16

Home: Rio de Janeiro, Brazil

Chapter 7

Mangroves on the coast of Brazil

The Andes are the longest range of mountains on Earth.

PACIFIC OCEAN

Mt. Aconcagua
22,834 ft (6,959 m)

Atacama Desert

A n d e s   M o u n t a i n s

Amazon Basin

Altiplano

Pampas

Rio de la Plata

The vast plains of the Pampas stretch from the Atlantic coast to the foothills of the Andes.

ATLANTIC OCEAN

Caribbean Sea

Orinoco River

Guiana Highlands

Amazon River

The Amazon River drains an area of about 2.7 million square miles.

Brazilian Highlands

Regional Flyover

Welcome aboard the fastest flight around South America ever! Your plane takes off from Bogotá, Colombia, high in the Andes. Traveling clockwise around the continent, you soon see the Brazilian rain forest—a vast green blanket veined with dark rivers flowing toward one huge river, the Amazon. This is the mighty Amazon basin, the rain forest lowlands that make up much of the continent.

As you fly down the east coast, you glimpse a river called the Rio de la Plata, flowing through the vast grasslands of the Pampas in Argentina.

When you reach the cold southern tip of the continent, your plane turns northward, following the Andes. You first see the Atacama Desert in Chile, wedged between the Andes and the Pacific Ocean, and then the Altiplano, a huge plain of level ground high up in the Bolivian Andes. After you cross the Equator in Ecuador, Colombia's parallel mountain ranges suddenly appear. As your plane lands in Bogotá, you count the number of countries you have seen—12!

In-Flight Movie

Take flight over South America and explore the region from the air.

my worldgeography.com

In-Flight Movie

275

Regional Overview
Human Geography

Origins of Diversity

South America's ethnic diversity grew from a series of migrations.

2 In the early 1500s, Europeans arrived to claim the land.

1 The earliest migration probably occurred before 11,000 B.C., when the ancestors of Native Americans arrived.

VENEZUELA

GUYANA

COLOMBIA

SURINAME

FRENCH GUIANA (France)

ATLANTIC OCEAN

3 Europeans brought enslaved Africans to labor in their colonies.

ECUADOR

EQUATOR 0°

10° N

5 During the 1800s, immigrants arrived from Japan, India, and other Asian countries.

PERU

BRAZIL

In many places, the different groups intermarried.

10° S

BOLIVIA

N
W E
S

PARAGUAY

TROPIC OF CAPRICORN

20° S

PACIFIC OCEAN

URUGUAY

30° S

CHILE

ARGENTINA

4 After the 1870s, immigrants from southern Europe arrived in southern Brazil, Argentina, Uruguay, Chile, and Paraguay.

40° S

0   400 mi
0   400 km
Lambert Azimuthal
Equal-Area Projection

50° S

110° W   100° W   90° W   80° W   70° W   60° W   50° W   40° W   30° W   20° W   10° W

my World IN NUMBERS

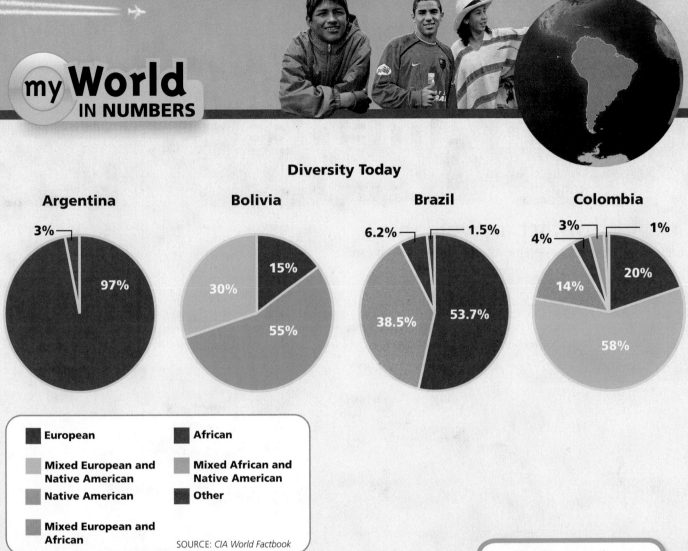

Diversity Today

Argentina
3%
97%

Bolivia
15%
30%
55%

Brazil
6.2%
1.5%
38.5%
53.7%

Colombia
4%
3%
1%
14%
20%
58%

Legend:
- European
- African
- Mixed European and Native American
- Mixed African and Native American
- Native American
- Other
- Mixed European and African

SOURCE: *CIA World Factbook*

Put It Together

1. Why is South America a place of such ethnic diversity?

2. Why do some South American nations have so many people of African descent?

3. Why do you think there are more people descended from Native Americans in Bolivia than in Argentina?

Data Discovery

Find your own data to make a regional data table.

Size Comparison

South America is much bigger than the United States.

my worldgeography.com Data Discovery

277

Chapter 5

Caribbean South America

Is conflict unavoidable?

ATLANTIC OCEAN

Caribbean Sea

Caracas

VENEZUELA

Lago Maracaibo

Orinoco River

Georgetown

Paramaribo

GUYANA

Cayenne

SURINAME

FRENCH GUIANA (France)

Quimbaya

Armenia

Bogotá

PACIFIC OCEAN

COLOMBIA

EQUATOR

10° N

0°

10° S

80° W

70° W

KEY
— National border
⊛ Capital city
○ Other city

0   200 mi
0   200 km
Lambert Azimuthal
Equal-Area Projection

Where in the World Is Caribbean South America?

Washington, D.C., to Armenia: 2,370 miles

Toy model of a popular vehicle in Colombia

my Story

Daniella's Coffee Run

Explore the Essential Question
- at **my worldgeography.com**
- using the **myWorld Chapter Activity**
- with the **Student Journal**

In this section, you'll read about Daniella, a girl who works as a tour guide on El Carriel, her family's coffee farm in Colombia. What does Daniella's story tell you about getting along with others?

Story by Richard Rapp for myWorld Geography Online

The quiet that blankets the lush green mountains is suddenly broken by the sound of an old pickup truck starting up. Daniella, a lively fifteen-year-old from the coffee region of Colombia, rushes to the vehicle. She has just finished her weekend work as a tour guide on her family's farm. Now she and her grandfather are about to drive into town. It is the harvest season and the pair are off to Quimbaya to sell part of this year's coffee crop.

The drive into town is short, and the scenery changes quickly. The soils in this part of Colombia are volcanic, which means the ground is very rich and fertile. Plantations and farms cover the hillsides. Closer to town, the plantations dotting the hills and valleys give way to one-family houses. Soon Daniella and her grandfather have arrived in the small but bustling downtown area, and the Plaza Bolívar—the square that is the central feature of almost every Colombian town and village.

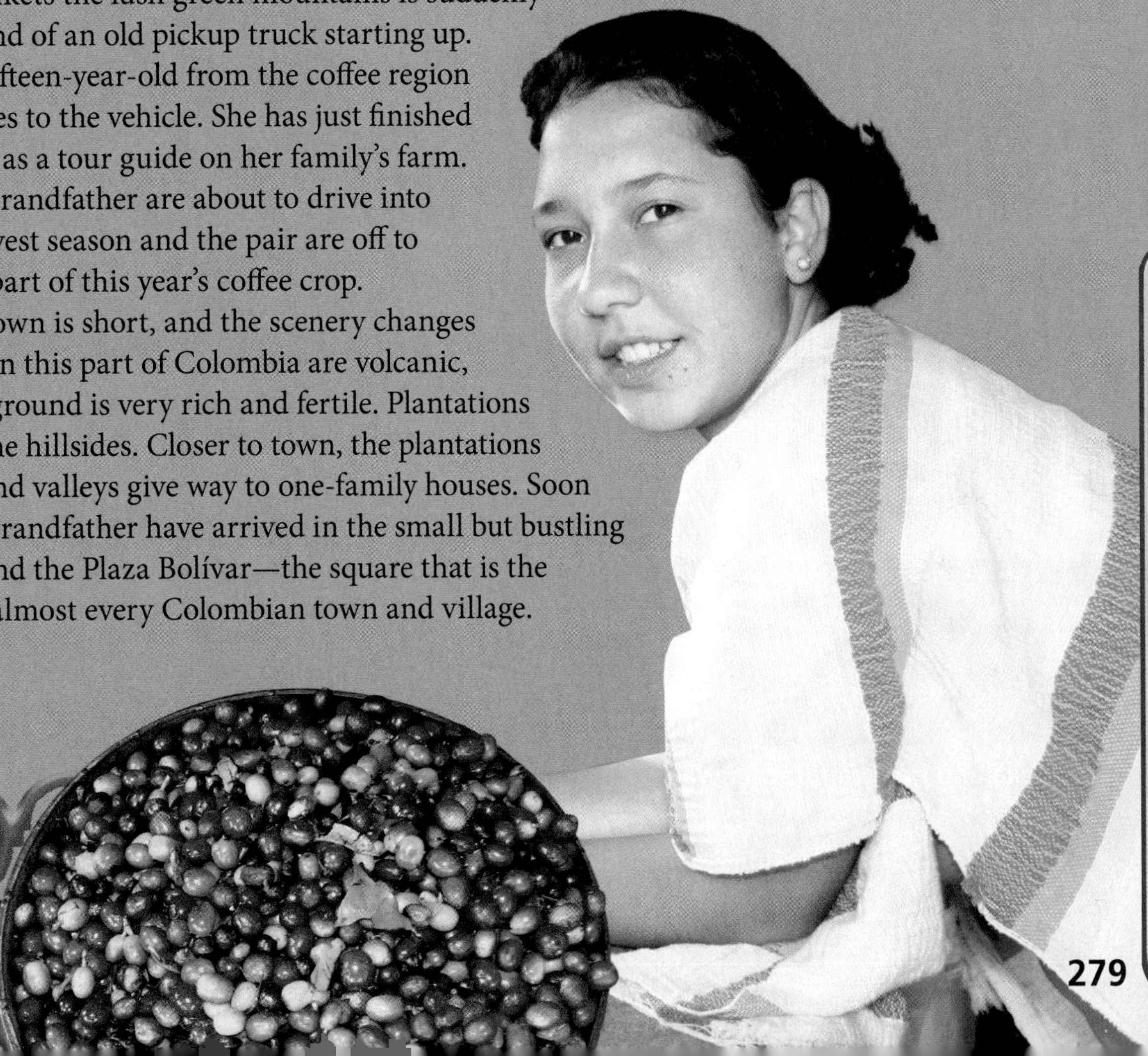

my worldgeography.com — On Assignment

Daniella the tour guide shows visitors a coffee plant.

Tourists arriving at the farm

Daniella and her grandfather wait to be paid for the coffee bean delivery.

While in Quimbaya, Daniella draws our attention to the tourists who have brought change to her region of Colombia.

"The farm has always been for growing coffee, and not only coffee, but for other crops like plantain and beans, too," explains Daniella. "But it isn't as easy as it used to be. . . . Then tourists started to come, and most locals thought that they could help us out economically and that we could enjoy each other as well."

Over the past two years El Carriel has undergone some changes. Handed down from her grandfather to her father, the coffee farm has expanded its activities to include tourism. New cabins have been built for the visitors. Her family is even planning to build a canopy line that will carry visitors through the treetops for a bird's-eye view of the farm and its surroundings.

During the week, Daniella lives in Armenia, where she goes to school. On weekends she travels from her home to work on the farm (near Quimbaya) as a tour guide. Here she educates tourists about the coffee process and

During the visit to Quimbaya, the beans are tested for quality.

Daniella fits in some bowling while in Quimbaya.

daily life on the farm. Daniella enjoys the people who come to learn about her region, even though sometimes these foreigners can be difficult to understand. She explains that "Sometimes it gets complicated due to the language difference. . . . But we always try to learn from one another."

Once in the marketplace, Daniella and her grandfather open their filled coffee sacks and have the beans tested for weight and quality. Then Daniella and her grandfather consult with the merchant over the price. After a little friendly haggling, all agree and set an amount. When paid, Daniella enjoys a quick game of bowling in the Quimbaya bowling alley. Then it's back to El Carriel.

On the farm, the heat of the afternoon gives way to a starry, early evening sky. The family all drink their last cup of coffee for the day as they chat. Daniella talks about her plans for the future. Although she hopes to become a cardiologist one day, she would still like to keep the farm in the family. Clearly enjoying the coffee produced here, she also explains why she enjoys the visitors, "We have conversations where we can learn about each other. . .besides making friends, I learn how they see things and then understand more about myself."

→ myStory Video

Learn more about Daniella by viewing a video about coffee farming in Colombia.

Meet the Journalist

Name Richard Rapp
Favorite Moment Waking up to the mountain view and looking forward to coffee and breakfast!

Chapter Atlas

 **Indiana**

6.3.1 Understand the countries and capitals of Europe and the Americas.

6.3.2 Use latitude and longitude to locate the capital cities of Europe and the Americas and describe the uses of locational technology.

6.3.7 Locate and describe the climate regions of Europe and the Americas and explain how and why they differ.

6.3.8 Identify major biomes of Europe and the Americas and explain how these are influenced by climate.

6.3.9 Identify current patterns of population distribution and growth in Europe and the Americas and evaluate factors that trigger migrations.

Visual Glossary

Key Terms • cordillera • Llanos • ecosystem • terraced farming

 Reading Skill: Label an Outline Map Take notes using the outline map in your journal.

Kukenan Mountain in Venezuela

Venezuelan dancer

Physical Features

Daniella lives in a coffee-growing area of Colombia. Colombia, along with Venezuela, Guyana, Suriname, and French Guiana, all border the Caribbean Sea, along the northern coast of South America.

In Colombia, the Andes Mountains, which extend up the west coast of South America, split into three ranges, known as **cordilleras.** Because the central range is volcanic, its fertile soil is good for coffee plants.

Between the cordilleras, the Cauca and the Magdalena rivers flow north

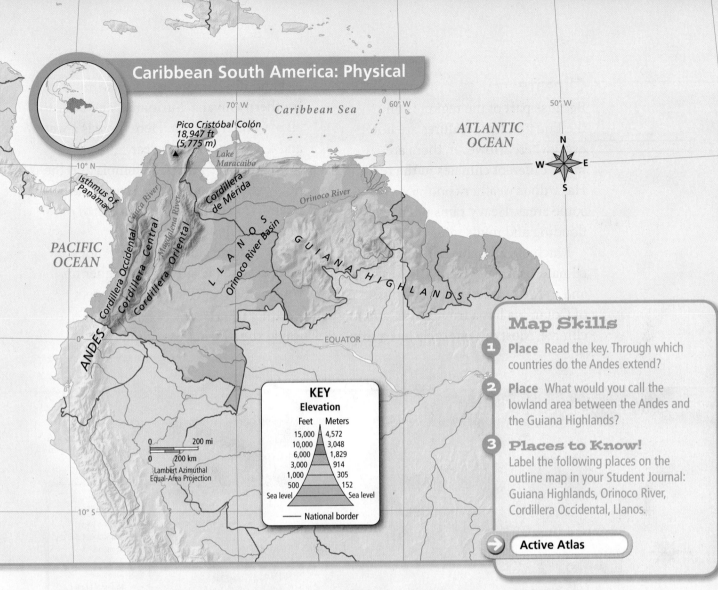

Caribbean South America: Physical

Caribbean Sea

ATLANTIC OCEAN

70° W

60° W

50° W

Pico Cristóbal Colón
18,947 ft
(5,775 m)

10° N

Lake Maracaibo

Isthmus of Panama

Cordillera de Mérida

Cauca River

Magdalena River

Orinoco River

PACIFIC OCEAN

Cordillera Occidental

Cordillera Central

Cordillera Oriental

L L A N O S

Orinoco River basin

G U I A N A   H I G H L A N D S

ANDES

0°

EQUATOR

200 mi

200 km

Lambert Azimuthal
Equal-Area Projection

10° S

KEY
Elevation

Feet	Meters
15,000	4,572
10,000	3,048
6,000	1,829
3,000	914
1,000	305
500	152
Sea level	Sea level

—— National border

Map Skills

1 **Place** Read the key. Through which countries do the Andes extend?

2 **Place** What would you call the lowland area between the Andes and the Guiana Highlands?

3 **Places to Know!** Label the following places on the outline map in your Student Journal: Guiana Highlands, Orinoco River, Cordillera Occidental, Llanos.

→ **Active Atlas**

through deep valleys toward the Caribbean Sea. The Cordillera Oriental, or eastern range, extends north to form the border of Venezuela. Another branch of this range stretches deep into Venezuela. This branch, called the Cordillera de Mérida, runs past Lake Maracaibo and extends along the Caribbean coast. The northern part of the Andes is an active volcanic area. Earthquakes often shake the region.

On the eastern side of the Andes, the mountains plunge down to lowland plains, or **Llanos,** in both Colombia and Venezuela. In the southeastern corner of Colombia, the Amazon rain forest creeps over the border from Brazil. In Venezuela, savannas and tropical rain forests cover the Orinoco River basin. The Orinoco is one of the longest rivers in South America.

In the southeast of Venezuela, the ground rises again to the Guiana Highlands, which extend through Guyana, Suriname, and French Guiana. Along the eastern coastlines you might see mangrove swamps and saltwater grasses.

Reading Check How would you describe the eastern coastline of Caribbean South America?

Climate

Because part of the region is on the Equator, temperatures are hot everywhere. However, there are many different climates in the region. Hazardous weather conditions occur in some areas. Heavy rains often lead to flooding and mudslides.

Much of Colombia has a tropical wet climate, especially along the west coast and in the southeast. The northwest coast of Columbia has a tropical wet and dry climate. Most of Venezuela has a tropical wet and dry climate, which also affects southern Guyana, Suriname, and almost all of French Guiana. Here there is a wet and a dry season each year.

The northern tip of Colombia and the northwestern coast of Venezuela have a semiarid climate. In the far north of Venezuela lies an arid desert.

The climate changes in the Andes according to elevation. The higher up you go, the cooler and wetter it gets.

Reading Check What kinds of climates would you find in this region?

Caribbean South America: Climate

Caribbean Sea

ATLANTIC OCEAN

Caracas

VENEZUELA

Georgetown

GUYANA

Paramaribo

Cayenne

SURINAME   FRENCH GUIANA (France)

Bogotá

PACIFIC OCEAN

COLOMBIA

Tropical wet

KEY
Climate
- Tropical wet
- Tropical wet and dry
- Semiarid
- Arid
- Maritime
- National border

0   200 mi
0   200 km

Lambert Azimuthal Equal-Area Projection

10° N

80° W   60° W   0°   EQUATOR   50° W

Arid

Maritime

Tropical wet and dry

Map Skills

1. **Location** Where would you find the hottest temperatures?

2. **Place** What kind of climate might you find in southern Colombia?

➜ Active Atlas

Ecosystems

If you traveled across Caribbean South America, you would pass through a variety of climate zones. You would also notice a different range of vegetation and animal life in each climate zone. The plants and animals that depend on each other and their environment for survival is called an **ecosystem.**

Along the Pacific coast of Colombia, warm temperatures and heavy rainfall have encouraged the growth of lush rain forests. <u>Unique</u> species of plants and animals thrive in these wet forests. Jaguars, coatimundi, giant anteaters, and tapirs hunt for food in this environment.

The Andes Mountains separate the western rain forests from one of the largest ecosystems in the region—the Llanos. Here grasslands and wetlands support many different kinds of plants and animals. Capybaras, the world's largest rodents, feed on plants along the waterways. In turn, anacondas, giant snakes that can grow to be 26 feet long, prey on the capybaras and other animals.

In the far eastern areas of the region, the Orinoco Delta supports an ecosystem that changes according to the season. During dry conditions, this area includes a mix of forests, wetlands, mangrove swamps, and grasslands. However, during the rainy season, most of the ground is flooded, providing good hunting for crocodiles and otters.

Reading Check What is an ecosystem?

unique, *adj.,* highly unusual, rare

myWorld Activity Caribbean Cruise Stopover

Animals of the Ecosystems

Each of these animals is part of a different ecosystem in Caribbean South America.

A scarlet ibis spreads its wings in the Orinoco delta.

The coatimundi of the Colombian rain forest belong to the raccoon family.

The capybaras of the Llanos may be big . . . but they'd better watch out for anacondas!

285

People and the Landscape

Human settlement and trade have always tied the region to the Caribbean world. Native Americans created a network of trade that linked the Caribbean islands to the mainland. Later, the Spanish created another economic web that connected all the lands of the Caribbean Sea.

Along the coast, Europeans established ports that prospered from the lively shipping trade. Settlers avoided areas farther inland because they feared diseases carried by insects. But the fertile soil and cooler temperatures of the highlands attracted settlement into the middle elevations.

In Colombia, European settlers reached the higher ground in the Andes by traveling through the river valleys between the cordilleras. However, east-west transportation and communication were difficult. The cordilleras isolated communities, so political unification was not easy.

unification, *n.,* the process of uniting

Reading Check What were the main areas of European settlement in the region?

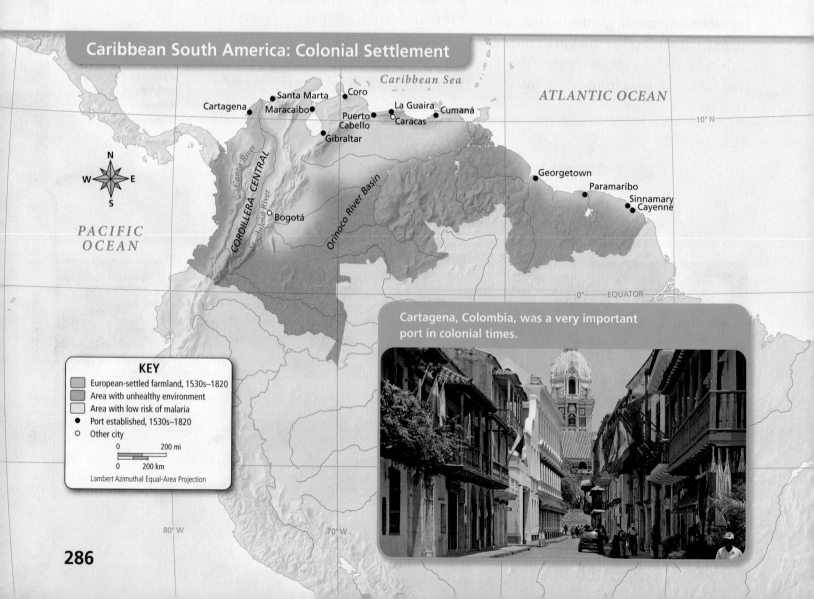

Caribbean South America: Colonial Settlement

Caribbean Sea

ATLANTIC OCEAN

Cartagena • Santa Marta • Coro
Maracaibo • Puerto Cabello • La Guaira • Cumaná
Gibraltar • Caracas

10° N

Cauca River
CORDILLERA CENTRAL
Magdalena River
O Bogotá
Orinoco River Basin

Georgetown
Paramaribo
Sinnamary
Cayenne

PACIFIC OCEAN

0° EQUATOR

KEY
- European-settled farmland, 1530s–1820
- Area with unhealthy environment
- Area with low risk of malaria
- • Port established, 1530s–1820
- ○ Other city

0   200 mi
0   200 km

Lambert Azimuthal Equal-Area Projection

80° W   70° W

Cartagena, Colombia, was a very important port in colonial times.

Where People Live

In Colombia, 80 percent of the population lives in the higher, cooler elevations of the Andes. Colombia's three largest cities—Bogotá, Medellin, and Cali—are all located here. For the most part, Colombia's eastern border is still covered by tropical rain forest. As in colonial days, the country's Caribbean coast has many busy ports.

Caracas, the capital of Venezuela, is by far the largest city in the region. Today Venezuela has one of South America's most urban societies. In fact, nine out of ten Venezuelans live in urban areas. In recent years, the country's huge population of urban poor has become a major political force.

Most people in Guyana, Suriname, and French Guiana live in the lowlands and along the coast. Guyana, Suriname, and French Guiana have small populations, in contrast to the heavily populated countries of Colombia and Venezuela.

Reading Check Where do most people live in the region?

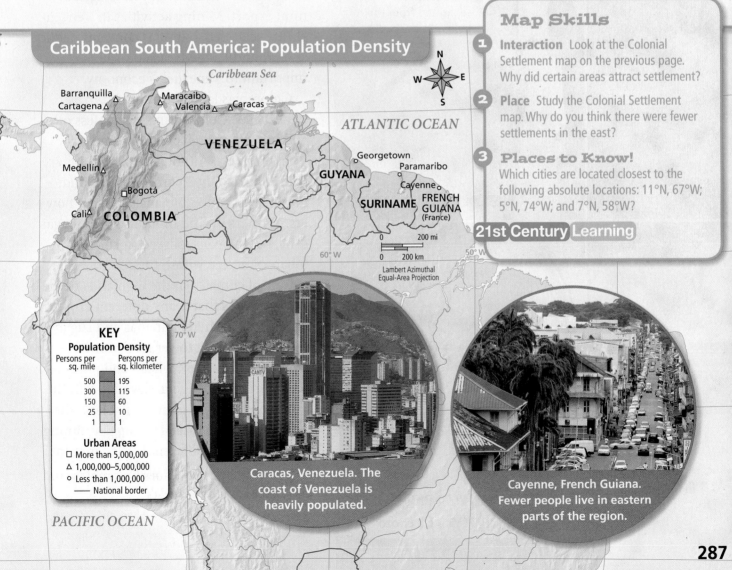

Caribbean South America: Population Density

Caribbean Sea

Barranquilla
Cartagena
Maracaibo
Valencia
Caracas

ATLANTIC OCEAN

VENEZUELA

Medellín

Georgetown
Paramaribo

GUYANA

Cayenne

Bogotá

SURINAME
FRENCH
GUIANA
(France)

Cali

COLOMBIA

0   200 mi
0   200 km

60° W   50° W

Lambert Azimuthal
Equal-Area Projection

70° W

KEY
Population Density

Persons per sq. mile	Persons per sq. kilometer
500	195
300	115
150	60
25	10
1	1

Urban Areas
☐ More than 5,000,000
△ 1,000,000–5,000,000
○ Less than 1,000,000
— National border

PACIFIC OCEAN

Caracas, Venezuela. The coast of Venezuela is heavily populated.

Cayenne, French Guiana. Fewer people live in eastern parts of the region.

Map Skills

1 **Interaction** Look at the Colonial Settlement map on the previous page. Why did certain areas attract settlement?

2 **Place** Study the Colonial Settlement map. Why do you think there were fewer settlements in the east?

3 **Places to Know!** Which cities are located closest to the following absolute locations: 11°N, 67°W; 5°N, 74°W; and 7°N, 58°W?

21st Century Learning

Coffee Production

Daniella's coffee farm is on the slopes of the Central Cordillera in Colombia. Here the combination of rich, volcanic soils and abundant rainfall is good for growing coffee. The coffee bean's journey from plant to cup is a long process.

THINK CRITICALLY Why does some of the best coffee come from Colombia?

1 The fruit of the coffee shrub is picked by hand.

2 The beans are separated from their pulp and washed.

3 The beans are dried in the sun.

4 The beans are roasted.

my Story Photo

How People Use Their Land

Along the coastal plains of Guyana, Suriname, and French Guiana, people grow crops for export. Large commercial farms produce sugar cane, bananas, and rice. They also export molasses, rum, and shrimp. Canals drain the soggy ground and provide fertile agricultural land.

In Venezuela, not much of the land is suitable for farming. The Orinoco River Valley floods during the wet season and is too dry at other times. Only 13 percent of Venezuela's labor force is involved in farming, and there is very little agricultural export. Mining activities in Venezuela are scattered, but oil is concentrated in and around Lake Maracaibo. Oil is very important to Venezuela's economy.

Colombia's land use differs from Venezuela's. Colombians extract less oil and minerals but export more agricultural products. Although Colombians are able to farm only 2 percent of the land, they export coffee, bananas, and cut flowers. Farmers in Colombia also grow sugar cane, cocoa beans, oilseed, corn, and tobacco for sale within the country. The variety of climates in the highlands of the Andes means that many different crops can be grown there. Bananas and sugar cane are grown at lower levels, while crops such as barley, wheat, and potatoes can grow at higher elevations. In the mountains, people gain the flat land they need through **terraced farming**—sculpting the hillside into different levels for crops.

Reading Check How does Colombia's land use differ from Venezuela's?

288

A Diverse Population

The region's population is ethnically and culturally diverse. Unlike many other regions of South America, Native Americans make up only a small percentage of the population. Many of the original people of the region died of European diseases. Over the centuries, the remaining population of Native Americans intermarried with Europeans. Their descendants are known as mestizos. But there was also intermarriage between Africans and Europeans as well as between Africans and Native Americans.

Although there was much intermarriage, many groups have remained ethnically distinct. Throughout the region are communities of Maroons, people descended from Africans who escaped slavery. These Africans fled into the rain forests where they joined with others for mutual protection.

After slavery ended in the 1800s, workers from around the world arrived to labor on the plantations. In Guyana and Suriname, the dominant ethnic group is made up of people descended from workers who migrated from India. There are also significant numbers of Chinese, and Javanese (from the Indonesian island of Java). In French Guiana, most of the population is of mixed European and African descent.

The variety of ethnic groups in the region has led to much cultural borrowing. In French Guiana, local dances reveal the influence of African, Indian, and French traditions. People in the former British colony of Guyana play cricket, while Venezuelans love baseball—thanks to cultural ties with the United States.

The region's location on the northern coast of South America has given it strong cultural connections with the Caribbean world. Today, this Caribbean heritage can be heard in some of the music of the region. It can also be seen in cultural traditions like Carnival. In the next section you will read how the region's unique cultural identity developed.

Reading Check What ethnic groups live in Caribbean South America?

Section 1 Assessment

Key Terms

1. Use the following terms to describe the geography of Caribbean South America: cordillera, Llanos, ecosystem, terraced farming.

Key Ideas

2. What are some features shared by all nations in this region?

3. What are some natural resources in this region?

4. Where does most of the population live in Caribbean South America?

Think Critically

5. **Draw Conclusions** Look at the population map. What factors explain these settlement patterns?

6. **Identify Central Issues** Why might some nations in this region have weaker economies than others?

Essential Question

Is conflict unavoidable?

7. How might geography be a divisive force in the region? Go to your Student Journal to record your answer.

289

History of Caribbean South America

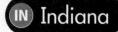 Indiana

6.1.4 Explain the development and organization of various systems in Europe and the Americas.

6.1.20 Analyze cause-and-effect relationships in history.

6.2.5 Discuss the impact of major forms of government in Europe and the Americas on civil and human rights.

Key Terms • El Dorado • caudillo • paramilitary • nationalize • austerity measure

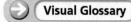 Visual Glossary

Reading Skill: Identify Main Idea and Details Take notes using the graphic organizer in your journal.

This gold figure was made in Colombia before the arrival of the Spanish. ▼

The world they had known was ending. Strange new illnesses were spreading. Tall ships patrolled the coasts. For the people of Caribbean South America, these were the first frightening signs that their lives were about to change.

For centuries, people had hunted, farmed, and fished throughout Caribbean South America. In the Andean highlands, the Chibcha had formed settled communities. In what is now Venezuela, the Arawak and Carib lived off the land and sea. Now these societies were under threat. Armored soldiers brought Spanish laws and taxes, while Christian missionaries preached a new religion. The invaders were everywhere, even in the rain forests where the Spanish hunted for treasure and a legendary gold-rich king called **El Dorado.**

Cultures Collide

Only a few years after conquering the Aztec Empire in Mexico, the Spanish were invading the lands to the south. In 1525 they settled the Colombian coast. By 1538 they had reached the Colombian highlands, where they founded Bogotá. Meanwhile, in what is now Venezuela, Spanish settlements spread through the highlands and along the coast. Rumors of El Dorado drew explorers up the Orinoco River in Venezuela. Although El Dorado was never found, the Spanish discovered plenty of gold in the highlands of Colombia.

Colonial Society The Spanish forced Native Americans to work in the gold mines and on coastal plantations that exported sugar, cacao, and tobacco. But millions of Native Americans died from mistreatment and disease. To replace them, the Spanish imported enslaved people from Africa. Many Africans did not accept a life of slavery. Some fought their masters or fled into the forests.

The Spanish had conquered such a huge empire in the Americas that they could not keep all of it under control. One of their weakest spots lay along the easternmost Caribbean coast of South America. There, English and Dutch pirates constantly threatened their shipping and their ports. In addition, rival European nations began colonizing coastal lands claimed by Spain. The Dutch, English, and French opened trading posts and settlements along the easternmost coast of the Caribbean. By the late 1700s, the British had a colony in Guyana, the Dutch controlled Suriname, and the French owned French Guiana.

Reading Check How did rival European powers gain a foothold in Spanish lands?

myWorld Activity
Shipwreck Discovery

Pirate Attacks in the Caribbean

The gold and silver of the Americas made Spain rich and filled the Caribbean with pirates. Wealthy Spanish ports suffered frequent pirate attacks in colonial times.

Culture Close-up

A pirate captain as pictured by the American illustrator Howard Pyle ▼

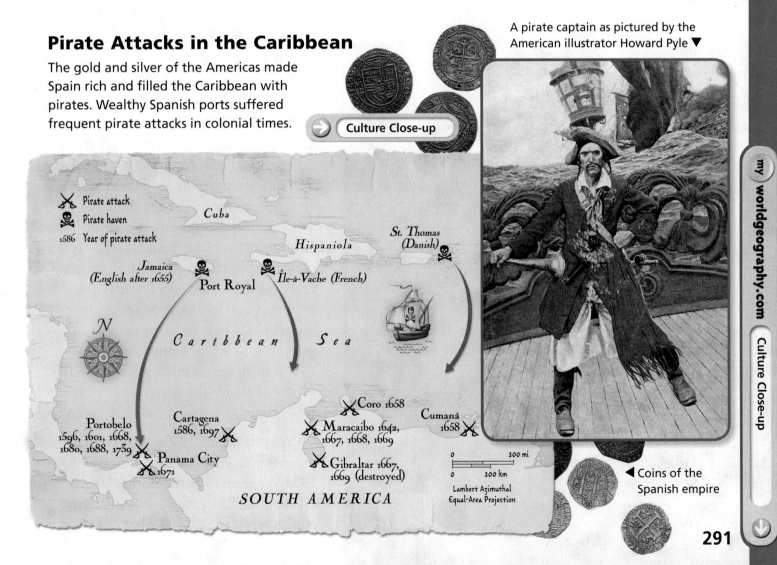

Map legend:
- ⚔ Pirate attack
- ☠ Pirate haven
- 1586 Year of pirate attack

Cuba

Hispaniola

St. Thomas (Danish) ☠

Jamaica (English after 1655)

☠ Port Royal   ☠ Île-à-Vache (French)

C a r i b b e a n   S e a

Portobelo 1596, 1601, 1668, 1680, 1688, 1739

Panama City 1671

Cartagena 1586, 1697

Coro 1658

Maracaibo 1642, 1667, 1668, 1669

Gibraltar 1667, 1669 (destroyed)

Cumaná 1658

SOUTH AMERICA

0   200 mi
0   200 km
Lambert Azimuthal Equal-Area Projection

◄ Coins of the Spanish empire

my worldgeography.com   Culture Close-up

The Fight for Independence

Members of the upper and middle classes were unhappy with Spanish rule. Although they owned the land, they wanted the right to trade with other nations throughout the world. They disliked being ruled by the Spanish-born peninsulares. Unlike colonial governments in North America, the Spanish colonial governments had no elected assemblies.

The rebels found a great leader in Simón Bolívar. Born in Venezuela, Bolívar dreamed of a new nation in which all people, including slaves, would be free. In 1805, he declared,

> ❝ I swear before you, I swear by the God of my fathers, I swear by my fathers, I swear by my honor, I swear by my country that I will not rest body or soul until I have broken the chains with which Spanish power oppresses us. ❞
> —Simón Bolívar, *Investor's Business Daily*

Bolívar kept his word. In 1811 Venezuela declared independence. Over the next decade, Bolívar fought Spanish and loyalist armies. With the help of patriots such as Colombia's Francisco de Paula Santander, Bolívar <u>liberated</u> other regions, creating several new nations.

Reading Check Why did the colonists want independence from Spain?

After Independence

The new nations were unstable. A small minority owned most of the land. In the new nations, **caudillos,** or dictators, soon emerged to control the governments.

The economies of the new nations were also weak. They were based on the export of just one or two products. Colombia's economy depended on a few exports, especially coffee. This dependence made the economy vulnerable to changes in prices on the world market.

Venezuela's economy was based on the export of cacao. Then, in the 1910s, an oil discovery led to an economic boom.

Oil Wealth In the 1900s, Venezuela prospered from its oil revenues. By 1928 Venezuela was the world's largest oil exporter. The government used the

liberate, *v.,* to free

Many towns in former Spanish colonies have a statue of Simón Bolívar. ▼

wealth to build roads and fund social services and welfare programs. Colombia also began to expand petroleum production into a key industry.

Political Conflict Despite the wealth that came from oil, much of the region was still poor. But attempts to redistribute land to those in need largely failed and led to civil conflict. In Colombia, a wave of political violence called La Violencia ("the violence") raged from 1948 to 1957.

In the 1960s, a new wave of conflict began in Colombia. Rebel armies began to form. Later, landowners responded by supporting **paramilitaries,** armed forces that are unauthorized by the government. Rebels and paramilitaries controlled large areas and forced people to pay them taxes. Both paramilitary and rebel groups funded their wars through the illegal drug trade. Fighting continues today, although the Colombian government claims that the situation is improving.

In 1976, the government of Venezuela **nationalized,** or took ownership of, the oil industry. Oil wealth funded social programs. But the country relied too much on oil revenues. A worldwide drop in oil prices brought about an economic decline in the 1980s. In early 1989, the government of President Carlos Andrés Pérez introduced **austerity measures,** or policies meant to save money. There were huge cuts in social services. An outraged public responded with riots and strikes. The nation was ripe for the political message of Hugo Chavez in the elections of 1998.

Chavez's government took control of the oil industry and used oil revenues to fund social programs. The government provided subsidized food and free healthcare. However, Chavez's popular policies angered the business community. As he gained more power, many feared that he was becoming a dictator. In the next section you will read how political conflicts like these are changing the region today.

Reading Check How did Venezuela use its oil revenues?

> **IN** Indiana
> **CONNECTIONS**
>
> Venezuela uses about
> **777,000**
> barrels of oil daily; Indiana uses more than
> **138,000,000**
> barrels of oil daily.

Section **2** Assessment

Essential Question

Is conflict unavoidable?

Key Terms

1. Use the following terms to describe the history of the region: El Dorado, caudillo, paramilitary, nationalize, austerity measure.

Key Ideas

2. What changes did Europeans bring to the region?

3. Who liberated the colonies in Caribbean South America?

4. What issues cause political tension in the countries of Caribbean South America?

Think Critically

5. **Make Inferences** Why were the liberated countries so unstable?

6. **Compare and Contrast** How did colonial governments in North America differ from those in South America?

7. What modern conflicts in Caribbean South America have their roots in colonial history? Go to your Student Journal to record your answer.

Union or Separation?

IN Indiana

6.1.21 Differentiate between fact and interpretation in historical accounts and explain historical passages.

6.1.23 Identify issues related to an event in Europe or the Americas and give arguments for and against that issue.

As they fought for independence, South American patriots argued over how to govern the liberated lands. Some, like liberator Simón Bolívar, wanted a strong central government. After independence, a nation called Gran Colombia was formed. Gran Colombia included territory that is now Colombia, Ecuador, Panama, and Venezuela. But geography and other factors made unification difficult. By the late 1820s, many Venezuelans were demanding their own nation. Analyze these excerpts to see the difficulties that arose in uniting these areas.

Caribbean Sea

PACIFIC OCEAN

GRAN COLOMBIA

Read the text on the right. Stop at each circled letter. Then answer the question with the same letter on the left.

Ⓐ **Analyze Cause and Effect** What does Bolívar think will happen if there are two different authorities?

Ⓑ **Infer** How does Bolívar think other countries will view the new smaller nations? Explain why.

Ⓒ **Draw Conclusions** How did Bolívar view a movement to break up this union? Explain why.

authorities, *n.,* governments

New Granada, *n.,* Colombia, Ecuador, Panama, and Venezuela

inspire, *v.,* to influence someone else

consideration, *n.,* respect

Bolívar on Unity

66 If we establish two independent <u>authorities</u>, one in the east and the other in the west, we will **Ⓐ** create two different nations which, because of their inability to maintain themselves as such, or even more to take their place among other nations, will look **Ⓑ** ridiculous. Only a Venezuela united with <u>New Granada</u> could form a nation that would <u>inspire</u> in others the proper <u>consideration</u> due to her. How can we think of dividing her **Ⓒ** into two? 99

—Simón Bolívar, Letter to Santiago Mariño, 1813

Simón Bolívar (1783–1830) ▶

294

Read the text on the right. Stop at each circled letter. Then answer the question with the same letter on the left.

D **Summarize** Why do the Venezuelans believe that union is impossible?

E **Form Opinions** Do you agree with the last statement? Explain why or why not.

Quito, *n.,* capital of Ecuador, also part of Gran Colombia

suitable, *adj.,* fitting, proper

customs, *n.,* traditions, ways of life

Venezuelans on Independence

66 **Venezuela ought not to remain united to New Granada and** <u>Quito</u>**, because the laws which are appropriate for those countries are not** <u>suitable</u> **for ours, which is completely different**

D in <u>customs</u>**, climate and products; and because government applied over a great area loses its**

E strength and energy. 99

—Declaration of Valencia, November 23, 1829

Analyze the Documents

1. **Compare Viewpoints** What most concerns Bolívar? What most concerns the Venezuelans? How do these viewpoints differ?

2. **Writing Task** Take the role of an advisor to Simón Bolívar, who has just read the Declaration of Valencia. Write a memo to Bolívar suggesting how he should reply to the leaders of the Venezuelan independence movement.

Section 3

Caribbean South America Today

IN Indiana

6.4.5 Compare the standard of living of various countries of Europe and the Americas today using GDP as an indicator.

6.4.6 Analyze current economic issues in the countries of Europe or the Americas using a variety of resources.

Key Terms • Latin America • subsidence • representative democracy • insurgent → **Visual Glossary**

Reading Skill: Compare and Contrast Take notes using the graphic organizer in your journal.

Daniella waves to visitors leaving her family's farm. ▼

my Story 📷 **Photo**

The solid ground around Daniella's farm sometimes trembles. The same volcanic forces that make the local soil so rich can also bring disaster. In 1999, Daniella's hometown of Armenia was destroyed by a terrible earthquake.

Like earthquakes in the Andes, political events sometimes shake the region. In Colombia, violent civil conflict has been raging for decades. In Venezuela, political changes are creating tension. Both Guyana and Suriname suffer from ethnic divisions.

Yet despite natural disasters and political conflict, Caribbean South America is a region full of energy and hope. Daniella's family, who turned to tourism for added income, is an example of how people in the region are working to improve their lives. Today, the nations of Caribbean South America are developing their economies while dealing with difficult political problems.

Diverse Cultures

Daniella lives in an area with strong Spanish influence. Yet the region of Caribbean South America as a whole is culturally quite diverse. The Spanish culture of Colombia and Venezuela differs from the culture of Guyana, Suriname, and French Guiana, where European and Asian influences mingle. Throughout the region there are also pockets of African and indigenous cultures.

Many writers have used the term **Latin America** to describe areas of the Americas influenced by the cultures of Spain, France, or Portugal—countries in which people speak languages descended from Latin. In the Caribbean countries of South America, the people of Colombia and Venezuela are overwhelmingly Catholic and speak Spanish. The population in French Guiana is mainly Catholic, and the official language is French rather than Spanish. Yet even in Latin cultures like these, music and dance are built on the complex rhythms of African music.

The countries that might be considered least Latin are Guyana and Suriname. The main language in Guyana is English, while in Suriname you might hear people speaking Dutch, English, or Surinamese. In both Guyana and Suriname, Hindustanis from India form the largest ethnic group, followed in number by those descended from enslaved Africans.

complex, *adj.,* complicated

Reading Check What are the major ethnic groups in this region?

Cultural Influences

The traditions of Caribbean South America reveal the diverse cultural influences in the region.

In **French Guiana,** African and French traditions merge in the carnival costumes of the Touloulous.

Venezuela's passion for baseball reveals the country's historical ties with the United States.

In **Suriname,** descendants of Indian immigrants celebrate Divali, the Hindu festival of light.

297

Environmental Problems

While each country in the region has different environmental challenges, all of them share one major problem—deforestation. Worldwide demand for wood products is encouraging companies to cut down trees. Large-scale commercial farming is also causing environmental damage. In this tropical region with many destructive insects, farmers are forced to use large amounts of pesticides. These pesticides are contaminating the soil and water.

restrict, *v.,* to limit

Venezuela also faces another kind of pollution—contamination from the oil industry. Industrial and oil processing plants have turned Lake Maracaibo into one of the most polluted areas in the region. Since the oil deposits are located under the lake, drilling has caused numerous spills and constant leakage. Because there is only a narrow channel connecting the lake to the ocean, most of this oil-polluted water is trapped in the lake. Decades of draining the underground oilfields is also causing land **subsidence,** or sinking of the ground. With the ground sinking, severe flooding is threatening both the oilfields and the people living around the lake.

Governments are making some efforts to solve environmental problems. Venezuela has passed the Organic Law of the Environment to protect its soils, forests, and water supplies. It has also tried to <u>restrict</u> logging and has begun reforestation by planting trees. In Colombia, the Pacific coastal area is now a protected ecosystem. Several nature reserves have been established in Suriname to protect wildlife. In Guyana, the Kaieteur National Park has been designated a conservation area.

Reading Check How is the oil industry affecting Venezuela's environment?

Air Pollution

Carbon dioxide (CO_2) is produced by the burning of coal, oil, and natural gas. Study the table to compare CO_2 emissions in the region.

Chart Skills

1. Which nation has higher levels of CO_2 emissions?

2. What might explain the difference in levels?

→ Data Discovery

Cars cause pollution in Venezuela. ▶

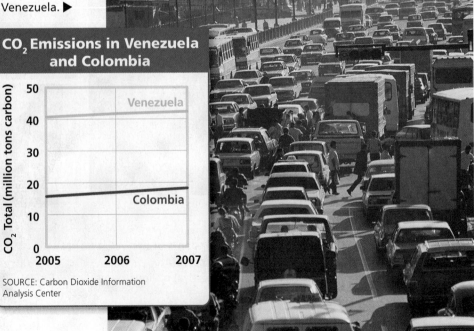

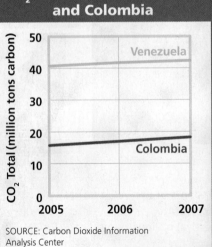

CO_2 Emissions in Venezuela and Colombia

CO_2 Total (million tons carbon)

Venezuela

Colombia

50
40
30
20
10
0

2005   2006   2007

SOURCE: Carbon Dioxide Information Analysis Center

Heads of State and Governments

Colombia

Colombia's President Juan Manuel Santos presides over a bicameral (two-house) Congress: Senate and Chamber of Representatives.

Venezuela

Venezuela's President Hugo Chávez Frías presided over a unicameral (one-house) National Assembly until his death in 2013. He was succeeded by Nicolás Maduro Moros.

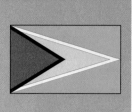

Guyana

Guyana's President Donald Ramotar governs with a unicameral National Assembly. The president is elected by simple majority vote.

Suriname

Suriname's President Desiré Delano "Dési" Bouterse was elected by a unicameral National Assembly.

French Guiana

In French Guiana French President François Hollande is head of state. The territory sends elected representatives to the French Parliament.

▲ The heads of state in Caribbean South America preside over varied governments.

Governments and Conflicts

All the countries in Caribbean South America are independent republics except French Guiana, which is considered part of France. Most of the nations in the region suffer from various tensions and conflicts.

Varied Governments Like the United States, Colombia has executive, legislative, and judicial branches of government. The Legislature is bicameral, which means that it has two "houses"—a Senate and a Chamber of Representatives. Two parties, the Liberals and Conservatives, compete for power.

In Venezuela, the new constitution of 1999 changed the system of government. The late president, Hugo Chávez Frías, reduced **representative democracy,** or democracy in which the people elect representatives to make the nation's laws. In Venezuela's new system of direct democracy, the people use referenda, or voting, to make or change laws.

Guyana is a democracy with a president and a National Assembly. The ruling party is supported by people of African descent, while the opposition party is favored by people of South Asian ancestry.

Suriname has a president and an elected National Assembly. As in Guyana, Suriname's political parties are divided along ethnic lines.

As its name suggests, French Guiana is not an independent nation. It is considered an overseas "department" of France and sends representatives to the French Parliament. Its people are French citizens who enjoy the same rights and social services as people in France.

my worldgeography.com Data Discovery

299

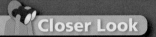

Politics in Venezuela

Although President Chavez died in 2013, he continues to influence his country. Read what ordinary Venezuelans have said about him.

THINK CRITICALLY Do you think that President Chavez helped or hurt Venezuela?

66 He is a communist and he's a disaster for Venezuela. . . . He sets the country's different groups against each other. 99

—Alicia Gomez, resident of Caracas*

▲ Anti-Chavez demonstration

66 What other president has ever taken the time to go into the shanty towns and meet the people? . . . This country has got huge oil wealth but so many of us still live in poverty. 99

—Jose Luis Arnal, resident of Caracas*

▲ Demonstration in support of President Chavez

*Quoted in "Rift in Venezuelan Society" from BBC.com

300

Conflicts and Tensions Ethnic tensions trouble the eastern parts of the region, such as Suriname and Guyana. In Suriname, warfare between South Asian and African ethnic groups has driven many Surinamese residents into neighboring French Guiana to seek refuge. In Guyana, the same two ethnic groups are also struggling for political power. The Guyanese tend to vote for public officials along racial lines.

In Colombia, the government has been fighting a civil war against **insurgents,** or rebels, for decades. The insurgents have long been able to hide in the remote forests and the mountainous terrain. Meanwhile, armed groups have formed to oppose the insurgents. Fighting between these two groups has brought suffering to civilians across the country. With military aid from the United States, the government of Colombia claims it is restoring order in this troubled land.

Political tensions are also running high in Venezuela after the death of Hugo Chavez. President Chavez wanted to narrow the large gap between the rich and the poor. However, his political actions have angered many landowners and businesspeople. They feel they no longer have a voice in how the resources of the country should be used.

Reading Check What are some tensions and conflicts in the region?

 myWorld Activity
Teaching Booklet

Economies

Caribbean South America is trying to diversify, or vary, its economies. The Venezuelan government is trying to create tourist and high-tech industries. However, Venezuela is still dependent on oil and natural gas exports.

President Chavez is trying to move away from a free-market economy and has begun to redirect revenues. For example, profits from oil enable the government to fund extremely low gasoline prices at the pumps. But Venezuelan oil revenues have been funding more than social programs. Since 2005, Venezuela has also been buying billions of dollars of military equipment from Russia.

Trade agreements among countries in this region are meant to eliminate tariffs and reduce unfair competition. The Organization of American States (OAS), formed in Bogotá in 1948, is one organization that promotes economic and cultural cooperation.

Although much of the region is poor, there is potential for economic growth.

▲ A rocket launch in French Guiana

Chart Skills

Which countries are the poorest in the region?

→ **Data Discovery**

Economies of Caribbean South America

Country	GDP per Capita
Colombia	$8,900
Venezuela	$13,500
Guyana	$3,900
Suriname	$8,900

SOURCE: *CIA World Factbook*

Guyana may soon profit from offshore oil. In French Guiana, the economy is helped by the European Space Agency, which has established a rocket launch site in the nation. Venezuela has its oil fields, while Colombia has rich resources of gold, coal, oil, and emeralds.

Reading Check What industries might help Venezuela to diversify its economy?

Section 3 Assessment

my worldgeography.com | Data Discovery

Key Terms

1. Use the following terms to describe life in Caribbean South America today: Latin America, subsidence, representative democracy, insurgent.

Key Ideas

2. How did the region become so ethnically diverse?

3. What are some natural resources of the region, and where are they located?

4. What environmental problems trouble the region?

Think Critically

5. Cause and Effect What economic forces contribute to deforestation?

6. Make Inferences Why are many business-people upset by the policies of Hugo Chavez?

Essential Question

Is conflict unavoidable?

7. What issues fuel conflicts in Caribbean South America? Go to your Student Journal to record your answer.

Civil Conflict in Colombia

IN Indiana

6.1.18 Create and compare timelines that identify people, events and developments in the history of Europe and the Americas.

6.1.22 Form research questions and use resources to present data on people, cultures and developments in Europe and the Americas.

Key Terms • guerrilla • land distribution • paramilitary group • collaborate

Colombia today is torn by civil conflict. Private armies roam the land, fighting over regions and resources. A weak central government has been unable to stop the violence. As warfare rages in the countryside, civilians are caught in the crossfire. Many have been murdered or kidnapped. Millions have fled to the cities or to other countries. This conflict has lasted more than four decades, and its roots lie deep in Colombia's geography and history.

A Divisive Landscape

Colombia's geography has always been an obstacle to national unity. Three Andean cordilleras, or mountain ranges, create massive north–south barriers. The cordilleras make communication and transportation inside Colombia very difficult. Other regions are far from the reach of government control. In many areas, there are few roads or settlements. To the west, the Pacific coast is covered with rain forest and swamp. In remote places like these, groups of **guerrillas**—soldiers who make surprise raids on their enemies—can operate freely.

Reading Check How has geography helped divide Colombia?

History of Inequality

Like many other former Spanish colonies, Colombia suffered from unequal **land distribution**, or ownership of land. For centuries, a tiny minority owned most of the land. This inequality led some to call for revolution. In politics, those who supported more equal distribution of wealth were termed *leftist*. Those who resisted such change were termed *rightist*.

◀ Memorial for those killed during a rebel attack on the Palace of Justice in Bogotá

302

Between 1948 and 1957, political groups fought in a bloody period known as La Violencia. In the late 1950s, levels of violence decreased. However, civil conflict flared up again in the 1960s.

In the mid-1960s, leftist rebel groups began to form. They hoped to overthrow the government and to improve the lives of the poor.

Reading Check What social problems were at the root of the rebellion?

Rise of the Rebels

Some rebel groups were influenced by events in Cuba. In 1959, Fidel Castro seized the government in that island nation. Soon after, he adopted communism. His success inspired rebels throughout Latin America.

Violence in Colombia grew during the 1970s and 1980s. The rebels kidnapped wealthy and powerful people, including government officials. They began selling illegal drugs to finance their operations.

While war raged in the countryside, fighting spread to the cities. In 1985, members of a rebel group invaded the Palace of Justice in Bogotá, holding dozens of people hostage. Government forces regained control of the building, but more than 100 people—including high-ranking judges—were killed in the battle.

Reading Check What world event influenced leftist groups in Colombia?

◀ ELN fighters unfurl their flag.

Chart Skills

Which rebel groups were formed by communists?

COLOMBIA

1965 Rebels form the National Liberation Army, or **ELN,** inspired and supported by Fidel Castro.

1966 Another group of communist rebels forms the Revolutionary Armed Forces of Colombia, or **FARC.**

1972 The **19th of April Movement,** or **M-19,** begins waging urban guerrilla war.

| 1960 | 1965 | 1970 | 1975 |

WORLD EVENTS

1959 Socialist leader Fidel Castro leads revolution in Cuba. His success encourages left-wing rebels throughout South America.

1961 Bay of Pigs invasion. Group of U.S.-trained, anti-communist Cubans fails in its attempt to invade Cuba.

1967 Cuban fighter Che Guevara is killed while trying to spread revolution in Bolivia. Cuban policy of exporting revolution comes to an end.

Che Guevara ▶

303

Rightist Reaction

The central government appeared too weak to stop the rebels. So landowners and others decided to take matters into their own hands. They formed rightist **paramilitary groups,** or private armies. Many of them later formed the United Self-Defense Groups of Colombia, or AUC. AUC forces raided rebel-held areas. Both sides punished people suspected of **collaborating,** or helping the enemy.

Many people, fearing for their lives, fled rural areas for the cities. They crowded into slums, where they lived in poverty, with poor sanitation and ill health.

Former President Andrés Pastrana, who was elected in 1998, launched a new strategy, called "Plan Colombia," to solve the nation's problems. President Pastrana gave FARC (the Revolutionary Armed Forces of Colombia) control of a large section of the country as long as the group joined talks to achieve a peace agreement.

FARC kept up its attacks, however. In 2002, Pastrana ordered the army to go after that rebel force once more.

Reading Check What effects did the growing violence have on the people of Colombia?

Paramilitary and Rebel Areas

By the 1990s, huge areas of Colombia were under the control of either the rebels or the paramilitary forces. The conflict forced thousands of ordinary Colombians from their homes.

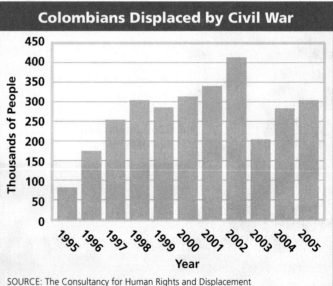

Colombians Displaced by Civil War

SOURCE: The Consultancy for Human Rights and Displacement

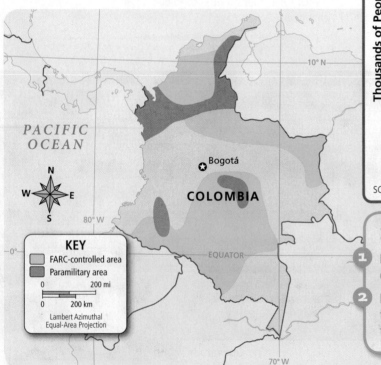

KEY

FARC-controlled area

Paramilitary area

0   200 mi

0   200 km

Lambert Azimuthal
Equal-Area Projection

Map Skills

1 **Location** Study the map. In which parts of the country are the rebels strongest?

2 **Interaction** In which year did the conflict force the largest number of people from their homes?

Signs of Progress?

In 2002, Alvaro Uribe Velez was elected president. He convinced the AUC to stop fighting. As a result, more than 30,000 fighters put down their weapons. About 14,000 members of FARC and the ELN (National Liberation Army) also agreed to give up their weapons.

Army and police units forced the rebels out of the cities. FARC weakened and no longer carried out large-scale attacks. ELN took part in talks with the government but, in the end, refused to give up.

Still, the get-tough policy had results. Murders, kidnappings, and other crimes fell dramatically.

In 2008, the government had more successes. FARC's leader died, weakening the group further. That summer, Colombian soldiers raided a FARC camp and freed 15 people the rebels had held hostage for years. Several high-ranking FARC leaders were killed, and many FARC fighters deserted the cause afterward.

As violence decreased, the economy grew and unemployment dropped. The government also adopted policies to help the poor.

Despite these promising signs, the situation in Colombia remains uncertain.

▲ Colombians demonstrate in favor of peace.

The old paramilitaries may be gone, but new armed groups have emerged. President Uribe calls these groups "criminal bands," but they cause the same kind of terror as the old paramilitaries.

The Colombian government is struggling to restore its authority in remote parts of the country. In a country so divided by its geography, this is no easy task. Only time will tell if President Uribe's policies are working.

Reading Check What signs of progress have appeared in recent years?

Assessment

1. How did developments in other countries influence events in Colombia?

2. How did attempts to end the violence lead to more violence?

3. What was the purpose of Pastrana's Plan Colombia?

4. Do you think that Colombia's government will bring peace? Explain why or why not.

5. What new conditions improved the situation in Colombia?

Chapter Assessment

Key Terms and Ideas

1. **Recall** Through which countries do the Andes extend?

2. **Explain** How do the **cordilleras** affect transportation in Colombia?

3. **Describe** What happened to the indigenous people of the region under Spanish rule?

4. **Recall** How did the legend of **El Dorado** encourage Spanish exploration of the region?

5. **Summarize** What social problems led to conflict in Colombia?

6. **Explain** What is causing **subsidence** around Lake Maracaibo?

7. **Discuss** What natural resources could help the economies of the region?

Think Critically

8. **Make Inferences** Why is it dangerous for a nation to base its economy on only one or two exports?

9. **Draw Conclusions** What factors explain settlement patterns in the region?

10. **Analyze Information** Why are some parts of this region more urbanized than others?

11. **Core Concepts: Migration** What factors drew immigrants to Caribbean South America?

Places to Know

For each place, write the letter from the map that shows its location.

12. **Bogotá**

13. **Cordillera Occidental**

14. **Orinoco River**

15. **Cayenne**

16. **Llanos**

17. **Caracas**

18. **Estimate** Using the scale, estimate the distance from Caracas to Bogotá.

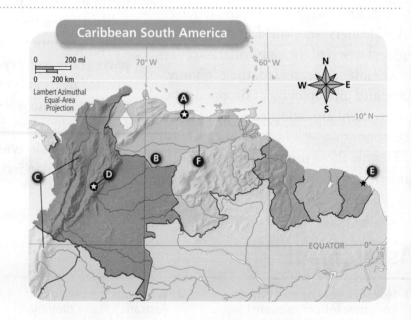

Caribbean South America

Essential Question
myWorld Chapter Activity

Hunt for Resources Follow your teacher's instructions to study the working conditions and political situation in each nation of Caribbean South America. Work with a group to choose the location of a new factory producing export goods somewhere in the region. Review the photograph and the information about the topic at each location. Then meet with your team and decide where to locate the factory. Prepare a report explaining why you have chosen this site.

21st Century Learning
Analyze Media Content

With a partner, choose one of the countries covered in this chapter. Then search online and through newspapers for articles about the political situation in that country. Discuss each article and decide whether the writer is for or against the government in power.

Document-Based Questions

Success **Tracker™**
Online at myworldgeography.com

Use your knowledge of Caribbean South America and Documents A and B to answer Questions 1–3.

Document A

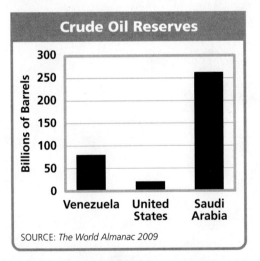

Crude Oil Reserves

Billions of Barrels

SOURCE: *The World Almanac 2009*

1. What does the information in Document A show about Venezuela's economy?

   A why Venezuela's economy is struggling

   B why petroleum is so important to Venezuela's economy

   C why Venezuela nationalized its oil industry

   D why Venezuela hopes to diversify its economy

Document B

" Venezuela has the largest oil reserves in the world. In the future Venezuela won't have any more oil—but that's in the 22nd Century."

—President Hugo Chavez, BBC News, April 2006

2. What does Document B reveal about how President Chavez regards Venezuela's oil reserves?

   A They are a resource that Venezuela can tap into forever.

   B They are a limited resource, but the country will be able to profit from them in the short term.

   C They are smaller than Saudi Arabia's.

   D They will only be useful in the next century.

3. **Writing Task** What do Documents A and B together reveal about Hugo Chavez's plans?

my worldgeography.com Self-Test

307

Chapter 6

The Andes and the Pampas

Essential Question

What are the challenges of diversity?

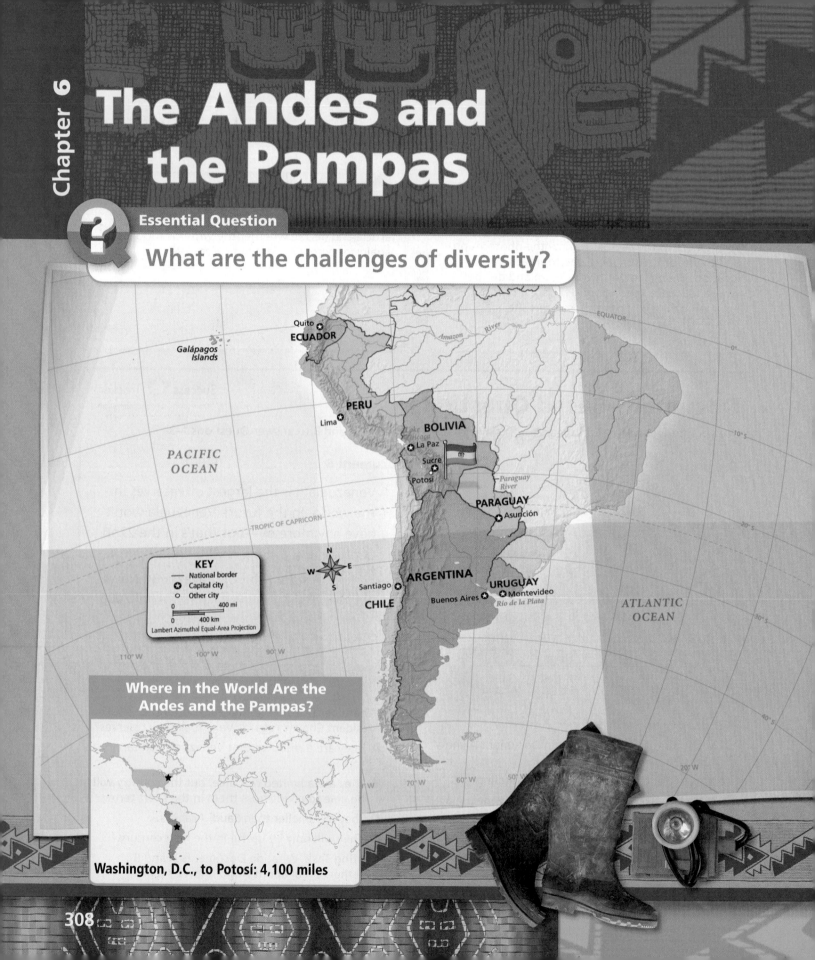

KEY

— National border
⊛ Capital city
○ Other city

0   400 mi
0   400 km
Lambert Azimuthal Equal-Area Projection

Where in the World Are the Andes and the Pampas?

Washington, D.C., to Potosí: 4,100 miles

my Story

Under the Rich Mountain

In this section, you'll learn about Omar and his struggle to earn a living under a mountain that once made an empire rich. **What does the story tell you about the diverse landforms and cultures of the Andes and the Pampas?**

Story by Neville Cole for myWorld Geography Online

Most days Omar follows the same routine: rising early, making his bed, eating breakfast, and heading off to work. He is only 14 years old but, like his father and grandfather before him, Omar is a miner. Six days a week Omar digs ore in the Paylaviri mine in Potosí, Bolivia. It's a typical story around here. Three of Omar's brothers are miners; so is his cousin, Frederico. In fact, almost all the men Omar knows have been miners at one time or another. Mining has a long and terrible history in this part of Bolivia, and Omar and Frederico must work under the mountain with the longest and most terrible mining history of them all—Cerro Rico, the "Rich Mountain."

At 15,827 feet, Cerro Rico towers over the town of Potosí like a pyramid. For more than 450 years, generations of miners have dug into this mountain to extract its incredible wealth of silver and tin.

Explore the Essential Question

- at **my** worldgeography.com
- using the **myWorld Chapter Activity**
- with the **Student Journal**

Omar at work

Omar at his father's grave

Omar and Frederico
pushing an ore cart

The locals say that so many tunnels have been carved into Cerro Rico that the mountain's heart is like Swiss cheese. The mine was discovered in 1544, and by 1600 it was producing half the world's silver, much of it sent to the Spanish king. But all that wealth came at a very high cost. More than 8 million people may have died here, either from mining accidents or as a result of illnesses caused by working underground. Omar knows this all too well. His own father became sick from breathing dust in the mine and died when Omar was ten.

"I hate going down into the mine," Omar says. "Every time I go into the mine I think it is the last time. I think I won't be coming out." Fortunately, working conditions are better today than they were years ago. The miners have formed a cooperative. They work together to make conditions safer.

Omar has to work for only a few hours each day, but those few hours are far from easy. "The work inside the mine is very tough. I have to run back and forth to dig ore. I also help my brothers or my cousin, Frederico, push the ore cart. It is very hot down underground. I have to carry enough water so that I don't get thirsty. You sweat a lot in the mine. It is very difficult work. You have to dig very hard and sometimes it is dangerous, especially when you have to use dynamite."

Omar and Frederico at the market

A game of soccer in the sun

After his father died, Omar's mother had to move away to find work. Working in the mine is the only way Omar and his brothers can make enough money to survive. "I make 250 Bolivianos, which is about 30 dollars per week. That's when I am lucky. Sometimes I only make 100 Bolivianos. . . . I give my brother some of that money to buy food for the house and sometimes I buy clothes. I also send my mother money to help raise my little brother."

Omar dreams that one day soon his life will change. He goes to school each afternoon after his shift at the mine. "I would like to become an architect when I grow up," he says. "I would like to build schools so other children all over the world can go to school too."

Despite all the hard work, Omar still finds time to have fun. On this day, he and Frederico stop by a soccer court to join a game. Frederico tackles the ball and moves it quickly down the court. Without even looking up, he switches direction and passes the ball to Omar on the wing. Omar makes a move back to the inside and drives the ball past the goalkeeper. For now Omar and Frederico are just two happy cousins celebrating a goal in the sun. Yet behind them looms the peak of Cerro Rico, reminding them that tomorrow morning they will be under the mountain once more.

➡ **myStory Video**

Learn more about Omar's life in the mine.

Meet the Journalist

Name Jorge Alborta
Favorite Moment Sharing Omar's good spirits despite his difficult life

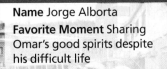

Chapter Atlas

 Indiana

6.3.1 Understand the countries and capitals of Europe and the Americas.

6.3.2 Use latitude and longitude to locate the capital cities of Europe and the Americas and describe the uses of locational technology.

6.3.7 Locate and describe the climate regions of Europe and the Americas and explain how and why they differ.

6.3.12 Compare the distribution and evaluate the importance of natural resources in Europe and the Americas.

6.3.13 Explain the impact of humans on the physical environment in Europe and the Americas.

→ Visual Glossary

Key Terms • subduct • Altiplano • El Niño • vertical climate zones

Reading Skill: Label an Outline Map Take notes using the outline map in your journal.

A horse and rider in the Andes

Physical Features

Omar lives in the Andes, the longest mountain range in the world. The Andes are the spine of South America, curving down the continent's west coast. To the west of the Andes lies the Pacific Ocean. This coast includes landforms such as the Atacama Desert. To the east of the Andes lie tropical rain forests. In the southeast, grassy plains spread out along the Rio de la Plata. These are the Pampas—vast fertile grasslands bustling with ranches and big commercial farms.

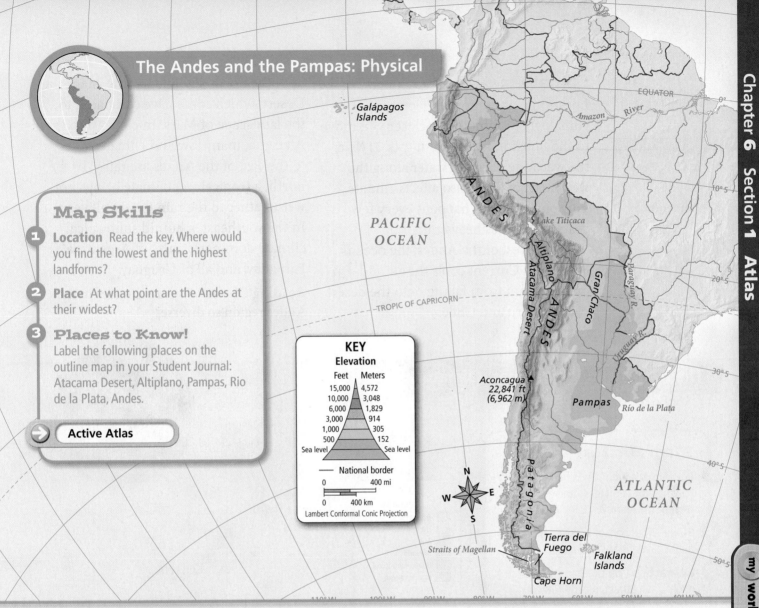

The Andes and the Pampas: Physical

Map Skills

1. **Location** Read the key. Where would you find the lowest and the highest landforms?

2. **Place** At what point are the Andes at their widest?

3. **Places to Know!** Label the following places on the outline map in your Student Journal: Atacama Desert, Altiplano, Pampas, Rio de la Plata, Andes.

Active Atlas

KEY
Elevation

Feet	Meters
15,000	4,572
10,000	3,048
6,000	1,829
3,000	914
1,000	305
500	152
Sea level	Sea level

— National border

0   400 mi
0   400 km
Lambert Conformal Conic Projection

Galápagos Islands

EQUATOR

Amazon River

PACIFIC OCEAN

ANDES

Lake Titicaca

Altiplano

Atacama Desert

ANDES

Gran Chaco

Paraguay R.

Uruguay R.

TROPIC OF CAPRICORN

Aconcagua 22,841 ft (6,962 m)

Pampas

Río de la Plata

Patagonia

ATLANTIC OCEAN

Straits of Magellan

Tierra del Fuego

Falkland Islands

Cape Horn

The Pampas stretch for some 250,000 square miles (647,000 square kilometers). This land was once covered by ten-foot-tall grass. The grassland extended over Patagonia (southern Argentina and Chile) and most of the lowlands. Today the area is an agricultural region. It is home to most of Argentina's population.

The Andes were formed as two tectonic plates called the Nazca Plate and the South American Plate collided slowly over millions of years. As the Nazca Plate was **subducted,** or tugged under, the force buckled up the South American Plate to form the Andes.

This 80-million-year-long crash has caused volcanic eruptions and earthquakes in the nations of the Andes.

The Andes include parallel chains of mountains called cordilleras. In Peru and Bolivia cordilleras flank a high plateau called the **Altiplano,** where Potosí is located. The Altiplano is rich in metals, such as silver, zinc, tin, and lead.

Reading Check How were the Andes formed?

Climate

Location is an important factor in climate. For example, the closer you move to the Equator, the hotter it gets. **El Niño,** the warming of ocean water along the west coast of Peru, also affects climate. This <u>phenomenon</u> happens every few years and causes heavy rain.

To the west of the Andes, the ocean's Humboldt Current cools the air and prevents rain from falling onto the desert coast of Peru and Chile.

phenomenon, *n.,* an event that can be scientifically described

In the north of Chile lies the Atacama Desert, which some have compared to the landscape of Mars. In contrast to the Atacama, many lowland climate zones to the east of the Andes are rainy. In the north, a tropical wet climate brings hot, wet weather to the rain forests all year. In the southeast, a humid subtropical climate dominates parts of Argentina, Paraguay, and all of Uruguay.

Reading Check Why are climates in the Andes region so diverse?

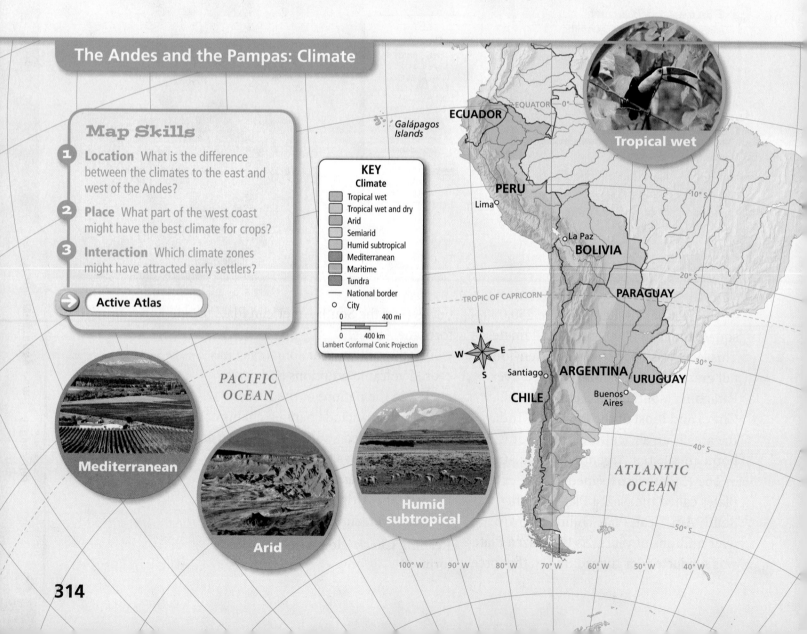

The Andes and the Pampas: Climate

Map Skills

1 **Location** What is the difference between the climates to the east and west of the Andes?

2 **Place** What part of the west coast might have the best climate for crops?

3 **Interaction** Which climate zones might have attracted early settlers?

→ **Active Atlas**

KEY
Climate
- Tropical wet
- Tropical wet and dry
- Arid
- Semiarid
- Humid subtropical
- Mediterranean
- Maritime
- Tundra
- National border
- ○ City

0   400 mi
0   400 km
Lambert Conformal Conic Projection

Tropical wet

Mediterranean

Arid

Humid subtropical

EQUATOR 0°
Galápagos Islands
ECUADOR
PERU
Lima
La Paz
BOLIVIA
PARAGUAY
TROPIC OF CAPRICORN
Santiago
ARGENTINA
URUGUAY
CHILE
Buenos Aires
PACIFIC OCEAN
ATLANTIC OCEAN
10° S
20° S
30° S
40° S
50° S
100° W   90° W   80° W   70° W   60° W   50° W   40° W

Ecosystems

In the Andes, climate and ecosystems vary. High rainfall in eastern Ecuador and Peru contrasts with dry conditions on the Pacific coast. In each climate zone a different ecosystem has developed. An ecosystem is the network of plant and animal life within a specific environment.

In the mountain highlands, climate is influenced by elevation as well as location. Near the Equator, the climate is hot and wet up to an altitude of 4,900 feet (1,494 meters). However, the higher up the mountains you travel, the cooler and wetter it gets. This creates a variety of ecosystems.

Temperature and rainfall determine the kind of vegetation that grows in a location. In the Andes farmers grow different crops at different elevations. The illustration that appears below shows a diagram of **vertical climate zones,** or climate zones that change according to elevation.

Reading Check Why are there so many ecosystems in the Andes?

Vertical Climate Zones

In the Andean highlands, climate changes according to altitude, or elevation. Because climate varies so much, farmers can grow a wide range of crops.

Chart Skills

1 Why would most settlements be located below the tree line?

2 Where is the best grazing land?

→ **Data Discovery**

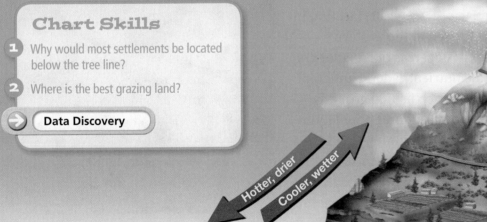

Hotter, drier

Cooler, wetter

Sea level

Snow Line
16,000 feet
Llamas, alpaca, vicuña

Tree Line
12,000 feet
Potatoes, wheat, barley, apples, corn, beans

6,000 feet
Coffee, corn

3,000 feet
Bananas, sugar cane, cacao

my **worldgeography**.com Active Atlas

IN Indiana
CONNECTIONS

In Argentina,
9.3% of the
country's GDP
comes from
agriculture.

In Indiana, about
2.2% of the
state's earnings
come from
agriculture.

myWorld Activity
A Poem of the Land

Land Use and Resources

In the Andes, there is surprisingly little good farmland. Tropical rain forests cover many areas east of the Andes. The Andes themselves are too mountainous for large-scale farming.

In places where people can farm, agricultural practices differ between the Andes and the Pampas. The farmers of Andean countries have to cope with difficult landforms. For example, in the Andes there are no large areas of flat land. So farming must take place on high plateaus and in narrow mountain valleys. However, an amazing variety of crops can be grown in these vertical climate zones: wheat, coffee, corn, vegetables, many different kinds of fruit, and thousands of kinds of potatoes.

Commercial, or large-scale, farming in the Andes is limited to the western foothills and the coastal areas of Ecuador and Peru. Here the nutrient-laden Humboldt Current provides rich fishing grounds. At higher altitudes, a poorer population labors in subsistence farming—farmers grow only enough to feed themselves and their families.

The open grasslands of the Pampas are ideal for cattle ranching, which attracted early settlers to the area. In colonial times settlers exported hides from Pampas cattle. Hides were shipped to Europe, via the huge Rio de la Plata estuary, or wide river mouth. Today, Buenos Aires in Argentina and Montevideo in Uruguay are the chief ports on this estuary. The Plata Basin, which includes Uruguay, Paraguay, northern Argentina, and eastern Bolivia,

is the site of commercial farming. Here large farms grow crops such as soybeans, corn, and wheat.

Bolivia lies roughly in the geographic center of this region. Because its territory includes both the Andean highlands and the lowlands of the east, it has examples of the kinds of farming seen in both the Andes and the Pampas. Subsistence farmers can be found in the Bolivian highlands, while large commercial farms spread over the eastern lowlands.

A Subsistence farming in the Andes

B Commercial farming on the Pampas

The natural resources of the Andes have attracted settlers for centuries. The Spanish mined gold, silver, and copper in the highlands of Peru and Bolivia. The mines at Potosí, where Omar works, once supplied huge quantities of silver that made the Spanish Empire rich.

Today people are using the resources and changing the landscape of the region in other ways. Hydroelectric dams are built to produce electricity by tapping the power of falling water. These dams can cause environmental damage to delicate ecosystems. In Chile the building of dams on the Bio-Bio River is flooding river valleys. It is also forcing Native Americans from their homes.

Fortunately, some new projects are less damaging to the landscape. The La Higuera project in the San Fernando Valley of Chile <u>generates</u> hydroelectricity from the natural flow of river waters.

generate, *v.,* to produce

Reading Check Where is the best agricultural land in the region?

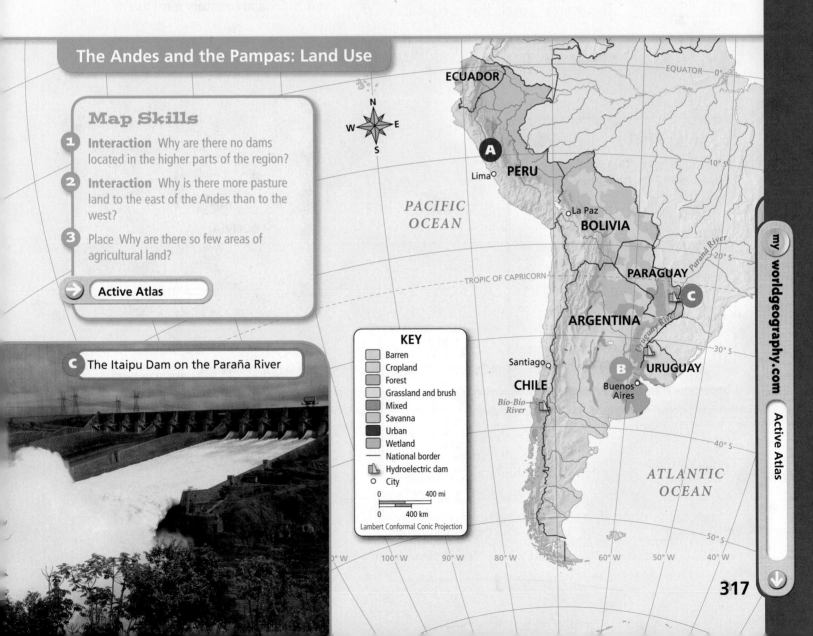

The Andes and the Pampas: Land Use

Map Skills

1. **Interaction** Why are there no dams located in the higher parts of the region?

2. **Interaction** Why is there more pasture land to the east of the Andes than to the west?

3. **Place** Why are there so few areas of agricultural land?

→ **Active Atlas**

C The Itaipu Dam on the Paraña River

KEY

- Barren
- Cropland
- Forest
- Grassland and brush
- Mixed
- Savanna
- Urban
- Wetland
- —— National border
- Hydroelectric dam
- ○ City

0 — 400 mi
0 — 400 km
Lambert Conformal Conic Projection

ECUADOR
EQUATOR — 0°
PERU
Lima
PACIFIC OCEAN
10° S
La Paz
BOLIVIA
Paraná River
20° S
TROPIC OF CAPRICORN
PARAGUAY
C
ARGENTINA
Uruguay River
30° S
Santiago
CHILE
B
URUGUAY
Buenos Aires
Bío-Bío River
40° S
ATLANTIC OCEAN
50° S
110° W 100° W 90° W 80° W 70° W 60° W 50° W 40° W

my worldgeography.com Active Atlas

People in the Andes and the Pampas

The region's population is unevenly distributed because of the variety of climates and landforms. There are few large cities in Paraguay, Ecuador, and Bolivia. Smaller populations live in rural areas, mountain valleys, grasslands, and in the tropical rain forests.

In earlier times settlers were attracted by the cooler temperatures and rich resources of the Andean highlands. Today most people live in coastal cities.

The largest city of the entire region is Buenos Aires, capital of Argentina, with a population of more than 12 million.

A dramatic ethnic divide exists between people in the Andes and in the Pampas. Almost all Argentina's people are of Spanish and Italian ancestry. Only 3 percent are indigenous and mestizo (people of mixed white and indigenous ancestry).

In contrast, the population of Andean countries such as Chile, Peru, Ecuador, and Bolivia are mainly a mixture

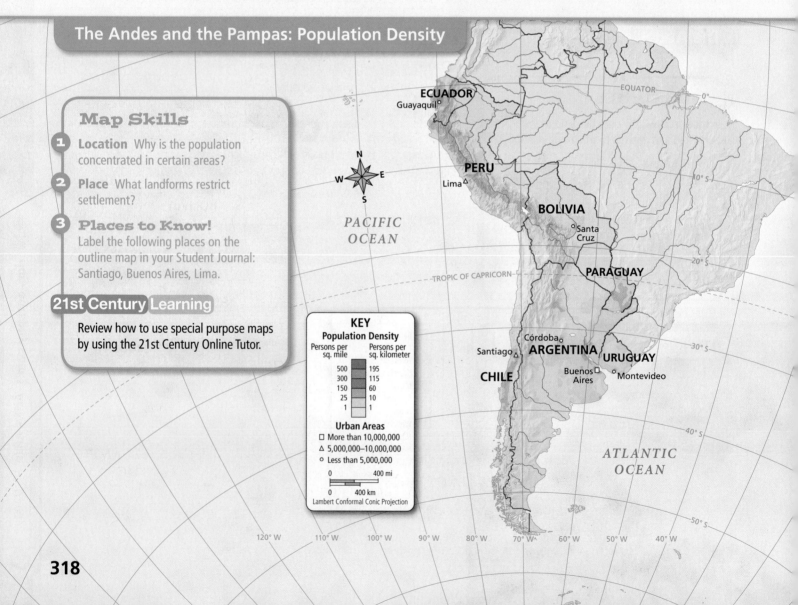

The Andes and the Pampas: Population Density

Map Skills

1. **Location** Why is the population concentrated in certain areas?

2. **Place** What landforms restrict settlement?

3. **Places to Know!** Label the following places on the outline map in your Student Journal: Santiago, Buenos Aires, Lima.

21st Century Learning

Review how to use special purpose maps by using the 21st Century Online Tutor.

KEY
Population Density

Persons per sq. mile	Persons per sq. kilometer
500	195
300	115
150	60
25	10
1	1

Urban Areas
□ More than 10,000,000
△ 5,000,000–10,000,000
○ Less than 5,000,000

0   400 mi
0   400 km
Lambert Conformal Conic Projection

318

of mestizos and Native Americans. However, in many places a small minority of people of Spanish descent hold on to economic and political power.

The Quechua, who are descendants of the Incas, still live on the southern Altiplano and in nearby mountains and speak the ancient Incan language. In Bolivia, indigenous people have recently won political power. This is a great achievement for groups who have suffered centuries of discrimination in their own land.

Reading Check **Where do most people live in the Andes and the Pampas?**

Geography and History

Physical geography has always played a central role in the history of this region. The Andes are difficult to cross. Societies and nations have always been isolated from one another. Even today, few east-west roads run through the Andes.

In the southeast, the fertile Pampas attracted settlement and helped create the wealth of Argentina. In parts of the Andes, the hot climate of the lowlands forced settlement up into the cooler highlands. It was there that the advanced civilization of the Incas developed. And it was also in the Andean highlands, in places such as Potosí, that the Spanish mined the silver that made them rich.

The Andes and the Pampas have also shaped history and culture in other ways. Just as in the American West, the wide open spaces of the Pampas bred a spirit of independence. It was the gauchos, or cowboys, of the Pampas who formed the cavalry when Argentina was fighting for independence.

The Andes also played an important part in the wars of liberation, when rebel armies climbed their heights to launch surprise attacks on royalist forces in Chile. In the next section you will read about the role geography played in the region's history.

Reading Check **How has geography affected history in the Andes and the Pampas?**

A gaucho on the Pampas ▼

Section 1 Assessment

Key Terms

1. Use the following terms to describe the geography of the region: subduct, Altiplano, El Niño, vertical climate zones.

Key Ideas

2. Why did the Andean highlands attract settlers?

3. In what ways are people changing the landscape today?

4. Where do most people live?

Think Critically

5. **Solve Problems** How have farmers adapted to the difficult landscape of the Andes?

6. **Draw Inferences** Why might there be many hydroelectric dams in the Andes?

Essential Question

What are the challenges of diversity?

7. How does the geographic diversity of the region determine where people live? Go to your Student Journal to record your answer.

History of the Andes and the Pampas

IN Indiana

6.1.1 Summarize the rise, decline, and cultural achievements of ancient civilizations in Europe and Mesoamerica.

6.1.4 Explain the development and organization of various systems in Europe and the Americas.

6.1.6 Identify trade routes and discuss their impact on the rise of cultural centers and cities in Europe and Mesoamerica.

6.1.20 Analyze cause-and-effect relationships in history.

Key Terms • immunity • criollo • mestizo • mercantilism • oligarchy

> **Visual Glossary**

Reading Skill: Analyze Cause and Effect Take notes using the graphic organizer in your journal.

Actors recreate the Inca festival of Inti Raymi.

> **Culture Close-up**

In 1532 a small group of Spanish soldiers trudged up into the highlands of the Inca Empire. They were astonished by what they saw. Here was a world full of unfamiliar plants and animals—llamas, potatoes, and guinea pigs bred for food. Even the air was different. Local people, who were used to breathing the thin air of the highlands, watched the invaders gasp for breath. The Spanish struggled on, driven by their hunger for treasure. It was as if they could sense the rich resources of the land.

The Spanish invasion is only one episode in the long story of the region. It is a story of trade, conquest, and the fight for riches.

Early History

Humans had lived throughout South America for at least 11,000 years. The first people may have come from the north, crossing the Isthmus of Panama before spreading through the continent. As they settled in different areas, they adapted to their environments. Some became hunter-gatherers, like the Pampa, who gave their name to the grasslands they roamed. Others farmed the highlands of the Andes. In the mountain valleys and plateaus they built villages, and in time, empires.

For thousands of years, civilizations had been developing in the Andes. Some societies adapted to the dry coastal deserts while others flourished high in the mountains. Native American communities grew different kinds of food at different altitudes. Trade routes helped distribute food. Fish from coastal settlements were traded for potatoes grown at higher levels.

In the 1400s, one Native American group, the Inca, began building a huge empire in the Andes. This empire was the largest in the Americas. It included the city of Machu Picchu, built high in the mountains. Many scholars believe it was a retreat for Inca rulers, but others think that this cultural center may have been used for religious purposes or as part of a trade network. The Inca was worshipped as a god. He ruled over a highly organized and productive society.

Reading Check **How did trade help early Andean societies survive?**

Closer Look   THE INCAS

The Incan empire stretched from what is now Ecuador to central Chile. Paved roads tied the empire together. Careful agricultural practices ensured a plentiful food supply.

THINK CRITICALLY **How did Incan organization keep the empire running smoothly?**

The Incan Empire in 1532

Machu Picchu

Cuzco

SOUTH AMERICA

PACIFIC OCEAN

ATLANTIC OCEAN

KEY

Incan Empire

Incan gold and silver attracted the Spanish. ▶

The Incas built many cities in remote places, such as Machu Picchu, shown here.

my worldgeography.com   Culture Close-up

321

The Colonial Period

In 1532, a Spanish soldier named Francisco Pizarro (frahn SEES koh pea SAHR oh) led 180 men into the Andean highlands in search of the Incas. He hoped to conquer their gold-rich empire.

Europeans Arrive The element of surprise was a key part of the Spanish plan. When Pizarro reached the Incan highlands, he tricked the Inca, Atahualpa (ah tuh WAHL puh), into visiting his camp. In a daring attack, the Spanish captured the Inca and later killed him in front of his people.

Although the Incas fought the invaders for <u>decades</u>, the conquistadors had several advantages. Their cavalry moved quickly in a land where no one had ever seen a horse. They also had deadlier weapons, such as steel swords and cannons. But the most powerful weapon that weakened the

decade, *n.,* a period of ten years

Incas was invisible. The people of South America had no **immunity,** or natural defense, against European diseases. Under these attacks, the mighty Incan Empire soon crumbled.

The Spanish divided the conquered lands into areas governed by viceroys. These viceroys ruled for Spain's king and queen. Spain's Roman Catholic Church worked to convert native peoples to Christianity. Meanwhile, the Spanish moved Native Americans from their homes and forced them to work. To expand this pool of workers, the Spanish imported enslaved people from Africa.

As the resources of the Andes created wealth for the Spanish Empire, a class system developed based on race. The Spanish who had been born in Spain, called peninsulares, were the ruling class. Spaniards born in the Americas were called **criollos**. The children of Spanish men who married indigenous women were called **mestizos**—of mixed race. At the bottom of society were Native Americans and enslaved Africans. As a result of disease and terrible working conditions, the indigenous population dropped by 90 percent by the end of the 1500s.

The Road to Revolution Spain kept a grip on the region's economy, which depended on exports to Europe. Resources such as gold and silver were shipped through the dazzling colonial capital of Lima, in what is now Peru. South American crops were also exported, including sugar and cacao.

The colonies were expected to trade only with Spain and not with one another.

Spanish conquistador ▶

Manufacturing was also discouraged. This was to make sure that Spanish colonists bought manufactured products only from Spain.

Wealth was unevenly distributed in the colonies. A small number of people owned most of the land. In addition, the peninsulares would not share political power with the criollos.

The criollos believed that Spanish control limited their economies. People were also inspired by the American and French revolutions. As Spain grew weaker from war with France, many in the Spanish colonies began preparing for rebellion.

When the fight for independence began in Venezuela in 1810, Simón Bolívar (see MOHN boh LEE vahr) emerged as military leader of the rebel-lion. For the next 20 years, Bolívar slowly <u>liberated</u> countries in the north of South America.

Meanwhile, in the south, Spain struggled to defeat another rebellion. There, José de San Martín (hoh SAY deh sahn marhr TEEN) fought for Argentina's independence. He knew that Spain would try to win back Argentina, as long as Spanish forces remained in South America. So San Martín took an army over the Andes to defeat Spanish forces in Chile. After San Martín rode north to liberate Lima, Peru, Bolívar went south to defeat the remaining royalist forces. The battle of Ayacucho in 1824 freed Peru. This was the last major battle in the fight for independence from Spain.

Reading Check **Why did the Spanish colonies rebel?**

liberate, *v.,* to free

Mercantilism

In colonial times, Spain set up the economic system of **mercantilism**. In this system, raw materials were sent to the mother country. In return, colonists were expected to buy Spanish products. *Who benefited most from this arrangement?*

myWorld Activity
Identity Game

❸ Ships set out from the Caribbean in a convoy to protect the treasure fleet from pirates.

Spain

❹ Ships returned with Spanish exports.

❷ The silver was carried over the Isthmus of Panama to the Caribbean.

Potosí

❶ Potosí, where Omar works today, was the world's greatest source of silver. The silver was sent to Spain via Panama.

South America after Independence

When José de San Martín retired from political life he warned the Peruvian Congress of dangers ahead:

> 66 The presence of a successful soldier . . . is dangerous to the States that have just been [created]. 99
>
> —José de San Martín

As San Martín predicted, military men soon seized control of the new nations.

From Instability to Export Boom The new countries were politically unstable. There was a wide economic gulf between rich and poor, with few people in the middle. The landowning criollos formed an **oligarchy,** a small group that holds political power. They made sure that other ethnic groups were not even allowed to vote. Caudillos, or strong men, took control of governments.

In Argentina, the gauchos, or cowboys, supported a caudillo named Juan Manuel de Rosas. In 1833 Rosas forced Native Americans from the southern Pampas and helped establish ranching there.

The new countries had weak economies. Most produced only a few exports, such as coffee or copper. If the market for one of these exports weakened, the country suffered.

However, starting around 1870 the nations of the "Southern Cone," Argentina, Paraguay, Uruguay, and Chile, began exporting more food to Europe and the United States. Immigrants from Italy and Spain arrived to take part in the boom. The location of resources influenced migration in other Andean nations as well. In the late 1800s Peruvian sugar plantations and mines attracted Asian immigrants from China and Japan.

Not everyone benefited from the export boom. Most remained poor. As a result of a war that began in 1879, Bolivia lost its mineral-rich coastline. Because of this, Bolivia could not participate in overseas trade. Today Bolivia is the poorest nation in the region.

Industrialization and Dictatorships In the early 1900s, the export boom ended and economies suffered. People in the region regretted becoming so dependent on exports. Now their goal was to make

Buenos Aires grew to resemble European cities such as Paris. ▼

the products that had previously been imported. So governments encouraged industrialization as a way of becoming economically independent.

Industrialization caused a population shift, as people migrated from the countryside to the cities. It also brought about political changes.

By the 1930s there were so many urban workers that they became a political force. They elected leaders such as Juan Perón of Argentina. Perón called for social justice, as well as economic independence from foreign powers. In 1970, in Chile, Salvador Allende (SAL vuh dawr ah YEN day) was also elected by appealing to workers and the poor. Peron and Allende nationalized industry and promised to redistribute land. In both countries, these changes caused fears that elected leaders were drifting towards communist policies. This fear sparked a terrifying reaction.

In 1973, military leaders overthrew Chile's President Allende. The military ended free speech and murdered tens of thousands of its opponents. A few years later in Argentina, the military seized control from President Peron. The military government murdered more than 10,000 Argentine citizens. Many people disappeared into secret prisons and torture centers and were never seen again. The mothers of some of those who had disappeared began holding weekly protests in Buenos Aires.

By the 1980s, people throughout the region were tired of military control. In Argentina the government tried to remain popular by starting a war to unite the country. Troops invaded the nearby Falkland Islands, which were claimed by Great Britain. When Argentina was defeated, the military lost face and fell from power. In Argentina, as in other nations of the region, democracy returned.

Democracy's revival did not solve all the region's problems. In the next section you will read how governments today are dealing with the legacy of the past.

Reading Check Why did governments encourage industrialization?

▲ Juan Peron's wife, Eva Peron, or "Evita," helped gain voting rights for women.

Section 2 Assessment

Key Terms

1. Use the following key terms to explain important events in the region's history: immunity, criollo, mestizo, mercantilism, oligarchy.

Key Ideas

2. How did Europeans change the physical and human geography of the region?

3. What resources made Spain so rich?

4. What changes were brought about by industrialization?

Think Critically

5. **Draw Conclusions** Why did Spain's colonial system lead to revolution?

6. **Draw Inferences** Why was reliance on exports bad for the region's economy?

Essential Question

What are the challenges of diversity?

7. How has the history of the region contributed to its ethnic diversity? Go to your Student Journal to record your answer.

The Incas

IN Indiana

6.1.1 Summarize the rise, decline, and cultural achievements of ancient civilizations in Europe and Mesoamerica.

6.1.21 Differentiate between fact and interpretation in historical accounts and explain historical passages.

6.1.23 Identify issues related to an event in Europe or the Americas and give arguments for and against that issue.

Various primary sources describe the Incan empire and its over-throw by Spanish invaders. In *Chronicles of the Incas*, Pedro de Cieza de León explains how the Incas organized their society. Sources like this are important because they provide eyewitness accounts of Incan life.

In *Letter to a King*, Huamán Poma records the events of the Spanish conquest. He describes the dramatic moment when the Spanish leaders Francisco Pizarro and Diego de Almagro captured the Inca Atahualpa.

▲ Incan gold figure

Two Incas discuss a quipu. ▼

Read the text on the right. Stop at each circled letter. Then answer the question with the same letter on the left.

A **Analyze Primary Sources** How did the Incas keep records?

B **Summarize** Why did the Inca rulers want this information?

C **Draw Conclusions** What does this excerpt tell you about Incan social organization?

quipu, *n.,* an Incan recording device made of knotted strings

Chronicles of the Incas

66 At the beginning of the new year the rulers of each village came to Cuzco [the Incan capital], bringing **A** their <u>quipus</u>, which told how many births there had been during the year, and how many deaths. In this way the Inca and the governors knew which of the Indians were poor, the women who had been widowed, whether they were able to pay their taxes, and how many men they could count on in the **B** event of war, and many other things **C** they considered highly important. 99

—Pedro de Cieza de León, *Chronicles of the Incas,* 1540

DEPOCITODELINGA COLL CA

Read the text on the right. Stop at each circled letter. Then answer the question with the same letter on the left.

D **Identify Main Ideas and Details** How did the Spanish justify their attack?

E **Summarize** Why were the Incas terrified of the Spanish?

F **Draw Conclusions** Why did the Spanish take Atahualpa prisoner?

musket, *n.,* an early type of gun

novelty, *n.,* something new or unusual

headlong, *adj.,* impulsive; rushed

Letter to a King

66 Pizarro and Almagro began to shout orders to their men, telling them to attack these Indians who rejected **D** God and the Emperor. The Spaniards began to fire their <u>muskets</u> and charged upon the Indians, killing them like ants. At the sound of the explosions and the jingle of bells on the horses' harness, the shock of arms and the whole amazing <u>novelty</u> of their attackers' appearance, the **E** Indians were terror-stricken. . . . They were desperate to escape from being trampled by the horses and in their <u>headlong</u> flight a lot of them were crushed to death. . . . Atahualpa Inca was pulled down from his throne without injury and became the prisoner of Pizarro and **F** Almagro.99

—Huamán Poma,
Letter to a King, about 1615

▲ An artist's idea of the attack on the Inca

Analyze the Documents

1. **Synthesize** Why might the capture of Atahualpa have been a mortal blow to the empire?
2. **Writing Task** How do you think the Spanish managed to conquer the Incan empire so easily? Explain your thinking.

Incan farmers sculpted the hillsides into terraces. ▼

The Andes and the Pampas Today

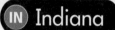 Indiana

6.2.7 Define and compare citizenship and the citizen's role throughout history in Europe and the Americas.

6.3.4 Describe and compare major cultural characteristics of regions in Europe and the Western Hemisphere.

6.4.2 Analyze how countries of Europe and the Americas have been influenced by trade in different historical periods.

6.4.6 Analyze current economic issues in the countries of Europe or the Americas using a variety of resources.

Key Terms • diversified economy • MERCOSUR • literacy • referendum • amend

→ **Visual Glossary**

Reading Skill: Summarize Take notes using the graphic organizer in your journal.

my Story 📷 **Photo**

Omar leaving the mine

O mar's Potosí is a town that has seen better days. Its poor narrow streets are a far cry from the wide elegant avenues of Buenos Aires, on the other side of the continent. If Omar traveled to that great city he would see a much wider range of wealth. However, he would still be able to speak the same language and recognize many of the city's customs and traditions.

The region in which he lives is a land of extremes. There is a wide range of income and a variety of climates and landforms. Great distances and obstacles divide communities. However, the nations of the Andes and the Pampas share a history and culture. Throughout the region, people struggle with similar problems and issues.

A Rich Culture

Much of the region's culture is based on the legacy of two groups, the Europeans and the Native Americans. In some places these cultures have merged. In Chile, for example, much of the population is mixed race. In other places, such as Argentina and Uruguay, European culture is very strong. European influences in these two countries produced new musical and dance forms, such as the tango.

Throughout the region there is a strong connection between landscape and culture. On the Pampas, the gaucho became the symbol of independent life. Meanwhile, in the distant Andes, a haunting music developed that combined Spanish stringed instruments with the ancient music of Native Americans.

The Spanish Inheritance Despite the ethnic diversity of the region, Spanish language and culture still dominate. The Catholic religion, as well as Spanish-style architecture, art, and dance can be found through most of the region today.

The Indigenous Revival A large population of mestizos and indigenous people influences culture in the Andes. Although native populations dropped dramatically over the centuries, today the textiles, music, and many languages of indigenous cultures have survived. In Bolivia, Peru, Ecuador, Chile, and Paraguay, people continue to follow traditional ways of life, such as raising llamas and alpacas for their wool.

In fact, native cultures in the Andes are reviving. Indigenous groups have also found new political power. The 2006 election of Bolivia's president, Evo Morales, brought <u>significant</u> change to the region. Morales is the first Native American to rule his country for 500 years. President Morales set about restoring indigenous peoples' rights. He redistributed income from Bolivia's natural gas industry to the poor. His actions are opposed by many people in the eastern regions of Bolivia. However, political events in Bolivia have strengthened Native American movements throughout South America.

significant, *adj.,* important

Reading Check How would you describe the culture of the Andes and the Pampas?

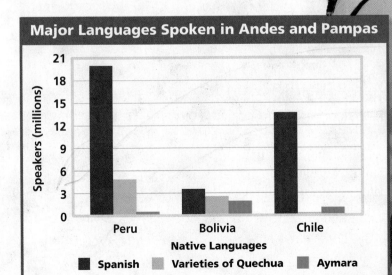

▼ Spanish speaker

▼ Quechua speaker

Major Languages Spoken in Andes and Pampas

Speakers (millions)

Peru   Bolivia   Chile

Native Languages

■ Spanish   ■ Varieties of Quechua   ■ Aymara

SOURCE: www.Ethnologue.com

Chart Skills

Which country has the highest percentage of speakers of Native American languages?

→ Data Discovery

Environmental Problems

Deforestation, the destruction of forests, is one of the major environmental problems of this region. The region's tropical rain forests include the Valdivian Forest in Chile. This forest is being destroyed at an alarming rate. In Peru, logging and gold mining are also damaging the tropical forest environment. In their search for gold, mining companies use heavy machinery to remove riverbanks and cut down forests.

Projects intended to boost an area's economy often threaten the environment. In Peru a road project is underway to connect the country's Pacific ports to a highway in Brazil. The highway will benefit the economy because it will increase commerce, or trade. But environmentalists argue that it will also attract more logging operations to the area.

Meanwhile, car exhaust in urban areas is a growing problem. Cities throughout the region are suffering from air pollution. In Santiago, Chile, smog forms as a steady upper layer of warm air traps cooler air close to the ground. Because of this, the exhaust from 600,000 vehicles cannot escape. These fumes are affecting health: hospitals report an increase in the number of children with breathing problems. Several attempts to reduce air pollution in Santiago have failed.

In Ecuador, oil pollution is damaging both rain forests and farmland. Waste from oil drilling seeps into water supplies and rivers. Cancer rates are unusually high in oil-polluted areas. Many suspect that there is a link between pollution and health problems.

Reading Check What environmental problems affect the Andes and the Pampas?

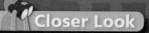

Closer Look

GLOBALIZATION AND the Environment

Economic globalization, the increase in world trade, is changing the scale of production in the region. Small farms are giving way to large commercial operations. Huge ships are dragging vast fishing nets through the seas. As human activities alter landscapes and ecosystems, people are debating the issue, using arguments like the ones on these pages.

THINK CRITICALLY Which point of view do you support?

Against Globalization

Chilean fishers protesting trawlers.

A fishing trawler unloads its catch.

- In Argentina, global demand for soybeans is turning forests and grasslands into cropland.
- Overfishing is reducing fish stocks in Peruvian waters.

Regional Economies

In general, the Southern Cone nations of Argentina, Chile, and Uruguay are the richest nations in the region. Paraguay and the Andean nations of Ecuador, Peru, and Bolivia are the poorest.

There are many obstacles to economic growth. For example, after the War of the Pacific in 1879, Bolivia lost its coastline and its access to overseas trade. Bolivia's economy has suffered ever since. Tariffs also are barriers to trade. However, today the nations of the region are overcoming these barriers.

Economic Growth Several countries now have more **diversified economies**—economies that depend on a range of exports or products. Today foreign <u>corporations</u> are investing in mining, petrochemicals, and transportation.

Tropical crops such as coffee, cacao, bananas, plantains (a kind of banana), and sugar cane are exported from Peru, Ecuador, and Bolivia. Countries with temperate climates such as Argentina, Chile, Paraguay, and Uruguay produce wheat, corn, grapes, apples, and pears.

Countries in the region are also strengthening economic ties with each other. A free-trade agreement was signed in 1991 by Brazil, Argentina, Uruguay, and Paraguay to form **MERCOSUR**, a trading bloc of South American countries. MERCOSUR is short for "Mercado Común del Sur," or Southern Common Market. Like the European Union, this trading bloc allows goods to be traded among its member countries without tariffs. Its goal is to allow goods, services, and people to move freely among its member states. The organization hopes

corporation, *n.,* company

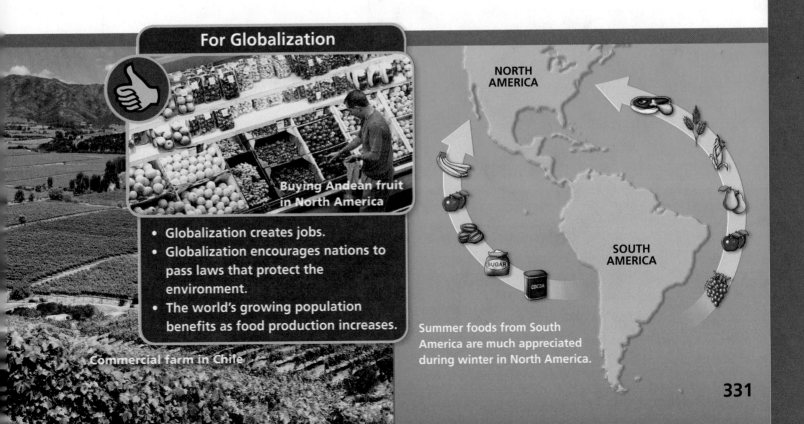

For Globalization

Buying Andean fruit in North America

- Globalization creates jobs.
- Globalization encourages nations to pass laws that protect the environment.
- The world's growing population benefits as food production increases.

Commercial farm in Chile

NORTH AMERICA

SOUTH AMERICA

Summer foods from South America are much appreciated during winter in North America.

331

to one day expand its free-trade zone to include all of South America.

The Andean Community of Nations is a similar trading agreement among Bolivia, Colombia, Ecuador, and Peru. It also recognizes members of MERCOSUR as associate members. In 2003, the U.S.-Chile Free Trade Agreement was signed. Within two years, trading obstacles were eliminated and Chile's productivity increased.

Argentina's economy is stronger than many of the Andean nations' economies. However, Argentina has suffered from the recent economic downturn.

Preparing for the Future Governments prepare for the economic future by investing in the education and health of their people. For example, Chile, where the government funds education, has high levels of **literacy**—the ability to read and write. In fact, most countries in the region have a literacy rate of more than 90 percent. The Andean nations of Peru and Bolivia have slightly lower rates.

To help combat poverty in the region, a new regional bank has been set up. The Banco del Sur, or Southern Bank, will fund economic and social projects. It will also support scientific projects.

Reading Check Which are the richer and the poorer nations in the Andes and the Pampas?

Trading Blocs in the Andes and the Pampas

KEY
- MERCOSUR
- Andean Community of Nations

South American Trade, 1999–2007

■ MERCOSUR ■ Andean Community of Nations

SOURCE: www.comunidadandina.org

Chart Skills

Which trading bloc exports more goods?

→ **Data Discovery**

The New Governments

Democracy has returned to the region today, and governments are working to protect civil rights. In Argentina, the people are determined that the time of terror will never return. In the words of Argentine writer Ernesto Sabato,

> 66 It is only democracy that can save a people from horror on this scale. 99
>
> —Ernesto Sabato

In Peru, democracy was strengthened when Alberto Fujimori, a former president, was charged with corruption and abuse of human rights, and sent to prison.

The nations of the Andes and the Pampas are once again democracies. Like the United States, they have constitutions and three branches of government (executive, legislative, and judicial).

In some democracies, voters decide whether a new constitution is to be accepted. This is done by **referendum**—people voting to reject or accept a law. Chile's return to democracy in 1990 was triggered by the 1989 referendum when Chile's citizens voted to **amend,** or make changes to, the constitution.

In Bolivia, the people have elected Evo Morales. President Morales is a Native American who champions social movements. However, the country remains divided—the poorer highland population supports the president while the richer lowland areas resist his policies.

Although such political tensions and social inequalities persist, the nations of the region are continuing a process of economic integration. The strengthening of democracy and closer economic ties are good signs for the future.

Reading Check What signs suggest that democracy is strengthening in the region?

myWorld Activity
Propaganda Poster

Bolivia's President Evo Morales greets supporters at his inauguration. ▶

Section 3 Assessment

Key Terms

1. Use the following terms to describe life in the region today: diversified economy, MERCOSUR, literacy, referendum, amend.

Key Ideas

2. What cultural features help unify the region?

3. What slows economic growth in the region?

4. What form of government followed military rule in Argentina?

Think Critically

5. **Synthesize** What is the link between environmental problems and global consumer demand?

6. **Draw Conclusions** What factors might explain poverty in the region?

Essential Question

What are the challenges of diversity?

7. In what ways have nations in the region tried to diversify their economies? Go to your Student Journal to record your answer.

Bolivia: A Divided Nation

IN Indiana

6.1.22 Form research questions and use resources to present data on people, cultures and developments in Europe and the Americas.

6.2.5 Discuss the impact of major forms of government in Europe and the Americas on civil and human rights.

Key Terms • peasant • land reform • autonomy

Bolivia is a large and diverse country. The highland Andes make up the western part. Lowland plains lie to the east. Bolivia's population is diverse too. Its people are a mixture of Native American and European ancestry. This mixture produces a rich culture. But ethnic differences also divide Bolivia. They help create social and economic inequality. This problem can be traced back to centuries of Spanish colonial rule.

Roots of Inequality

Spain conquered the area we now call Bolivia in the 1530s. The Spanish mined rich deposits of silver. They also created large landed estates, called haciendas. Bolivia's natural wealth brought great riches to Spain.

Class System The Spanish set up a class system based on ethnicity. Colonists who had been born in Spain occupied the top level of society. They controlled most of the wealth and all of the political power. Under them were ranked criollos (people of Spanish ancestry born in the Americas) and mestizos (people of mixed European and Native American ancestry). At the bottom were the Native American peoples, mostly Quechua and Aymara.

Although Native Americans made up the vast majority, they had almost no rights. They were forced to work on haciendas and in mines such as the famous silver mine at Potosí. They suffered from poverty and discrimination. They received no education or other social benefits.

Bolivia won independence in 1825, but for the majority of the population very little changed. Military dictators took power in violent takeovers. They ruled for their own personal gain. Society remained unequal, with criollos at the top and native peoples at the bottom.

Bolivian mestizo couple of the 1700s ▼

Economically, Bolivia remained poor and unstable. Prosperity did not come to the new nation. The mines slowly produced less silver. Towns such as Potosí, which had once been wealthy, began to slide into poverty. As the result of a war, Bolivia lost its coastline. This meant that Bolivia lost its ability to trade by ship with other nations.

Native Americans formed a huge class of **peasants,** or poor farmers who farmed small plots of land. The new country had few exports and very little trade. Because of this, the Bolivian government had to rely on money raised by taxing the peasants. This only increased the poverty in the land.

Land Reform In 1952 a group of reformers staged a successful revolution. The new government began to make changes. It brought benefits to the poor. It gave Native Americans the right to vote and provided rural education. It also began a **land reform** program to redistribute land. It broke up haciendas and gave the land to poor farmers. The government also nationalized the three largest tin-mining companies.

Military leaders took power again in the 1960s. The reform period came to an end. But poor Bolivians never forgot the gains they had made.

Reading Check How did colonial rulers create an unequal society?

The mountain known as Cerro Rico at Potosí, site of an important colonial silver mine ▼

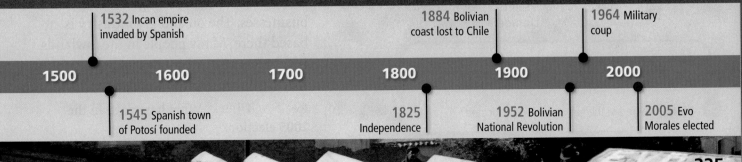

Bolivian History

1532 Incan empire invaded by Spanish

1884 Bolivian coast lost to Chile

1964 Military coup

1500	1600	1700	1800	1900	2000

1545 Spanish town of Potosí founded

1825 Independence

1952 Bolivian National Revolution

2005 Evo Morales elected

335

A Divided Society

Most of the indigenous population lives in the Andean highlands (to the west). Gas and oil resources are located in the eastern lowlands, where many people of Spanish ancestry live.

Bolivian Resources

KEY
- Gas field
- Mine
- Oil field
- National border
- Department border

0   200 mi
0   200 km

Lambert Conformal Conic Projection

Pando

Beni

La Paz

BOLIVIA

Cochabamba

Santa Cruz

Oruro

Chuquisaca

Potosí

Tarija

Bolivia Election Results

★ La Paz

★ Sucre

- MAS majority
- Podemos majority

In the election of 2005, the poorer peoples of the west supported Morales and his MAS party (Movimiento al Socialismo, "Movement toward Socialism"). The richer population in the east voted against Morales by supporting Podemos (Poder Democrático y Social, "Social and Democratic Power").

Map Skills

1. **Place** Compare the maps. What divisions do you see?

2. **Place** Where are the gas and oil fields located?

Indigenous Revival

In the 1980s, Bolivia finally returned to civilian rule. Bolivians who were indigenous, or native to the region, began to demand their rights. Many Bolivians became aware of their country's native heritage. As one mestizo student said, "We realize that these are *our* cultural roots and that they are something to be proud of."

Election of Evo Morales In 2005 Bolivia elected its first indigenous head of state since the Spanish Conquest—Evo Morales. President Morales won 54 percent of the vote. Other Native Americans won seats in congress. Morales took office in a ceremony rich in Quechua and Aymara traditions. He made native rights and culture a high priority. He also appointed various native officials to his cabinet.

After his election, President Morales also called for a new constitution. This document declared all of Bolivia's native tongues to be official languages.

Divided Opinions These changes were popular among Native Americans in the country's western highlands. But they were not popular among Bolivians in the eastern lowlands. The lowlands include the richest part of the country. They are home to the country's largest farms and businesses. The oil and gas industry is based there. Many people in the lowlands felt threatened by Morales's government, which favored higher taxes on the rich.

Reading Check What happened in the 2005 election?

Bolivia Today

As president, Morales worked to bring changes to Bolivia. He vowed to reduce poverty and discrimination. He helped give native communities, called ayllus, a voice in government. Morales also placed the country's energy resources under national control. Previously, foreign companies controlled Bolivia's oil and gas fields.

In response to these changes, protests broke out in the eastern plains. Leaders there said that the government did not represent their interests. They feared it would take away their rights. They called for local **autonomy**—the right to make their own political decisions. So four of Bolivia's wealthier provinces held referenda, or voted, in support of more political independence from the government. However, the government refused to recognize the results of these referenda.

This regional conflict divided Bolivia. It raised new threats to the country's stability. In August 2008 there was violence in the lowland city of Santa Cruz as people protested against the reforms of President Morales.

However, in early 2009 Bolivians voted on the new constitution, which permits land reform and gives more power to the Native American majority. The constitution also grants the president the right to a second term in office. Although 61 percent of voters approved the constitution, it was rejected by voters in the lowlands. It seems that Bolivia is still a land divided by geography, resources, and race.

▲ Bolivians celebrate after voters approved the new constitution.

Reading Check Why did many easterners oppose the new government?

Assessment

1. How did the colonial class system cause inequality in Bolivia?

2. What effects did the 1952 revolution have on Native American rights?

3. Why was the 2005 election important?

4. What current issues divide Bolivia?

5. What changes did the 2009 constitution introduce?

Chapter Assessment

Key Terms and Ideas

1. **Discuss** How has physical geography determined settlement patterns?

2. **Explain** How does **El Niño** affect climate?

3. **Summarize** How did Spain benefit from **mercantilism**?

4. **Explain** For what economic reasons did the Spanish colonies rebel against Spain?

5. **Summarize** Why have countries tried to achieve **diversified economies**?

6. **Cause and Effect** What effect has globalization had on the region?

7. **Recall** Why are nations in South America forming trading blocs?

Think Critically

8. **Analyze Information** What factors play a divisive role in this region?

9. **Identify Evidence** How have this region's resources affected its history? Support your answer with evidence from the chapter.

10. **Draw Conclusions** What modern problems in this region can be traced back to colonial times?

11. **Core Concepts: Migration** How have human migrations changed settlement patterns in the region?

Places to Know

For each place, write the letter from the map that shows its location.

12. **Andes**

13. **Atacama Desert**

14. **Rio de la Plata**

15. **Santiago**

16. **Pampas**

17. **Buenos Aires**

18. **Estimate** Using the scale, estimate the distance between Buenos Aires and Santiago.

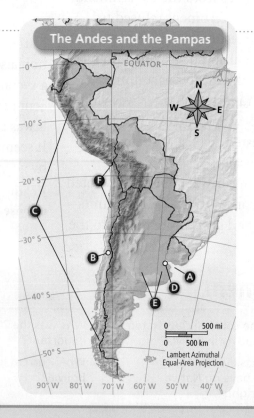

The Andes and the Pampas

Essential Question
myWorld Chapter Activity

Grant Report Follow your teacher's instructions to study problems faced by each country in the region. Review photographs and information about each topic. Then meet with your team and decide what kind of grant to recommend for your country before writing your recommendation.

21st Century Learning
Give an Effective Presentation

With a partner, look back over the chapter and choose a landform that has been important in the region's history. Work together to develop a presentation on the importance of this landform. Make a checklist to evaluate each other's performance: maintain good posture, pause at important points, and use expressive body language.

Document-Based Questions

Success Tracker™
Online at myworldgeography.com

Use your knowledge of the Andes and the Pampas and Documents A and B to answer questions 1–3.

Document A

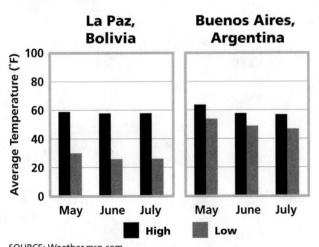

SOURCE: Weather.msn.com

Document B

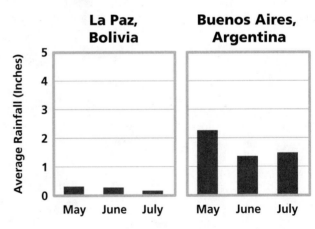

SOURCE: Weather.msn.com

1. What does document A tell you about the difference between the climates of La Paz and Buenos Aires in May, June, and July?

   A La Paz is much hotter than Buenos Aires.

   B Buenos Aires is hotter than La Paz.

   C Temperatures in La Paz vary more than temperatures in Buenos Aires.

   D Buenos Aires is much colder than La Paz.

2. Document B shows that in May, June, and July

   A La Paz is wetter than Buenos Aires.

   B Buenos Aires is wetter than La Paz.

   C La Paz receives no rain.

   D Buenos Aires receives no rain.

3. **Writing Task** Explain what the two documents tell you about the climate in the region.

myworldgeography.com | Self-Test

Chapter 7

Brazil

Who should benefit from a country's resources?

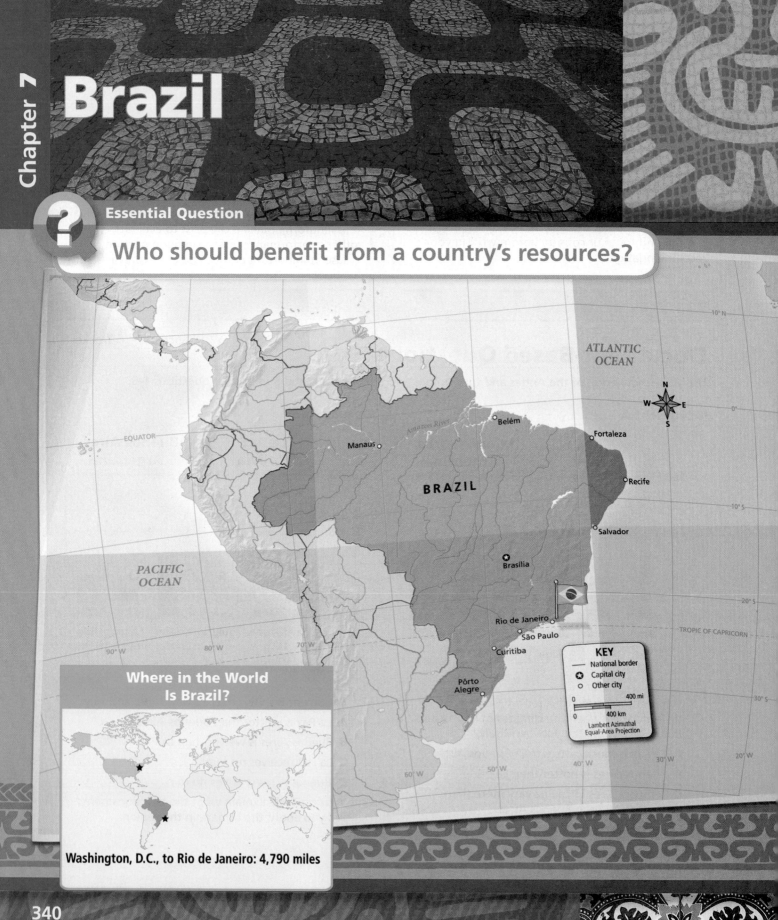

ATLANTIC OCEAN

Belém

Fortaleza

EQUATOR

Manaus

Amazon River

Recife

BRAZIL

Salvador

PACIFIC OCEAN

★ Brasília

Rio de Janeiro

São Paulo

Curitiba

TROPIC OF CAPRICORN

Pôrto Alegre

KEY

— National border
★ Capital city
○ Other city

| 0 | 400 mi |
| 0 | 400 km |

Lambert Azimuthal
Equal-Area Projection

Where in the World Is Brazil?

Washington, D.C., to Rio de Janeiro: 4,790 miles

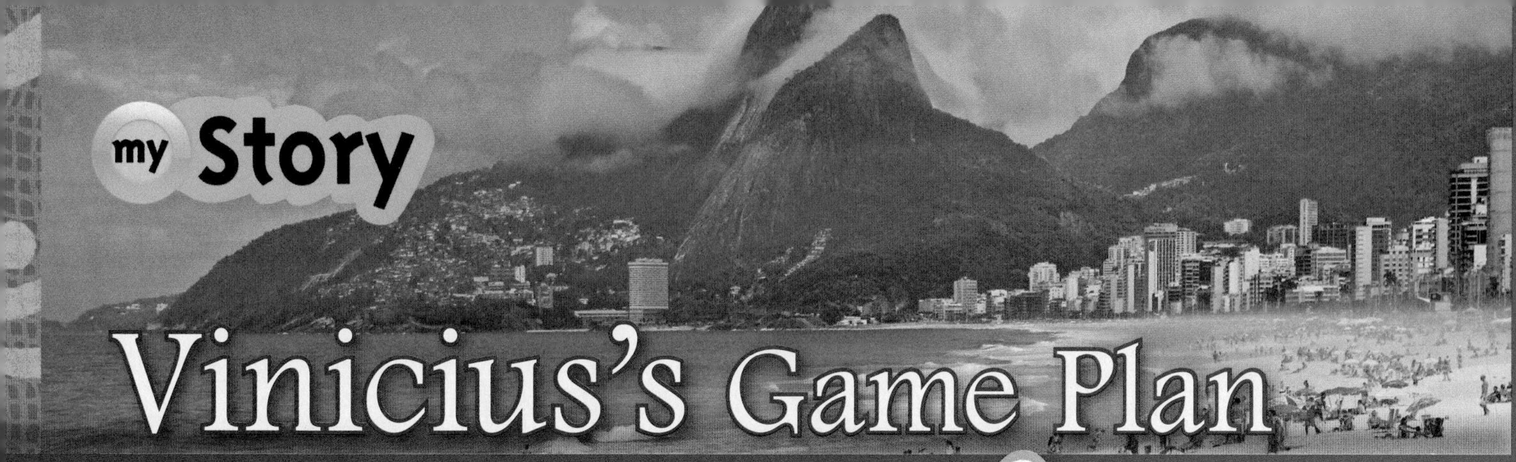

my Story

Vinicius's Game Plan

Explore the Essential Question

- at my worldgeography.com
- using the **myWorld Chapter Activity**
- with the **Student Journal**

In this section you'll read about Vinicius, a young Brazilian soccer player who hopes that success in sports will lead to a better life for him and his family. What does Vinicius's story tell you about life in Brazil?

Story by Bindu Mathur for myWorld Geography Online

It's a loud and thrilling Sunday afternoon at Maracanã Stadium in Rio de Janeiro, Brazil. Maracanã is the biggest soccer stadium in South America, and forty thousand fans are cheering for Flamengo, the most popular team in Brazil.

Flamengo is ahead by three goals, and the crowd has gone wild. The team's supporters are cheering, singing, and dancing to the traditional beats of the Brazilian samba. Dressed in their team's colors, they fill the stands with a loud and rippling sea of red and black.

But in the midst of all this excitement, one 16-year-old Flamengo supporter stays quiet. Vinicius is too busy studying the players' techniques. That's because for Vinicius soccer is not just a game—it's a passport to a better life for him and his family.

Two years ago, Vinicius was selected from thousands of young hopefuls to play for Flamengo's youth division. This was the first step in a process that might lead to a

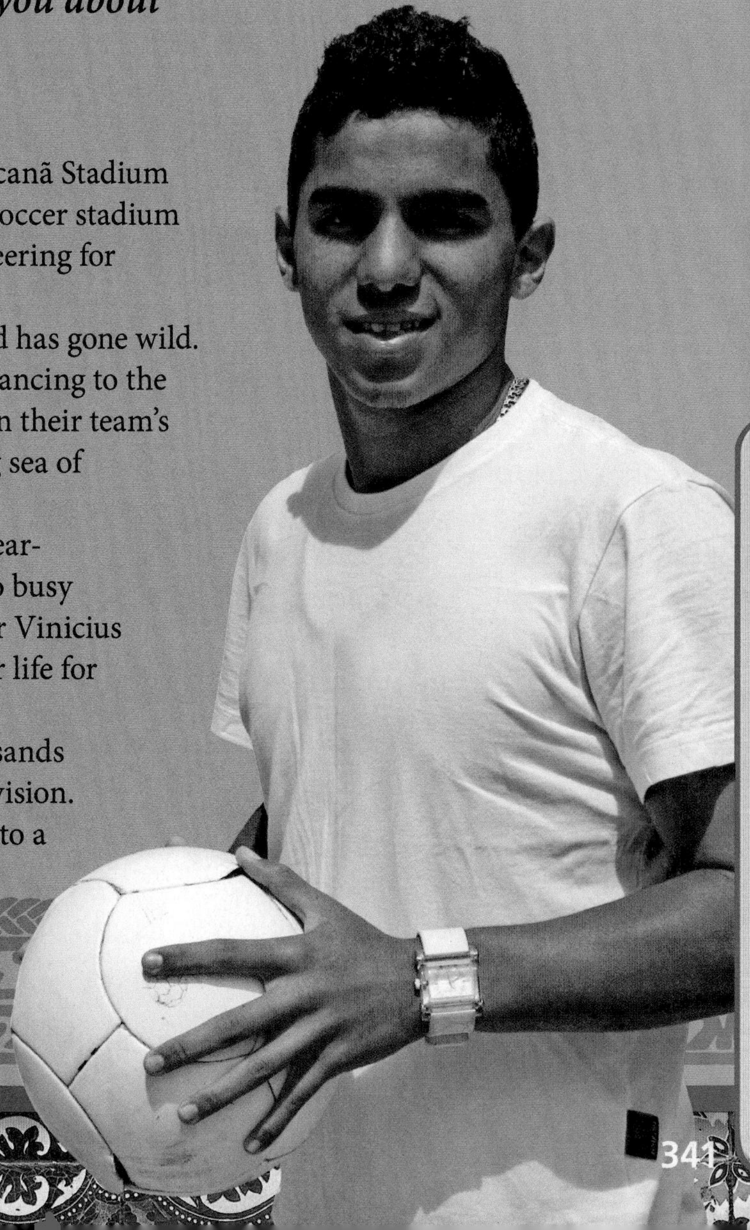

Vinicius captures the spectacular landscape of Rio de Janeiro.

Vinicius strolls down the beach during his free time.

professional contract. Playing for the Flamengo team could make Vinicius a star.

Vinicius says, "It's so exciting to come to the stadium and see the professionals on the field, because I hope that will be me in the future, playing for a huge cheering crowd shouting my name. It is my ultimate dream!"

The next day, the whistle blows at the Flamengo training facility near Rio. Forty boys age 14 to 17 dressed in red and black uniforms are running drills with a coach. Vinicius is there, the only player with a Mohawk hairstyle, taking up his position as a forward on the team.

These boys were selected from all over Brazil, and here they undergo a rigorous training routine. For six days a week, physical exercise begins at seven o'clock in the morning and is followed by soccer training. Then there's time for a traditional lunch of arroz feijão (rice with black beans) and rest until the next day's practice.

For Vinicius, pursuing his dream has meant sacrifice. He moved far from his hometown of Belém, more than 1,500 miles north of Rio de Janeiro. Belém is located in the huge Amazon rain forest. He left behind his mother, who works as a secretary, and his father, a math teacher.

Vinicius loves the rain forest and regrets its ongoing destruction. "There are many green areas, trees, and rivers. But people are destroying it. There are trees that are over a hundred years old, but people are cutting the trees for wood and also polluting the rivers."

His new life away from home has not been easy. In the southeastern city of Rio de Janeiro, Vinicius has faced prejudice against people from the North, which is a poor region. "Some people called me names when I first arrived. It was upsetting," he explains. "And I really miss my family. I have cried several times, but I remember that I am here hoping to give them a better life."

Brazil is a country with widespread poverty and a huge gap between rich and poor. For young people from poorer families, success at sports is one of the few ways to achieve a more comfortable life.

For now, Rio will be his home as he waits to find out whether he will advance to the next level of the Flamengo youth team. Rio is world famous for its beaches and tourist attractions, but Vinicius doesn't

A typical Brazilian meal of chicken, rice, and black beans

Vinicius shows off some fancy footwork at training.

Flamengo supporters gather outside the stadium.

get much time to see the sights. When he's not busy training, he goes to night classes to complete his high school diploma so he can enter a university.

"Some players do sign a professional contract, but there are those who don't succeed, or who get injured, so I think it is important to have a 'Plan B.' I am thinking of studying physical education at university," he says.

Back on the soccer field, the head coach announces the selections for the following year. Some of the boys put on a brave face when they discover they haven't made the list.

But Vinicius has a big smile. Although he has not been offered a professional contract, he's been invited back for another year on the youth team and is one step closer to his dream.

"If I become professional one day, it will be worth all of this sacrifice of being far from home," he grins.

myStory Online

Join Vinicius as he shows you more about his life in Rio.

Meet the Journalist

Name Bindu Mathur
Favorite Moment Watching Vinicius's reactions to the game in Maracanā stadium.

343

 **Indiana**

6.3.1 Understand the countries and capitals of Europe and the Americas.

6.3.3 Describe and compare major physical characteristics of regions in Europe and the Americas.

6.3.7 Locate and describe the climate regions of Europe and the Americas and explain how and why they differ.

6.3.8 Identify major biomes of Europe and the Americas and explain how these are influenced by climate.

6.3.14 Explain how nature has impacted the physical environment and human populations in areas of Europe and the Americas.

Visual Glossary

Key Terms • Amazon basin • savanna • canopy • favela

 Reading Skill: Label an Outline Map Take notes using the outline map in your journal.

◀ View of Sugar Loaf Mountain and Rio de Janeiro

Boy practicing capoeira, the Brazilian dance and martial art

Physical Features

Vinicius lives in Brazil—the fifth-largest country in the world. Brazil covers nearly half of South America. It shares a border with almost every other country on the continent. Because the country is so large, it includes a wide variety of landscapes.

Brazil's best-known physical feature is the Amazon River. This mighty river flows east from the Andes for about 4,000 miles. It passes through the Amazon lowlands of northern Brazil before it empties into the Atlantic Ocean, near Vinicius's hometown of Belém. The Amazon helps drain the continent.

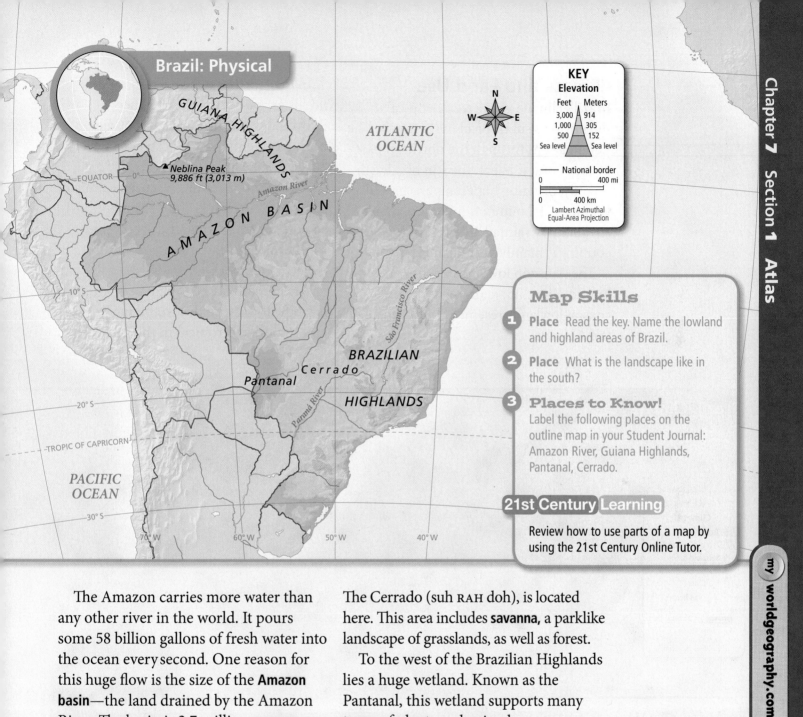

Brazil: Physical

GUIANA HIGHLANDS

▲ Neblina Peak
9,886 ft (3,013 m)

EQUATOR 0°

Amazon River

A M A Z O N   B A S I N

ATLANTIC OCEAN

São Francisco River

BRAZILIAN

Cerrado

Pantanal

HIGHLANDS

Paraná River

10° S

20° S

TROPIC OF CAPRICORN

PACIFIC OCEAN

30° S

70° W   60° W   50° W   40° W

KEY

Elevation

Feet	Meters
3,000	914
1,000	305
500	152
Sea level	Sea level

—— National border

0 _____ 400 mi

0 _____ 400 km

Lambert Azimuthal
Equal-Area Projection

N   E   S   W

Map Skills

1 **Place** Read the key. Name the lowland and highland areas of Brazil.

2 **Place** What is the landscape like in the south?

3 **Places to Know!** Label the following places on the outline map in your Student Journal: Amazon River, Guiana Highlands, Pantanal, Cerrado.

21st Century Learning

Review how to use parts of a map by using the 21st Century Online Tutor.

The Amazon carries more water than any other river in the world. It pours some 58 billion gallons of fresh water into the ocean every second. One reason for this huge flow is the size of the **Amazon basin**—the land drained by the Amazon River. The basin is 2.7 million square miles (7 million square kilometers).

The Amazon lowlands are vast. But highlands cover more of the country. North of the Amazon River are the Guiana Highlands, which include Neblina Peak, Brazil's highest point. To the south are the Brazilian Highlands. This region of plateaus and hills contains mineral resources.

The Cerrado (suh RAH doh), is located here. This area includes **savanna,** a parklike landscape of grasslands, as well as forest.

To the west of the Brazilian Highlands lies a huge wetland. Known as the Pantanal, this wetland supports many types of plants and animals.

A strip of low-lying land hugs Brazil's Atlantic coast. These Atlantic lowlands narrow farther south, where the Brazilian Highlands crowd the coast for some 1,600 miles. Still farther south, the lowland region widens again.

Reading Check Where does the Amazon River begin, and where does it end?

myWorldActivity
A Sculptor's Brazil

Climate and Land Use

Brazil's climate varies from tropical in the north to subtropical in the south. The Equator runs through the northern part of the country. There, the sun hits Earth directly, bringing high temperatures all year long. Humidity is high, too, thanks to the heavy rainfall. The rest of the country is mainly humid and rainy.

The Amazon lowlands are hot and humid. The climate in the northern coastal lowlands resembles the climate of the Amazon.

In the Northeast, heavy rains and floods arrive during the summer (November to April). In parts of the northeast, temperatures can rise above 100°F (38°C).

As you move south, the coastal climate starts to change. It is still humid but not so hot. Air from Antarctica cools the southern coast in the winter months (May to October).

The climate of the Brazilian Highlands is tropical wet and dry in the north and humid subtropical in the far south.

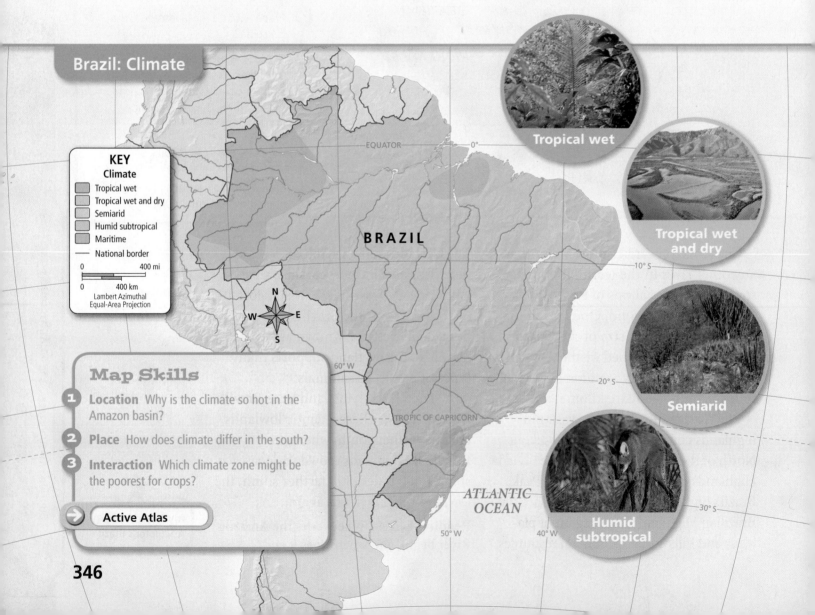

Brazil: Climate

KEY
Climate
- Tropical wet
- Tropical wet and dry
- Semiarid
- Humid subtropical
- Maritime
- National border

0   400 mi
0   400 km
Lambert Azimuthal
Equal-Area Projection

EQUATOR   0°

BRAZIL

N
W   E
S

60° W

10° S

20° S

TROPIC OF CAPRICORN

ATLANTIC
OCEAN

50° W   40° W   30° S

Tropical wet

Tropical wet and dry

Semiarid

Humid subtropical

Map Skills

1. **Location** Why is the climate so hot in the Amazon basin?

2. **Place** How does climate differ in the south?

3. **Interaction** Which climate zone might be the poorest for crops?

→ **Active Atlas**

However, the climate also varies with elevation. Higher areas are cooler.

In the rich soil of southern and southeastern coastal areas, farmers grow a wide variety of crops such as coffee, oranges, soybeans, and other foods.

The northeast is a hot region, where rainfall is limited to the summer months. In this dry landscape, cattle ranching dominates. Drought and the growth of huge commercial farms have forced many farmers to migrate out of the region.

Ranchers raise cattle on the grasslands of the Brazilian Highlands. These highlands produce iron ore, bauxite, and gold.

Forests cover more than half the country and produce rubber, palm oil, and timber. Hardwood trees provide good lumber for furniture, flooring, and other products. As more and more roads have been built across the Amazon basin, loggers have increased their harvesting of the region's vast reserves of hardwoods.

With all the water in Brazil, it is not surprising that many hydroelectric dams have been built or planned. The largest of these is the Itaipu Dam, which generates electric power for both Brazil and Paraguay.

Some soils in the Amazon are good for farmland. The sediments washed down from the Andes enrich some areas. However, attempts to turn many other forestlands into farmland have failed. When the rain forests are cut down, the land is fertile only for a short time. Most of the nutrients in the soil come from the leaves that fall to the ground. When the trees are cut down, the soil loses fertility.

Reading Check What part of Brazil experiences drought and floods?

Brazil: Land Use

KEY

Brush
Cropland
Forest
Grassland
Mixed
Savanna
Urban
Wetland
— National border
Farming
Forestry
Grazing
○ City

0   400 mi
0   400 km
Lambert Azimuthal
Equal-Area Projection

Map Skills

1. **Place** Compare this map to the map on the previous page. What connection do you see between climate and land use?

2. **Interaction** What might explain the lack of farming in certain areas?

3. **Places to Know!** Label the following places on the outline map in your Student Journal: São Paulo, Rio de Janeiro.

Active Atlas

my worldgeography.com   Active Atlas

Ecosystems

An ecosystem is a kind of web of living things that are tied to one another and to their environment.

One kind of ecosystem can be found along Brazil's northeast coast. Here mangrove forests shelter a variety of species. In turn, sea grasses and coral reefs protect the forests from the ocean's waves.

In the semiarid northeast, rainfall is low. Here the ecosystem includes scrub vegetation and a variety of animals that can survive <u>periods</u> of drought.

In contrast to the semiarid ecosystem of the northeast, the rain forest ecosystem of the Amazon lowlands teems with life. The rain forest shelters the largest variety of plant species in the world. The rain forest is also home to an amazing number of animal species.

Most of this animal life is found high in the upper leaves of rain forest trees. This level is called the **canopy.** The canopy is like a leafy tent. It prevents most of the sun's rays from reaching the ground. The fruit that hangs in the branches of the canopy attracts animals.

Most rain forest soil is not rich. This is because most nutrients in the forest are stored in the trees. As leaves fall to the ground, heat, moisture, and insects speed up decay. Nutrients are absorbed through the tree roots and distributed to leaves and branches. In time the trees' leaves drop back to the floor. This process creates a constant cycle of growth and decay.

period, *n.,* a portion of time

Amazon Flooding

During the rainy season, the Amazon basin fills with rainwater rushing down from the Andes Mountains and the Guiana Highlands.

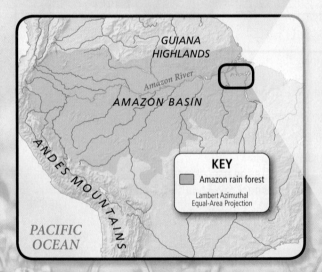

GUIANA HIGHLANDS

Amazon River

AMAZON BASIN

ANDES MOUNTAINS

PACIFIC OCEAN

KEY
Amazon rain forest
Lambert Azimuthal Equal-Area Projection

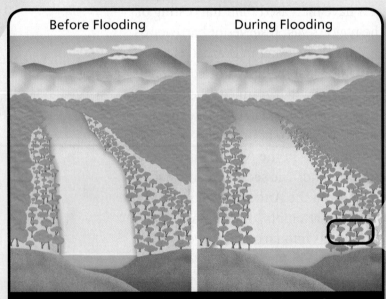

Before Flooding | During Flooding

These seasonal floods change the landscape of the rain forest. In some parts of the forest, water levels rise near the treetops.

Although the Amazon lies near the Equator and does not experience great changes in seasons, many river areas are affected by seasonal flooding. When rains fall to the north and south of the Equator, waters pour into the Amazon basin. This causes land along the river to flood. Permanently flooded forests are known as igapo (ee GAP poh). Seasonally flooded forests are called varzea (VAR zee ah). As the waters rise—up to 40 feet—fish swim into areas that they would not normally visit. At such times, the ecosystems of the river and the forest merge, as trees depend on fish to eat their fruit and spread their seeds.

The igapo is full of fish such as the piranha, whose teeth can shred flesh quickly. Many animals have adapted to this wet landscape. The jaguar is able to climb into the canopy, swim, and it even attacks caimans, or Amazon crocodiles.

adapt, *v.,* to adjust to a changed situation

Reading Check What causes flooding in the Amazon lowlands?

Culture Close-up

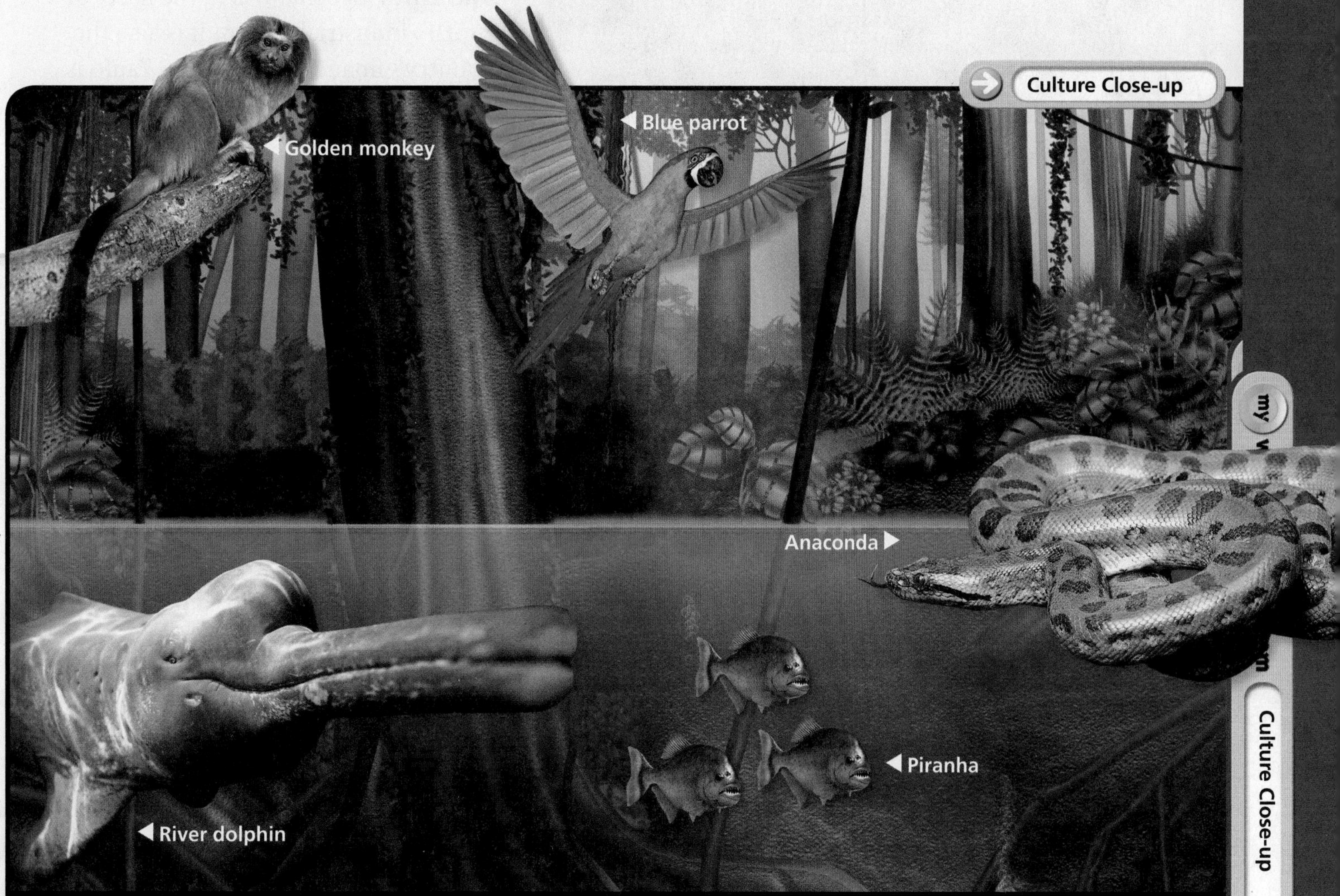

◄ Golden monkey

◄ Blue parrot

Anaconda ►

◄ River dolphin

◄ Piranha

Culture Close-up

During flooding, land and water ecosystems merge. Fish eat the fruit that falls from the trees and help spread the seeds. Animals like the river dolphin and piranha swim into areas that are normally dry.

Population Density

Today the population of Brazil is almost 200 million. However, this population is not spread evenly throughout the country. As you can see from this satellite photo, more than 80 percent of Brazilians live near the coast.

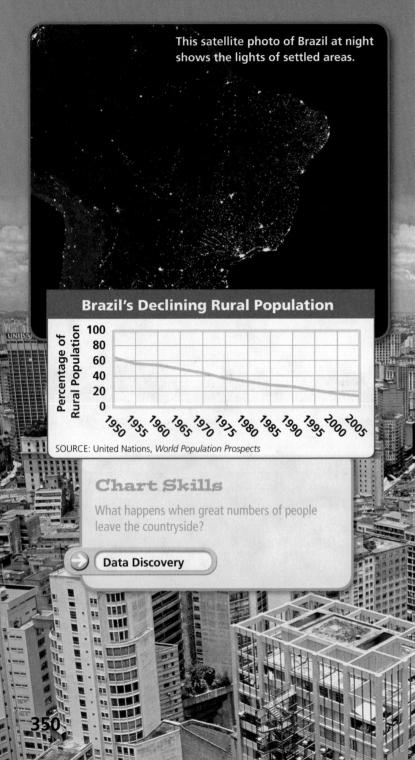

This satellite photo of Brazil at night shows the lights of settled areas.

Brazil's Declining Rural Population

SOURCE: United Nations, *World Population Prospects*

Chart Skills

What happens when great numbers of people leave the countryside?

→ **Data Discovery**

People in Brazil

Brazil has a large and diverse population. Brazil's largest city, São Paulo, has about 19 million people. Some 12 million live in the second-largest city, Rio de Janeiro.

Great Diversity Brazil is ethnically diverse. For centuries, people of European, African, and Native American ancestry have been marrying one another. Today, Brazilians share the same language and many other cultural traits.

The Cities São Paulo is in the heart of Brazil's industrial region. It is also the country's financial center. São Paulo is close to the port of Santos, which handles the highest volume of shipping in all of Latin America.

Coastal cities are overcrowded. For this reason, the government has long tried to encourage Brazilians to settle the country's vast interior. To help achieve this goal, in 1956 the government began building a brand-new capital city, called Brasília, well inland.

Manaus, with a population of 1.6 million people, is another large inland city. It is located deep in the Amazon rain forest. Manaus began as a rubber manu-facturing center in the 1800s. Today, Manaus is Brazil's only free trade zone that allows the production of goods. In Manaus, foreign companies can manufac-ture goods without having to pay tariffs, or taxes on imports, to the government.

Rich and Poor Brazilian cities all have a similar layout. The business district and the richer neighborhoods occupy the city center. The outskirts of the city are filled with slums called **favelas.** These poor neighborhoods keep growing, as people migrate from rural to urban areas in search of jobs and a better life.

Most of the favelas are built on hillsides. Some favela houses are built of bricks. Others are built of materials gathered from waste dumps. Favelas usually have no paved roads, electricity, piped water supply, toilets, or sewers. It is estimated that more than 14 million people live in the favelas of Brazilian cities.

The gap between rich and poor in Brazil is one of the widest in the world. An estimated 10 percent of Brazilians own more than 70 percent of the land and control more than half of the country's wealth.

Since 1980, poverty has increased by 50 percent. The continued presence of poverty in such a modern country has outraged many Brazilians.

66 We have two countries here under one flag, one constitution, and one language. One part of Brazil is in the twentieth century, with high-technology computers and satellite launches. And, beside that, we have another country where people are eating lizards to survive. 99

—Wilson Braga, governor of
Paraiba state, 1985

In addition to poverty, Brazilians of African ancestry often suffer from racial discrimination. However, the country is unique in the amount of racial mixing in the general population. Brazil is a new kind of society that is both multiethnic and multicultural. In the next section you will read about the events that helped create this dynamic new society.

Reading Check Where do most Brazilians live?

Favela in
Rio de Janeiro ▼

Section 1 Assessment

Essential Question

Key Terms

1. Use the following terms to describe the geography of the region: Amazon basin, savanna, canopy, favela.

Key Ideas

2. What physical features have kept Brazilians from settling inland?

3. How does the climate in Brazil's northeast differ from the climate in the rest of the country?

4. In Brazil's cities, where are wealthy and poor neighborhoods usually located?

Think Critically

5. **Draw Inferences** Road building speeds up destruction of the Amazon rain forest. Why might this be so?

6. **Solve Problems** What factors might persuade people to move to an inland city?

Who should benefit from a country's resources?

7. Where are some of Brazil's resources located? Explain. Go to your Student Journal to record your answer.

History of Brazil

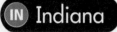 **Indiana** · **6.1.4** Explain the development and organization of various systems in Europe and the Americas. **6.1.11** Compare and contrast various colonies in the Americas. **6.1.20** Analyze cause-and-effect relationships in history.

Key Terms • brazilwood • export economy • boom and bust cycle
• abolitionist • coup

Visual Glossary

 Reading Skill: Sequence Take notes using the graphic organizer in your journal.

On March 7, 1808, the people of Rio de Janeiro awoke to an extraordinary sight. A fleet of Portuguese ships was approaching the harbor. On board were refugees from war-torn Europe. But unlike many refugees, these people were not poor. In fact, the new arrivals were members of the Portuguese royal family. For the next 13 years, Rio de Janeiro would be their home.

Rio welcomed more and more wealthy refugees as the Portuguese government and aristocracy arrived to seek safety. The arrival of the royal family changed Brazilian history. Suddenly a remote colony became the most important location in the Portuguese empire.

Brazil has always been a different kind of place. Unlike most countries in South America, Brazil was colonized by Portugal. Its people speak Portuguese rather than Spanish. In contrast to neighboring Spanish colonies, Brazil achieved independence fairly peacefully. Its history is unique for another reason as well—because for about 80 years it was the only empire in the Americas.

Cultures Meet

In A.D. 1500, Portuguese explorers first set foot on the land we know today as Brazil. This land was home to several million native people. Most of them were located along the heavily forested coast and in the Amazon basin. Native American tribes had adapted to Brazil's various environments. Some lived by hunting or fishing and gathering. Others had turned to farming.

◀ Woman in traditional costume, Bahia, Brazil

Language Lesson

Land Claims Portuguese explorers arrived to claim the land. In the Treaty of Tordesillas of 1494, Spain claimed all American lands west of a set line of longitude. Portugal claimed lands to the east and began colonizing Brazil.

The Portuguese first established trading posts on the northeast coast. The Portuguese traded with the Native Americans for **brazilwood,** a wood that produces a red dye. This wood gave Brazil its name. The Portuguese set up an **export economy,** an economy based on exports.

Next, the Portuguese developed another export crop, sugar. They began forcing Native Americans into slavery to work on sugar cane plantations. But native peoples either fled or died of the European diseases brought by the settlers.

Africans Arrive To replace the Native Americans, the Portuguese brought enslaved Africans to labor on sugar cane plantations and later in the gold and diamond mines of Minas Gerais.

Of the estimated 10 million enslaved Africans brought to the Americas, as many as 3 to 4 million ended up in Brazil. African culture helped shape Brazil's culture. Traditions such as capoeira, a blend of martial arts and dance, have strong African features. By the time slavery was outlawed in 1888, many Africans, Native Americans, and Portuguese had adopted one another's customs and intermarried.

Brazil's slave-based economy was part of a mercantile system. In mercantilism, colonies benefit the parent country. Brazilians were expected to export products only to Portugal. They were not allowed to trade with other countries.

An Independent Brazil The seeds of Brazil's independence were planted in 1807, when the French emperor Napoleon invaded Portugal. To escape Napoleon, Portugal's royal family fled to Brazil and governed from there.

IN Indiana CONNECTIONS

Brazilwood was Brazil's earliest top export. Today, medical products are Indiana's top export.

myWorldActivity Timeline Inquiry

The Uninvited Guests

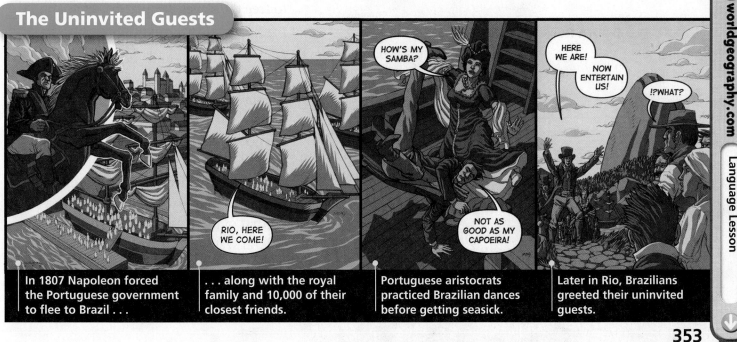

In 1807 Napoleon forced the Portuguese government to flee to Brazil . . .

. . . along with the royal family and 10,000 of their closest friends.

Portuguese aristocrats practiced Brazilian dances before getting seasick.

Later in Rio, Brazilians greeted their uninvited guests.

Boom and Bust

For centuries the Brazilian economy depended on one or two main export products. When foreign demand for the product was high, Brazil's economy boomed. But when demand fell, the economy suffered a decline, or a "bust."

THINK CRITICALLY **Study the timeline and the map. What export came from western Brazil and when?**

KEY

- Brazilwood
- Sugar cane
- Gold
- Diamonds
- Coffee
- Rubber

Boom Period for Each Export

- 1879–1912 (Rubber)
- 1550–1650s (Sugar cane)
- 1729–1870 (Diamonds)
- 1500–1550 (Brazilwood)
- 1695–1775 (Gold)
- 1840–1930 (Coffee)

1500 1600 1700 1800 1900 2000

Enslaved Africans worked on coffee plantations

After slavery ended, European immigrants arrived to seek work.

The king returned to Portugal in 1821. His son, Pedro I, stayed in Brazil. In 1822, Pedro declared that Brazil was no longer part of Portugal. He made himself emperor of an independent Brazil.

By this time, Brazilians had begun growing coffee. By the mid-1800s, coffee exports were the main source of revenue for Brazil's economy. Coffee was the latest "star" product in a **boom and bust cycle**—a period of strong economic growth followed by a period of sharp decline.

Reading Check What three cultures came together in Brazil?

The New Brazil

In the late 1800s, coffee had brought such wealth that coffee planters were politically powerful. They challenged the government, which was controlled by the owners of the sugar plantations. The coffee planters wanted a republic. Meanwhile, **abolitionists,** or people who wanted to end slavery, were campaigning to free the slaves.

Freedom and Republic Under pressure from republicans and abolitionists, the old Brazil was swept away. In 1888, all the slaves were freed. A year later, Brazil's military staged a **coup**—an overthrow of the government. The empire ended, and a republic took its place.

New leaders drew up a constitution. They formed a government based loosely on that of the United States. It was a federal system with an elected president.

During the republic, power shifted from the sugar plantations of the northeast to the coffee growers of the southeast. In fact, some of the first leaders of the republic were known as "coffee presidents."

Throughout the 1900s, the republic faced many challenges. Brazil's economy was hurt when demand for rubber (from the Amazon basin) declined. Coffee continued to carry the economy until the Great Depression began in 1929. Then coffee prices fell sharply in world markets.

As coffee lost its value, new groups challenged the power of the coffee elites. In 1930 Getúlio Vargas overthrew the government. Vargas appealed to the huge numbers of workers now crowding the cities. He tried to encourage manufacturing, so that Brazil would not be so dependent on foreign goods. During the 1930s his dictatorship stifled democracy but brought in many changes, such as giving women voting rights. Vargas continued to be a powerful figure in Brazilian politics for 24 years.

In the second half of the 1900s, Brazil's government was controlled mainly by dictators or the military. During this time, highways were constructed, and the new capital, Brasília, was built. By the early 1980s, Brazil had become one of the world's most important industrial nations. However, all this progress came at a terrible price for democracy. Many thousands of people were arrested for opposing government policies. Only in 1990 was democracy <u>restored</u>.

Reading Check What type of government did Brazil adopt after the empire fell?

restore, *v.,* to bring back

Government buildings in Brazil's futuristic capital, Brasília ▼

Section 2 Assessment

Key Terms

1. Use the following key terms to explain important events in the region's history: brazilwood, boom and bust cycle, abolitionist, coup.

Key Ideas

2. What crop did enslaved Native Americans help produce?

3. Why did the Portuguese replace Native American slave labor with African slave labor?

4. What products went through periods of boom and bust?

Think Critically

5. **Draw Inferences** How might Brazil's history have been different if the coastal Indian groups had united to resist the Europeans?

6. **Synthesize** What headline might have appeared in U.S. newspapers after the coup in Brazil in 1889?

? Essential Question

Who should benefit from a country's resources?

7. Did the export of sugar and other valuable resources from Brazil benefit all the people in the colony? Explain. Go to your Student Journal to record your answer.

Describing Brazil's Landscape

IN Indiana

6.1.21 Differentiate between fact and interpretation in historical accounts and explain historical passages.

6.3.14 Explain how nature has impacted the physical environment and human populations in areas of Europe and the Americas.

Many Brazilian writers and artists have described or shown what life is like on the land. The Brazilian writer Euclides da Cunha (oo klee des dah KOON yah), in his book *Rebellion in the Backlands*, describes how drought develops in the northeast and what effects it has on the landscape. Although the description was published in 1902, these weather patterns continue today.

In his painting *Coffee,* Candido Portinari depicts farming activity in 1935. When you have finished studying the painting, compare it to the photograph that appears below it.

▲ Brazilian writer Euclides da Cunha

A dry river bed in northeast Brazil ▼

Read the text on the right. Stop at each circled letter. Then answer the question with the same letter on the left.

Ⓐ Compare and Contrast To what is the drought compared?

Ⓑ Analyze Cause and Effect Why don't October rains bring relief?

Ⓒ Identify Main Idea and Details What images does the author use to paint a vivid picture of the dry landscape?

inexorably, *adv.,* unable to be stopped

caatinga, *n.,* the landscape and plants in the dry northeast of Brazil

The Drought

❝ The symptoms of the drought are not long in appearing; they come in a series, one after another, <u>inexorably</u>, like those of some cyclic **Ⓐ** disease. . . . The brief period of October rains, the chuvas do cajú, goes by, with numerous showers **Ⓑ** that are quickly evaporated in the parched air, leaving no trace behind them. The <u>caatingas</u> are "mottled," here, there, and everywhere, speckled with grayish-brown clusters of withered trees . . . and the water **Ⓒ** level in the pits slowly sinks. ❞

—Euclides da Cunha, *Rebellion in the Backlands*

Answer each question about the painting.

D **Identify Evidence** What does the painting reveal about the landscape and climate of the region shown?

E **Summarize** What does the painting tell you about the life of plantation workers?

F **Draw Inferences** Why is one man dressed differently from the others? What do his clothes and his gesture reveal about him?

Coffee by Candido Portinari, 1935 ▶

Coffee pickers on a plantation in southeast Brazil in the early 1900s ▼

Analyze the Documents

1. **Compare Viewpoints** What similarities do you notice as you compare the text and the painting? Explain.

2. **Writing Task** Write a description of the painting *Coffee*, using some of the words and phrases from "The Drought."

Brazil Today

IN Indiana

6.2.7 Define and compare citizenship and the citizen's role throughout history in Europe and the Americas.

6.3.4 Describe and compare major cultural characteristics of regions in Europe and the Western Hemisphere.

6.3.13 Explain the impact of humans on the physical environment in Europe and the Americas.

6.4.4 Describe how different economic systems in Europe and the

Americas answer the basic economic questions.

Key Terms • ethanol • urban planning • market economy • social services

Visual Glossary

Reading Skill: Summarize Take notes using the graphic organizer in your journal.

Soccer is a matter of national pride in Brazil. Brazilian soccer players are among the best in the world. The Brazilian men's team often wins the World Cup, the top international soccer tournament.

If Vinicius is offered a contract to play on the Flamengo team, he could be on the road to stardom. But Vinicius knows that for now, he has to have an alternative plan for his life. So if he doesn't make the Flamengo team, he plans to enroll in a university. Whatever happens, Vinicius is looking forward to the future with excitement. He is a good symbol of a young nation full of hope and energy.

Brazil today is a country with a lively culture, a strong economy, and rich natural resources. It is a country eager to play a leading role in the region—and in the world. However, Brazil also faces enormous challenges, such as poverty and environmental damage. Can Brazil close the gap between rich and poor? Can the country protect its rain forest and keep its economy growing?

A Rich Culture

The richness of Brazilian culture grew as different ethnic groups influenced one another's customs over the centuries. After more than 400 years of intermarriage between Africans, Europeans, Native Americans, and others, almost half of Brazil's people are of mixed racial ancestry. The long cultural exchange has also produced new kinds of religious worship as well as one of the biggest parties in the world—Carnival.

my Story **Photo**

◄ Vinicius on his tour of Rio

Carnival Nothing on Earth is quite like Carnival. This festival—several days of parades, music, and dance—releases the energy and creativity of Brazilian culture. Like much else in Brazil, Carnival also represents a blending of European and African traditions. The festival is held before the Christian season of Lent, a 40-day period of fasting that leads up to Easter. Traditionally, Christians hold a feast—Carnival—before beginning their fast. This European custom mingled with African music and dance and became the festival that Brazilians enjoy today.

Ethnic Groups African heritage remains strong in Brazil. This is especially true along Brazil's northeast coast, where enslaved Africans first arrived. People of European descent live throughout Brazil, although immigrants from Europe have tended to settle in the south. Native peoples, too, live in all parts of Brazil, while many Native American communities survive in the rain forests.

Religion and Family Life The Portuguese introduced Roman Catholicism to Brazil. Today, a large majority of the population remains Catholic. However, religious diversity is increasing. Various Protestant churches have gained followers in recent years. Japanese, Chinese, and Korean immigrants have brought Buddhism to Brazil. There are also small populations of Mormons, Jews, Muslims, and followers of traditional African religions.

Reading Check What groups and traditions have shaped Brazilian culture?

Closer Look

Carnival

Carnival combines the religious traditions of southern Europe with the music and dance of Africa and the Americas. During the festival, people dance to the music of the samba, which draws on Native American, African, and Portuguese styles of music and dance.

THINK CRITICALLY **In what ways is Carnival a multicultural event?**

The float that appears below commemorates 100 years of Japanese immigration to Brazil. ▼

Carnival costumes and floats can be dazzling.

Environmental Issues

Like all modern countries, Brazil is trying to deal with urban pollution. Vehicle exhaust and factories spew pollutants into the air and water. But Brazil's main environmental issue involves the rain forest.

The Amazon rain forest is a unique place that helps support life on Earth. Its trees absorb carbon dioxide (a major part of vehicle exhaust) and produce oxygen for all living things to breathe. The rain forest is also a vast natural pharmacy. Many modern medicines have come from tropical rain forests.

However, the Amazon's ecosystem is being destroyed. Humans are cutting down its trees for timber or to clear land for farms and ranches. They are mining its streams for gold and are damming its rivers to <u>generate</u> electricity.

The Amazon is a vast region, and most of it is still healthy. Today, Brazil's government is taking steps to defend the rain forest from too much development. The president has imposed fines on lawbreakers. Hundreds of federal police have been sent to stop the destruction. The government has also created large conservation areas.

Unfortunately, much of the destruction is taking place in Brazil's remote areas, or frontiers, and frontiers are always difficult to patrol. As long as there is a worldwide demand for products such as soybeans, meat, and wood, the rain forest will be under threat.

Although rain-forest destruction is a problem in the Amazon, Brazil is continuously searching for other solutions. Brazil has found an alternative fuel for its cars. **Ethanol,** a fuel that can be made from sugar cane, is enabling the country to reduce its dependence on oil.

Brazil's southeastern city of Curitiba is another success story. In Curitiba, careful **urban planning**—the planning of a city— has reduced car traffic and trash while creating a parklike environment. Today Curitiba is admired throughout the world. Many consider it a new kind of "green city" that is less harmful to the environment than other cities.

Reading Check Why is it important to protect the Amazon rain forest?

generate, *v.,* to produce

Satellite pictures of the same area show rain-forest destruction between 1990 and 2000. ▼

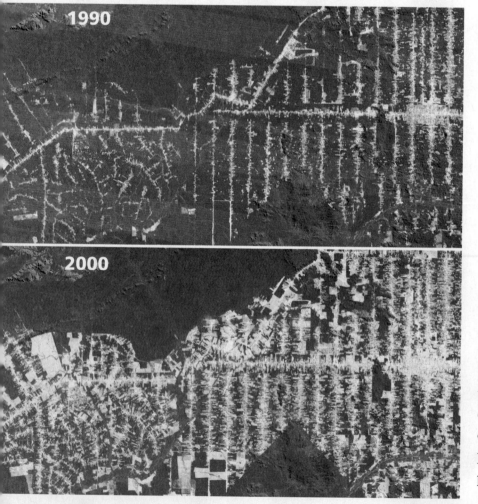

1990

2000

360

Closer Look

Curitiba: Green City of the Future

In the late 1900s, Curitiba's leaders realized that the city was growing too quickly. So the city adopted a plan to solve the problems of urban growth and help the environment. Curitiba's plan has been a popular success. The city has become a world-famous model of "green," or environmentally friendly, urban planning.

THINK CRITICALLY **If you were an urban planner, how would you make your own community greener?**

Problem Large populations create trash in urban centers.

Problem Increasing numbers of cars cause pollution and traffic congestion.

Problem Building on wetlands damages habitats and worsens flooding.

Curitiba's Solution Recycling programs keep the streets clean.

Curitiba's Solution Improve the public transportation system. Some streets are set aside for buses only. Other streets are set aside for pedestrians.

Curitiba's Solution Allow only parkland and lakes along the waterways to absorb floodwaters.

Chart Skills

1 Which region is Brazil's largest trading partner?

2 What is the largest segment of the Brazilian economy?

Data Discovery

Destination of Brazilian Exports

17.8%
25.9%
14%
18.9%
23.4%

- Latin America and the Caribbean
- European Union
- Asia (except Middle East)
- United States, including Puerto Rico
- Others

SOURCE: Banco Central do Brasil

Brazil's Economy

5.5%
28.7%
65.8%

Percentage of GDP in 2007

- Agriculture
- Industry (such as steel, aircraft, chemicals, vehicles)
- Services (such as mail, banking, computing)

SOURCE: U.S. Department of State

A Growing Economy

Brazil has a **market economy,** in which the prices of goods are set by demand, not by the government. Brazil's economic growth is no longer dependent on a single crop or product as it was in the past. Today, the economy has diversified. Agriculture is just one part of Brazil's modern industrial economy—the largest economy in South America.

Resources and Manufacturing Brazil's geography provides a wealth of natural resources to support economic growth. Mineral resources include iron, manganese, and tin, as well as widespread oil and natural gas deposits. In addition, the Amazon basin is a source of timber, rubber, diamonds, and gold.

Brazil's main manufacturing region lies in the Southeast, between São Paulo and Rio de Janeiro. Vehicle manufacturing for the Brazilian market is a major industry. Foreign automakers have also built factories here.

Farming and Free Trade Brazil is still one of the world's major exporters of coffee. The country continues to grow a huge amount of sugar cane. Today most sugar cane is converted into ethanol, a cheaper alternative to gasoline. Recently, Brazil has also become the world's largest grower and exporter of soybeans.

Brazil is part of a trade organization that includes the nations of Argentina, Paraguay, and Uruguay. This organization is called MERCOSUR, which is short for Mercado Común del Sur, or Southern Common Market. MERCOSUR allows member countries to trade freely with one another, without tariffs.

Reading Check How has Brazil diversified its economy?

myWorldActivity
Challenges for Brazil

362

Government for the People

Brazil has been independent since 1889. But it has not always been a democracy. As you have read, starting in the 1930s Brazil was ruled by dictators or the military. However, in 1990 democracy was restored.

Branches of Government The <u>structure</u> of Brazil's national government is similar to that of the United States. A president heads the executive branch. Two houses make up the legislative branch, called the National Congress. The highest court in the judicial branch is the Federal Supreme Court. The president and members of the legislature are elected by the people. The minimum voting age is 16.

Balancing Growth and Social Needs Despite Brazil's growing economy, poverty remains widespread. Too many people in both rural and urban areas lack good housing, schools, hospitals, and police and fire protection. A wide gap exists between the poverty of the north and the wealth of the south. But dealing with problems such as these takes money. Much of that money must come from taxes.

Business owners claim that taxes slow growth. Others, like President Lula, want to redirect Brazil's oil wealth into **social services**—programs designed to help the poor. Speaking of the oil recently discovered off the coast, President Lula said,

> 66 It is the wealth of the country, it is the wealth of 190 million Brazilians, and we have to use this wealth to help the poor of the country. 99
>
> —President Lula da Silva, BBC News, August 5, 2008

structure, *n.,* organization

Looking Toward the Future With its newfound oil fields and its increasing production of ethanol, Brazil is on its way to energy independence. This country, which is already an industrial giant, is also becoming an agricultural superpower. But only time will tell if Brazil will use its resources wisely—lifting millions out of poverty and into a brighter future.

Reading Check What is the basic structure of Brazil's national government?

Section 3 Assessment

Essential Question

Key Terms

1. Use the following terms to describe life in Brazil today: ethanol, urban planning, market economy, social services.

Key Ideas

2. Which ethnic traditions are the main influences on Brazilian culture today?

3. What is the most serious environmental issue facing Brazil?

Think Critically

4. **Solve Problems** Why doesn't Brazil simply outlaw all development in the Amazon basin?

5. **Identify Evidence** What are some strengths of the Brazilian economy?

Who should benefit from a country's resources?

6. What is the debate in Brazil over how to use the country's oil wealth? Go to your Student Journal to record your answer.

Destruction of the Amazon Rain Forest

IN Indiana

6.1.22 Form research questions and use resources to present data on people, cultures and developments in Europe and the Americas.

6.4.6 Analyze current economic issues in the countries of Europe

or the Americas using a variety of resources.

6.4.7 Identify economic connections between the community and the countries of Europe or the Americas

and identify job skills needed to be successful in the workplace.

6.4.8 Identify how societies deal with externalities in Europe or the Americas.

Key Terms • slash-and-burn • habitat • biodiversity

Most of the Amazon rain forest lies in Brazil. That gives the country a huge responsibility. The rain forest is vital to the health of the planet. It protects a huge number of plant and animal species. It also shelters many native peoples. For the sake of the entire world, Brazil must protect this forest environment. That is not an easy job. The Amazon rain forest is being attacked from several directions. It is rapidly being destroyed.

Causes of the Destruction

Rain forests everywhere are steadily disappearing. For the most part, humans are to blame. In Brazil, the Amazon rain forest offers a wealth of natural resources. Humans exploit those resources. That is, they use the resources for their own benefit.

Amazon Resources Loggers make a big profit from selling the Amazon's trees. To transport the wood, loggers build roads. These roads open the rain forest to farmers, ranchers, miners, and others.

Logging operation in Brazil ▼

Farmers and ranchers use the land to produce food. They often employ **slash-and-burn** methods to clear the land for planting. They cut down all the vegetation in an area and burn it. But the soil of the Amazon basin—the area drained by the Amazon River—is not very fertile. A plot often produces crops or grasses for cattle grazing for only a few years before the farmer or rancher has to move on.

Global agricultural firms have found that land is cheap in the Amazon basin. In recent years, huge soybean farms have begun to appear on rain forest land. Even larger areas have been cleared for cattle ranches.

Brazil's previous governments are partly responsible for all this destruction of the rain forest. In the 1970s, the military rulers saw the Amazon as an empty region waiting to be developed. They encouraged farmers and ranchers to resettle in the Amazon. They did not care when environmental laws were broken. Brazilians needed food, and those farmers and ranchers produced it.

Reading Check What activities contribute greatly to the destruction of the Amazon rain forest?

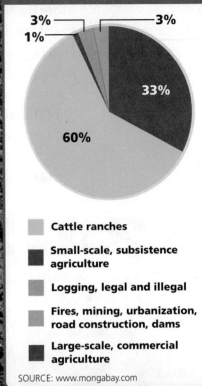

Causes of Deforestation in the Amazon, 2000–2005

3%
1%
3%
33%
60%

- Cattle ranches
- Small-scale, subsistence agriculture
- Logging, legal and illegal
- Fires, mining, urbanization, road construction, dams
- Large-scale, commercial agriculture

SOURCE: www.mongabay.com

Aerial view showing destruction

365

Effects of the Destruction

The rain forest is disappearing rapidly. More than 4,000 square miles of rain forest are destroyed each year. That's an area larger than the Florida Everglades. Since the 1960s, about one fifth of the Amazon rain forest has been cut down.

Fortunately, this deforestation is taking place largely along the edges of the Amazon basin. In the heart of the region, the rain forest remains mostly intact.

Everyone's Loss The process of destruction always follows the same cycle. As workers start clearing the forest, first the animals run away. After the trees have been removed, the remaining plants are cut and burned. Farmers or ranchers may cultivate the area for one or two years. Then they leave. The soil is exhausted.

The rain forests cover just two percent of the surface of the Earth, but they contain half of Earth's plant and animal species.

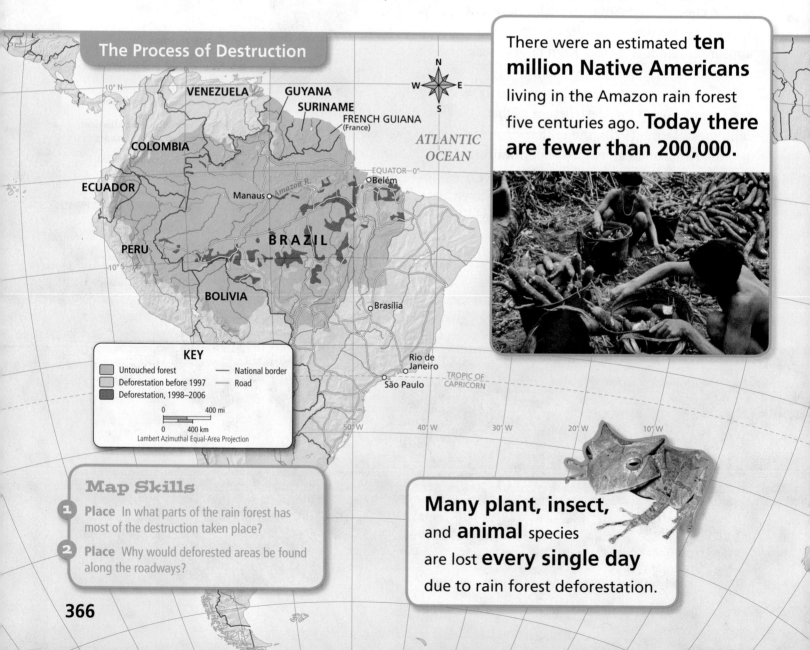

The Process of Destruction

VENEZUELA
GUYANA
SURINAME
FRENCH GUIANA
(France)
COLOMBIA
ATLANTIC
OCEAN
ECUADOR
EQUATOR—0°
Belém
Manaus
Amazon R.
BRAZIL
PERU
10° S
BOLIVIA
Brasília
Rio de Janeiro
São Paulo
TROPIC OF CAPRICORN
10° N
0°

KEY

Untouched forest	National border
Deforestation before 1997	Road
Deforestation, 1998–2006	

0   400 mi
0   400 km
Lambert Azimuthal Equal-Area Projection

There were an estimated **ten million Native Americans** living in the Amazon rain forest five centuries ago. **Today there are fewer than 200,000.**

Map Skills

1 **Place** In what parts of the rain forest has most of the destruction taken place?

2 **Place** Why would deforested areas be found along the roadways?

Many plant, insect, and **animal** species are lost **every single day** due to rain forest deforestation.

These forests provide a **habitat**—a natural environment—for those plants and animals.

Widespread deforestation reduces the forest's **biodiversity,** or variety of organisms. This affects all life in the forest, including human life. Some 200,000 Native Americans still live in the Amazon basin today. Their way of life may disappear with the rain forest.

A Growing Threat The threat to humans goes far beyond Brazil. Rain forest plants may provide medicines to treat diseases. The Amazon also contains some 70 billion tons of carbon, stored in its plants. Slash-and-burn agriculture releases this carbon dioxide gas into the atmosphere. This gas contributes to climate change, the gradual rise in temperature that scientists predict will change much of Earth's climate.

Reading Check Why would forest destruction threaten human beings?

Responses to the Destruction

Brazilians have long argued about the rain forest. Some want to preserve the rain forest in its natural state. Others want to develop its many resources.

Protecting the Land The government has passed laws to protect the environment. In fact, much of the destruction is now illegal. But loggers, sometimes aided by corrupt government officials, keep cutting down trees without permission. Farmers and ranchers have moved onto protected lands.

Since 2003, Brazil's government has tightened rules for logging, ranching, and farming in the Amazon basin. In 2008, the government announced that, by 2018, it would reduce the amount of forest destroyed each year by half.

Reading Check How has Brazil's government responded to rain forest destruction since 2003?

▲ Sloths like this one feed on fruits and leaves in the rain forest canopy.

Assessment

1. How do logging roads contribute to the destruction of the Amazon rain forest?

2. How did Brazil's former government help cause the destruction of the rain forest?

3. Is the entire rain forest at risk of disappearing? Explain.

4. Why is the loss of biodiversity in the Amazon a threat to humans?

5. What are the two opposing arguments in Brazil's debate over the fate of the Amazon rain forest?

Chapter Assessment

Key Terms and Ideas

1. **Summarize** What kind of landforms can be found in Brazil?

2. **Discuss** What causes the floods in the **Amazon basin**?

3. **Recall** What language is spoken in Brazil today?

4. **Explain** What happens during a **boom and bust cycle**?

5. **Describe** Why is Carnival a good symbol of Brazil's multicultural society?

6. **Summarize** Why is Brazil developing the fuel **ethanol** into a major industry?

7. **Discuss** In what ways has Brazil diversified its economy?

Think Critically

8. **Make Inferences** Why are Brazilian cities growing so rapidly?

9. **Draw Conclusions** What are the dangers of an export economy?

10. **Categorize** What are some of Brazil's strengths and problems?

11. **Core Concepts: Migration** How did migration help shape Brazilian culture?

Places to Know

For each place, write the letter from the map that shows its location.

12. **Guiana Highlands**

13. **Manaus**

14. **Rio de Janeiro**

15. **Amazon River**

16. **Pantanal**

17. **São Paulo**

18. **Estimate** Using the scale, estimate the distance between São Paulo and Rio de Janeiro.

Essential Question

myWorld Chapter Activity

Job Search Follow your teacher's instructions to study the resources in each of Brazil's regions. Join a national team traveling to each location in the classroom. Review the photograph and the information about the topic at each location. Then meet with your team and decide where you would like to live. Create a résumé that presents your skills.

21st Century Learning

Search for Information on the Internet

With a partner, search for sites that give information on the Brazilian economy today. Before you begin, brainstorm the kind of key words that might help your search, such as *Brazilian trade*, *Brazilian manufacturing*, and so forth.

Success Tracker™
Online at myworldgeography.com

Document-Based Questions

Use your knowledge of Brazil and Documents A and B to answer Questions 1–3.

Document A

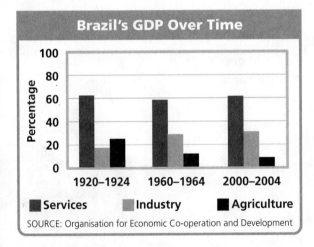

Brazil's GDP Over Time

Percentage

■ Services　■ Industry　■ Agriculture

SOURCE: Organisation for Economic Co-operation and Development

Document B

" I come from a country and also a continent whose identity is in the making. We're a very young culture, and I think that things are not yet crystallized."

—Walter Salles, Brazilian film director

1. What does the information in Document A reveal about Brazil's economy?

    A Industry has become less important than agriculture.

    B Industry has become more important than agriculture.

    C Services are the least important sector of the economy.

    D Industrial production has fallen since the 1920s.

2. When Walter Salles says that things in Brazil are not yet crystallized, he means which of the following?

    A Brazil has no more crystal mines in operation.

    B Brazilian culture was formed centuries ago.

    C Brazilian culture is still being created.

    D Brazilian culture does not exist.

3. **Writing Task** Explain why Documents A and B show that Brazil is still changing.

myworldgeography.com　Self-Test

Mapping Life Expectancy

Your Mission Research life expectancy data on the Internet and present your findings on an annotated map and in an oral report. Divide into five teams: one mapping team and four research teams. Work together to prepare the map and report.

Do you think that you will reach the age of 100? Life expectancy depends on many factors. In general, people in developed nations live longer than people in developing nations. The factors that have a large impact on life expectancy include the quality of public health, medical care, and eating habits.

Life expectancy drops sharply in countries with high rates of infant mortality. Suppose a country has a life expectancy of 70 years for people who live past their first birthday but a 10 percent infant mortality rate. The overall life expectancy for that country would drop to 63. Life expectancy also differs for males and females.

10years
20years
40years
60years

STEP 1

Complete Specialized Tasks.

The mapping team will draw and label a large political map of South America. The four research teams should use reliable podcasts or Web sites (suggested by your teacher) to find specific statistics for each country in the region. Statistics to be researched are immunization, access to clean water, infant mortality rates, and male life expectancy and female life expectancy.

STEP 2

Annotate the Map.

Each research team should discuss its findings. The teams should try to find trends or analyze the data and draw conclusions. Consider, for example, the connection between life expectancy and access to clean water. Then use captions, graphs, or photographs to annotate the political map drawn by the mapping team. Groups should cooperate as they fill in the map with their research.

STEP 3

Regroup and Prepare Oral Reports.

After the map is finished, students should return to their original teams. Each team will work together as a group to prepare an oral report summarizing the overall findings. In your report, define key terms, give your sources, and note the date of the information you found. Try to draw conclusions about why life expectancy varies among the populations of South America.

Regional Overview

Europe and Russia

The many countries of Europe plus Russia reach from the Atlantic Ocean to the Pacific Ocean. Russia spreads over two continents, Europe and Asia. More than 590 million people live in Europe with another 140 million in Russia. Most live in urban areas. More than 230 languages are spoken here, such as English, French, Spanish, Basque, Greek, Finnish, and Russian.

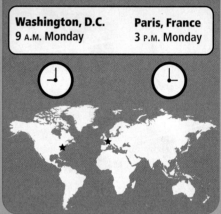

What time is it there?

Washington, D.C.	Paris, France
9 A.M. Monday	3 P.M. Monday

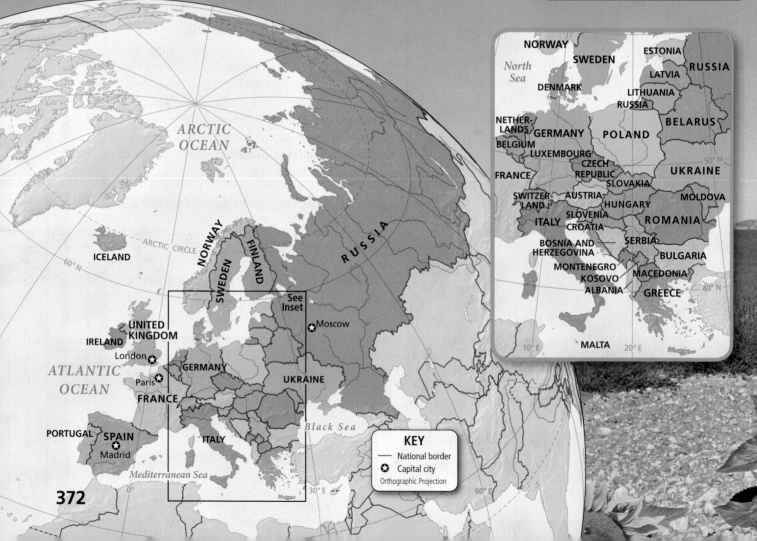

KEY
— National border
✪ Capital city
Orthographic Projection

372

my worldgeography.com

Plan your trip online by doing a Data Discovery Activity and watching the myStory Videos of the region's teens.

my Story

Yasmin

Age: 18

Home: Bjärred, Sweden

Chapter 10

my Story

Serhiy

Age: 16

Home: Bezpalche, Ukraine

Chapter 11

my Story

Boris

Age: 15

Home: Moscow, Russia

Chapter 12

A field of sunflowers and lavender in France

Regional Overview
Physical Geography

ARCTIC OCEAN

The Alps are rugged mountains that have their own snowy climate, perfect for winter sports like skiing.

Scandinavia is a long, narrow peninsula that extends from the northernmost part of Europe.

Ural Mountains

Northwestern Highlands

Scandinavia

Baltic Sea

North European Plain

Carpathian Mountains

Black Sea

ATLANTIC OCEAN

North Sea

Balkan Peninsula

Alps

Adriatic Sea

Mont Blanc
15,774 ft (4,808 m)

Mediterranean Sea

Iberian Peninsula

Siberia

Caspian Sea

The West Siberian Plain borders the world's largest steppes region, an extensive area of cold and dry grasslands.

Regional Flyover

Suppose you fly in an airplane across Europe and Russia. If you began over the Atlantic Ocean, you would first notice that Europe is a giant peninsula stretching westward from a larger landmass. From it extend many smaller peninsulas, so that the whole continent of Europe is sometimes called the "peninsula of peninsulas."

Next, you might notice two important mountain ranges. The Alps stretch in an east-west arc through central Europe. Flying east, you would see a north–south mountain range called the Urals. These mountains form the traditional border between European Russia and Asiatic Russia.

The North European Plain sweeps east–west across Europe into European Russia. These lowlands have had both benefits and drawbacks for the region. The flat land is good for settlement and farming. It has also been a gateway for invading armies throughout history.

In-flight Movie

Take flight over Europe and Russia and explore the region from the air.

my worldgeography.com In-flight Movie

375

Regional Overview
Human Geography

Europe About 1890
Europe was composed of large empires at the end of the 1800s.

London about 1890

Europe Today
In the 1900s, large empires fell, leading to the creation of many smaller countries.

London today

Where People Live

Throughout history, the population density of Europe has been high because of its temperate climate, miles of coastline and rivers, and acres of good farmland.

Russia, on the other hand, is the largest nation on Earth, but about 80 percent of the population live in the smaller, European part of the country. This is because only about 7 percent of Russia's land is good for farming, and its harbors are blocked by ice for months. Russia is a land of extremes—harsh climate, rugged terrain, and great distances.

my World IN NUMBERS

Sweden

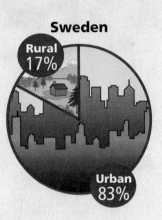

Rural 17%

Urban 83%

France

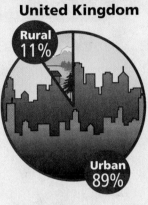

Rural 24%

Urban 76%

United Kingdom

Rural 11%

Urban 89%

Italy

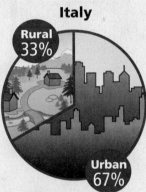

Rural 33%

Urban 67%

Ukraine

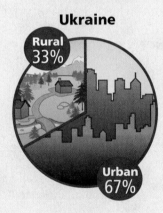

Rural 33%

Urban 67%

Russia

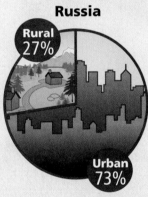

Rural 27%

Urban 73%

SOURCE: United Nations Secretariat, Population Division

Put It Together

1. Which mountain range separates European Russia from Asiatic Russia?

2. In what ways has the physical geography of Europe and Russia affected where people live and work?

3. True or false: According to the graphs above, Europe and Russia are mostly rural. Explain your answer.

→ **Data Discovery**

Use your own data to make a regional data table.

Size Comparison

The land area of Europe and Russia is more than 150% larger than that of the United States.

Chapter 8

Ancient and Medieval Europe

? Essential Question

What are the challenges of diversity?

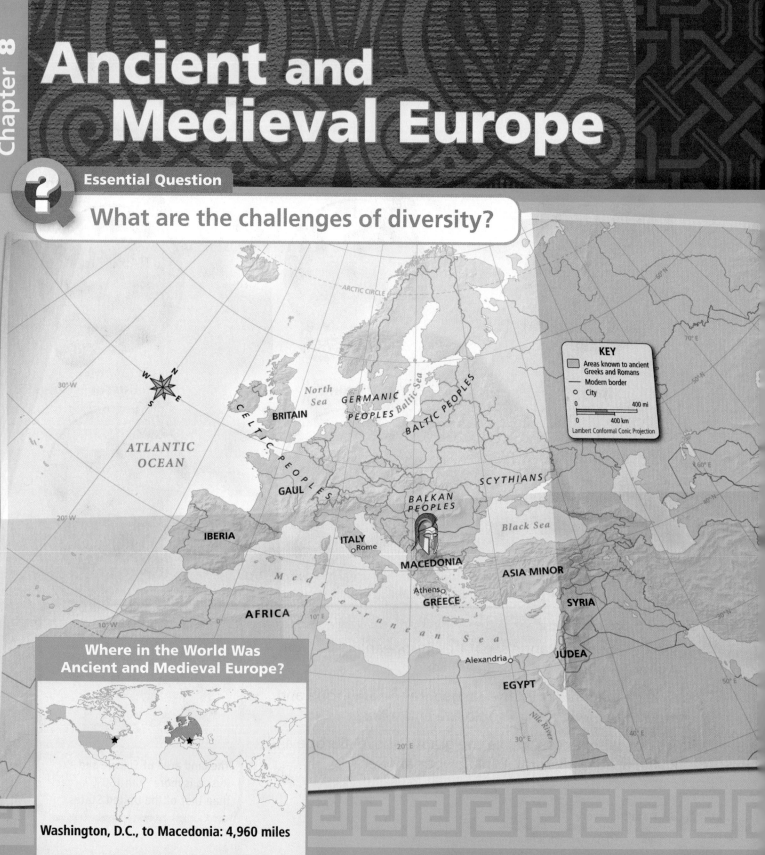

KEY
- Areas known to ancient Greeks and Romans
- Modern border
- ○ City

400 mi

400 km

Lambert Conformal Conic Projection

ARCTIC CIRCLE

ATLANTIC OCEAN

North Sea

Baltic Sea

GERMANIC PEOPLES

BALTIC PEOPLES

CELTIC PEOPLES

BRITAIN

GAUL

IBERIA

ITALY
○ Rome

BALKAN PEOPLES

MACEDONIA

SCYTHIANS

Black Sea

Mediterranean Sea

AFRICA

Athens ○
GREECE

ASIA MINOR

SYRIA

JUDEA

Alexandria ○

EGYPT

Nile River

Where in the World Was Ancient and Medieval Europe?

Washington, D.C., to Macedonia: 4,960 miles

my Story

A Prophecy Fulfilled

Explore the Essential Question

- at my worldgeography.com
- using the **myWorld Chapter Activity**
- with the **Student Journal**

In this section, you'll read about Alexander the Great, a Macedonian warrior who conquered much of the world known to the ancient Greeks. What does Alexander's story tell you about life in the ancient Greek world?

Story by Michael Chatlien for myWorld Online

In 334 B.C., Alexander the Great led his army from Europe into Asia. His troops came from Macedonia and Greece. Alexander wanted to defeat the Persian forces led by Darius III. The two armies met at the Granicus River in present-day Turkey. With 75,000 troops, Darius III seemed to have the advantage. Alexander had only 35,000 soldiers. Even so, he felt that he was destined to defeat Darius and conquer Asia. Indeed, his upbringing prepared him to become a great ruler.

Alexander's father was Philip II, the king of Macedonia. His mother was Olympias, a princess from western Greece. Olympias taught Alexander that he was descended from the great warrior Achilles. And Philip convinced his son that Macedonian kings were descended from the god Hercules.

At age 12, Alexander tamed Bucephalus. The name means "ox's head" and refers to the wild horse's massive head.

my worldgeography.com | On Assignment

The Greeks perfected the phalanx, a wedge-shaped battle formation.

The Persian king Darius faced Alexander in battle three times.

"There is no part of my body remaining free of wounds. I have been wounded with the sword, shot with arrows, and hit with stones for the sake of your lives, your glory, and your wealth."

The respected philosopher Aristotle taught the young Alexander. From him, Alexander learned about science, the arts, and politics. While he studied, he also trained in sports and combat. When Alexander's father Philip conquered Greece, Alexander commanded a division in his father's army.

Philip then wanted to invade Asia, but his plans were cut short when a bodyguard murdered him. So at the age of 20, Alexander became king of Macedonia and Greece. Two years later, he invaded the Persian Empire, seeking to be ruler of Asia as well.

At the shores of the Granicus River, Alexander readied his troops for combat. It would be the first of three battles against the Persians. The Greek historian Arrian described how both armies waited at the edge of the river ready to attack. Alexander shouted for his men to show courage:

66 Alexander leaped upon his steed, ordering those about him to follow, and exhorting [urging] them to show themselves valiant men. 99

The cavalry attacked first, with warriors and horses moving in a phalanx formation. Archers and spear throwers then joined in to support the assault.

Alexander raises his sword to cut apart the Gordian knot.

Alexander is said to have wept when he looked out over his empire, sad because there were no more worlds to conquer.

Next the foot soldiers joined in and dealt the crushing blow. The modern historian Robin Lane Fox describes Alexander's army in combat:

66 Nobody who faced them ever forgot the sight; they kept time to their roaring of the Greeks' ancient war cry, Alalalalai; their scarlet cloaks billowed, and the measured swishing of their sarissas [long pikes], up and down, left and right, seemed to frightened observers like the quills of a metal porcupine. 99

The Greeks crushed the Persians. Darius and his troops retreated eastward. Alexander needed more troops, so he set off to find new recruits to join his army. On his march, Alexander came upon the legendary Gordian knot. This knot was tied to an ox cart. An ancient prophecy stated that the person who untied the knot would rule Asia. Alexander first tried to undo the huge knot and could not. Frustrated, he drew his sword and cut it with one stroke. This may not be a true story, but Alexander did go on to fulfill the prophecy.

Later, at the battle of Issus, the Greeks were again victorious. Darius escaped, but he offered Alexander a peace treaty. He said he would give Alexander a large sum of money and the Persian lands west of the Euphrates River. Alexander's general Parmenio advised his commander to accept the terms—but Alexander had greater ambitions.

He faced Darius again at Gaugamela. With a third victory here, Alexander took control of much of Southwest Asia. It was still not enough— Alexander wanted India.

After eight long years of marching and fighting, the army reached the western border of India. Alexander's troops had become homesick and wanted to turn back. Coenus, an old commander, gathered his courage as he spoke for his fellow soldiers,

66 Do not lead us now against our will. . . .But, rather, return of your own accord to your own land. . .and carry to the home of your fathers these victories great and small. 99

Alexander reluctantly agreed to return to Macedonia, but he would not make it home. He died of a mysterious illness at Babylon in 323 B.C.

Alexander's empire stretched from Macedonia and Greece in the west to the borders of India in the east. This region included much of the world that was known to the ancient Greeks. Indeed, the prophecy of the Gordian knot had come true.

→ **myStory Video**

Join Alexander the Great as he conquers a vast empire.

my worldgeography.com myStory Video

Ancient Greece

IN Indiana

6.1.1 Summarize the rise, decline, and cultural achievements of ancient civilizations in Europe and Mesoamerica.

6.1.20 Analyze cause-and-effect relationships in history.

6.2.1 Compare and contrast forms of governments in Europe and the Americas throughout history.

6.2.2 Explain how elements of Greek direct democracy and Roman representative democracy are present in modern systems of government.

6.4.2 Analyze how countries of Europe and the Americas have been influenced by trade in different historical periods.

Key Terms • city-state • direct democracy • oligarchy • philosophy • cultural hearth

Visual Glossary

Reading Skill: Label an Outline Map Take notes using the outline map in your journal.

The civilization of ancient Greece has had a great effect on today's world. Democratic government traces its roots back to this civilization. Modern science began with the ancient Greek thinkers. In the arts and architecture, ancient Greek ideas remain strong today.

The Aegean World

Greece is a peninsula and a group of islands that jut out from southern Europe into the Mediterranean Sea. The Aegean World also included the islands of Crete and Rhodes, and the lands of Ionia.

Physical Geography The Greek peninsula is a mountainous area with an irregular coastline. The land is rugged and mostly rocky. Only small valleys near the coast have fertile soil. In general, the climate in this region is warm and dry. Summers tend to be hot and dry and winters mild.

The seas around Greece are full of fish. Because they had so little farmland, the ancient Greeks depended on the sea for their food. The mountains contain large amounts of marble and limestone. The ancient Greeks used these resources to construct buildings.

Greek Settlements The ancient Greeks mostly settled in valleys with fertile soil near the coast. There they set up farms and fished. Mountains or bodies of water often separated these settled areas. As a result, each settled area tended to develop its own independent spirit.

Reading Check What were some of the natural resources found in ancient Greece?

A Minoan ceremonial object in the shape of a bull's head ▼

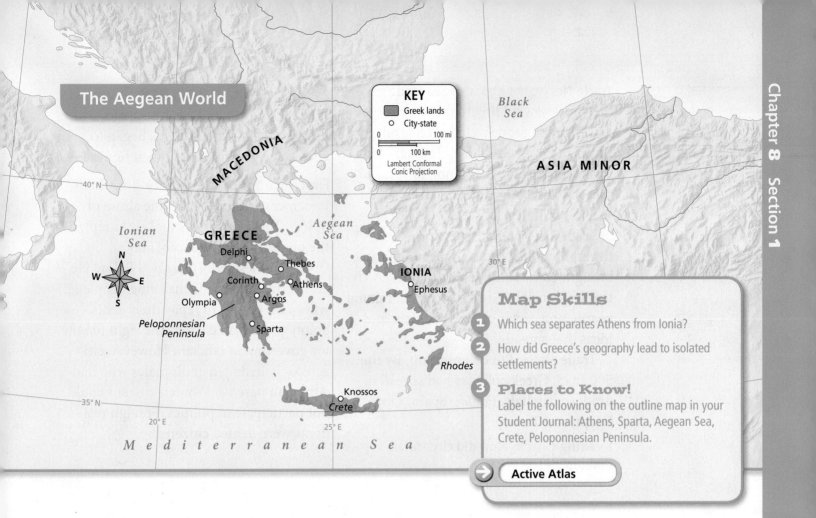

The Aegean World

KEY
- Greek lands
- ○ City-state

0 — 100 mi
0 — 100 km
Lambert Conformal
Conic Projection

Black Sea

MACEDONIA

ASIA MINOR

Ionian Sea

GREECE

Aegean Sea

Delphi

Thebes

Corinth

Athens

Olympia

Argos

Peloponnesian Peninsula

Sparta

IONIA

Ephesus

Rhodes

Knossos

Crete

M e d i t e r r a n e a n   S e a

40° N

30° E

35° N

20° E

25° E

Map Skills

1. Which sea separates Athens from Ionia?
2. How did Greece's geography lead to isolated settlements?
3. **Places to Know!**
   Label the following on the outline map in your Student Journal: Athens, Sparta, Aegean Sea, Crete, Peloponnesian Peninsula.

→ **Active Atlas**

The Rise of City-States

In prehistoric times, two civilizations developed in the Aegean region. The people called the Minoans lived on Crete and many other islands. The Mycenaeans (my suh nee uns) lived on the Greek mainland.

Minoans and Mycenaeans Around 3000 B.C., the Minoan civilization emerged on the island of Crete. The Minoans were skilled sailors who developed a writing system. They traded with mainland Greece, Egypt, and Sicily.

Around 1400 B.C., Mycenaeans from the mainland conquered the Minoans. They borrowed the Minoan system of writing and built <u>fortified</u> towns. Around 1200 B.C., the Mycenaean civilization collapsed for unknown reasons.

City-States Form The many fortified towns in Greece gradually developed into city-states. A **city-state** is a city or town that controls surrounding villages and farmland nearby.

Each city-state was independent and often fought frequently with other city-states. Many city-states were aristocracies run by wealthy landowners. The word *aristocracy* means "rule by the best people." Laws were based on tradition.

In many city-states, farmers and merchants rebelled against the aristocrats. To restore order, tyrants took control. A tyrant is a leader who gains total power by force. In some areas, the tyrants were replaced by an **oligarchy,** or government in which a small group of people rule.

fortified, *adj.,* strengthened by walls

Trade Networks Expand Sea trade gave the Greeks a vital link to the outside world. Trade goods included olive oil, gold, silver, and iron. Greek merchants traded with people from Asia Minor, Egypt, and Mesopotamia. As trade expanded, so did the power of the city-states.

Trade also spread Greek culture throughout the Mediterranean region. It brought cultural influences to Greece. In this way, ancient Greece became a **cultural hearth,** or a center of new practices and ideas that spread.

Trade also led to colonization. By the 500s B.C., Greek colonies had spread to modern day Italy, France, Spain, Libya, Egypt, and Turkey.

Reading Check How did city-states develop?

Athenian Democracy

As Greek power and wealth spread, its largest city-state, Athens, began to encourage political freedom at home.

First Stirrings of Democracy In Athens, reformers wanted to stop the abuse of power. These reformers looked to replace the oligarchy with a democracy.

One of these reformers was Solon. He ended the practice of enslaving people who were unable to repay their debts. Solon granted all citizens the right to vote for government officials. However, citizens only included adult males who had Athenian parents. Women citizens could not participate in politics. Foreign residents were denied citizenship.

Closer Look

Rulers of the Seas

At the height of Greek civilization, the Athenian navy ruled the seas. The Greek trireme (Latin for "three oars") was powered by 170 oarsmen sitting on three levels in the ship's hull. These wooden ships were expensive to build, and the oarsmen required years of training. The trireme's oarsmen made the ships fast. In his epic poem *The Odyssey,* Homer said of the Greeks, "Their ships are swift as a bird or a thought." The bronze ram made the trireme the most deadly ship on the Mediterranean.

Today, Greek fishermen still paint eyes on their ships' bows for good luck, just as their ancient ancestors did.

Greek triremes used a bronze ram to damage enemy ships.

In the mid-400s B.C., the statesman Pericles made more democratic reforms in Athens. For example, he set up salaries for public officials so that poor people could serve in government. Pericles famously said,

66 Here each individual is interested not only in his own affairs but in the affairs of the state as well. 99

Athenian Direct Democracy Under Pericles, Athens became the world's first **direct democracy.** In direct democracy, citizens take part directly in the day-to-day affairs of government. Today, in most democratic countries, such as the United States, people instead participate in government through elected representatives.

However, there are some examples of direct democracy-style governments in the modern world. One of these is in Switzerland, where citizens have the ability to vote on federal laws. Another is the town hall style of city government used in many communities in the New England region of the United States.

Reading Check What reforms did Solon propose?

Life in Ancient Greece

The period between the end of the Persian Wars and the death of Alexander (about 500 B.C.–323 B.C.) is called the classical period. It was a time of great advances in learning and art. Athens, named for the goddess of wisdom, was the most important cultural center of classical Greece.

The Greeks were also skilled sea traders. Trade ships were usually powered by a single square sail. The wooden ships were durable, and some lasted as long as 80 years. Pirates and shipwrecks were constant threats. The Greeks most commonly traded olive oil, wine, and almonds.

THINK CRITICALLY How was slavery connected to Greek naval power?

The Greeks have cultivated olives for thousands of years. The ancient Greeks exported olive oil in clay vessels like the one below.

myWorldActivity
Let's Make a Trade

385

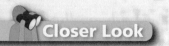
A New Form of Government and Justice

The Athenians called their political system *demokratia,* which means "rule by the people." This political system affected law-making as well as the courts. There were no professional judges or lawyers in Athens. Every citizen had the right to bring another citizen to trial or to serve on a jury. Some of the most basic elements of modern democracy originated in Athens, including majority rule, civic debate, judgment by jury, and the rule of law.

THINK CRITICALLY **Why is civic debate important in a democracy?**

The kleroterion was used to select jurors at random. Random selection ensured fairness. ▼

Bronze juror tickets with jurors' names were inserted into the slots of the kleroterion. ▶

Citizens of Athens
(Men of at least 18 years of age whose parents were Athenian)

Ecclesia
(Citizens' assembly; debated laws and important decisions)

Magistrates (9)
(Elected by the Ecclesia; applied the laws)

Boule (Council of 500)
(Chosen at random; debated important decisions and negotiated with foreign states)

People's Court (6,000 jurors)
(Selected at random; judged those who violated the laws)

Greek Religion The Greeks believed in many deities, or beings with supernatural powers. These gods and goddesses ruled over different areas of human life and the natural world. The chief god was Zeus, who ruled from his home on Mount Olympus. He was lord of the sky and rain.

The Greeks had no book or manuscripts to explain their religion. Rather, they used mythology, or a collection of stories told about history or gods. To honor the gods, the Greeks made beautiful statues in marble and built magnificent temples.

Love of Wisdom The Greeks also studied **philosophy,** or "love of wisdom." Greek scholars applied logic, or reason, to a study of knowledge and the world.

The Greek philosopher Plato wrote about government, ethics, and religion. Other important philosophers were Plato's teacher, Socrates, and Aristotle, Plato's student. In *Poetics,* Aristotle said,

> 66 Poetry, therefore, is a more philosophical and a higher thing than history: for poetry tends to express the universal, history the particular. 99

The ancient Greeks also investigated science and mathematics. People used to believe that the sun circled Earth. Using mathematics and careful observation, the astronomer Aristarchus (a ris TAHR kus) concluded that Earth circled the sun. Almost 2,000 years passed before scientists widely accepted this idea.

The Greeks also studied the past, but they did more than simply record events. The historian Herodotus is known as the father of history because he was the first to note events and analyze them. Two of ancient Greece's most important historians were also soldiers. Thucydides wrote the history of the Pelopponesian Wars, while Xenophon recorded Greek history as well as the sayings of Socrates.

Arts and Leisure The ancient Greeks developed a rich literary tradition, especially in poetry and drama. The playwrights Aeschylus, Sophocles, and Euripides wrote great tragedies, or serious works that have flawed heroes. Aristophanes' plays were comedies that often poked fun at Greek society.

The ancient Greeks made many advances in architecture. The most impressive type of public building in classical Greece was the temple. It consisted of a long chamber that housed a statue of a god or goddess. Columns surrounded the chamber. The most famous Greek temple is the Parthenon in Athens.

Greeks held public festivals to honor their gods. One such festival at Olympia was held every four years to honor Zeus. City-states would send their best athletes to compete in these festivals, which were known as the Olympic Games. Athletes from all over Greece competed in running, wrestling, and jumping.

Public and Private Life Though the public buildings in ancient Greece were impressive, most people lived in simple homes of mud bricks. They ate simple meals of bread, cheese, olives, and fish. Very few people ate meat since there was little space in which to raise <u>livestock</u>.

▲ On this ancient Greek vase, harvesters use sticks to knock olives from the trees.

livestock, *n.,* farm animals raised for food and profit

387

At the heart of the Greek city lay the agora, a public space that included the council-house, religious shrines, and the marketplace. Most of those who gathered in the agora were freemen, discussing politics or bargaining for goods and services.

These freemen were generally upper-class leaders of social and political life. The upper class included aristocrats, wealthy landowners, and, later, successful merchants. As free residents and citizens, they possessed more rights than anyone else.

For the most part, women ran the home. Women had few rights. They could not vote or own property. Some women served as priestesses in temples.

Slavery One third of the population of Athens were slaves. These people were owned by someone else and did not have the same rights as free people. Many slaves were captured during wartime or were children whose parents had been enslaved. Slaves did most of the hard labor in ancient Greece. A slave might be able to buy his or her freedom or obtain it from a grateful master.

Reading Check How did the Greeks influence the study of history?

Conflict and Decline

At sea, Athens' navy was superior. On land, Sparta's army challenged Athens.

Soldiers Rule Sparta The Spartans devoted themselves to military might from an early age. As adults, Spartan warriors were expected to put their military careers before wives and families.

A gold coin on which Alexander is portrayed as Ares, the god of war. ▼

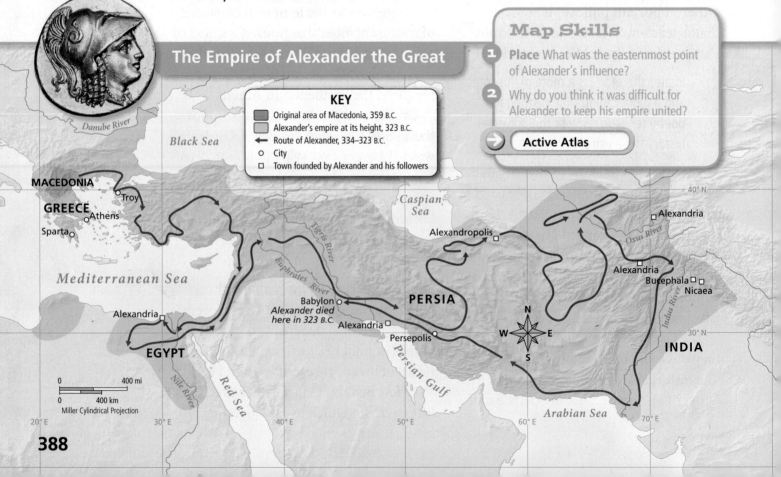

The Empire of Alexander the Great

KEY
- Original area of Macedonia, 359 B.C.
- Alexander's empire at its height, 323 B.C.
- ← Route of Alexander, 334–323 B.C.
- ○ City
- □ Town founded by Alexander and his followers

Map Skills

1. **Place** What was the easternmost point of Alexander's influence?

2. Why do you think it was difficult for Alexander to keep his empire united?

➡ **Active Atlas**

Danube River
Black Sea
MACEDONIA
Troy
GREECE
Athens
Sparta
Caspian Sea
40° N
Alexandria
Alexandropolis
Oxus River
Tigris River
Mediterranean Sea
Euphrates River
Alexandria
Bucephala
Nicaea
Indus River
Babylon
Alexander died here in 323 B.C.
PERSIA
Alexandria
N
Persepolis
W   E
30° N
Alexandria
EGYPT
S
INDIA
400 mi
0   400 km
Miller Cylindrical Projection
Nile River
Red Sea
Persian Gulf
Arabian Sea
70° E
20° E   30° E   40° E   50° E   60° E

Spartan women enjoyed more freedom than the women of Athens. They could own land and take part in business.

The city-state of Sparta was governed by an oligarchy led by the army. At the top of Spartan society were aristocrats who were also professional military men. Unlike the citizens of Athens, the people of Sparta played a much smaller part in government.

The Persian Wars War was frequent among the Greeks, but an outside threat united the city-states. That threat was the invading Persian army led by Darius, the king of Persia.

The Greek army met the Persians first at the Battle of Marathon. The Greeks surrounded the Persians, and the enemy fled to their ships in the Aegean Sea.

Darius's son Xerxes commanded the Persians in the second war with the Greeks. As allies, the Spartans joined the Greeks to stop the Persians at Thermopylae. Finally, Xerxes sailed for home after losing thousands of men and more than 200 ships in the Battle of Salamis.

Decline of the City-States In spite of their alliance, these two city-states remained enemies. War broke out between Athens and Sparta in 431 B.C. It was called the Peloponnesian War and continued off and on for 27 years. Athens was at last defeated, ending the golden age of this once-great city-state. The war also hurt other city-states around Greece, toppling governments and damaging trade. Greek culture did not end, but ongoing conflict kept it from reaching the unity or stability that had made it strong.

Spread of Greek Culture As you read at the beginning of this chapter, Alexander conquered most of the world known to the ancient Greeks. Greek culture eventually spread across southwest Asia, southern Europe, and North Africa. Today, the impact of Greek culture remains strong in democratic forms of government as well as in art and architecture.

Reading Check Which common enemy united Athens and Sparta?

As king, Alexander was popular and much loved. He died of an unknown illness at age 32. ▼

my worldgeography.com   Active Atlas

Section 1 Assessment

Essential Question
What are the challenges of diversity?

Key Terms

1. Use each of the following terms in a sentence: city-state, cultural hearth, direct democracy, philosophy.

Key Ideas

2. Where did most of the ancient Greeks settle?

3. Name some of the democratic reforms made during the golden age of Athens.

4. How did the Greeks defeat the Persians?

Think Critically

5. **Draw Conclusions** How were Sparta and Athens similar and different?

6. **Draw Inferences** Do you think Aristotle was influenced by Plato and Socrates? Explain why or why not.

What are the challenges of diversity?

7. How did the diversity of Alexander the Great's Empire affect Greek culture? Go to your Student Journal to record your answer.

389

Ancient Greek Literature

IN Indiana

6.1.1 Summarize the rise, decline, and cultural achievements of ancient civilizations in Europe and Mesoamerica.

6.1.21 Differentiate between fact and interpretation in historical accounts and explain historical passages.

Ancient Greece produced a wealth of literature that influenced later cultures. Greek plays and works of philosophy are still read today. Storytelling also played a large role in Greek literature. *Aesop's Fables* is a collection of short tales that teach a moral by telling a story, usually about animals. Perhaps the most famous pieces of all Greek literature are the two epic poems by Homer—*The Iliad* and *The Odyssey*. An epic poem is a long poem that tells a story about heroes. In *The Odyssey*, the warrior Odysseus encounters many dangers as he tries to return home after the Trojan War.

▲ A portrait believed to be of the ancient Greek poet Sappho

Stop at each circled letter on the right to think about the text. Then answer the question with the same letter on the left.

Ⓐ **Solve Problems** What problem is the dog making for the oxen?

Ⓑ **Identify Evidence** What detail shows that the dog is being cruel, rather than trying to protect something he needs?

Ⓒ **Synthesize** How does the moral at the end relate to the fable?

The Dog in the Manger

❝A Dog lay in a <u>manger</u>, and by his growling and snapping prevented Ⓐ the oxen from eating the hay which had been placed for them. 'What a selfish Dog!' said one of them to his Ⓑ companions; 'he cannot eat or sleep in the hay himself, and yet refuses to allow those to eat who can.' People often <u>begrudge</u> others what Ⓒ they cannot enjoy themselves. ❞

—Aesop, *Aesop's Fables*, translated by George Fyler Townsend

manger, *n.,* a box that holds food for cattle or horses

begrudge, *v.,* to give reluctantly

Diego Velázquez's 1640 portrait of Aesop shows the ancient Greek author as a modest man holding a book of his fables. ▶

Stop at each circled letter on the right to think about the text. Then answer the question with the same letter on the left.

D Categorize Is the speaker giving Odysseus a warning or a recommendation? How do you know?

E Draw Conclusions What happens to men when they first hear the cry of the Sirens?

F Identify Evidence What happens to the men the Sirens bewitch? What evidence proves this?

Siren, *n.,* a mythical creature, part bird and part woman, who lures sailors to their death on the rocks

bewitch, *v.,* to cast a spell over

loll, *v.,* to relax in a leaning position

flay, *v.,* to strip off or to skin

The Sirens' Song

66 Listen with care
D to this, now, and a god will arm
    your mind.
Square in your ships' path are <u>Sirens</u>, crying
beauty to <u>bewitch</u> men coasting by;
woe to the innocent who hears that sound!
He will not see his lady nor his children
in joy, crowding about him, home from sea;
E the Sirens will sing his mind away
    on their sweet meadow <u>lolling</u>.
F   There are bones
of dead men rotting in a pile beside them
and <u>flayed</u> skins shrivel around the spot. 99

—Homer, *The Odyssey,*
translated by Robert Fitzgerald

An ancient Greek vase showing Odysseus resisting the call of the Sirens ▼

Analyze the Documents

1. **Synthesize** What do the dog in the fable and the Sirens have in common?
2. **Writing Task** Write your own fable to teach a lesson.

The ancient Greeks also enjoyed plays performed at outdoor theatres like this one in Taormina. ▼

Ancient Rome

IN Indiana

6.1.1 Summarize the rise, decline, and cultural achievements of ancient civilizations in Europe and Mesoamerica.

6.1.2 Describe and compare the beliefs, the spread and the influence of religions throughout Europe and Mesoamerica.

6.2.2 Explain how elements of Greek direct democracy and Roman representative democracy are present in modern systems of government.

6.4.1 Give examples of how trade related to key developments in the history of Europe and the Americas.

6.4.2 Analyze how countries of Europe and the Americas have been influenced by trade in different historical periods.

Key Terms • patrician • plebeian • representative democracy • Pax Romana • aqueduct

Visual Glossary

Reading Skill: Sequence Take notes using the graphic organizer in your journal.

◄ Livia, wife of the Roman emperor Augustus, shown as Ceres, the goddess of grains.

Historians are not sure about the origins of ancient Rome. One legend says it was founded by Aeneas, the Greek hero of Virgil's poem *The Aeneid*. Aeneas is said to have escaped after the Trojan War and traveled to Latium. There, he married a princess and founded the town that would become Rome.

We do know that by the 700s B.C., a shepherd people called the Latins lived in central Italy. From their simple villages came a great empire.

The Roman Republic

Around 1000 B.C., the Latins settled near the Tiber River in central Italy. This river gave them access to the sea. The region also had fertile soil and marble and limestone for building. The surrounding hills protected the settlement. The Latins named the village Rome.

Etruscan Influence To the north lived the Etruscans, an advanced group of artists, builders, and sailors. In their sea travels, the Etruscans had learned things from many other cultures, including the Greeks.

The Etruscans expanded into Latium, ruling with the consent of the Romans. The presence of the Etruscans added much to Roman society and its government. The Etruscans introduced a writing system that they adapted from the Greeks. This formed the basis of the Latin alphabet that we use today. In addition, the Etruscans brought a strong military tradition to Rome, including the use of the Greek phalanx formation. Roman cities were improved through Etruscan methods of paving streets and using stone arches to support heavy structures such as bridges.

From Kingdom to Republic In 509 B.C., the Romans overthrew the Etruscan kings and established a republic. A republic is a government without king or emperors.

The republic had a Senate and a citizens' assembly, which it adopted from the Etruscans. The assembly was divided into two groups: the **patricians** and the **plebeians.** The patricians were wealthy aristocrats. The plebeians were all the remaining citizens. A patrician's vote counted for more than a plebeian's vote. The assembly elected two consuls, who led the government. A group of 300 wealthy citizens were appointed to serve in the Senate, which passed the laws.

In the early 400s B.C., after many protests, the plebeians gained the right to have representatives called tribunes. A tribune could overturn the act of any public official that was unjust to any citizen. Then the plebeians were given their own assembly. Eventually, the plebeians' votes counted as much as the patricians' votes.

During a crisis, the power of government was given to a dictator. The Roman statesman Cicero describes the role of dictator.

> 66 [W]hen a serious war or civil [disagreements] arise, one man shall hold, for not longer than six months, the power which ordinarily belongs to the two consuls . . . he shall be 'master of the people.' 99

Roman Law The Romans wrote down their laws, the Twelve Tables, around 450 B.C. With written laws, people would know their rights and duties rather than rely on customs that could be ignored.

The Roman government was considered a **representative democracy,** meaning that elected representatives made the political decisions. This system prevented any one individual from gaining too much power. It differed from Athenian direct democracy. The republic of Rome influenced representative governments throughout the world, including, centuries later, that of the United States.

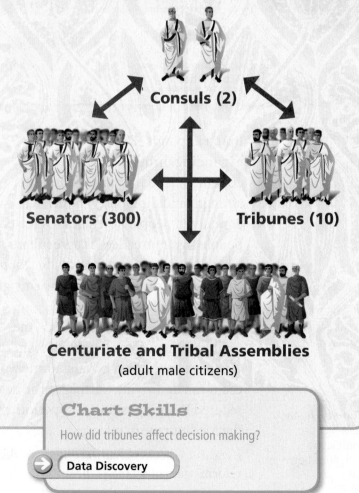

Roman Checks and Balances

Some modern democracies still use the system of checks and balances devised in ancient Rome. This system ensures that no one branch of the government becomes too powerful.

Consuls (2)

Senators (300)

Tribunes (10)

Centuriate and Tribal Assemblies
(adult male citizens)

Chart Skills

How did tribunes affect decision making?

Data Discovery

The Roman Empire

BRITAIN

London

ATLANTIC OCEAN

GAUL

GERMANY

Lyon

Danube R.

DACIA

SPAIN

ITALY

Black Sea

Toledo

Rome

THRACE

Byzantium

Cádiz

ASIA MINOR

MESOPOTAMIA

Athens

MAURETANIA

Carthage

GREECE

SYRIA

AFRICA

Mediterranean Sea

JUDEA

Alexandria

ARABIA

EGYPT

Red Sea

TROPIC OF CANCER

KEY

Roman Empire, A.D. 117

○ City

0   500 mi

0   500 km

Lambert Conformal Conic Projection

Map Skills

1 Estimate Using the scale bar, find how far the Roman Empire stretched from west to east.

2 Interaction How might the Mediterranean Sea have helped unify the empire?

→ **Active Atlas**

▲ This column commemorates the emperor Trajan's victories in the Dacian Wars (A.D. 100–106).

diplomacy, *n.,* the art and practice of conducting negotiations between nations

Rome Expands Rome set about expanding through alliances and conquests. The Romans used military strength and <u>diplomacy</u> to turn conquered people into allies. Defeated people signed treaties, or agreements, in which they promised to provide troops to Rome. In this way, the Roman army grew to be the largest force in Italy.

During the 200s and 100s B.C., the mighty Roman army fought its main rival, Carthage, in the Punic Wars. Rome won each war, destroying Carthage. The defeat secured Rome's position of superiority in the Mediterranean region.

Reading Check What were some of the reforms gained by the plebeians?

Rome Becomes an Empire

By 100 B.C., the republic was becoming unstable. After several revolts, the republic came under the control of dictators and military leaders.

Beginnings of Empire In the 50s B.C., Julius Caesar conquered Gaul, land that is much of present-day France and Belgium. He then invaded Italy and made himself the sole ruler of Rome and its territories. Hoping to restore the republic, aristocrats assassinated Caesar.

The result was chaos and the end of the republic. Caesar's nephew Octavian eventually emerged as the victor. He took the name Augustus and became the first Roman emperor in 27 B.C.

The Empire Unifies The rule of Augustus started a period of stability known as the **Pax Romana** (Roman Peace). This period lasted for about 200 years.

Rome set up colonies in conquered areas. Many Roman citizens migrated to these colonies. Some of the people conquered by the Romans became citizens. The spread of Roman law helped to unify the empire. The empire was also united by a network of roads that helped soldiers move and keep order.

Trade along Roman roads and across the seas also stabilized the empire. The use of coins made trade easier. The empire gained wealth from trade and tributes paid by <u>provinces</u>. Tributes were a type of taxation.

Gradually, wealthy Romans came to admire Greek culture. Greek books were copied and sold widely. Learned Romans read both Latin and Greek. Greco-Roman culture was spread throughout the empire with colonies in Gaul, Spain, and North Africa. In addition to cultural influences, Roman colonists received Roman citizenship and lived under Roman law.

Reading Check What was the result of Caesar's assassination?

Life in Ancient Rome

The basic social unit in ancient Rome was the family. The father had complete control over the family and the home.

Roman women worked in the home. They could not vote or participate in politics. Gradually, Roman women did gain more rights. Emperors' wives, such as Livia and Julia Agrippina, also influenced politics in Rome.

Slavery in Ancient Rome About one third of the people in Rome were slaves. The economy depended on their work.

Sometimes, a slave could buy his or her freedom. Freed slaves were allowed to become citizens. Household slaves sometimes became trusted companions. Other slaves led short, brutal lives. Some worked in copper or tin mines. Gladiator slaves faced death in arena matches in the Colosseum. Slaves also worked as farmers or as rowers on Roman warships.

myWorldActivity
What's the News in Rome?

province, *n.,* country or region under control of a larger government

One important Roman innovation was the **aqueduct,** a channel that moves water over great distances.

395

Roman Religion Romans worshiped many deities, some of whom were adopted from the Greeks and the Etruscans. In Rome, religion was tied closely to political life and emperors were sometimes worshiped as gods.

Roman Achievements Like the Greeks, Romans made statues in marble. Roman literature includes poetry by Virgil and Horace, and essays by Cicero. Architects perfected the arch and invented concrete to build temples and public buildings.

In Roman Egypt, Ptolemy (TAH luh mee) calculated the size and distance of the sun and the paths of the stars and planets across the sky. The Greek Galen discovered how parts of the body worked.

Reading Check What elements helped to unify the Roman empire?

Judaism and Christianity

The Jews of Judea lived in an area that came under direct Roman rule in A.D. 63. In the centuries before the Roman empire, the Jews had spread to Egypt and to other parts of southwest Asia. The Jews believed in one God. This belief is called monotheism. The Romans, who believed in many gods, did not usually force them to change their practices.

Jews Flee Harsh Rule Some Jews, however, felt Roman rule and taxes were too harsh. They rebelled. The Romans struck back harshly and destroyed the Jewish Temple in Jerusalem in A.D. 70.

The Romans killed many thousands of Jews. Other Jews left the ruined province for other parts of the empire. Many moved to Italy and other parts of Europe.

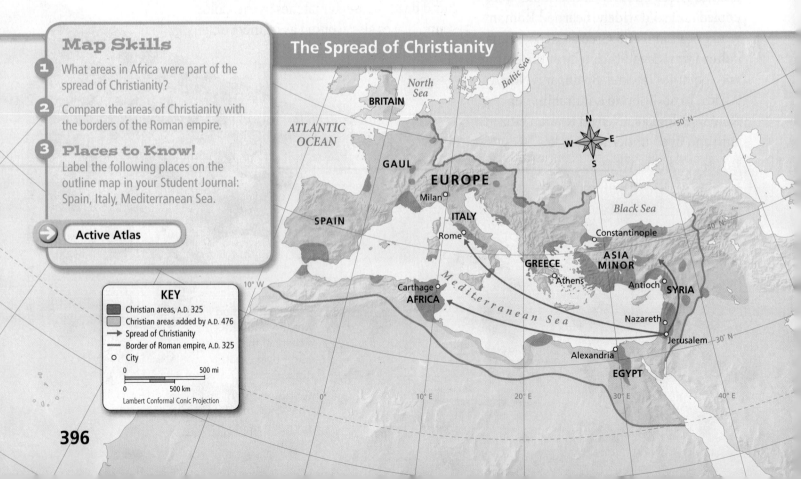

Map Skills

1 What areas in Africa were part of the spread of Christianity?

2 Compare the areas of Christianity with the borders of the Roman empire.

3 **Places to Know!** Label the following places on the outline map in your Student Journal: Spain, Italy, Mediterranean Sea.

→ **Active Atlas**

The Spread of Christianity

KEY
- Christian areas, A.D. 325
- Christian areas added by A.D. 476
- → Spread of Christianity
- — Border of Roman empire, A.D. 325
- ○ City

0   500 mi
0   500 km
Lambert Conformal Conic Projection

Birth and Spread of Christianity Around 4 B.C., a Jew named Jesus was born in Judea. He grew up in Nazareth and learned to be a carpenter.

When he was 30 years old, he became a religious teacher. Jesus preached that there was only one God. Many of his followers believed that Jesus was the Messiah. Jews believed that a leader called the Messiah would bring them freedom. The name Christ comes from the Greek word for messiah. Jesus's followers later came to be known as Christians. Jesus's teachings formed the basis for a new religion, Christianity.

Christianity gradually spread across the Roman empire and into neighboring lands. For more than 200 years, Christians faced harsh treatment from the Roman government. Then, in A.D. 312, Roman emperor Constantine I became a Christian. Over the next 100 years, Christianity spread across much of Europe, and most Romans became Christians.

Reading Check Why did the Jews want to flee Roman rule?

The Western Empire Falls

Historians are not sure what caused the fall of the Roman empire. One theory proposes that the Romans used so many everyday objects made of lead that people may have sickened and died from lead poisoning. Most likely the collapse came from several factors.

Instability and Division From A.D. 235 to A.D. 284, there were 60 men who declared themselves emperor. Prices increased, taxes rose, and disease reduced the population. The Roman army weakened as it came to depend more on mercenaries, or soldiers who fought for money rather than for loyalty to a leader or nation.

Diocletian eventually divided the empire into eastern and western lands to make it easier to govern. Constantine moved the capital east, renaming it Constantinople. The Eastern Roman empire went on to thrive as the Byzantine empire, while the west fell to Germanic invaders.

Reading Check Identify one factor that led to the fall of the Roman empire.

Invaders!

▶ **378** Visigoths defeat the Roman army.

▶ **406** Vandals attack Gaul.

▶ **410** Visigoths sack Rome.

▶ **441** Attila (above) and the Huns begin to invade the empire.

▶ **450** Angles, Saxons, Jutes invade Britain (traditional date).

▶ **476** Rome falls to the Germanic leader Odoacer.

Timeline

my worldgeography.com Timeline

Section 2 Assessment

Essential Question

Key Terms

1. Define each of these key terms with a complete sentence: patrician, plebeian, representative democracy, Pax Romana, aqueduct.

Key Ideas

2. Why was Julius Caesar assassinated?

3. How did the conversion of Constantine I affect religion in Europe?

4. Name three elements that led to the fall of the Roman empire.

Think Critically

5. Compare and Contrast How did Roman democracy differ from ancient Greek democracy?

6. Problem Solving If you were in charge of the Roman empire, how would you prevent it from collapsing? List at least three ways.

What are the challenges of diversity?

7. How did the Romans use citizenship to unify a diverse empire? Go to your Student Journal to record your answer.

The Fall of the Roman Empire

IN Indiana

6.1.1 Summarize the rise, decline, and cultural achievements of ancient civilizations in Europe and Mesoamerica.

6.1.23 Identify issues related to an event in Europe or the Americas and give arguments for and against that issue.

For centuries, scholars have wondered why the powerful Roman empire collapsed. In its final years, the Roman empire was weakened by economic, military, political, and social problems. In the 1700s, the English historian Edward Gibbon wrote that Rome fell to stronger Germanic invaders. For generations, his ideas were unquestioned. Today, most historians agree that many factors led to the collapse of the empire. The topic remains popular with researchers and historians who continue to propose new ideas about what weakened the once-mighty empire.

▲ This Roman coin depicts Mars, the god of war.

Stop at each circled letter on the right to think about the text. Answer the question with the same letter on the left.

Ⓐ **Draw Conlusions** How does Gibbon believe the Romans viewed their situation? Might he have been correct? Explain.

Ⓑ **Identify Bias** What was Gibbon's view of the northern tribes? How can you tell?

Ⓒ **Draw Inferences** What were the "fruits of industry," and why would the northern tribes want them?

voracious, *adj.,* extremely hungry

ravish, *v.,* to seize and carry away by force

barbarian, *adj.,* those considered uncivilized by the ancient Greeks and Romans

Numerous Enemies

❝ The Romans were ignorant of
Ⓐ the extent of their danger, and the number of their enemies. Beyond the Rhine and Danube, the northern countries of Europe and Asia were filled with [a great many] tribes of hunters
Ⓑ and shepherds, poor, <u>voracious</u>, and turbulent [agitated]; bold in arms, and impatient to <u>ravish</u> the
Ⓒ fruits of industry. The <u>Barbarian</u> world was agitated by the rapid impulse of war. ❞

—Edward Gibbon,
The History of the Decline and Fall of the Roman Empire, 1776–1788

In this marble relief, a Germanic swordsman defends himself against a Roman warrior. ▼

Stop at each circled letter on the right to think about the text. Then answer the question with the same letter on the left.

D **Draw Conclusions** What does "the decay of their bodies and health" mean?

E **Draw Inferences** Why did the Romans use so much lead?

F **Synthesize** If most people in an empire accidentally ingested something that damaged their health, how might this have affected the empire as a whole?

chronic, *adj.,* occurring often and lasting a long time

metallurgist, *n.,* a person who works with metals

ingest, *v.,* to take food or chemicals into the body

Lead Poisoning

66 In 1983, Jerome O. Nriagu, an environmental scientist . . . theorized that the decline of the empire had its roots not in the decay of Roman ideals and morality, but in the **D** decay of their bodies and health. The cause of this decay, Nriagu wrote, was <u>chronic</u> lead poisoning. A soft gray metal that is **E** plentiful in nature, lead was used by the Romans to make many household items. Roman <u>metallurgists</u> blended lead with tin to make a silver-gray metal known as pewter. Craftsmen used the handsome metal to make cups, plates, spoons, cooking pots, **F** and wine vessels. . . . What the Romans did not know is that lead is one of the most poisonous metals a person can <u>ingest</u>. 99

—Bradley Steffens,
The Fall of the Roman Empire, 1994

Analyze the Documents

1. **Categorize** According to these documents, what was a danger within the empire and what was a danger outside the empire?

2. **Writing Task** Make an outline for a persuasive essay in which you try to convince people in the Roman empire to make changes to save themselves.

▲ Lead keys from ancient Rome

Early Middle Ages

IN Indiana

6.1.3 Explain the continuation and contributions of the Eastern Roman Empire after the fall of the Western Roman Empire.

6.1.4 Explain the development and organization of various systems in Europe and the Americas.

Visual Glossary

Key Terms • schism • lord • vassal • feudalism • manorialism

Reading Skill: Summarize Take notes using the graphic organizer in your journal.

▼ The emperor Justinian ruled the Byzantine empire from 527 to 565.

After the fall of the Roman empire, a new age dawned in Europe. This age is often called the medieval period or Middle Ages. The word *medieval* comes from the Latin words for "middle" and "age." Historians use this term because the medieval period is beween the ancient and modern periods of European history.

The Byzantine Empire

As the Western Roman empire declined, power shifted east. The Eastern Roman empire remained strong. Its capital, Constantinople, grew rich on trade. Historians refer to the surviving eastern empire as the Byzantine empire.

Emperor Justinian's Rule Justinian ruled as an autocrat, or a single ruler with absolute power. He ruled both the empire and the Christian Church. Under Justinian, the empire expanded through conquest and trade. Justinian's wife Theodora served as his close advisor and, in effect, co-ruler. One of Justinian's greatest acts as emperor was to organize Roman laws into one code, called Justinian's Code. By the 1100s, these laws had reached Western Europe and helped monarchs unify their power. These laws remain part of many countries' laws.

Byzantine Christianity Since early Christian times, leaders called patriarchs had led the Christian churches in different regions. In the west, the head of the Church was the patriarch of Rome, known as the pope. The pope claimed the power to lead all Christians.

In the east, the highest official was the patriarch of Constantinople. This patriarch obeyed the Byzantine emperor. Unlike Christian priests in Western Europe, the Byzantine clergy had the right to marry. Greek, not Latin, was the language of the eastern Church.

A New Alphabet During Roman times, a people called the Slavs lived in what is now Poland, Belarus, and Ukraine. The Slavs had been farmers and traders for centuries. This commerce brought them in contact with the Byzantine empire.

In about 863, two Byzantine Greeks, the brothers Cyril and Methodius, traveled to Eastern Europe to bring Christianity to the Slavs. While there, they translated the Greek Bible into a Slavic language. This translation let people learn about Christianity in a language they understood. The brothers invented the Cyrillic alphabet. This alphabet combined Greek and Latin letters to express the sounds in the Slavic languages. In this way, writing and Christianity spread among the Slavic peoples. Today, people in Eastern Europe—as well as some in Russia and Mongolia—write in the Cyrillic alphabet.

Christianity Splits Gradually, the two branches of Christianity grew more divided. The Eastern church rejected the pope as leader of all Christians. Finally, the church went through an official **schism** (SIZ um), or split, called the Great Schism of 1054. The Byzantine church became the Eastern, or Greek, Orthodox church. The Western church became the Roman Catholic Church. These churches remain divided today.

The Byzantine Empire Falls By the time of the Great Schism, the Byzantine empire had begun to weaken. The emperors lost their lands to invaders such as the Arabs. Arabs conquered most of the Byzantine lands in North Africa and southwest Asia during the 600s. The Arabs were Muslims, or followers of Islam, a new religion. Like Judaism and Christianity, Islam was based on the worship of one God.

In addition, powerful merchants from the Italian city-state of Venice took control of important Byzantine trade routes. Then,

myWorldActivity
Write in Cyrillic

Cyril and Methodius, whom Christians revere as saints, hold religious documents writtten in Cyrillic. *How did this alphabet get its name?* ▼

401

in 1453, the Ottoman Turks captured Constantinople. This meant the end of the Byzantine empire. The Turks changed the city's name to Istanbul. They also introduced Islam and made Istanbul a center of Muslim culture.

Byzantine Achievements Building on Greco-Roman culture, the Byzantine empire lasted for almost 1,000 years. Its artists advanced art and architecture. Its scholars preserved ancient learning. One such scholar was Anna Comnena, the first important female historian in the west. The Byzantine <u>legacy</u> led to Europe's later cultural flowering, the Renaissance.

legacy, *n.,* something transmitted or received from a predecessor

Reading Check What did Cyril and Methodius achieve?

New Kingdoms in Europe

By around A.D. 450, Germanic tribes had taken control of most of the Western Roman empire.

Germanic Tribes Take Control Different tribes controlled the various parts of the region. A Germanic tribe called the Visigoths settled in Spain. The Angles, Jutes, and Saxons—later known as the Anglo-Saxons—took over most of Britain. And the Franks set up a kingdom in Gaul, in present-day France and Belgium.

Within each of these kingdoms, people were loyal only to their local leader. As a result, the idea of a central government disappeared.

Rise of the Franks A king of the Franks named Clovis defeated the last Roman commander in 486. He then established a kingdom that stretched from the Rhine region in the east to the Pyrenees Mountains in the west. Later, this area was named France after the Franks.

After Clovis's death, his kingdom was divided into smaller kingdoms. In the early 700s, however, the Frankish ruler Charles Martel united these kingdoms.

Charlemagne During the 770s, Charles Martel's grandson, Charlemagne (742–814), became king of the Franks. He conquered much of Western Europe and expanded the Frankish empire.

Charlemagne strongly supported the Catholic Church. He believed that by converting people to Christianity all across his growing empire, he could unite and strengthen it. Pope Leo III crowned Charlemagne Holy Roman Emperor in 800.

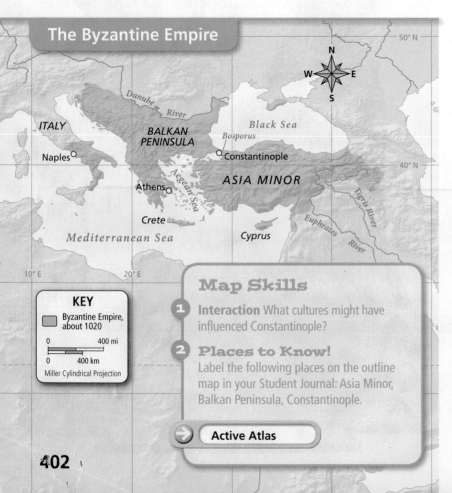

The Byzantine Empire

ITALY

Naples

Danube River

BALKAN PENINSULA

Black Sea

Bosporus

Constantinople

ASIA MINOR

Athens

Aegean Sea

Crete

Mediterranean Sea

Cyprus

Euphrates River

Tigris River

50° N

40° N

N W E S

10° E   20° E

KEY

Byzantine Empire, about 1020

0   400 mi
0   400 km
Miller Cylindrical Projection

Map Skills

1 **Interaction** What cultures might have influenced Constantinople?

2 **Places to Know!** Label the following places on the outline map in your Student Journal: Asia Minor, Balkan Peninsula, Constantinople.

Active Atlas

This was important because a Christian pope had crowned a Germanic ruler as a successor to Roman emperors.

Charlemagne reestablished the rule of law, which had weakened after the fall of Rome. For example, he declared that judges should base their decisions on accepted laws. He also set up a school at his palace, though he himself could not write. This school attracted scholars from all of Europe.

After Charlemagne's death, the empire was divided among his sons. Some of these lands later became the modern countries of France and Germany.

Vikings and Magyars During the 800s and 900s, Viking invaders made terrifying raids along the coasts and rivers of Europe. The Vikings came from Scandinavia in northern Europe. They conquered parts of what are now England, Scotland, Ireland, France, and Ukraine. The Vikings who settled in France were called Normans. The Normans later conquered England.

Viking and Norman invaders also helped shape powerful kingdoms in England and in Ukraine. The kingdom in Ukraine, called Kievan Rus, adopted Eastern Christianity. The modern nations of Ukraine, Belarus, and Russia grew out of Kievan Rus.

During the 900s, a people called the Magyars conquered what is now Hungary. They made fearsome raids into Germany, Italy, and other parts of Western Europe. Around 1000, the Magyars converted to Christianity. The Magyars formed the kingdom of Hungary.

Christian Life The Christian church and its teachings were the center of medieval life. The church sent people across Europe to spread Christianity and gain new members. Gradually, most pagans in Europe converted to the Christian religion. A pagan was someone who worshiped more than one god. Although Western Europeans were divided politically, the Catholic Church united them through religion. Eastern Europeans were united through the Eastern Orthodox Church. *Orthodox* means following traditional or established beliefs.

Statue of Charlemagne ▼

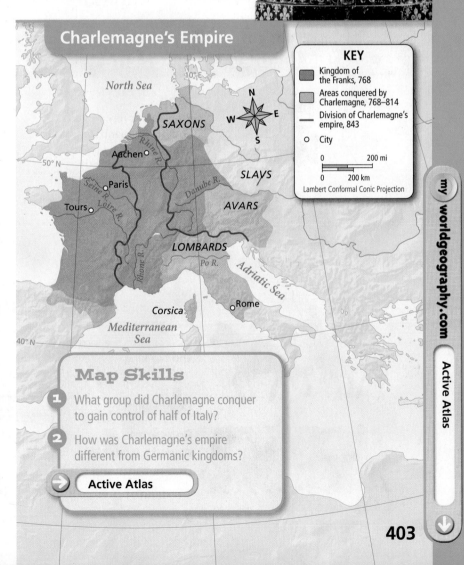

Charlemagne's Empire

KEY

■ Kingdom of the Franks, 768
■ Areas conquered by Charlemagne, 768–814
— Division of Charlemagne's empire, 843
○ City

0   200 mi
0   200 km
Lambert Conformal Conic Projection

Map Skills

1 What group did Charlemagne conquer to gain control of half of Italy?

2 How was Charlemagne's empire different from Germanic kingdoms?

→ **Active Atlas**

my **worldgeography**.com

Active Atlas

403

manuscript, *n.,* a document written by hand

Male Christian religious people called monks lived in monasteries, secluded communities focused on prayer and service. These monks made copies of the Bible and Greek and Roman works. They helped to preserve valuable <u>manuscripts</u>, many of which contained ancient learning.

Women joined religious orders as nuns. Some nuns became abbesses, or heads of female religious communities. The German abbess Hildegard of Bingen wrote poems and music inspired by her visions of God.

Reading Check What were some of Charlemagne's reforms?

Feudalism and Manorialism

As you have read, during the late Roman empire, people began to accept the protection and control of landowners from the nobility. In the Middle Ages, barbarians and other warriors took control of most of the land. They offered protection to the peasants, or small farmers, living on the land in return for service. Each landowning warrior pledged loyalty to a tribal leader called a **lord,** or to the king. A lord was a man who controlled large areas of land. In return for the warrior's service, the lord or king offered protection.

How Feudalism Worked As time went by, kings granted land to lords in return for service. Lords, in turn, granted land to noble soldiers called knights in return for military service. A noble who received the land was called a **vassal.** The system of rights and duties connecting lords and vassals was called **feudalism.**

The lord promised to protect his vassals. In return, the vassals provided military support and money or food for their lord. The peasants were subject to both lords and vassals. Lords and vassals also had trained warriors called knights to serve them.

Lords sometimes quarreled over territory. In these conflicts, a vassal and his knights would help their lord in battle.

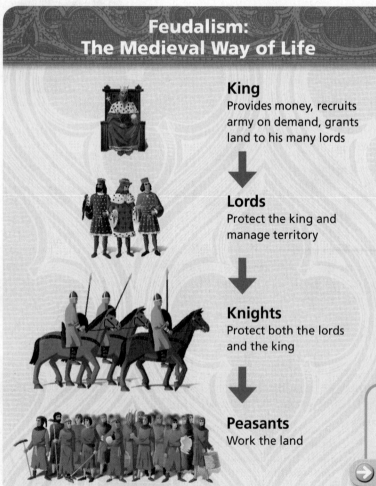

Feudalism: The Medieval Way of Life

King
Provides money, recruits army on demand, grants land to his many lords

Lords
Protect the king and manage territory

Knights
Protect both the lords and the king

Peasants
Work the land

Chart Skills

Describe the relationship between the king and the peasants in feudalism.

Data Discovery

By the end of the early Middle Ages, feudalism had spread across both Western and Eastern Europe. Feudalism was supported by an economic system called manorialism.

How Manorialism Worked The economic relationship that existed between lords or knights and peasants was called **manorialism.** The center of the system was the manor, a huge estate that included the lord's house or castle, farmland, pastures, peasants, and possibly a village. Many of the peasants who lived on the manor were serfs, or people who belonged to the estate as laborers. They were not slaves, but they were not free to move, marry, or buy land without the lord's permission.

Each manor was self-sufficient, supplying all the food, clothing, and shelter needed by both the lord and peasants. Peasants and their lords were thus dependent on one another.

The wife of the lord was called a lady. She attended to domestic chores and managed the servants. Literacy was not common even among noblewomen. Ladies had few rights. Some lords chose a wife for her dowry, or a payment of money and land provided at the time of marriage. In most parts of Europe, women could own land. When a woman's parents died, however, their land passed to the oldest brother in many countries.

Peasants led hard lives working from sunup to sundown. Their diets seldom varied and disease was common.

Reading Check What was the knight's role in feudalism?

Culture Close-up

▲ Peasants farmed their own plots of land as well as those of the lord.

Section **3** Assessment

Essential Question

Key Terms

1. Write a short paragraph showing how these key terms are related: lord, vassal, feudalism.

Key Ideas

2. What was Justinian's Code?

3. How did medieval monks preserve ancient learning?

4. What was feudalism?

Think Critically

5. **Categorize** Draw a table of three rulers who tried to unify Western Europe after the fall of the Roman empire. Under each ruler, list his ethnic group, time of rule, and accomplishments.

6. **Draw Inferences** Do you think peasants often traveled far from the manor? Explain why or why not.

What are the challenges of diversity?

7. How did cultural differences between the East and the West affect the Christian church? Go to your Student Journal to record your answer.

Learned Women of the Middle Ages

IN Indiana   **6.1.21** Differentiate between fact and interpretation in historical accounts and explain historical passages.

Most medieval women had limited roles. Peasant women worked in the fields or as servants. Noble women tended their husbands' manors. Women were not expected to become writers or teachers, but some did so anyway. Hildegard of Bingen was an educated noblewoman who became the abbess of a religious order. She had visions that she said were from God, and she wrote essays, poems, and songs. Christine de Pisan was a Venetian woman who lived in Paris. After her husband died, she made a living by copying manuscripts and by writing poems and books on women's behavior.

▲ A medieval woman uses scissors to cut cloth.

This medieval image shows Hildegard receiving divine visions in the form of flames. ▼

Stop at each circled letter on the right to think about the text. Then answer the question with the same letter on the left.

A **Categorize** What kind of story does the first sentence make you anticipate? Explain.

B **Draw Conclusions** Who or what affects the motion of the feather?

C **Draw Inferences** Who is the air and who is the feather? Explain what this reveals about Hildegard of Bingen.

adorn, *v.,* decorate

vestment, *n.,* ceremonial clothing

of its own accord, *adv. phrase,* on its own

borne, *v.,* carried

A Feather on the Breath of God

66 Listen now: a king sat on his throne, high

A pillars before him splendidly <u>adorned</u> . . . . They showed the king's <u>vestments</u> in great honor everywhere. Then the king chose to lift a small feather from the

B ground, and he commanded it to fly just as the king himself wished. But a feather does not fly <u>of its own accord</u>; it is <u>borne</u> up by the air. So too I am. . . . I depend entirely on God's help. 99

C —Hildegard of Bingen, letter written in 1148

Stop at each circled letter on the right to think about the text. Then answer the question with the same letter on the left.

D **Solve Problems** What should a housewife do if she has more food than her family can eat?

E **Draw Conclusions** Why is it important not to give away anything that is stale or damaged?

F **Synthesize** According to Christine de Pisan, what is the best kind of charity?

indigent, *n.,* poor people

charity, *n.,* the giving of money or help to those in need

alms, *n.,* money and goods given to the poor

childbed, *n.,* the bed of a woman who is giving birth to a child

The Wise Housewife

66 This wise woman will take great care that no food goes bad around her house, that **D** nothing goes to waste that might help the poor and <u>indigent</u>. If she gives them to the **E** poor, she will ensure that the leftovers are not stale and that the clothes are not moth-eaten. [I]f she loves the welfare of her soul **F** and the virtue of <u>charity</u>, she will not give her <u>alms</u> only in this way, but with the wine from her own cellar and the meat from her table, to poor women in <u>childbed</u>, to the sick, and often to her poor neighbors. 99

—Christine de Pisan,
The Treasure of the City of Ladies,
translated by Sarah Lawson

Christine de Pisan instructing a young man ▶

Analyze the Documents

1. **Compare Viewpoints** Which of these writers was more concerned with practical matters and which was more concerned with spiritual matters?

2. **Writing Task** Decide what kind of an essay you would write about these two learned women. Then write the thesis statement you would use in the essay.

407

High and Late Middle Ages

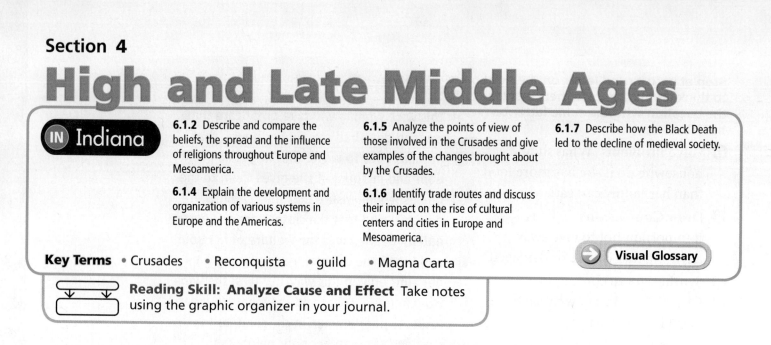

IN Indiana

6.1.2 Describe and compare the beliefs, the spread and the influence of religions throughout Europe and Mesoamerica.

6.1.4 Explain the development and organization of various systems in Europe and the Americas.

6.1.5 Analyze the points of view of those involved in the Crusades and give examples of the changes brought about by the Crusades.

6.1.6 Identify trade routes and discuss their impact on the rise of cultural centers and cities in Europe and Mesoamerica.

6.1.7 Describe how the Black Death led to the decline of medieval society.

Visual Glossary

Key Terms • Crusades • Reconquista • guild • Magna Carta

Reading Skill: Analyze Cause and Effect Take notes using the graphic organizer in your journal.

◀ Knights wore suits of armor such as this one during the Middle Ages.

By 1000, feudalism had stabilized Europe and the population was growing. Universities formed, merchants gained power, and farming techniques improved. This period is called the High Middle Ages. It lasted until the early 1300s. During the Late Middle Ages, however, wars, disease, and famine hit Europe hard. As a result, the the feudal system weakened and collapsed.

The Crusades and the Wider World

By 1081, the Seljuk Turks had overrun much of the Byzantine empire. These people had migrated from Central Asia, and when they reached the Middle East, they converted to Islam. As they conquered new lands, they converted the defeated peoples to Islam.

The Turks also took control of Palestine. This region was sacred to Jews, Christians, and Muslims. It was known to Christians as the Holy Land. Many Christians in Europe objected to Muslim control of the Holy Land.

The Holy Wars Begin In 1095, Pope Urban II urged church leaders to organize the **Crusades,** a series of military expeditions to free the Holy Land from Muslim rule. At the Council of Clermont, named for the town in France where it was held, Pope Urban II urged people of all classes to unite to take back Jerusalem in a holy war,

66 You common people who have been miserable sinners, become soldiers of Christ! You nobles, do not [quarrel] with one another. Use your arms in a just war! Labor for an everlasting reward. 99

The First Crusade

North Sea

Baltic Sea

HOLY ROMAN EMPIRE

Paris
Metz
Regensburg

FRANCE

HUNGARY

Genoa
Venice

Black Sea

BYZANTINE EMPIRE

Rome

Constantinople

KINGDOM OF SICILY

ARMENIA

Antioch

Mediterranean Sea

Jerusalem

KEY

→ First Crusade, 1096–1099

○ City

0   250 mi
0   250 km

Lambert Conformal Conic Projection

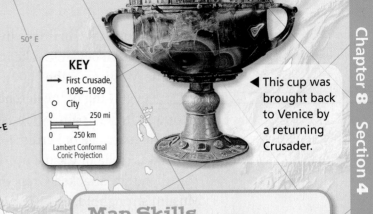

◄ This cup was brought back to Venice by a returning Crusader.

Map Skills

1 **Movement** Through which city did all First Crusade routes pass to reach Jerusalem?

2 **Places to Know!** Label the following places on the outline map in your Student Journal: Rome, France, Venice, Black Sea.

Active Atlas

Europeans responded to the pope's call for different reasons. Some went to war for religious reasons. They believed that God wanted the Holy Land to be Christian. Others had more worldly reasons. Some knights wanted to win new possessions in the Holy Land. Others wanted the status that came from military success. Of course, Muslims in the Holy Land wanted it to remain Muslim. They did not want foreign Christian rulers.

By the summer of 1096, a large European army had formed and headed for the Holy Land. This force captured Jerusalem, and Christian leaders divided Palestine into four states. Many Muslims in the region faced brutal treatment. Then European leaders sent a second Crusade to the Holy Land. Internal quarrels weakened this force, and Muslims defeated them.

In 1187, the Muslim leader Saladin recaptured Jerusalem. Further Crusades were attempted but failed. These conflicts led to bitter feelings between Christians and Muslims that have lasted to this day.

Muslims in Spain By 718, Muslims had conquered most of Spain. Spanish Christians controlled only a small area in northern Spain. During Muslim rule, many Spanish people converted to Islam. Muslim leaders also tolerated the practice of Judaism and Christianity.

Muslims made important advances in mathematics and medicine. They studied the learning of the ancient Greeks and Romans. In addition, they built beautiful mosques and palaces. During the 900s, Córdoba became a center of Muslim culture. Muslim influence helped shape art and literature in Christian Spain.

expel, *v.,* to force someone to leave a place

The Reconquista Christians living in northern Spain began to take back land from the Muslims in the 1000s. This was the beginning of the **Reconquista,** or reconquering of Spain by Christians. In 1469, the marriage of Ferdinand of Aragon and Isabella of Castile united Spain. Together, they attacked Granada, the last Muslim stronghold, in 1492. Granada fell and the Reconquista was complete.

Under Ferdinand and Isabella, the religious tolerance that had existed under the Muslims came to an end. A Church court called the Inquisition was set up to try to punish people who practiced religions other than Christianity. Some Jews and Muslims were burned at the stake.

Over time, more than 150,000 Jews and Muslims fled or were <u>expelled</u> from Spain, among them some of the most skilled and educated people in the nation.

Effects of the Crusades The Crusades had a lasting impact on society. Returning crusaders increased trade, bringing back exotic spices and fabrics from the Middle East (Southwest Asia and North Africa). Much of this trade used money rather than barter, or the exchange of one good for another.

People also gained a broader view of the world and discovered new ideas. Sailors learned to use the magnetic compass and the astrolabe, a device that measured the position of the sun, moon, and stars.

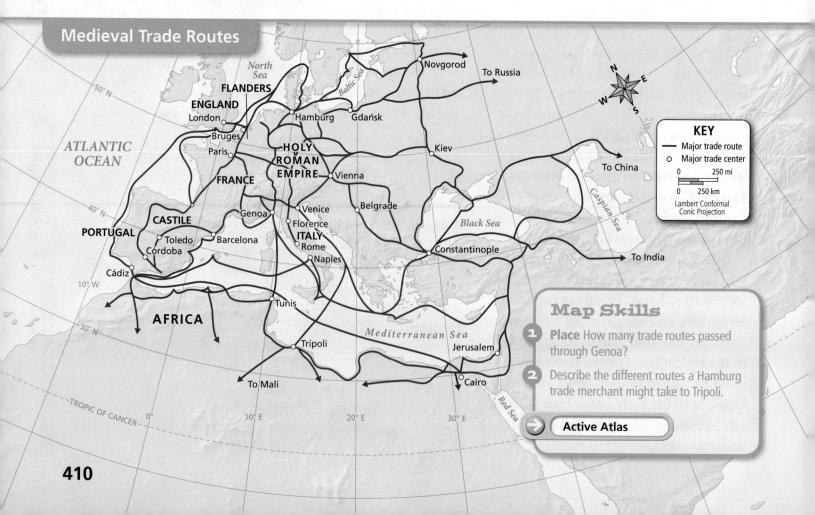

Medieval Trade Routes

KEY

— Major trade route
○ Major trade center

0 — 250 mi
0 — 250 km
Lambert Conformal Conic Projection

Map Skills

1 **Place** How many trade routes passed through Genoa?

2 Describe the different routes a Hamburg trade merchant might take to Tripoli.

Active Atlas

410

myWorldActivity
Trade Spices Up Life

In this way, sailors could know their position on Earth's surface out of sight of land.

The compass and astrolabe were among the new ideas or technologies that Europe gained from contact with the Muslim world. Europeans also learned to make gunpowder and paper from Muslims, although these technologies first developed in China.

Muslims had preserved much of the learning of the ancient Greeks and Romans. Muslims also studied ancient Indian learning. Muslims drew on this ancient learning to make advances in science and mathematics. They passed this knowledge on to medieval Europeans.

Reading Check How did the Crusades increase trade?

The Rise of Cities

During the 1000s, more and more people moved from manors to cities. Many factors led to this migration.

Farming Improves During the Middle Ages, farmers found ways to improve agriculture. They gained more cropland by draining swamps and clearing forests. They also developed the horse collar and harness so horses instead of oxen could be used to plow fields. Horses plowed faster than oxen. In this way, they could plant more, harvest more, and even have surplus, or extra, crops.

As the food supply increased, people became healthier. Peasants were able to earn extra money by selling surplus crops. Some used this money to buy their freedom from their lord. Freed peasants sometimes moved to cities and towns.

Technology Develops While Europeans learned new technologies from the Muslims, they also developed new skills and products of their own. Among these were clocks, eyeglasses, and upright windmills. Military technologies like plate armor and cannons made the armies strong. Engineering advances let Europeans build soaring cathedral towers.

Commerce Begins In towns, many peasants learned special skills as craft workers. They specialized in leather goods or gold objects and sold these goods in their shops or at local markets or trade fairs.

Some merchants sold these goods along trade routes throughout Europe and Asia. They exchanged both goods and ideas. Some expanded commerce by setting up banks and issuing loans.

The winged lion on top of the column is the symbol of the city of Venice. *What evidence do you see of the city's history in this modern photograph?* ▼

my worldgeography.com

Active Atlas

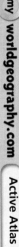

411

The Italian Trade Centers The port of Venice was a busy place. Ships from Constantinople arrived loaded with gold, silks, and spices. Traders loaded these goods onto mules and began the trek to markets in Northern Europe.

The city-state of Venice was only one of the new commerce centers in present-day Italy. Cities such as Florence, Genoa, and Naples also served as hubs for goods coming into Europe.

The New Merchant Class As people moved to towns, many towns grew into cities. In urban areas, a person could earn a good living by working as a merchant, an artisan, or a craftsperson. As a result, the group of people who earned more than peasants grew.

Language Lesson

King John signs the Magna Carta. A copy of the original document is above.

This group became known as the middle class since they still ranked below the nobles. As their numbers increased, so did their political and economic power.

For protection, merchants and craftspeople formed **guilds.** A guild is an association of people who have a common livelihood. Guilds protected members from unfair business practices. They also set prices and wages. Women could sometimes become guild members. They often specialized in needlecraft and papermaking. Women were also active in the silk and wool trades.

City Life Develops As cities grew, they spread outward—and upward. People needed more living space and built homes with two or three stories. In the largest cities, a church called a cathedral formed the center of the city. These cathedrals became centers of learning and city life.

Weekly market stalls were replaced by permanent shops, though hawkers still rolled through the streets with their carts. There were no sewers or garbage collection, so medieval streets could be dirty as well as noisy and crowded.

Reading Check Why were medieval city craftsmen known as a middle class?

Limiting the King's Power
During the High Middle Ages, the power of kings was put to the test.

Normans Conquer England During the 1000s, England was fairly prosperous with good agricultural land. William, duke of Normandy in northern France, believed himself to be heir to the English throne.

When it was given to an Anglo-Saxon noble named Harold, William invaded England with a huge army. He defeated Harold at the Battle of Hastings in 1066. William was crowned king of England and became known as William the Conqueror.

At the time, most of the people in England were Anglo-Saxon. The Normans treated them as inferiors. Many Anglo-Saxon lords tried to revolt, but after several years, William <u>subdued</u> them. Over time, the Normans and Anglo-Saxons intermarried, becoming one people.

Magna Carta After William's death, kings often struggled with lords for control of England. During the early 1200s, King John demanded large amounts of money without consulting the lords. He also set severe penalties for minor crimes.

Lords and church leaders rebelled. Soon, they forced King John to sign a charter called the **Magna Carta.** This was a document that limited the English king's power. The Magna Carta helped lead to more democratic government in England.

By the late 1200s, King Edward I expanded his meetings with lords and church leaders to include town representatives. These meetings came to be called the Model Parliament. They were the beginning of England's Parliament, its legislative or lawmaking assembly. Royal courts made rulings based on earlier cases. The courts created a body of common law, which was applied equally in any part of a country.

Hundred Years' War In the 1330s, the French attempted to take over an English-held province in southwest France. This conflict started a series of wars between France and England known as the Hundred Years' War (1337–1453).

By 1428, the English had taken over northern France. In Orleans, a peasant girl named Joan of Arc appeared. She claimed that she had been told by God to lead the French army into battle. In desperation, the French king agreed. The 17-year-old Joan led the army to victory. However, the next year, the English captured Joan and she was burned at the stake as a witch.

New weapons developed at this time changed warfare. The English longbow launched arrows that pierced the armor of French knights. In addition, gunpowder and cannons became common. Cannons could destroy castle walls. In this way, two of the major defenses of feudal lords—knights and castles—became much less effective.

subdue, *v.,* to bring under control

At the right, the English soldiers use longbows, while the French at the left use crossbows. *How might cannons be used in this scene?* ▼

Flea-ridden rats from ships reached land and transmitted the plague germs. ▼

Closer Look

The Black Death

Europe's busy ports unloaded more than trade goods or returning Crusaders. They also brought rats covered with the fleas that carried germs for the deadly bubonic plague. Flea-covered rats thrived in filthy medieval cities, and the plague spread quickly to the countryside. People knew very little about how disease was spread. Physicians were powerless to treat the victims. Gravediggers could not keep up with the number of dead. Many people believed that the plague was a punishment from God for their sins.

THINK CRITICALLY **Why do you think the Black Death caused such fear?**

Doctors wore masks to protect against the "evil air" that they thought caused disease. The beak held spices that did little to disguise the smell of sickness and death. ▶

This medieval image shows the fear that people felt during the time of the plague—death might claim a person at any time. ▼

414

The French finally won the Hundred Years' War. The war led England and France down two different paths. The French increased the power of the monarchy. The English increased Parliament's "power of the purse," or its financial role in government.

Reading Check What did the Magna Carta do?

Medieval Society Weakens

Improvements in farming during the High Middle Ages caused Europe's population to grow. By the 1300s, the population had outgrown the food supply. When harvests, or crops gathered for food, were low, people experienced famines. Famines are times of hunger and starvation. Famines were just one of the hardships that increasingly weakened medieval society.

Famine Strikes In 1315, bad weather caused poor harvests in Europe. These conditions continued for two more years. By that time, many Europeans were starving. Historians estimate that about ten to fifteen percent of the population died during the winter of 1317.

The Black Death Arrives As the famines continued in later years, the constant hunger made people sickly. In 1347, Europe faced a terrible epidemic, or a widespread outbreak of disease. Because people were already weakened from poor nutrition, the epidemic was disastrous. The disease was bubonic plague, or the Black Death. Victims suffered swelling and extreme pain. Death came quickly, usually in a matter of days.

Michael Platiensis, an eyewitness, described the disease,

> 66 Those infected felt themselves penetrated by a pain . . . Then there developed on the thighs or upper arms a boil. . . .This infected the whole body, . . . [three days later], there being no means of healing it, and then the patient expired. 99

Physicians had many theories about what caused the plague, all of them wrong. They tried several cures, but nothing worked. Some people falsely blamed the plague on Jews or beggars. These accusations spread, and, in some cites, thousands of Jews were tortured and killed.

By the time the Black Death ended in the early 1400s, the medieval world had begun to change. About 25 million Europeans died from the plague—from one quarter to one third of the population. The dead came from all levels of society, rich and poor. Suddenly, Europe faced a labor shortage. The disease also caused religious turmoil as many of the faithful began to have doubts.

Decline of Medieval Europe War, famine, and the Black Death changed medieval Europe profoundly. With millions of workers dead, production declined and food shortages were common. Economic uncertainty led to social upheaval. Important social structures such as manorialism and feudalism began to break down.

In manorialism, the labor of the peasant was vital. Following the plague, however, peasants began to leave the manors. In order to convince them to stay, lords offered for the first time to pay them wages. Some lords converted cropland to pastures for raising sheep. Some peasants still left the manors seeking higher wages or moving to cities.

Feudal lords found it harder to defend themselves against new weapons such as guns and cannons. In the cities, feudal influence weakened against wealthy merchants and powerful guilds. However, spurred by fresh ideas, a new age called the Renaissance was about to begin.

Reading Check How did the Black Death change Europe?

Indiana CONNECTIONS

The Spanish influenza, the worst epidemic in U.S. history, infected **28%** of the population, including **350,000** Indiana residents.

Section 4 Assessment

Essential Question

What are the challenges of diversity?

Key Terms

1. Use each of the following terms in a sentence: Crusades, Reconquista, guild, Magna Carta.

Key Ideas

2. Why did the middle class grow during the High Middle Ages?

3. What were some of the main results of the Crusades?

4. How did the Great Famine and the Black Death lead to the decline of feudalism?

Think Critically

5. **Draw Inferences** How do you think feudal lords felt about the growth of cities? Explain.

6. **Draw Conclusions** How might the Hundred Years' War affect nation-building in France and England?

7. How did diversity have both positive and negative effects on Spain? Go to your Student Journal to record your answer.

Chapter Assessment

Key Terms and Ideas

1. **Compare and Contrast** How is an **oligarchy** different from a **direct democracy**?

2. **Recall** What was the job of a tribune in the ancient Roman Republic?

3. **Compare and Contrast** What are some similarities and differences between the government of ancient Athens and that of the Roman Republic?

4. **Discuss** Did **manorialism** encourage trade? Why or why not?

5. **Describe** How did Christianity spread during the early Middle Ages?

6. **Recall** How did William the Conqueror gain the English crown?

7. **Explain** How was the **Reconquista** connected to the Spanish Inquisition?

Think Critically

8. **Determine Relevance** How did the Pax Romana lead to stability across the Roman empire?

9. **Test Conclusions** Why do you think Sparta was able to take control of the Peloponnesian Peninsula and defeat Athens? Support your answer with evidence from the chapter.

10. **Analyze Information** About 25 million Europeans died from the Black Death. Name three factors that contributed to this huge death toll.

11. **Core Concepts: Economics** How did economics contribute to the decline of feudalism?

Places to Know

For each place, write the letter from the map that show its location.

12. Athens
13. Constantinople
14. Spain
15. Venice
16. Rome
17. Sparta
18. **Estimate** Using the scale, estimate how far Constantinople was from Rome.

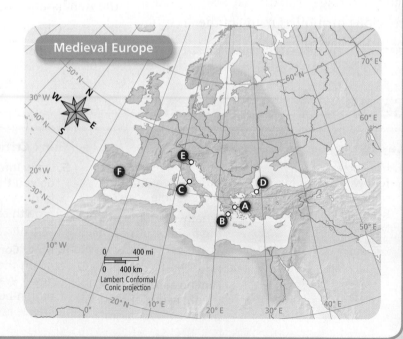

Medieval Europe

my worldgeography.com Self-Test

Essential Question

myWorld Chapter Activity

Piecing Together the Past Choose one image from the chapter activity cards. Follow your teacher's instructions and do your own field research to find similar objects in other European cultures. Then write a caption for each object you find, summarizing how it reflects diversity in European culture.

21st Century Learning

Generate New Ideas

Write Dialogue Write a scene in which Joan of Arc tries to convince the king to let her lead the French army into battle. Include:
- Joan's visions
- the king's desperation
- the city of Orleans
- the English army
- the French army

Document-Based Questions

Success Tracker™
Online at myworldgeography.com

Use your knowledge of the Middle Ages and Documents A and B to answer Questions 1–3.

Document A

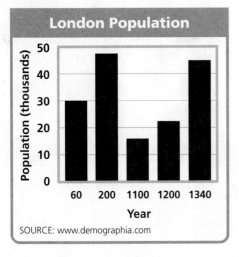

London Population

SOURCE: www.demographia.com

Document B

" Each trade occupied its own quarter—butchers and tanners around the Châtelet, money-changers, goldsmiths, and drapers on the Grand Pont, scribes, illuminators, and parchment- and ink-sellers on the left bank around the University [of Paris]."

— Historian Barbara Tuchman describing Paris during the High Middle Ages

1. Which of the following might explain the drop in London's population from A.D. 200 to A.D. 1100?

   A decline of Greece, rise of feudalism

   B decline of Greece, rise of trade

   C decline of Rome, rise of feudalism

   D decline of Rome, rise of trade

2. Based on Document B, which of the following best describes Paris during the High Middle Ages?

   A an economically busy city with few craft workers

   B an economically busy city with many craft workers

   C an economically quiet city with few craft workers

   D an economically quiet city with many craft workers

3. **Writing Task** Describe details in Document B that show prosperity in medieval Paris.

417

Chapter 9

Europe in Modern Times

? **Essential Question**

What makes a nation?

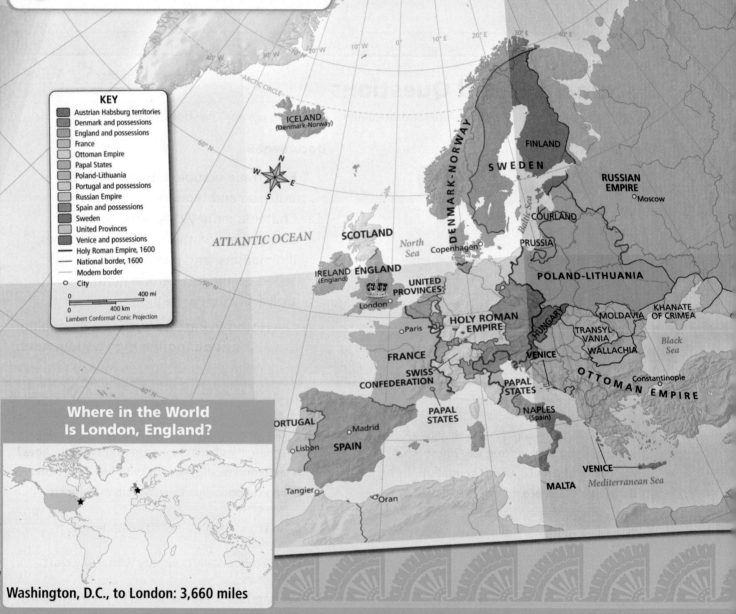

KEY
- Austrian Habsburg territories
- Denmark and possessions
- England and possessions
- France
- Ottoman Empire
- Papal States
- Poland-Lithuania
- Portugal and possessions
- Russian Empire
- Spain and possessions
- Sweden
- United Provinces
- Venice and possessions
- —— Holy Roman Empire, 1600
- —— National border, 1600
- —— Modern border
- ○ City

0   400 mi
0   400 km
Lambert Conformal Conic Projection

ATLANTIC OCEAN

ARCTIC CIRCLE

ICELAND
(Denmark-Norway)

DENMARK-NORWAY

SWEDEN

FINLAND

RUSSIAN EMPIRE
○ Moscow

Baltic Sea

COURLAND

PRUSSIA

SCOTLAND

North Sea

Copenhagen ○

POLAND-LITHUANIA

IRELAND
(England)

ENGLAND

UNITED PROVINCES

London ○

HOLY ROMAN EMPIRE

○ Paris

HUNGARY

MOLDAVIA

KHANATE OF CRIMEA

TRANSYL-VANIA

FRANCE

VENICE

WALLACHIA

Black Sea

SWISS CONFEDERATION

PAPAL STATES

OTTOMAN EMPIRE

○ Constantinople

PORTUGAL

PAPAL STATES

NAPLES
(Spain)

Madrid ○

VENICE

○ Lisbon

SPAIN

MALTA

Mediterranean Sea

Tangier ○

○ Oran

Where in the World Is London, England?

Washington, D.C., to London: 3,660 miles

my Story
The Battle of the Spanish Armada

Explore the Essential Question ...

- at my worldgeography.com
- using the myWorld Chapter Activity
- with the Student Journal

In this section, you'll read about Queen Elizabeth I of England and the defeat of the great Spanish Armada. What does Elizabeth's story tell you about life in early modern Europe?

By Ruth Hull Chatlien for myWorld Online

In 1588, Europe's greatest power, Spain, prepared to attack the smaller kingdom of England. The Spanish army gathered supplies and horses for an invasion. The Spanish soldiers were to travel to England on barges. At the same time, a fleet of 130 Spanish ships, the Armada, gathered to protect the barges. The Spanish Armada used massive galleons, huge ships that rode high in the water and were clumsy to maneuver. The English captains manned "race ships." These were smaller, faster, and much easier to handle.

On the English shore, the troops gathered at Tilbury to hear their queen. This was a time when few women held power, but Elizabeth had earned her people's respect. The English people also loved their queen. At Tilbury, she knew that she had to prepare the troops to meet the Spanish, the best fighters of the day.

> I know I have the body but of a weak and feeble woman, but I have the heart of a king, and of a king of England, too.

my worldgeography.com **On Assignment**

419

In 1587, Elizabeth's advisors convinced her to order the death of her cousin, Mary, Queen of Scotland. They saw Mary, a Catholic, as a threat to Elizabeth, a Protestant.

Elizabeth and trusted court advisors planned the strategy for the battle with the Spanish navy.

Spain's attack against England happened in a time of religious conflict between Catholics and Protestants. Catholicism had been the main religion of Western Europe until the early 1500s. At that time, some Christians left the Roman Catholic Church and started their own Protestant churches.

Spain's king, Philip II, was a very religious man who wanted to restore Catholicism to all of Europe. Elizabeth, who was a Protestant, urged Philip to let Protestants in the Netherlands practice their religion. At that time, the Netherlands was a Spanish possession.

Philip also believed that he should be king of England because he had been married to Mary I. Mary was Elizabeth's half-sister who ruled England before her death in 1558. Religious strife had shaken England ever since Henry VIII, father of Elizabeth and Mary, broke with the Catholic Church and started the Protestant Church of England.

As queen, one of Protestant Elizabeth's earliest acts was to order a compromise with Catholics. Unlike Philip, she did not want to force people to share her religion. "I have no desire to make windows into men's souls," she said. Her wise actions prevented civil war in England, although tension remained throughout her reign.

Spain and England were also rival empire-builders. England wanted an empire and colonies like those of Spain. Those colonies had brought fabulous wealth, such as gold and silver, to Spain. English ships had attacked Spanish ships and taken their gold and silver.

As the Spanish Armada set sail, the huge fleet appeared to be invincible, or unbeatable. Yet, the Spanish had several weaknesses. Besides sailing heavier ships, the Spanish captains had no maps of the coasts of Scotland or Ireland. The Spanish soldiers were brave fighters, but in the use of cannon, they lagged behind their rivals. In addition, food stores had been loaded too early and were rotting. Water barrels leaked, and cannon balls were poorly made or the wrong size. In addition, there were discipline problems on board the Spanish ships.

The Spanish were sure that they would win and saw the battle as a holy war. Philip even had the ships' sails painted with the cross of St. George, the symbol of the medieval Crusaders. In spite of the seeming advantage of the Spanish, Elizabeth predicted,

66 Let tyrants fear. . . .We shall shortly have a famous victory over these enemies of my God, of my kingdom, and of my people. 99

The Spanish navy had helped make Spain a wealthy global empire. But the Spanish sailed old-fashioned, slower ships. Their loss to England changed sea warfare and the fortunes of Spain.

As the Spanish Armada neared the coast of England, the English fleet moved into position. For several days, the English managed to keep the Spanish ships at a distance.

At midnight, the English sent fireships loaded with explosives into the midst of the Spanish fleet. The Spanish commanders were forced to cut the ships' anchor cables and sail out to sea to avoid catching fire. The Spanish formation became disorganized, and the English took advantage of the confusion to attack at dawn. A decisive battle took place, and the losses to Spain far outweighed those of England. Spanish domination of the seas had ended.

The English felt this victory proved that God was on their side. English admirals received a medal that said, "God blew and they were scattered." This victory at sea was one of the greatest triumphs of Elizabeth's reign.

myStory Online

Join Elizabeth and her advisors as they plan the battle against the Spanish Armada.

421

New Ways of Thinking

IN Indiana

6.1.2 Describe and compare the beliefs, the spread and the influence of religions throughout Europe and Mesoamerica.

6.1.6 Identify trade routes and discuss their impact on the rise of cultural centers and cities in Europe and Mesoamerica.

6.1.8 Compare the diverse perspectives and people that brought about the Renaissance in Europe.

6.1.9 Analyze the interconnections in the exchanges of the European Renaissance that led to the Scientific Revolution, voyages of discovery and imperial conquest.

6.1.12 Describe the Reformations and their effects on European and American society.

Key Terms • Renaissance • humanism • perspective • Reformation • Catholic Reformation

Visual Glossary

Reading Skill: Label an Outline Map Take notes using the graphic organizer in your journal.

Leon Battista Alberti drew on ancient models for his Renaissance church, Santa Maria Novella, in Florence, Italy.▼

The Late Middle Ages brought many changes to Europe. Feudalism came to an end. Farmers began producing more agricultural goods than they needed. Trade increased. These changes led to a new age in European history called the **Renaissance,** or "rebirth," a time of a renewed interest in art and learning.

The Italian Renaissance

Italy is a peninsula in southern Europe. Italy had been the center of the Roman Empire. This classical influence contributed to the Renaissance.

Trade Grows and Cities Compete Italian traders brought silks and spices back from Asia. They sold these in Italian cities such as Genoa, Venice, Naples, and Florence. These cities were major trade centers. In the markets, people exchanged coins of different lands. Merchants adopted a system to deposit money and write checks. These practices became the basis of modern banking.

Unlike the kingdoms of other parts of Europe, Italy was divided into city-states. These city-states were often ruled by one powerful family. In addition to ruling families, city-states were dominated by a wealthy merchant class. City-states fought often. They invented taxes on property and income and other ways to finance their wars.

Old and New Ideas Inspire Trade brought Europeans into contact with the learning of Asia and the Muslim world. For example, Muslim mathematician Al-Khwarizmi (al KWAHR iz mee) had used Hindu-Arabic numerals and developed algebra in the 700s. Muslim scholars had copied and preserved works from ancient Greece and Rome. Many of these had been lost in Europe. Europeans also learned Chinese techniques such as block printing and papermaking.

During the Renaissance, European scholars took an interest in ancient Greek and Roman ideas. This was the beginning of **humanism,** or the study of secular, or nonreligious, subjects such as history and philosophy. Humanists emphasized individual accomplishment and serving the people of this world instead of focusing on religion.

Art Copies Nature Medieval artists had focused on teaching spiritual lessons. As a result, their art was symbolic, not realistic. In contrast, the Greeks and Romans had honored nature and tried to make their art lifelike. Renaissance artists imitated the realism of classical art.

Art changed in two major ways during the Renaissance. First, artists studied the human body so that they could create lifelike statues and paintings. Second, Renaissance painters used **perspective,** a technique that allows artists to portray a three-dimensional space on a flat surface.

Artists Michelangelo and Leonardo da Vinci both created Renaissance masterpieces. Michelangelo carved sculptures, such as the statue *David*. He also painted scenes from the Bible on the ceiling of the Sistine Chapel in Rome. Leonardo painted the famous portrait *Mona Lisa*. He also drew thousands of diagrams of ideas for inventions. Architect Filippo Brunelleschi (fee LEEP po broo nel LES kee) used classical features such as domes, columns, and arches in his buildings.

Reading Check What did humanists emphasize?

A New Perspective

For *The Last Supper* (1495–1497), Leonardo used perspective to make the painting as realistic as possible. *How did Leonardo use perspective to focus on the figure of Jesus?*

423

Gutenberg's Press

Gutenberg and his pressmen examine a newly printed page (above). The page at the left was copied out by hand. The page at the right was printed using movable type. *How did Gutenberg's printing press change books?*

The Northern Renaissance

A network of land and sea trade routes linked the city-states of Italy with the kingdoms and small states of Northern Europe. These northern lands included England, Germany, and Flanders (a region now divided between France and Belgium). Like Italy, Germany and Flanders were divided into small, competitive states.

Northern Cities Grow Improved ships made traveling by sea faster than traveling overland. As a result of <u>rapid</u> sea travel, trade between northern and southern Europe increased. Trade also increased within northern Europe. Some northern towns decided to form trade associations so they could have more influence over trade. For example, the Hanseatic (han see AT ik) League was a group of more than 60 towns in Germany and other lands. They worked together to improve trade among members.

Cities and countries began to specialize in the production of certain goods. The countries of England, France, and Flanders produced cloth. Northeastern Europe produced grain. Germany, Hungary, and Austria mined copper, iron, gold, and silver. Trade helped northern cities such as London, Paris, Brugge (BROOG uh), and Lyon grow. A middle class of traders and craftsmen developed. Middle-class people were wealthier than peasants and could buy more goods. This encouraged trade.

Renaissance Ideas Spread Renaissance ideas spread to northern Europe in several ways. First, traders brought the new ideas with them. Second, rulers such as King Francis I of France invited Renaissance scholars and artists to visit their courts. Third, many northern nobles and wealthy members of the middle class traveled to Italy for their education. While in Italy, they learned about Renaissance ideas.

rapid, *adj.,* fast

myWorld Activity
A Life-Changing Product

New technology helped spread knowledge. In the 1400s, German craftsman Johannes Gutenberg invented the printing press. Gutenberg made movable type, or pieces of metal formed into letters of the alphabet. He then printed pages by using a machine to squeeze paper against inked type. Before the printing press, the only way to reproduce writing was by hand. The press made it possible to create copies of books much faster than ever before. As more books became available, more people learned to read.

Renaissance ideas began to influence northern artists and writers. Flemish artist Pieter Bruegel (PEA tur BROO gel) the Elder painted lively scenes of peasant life. German artist Albrecht Dürer (AHL brekt DYOOR ur) used Italian techniques of realism and perspective to create life-like paintings.

The English playwright William Shakespeare wrote brilliant plays seen as key works of Renaissance humanism. In his play *Hamlet*, he expressed the Renaissance view of human potential:

> 66 What a piece of work is a man, how noble in reason, how infinite in faculties, in form and moving, how express and admirable in action, how like an angel in apprehension, how like a god! 99

Shakespeare's work remains popular today, both on stage and in movies.

Some northern writers, known as Christian humanists, combined classical and religious studies. The Dutch scholar Erasmus (ih RAZ mus) studied the New Testament in its original Greek language. He suggested the Catholic Church make changes, such as teaching in modern languages instead of Latin. The English humanist Thomas More wrote about an ideal society in his book *Utopia*. Today, we use the word *utopia* to mean a place of perfection in laws and society.

Reading Check Who spread Renaissance ideas to Northern Europe?

Above, a diagram shows the structure of the Globe Theatre.

At the right, modern actors perform a play by Shakespeare in London's Globe Theatre, an authentic replica of the theater where these plays were first performed.

425

The Protestant Reformation

During the Renaissance, humanism led Europeans like Erasmus to think critically about the Catholic Church. Some learned Europeans began to read the Bible and interpret it for themselves instead of simply following the Church's interpretation.

Criticisms of the Church Some Europeans began to believe that the Church did not uphold the Bible's teachings. Some felt that Church leaders were corrupt. Others thought that the Church had become too rich, or that it was too involved in politics.

The Inquisition also led to criticism. The Inquisition was a church court set up to try people accused of heresy, or religious belief contrary to established Church teachings. The Church gained wealth by taking property from people accused of heresy.

Early critics of the Church, such as John Wycliffe, Jan Hus (yahn hous), and Girolamo Savonarola (jee ROH lah moh sah voh nuh ROH lah), risked their lives by speaking out. Church leaders executed both Hus and Savonarola, yet the calls for reform did not end.

The printing press helped spread the desire for change. As books grew more common, more people were able to read the Bible and scholarly works. People formed their own ideas about religion. More people questioned Church teachings.

Luther Calls for Reform The Church made money by selling indulgences, or pardons for sin. A German monk named Martin Luther studied the Bible and came to believe that people could neither buy nor earn pardon for sin. In 1517, Luther drafted the 95 Theses, a list of arguments against indulgences. He sent the list to to a church official who called for an investigation of Luther's beliefs. Luther's call for reform started the **Reformation,** a religious movement in which calls for reform led to the emergence of non-Catholic, or Protestant, churches.

Comparing Catholicism and Lutheranism

	Catholicism	Lutheranism
Salvation	Faith and good works bring salvation.	Faith alone brings salvation.
Sacraments	Priests perform the seven sacraments, or rituals.	Accepts some sacraments, but rejects others because they lack Biblical grounding.
Head of the Church	The pope, together with the bishops	Elected councils
Importance of the Bible	Bible is one source of truth; Church tradition is another.	Bible alone is the source of truth.
Interpretation	Bible is interpreted by priests according to tradition and Church leadership.	People read and interpret the Bible for themselves.

Chart Skills

Note the differences in the heads of the two churches. Why was this difference important?

Data Discovery

Luther believed that religious salvation came only from faith. He also believed that the Bible—not the Church—was the only true authority for Christian life. He encouraged ordinary people to study the Bible. People began Lutheran churches based on Luther's teachings.

Other Protestants took the movement even further. In his book *Institutes of the Christian Religion*, John Calvin offered an explanation of Protestant beliefs. His main theme is the belief that God has complete control over the universe. Calvin also stressed morality and hard work.

The Reformation began a series of events in which churches continued to split up over various disagreements. One new group of Protestants, the Anabaptists, baptized only adults. Other new churches included the Baptists, the Mennonites, and the Quakers. In the 1700s, English clergyman John Wesley founded the Methodist Church.

The Reformation and Government

During this time period, many European rulers forced their people to follow the ruler's religion. Catholics and Protestants felt certain that their own beliefs were the only correct <u>doctrines.</u> Many people did not think other views should be allowed. Sometimes, state churches punished people of other faiths. Such abuses of religious power later led the authors of the U.S. Constitution to call for the separation of church and state.

doctrine, *n.*, teaching or principle

Protestant and Catholic Europe

Map Skills

1 **Place** Which country was Anglican?

2 **Movement** To which areas did Protestant (Anglican, Lutheran, or Calvinist) churches spread?

3 **Places to Know!** Label the following places on the outline map in your Student Journal: England, Wittenberg, Scotland, Sweden, Paris, Spain.

→ **Active Atlas**

KEY

- Mainly Roman Catholic
- Mainly Anglican
- Mainly Lutheran
- Mainly Calvinist
- Eastern Orthodox
- Eastern Orthodox with Muslim minorities
- — Border as of 1600

0   400 mi
0   400 km
Lambert Conformal Conic Projection

Map labels: SWEDEN, NORWAY, SCOTLAND, ATLANTIC OCEAN, North Sea, IRELAND (England), DENMARK, Baltic Sea, ENGLAND, Woodstock, London, Münster, Wittenberg, POLAND-LITHUANIA, Wartburg, Paris, Worms, HOLY ROMAN EMPIRE, FRANCE, Augsburg, Geneva, Trent, HUNGARY, VENICE, Venice, Black Sea, OTTOMAN EMPIRE, PORTUGAL, SPAIN, Corsica, PAPAL STATES, Rome, Adriatic Sea, NAPLES (Spain), Sardinia, Mediterranean Sea, Sicily, 50° N, 40° N

427

Each of the small states in Germany followed the religion of its ruler. Some German princes remained Catholic, while others became Lutheran. Religious conflict in Germany was a cause of the Thirty Years' War. The war raged in central Europe from 1618 to 1648. The fighting left Germany in ruins.

Religion in England Religion also played a major role in English politics. King Henry VIII wanted to have sons to rule after him, but he and his wife Catherine of Aragon had only one child who survived infancy—a daughter. Henry,

who was Catholic, asked the pope to allow him to end his marriage. The pope refused. In response, Henry declared that England was no longer under the authority of the pope. Instead, Henry formed a new church, the Church of England. This church is also called the Anglican church. As head of the Church of England, Henry ended his marriage.

Henry went on to have five more wives, one more daughter, and one son. Each of his three children later ruled England in turn. When power changed hands, England went from Protestant to Catholic, and finally, under the rule of Elizabeth I, to Protestant again.

Reading Check How did Martin Luther begin the Reformation?

The Catholic Reformation

Even after the Protestant Reformation, millions of Europeans remained Catholic. The Catholic Church was especially strong in Italy and Spain. In response to reformers' criticisms, the Church began to make changes. These changes, which helped keep Catholicism strong, are called the **Catholic Reformation.**

The Catholic Church Responds When Luther posted his 95 Theses, Pope Leo X did not take the event very seriously. He believed that the calls for change would soon end. However, the pope did excommunicate Luther—that is, he banned Luther from the Catholic Church.

In 1545, Pope Paul III took action against the Reformation. He called Church leaders to the Council of Trent where they rejected several key Protestant beliefs.

A New Church

CATHERINE of ARRAGON

Henry VIII broke with the pope to divorce Catherine of Aragon (above). Even though he was head of the Church of England, he never abandoned the Catholic faith.

First, it decided that only the Catholic Church and its leaders could interpret the Bible. Second, the council declared that Church tradition was just as important a guide for Christian life as the Bible. Third, the council decided that both faith and good deeds were needed for salvation.

The Church Renews Itself Over time, the Catholic Church ended many of the abuses that Protestants had criticized. This helped Catholics remain loyal to the faith. Also, Catholic mystics such as John of the Cross and Teresa of Avila wrote inspiring works about their faith. Mystics are people who aim to experience the presence of God.

In addition, Ignatius (ig NAY shus) of Loyola helped the Church gain new strength. Loyola wrote a set of spiritual exercises that became the basis for the Jesuit order of priests. The Jesuits were disciplined and well trained. They became educators in Catholic schools. Many became missionaries. Sending Jesuits and other Catholic missionaries to Asia, Africa, and the Americas was another part of the Catholic Reformation. Catholic leaders believed that spreading their faith around the world would help to strengthen the church at home. As a result, Catholicism grew in many European colonies.

Reading Check How did Ignatius of Loyola help strengthen Catholicism?

> **myStory Online**

Queen Elizabeth rallies the troops at Tilbury.

Section 1 Assessment

Essential Question

What makes a nation?

Key Terms

1. Explain how the following terms affected European life in the period covered in this section: Renaissance, Reformation, Catholic Reformation.

Key Ideas

2. What cultures helped to shape the Renaissance?

3. How did the Renaissance help cause the Reformation?

4. What were two Catholic responses to the Reformation?

Think Critically

5. **Compare and Contrast** How were Italy and Germany alike and different?

6. **Synthesize** How did the printing press affect the spread of Protestantism?

7. **Analyze Cause and Effect** How did trade expand knowledge?

8. How might a desire to build a stronger nation affect a ruler's decision to become a Protestant or a Catholic? Go to your Student Journal to record your answer.

429

Renaissance Views of Rulers

IN Indiana

6.1.8 Compare the diverse perspectives and people that brought about the Renaissance in Europe.

6.1.21 Differentiate between fact and interpretation in historical accounts and explain historical passages.

6.1.23 Identify issues related to an event in Europe or the Americas and give arguments for and against that issue.

The Renaissance brought an increased emphasis on secular, or non-religious matters, such as how to govern. Before the Renaissance, most thinkers had focused on religious matters. The Renaissance princes who ruled Italian city-states sought advice on the practical aspects of government. Niccolò Machiavelli's *The Prince* provided just such a guide for Renaissance rulers, though it had little say about what was good for society. In England, Thomas More wrote *Utopia* to express his ideas about the perfect society. These two Renaissance writers offered very different portraits of the ideal ruler.

▲ A medal with a portrait of Queen Elizabeth I

Portrait of Machiavelli ▼

Stop at each letter on the right to think about the text. Then answer the question with the same letter on the left.

A **Categorize** According to Machiavelli, what are the two possible ways for subjects to feel about their ruler?

B **Analyze Primary Sources** What emotion does Machiavelli think rulers should inspire, and why?

C **Identify Bias** How does Machiavelli's view of human nature shape his view of how to rule? Explain.

dispense with, *v.,* to get rid of

assert, *v.,* to argue, claim

fickle, *adj.,* not reliable or loyal

covetous, *adj.,* greedy

Feared Rulers

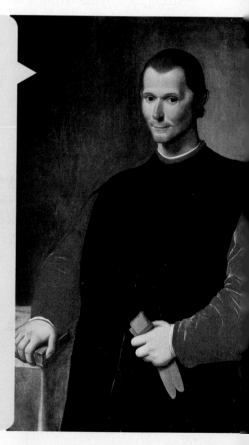

❝ . . . [A] question arises:
A whether it be better to be loved than feared or feared than loved? It may be answered that one should wish to be both, but, because it is difficult to unite them in one person, it is much
B safer to be feared than loved, when, of the two, either must be <u>dispensed with</u>. Because this is
C to be <u>asserted</u> in general of men, that they are ungrateful, <u>fickle</u>, false, cowardly, <u>covetous</u>. . . . ❞

—Niccolò Machiavelli,
The Prince, 1513,
translated by W. K. Marriott

Stop at each letter on the right to think about the text. Then answer the question with the same letter on the left.

Ⓓ Draw Conclusions In More's ideal world, what kind of character do magistrates have?

Ⓔ Analyze Cause and Effect How do the people respond to the rule of the magistrates?

Ⓕ Draw Inferences What do you think the sheaf of grain stands for? Explain what it says about the role of the prince.

zealously, *adv.,* eagerly

magistracy, *n.,* the position of a magistrate, a powerful legal official

exact, *v.,* to get by force

diadem, *n.,* crown

sheaf, *n.,* bunch

Ideal Rulers

❝ Any man who campaigns too <u>zealously</u> for a <u>magistracy</u> is sure to fail. They live together harmoniously
Ⓓ and the magistrates are never proud or cruel. Instead they are called fathers, and deservedly. Because the magistrates do not <u>exact</u> honor from people against their will, the
Ⓔ people honor them willingly, as they should. Not even the prince has the distinction of robe or <u>diadem</u>; he
Ⓕ is known only by a <u>sheaf</u> of grain carried before him. In the same way the priest is known by a wax candle. ❞

—Thomas More, *Utopia,* 1516, translated by H.V.S. Ogden

▲ Portrait of Thomas More by Hans Holbein

This statue of Grand Duke Ferdinando I de' Medici portrays the kind of Renaissance ruler that Machiavelli described. ▶

Analyze the Documents

1. **Compare Viewpoints** How are Machiavelli's and More's ideas about rulers similar and different?

2. **Writing Task** Write a letter to the U.S. president. Recommend that government officials be required to study either *The Prince* or *Utopia,* and explain why. Include a sentence stating why you decided against the other work.

Europe Expands

IN Indiana

6.1.6 Identify trade routes and discuss their impact on the rise of cultural centers and cities in Europe and Mesoamerica.

6.1.9 Analyze the interconnections in the exchanges of the European Renaissance that led to the Scientific Revolution, voyages of discovery and imperial conquest.

6.1.10 Explain the outcomes of European colonization on the Americas and the rest of the world.

6.1.11 Compare and contrast various colonies in the Americas.

6.2.4 Define the term nation-state and describe their rise headed by monarchs in Europe from 1500 to 1700.

Key Terms • cartography • caravel • plantation • northwest passage • triangular trade • absolutism

Visual Glossary

Reading Skill: Sequence Take notes using the graphic organizer in your journal.

A modern replica of English explorer Sir Francis Drake's ship *Golden Hind*

By 1300, innovations such as navigational charts, triangular sails, and magnetic compasses had made sailing easier. These new technologies also helped Renaissance mapmakers develop **cartography,** the science of making accurate maps and globes. A new age of exploration was about to begin.

The Age of Exploration

During the 1300s, Italian merchant Marco Polo published a book about his travels in China and India. His descriptions of the wealth and wonders of Asia increased European interest in the continent.

Portugal Sets Sail Portugal led the search for a sea route to Asia. The Portuguese sailed **caravels,** small, triangular-sailed oceangoing ships. Henry the Navigator, a Portuguese prince, paid for voyages to Asia and helped train explorers in navigation.

Throughout the 1400s, Portuguese ships explored the west coast of Africa by sailing farther and farther south. In 1488, Bartolomeu Dias became the first explorer to travel around the southern tip of Africa. In 1497, Vasco da Gama reached India. During the first half of the 1500s, the Portuguese established trading centers in India, Southeast Asia, and China. They enabled Portugal to end Italy's control over trade with Asia.

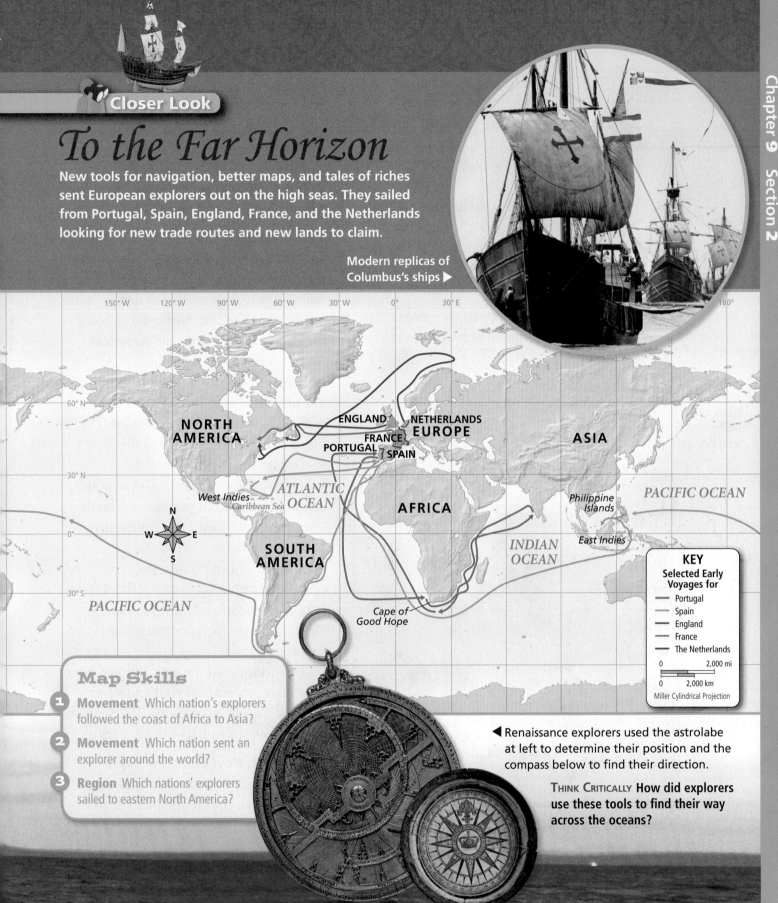

Closer Look

To the Far Horizon

New tools for navigation, better maps, and tales of riches sent European explorers out on the high seas. They sailed from Portugal, Spain, England, France, and the Netherlands looking for new trade routes and new lands to claim.

Modern replicas of Columbus's ships ▶

KEY
Selected Early Voyages for
— Portugal
— Spain
— England
— France
— The Netherlands

0   2,000 mi
0   2,000 km
Miller Cylindrical Projection

Map Skills

1 **Movement** Which nation's explorers followed the coast of Africa to Asia?

2 **Movement** Which nation sent an explorer around the world?

3 **Region** Which nations' explorers sailed to eastern North America?

◀ Renaissance explorers used the astrolabe at left to determine their position and the compass below to find their direction.

THINK CRITICALLY How did explorers use these tools to find their way across the oceans?

finance, *v.,* to raise or provide funds

Reaching the Americas Italian explorer Christopher Columbus promised to reach Asia by sailing westward across the Atlantic. Spain's rulers agreed to <u>finance</u> his voyage. They wanted to take part in the rich Asian spice trade.

In October 1492, Columbus and his crew made landfall in the Caribbean. He believed he had reached the Indies—islands in Southeast Asia—so he called the native people Indians. He later wrote:

> 66 They came to the ship in canoes, … some of them large enough to contain forty or forty-five men. 99

Columbus did not reach Asia, but he helped Spain start an empire in the Americas.

Reading Check Why did Portugal and Spain look for water routes to Asia?

This painting from India shows Europeans (bottom left) bringing gifts to the Indian ruler. *Why might Europeans bring gifts?* ▼

An Age of Empires

The age of exploration was also an age of imperialism, or empire-building. European countries expanded their empires by taking over other lands as colonies. These colonies made European nations wealthy and powerful.

Spain Conquers the New World Many Spanish explorers followed Columbus to the Americas. In 1513, Vasco Nuñez de Balboa (VAHS koh NOO nyes deh BOH uh) became the first European to reach the Pacific Ocean from the Americas. This proved that he was not in Asia. The explorer Amerigo Vespucci (ah meh REE goh ves POOH chee) believed that explorers had found a "New World." A mapmaker at the time called the New World *America* after Vespucci.

Spain sent conquistadors, or conquerors, to the Americas to seize new lands. They used gunpowder, a Chinese invention, to help them conquer native peoples. On the Caribbean islands, the Spanish set up **plantations,** or large commercial farms.

In Mexico, Spanish troops under Hernán Cortés took control of the Aztec Empire. In Peru, troops under Francisco Pizarro conquered the Inca Empire. Spain took huge amounts of gold and silver from its American colonies. The Spanish empire covered much of the Americas.

Establishing New Colonies Explorers also searched for a **northwest passage,** a route between the Atlantic and Pacific Oceans along the northern coast of North America. They hoped to increase trade with Asia by finding a faster sea route.

The Columbian Exchange

Columbus's landing in America changed life around the world. European ships brought animals, food plants, and diseases that transformed life there. In turn, Europeans brought back new foods and other products.

Diagram Skills

Explain in your own words how this diagram shows the Columbian Exchange.

→ **Data Discovery**

Foods such as corn and cocoa were unknown in Europe. ▶

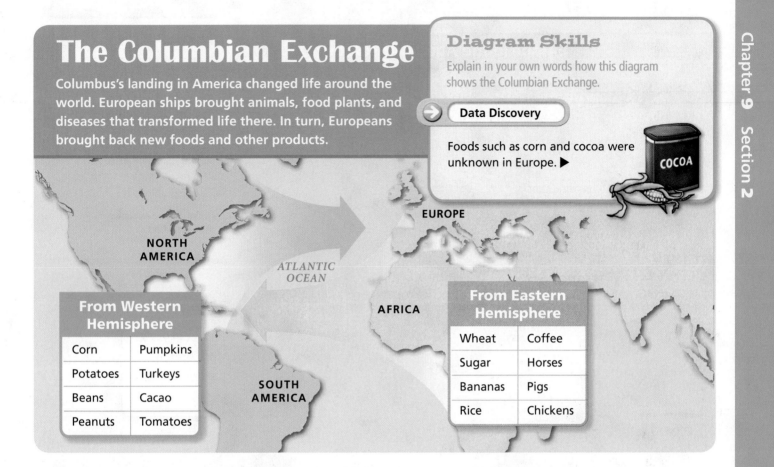

NORTH AMERICA

EUROPE

AFRICA

SOUTH AMERICA

ATLANTIC OCEAN

COCOA

From Western Hemisphere

Corn	Pumpkins
Potatoes	Turkeys
Beans	Cacao
Peanuts	Tomatoes

From Eastern Hemisphere

Wheat	Coffee
Sugar	Horses
Bananas	Pigs
Rice	Chickens

Explorers never found a northwest passage, but others established new colonies in North America. Both England and France claimed lands in eastern North America. They also traded with Native Americans for furs to take back to Europe.

By the mid-1700s, England had a group of colonies stretching down the Atlantic coast of North America. Early settlements included Jamestown in Virginia and Plymouth Colony in New England. The Netherlands had also founded North American colonies, but the English took them over.

The Dutch, English, and French had colonies in other regions. The Dutch controlled land in the East Indies. England and France had additional colonies in India.

England also founded colonies in Australia during the early 1800s. Most of these colonies began as places to send people convicted of crimes. By the late 1800s, though, most colonists in Australia were not criminals. Those colonists went to Australia to make a living in agriculture, mining, or in Australia's growing cities.

Plantation Agriculture Plantations in the Caribbean and southeastern North America produced crops such as sugar and tobacco. Plantation agriculture required huge numbers of workers. At first, landowners used Native Americans, but they fell ill from European diseases. Europeans began to bring enslaved Africans to do this work.

convict, *v.,* to find or prove guilty

my **worldgeography.com** (Data Discovery)

myWorld Activity
Sailing for Riches

Europe in the Age of Absolutism

ICELAND (Denmark)

SCOTLAND

North Sea

IRELAND (England)

NORWAY (Denmark)

SWEDEN

Stockholm

Moscow

RUSSIA

ENGLAND

London

NETHERLANDS

DENMARK

PRUSSIA (Brandenburg)

POLAND

Warsaw

SPANISH NETHERLANDS (Spain)

BRANDENBURG

Berlin

Paris

SMALL GERMAN STATES

Prague

ZAPOROZHIA

ATLANTIC OCEAN

FRANCE

Vienna

AUSTRIA-HUNGARY

Black Sea

SWITZERLAND

MILAN (Spain)

VENICE

SMALL ITALIAN STATES

PAPAL STATES

Rome

NAPLES (Spain)

Constantinople

OTTOMAN EMPIRE

PORTUGAL

Madrid

Lisbon

SPAIN

Mediterranean Sea

MOREA (Venice)

Map Skills

1. **Location** Which large country separated Spain's possessions?

2. **Place** Why might Spain have had trouble controlling its European empire?

3. **Places to Know!** Label the following places on the outline map in your Student Journal: Paris, Constantinople, London, Poland.

Active Atlas

KEY

— Border as of 1700

0 — 400 mi

0 — 400 km

Lambert Conformal Conic Projection

▲ A china vase made in the 1700s for King Augustus II the Strong, Elector of Saxony and King of Poland

In time, a system known as the triangular trade developed. The **triangular trade** was a three-stage pattern of Atlantic trade that carried goods and enslaved people between Europe, Africa, and the Americas. In the first stage, Europeans shipped manufactured goods from Europe to Africa. These goods were traded for slaves and gold. In the second stage, ships carried enslaved Africans to the Americas. In the third stage, ships carried sugar and other agricultural products back to Europe. Trade winds and ocean currents helped ships along this trade route.

Reading Check Why did European nations compete for colonies?

An Age of Absolutism

During this time, European nations grew in size and power to become nation-states. A nation-state is a region that shares a government and is independent from other states. Monarchs during this time felt that God had chosen them to rule, a belief called the divine right of kings. They also believed in absolutism. **Absolutism** is a political system of centralized and unlimited government power.

Absolute Power in Spain Perhaps the most powerful monarch in Europe was Spain's Philip II. Philip kept firm control over the Spanish empire. As he once said, "It is best to keep an eye on everything."

Philip was a Catholic, and he used his power to back Catholicism throughout Europe. Conflict between Catholics and Protestants led to fighting in the Spanish Netherlands.

Spain also came into conflict with England. King Philip wanted to end English attacks on Spanish ships carrying gold and silver from the Americas. He also wanted to force England, a Protestant country, to return to the Catholic Church. But, as you have read, in 1588, the English navy defeated a Spanish navy fleet, called the Armada.

The Sun King Just as the sun is the center of the solar system, Louis XIV was the center of the French government. Known as the Sun King, he centralized power around the throne. In fact, Louis believed he was so important that he said "L'état, c'est moi," meaning "I am the state."

Louis wanted to make France the greatest nation in Europe. He spent years building the biggest palace in Europe at Versailles. He encouraged the growth of industry and built canals and roads. He sent the French army to build colonies in Asia and the Americas. Under Louis, France was at war almost constantly.

Prussia and Austria In 1740, Prussia seized Austrian territory in what is now Poland. That same year, Austrian Empress Maria Theresa began her 40-year rule, making Vienna a cultural center.

Although both Austrian and Prussian rulers were absolutists, Prussia practiced religious tolerance. Both struggled for years to control Central Europe.

Reading Check How did European rulers use their power?

King Louis XIV wears robes decorated with golden fleurs-de-lis, a symbol of France.
▼

Section 2 Assessment

Essential Question

What makes a nation?

Key Terms

1. Write complete sentences to define each of the following terms: cartography, plantation, northwest passage, triangular trade, absolutism

Key Ideas

2. Why did Spain support Columbus's voyages of exploration?

3. Which three European nations established colonies in eastern North America?

4. Why did European powers create colonies in the Americas?

Think Critically

5. **Identify Bias** What did the actions of Europeans reveal about their attitudes toward non-Europeans?

6. **Draw Inferences** How would Spain's discovery of huge quantities of silver and gold in the Americas affect relations with other European nations?

7. **Identify Evidence** How did absolutism help monarchs build power at home and abroad?

8. How might wars among European powers have helped build loyalty to the new nation-states? Go to your Student Journal to record your answer.

The Colonies of Spain, Portugal, France, and Great Britain

6.1.11 Compare and contrast Spanish, Portuguese, French, and British colonies in the Americas.

Portugal, Spain, France, and Great Britain all established colonies in North and South America. In this section, you will learn that these European colonies had some similarities, but also some important differences.

Reasons for Colonization

European nations founded colonies in the Americas for many reasons. First, most of their leaders followed policies of mercantilism. They thought nations could become stronger by expanding trade and were especially interested in precious metals found in North and South America. Leaders in Portugal, Spain, France, and Great Britain all wanted American colonies to gain these natural resources.

Religion was another reason Europeans founded colonies. The Catholic countries of Portugal, Spain, and France wanted to spread their religion throughout the world. They sent missionaries to convert native peoples in their colonies. In Great Britain, the Anglican Church was the established religion. Some British colonies, such as Plymouth and Massachusetts Bay Colony, were founded by dissenters of the Anglican Church who wanted to create new communities where they could freely practice their religious beliefs.

Reading Check What were two reasons that European nations established colonies in the Americas?

Some Europeans, such as these Pilgrims coming ashore in Plymouth, Massachusetts, founded colonies for religious reasons. ▶

Locations of Colonies

After Spain and Portugal began voyages of exploration, the two countries signed the Treaty of Tordesillas to divide up land claims. According to this 1494 treaty, Spain claimed all territory west of the line of latitude at 46° 30 W, and Portugal claimed all territory east of that line. As a result, Portugal's only American colony was present-day Brazil. Spain claimed a vast amount of territory in South and Central America, as well as parts of the Caribbean, present-day Florida, and southwestern North America.

France's colonies in the Western Hemisphere were limited to North America and the Caribbean. New France, the largest French colony, was located in eastern Canada along the St. Lawrence River and south through the Ohio River valley and along the Mississippi River to the Gulf of Mexico. Great Britain's colonies were also in North America and the Caribbean. They claimed land in western Canada and along the east coast of the United States.

Reading Check Why was the Treaty of Tordesillas important?

Spain, Portugal, France, and Great Britain all had colonies in the Americas. Spain claimed more land than any of the other European nations. ▶

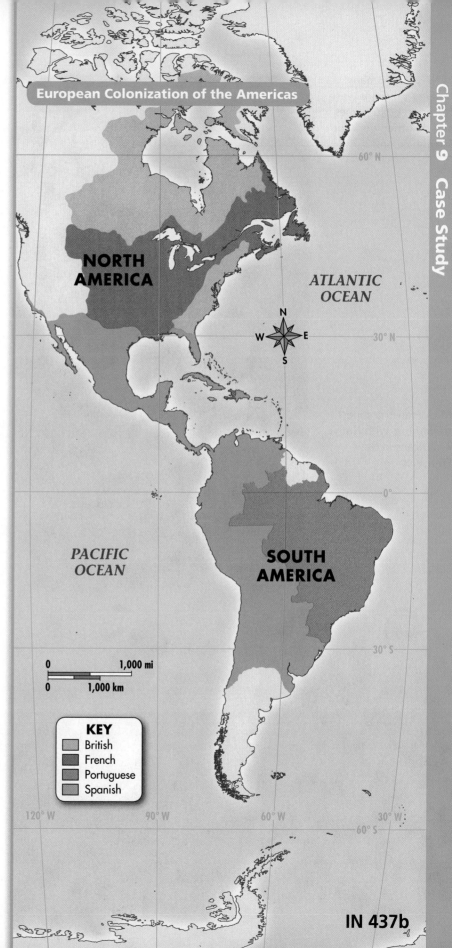

European Colonization of the Americas

NORTH AMERICA

ATLANTIC OCEAN

PACIFIC OCEAN

SOUTH AMERICA

60° N

30° N

0°

30° S

60° S

120° W   90° W   60° W   30° W

0   1,000 mi
0   1,000 km

KEY
British
French
Portuguese
Spanish

In New Spain, many Native Americans were forced to build homes and do other work for Spanish colonists. ▶

Most French trappers traded furs with Native Americans in New France. ▼

Settlement Patterns and Relations with Native Americans

In Brazil, many Portuguese colonists were aristocrats, or privileged members of the ruling class, who forced Native Americans and enslaved Africans to work on sugar and tobacco plantations. More enslaved Africans were sent to Brazil than any other American colony. In addition to enslaving Native Americans, Portuguese colonists also tried to convert them. Jesuits, a group of Catholic missionaries, set up missions and villages for converted Native Americans.

In Spanish colonies, settlers often built large cities, such as Mexico City, where the colonial government was based. Relations between Spanish colonists and Native Americans were similar to those in Portuguese colonies. Catholic priests established missions, while aristocratic settlers forced Native Americans to work in mines or on plantations.

French colonies had a different goal than Spanish or Portuguese colonies. As a result, French settlers had different relations with Native Americans. New France had fewer permanent settlers, and instead, the colony's main economic activity was the fur trade. Native Americans were important trading partners for French colonists. Because of this, French colonists had better relations with Native Americans than the Spanish or Portuguese did.

The 13 British colonies each had their own governments, economic activities, and settlement patterns. In New England, many settlers lived in towns or on small farms. In the southern colonies, where the geography was well suited to agriculture, colonists established some large plantations. Settlers throughout the British colonies clashed with Native Americans and over time forced them to move west, out of the region. To meet their labor needs, British colonists generally imported enslaved Africans rather than enslaving Native Americans.

Though relations with Native Americans differed across European colonies, they shared one common element: disease. Europeans brought diseases to the Western Hemisphere which killed huge numbers of Native Americans in both North and South America. Of all of the effects of European colonization, this one was the most significant, and for Native Americans, the most destructive.

Reading Check Which country received the largest number of enslaved Africans?

In the British colony of Virginia, the climate allowed colonists to grow tobacco, as shown here. ▼

Assessment

1. What role did religion play in the establishment of European colonies in the Americas?

2. What was the most significant difference between the Spanish colonies and the French colonies?

3. What are two ways that the Spanish colonies and the Portuguese colonies were similar?

4. If there had not been a shortage of labor in the American colonies, do you think Native Americans' experience with Europeans would have been different? Explain.

IN 437d

An Age of Revolutions

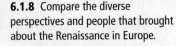

IN Indiana

6.1.8 Compare the diverse perspectives and people that brought about the Renaissance in Europe.

6.1.13 Explain the origin and spread of ideals associated with the Age of Enlightenment/Age of Reason.

6.1.14 Describe the Industrial Revolution and explain the impact of these changes.

6.2.1 Compare and contrast forms of governments in Europe and the Americas throughout history.

6.2.3 Examine key ideas of documents that placed limits on the English monarchy and how they have affected the shaping of other governments.

Visual Glossary

Key Terms • Scientific Revolution • Enlightenment • English Bill of Rights • French Revolution • Industrial Revolution

Reading Skill: Analyze Cause and Effect Take notes using the graphic organizer in your journal.

London's Royal Greenwich Observatory was established in the 1600s to study the stars and navigation. ▼

Medieval scholars had relied on religion and ancient writings to explain the world. But Renaissance thinkers questioned these old beliefs. Instead, they relied on logic, reason, and observation. Their ideas would transform science, government, and the economy.

A Scientific Revolution

During the Renaissance, scholars began studying the world around them. This led to the **Scientific Revolution,** a series of major advances in science during the 1500s and 1600s.

Science Changes Over time, scholars developed new ways to approach science. Francis Bacon taught that scientists should observe and interpret facts. René Descartes (ruh NAY day KAHRT) stressed the use of logic, or reason, to form scientific theories. Isaac Newton believed in testing theories using the scientific method, or controlled experiments.

Scientists Make Discoveries Medieval scientists believed that the sun, planets, and stars orbited, or circled, Earth. This theory was part of Catholic teachings. But in 1543, Polish astronomer Nicolaus Copernicus argued that the planets orbit the sun.

Italian astronomer Galileo Galilei (gal uh LAY oh gal uh LAY ee) agreed with Copernicus. Galileo published evidence that Earth circled the sun. In 1633, the Catholic Church put Galileo on trial for contradicting Church teaching. To save his life, Galileo signed a confession stating that his books were wrong.

Advances in Science

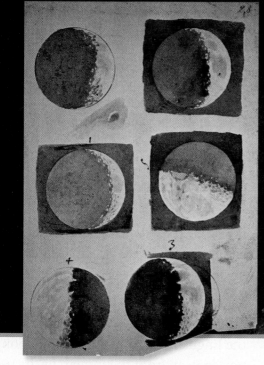

◄ Galileo sketched these phases of the moon that he saw through a telescope. In the background is a modern photograph of the moon.

The Scientific Method

Step One
State the problem.

Step Two
Gather information about the problem.

Step Three
Form a hypothesis, or educated guess.

Step Four
Experiment to test hypothesis.

Step Five
Record and analyze data.

Step Six
State a conclusion.

Step Seven
Share conclusions.

The English scientist Isaac Newton studied how the physical world worked. He described gravity and explained how objects moved in space.

Results of Discovery Scientific and technological advances improved life. Agricultural advances led to larger harvests. Inventors built instruments to measure longitude, latitude, and speed. The work of astronomers resulted in a more accurate calendar.

Thomas Newcomen and James Watt invented steam engines. Alessandro Volta and Michael Faraday conducted electrical experiments. Electricity and steam later became important energy sources.

Reading Check How did the scientific method change science?

The Enlightenment

The **Enlightenment** was a movement during the 1600s and 1700s to apply observation and reason to human affairs. The movement drew on the success of the Scientific Revolution.

Philosophers Study Society Enlightenment thinkers believed that nothing was beyond the human mind. Some studied the nature of reality. Many wrote about society and government. Thomas Hobbes believed that people were selfish and <u>greedy</u> and needed a strong ruler. Hobbes painted this picture of life without a strong ruler in his book *Leviathan*:

> 66 There is … continual fear and danger of violent death, and the life of man [is] solitary, poor, nasty, brutish, and short. 99

greedy, *adj.,* having a strong desire for wealth and possessions

439

myWorld Activity
Long Live the Revolution

consent, n.,
agreement or
approval

With their emphasis on reason, some philosophers questioned church teachings and even founded new religious groups. Others had political views that shaped modern democracy. John Locke wrote that people are born with the right to life, liberty, and property. Charles-Louis Montesquieu (MAHN tus kyoo) believed that the powers of government should be separated into branches. Jean-Jacques Rousseau (roo SOH) said that government depends on the people's <u>consent.</u> These ideas later shaped Americans' views of government.

Enlightened Rulers A few European rulers were influenced by Enlightenment ideas about government. Frederick II of Prussia improved education and outlawed torture. Joseph II of Austria ended serfdom, a system in which peasants were forced to work for a noble.

These reforms were limited. For example, Frederick II promoted religious tolerance but allowed discrimination against Jews. Frederick and other absolute monarchs kept firm control over their people.

Reading Check How did Enlightenment thinkers shape democracy?

Democratic Revolutions

The political ideas of the Enlightenment helped shape modern government. They also led to a period of violent change.

Changes in England During the 1600s, the English Parliament gradually took power away from the monarchy. In 1628, Parliament forced King Charles I to sign the Petition of Right. This document ended illegal taxation and imprisonment.

A civil war began in 1642. In 1649, Parliamentary forces executed the king. England became a commonwealth, or a republic.

Over the next 40 years, Charles I's sons regained the throne but had renewed conflicts with Parliament. Parliament then gave the throne to William and Mary in 1689, under the condition that they sign the English Bill of Rights. The **English Bill of Rights** was an act that limited the power of the monarch and listed the rights of Parliament and the English people. England's absolute monarchy had come to an end.

The Magna Carta Paves the Way

Magna Carta (1215)
The king and nobles must respect the law.

A Struggle for Democracy (1295–1641)
Representatives of the English people struggle with kings for power.

English Revolution and Restoration (1641–1688)
The monarchy is abolished and Parliament rules England as a republic. The monarchy is restored in 1660. Conflicts between the king and Parliament resume.

English Bill of Rights (1689)
King William and Queen Mary agree to the English Bill of Rights. The Bill of Rights ensures the superiority of Parliament over the monarchy.

American Declaration of Independence (1776)
The monarchy is abolished and replaced with a democratic government in the United States.

How does this flowchart show the changing relationship of government and the people?

440

Revolution in France In France, society was divided into three groups called estates: clergy (the First Estate), nobles (the Second Estate), and common people (the Third Estate). Most French people were in the Third Estate. They paid heavy taxes and had few rights.

Enlightenment ideas inspired some French people to demand a voice in government. However, King Louis XVI refused to give up any of his powers. On July 14, 1789, a mob stormed the Bastille, a Paris prison. This marked the start of the **French Revolution,** a political movement that removed the French king from power and formed a republic.

The Revolution took a brutal turn. During the Reign of Terror in 1793 and 1794, the republic's government killed thousands of its opponents.

Napoleon Takes Power Meanwhile, Napoleon Bonaparte rose quickly in the French army. In 1799, he took power in France as a dictator.

Napoleon wanted to create a mighty French empire. In the Napoleonic Wars, he conquered much of Europe. His invasion of Russia proved disastrous, however. The French army was weakened, and Napoleon was defeated in 1815.

Revolution Spreads French domination led to growing nationalism, or devotion to one's country. Many Europeans also wanted greater democracy. In 1848, revolutions broke out across Europe. By 1871, both Germany and Italy had become unified nations.

Reading Check What caused the French Revolution?

The Reign of Terror

The promise of the French Revolution quickly soured. What had been a revolution calling for brotherhood and liberty turned into a civil war. Respected leaders such as Robespierre became feared tyrants.

A French mob storms the Bastille. ▼

Robespierre, who sentenced hundreds to the guillotine, was executed himself in 1794. ▼

The French Republic's government used the falling blade of the guillotine (right) to silence opponents. ▶

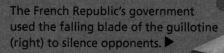

Culture Close-up

my **worldgeography**.com   Culture Close-up

Life in the Industrial Age

The Industrial Revolution has been chronicled in art, literature, and photography. It transformed life and society across Europe. Industrialization had both positive and negative aspects. Its innovations remain part of modern life.

- **Widespread pollution from factories**
- **Long work hours, child labor common**
- **Overcrowded living conditions**

The Industrial Revolution

Alongside these political revolutions, a different kind of revolution began. The **Industrial Revolution** was a shift from hand tools driven by animal or human power to large-scale machinery powered by fuels or natural forces. It led to a growth of cities and large organizations and to rapid changes in technology. The Industrial Revolution began in Britain but soon spread to the rest of Europe.

Technology Changes Industry Before the Industrial Revolution, most people were farmers. Others worked at home. There, they used hand tools to make cloth, leather goods, and other items.

In England in the mid-1700s, this process began to change. Fast, new machines in factories began to do much of the work once done by people in their homes. The textile industry was the first to change. Inventors developed machines for spinning thread and weaving cloth.

Transportation also changed. Coal and steampower made steamboats and locomotives possible. These ships and trains carried raw materials to factories. They brought finished goods to distant markets.

Industry Changes Landscapes

Entrepreneurs, or people who start businesses, built factories in areas that had a labor supply, resources such as coal, and good transportation. Towns without access to coal and iron or to transportation often did not industrialize.

Industrial towns grew quickly as workers moved there for jobs in factories. This rapid growth caused problems such as housing shortages. People had to live in crowded apartment buildings. Many people had no access to clean water.

Cities could not dispose adequately of waste, and coal-burning factories polluted the air. Diseases spread rapidly in these crowded, dirty conditions. Working conditions in factories were difficult. Factories and mines often hired young children to work dangerous jobs.

Trade Grows Workers in factories produced far more goods than individual workers ever had. Industrialized nations needed new places to sell these products. Many of the new markets were in European colonies in Africa and Asia. Colonies also provided raw materials for European manufacturers.

IN Indiana **CONNECTIONS**

Between 1800 and 1840, Indiana's population grew from **5,641** to **685,866**.

- Better public education and social reforms
- Improvements in healthcare, public hygiene
- Advances in arts and sciences

Positive Effects The Industrial Age also brought improvements. During this period, doctors and scientists made advances in research and medicine. Louis Pasteur and Robert Koch discovered that germs caused disease. Researchers found ways to cure or prevent illness. Cities built sewer systems to dispose of waste and prevent disease. Inventors developed ways to use electric power.

Because production was more efficient, the cost of goods went down. With the number of jobs increasing and the price of products decreasing, people could afford to buy more goods. For example, people began to wear clothing made in factories instead of at home. Middle-class families purchased new labor-saving devices, such as sewing machines. As a result, the standard of living—or the level of comfort—rose for millions of people.

Another positive change was greater access to primary school education. Where once only some boys had attended school, now girls too could receive an education.

Reading Check How did life change during the Industrial Age?

Section 3 Assessment

Key Terms

1. Using full sentences, describe how each of the following terms relates to social and political change: Scientific Revolution, Enlightenment, English Bill of Rights, French Revolution, Industrial Revolution.

Key Ideas

2. How did the Industrial Revolution transform methods of manufacturing goods?

3. What did Isaac Newton contribute to the Scientific Revolution?

4. How did the Scientific Revolution influence Enlightenment thought?

5. How did the Enlightenment affect rulers' ideas?

Think Critically

6. **Categorize** Which of the events discussed in this section would you call political revolutions and which would you call cultural revolutions?

7. **Synthesize** How did the Enlightenment change governments in Europe?

Essential Question

What makes a nation?

8. How did the Napoleonic Wars encourage nationalistic feelings in Europe? Go to your Student Journal to record your answer.

The Rise of Liberalism, Conservatism, and Socialism

IN Indiana **6.1.16** Identify individuals, beliefs, and events that represent various political ideologies during the nineteenth and twentieth centuries and explain their significance.

English philosopher John Locke was a leading proponent of the political ideology of liberalism. ▼

The increased number of factories, such as these in France, changed the way that many people thought about society. ▼

European Political Ideologies

In the late eighteenth and early nineteenth centuries, European and American societies were radically transformed. The American and French Revolutions altered the relationship between people and their governments. At the same time, the Industrial Revolution changed the way that many people earned their living. These political and economic changes created problems for society, such as harsh living and working conditions for laborers, unrelenting poverty, and disorder. To solve these problems, writers, thinkers, and politicians, including John Locke, Edmund Burke, and Karl Marx, developed political ideologies, or systems of thought and belief.

Liberalism Liberalism was a political ideology that developed in reaction to the tyrannical monarchies that existed in many European countries, including Great Britain and France. Liberalism is the belief that individuals' freedoms should be protected and the government should be limited. Liberal ideals led to the growth of representative government during the eighteenth and nineteenth centuries.

John Locke was a British philosopher whose work reflected liberal ideas. Locke believed that rulers' power should come from the consent of the people they governed. He also believed in freeing people from the strong institutions of the church and the government. His ideas became the basis of the U.S. Constitution, and also led to changing laws in Europe, especially in France and England. These laws gave more power to the elected branches of government and expanded the number of people who had the right to vote.

One aspect of liberalism is *laissez-faire* economics. The term means "leave things alone" or "don't interfere." This idea, championed by the British writer Adam Smith, says that when individuals work for their own economic gain, society as a whole benefits. As a result, governments should not interfere in the economy. This was partly a reaction to the ideals of mercantilism, which had widespread support in the sixteenth and seventeenth centuries. *Laissez-faire* supporters believed in free trade and no tariffs.

Reading Check Why is John Locke an important historical figure?

Conservatism

Conservatism developed in the eighteenth century as a reaction to some of the political changes occurring throughout Europe, especially the French Revolution of 1789. Conservatism is a political ideology that stresses maintaining existing political structures. Conservatives believed in gradual, not rapid, change in government and society.

One early conservative thinker was Edmund Burke. An eighteenth-century British politician, Burke supported a representative government, but strongly believed in the authority of institutions such as the monarchy and a strong church. In addition to these views, conservatives generally supported tariffs to protect the manufacturers of local goods.

Reading Check What did Edmund Burke believe about social and political change?

Edmund Burke, another English philosopher, spoke out in support of conservative ideals in the eighteenth century. ▼

Socialism

During the nineteenth century, the Industrial Revolution created harsh living and working conditions for laborers, while at the same time making factory owners very wealthy. It seemed that *laissez-faire* economics was no longer working, so many people demanded better working conditions and more workers' rights.

At this time, a new ideology, socialism, gained strength. Socialism was the belief that workers, rather than private individuals, should control the means of production of goods and services, so that they would gain some of the wealth that was being created. The early socialists believed in a mix of public and private ownership.

One of the founders of socialism was Robert Owen, a Scottish factory owner who ran mills in New Lanark, Scotland, and created a community for workers there. He tried to improve workers' lives, providing them with good wages, education, and housing.

Conditions in factories such as this one led many people to oppose old economic policies and support socialism. ▼

◀ The ideas of Karl Marx and Friedrich Engels led peasants in Russia to overthrow their government in the Russian Revolution of 1918.

Many socialists wanted increased voting and political rights for workers. Louis Blanc, one of the most prominent French socialists, thought that the state should organize factories to guarantee employment for all adult citizens.

After 1848, socialism was influenced by more radical critics of industrial society. Two of those critics were Karl Marx and Friedrich Engels. These two men believed that the Industrial Revolution created class differences and that those differences would lead to conflict. Eventually, they believed that workers would revolt and take over ownership of property. Marx and Engels explained their ideas in a pamphlet called ìThe Communist Manifesto.î Their ideas have influenced socialists and communists throughout the nineteenth and twentieth centuries.

Reading check What conditions contributed to the rise of socialism?

Assessment

1. What made liberalism an important ideology in the eighteenth century?

2. What impact did *laissez-faire* economics have on laborers and factory owners in the nineteenth century?

3. How did the Industrial Revolution lead to increased support for socialism?

Section 4

Wars and Hardship

IN Indiana

6.1.16 Identify individuals, beliefs and events that represent various political ideologies during the 19th and 20th centuries and explain their significance.

6.1.20 Analyze cause-and-effect relationships in history.

6.2.1 Compare and contrast forms of governments in Europe and the Americas throughout history.

6.2.5 Discuss the impact of major forms of government in Europe and the Americas on civil and human rights.

Key Terms • World War I • Great Depression • communism • fascism • World War II • Holocaust

Visual Glossary

Reading Skill: Compare and Contrast Take notes using the graphic organizer in your journal.

Fighter pilots engage in a dramatic dogfight during World War I.

When the 1900s began, large multinational empires controlled central Europe. A series of alliances linked Europe's great powers into competing blocs.

The Great War: World War I

World War I (1914–1918), or the Great War, was the first modern global conflict. It involved most of Europe, the United States, Canada, and many parts of Africa and Asia.

Causes of War World War I had four main causes: nationalism, imperialism, militarism, and alliances.

- **Nationalism**—Nationalism, or devotion to one's nation or people, sometimes led to hostility toward other nations.
- **Imperialism**—European imperial powers competed to extend their empires by seizing territory to add to their colonies in Africa and Asia.
- **Militarism**—For decades, European countries had been building up military power and adopting warlike attitudes.
- **Alliances**—In a complex system of alliances, many European countries had agreed to defend one another from attack. These alliances pulled nations into the war.

War Breaks Out In June 1914, a Serbian nationalist killed the Austrian archduke. Austria-Hungary declared war on Serbia. One by one, the major European powers entered the war to support their allies. The fighting later spread overseas.

In Europe, armies fought on two fronts. On the Western Front, Germany battled the Allied Powers—France and Britain. Soldiers lived in a network of trenches dug into the earth. For years, they gained little ground. On the Eastern Front, Germany and Austria-Hungary fought Russia. But when the Russian Revolution began in 1917, Russia pulled out of the war.

In 1917, the United States entered the war on the side of the Allies. U.S. troops helped force the Germans out of France. Exhausted, Germany sought a truce, and the war ended on November 11, 1918.

Consequences of War The Allies forced Germany to sign the Treaty of Versailles. The treaty <u>humiliated</u> Germany. It made Germany give up territory and pay huge reparations, or sums for war damage.

Other treaties carved up Austria-Hungary into several new nations, ended the Ottoman Empire, and created new countries. For example, Yugoslavia was a federation of Slavic republics, including Serbia. Poland was shaped from parts of Germany, Austria-Hungary, and Russia. The maps below show these changes.

Reading Check **What were the four main causes of World War I?**

humiliate, *v.,* to embarrass or to reduce a person's feeling of self-worth

Map Skills

1 **Region** How did Europe change after World War I?

2 **Place** What areas of Europe changed the most? Why do you think this happened?

→ Active Atlas

Europe Before and After World War I

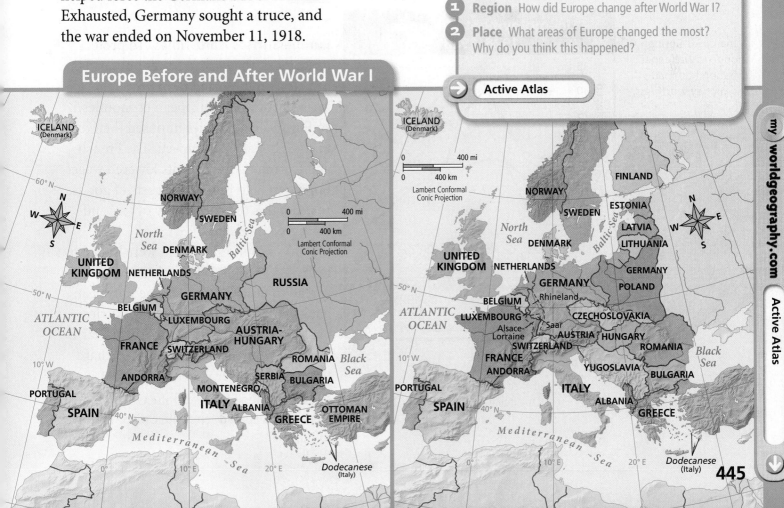

The Great Depression

Germany had lost land, people, and resources. At the same time, Germany owed billions of dollars in reparations. The government printed money to try to make these payments. As a result, German money lost value. The price of goods increased rapidly during a period of inflation. Many Germans lost their savings. This caused unrest and political instability in Germany.

A Global Financial Crisis Develops

During the 1920s, the American economy had grown dramatically. At same time, prices on the U.S. stock market rose.

Many Americans bought stocks, some with borrowed money, hoping to make a profit as the prices of stocks increased.

At first, stock prices soared. Then stocks leveled off and fell. Nervous lenders demanded repayment. Investors sold stocks to repay the loans. Heavy selling drove prices down quickly. In October 1929, the U.S. stock market collapsed.

Many investors lost fortunes selling their stocks for much less than they had paid. People and businesses who had borrowed money could not repay their debts. Soon, banks failed and businesses closed. As a result, millions of people were out of work. This was the beginning of the **Great Depression,** a deep, worldwide economic <u>slump</u> that lasted through the 1930s. It caused hardship around the world.

Europe Suffers Hard Times To protect its farmers, the United States put tariffs, or taxes, on imported farm products. These tariffs hurt European economies, so European countries imposed their own tariffs. Global trade slowed. The French and German governments lowered wages, hoping to help reduce the costs of goods. Instead, this only angered workers and increased hardship.

Banks around the world were linked by loans. As a result, U.S. banking problems spread to other nations. Some European banks failed. Most European countries had not yet recovered from World War I. These new financial troubles made hard times even harder.

Reading Check How did the Great Depression spread from the United States to Europe?

slump, *n.,*
a marked decline

A man uses German money as wallpaper. Inflation had made the money worthless.
▼

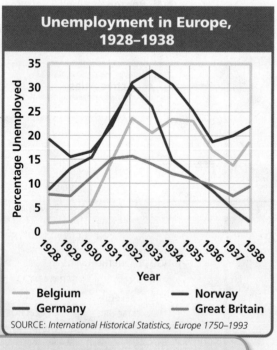

Unemployment in Europe, 1928–1938

Percentage Unemployed vs Year (1928–1938)

SOURCE: *International Historical Statistics, Europe 1750–1993*

— Belgium   — Norway
— Germany   — Great Britain

Chart Skills

In which years did each European nation on the graph experience the highest unemployment?

Data Discovery

A War of Ideas

After World War I, antidemocratic leaders took power in Italy, Germany, and other European countries. Those governments took control of daily life.

The Rise of Communism The 1917 Russian Revolution led to the formation of the communist government of the Soviet Union. **Communism** is an economic and political system in which the state, run by a Communist Party, takes over industry and farmland and controls most organizations.

Communism promised to share wealth among all workers. During the Great Depression, workers across Europe found this promise very appealing.

Fascism in Italy and Spain In Italy, nationalist pride led to fascism. **Fascism** is a political system that stresses national strength, military might, and the belief that the state is more important than individuals. Fascists use propaganda and violence to achieve goals and believe that a dictator—a leader with unlimited powers—should rule. In the 1920s, fascist Benito Mussolini took power in Italy. He promised to build a strong Italian empire. During the 1930s, fascists under Francisco Franco took control of Spain.

Nazis Take Power in Germany Many Germans resented the Treaty of Versailles and blamed it for their hardships. Some blamed Germany's democratic government for obeying the treaty.

Adolf Hitler had served in the German army during World War I. Like many other Germans, he felt that Germany had been treated unfairly after the war.

Hitler came to lead a small, fascist German political party, the Nazi Party. Hitler's ideas included extreme nationalism, racism, and anti-Semitism, or prejudice against Jews. Hitler unfairly blamed Jews for Germany's economic problems.

In 1923, the Nazis tried and failed to overthrow the government. Hitler was jailed, but worked after his release to rebuild the Nazi Party. Amid the Great Depression, the Nazis gained strength in the early 1930s. In 1932, the Nazis won more votes than any other party, but less than a majority of votes. Nonetheless, in 1933, Hitler became head of Germany's government.

Understanding Political Systems			
	Democracy	**Communism**	**Fascism**
Individuals and the State	Individuals' rights are more important than government interests.	Government interests are more important than individuals' rights.	Government interests are more important than individuals' rights.
Values	Freedom, individuals' rights, justice	Obedience, discipline, economic security	Obedience, discipline, national pride, military power
Government	The people and their elected representatives make decisions; control of people's lives is minimal.	Communist party makes all decisions; extreme control of all aspects of life.	Fascist party controls all aspects of life; government is permanent and necessary for national progress.

Chart Skills

Compare the values associated with fascism to those of democracy and communism.

Data Discovery

▲ Flag of Italy under fascism

447

▲ The Nazis forced Jewish people to wear yellow stars for identification.

Once in power, Hitler ruled as a dictator. He controlled every aspect of German life, using secret police to spy on people. Hitler imprisoned or killed his opponents. Because Germany's economy improved under the Nazis, many Germans accepted Nazi rule.

The Nazi government passed a number of laws against Jews, eliminating their rights as citizens. In 1938, Nazis led anti-Jewish riots in Germany and Austria. For 48 hours, Nazis systematically destroyed Jewish synagogues and Jewish businesses. Nazi hatred toward Jews later led to the Nazi "Final Solution," the plan to murder all Jews.

Reading Check Why were the German people attracted to the Nazi Party?

World War II

Under Adolf Hitler, Germany built a powerful army and formed an alliance with Italy and Japan. These countries were called the Axis Powers. Britain and France formed the Allied Powers, later joined by the United States and Soviet Union.

War Begins Hitler wanted to build a mighty German empire across Europe. In 1938, German troops occupied Austria and seized part of Czechoslovakia. Germany and the Soviet Union then secretly agreed to divide Poland between them. On September 1, 1939, Germany invaded Poland. Two days later, Britain and France declared war on Germany. **World War II,** the second major global conflict of the 1900s, had begun.

War in Europe By the end of 1940, Germany's powerful armies had conquered much of Europe. Italy attacked North Africa. At first, Britain fought on alone, with the help of some military aid from the United States.

The German air force repeatedly bombed British military targets and civilian areas, but the British did not give up.

Wartime Opponents, 1942

KEY
- Allied territory, 1942
- Axis territory, 1942
- Neutral territory, 1942
- Borders as of 1938

0   400 mi
0   400 km
Lambert Conformal Conic Projection

North Sea

Baltic Sea

ATLANTIC OCEAN

North Sea

Black Sea

Mediterranean Sea

60° N
50° N
40° N
10° W
0°
10° E
20° E
30° E
40° E

N W E S

Map Skills

Place Who controlled more of Europe in 1942, the Allies or the Axis Powers?

→ **Active Atlas**

British Prime Minister Winston Churchill inspired the people with stirring speeches:

> 66 We have before us many, many long months of struggle and of suffering. You ask, what is our policy? I will say: It is to wage war, by sea, land and air, with all our might and with all the strength that God can give us. 99

In June 1941, Germany broke its earlier agreement and invaded the Soviet Union. The Soviet Union joined the Allied Powers. Soviet resistance, brutal winter weather, and a lack of supplies finally forced Germany to retreat in 1943.

America Enters the War In late 1941, Japan bombed Pearl Harbor, a U.S. naval base in Hawaii. This pushed the United States into the war. American forces helped the Allies defeat Italy.

With U.S. help, the Allies pushed back into western Europe. On June 6, 1944, D-Day, more than 150,000 Allied troops invaded German-occupied France. The Allies slowly forced German troops back across France into Germany. At the same time, Soviet troops invaded Germany from the east. Germany surrendered on May 7, 1945. World War II ended later that year with Japan's surrender to the United States.

Effects of the War Approximately 17 million European soldiers died in World War II. Millions of civilians died as well. Many civilian deaths occurred in the **Holocaust,** the mass murder of Jews by the Nazis during World War II. The Nazis murdered 6 million Jews and another 5 million people from other groups.

After the war, Europe's cities, roads, and farms lay in ruins. Much of the continent needed to be rebuilt.

Reading Check How were the Allied forces able to win World War II?

World at War

- ▶ **1914** World War I begins.
- ▶ **1918** World War I ends.
- ▶ **1919** The Treaty of Versailles
- ▶ **1939** Germany invades Poland; France and Britain declare war on Germany. World War II begins.
- ▶ **1941** The United States enters the war.
- ▶ **1945** Germany and Japan surrender. World War II ends.

➜ Timeline

Section 4 Assessment

Key Terms

1. Define each of the following terms using a complete sentence: World War I, Great Depression, communism, fascism, World War II, Holocaust.

Key Ideas

2. Whom did the Nazis murder during the Holocaust?

3. How did competition among nations contribute to World War I?

4. How did the Great Depression affect Europe?

5. Which nations defeated the Axis Powers in World War II?

Think Critically

6. **Problem Solving** How did Germany's situation after World War I help cause the next world war?

7. **Compare Viewpoints** How might French citizens have felt about the Treaty of Versailles? Compare their viewpoint to that of German citizens.

? Essential Question

What makes a nation?

8. Why did so many nations gain independence after World War I? Go to your Student Journal to record your answer.

The World Wars in Art

IN Indiana

6.1.21 Differentiate between fact and interpretation in historical accounts and explain historical passages.

6.1.23 Identify issues related to an event in Europe or the Americas and give arguments for and against that issue.

Eyewitness accounts make the experience of battle frighteningly real. Ancient historians like Herodotus recorded the heroism of the Greeks against the Persians. In 1812, Philippe Paul de Ségur remembered Napoleon's "skeletons of soldiers" as the French army returned in defeat from Russia. But few accounts of war have been as powerful as those left by the poets, novelists, and artists who experienced World War I and World War II. Not only did they write about fighting the enemy on the battlefield, but these artists also recorded the horrors of the Holocaust.

▲ A poppy worn in remembrance of war veterans

Stop at each letter on the right to think about the text. Then answer the question with the same letter on the left.

Ⓐ **Identify Evidence** What do the crosses indicate?

Ⓑ **Synthesize** Who is the narrator and how did he come to be in Flanders?

Ⓒ **Draw Inferences** Why does the poet use the image of a relay race here?

scarce, *adv.*, hardly or barely

quarrel, *n.*, disagreement, dispute

foe, *n.*, enemy

In Flanders Fields

66 In Flanders fields the poppies blow
Ⓐ Between the crosses row on row,
That mark our place; and in the sky
The larks, still bravely singing, fly
<u>Scarce</u> heard amid the guns below.

Ⓑ We are the Dead. Short days ago
We lived, felt dawn, saw sunset glow,
Loved and were loved, and now we lie
In Flanders fields.

Take up our <u>quarrel</u> with the <u>foe</u>:
Ⓒ To you from failing hands we throw
The torch; be yours to hold it high.
If ye break faith with us who die
We shall not sleep, though poppies grow
In Flanders fields. 99
—Lieutenant Colonel John McCrae, M.D., after the Battle of Ypres, Belgium, 1915

British soldiers walk across the battlefield near Ypres during World War I.

Stop at each letter on the right to think about the text. Then answer the question with the same letter on the left.

D **Synthesize** How many times does the word "and" appear in the first sentence? How does this affect the way you read it?

E **Summarize** Why does mixing up the shoes seem so "crazy" to the narrator?

F **Draw Conclusions** Why does the German watch "with interest" how the men react to the cold?

heap, *n.,* pile

writhe, *v.,* to twist and turn

Heaps of Shoes

66 Now another German comes and tells us to put the shoes in a certain corner, **D** and we put them there, because now it is all over and we feel outside this world and the only thing is to obey.

Someone comes with a broom and sweeps away all the shoes, outside **E** the door in a <u>heap</u>. He is crazy, he is mixing them all together, ninety-six pairs, they will be all unmatched.

The outside door opens, a freezing wind enters and we are naked and cover ourselves up with our arms. The wind blows and slams the door; the German reopens it and stands **F** watching with interest how we <u>writhe</u> to hide from the wind, one behind the other.

Then he leaves and closes it. 99

—Primo Levi, *Survival in Auschwitz,* 1958

Piles of shoes taken from prisoners sent to the concentration camp at Auschwitz ▼

Analyze the Documents

1. **Compare and Contrast** Both the poem and the text above show courage and bravery. Compare and contrast how each source does this.

2. **Writing Task** Write a short poem in reaction to either "In Flanders Fields" or to the excerpt from *Survival in Auschwitz.*

Rebuilding and New Challenges

 **Indiana**

6.2.1 Compare and contrast forms of governments in Europe and the Americas throughout history.

6.2.6 Describe the functions of international political organizations in the world today.

6.3.9 Identify current patterns of population distribution and growth in Europe and the Americas and evaluate factors that trigger migrations.

6.3.13 Explain the impact of humans on the physical environment in Europe and the Americas.

Key Terms • Cold War • Marshall Plan • Berlin Wall • European Union (EU)

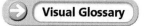 **Visual Glossary**

Reading Skill: Identify Main Ideas and Details Take notes using the graphic organizer in your journal.

When World War II ended, Soviet troops occupied most of Eastern Europe. The Soviet Union set up communist governments there. U.S. troops backed democratic governments in Western Europe.

Cold War and Division

The United States and Britain wanted to stop the Soviet Union from spreading communism. The result was the **Cold War**, a long period of hostility between the Soviet Union and the democratic West.

To encourage democracy and oppose communism, the United States created the **Marshall Plan**, a U.S. recovery plan that offered money to help European countries recover from the war. This money helped Western Europe rebuild.

A woman walks down a bombed-out street in Warsaw, Poland, in 1946. ▼

International Cooperation After World War II, many nations joined together to form the United Nations (UN). The UN's main task was to safeguard world peace. The UN later went on to help people cope with disasters and poverty.

The Berlin Wall Goes Up The Cold War divided Europe between Soviet-controlled, communist Eastern Europe and democratic Western Europe, mostly allied with the United States. This split ran roughly along the line where the troops of the Western Allies met the Soviet troops at the end of World War II.

This dividing line ran right through the center of Germany. The Soviets occupied East Germany, which became communist. West Germany, occupied by the Western Allies, became a democracy.

The Soviets and Western Allies also divided Germany's capital, Berlin, located within East Germany. In 1948, the Soviets blocked land and sea access to West Berlin. The United States and Britain flew supplies into Berlin for 11 months until the Soviets lifted the blockade.

About 2.5 million East Germans fled to the West by crossing into West Berlin. In 1961, East Germany built a wall around West Berlin to prevent escapes. The **Berlin Wall** <u>symbolized</u> Cold War divisions.

The Democratic West Unites Helped by American aid, Western Europe's economy recovered quickly. By 1951, factories were producing more than ever. Nations such as Italy adopted democracy. Meanwhile, European nations were forced to give up their colonies. For example, Britain made India and other colonies independent.

▲ This 1962 nuclear explosion at a U.S. testing site was part of a Cold War arms race with the Soviet Union.

In 1949, the United States and Western European countries formed a military alliance called the North Atlantic Treaty Organization (NATO). The United States was NATO's strongest member. After the war, the United States and the Soviet Union became the world's dominant nations, or superpowers.

Communists Control the East The Soviet Union viewed Eastern European countries as satellites, or dependent countries. In response to NATO, the Soviet Union and its satellites formed a military alliance called the Warsaw Pact in 1955. Eastern Europe had weak, state-controlled economies.

The Soviets often used force to control Eastern Europe. In 1956, Soviet forces invaded Hungary and blocked democratic change. In 1968, Soviet troops crushed a reform movement in Czechoslovakia.

Reading Check How did the Soviet Union gain and keep control of Eastern Europe?

symbolize, *v.,* to represent or express something

453

Closer Look

In 1946, Winston Churchill, former British prime minister, said "[A]n iron curtain has descended across the Continent." During the Cold War, the Iron Curtain was a fortified set of defenses between the democratic west and the communist east. East of the Iron Curtain, West Berlin was surrounded by the Berlin Wall, a concrete barrier that prevented East Germans from moving to democratic West Berlin.

THINK CRITICALLY How might Germans have felt about the Iron Curtain?

Map Skills

1 **Location** What nation was divided by the Iron Curtain?

2 **Places to Know!**
Label these places on the outline map in your Student Journal: Romania, Belgium, Greece, Portugal, Italy.

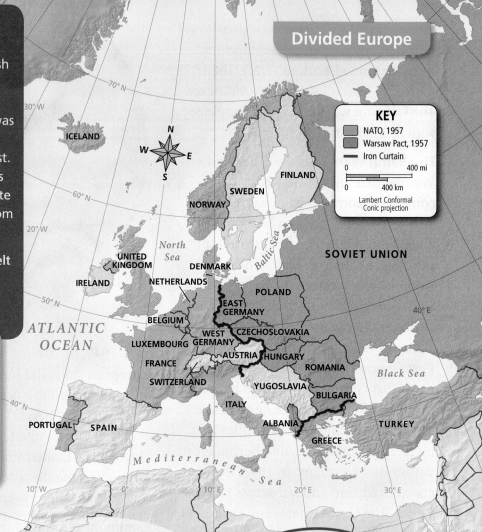

KEY
- NATO, 1957
- Warsaw Pact, 1957
- Iron Curtain

0   400 mi
0   400 km
Lambert Conformal Conic projection

ICELAND
NORWAY
SWEDEN
FINLAND
SOVIET UNION
North Sea
Baltic Sea
UNITED KINGDOM
DENMARK
IRELAND
NETHERLANDS
POLAND
EAST GERMANY
BELGIUM
WEST GERMANY
CZECHOSLOVAKIA
LUXEMBOURG
ATLANTIC OCEAN
FRANCE
AUSTRIA
HUNGARY
SWITZERLAND
ROMANIA
Black Sea
YUGOSLAVIA
BULGARIA
ITALY
ALBANIA
TURKEY
GREECE
PORTUGAL
SPAIN
Mediterranean Sea

Below, Greek children receive food supplied by the Marshall Plan. At right, construction of the Berlin Wall begins in 1961.

454

The European Union

Long-standing hostility between Germany and France played a role in fueling Europe's wars. After World War II, West German and French leaders searched for a way to exist in peace.

Forming a Community In 1951, France and West Germany agreed to coordinate their coal and steel production. This would tie the countries economically and help to prevent future wars. Italy, Belgium, Luxembourg, and the Netherlands also signed the agreement.

In 1957, those six countries formed the European Economic Community, or Common Market. This was a free trade zone. It let manufactured goods and services move freely among the countries. Trade increased dramatically.

Toward a Unified Europe Six more countries had joined the Common Market by 1986. The Common Market nations signed the Maastricht Treaty in 1992. This treaty created the **European Union (EU),** an economic and political partnership. Starting in 1995, an open-borders policy allowed people to move freely among many EU nations.

In 2002, most EU nations adopted a single currency called the euro. A currency is a unit of money, like the dollar. Sharing a common currency made trade easier. However, some countries rejected the euro so that they could keep control of their money. In 2003, a treaty let Eastern European countries join the EU. By 2008, the EU had grown to include 27 nations.

Reading Check Why did West Germany and France form a common market?

Democracy Spreads East

By the 1980s, communism was failing. Weak Soviet and Eastern European economies could not compete with Western market economies.

Communism Fails In Eastern Europe, government officials planned what farms should grow and what factories should produce. Officials made decisions based on the state's wishes rather than people's needs. For example, they made tanks instead of home appliances. Second, people had no motive to work hard because the government limited their pay. As a result of these two problems, communist countries often had shortages of food and consumer goods.

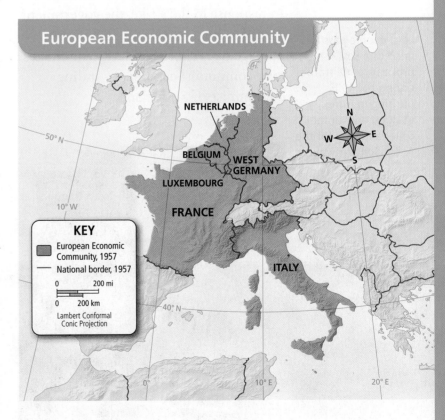

European Economic Community

NETHERLANDS
BELGIUM
LUXEMBOURG
WEST GERMANY
FRANCE
ITALY

50° N
10° W
40° N
0°
10° E
20° E

KEY

■ European Economic Community, 1957
— National border, 1957

0 ___ 200 mi
0 ___ 200 km

Lambert Conformal Conic Projection

455

In 1985, Mikhail Gorbachev became the new leader of the Soviet Union. Gorbachev was younger than other leaders and more open to change. In the late 1980s, Gorbachev began to loosen government control within the Soviet Union. He supported greater democracy, particularly in the Soviet satellites of Eastern Europe. Gorbachev also gave Eastern European countries more freedom to choose their own way.

A Democratic Revolution Spreads In 1980, a Polish shipyard workers' union called Solidarity went on strike. The Polish government granted some union demands and the union head, Lech Walesa (lek vah WEN suh), became a hero. Solidarity went on strike again in 1988. In response to the strike, the government agreed to hold free elections. Voters courageously chose Solidarity candidates over communist candidates, ending communist rule in Poland.

Poland's example inspired other countries. In Czechoslovakia, thousands of people protested the communist government in 1989. In response to the protests, the government agreed to give up power. This peaceful <u>transfer</u> of power is known as the Velvet Revolution. In free elections later that year, Czechoslovakians elected writer Vaclav Havel (VAHTS lahv HAH vul) president. Havel described his people's experience.

> 66 People have passed through a very dark tunnel at the end of which there was a light of freedom. 99
>
> —Vaclav Havel, 1990

Romania overthrew its communist government in 1989, but its communist dictator killed many protesters before giving up power. Hungary's Communist Party went out of existence, and in 1990 the country elected a non-communist government. Bulgaria also held its first free elections in 1990.

Germany Reunifies During 1989, East Germans began protesting for democratic change. East Germany's communist government at first refused to make changes. The government then began to respond to some protester demands.

Finally, on November 9, 1989, East German border guards opened the gates of the Berlin Wall. East and West Germans rushed to greet each other.

Demands for reform led to free elections, which removed the communist government from power in 1989. A year later, on October 3, 1990, the two halves of Germany were reunified.

transfer, *n.,* a carrying over of something from one situation to another

**myWorld Activity
Tear Down This Wall**

Left, people pass the head of a Soviet ruler broken from a statue during the 1956 uprising in Hungary; at right, a volunteer collects money for the Polish Solidarity party.

The Soviet Union Falls Nationalism and the desire for reform rocked the Soviet Union. In 1990, the Soviet republic of Lithuania demanded independence. The Soviet army invaded Lithuania.

Soviet citizens took to the streets to protest the invasion. The army refused to fight the people. In 1991, the Soviet Union broke apart into 15 new nations, including Moldova, Ukraine, Belarus, Lithuania, Latvia, and Estonia in Eastern Europe. The largest post-Soviet nation was Russia.

Reading Check **How did Eastern Europe gain freedom from communism?**

THE WALL COMES DOWN

During the late 1980s, communist governments across Eastern Europe followed the lead of the Soviet Union. They began to allow their opponents to speak more freely. Some scheduled free elections. East Germany's government resisted these changes. In the fall of 1989, however, East German people began to hold peaceful protests. The protesters said they wanted democracy. East German leaders knew that the Soviet Union was no longer willing to put down peaceful protests. When border guards opened the Berlin Wall on November 9, 1989, Germans on both sides began to knock it down.

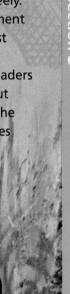

> **66 We are the people! 99**
> —Chant of East German democracy protesters, 1989

▲ In this 1990 political cartoon, Soviet leader Mikhail Gorbachev is pictured as Humpty Dumpty sitting on a crumbling wall with the symbol of the Soviet Union. *What does this cartoon mean?*

▲ In 2004, terrorists bombed this train in Spain. In the inset, a London man reads about the 2005 terrorist bombings in that city.

Europe Faces Challenges

After reunifying, Germany struggled economically. East German factories were outdated and inefficent, and many went out of business. Unemployment soared in eastern Germany. Some citizens failed to adapt to the market economy, which required initiative and hard work.

Integrating the East After the collapse of communism, Europe worked to rebuild ties between East and West. The EU opened membership to Eastern European nations who could show that they had democratic governments and strong market economies. Most eastern nations had to make reforms before joining the EU. Even so, their economies often remained weak due to problems similar to those in eastern Germany.

Communist rule had not prepared people for democracy either. Many people in formerly communist lands did not trust their leaders. Government corruption had been widespread under communist rule and remained a problem.

International Issues In the late 1900s, a global economy developed as foreign trade and multinational corporations grew. The EU began to consider issues such as free trade with nonmember nations.

Incidents of international terrorism also scarred Europe. In 2004, the terrorist group al-Qaeda exploded bombs on commuter trains in Madrid, Spain, killing nearly 200. Afterward, European countries worked together to fight terrorism.

Immigration was another challenge. When Eastern European countries joined the EU, thousands of Eastern Europeans moved to western European countries for work. Many Western Europeans resented the newcomers. In addition, immigrants from Africa and Asia, some of them illegal, poured into Europe. Some Europeans began to fear that immigrants would take their jobs. Europeans and their leaders had to find ways to accommodate growing populations with customs and languages from outside of Europe.

Wind farms such as this one off the coast of Denmark make Europe a world leader in alternative energy sources.

Energy and the Environment Because of its industry, Europe has long fought pollution. For example, it has tried to reduce the air pollution that causes acid rain, which kills forests. The EU also signed the Kyoto Protocol, an agreement to reduce the emission of greenhouse gases that contribute to climate change.

Europe also aims to reduce its dependence on foreign oil. The EU is trying to reduce energy consumption, switch to cleaner forms of transportation, and use renewable energy such as wind and bio-fuels.

Reading Check What economic challenges did Eastern Europe face after the collapse of communism?

Section 5 Assessment

Essential Question

What makes a nation?

Key Terms

1. Using complete sentences, describe how each of the following terms relates to consequences from World War II: Cold War, Marshall Plan, Berlin Wall, European Union.

Key Ideas

2. What kind of partnership is the European Union?

3. Why did the Soviet Union set up communist states in Eastern Europe?

4. Which two countries began the movement to create a European Union and why?

5. How did change in the Soviet Union clear the way for democracy in Eastern Europe?

Think Critically

6. **Draw Conclusions** Why did Western Europe develop stronger economies than Eastern Europe?

7. **Make Decisions** What decisions do you think the German government could make to improve the economy of the former East Germany?

8. Why do you think East and West Germans still felt that they belonged to a single nation even after more than 40 years apart? Go to your Student Journal to record your answer.

Democracy in Eastern Europe

IN Indiana **6.1.21** Differentiate between fact and interpretation in historical accounts and explain historical passages.

Democracy developed more slowly in Eastern Europe than in Western Europe. Large empires such as Russia and Austria controlled much of the region for centuries. The rulers of these empires did not allow the region's different peoples to form their own independent countries. In Hungary, the nationalist Lajos Kossuth (LAH yohsh KAW shoot) fought unsuccessfully to free his country from Austrian control during the revolutions of 1848. Vaclav Havel became president after Czechoslovakia threw off communist rule in 1989.

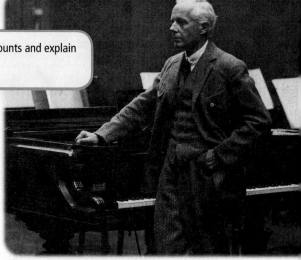

▲ Hungarian composer Béla Bartók fled the Nazi regime in 1940 to live in the United States.

Hungarian revolutionary Lajos Kossuth ▼

Stop at each letter on the right to think about the text. Then answer the question with the same letter on the left.

A **Draw Conclusions** What was the Hungarian cause that Kossuth mentioned here?

B **Compare Viewpoints** How did some other people view Hungary's cause? Explain how that compared to Kossuth's view.

C **Identify Main Ideas and Details** What did Kossuth compare a salad to? Explain how the detail "leaf by leaf" relates to this idea.

consideration, *n.,* careful thought

despotism, *n.,* government by a ruler with absolute power

The Cause Of One Country

❝ I first heard my humble claims contradicted, by telling me that the

A cause of Hungary was not worthy of much <u>consideration</u>—because,

B after all, it is only the cause of one country. . . . Let me tell those who don't care about the violation of the law of nations in Hungary . . . let me tell them that the freedom and independence of the world is

C like the salad—not even the jaws of <u>despotism</u> can swallow at once— but only leaf by leaf. ❞

—Lajos Kossuth, "Speech at the Pittsburgh Banquet," 1852

Stop at each letter on the right to think about the text. Then answer the question with the same letter on the left.

D Categorize What were some of the sacrifices people made to gain freedom?

E Analyze Cause and Effect Why did the government persecute some people?

F Solve Problems What do you think Czechs and Slovaks today can do to make sure past sacrifices are not forgotten?

perish, *v.,* to die, especially a violent or early death

totalitarian, *adj.,* describing a government in which a dictator or one political party has complete control of the country

persecute, *v.,* to harass or subject to unfair treatment because of race, religion, ethnic origin, or political beliefs

The Price Of Freedom

❝ We had to pay, however, for our present freedom. Many citizens **D** perished in jails in the 1950s, many were executed, thousands of human lives were destroyed, hundreds of thousands of talented people were forced to leave the country. Those who defended the honor of our nations during the Second **E** World War, those who rebelled against totalitarian rule and those who simply managed to remain themselves and think freely, were **F** all persecuted. We should not forget any of those who paid for our present freedom in one way or another. ❞

—Vaclav Havel,
"New Year's Address to the Nation,"
January 1, 1990

Above, Czechoslovak president Vaclav Havel; below, demonstrators carry Czechoslovak flags in Prague during the Velvet Revolution in 1989.

Analyze the Documents

1. **Synthesize** According to Kossuth and Havel, what forces made it difficult to establish democracy in Eastern Europe?

2. **Writing Task** Write an opening paragraph on the topic *Eastern Europe's Fight for Democracy.* Include details from the two speeches in your paragraph. If you use a direct quote, be sure to format it correctly.

461

Chapter Assessment

Key Terms and Ideas

1. **Discuss** How did **humanism** help lead to the Reformation?

2. **Summarize** In what ways did art change during the **Renaissance**?

3. **Compare and Contrast** What different routes did Portugal and Spain take when trying to find a way to reach Asia during the Age of Exploration?

4. **Recall** What Renaissance attitudes helped bring about the Scientific Revolution?

5. **Explain** How did the **Industrial Revolution** change where people lived?

6. **Compare and Contrast** What did the English Civil War and the **French Revolution** have in common?

7. **Explain** How did **World War I** change the map of central and eastern Europe?

8. **Describe** What emotions did East Germans and West Germans experience when the **Berlin Wall** was opened? How do you know?

Think Critically

9. **Draw Conclusions** How did geography contribute to Italy's role in beginning the Renaissance?

10. **Distinguish Between Fact and Opinion** Thomas Hobbes described life without strong government as "poor, nasty, brutish, and short." Is that a fact or an opinion? Explain.

11. **Identify Evidence** Use evidence from the text to describe how World War I was a global war.

12. **Drawing Inferences** How was the Cold War like a war even though the United States and the Soviet Union never engaged in battle?

13. **Problem Solving** Turn again to the last red heading in Section 5. Which of the problems described in the blue headings should be Europe's first priority? Support your answer with examples from the text.

Places to Know

For each place, write the letter from the map that shows its location.

14. Berlin

15. London

16. Rome

17. Romania

18. Belgium

19. Constantinople

20. Portugal

21. **Estimate** Using the scale bar, estimate how far fighter pilots flew between Berlin and London during World War II.

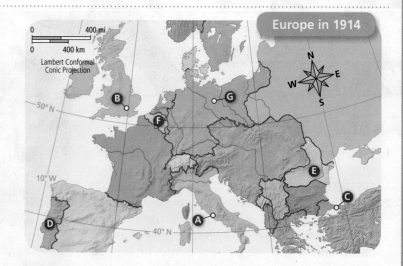

Europe in 1914

Essential Question

myWorld Chapter Activity

Technology Then and Now Follow your teacher's instructions to examine different kinds of technology that developed in early modern Europe. This technology may be related to advances in science or medicine, warfare, industry, or transportation. At the time, these inventions were cutting-edge technology. Make an illustrated poster linking these examples of past technology to current examples of technology.

21st Century Learning

Communication

Summarize Write an essay arguing for or against adding new Eastern European members to the European Union. Include
- the benefits of adding these members
- the drawbacks of adding these members
- the economic and political impact of adding these members
- your opinion
- two reasons in support of your opinion

Document-Based Questions

Success Tracker™
Online at myworldgeography.com

Use your knowledge of early modern Europe and Documents A and B to answer Questions 1–3.

Document A

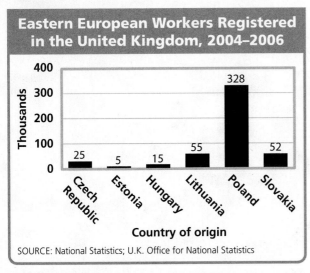

Eastern European Workers Registered in the United Kingdom, 2004–2006

Thousands — Country of origin: Czech Republic 25, Estonia 5, Hungary 15, Lithuania 55, Poland 328, Slovakia 52

SOURCE: National Statistics; U.K. Office for National Statistics

1. Which country shown here had the most workers registered in the United Kingdom?

A Estonia

B Latvia

C Poland

D Slovakia

Document B

" It's my dream to return to Poland, but not for 30 percent of my salary. So many have gone west [that] to return, they might not have to receive equal pay, but certainly more than now."

—Jacek Cukrowski,
"Where have all our migrants gone? Eastern Europe wants them back,"
Christian Science Monitor

2. What would convince Cukrowski to return to Poland?

A more salary than he earns in the West

B a better salary than Polish workers earn now

C exactly the same salary that Polish workers earn

D 30 percent of the salary that he earns in the West

3. Writing Task If Eastern Europeans keep moving to Western Europe for jobs, how might Eastern Europe's economy be affected? Explain.

my worldgeography.com Self-Test

463

Chapter 10

Western Europe

Is it better to be independent or interdependent?

KEY

— National border
✪ Capital city
○ Other city

| 0 | 400 mi |
| 0 | 400 km |

Lambert Conformal Conic Projection

**Where in the World
Is Western Europe?**

Washington, D.C., to Lund: 4,060 miles

464

my Story

Europe at Her Doorstep

Explore the Essential Question
- at my worldgeography.com
- using the myWorld Chapter Activity
- with the Student Journal

In this section, you'll read about Yasmin, a young woman living in Sweden who has family in Spain and Pakistan. What does Yasmin's story tell you about life in Western Europe today?

By Jake Johnson for myWorld Online

Yasmin straps on her dancing shoes. She glances in the mirror, adjusts her dress, and taps her way into the dance studio. With a rose in her hair and a colorful shawl stretched between her hands, Yasmin practices flamenco, a traditional Spanish dance. Inside the studio, the music makes Yasmin think of the warm Mediterranean while Sweden's winter winds blow outside.

Yasmin was born in Madrid, Spain, but she lives with her family in the coastal town of Bjärred in southern Sweden. Her father, Asif, is Pakistani and Spanish. Her mother, Monica, is Finnish and Swedish. Yasmin uses both of her parents' last names as a part of her heritage.

Yasmin's father Asif left Spain to work in Sweden in 1995. At that time, Sweden had just become a member of the European Union (EU). EU member countries allow people to move across borders without passports or complicated documents. Asif decided to try life in Sweden where more jobs were available. So, at age six Yasmin, along with her sister Sabina and brother Daniel, moved to frosty Sweden—a completely different world from Spain.

Yasmin remembers that she wasn't ready for the change in cultures. "At first, I was very different from the Swedish girls.

Yasmin with her father and mother

Yasmin stands in front of Lund's medieval cathedral.

In general, Swedes are much more quiet than Spaniards. I spoke very loud . . . I was a Spanish girl, and I yelled and ran around everywhere. I was more like the Swedish boys."

At home, Yasmin speaks Spanish with her father and Swedish with her mother. Everyone also speaks English. "The language that we speak is similar to the foods we eat. It is very mixed up," laughs Yasmin. She adds, "Sometimes we mix up our languages, even though our parents say we shouldn't. It's just easier to find the word you are looking for in another language. We even mix up languages within one sentence—but we all understand each other."

Even the family meal is a cultural medley. "We make it up as we go," explains Asif as he dices potatoes. He is making a Pakistani dish called alu gosht, a sort of a beef stew. Yasmin explains that this alu gosht includes Spanish olive oil, Swedish potatoes, and Chinese rice. The olive oil comes from the family's own olive trees in Spain!

Yasmin enjoys cooking and shopping at the farmers' market.

Yasmin attends classes in linguistics at Lund University.

The strait of Öresund separates Sweden from Denmark.

One of Yasmin's favorite possessions is her video camera. She has made several videos, including many that documented her trip to meet family in Pakistan. Music is also important to Yasmin, and she can play the piano, the flute, and the guitar.

Most days, Yasmin rides the bus to Lund to attend university classes. Lund is a medieval city full of gothic architecture and winding streets. Higher education is free in Sweden, so students from all over the world come to Lund University. Yasmin has many interests such as film and architecture, but she hasn't decided on a major.

One of Yasmin's new hobbies is tae kwon do, a form of martial arts that developed in Korea. At a dojo (a martial arts training school) near the university, she puts on a white uniform and her blue belt. Barefoot, Yasmin and a partner practice a complex routine designed for self-defense.

"Tae kwon do has a philosophy of peace," Yasmin says, "that teaches me to have the right mindset in order to be able to do the sport correctly."

Back in Bjärred, Yasmin walks along the beach. It's cold and windy, but beautiful. Bjärred is famous for its 500-meter pier into the strait of Öresund. It is the longest pier in the country. At the end of the pier is the Bjärred Kallbadhus (bath house). In the winter, people dive from the sauna there into the icy waters of the Öresund. Walking over the snow-covered dunes, Yasmin thinks about how much she cherishes the blazing sun of Spain. At the same time, she looks forward to ice-skating near her home in Sweden. Whether she's ice-skating, studying, or making a video, Yasmin has many choices, since Europe is at her doorstep.

Meet the Journalist

Name Jake Johnson
Favorite Moment Dinner with Yasmin's family

→ **myStory Video**

Join Yasmin as she shows you about life in her city.

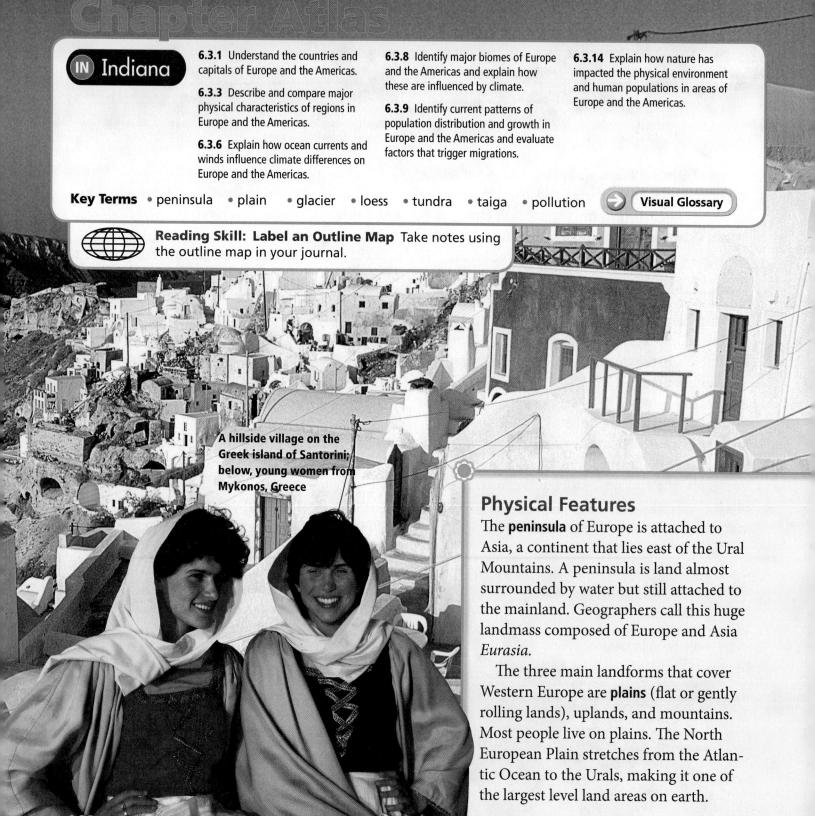

IN Indiana

6.3.1 Understand the countries and capitals of Europe and the Americas.

6.3.3 Describe and compare major physical characteristics of regions in Europe and the Americas.

6.3.6 Explain how ocean currents and winds influence climate differences on Europe and the Americas.

6.3.8 Identify major biomes of Europe and the Americas and explain how these are influenced by climate.

6.3.9 Identify current patterns of population distribution and growth in Europe and the Americas and evaluate factors that trigger migrations.

6.3.14 Explain how nature has impacted the physical environment and human populations in areas of Europe and the Americas.

Key Terms • peninsula • plain • glacier • loess • tundra • taiga • pollution ➔ **Visual Glossary**

Reading Skill: Label an Outline Map Take notes using the outline map in your journal.

A hillside village on the Greek island of Santorini; below, young women from Mykonos, Greece

Physical Features

The **peninsula** of Europe is attached to Asia, a continent that lies east of the Ural Mountains. A peninsula is land almost surrounded by water but still attached to the mainland. Geographers call this huge landmass composed of Europe and Asia *Eurasia.*

The three main landforms that cover Western Europe are **plains** (flat or gently rolling lands), uplands, and mountains. Most people live on plains. The North European Plain stretches from the Atlantic Ocean to the Urals, making it one of the largest level land areas on earth.

Western Europe: Physical

ARCTIC OCEAN

ARCTIC CIRCLE

Iceland

Norwegian Sea

Scandinavian
Peninsula

ATLANTIC
OCEAN

60° N

North
Sea

Baltic Sea

Great
Britain

Ireland

North European Plain

50° N

Central Uplands

A l p s

Pyrenees

Adriatic Sea

Italian Peninsula

Balkan Peninsula

40° N

Iberian
Peninsula

Sardinia

Mediterranean Sea   Sicily

*Aegean
Sea*

10° W   0°   10° E   20° E   30° E

KEY
Elevation

Feet	Meters
6,000	1,829
3,000	914
1,000	305
500	152
Sea level	Sea level

— National border

0 ———————— 400 mi
0 ———————— 400 km
Lambert Conformal Conic Projection

Map Skills

1 **Region** Which part of Western Europe has the highest elevation?

2 **Interaction** Why might fishing be such a large industry in Scandinavia?

3 **Places to Know!**
Label the following places on the outline map in your Student Journal: Iberian Peninsula, Ireland, Alps, Mediterranean Sea, North Sea.

Active Atlas

Most of northern Europe lies on the Scandinavian Peninsula, between the Arctic Ocean, the North Sea, and the Baltic Sea. The west coast of Norway features dramatic fiords, or long, narrow, deep inlets of the sea. In Scotland, similar inlets, as well as lakes, are called lochs.

The Central Uplands in the center of southern Europe consist of mountains and plateaus, or raised areas of level land bordered by steep slopes.

The Alps stretch from France to Eastern Europe. Streams formed by **glaciers,** slow-moving masses of ice and snow, flow out of the Alps. These streams feed the Rhine River and the Danube River.

To the south is the warmer Mediterranean region. This region is named for the Mediterranean Sea nearby. Days are sunny and the climate is generally temperate. Here the land is mountainous peninsulas with narrow, <u>fertile</u> plains.

Active volcanoes may be found in Italy, Greece, and Iceland. At times, volcanic activity has led to earthquakes and tsunamis (tidal waves). Since ancient times, earthquakes have been widespread in the Mediterranean countries.

fertile, *adj.,* rich in nutrients; able to grow many plants

Reading Check What landform divides Europe from Asia?

Climate and Ecosystems

Most Western Europeans enjoy a mild climate because the Atlantic Ocean carries warm ocean water from the tropics to Europe's western coast. This water warms the air, bringing mild winters to places as far north as Scandinavia.

Most of Western Europe is located in the temperate zone, although its northern edges reach to the Arctic region. Land close to the Mediterranean Sea has wet winters and dry summers.

In ancient times, forests covered most of Western Europe. Today, people have replanted some forests, but most of the land has been cleared for cities, farms, and industry. One of north central Europe's natural resources is **loess,** a rich soil made of fine sediment deposited by glaciers and spread by centuries of wind.

Northern Scandinavia has few forests because of its Arctic climate. The Arctic **tundra** is a plant community made up of grasses, mosses, herbs, and low shrubs.

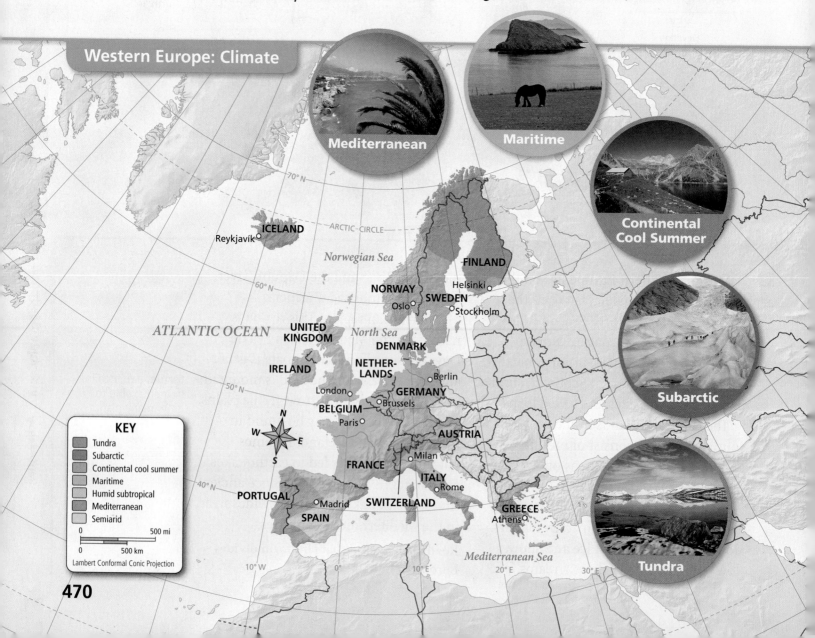

Western Europe: Climate

Mediterranean

Maritime

Continental Cool Summer

Subarctic

Tundra

ICELAND
Reykjavík

ARCTIC CIRCLE

Norwegian Sea

FINLAND
Helsinki

NORWAY
Oslo

SWEDEN
Stockholm

ATLANTIC OCEAN

North Sea

UNITED KINGDOM

DENMARK

IRELAND

NETHER-LANDS

Berlin

London

GERMANY

BELGIUM
Brussels

Paris

AUSTRIA

FRANCE

Milan

ITALY
Rome

PORTUGAL
Madrid

SWITZERLAND

GREECE
Athens

SPAIN

Mediterranean Sea

KEY

- Tundra
- Subarctic
- Continental cool summer
- Maritime
- Humid subtropical
- Mediterranean
- Semiarid

0   500 mi
0   500 km
Lambert Conformal Conic Projection

N
W   E
S

70° N
60° N
50° N
40° N

10° W
0°
10° E
20° E
30° E

Trees are unable to grow here because it is too cold and dry. The **taiga,** a thick forest of coniferous trees, lies south of this zone. It extends from Scandinavia east across Eurasia for thousands of miles.

Mediterranean vegetation is a mix of small trees, forests, shrubs, and grasses. Trees and shrubs here must be hardy enough to survive the dry summer season.

Reading Check Contrast taiga vegetation with that of the Mediterranean region.

A Diverse Continent

In general, the nations of Western Europe have a high standard of living. Almost all Western Europeans can read and write. This region has strong education systems. There is a direct connection between good education and a high standard of living.

Across Western Europe, people speak a variety of different languages. About half of the people in Europe speak English and their native languages or dialects.

dialect, *n.,* a regional variety of a language

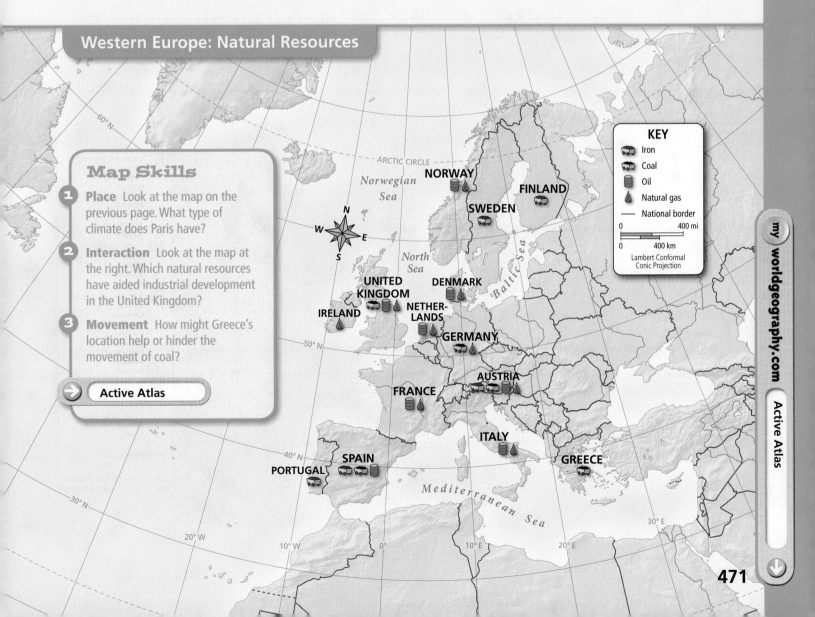

Western Europe: Natural Resources

Map Skills

1 Place Look at the map on the previous page. What type of climate does Paris have?

2 Interaction Look at the map at the right. Which natural resources have aided industrial development in the United Kingdom?

3 Movement How might Greece's location help or hinder the movement of coal?

Active Atlas

KEY
- Iron
- Coal
- Oil
- Natural gas
- National border

0   400 mi
0   400 km
Lambert Conformal
Conic Projection

NORWAY

Norwegian Sea

SWEDEN

FINLAND

ARCTIC CIRCLE

North Sea

Baltic Sea

UNITED KINGDOM

DENMARK

IRELAND

NETHER-LANDS

GERMANY

AUSTRIA

FRANCE

ITALY

SPAIN

GREECE

PORTUGAL

Mediterranean Sea

60° N

50° N

40° N

30° N

20° W

10° W

0°

10° E

20° E

30° E

my worldgeography.com Active Atlas

Language is part of culture. Sometimes, language unites those from different cultures. For example, when North Africans move to France, they encounter a different culture. But many North Africans speak French. This makes the transition to a new life a little easier.

When European Union (EU) leaders meet to discuss economics or energy policy, they often conduct business in English. This helps make discussion and decision-making easier. The European Union has 27 member nations and 23 official languages, but it is easier if everyone speaks the same language.

Europe is a region of many different cultures. For 2,000 years, Christianity has been the dominant religion. A large Jewish population has also lived there continuously. Since World War II, people from around the world have moved to Europe for jobs and education. They brought different religions, languages, and customs. When people move to a new country, they often take on parts of its cultures. At the same time, newcomers have introduced Western Europeans to new ideas and customs.

Reading Check How many official languages are there in the European Union?

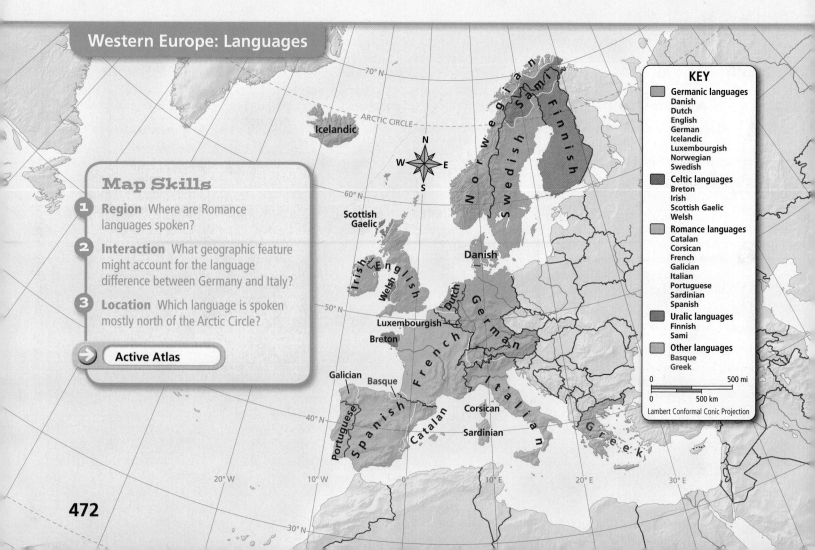

Western Europe: Languages

Map Skills

1 Region Where are Romance languages spoken?

2 Interaction What geographic feature might account for the language difference between Germany and Italy?

3 Location Which language is spoken mostly north of the Arctic Circle?

Active Atlas

KEY

Germanic languages
Danish
Dutch
English
German
Icelandic
Luxembourgish
Norwegian
Swedish

Celtic languages
Breton
Irish
Scottish Gaelic
Welsh

Romance languages
Catalan
Corsican
French
Galician
Italian
Portuguese
Sardinian
Spanish

Uralic languages
Finnish
Sami

Other languages
Basque
Greek

0   500 mi
0   500 km
Lambert Conformal Conic Projection

Where People Live and Work

Western Europe's geography shapes where and how people live. This region is largely urban and industrialized.

In Western Europe, most of the population lives within 100 miles of the coast. This is because being close to water offers many opportunities for trade. Europe's major rivers, the Danube and the Rhine, carry goods and people. They also carry large quantities of water. Western European highways often follow river routes to connect towns and cities that have grown along these rivers.

In northern Europe, people live near the coast. Even in Arctic climates, being near the ocean offers milder weather. Inland, <u>vast</u> empty areas separate towns and villages. Settlement is sparse because these areas are cold and dry.

In Southern and Central Europe, population is more evenly spaced. In the temperate climate of Italy, population is densest near the coast. People also live in large numbers inland as well.

In general, people do not choose to live in high mountains and marshy wetlands. Instead, they tend to settle in low, sunny, warm places close to water. Natural resources such as water, minerals, and rich farmland also attract people.

A recent report by the European Union addressed climate change trends. This report noted changes such as the melting of glaciers in the Arctic Ocean and drier conditions in the Mediterranean area of Southern Europe. Changes in climate may affect crop yields, water levels in rivers, and human health.

As a highly industrialized region, Western Europe has experienced air and water **pollution.** Pollution is harmful material released into the environment. One result of air pollution is acid rain. This occurs when exhaust from industries mixes with moisture in the air. This precipitation then falls as acid rain. It has damaged historic buildings, bridges, cathedrals, and monuments across Western Europe. Over the years, acid rain has also damaged forests and freshwater lakes.

Water pollution may result from chemical spills. A chemical spill is an accidental release of toxic or dangerous materials.

vast, *adj.,* very great in size, number, or quantity

myWorld Activity
Danube Cleanup

ENVIRONMENTAL CHALLENGES IN WALES

Over a period of 30 years, this forest has been destroyed by acid rain, due to the air pollution from nearby industrial plants.

Workers spread chemicals to clean up an oil spill on a Welsh beach. *What might be likely causes for the pollution shown in each photograph?*

my worldgeography.com   Active Atlas

473

One of Western Europe's busiest waterways, the Rhine River, was once one of the region's most polluted. From the 1950s to the 1970s, industrial waste flowed into the river. Fish disappeared from it and swimmers avoided it. A cleanup effort was launched, but in 1986, a chemical spill reversed years of effort. A chemical factory fire in Switzerland led to 30 tons of toxic chemicals being washed into the river as firefighters fought the blaze. Within 10 days, the pollution traveled the length of the Rhine to the North Sea. Today, the Rhine is much cleaner and fish are returning to swim in it again.

Reading Check How have Europe's coasts and waterways affected settlement?

The Urban Continent

Europe has been called the "urban continent" because so many people live in urban areas. An urban area may include a city and its surrounding suburbs. In the United Kingdom, for example, almost nine out of ten people live in cities.

Most countries in Western Europe have dense populations clustered in small land areas. To preserve land for growing food, for forests, and for recreation, most countries set strict limits on the expansion of cities and suburbs. This means that the region's cities tend to be tightly packed with people. Very few Europeans live in single-family houses with yards. Instead, most live in apartment buildings.

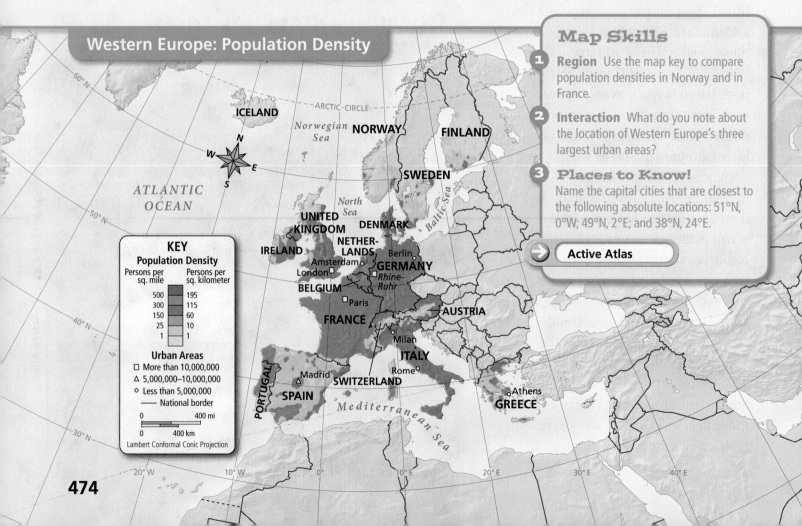

Western Europe: Population Density

Map Skills

1 **Region** Use the map key to compare population densities in Norway and in France.

2 **Interaction** What do you note about the location of Western Europe's three largest urban areas?

3 **Places to Know!** Name the capital cities that are closest to the following absolute locations: 51°N, 0°W; 49°N, 2°E; and 38°N, 24°E.

Active Atlas

KEY
Population Density

Persons per sq. mile	Persons per sq. kilometer
500	195
300	115
150	60
25	10
1	1

Urban Areas
□ More than 10,000,000
△ 5,000,000–10,000,000
○ Less than 5,000,000
— National border

0   400 mi
0   400 km
Lambert Conformal Conic Projection

In order to reach their jobs, schools, and other activities, most Europeans use public transportation. Over time, urban areas have built up dense public transportation networks. Train, subway, trolley, and bus services connect neighborhoods and cities all over Europe.

Germany's Rhine-Ruhr region is one of Europe's largest urban areas. Five cities there have more than 500,000 inhabitants. Contrast that with Greenland, a territory of Denmark and the world's largest island. Greenland is six times as large as all of Germany, but has a population of only about 58,000 people.

European governments favor public transportation over driving by setting high taxes on gasoline. Gasoline in Europe can cost twice as much as gasoline in the United States. While most families in Western Europe have a car, they may use it only for occasional trips to the countryside or to a regional shopping center.

Reading Check Why are Europe's cities so crowded?

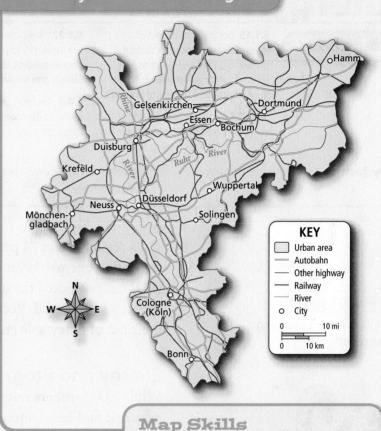

Germany's Rhine-Ruhr Region

KEY
- Urban area
- Autobahn
- Other highway
- Railway
- River
- ○ City

0   10 mi
0   10 km

Map Skills

The Rhine-Ruhr region is a transportation and industrial hub for the entire continent. What are the different forms of transportation available?

→ **Active Atlas**

Section 1 Assessment

Key Terms

1. Use each of the following terms in a sentence: peninsula, loess, tundra, pollution.

Key Ideas

2. What is Eurasia?

3. How does geography affect settlement patterns?

4. Why do some countries restrict urban growth?

Think Critically

5. **Compare and Contrast** Look at the physical map and the climate map in this section. Why is there more farming in France than in Scandinavia?

6. **Draw Conclusions** How does keeping a river like the Rhine clean benefit Western Europe?

Essential Question

Is it better to be independent or interdependent?

7. Look at the languages map in this section. Do you think the number of languages spoken by EU members helps or harms Western Europe? Go to your Student Journal to record your answer.

475

Energy for the Future

IN Indiana

6.1.15 Describe the impact of industrialization and urbanization on people's lives and on trade and cultural exchange between Europe and the Americas and the rest of the world.

6.1.17 Discuss the benefits and challenges related to the development of a highly technological society.

6.1.22 Form research questions and use resources to present data on people, cultures and developments in Europe and the Americas.

6.4.6 Analyze current economic issues in the countries of Europe or the Americas using a variety of resources.

6.4.7 Identify economic connections between the community and the countries of Europe or the Americas and identify job skills needed to be successful in the workplace.

6.4.8 Identify how societies deal with externalities in Europe or the Americas.

Key Terms
- renewable energy
- biofuel
- nonrenewable energy
- wind turbine
- fossil fuel
- hydropower

In Italy, a man cooks using a solar reflector. ▼

In a region where 74 percent live in areas of high energy use such as cities, energy consumption is a hot topic. The European Union (EU) has promoted the use of **renewable energy,** or energy sources that can be replaced. Recently, EU member nations decided to boost their use of renewable energy sources by 20 percent by the year 2020.

Energy and Progress

While EU members might agree that it is important to conserve energy and find new sources of energy, changing energy policy raises concerns. Not every EU member can afford to invest in alternative energy sources.

In some cases, a nation's history affects its energy policy. Poland, for example, has long depended on heavy industry that burns coal as fuel. Changing to technologies that use renewable energy would be expensive for Poland and would take many years to develop. Other EU members such as Sweden and Denmark have long used "green energy" (clean, efficient, renewable energy) and can more easily meet the EU energy goal.

Concerns about energy consumption generally come as a society reaches a certain level of progress. During the Industrial Revolution, for example, Manchester, England, a center for textile manufacturing, grew quickly as thousands moved there for jobs at coal-powered factories. Over the years, coal pollution left a coating of black smoke everywhere. People died from lung diseases after breathing coal smoke all their lives. Eventually, people realized using pollution-causing fuels affected human health and the environment.

Reading Check Why might some nations have trouble meeting the European Union's energy goal?

Power to the People

Everyday energy comes in many forms: gasoline for cars, natural gas for heating and cooking, or coal for the generation of electric power. Each of these forms of energy is made from fossil fuels and is **nonrenewable energy,** or energy that cannot be replaced. **Fossil fuels** come from carbon-based organic material that took millions of years to form. Nuclear energy, which comes from the metal uranium, is also considered nonrenewable.

Scientists have been able to find new ways to collect energy: wood, crops such as corn, and even weeds for **biofuels** (fuel from organic material), wind and water for electricity, or energy from the sun that solar cells can convert into electricity. These are all forms of renewable energy.

The EU Common Energy Policy seeks ways to bring more energy to its growing population without damaging the environment. Supporters of the policy also want the EU to become less dependent on energy from other parts of the world, such as Russia or Southwest Asia.

Reading Check Why are fossil fuels considered nonrenewable?

EU Energy Imports

Coal
Oil
Gas
Nuclear

0 25 50 75 100
Percentage of Fuel Imported
SOURCE: European Commission

Harnessing Energy

Whether renewable or nonrenewable, energy must be harnessed and processed before it reaches customers. Utility companies use different technologies to turn energy sources into forms of energy for homes, offices, and businesses.

This race-car driver uses biofuel made from crops grown on her family's farm in England. ▶

Coal
Oil and gas
Wind
Nuclear
Hydro-power

Utility company
Power grid
Customer

Chart Skills

How can utility companies help customers use more renewable energy?

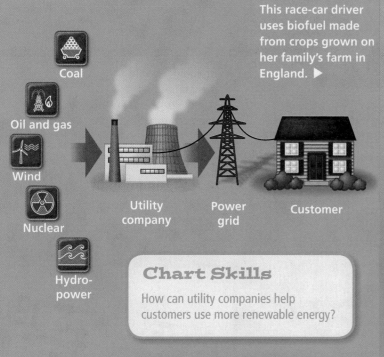

477

Energy Choices

As EU members discuss how to reach their 2020 energy goal, they will learn more about the types of renewable energy sources available. They will also weigh the advantages and disadvantages of these alternative forms of energy. *Choose one form of energy below and make a case for its use.*

 Sun Solar energy is collected by special panels and used for heating and electricity.

 Wind **Wind turbines,** or giant windmills, use large blades to collect the wind's energy. A generator on the turbine turns the mechanical energy into electricity. A cable transfers the electricity to a transmission line.

Ocean Heat from the sun on the ocean can be harnessed for thermal energy, while tides and waves may provide mechanical energy.

 Water **Hydropower,** or energy harnessed from flowing water, is converted into electricity.

 Biofuel Biofuel is energy gathered by processing organic matter from food crops such as corn, sugar cane, or beets, or industrial waste from wood or paper mills.

Hydrogen Hydrogen is present in many compounds (water and biofuels) and can be used to store energy or to transfer it from place to place.

Earth Earth's internal heat, geothermal energy, can be tapped for heating and cooling buildings.

▲ Wind farms are a growing source of energy in Europe.

Food or Fuel?

People As populations grow, so does the need for food and fuel.

Farms Farmers receive subsidies to grow biofuel crops, but that means fewer crops for food.

Prices Biofuels might cost less to consumers, but production can lead to higher food prices and hunger in poorer countries.

Weather Poor harvests of biofuel crops can lead to increased use of fossil fuels, higher food prices, and food shortages.

 In Spain, people dressed in corn costumes protest using food crops to produce fuel. ▶

FUEL $1.25 PER GALLON

▲ Advocates believe that access to more biofuels will reduce fuel prices.

FAMINE ZERO

ANTES COMESTIBLES QUE COMBUSTIBLES

Learning an Energy Lesson

In 2009, a dispute between Ukraine and Russia led to a three-week interruption of natural gas supplies to Europe. During one of the coldest winters in years, Europeans had to find other ways to stay warm. Schools closed and people used wood fires to heat their homes. Some people froze to death due to lack of heat.

The Russia-Ukraine pipeline supplies 80 percent of the EU's natural gas. Following the 2009 shortage, Europeans realized that they had become too dependent on a single energy source. This event also drew attention to the need to expand renewable energy sources.

Reading Check What event highlighted Europe's energy dependence?

Sharing the Burden

Members of groups like the EU share the benefits as well as the challenges of energy policy. Wealthier nations such as Germany, Denmark, France, and Spain use more renewable energy because they have invested in renewable technologies for many years. France, for example, leads the EU in biofuel production because it has many farms. Spain, with its windy hillsides and plains, is second in wind-energy production.

Some EU members have smaller economies and cannot contribute to the EU energy policy as much as wealthier nations. People in wealthier nations might see the expectation that they spend more on renewable energy as unfair. Some of the newer (and poorer) EU member nations have only recently been able to shift their attention from economic development to energy consumption.

Energy policy must also balance food and energy needs. If European farmers commit too much of their land to crops that will be used for biofuels, there will be less food for people to eat. These crops (corn, soybeans, wheat, and beets) could become scarce and prices could rise.

There is also a concern that land needed for housing or farms might instead be dedicated to energy production. In addition, there could be environmental damage as fossil fuel production expands to forested areas or to ocean drilling sites.

European individuals, companies, and governments are working to resolve these issues. Poorer nations want more economic growth. Europeans must balance that desire with the goals of energy independence and lower pollution.

Reading Check What could happen if more European farmers grew corn for biofuel instead of food?

Assessment

1. Name and define four kinds of renewable energy.

2. In what ways might energy investment differ among EU member nations?

3. How does Spain's geography allow it to be a leader in wind-energy production?

4. What is the primary goal of the EU Common Energy Policy?

5. Write a short paragraph outlining the advantages and disadvantages of growing crops such as corn for biofuel rather than food.

Northwestern Europe Today

IN Indiana

6.2.7 Define and compare citizenship and the citizen's role throughout history in Europe and the Americas.

6.3.9 Identify current patterns of population distribution and growth in Europe and the Americas and evaluate factors that trigger migrations.

6.3.10 Explain the ways cultural diffusion, invention, and innovation change culture.

6.3.12 Compare the distribution and evaluate the importance of natural resources in Europe and the Americas.

6.4.5 Compare the standard of living of various countries of Europe and the Americas today using GDP as an indicator.

Key Terms • constitutional monarchy • Parliament • cradle-to-grave system • gross domestic product (GDP) • cultural borrowing

→ **Visual Glossary**

Reading Skill: Sequence Take notes using the graphic organizer in your journal.

Beefeaters are ceremonial guards at the Tower of London. ▼

You might be surprised to learn that England has a queen, yet it also has a long history of democracy. During the summers in northern Scandinavia, there is sunshine at midnight. How can this be? The nations of Northwestern Europe are worth a closer look.

The United Kingdom and Ireland

The United Kingdom, or Britain, is an island nation made up of several regions. England, Wales, and Scotland are located on the largest island, Great Britain. Northern Ireland, on the nearby smaller island of Ireland, is also part of the United Kingdom. Most of this island is the independent nation of Ireland.

British Government You have read about King John signing the Magna Carta in 1215. This document limited the power of the king and gave rights to his people. It was the beginning of democratic government in England. Today, the British government is a **constitutional monarchy.** This means the monarch is the ceremonial leader, but Parliament makes the laws. Unlike the U.S. Constitution, the British constitution is not a single document, but a group of laws and court decisions. The symbolic head is Queen Elizabeth II, who symbolizes Britain's nationhood.

The British legislature, or **Parliament,** is located in London, England. It is made up of the House of Lords and the House of Commons. At one time, members of the House of Lords inherited their seats. Today, Parliament is moving toward a combination of elected and appointed members in both houses. These members are composed of high-ranking clergy, judges, and national leaders. The head of the majority party in the House of Commons is the prime minister, the true head of the British government.

Since the 1990s, some lawmaking power has moved from a national to a regional level. Scotland has its own Parliament and government that handles laws specific to that country. The Welsh National Assembly can pass laws that directly affect Wales. Northern Ireland also has a separate assembly with its own powers.

The official language of the United Kingdom is English. Some people also speak Welsh, Irish, or Scottish Gaelic. Thousands of immigrants come to Britain every year. Many come from countries that were once part of the British empire.

Prosperity and Partnerships Britain and Ireland both have a high standard of living and strong economies. In the past, Britain owed its wealth to iron and steel, textiles, and shipbuilding. Today, Britain is part of a global economy. The British work with international partners in finance and banking, high-technology fields, and service industries. Entrepreneurs, or people who start businesses, have had much success in Northwestern Europe.

One Nation, Four Countries

Known as the United Kingdom of Great Britain and Northern Ireland, these four countries act together on matters such as foreign policy. However, they act independently with regard to EU involvement and legal issues.

Map Skills

How might giving more power to regional governments strengthen the United Kingdom?

Active Atlas

The United Kingdom and Ireland also benefit from being in the European Union. The European Union (EU) is an organization of European nations that promotes free movement of goods and people across borders. Ireland and Britain can trade with other member nations in an open market. There are no tariffs, or taxes, on goods imported from other member nations. Without tariffs, goods and services move freely. The EU has its own currency, the euro. Ireland uses the euro, but Britain does not. The British currency is the pound.

currency, *n.,* a system of money, especially the bills and coins, used in a country

481

A Tourist Destination Britain is the world's sixth most popular travel destination. Many people visit Britain because of their <u>heritage</u>. Americans, for example, often travel to the United Kingdom to revisit the homes of their English, Irish, Scottish, or Welsh ancestors.

heritage, *n.,* something possessed as a result of one's natural situation or birth

Tourists flock to famous places such as London's Buckingham Palace. They also visit ancient and historic sites such as Stonehenge and Shakespeare's hometown, Stratford-upon-Avon. Ireland draws visitors to its prosperous cities and green rural areas. Fishing is popular in Scotland's rivers. History lovers visit Welsh castles and villages.

Reading Check How has EU membership promoted economic development in Britain and Ireland?

The Scandinavian Countries

Denmark, Finland, Iceland, Norway, and Sweden make up the area known as Scandinavia. Life near the Arctic Circle is chilly, but full of variety.

Cradle-to-Grave Benefits Sweden, Norway, and Denmark are constitutional monarchies much like the United Kingdom. Each monarch is mainly a symbolic leader. Political decisions are made by an elected parliament. Finland is a democratic republic with a president. All are members of the EU except Norway. Norway has voted to remain outside the EU for several reasons. Some Norwegians feel that the EU's structure is not democratic. They also want to keep Norway's economic and political freedom.

The Cradle-to-Grave System

This system of social services originated after World War II in response to postwar hardships. Funding for the system comes from high taxes, such as payroll taxes and sales tax. These taxes fund benefits such as universal healthcare, education, and pensions.

Chart Skills

How does this diagram show advantages and disadvantages of the cradle-to-grave system?

Data Discovery

**myWorld Activity
Cradle to Grave?**

PAYCHECK

Monthly pay $5,000.00

Payroll taxes $2,600.00

TAKE HOME $2,400.00

Sales Tax

Social Services
Pensions
Healthcare
Unemployment
College tuition

The Scandinavian governments have a **cradle-to-grave system,** a system of basic services for citizens at every stage of life. It covers healthcare, education, and retirement. Benefits are funded through taxes. Because people believe this system is important, they are willing to pay high taxes for it. In Sweden, people pay on average almost 60 percent of their income in taxes. Clothing and food are also expensive due to taxes. On the other hand, healthcare costs and rents are low.

Fish, Forests, and Phones In the past, the Scandinavian countries depended on farming. Agriculture and dairy farming are still important in Denmark, where the climate is warmer. Today, the economies of these countries rely on multinational corporations, high-technology industries, and exports. Finland, for example, is a leading manufacturer of mobile telephones.

Scandinavia's geography also affects the economy. Miles of coastline and acres of forests supply the fishing and lumber industries. Oil production in the North Sea also helps this region maintain a high standard of living. Membership in the EU opens Denmark, Finland, and Sweden to free trade and global markets.

Located near the Arctic Circle, the northernmost Scandinavian cities have what are called white nights. From May to July, the sun appears on the horizon for almost 24 hours a day. This is because the northern hemisphere is tilted toward the sun at that time of year.

Reading Check Why do people in Sweden pay high taxes?

SCANDINAVIA: LAND OF THE VIKINGS

The gods, giants, and elves of ancient Scandinavian myths remain popular today. The adventures of the Norse warriors known as the Vikings left marks on territory from England to Russia. In modern times, Scandinavia has been known for its famous scientists and artists. These nations also have a long record of gender equality and human rights. *Why might people build replicas of ancient ships today?*

Danish carpenter Ole Kirk Christiansen invented one of the world's most popular children's toys. ▼

The dala horse was once a toy, but has become a symbol of Sweden. ▼

Modern-day replica of a Viking ship ▶

my **worldgeography**.com   Data Discovery

Life in Northwestern Europe

Aspects of daily life in northwestern Europe are changing rapidly.

Living With Technology With almost universal access to the Internet, cellphones, and television, faraway places are much nearer. Life has become more fast-paced. Technology has changed how people work in surprising ways. Danish farmers use modern technology to produce healthier food. Scientists in Norway have discovered new ways to preserve water supplies.

Finland uses more than 3 percent of its **gross domestic product** for technology research and development. Gross domestic product (GDP) is the total value of all goods and services produced and sold in a country in a year.

transportation, *n.,* a means of carrying people or goods from one place to another

In this region, finding ways to save energy is important. Due to its cold climate, Finland uses a great deal of energy for heating. One way to reduce energy use is driving cars with better gas mileage. Finland has passed a law raising taxes for cars with poor gas mileage. The owners of cars with higher gas mileage pay less in taxes.

Living in Cities Many of the large cities in this region are capital cities: London, Dublin, Copenhagen, Oslo, Stockholm, and Helsinki. These cities are centuries old and rich in history and culture.

London has museums and palaces, and Stockholm has historic city squares. In Dublin, people lunch at pubs, while in Helsinki they relax in saunas. Most people use public <u>transportation</u> rather than their cars for daily travels.

A United Kingdom woman paints figures for a company that exports tableware and gifts. ▼

Chart Skills

Compare Norway's GDP with the world average.

→ **Data Discovery**

GDP per Person, Northwestern Europe

GDP per Person (thousands)	

Iceland — ~$41
Ireland — ~$46
Norway — ~$53
United Kingdom — ~$35
World Average — ~$10

SOURCE: *CIA World Factbook, 2008*

Living Together Northwestern Europe is a region of many ethnic groups due to a large immigrant population. Some immigrants have lived there for generations. Others have come more recently.

The EU's open-border policy has also let people move between nations. In this chapter's myStory, you read about how the policy lets Yasmin move easily about Europe for family trips and education.

It is common to see people from the Caribbean, India, Pakistan, Turkey, or Somalia here. These newcomers face many challenges. To find jobs, they must learn how to get around. They may have to learn a language different from their parents' language.

Some immigrants have religious beliefs that <u>conflict</u> with local customs. For example, there is a significant Muslim population in Norway. Muslims have certain religious beliefs about food preparation. These beliefs can lead to higher prices in markets and restaurants—whether or not customers are Muslim.

▲ This London restaurant owner offers food from India, where he grew up.

conflict, *v.,* to clash or to be in opposition

Immigrants may also take part in **cultural borrowing,** an exchange that takes place when groups come into contact and share ideas, language, customs—and even food. Many Londoners enjoy eating at Indian or Ethiopian restaurants. In Copenhagen, people have grown to love Turkish coffee or food that mixes traditional Danish ingredients with those of France or Japan.

Reading Check What is one way that Finland tries to reduce energy use?

Section 2 Assessment

Key Terms

1. Use the following terms to describe Northwestern Europe today: constitutional monarchy, cradle-to-grave system, cultural borrowing.

Key Ideas

2. How has a long history of democracy affected Northwestern Europe?

3. Describe how technology has changed daily life for Northwestern Europe.

4. What sorts of challenges do immigrants face in a new country?

Think Critically

5. **Draw Conclusions** How does the EU open market benefit member nations?

6. **Categorize** Name three industries that developed because of Scandinavia's geography.

Essential Question

Is it better to be independent or interdependent?

7. What are the benefits of cultural borrowing? What might be some of the challenges? Go to your Student Journal to record your answer.

West Central Europe Today

 Indiana

6.2.6 Describe the functions of international political organizations in the world today.

6.3.4 Describe and compare major cultural characteristics of regions in Europe and the Western Hemisphere.

6.3.9 Identify current patterns of population distribution and growth in Europe and the Americas and evaluate factors that trigger migrations.

6.3.13 Explain the impact of humans on the physical environment in Europe and the Americas.

6.4.7 Identify economic connections between the community and the countries of Europe or the Americas and identify job skills needed to be successful in the workplace.

Key Terms • privatization • gross national product (GNP) • polders • reunification → **Visual Glossary**

Reading Skill: Identify Main Ideas and Details Take notes using the graphic organizer in your journal.

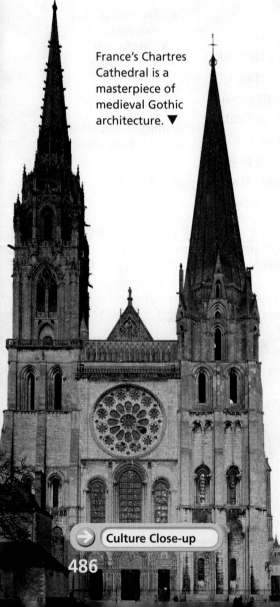

France's Chartres Cathedral is a masterpiece of medieval Gothic architecture. ▼

→ **Culture Close-up**

Rich in culture, the nations of West Central Europe include some of the largest and most prosperous on the continent. Most are members of the European Union, an organization that plays a major role in life in this region.

At the Center of the European Union

West Central Europe includes Austria, Belgium, France, Germany, Liechtenstein, Luxembourg, Monaco, the Netherlands, and Switzerland. All have joined the European Union (EU) except Switzerland, Liechtenstein, and Monaco. Why have some countries joined the EU while others have not?

EU membership is similar to playing on a school sports team. Each team member has different abilities or strengths, but the team works best when its members work together.

Just as not all students take part in sports, not every country in Europe is a member of the EU. Some countries do not meet certain guidelines. Some want to be members in certain ways, but not in others. Germany and France are the largest EU countries by population. They make up almost one third of the entire EU population. Some critics say that larger countries have more power in the EU government. If a country has more power, it can influence EU laws in its own favor. However, the EU has policies in place so that members work together.

Reading Check How might a larger nation influence laws in an alliance such as the European Union?

486

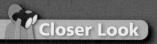

Closer Look

UNDERSTANDING THE EUROPEAN UNION

In the 1950s, European leaders wanted to ensure that world war would never happen again. In 1957, Belgium, Germany, France, Italy, Luxembourg, and the Netherlands formed the European Economic Community (EEC). Their main goal was economic unity through a single market.

The EEC later became the EU, which today consists of 27 member nations. The EU works to expand prosperity, to spread democracy, and to defend human rights and the rule of law. The EU single market system has removed trade barriers and raised standards of living. However, the EU has drawn criticism over powers given to unelected officials.

THINK CRITICALLY What are some advantages to having a single currency throughout several nations?

Council of Ministers
(represents national governments)

European Union

European Parliament
(represents the people)

European Commission
(represents collective EU interests)

◀ The euro is the EU currency.

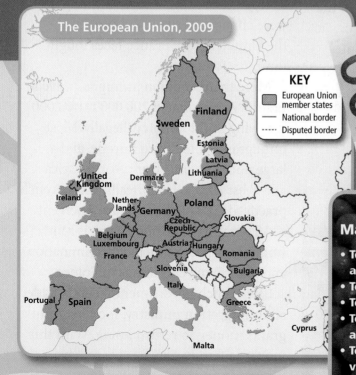

The European Union, 2009

KEY

- ▢ European Union member states
- ─── National border
- ----- Disputed border

Finland
Sweden
Estonia
Latvia
Lithuania
United Kingdom
Denmark
Ireland
Netherlands
Germany
Poland
Belgium
Luxembourg
Czech Republic
Slovakia
France
Austria
Hungary
Romania
Slovenia
Bulgaria
Italy
Portugal
Spain
Greece
Cyprus
Malta

Before France adopted the euro, signs showed prices in the national currency (French francs) as well as euro. ▶

Main Aims of the EU

- **To form a closer union among Europeans**
- **To remove trade barriers**
- **To improve the environment**
- **To fight terrorism, crime, and illegal immigration**
- **To give Europe a stronger voice in the world**

IN Indiana CONNECTIONS

72% of Indiana's population lives in urban areas; the same percentage of Europe's population lives in urban areas.

France: History and Diversity

Known for its rich heritage, France has taken a leading role in the EU. The changing face of France presents many challenges.

The French Economy France has fertile soil, a mild climate, and large areas of level land. Its farms, dairies, and vineyards produce wines, cheeses, and grains. The EU ensures that these products reach people around the world.

However, France's largest industry is tourism. Around 75 million tourists a year come to see historic sites and scenic landscapes. French cities attract shoppers and art lovers. Some tourists come just to eat French cuisine!

France is a republic with a strong centralized government. In the past, the government owned many industries such as airlines, banks, and telecommunications. Much of that has changed due to **privatization,** or private ownership of businesses.

Algerian-born Zinédine Zidane (center) played for the French national soccer team, a team known for its ethnic diversity. ▼

City of Light Paris, the capital of France, is known as the City of Light. It is the nation's cultural and economic center. Paris straddles the Seine River and is home to more than 2 million people. Its entire urban area covers around 890 square miles (2,300 square km) and is home to 12 million people.

Parisians live among Gothic churches, baroque palaces, elaborate gardens, and modern skyscrapers. Some Parisians work for the EU as their nation helps shape its policies.

The New Face of France In 2005, two North Africans youths were killed after a police chase in a Paris suburb. This event touched off riots all over France. In 2006, some French people held an anti-immigration protest, saying immigrants were changing French culture. Like the United States, France faces tough immigration issues.

More than 5 million immigrants live in France. An estimated 200,000 to 400,000 are living in the country illegally. Most immigrants come from Europe, and a large number come from North Africa and West Africa. Historically, most French practiced Catholicism. Today, 5 percent to 10 percent of the population is Muslim. Immigrants often face job discrimination and poor living conditions in France.

The French government recently added an immigration ministry. It offers immigrants money to return home. With this money, a family may be able to have a better life in its native country.

Reading Check How have immigrants changed religious life in France?

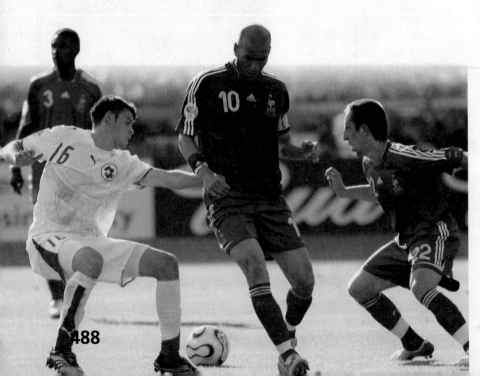

The Low Countries

Belgium, Luxembourg, and the Netherlands form the Low Countries. These countries are small in size, but they are politically and economically powerful.

Belgium: EU Headquarters Belgium serves as the political hub of Europe. Both the EU and NATO have their headquarters in the capital of Brussels. NATO is a military alliance that includes the United States, Canada, and many European nations.

Belgium is a constitutional monarchy. The country has few natural resources, so it relies on trade. It has a high standard of living and a high **gross national product (GNP),** which is the annual income of a nation's companies and residents. Almost 97 percent of Belgians live in cities.

Belgium is made up of three regions. In Flanders in the north, people speak a form of Dutch called Flemish. In Wallonia in the south, they speak French. In the third region around Brussels, people speak both French and Flemish. Periodically, some Flemish call for independence, but most Belgians prefer a united country.

Landlocked Luxembourg Luxembourg is a tiny landlocked country, one of Europe's oldest and smallest. It is a constitutional monarchy as well as a member of the EU and NATO.

Most of its citizens speak French, German, and Luxembourgish, a German dialect. Its key industries are banking and media. Because of its strict banking laws, people around the world use Luxembourg banks.

The Netherlands: A Fragile Balance The Netherlands is also known as Holland. Its people are Dutch. The Netherlands has a long history as a sea-trading nation.

More than half of the Netherlands is below sea level. For centuries, the Dutch have been working to hold back the sea. One way is to build dikes—levees or long dams—to keep out water. With dikes, the Dutch can live on **polders,** or areas of land reclaimed from lake bottoms or the seabeds. The famous Dutch windmills power pumps to drain water from land.

The Dutch live in a <u>fragile</u> balance with their environment. Industry and consumers produce air pollution. As the Dutch population has grown in urban areas, more rural land is needed for human use. Wildlife habitats may be threatened. Water pollution is also a concern because three of Europe's major rivers flow through the Netherlands.

Reading Check How do the Dutch use windmills?

myWorld Activity
Make a Travel Poster

fragile, *adj.,* easily broken or destroyed

The Dutch windmill aids in irrigation for farming. Some farmers also live in windmills. ▶

489

Germany: Industrial Giant

Germany has the largest population in the EU and Western Europe. Its economy is one of the world's largest.

A United Germany When the Berlin Wall came down in 1989, it marked the end of the split between East Germany and West Germany. **Reunification,** or the process of becoming unified again, brought many changes. Many East Germans "voted with their feet." They left the east and went west for a better life.

Germany is a member of international organizations such as the EU and NATO. Germany also joins other nations for international meetings about global economic issues. Through its membership in the Organization for Security and Co-operation in Europe (OSCE), Germany helps keep the region safe.

A Rich Culture German culture includes some of the world's finest music, art, poetry, films, and literature. Germans have also been leaders in the study of botany, mathematics, and military technology.

Modern German culture remains colored by the painful memories of World War II and the Holocaust, in which Nazis murdered six million European Jews and other innocent people. That troubled period partly resulted from excessive nationalism.

While many Germans feel proud of their nation, they want to avoid the mistakes of the past. They believe that one way to ensure a better future is through education. The country ranks high in the number of university professors, published book titles, and Nobel laureates.

Leading German Exports, 2005

Export	Percent of Total Exports	Value in Euros (billions)	Value in U.S. Dollars (billions)
1. Automobiles	17.4	155.12	183.72
2. Machinery	12.5	111.62	132.20
3. Chemicals	11.4	101.91	120.70
4. Metals	5.6	50.27	59.54
5. Electrical machinery	4.4	39.10	46.31

SOURCE: Federal Statistical Office, Federal Republic of Germany

Heat lamps are used to dry paint on a new car at a German automobile factory. ▼

Chart Skills

Data Discovery

Compare the value of Germany's top export with its third-largest export.

490

Building Tolerance Like the rest of Europe, West Germany <u>recruited</u> guest workers from nearby poorer countries to address the postwar labor shortages of the 1950s. Today, immigrants still come to Germany from these same regions: Turkey, the Middle East, and Eastern Europe. Other immigrants are of German descent and are returning to Germany after generations of living in Poland or Romania.

Because of its past and its diverse population, modern Germany encourages tolerance. However, conflict still occurs. Anti-immigrant and anti-Semitic groups such as the neo-Nazis have staged violent marches. Many Turks, Germany's largest immigrant group, claim that they often encounter racism and prejudice. Even popular Turkish soccer players say they have been taunted because they are not "real Germans." German leaders continue to encourage open-mindedness.

Reading Check What are some reasons that immigrants have moved to Germany?

Austria and Switzerland

Austria shares a language as well as economic and cultural ties with Germany. Austria was once the center of the Austro-Hungarian empire. Its size was dramatically reduced during the two world wars. When Soviet occupation ended in 1955, Austria has become a prosperous democracy. Tourism is a top industry in this country, famous for its Alpine scenery and ski resorts.

Switzerland is one of the world's oldest democracies. It has a long history of neutrality, or not taking sides in wars. This neutrality has led to Switzerland's uneasy relationship with international organizations such as the United Nations. Switzerland did not formally join the UN until 2002. Some people believe joining the UN will help the nation to grow. Other worry that membership will damage Switzerland's neutrality.

Reading Check What industry contributes to the economies of both Alpine nations?

recruit, *v.,* to increase or maintain the number of

Winter sports enthusiasts keep tourism a top industry in both Austria and Switzerland. ▼

Section 3 Assessment

Key Terms
1. Write a one-sentence definition of each of the following terms: gross national product, privatization, polders.

Key Ideas
2. Most of the immigrants in France and Germany come from which regions?
3. Give some examples of the cultural heritage in West Central Europe.

Think Critically
4. **Identify Evidence** What actions of the Dutch suggest that the country has a high population density?
5. **Draw Inferences** How might Switzerland's history of neutrality have affected its history?

Essential Question
Is it better to be independent or interdependent?
6. Why might EU membership appeal to smaller countries? Go to your Student Journal to record your answer.

A Sense of Identity

Indiana **6.1.21** Differentiate between fact and interpretation in historical accounts and explain historical passages.

▲ Yasmin is a European of Spanish, Pakistani, and Finnish heritage.

Nationalism has played a major role in European history. While national pride can be positive, it has also caused destructive wars that tore Europe apart. After World War II, European leaders founded the European Union (EU) to promote political and economic cooperation. Anyone who is a citizen of an EU nation also has European citizenship. But what is European citizenship? Will it ever replace national identity? In these passages, Nicole Fontaine, former President of the European Parliament, and Leszek Kolakowski, a Polish historian, express different views.

A girl draws the EU flag with chalk. ▶

Stop at each letter on the right to think about the text. Then answer the question with the same letter on the left.

Ⓐ **Draw Conclusions** What is the relationship between Community, or EU, law and the laws of the separate nations?

Ⓑ **Categorize** Which of these trappings of citizenship are mostly symbolic?

Ⓒ **Summarize** How does Fontaine define European citizenship?

institutional, *adj.,* related to institutions, or established organizations

trapping, *n.,* a thing usually associated with something

underpin, *v.,* to act as a foundation for

bulk, *n.,* a large part, or the largest part

Sharing a European Identity

❝ Not only do Europeans enjoy the <u>institutional</u> <u>trappings</u> of citizenship such as a common flag, a common anthem, Community law <u>underpinning</u>
Ⓐ and directing the vast <u>bulk</u> of national legislation, a form of common government, . . . and of course,
Ⓑ a common currency which in less than two years' time will be the only currency to be found in our wallet:
Ⓒ we share something else as citizens, namely the right to vote and to stand for election. ❞

—Nicole Fontaine, President of the European Parliament, speech of January 29, 2000

492

Stop at each letter on the right to think about the text. Then answer the question with the same letter on the left.

D **Identify Main Ideas and Details** What two forces does Kolakowski think stand in the way of unification?

E **Analyze Cause and Effect** Why does he think many people distrust attempts to unify Europe?

F **Summarize** How does Kolakowski think that European identity could relate to national identity?

complex, *adj.,* having many different pieces
separatist, *adj.,* in favor of remaining apart
xenophobic, *adj.,* afraid of foreigners
wary, *adj.,* cautious, suspicious

Is a European Identity Possible?

66 The question of national identity is endlessly <u>complex</u>. Given the extent to which progress towards unification has been accompanied by a rise in <u>separatist</u> and <u>xenophobic</u> tendencies,

D it is too soon to talk about the end of the nation state. And modern attempts—made by Napoleon, by Hitler, by Moscow—to unify Europe

E by force have made the various peoples of the continent <u>wary</u>. But assuming that national identities will persist, can a European identity be built alongside them or over

F them? Is there such an identity, and if not, is it desirable? Is there, or can there be, such a thing as European patriotism? 99

—Leszek Kolakowski,
"Can Europe Happen?"
The New Criterion, May 2003

▲ Dairy farmers drove their tractors in the streets during a 2009 protest against EU milk pricing policies.

Analyze the Documents

1. **Identify Bias** Is Fontaine or Kolakowski more likely to have a biased view of European identity? Explain.

2. **Writing Task** Write your own definition of national identity. Name the qualities that define your own national identity.

◀ Flags at the European Parliament in Strasbourg, France

493

Southern Europe Today

IN Indiana

6.3.4 Describe and compare major cultural characteristics of regions in Europe and the Western Hemisphere.

6.3.10 Explain the ways cultural diffusion, invention, and innovation change culture.

6.4.5 Compare the standard of living of various countries of Europe and the Americas today using GDP as an indicator.

6.4.6 Analyze current economic issues in the countries of Europe

or the Americas using a variety of resources.

Key Terms • Iberian Peninsula • cultural diffusion • diversify
• deportation

→ **Visual Glossary**

Reading Skill: Analyze Cause and Effect Take notes using the graphic organizer in your journal.

The nations of Southern Europe have enjoyed especially strong growth as members of the European Union. Today, these nations face some of the region's greatest challenges.

A Region of Tradition

Spain, Portugal, Italy, and Greece have an ancient history of civilization. This rich past lives on in traditions that still shape the region today.

The Legacy of Empire Although the ancient Greeks and Romans lived thousands of years ago, their legacies remain. The idea of democracy—that citizens should have a voice in government—began in ancient Greece. The protection of people's rights regardless of wealth or class began in ancient Rome. Today, the European Union (EU) assures members of its commitment to these same ideas. The 12 stars on the EU flag and the EU motto, "United in diversity," tell of the goals of fairness and solidarity, or an attitude shared by a group.

Most of the languages spoken in Southern Europe originated in ancient Greek or Latin. The **Iberian Peninsula** (Spain, Andorra, and Portugal) remains a center of culture and commerce as it has since the Age of Exploration. Farmers and shepherds here live as they have for centuries. The cities of Southern Europe have cathedrals and palaces, many of which date back to the Middles Ages or the Renaissance.

◀ The Leaning Tower of Pisa, in Italy

Centuries of trade have influenced the artistic traditions of Southern Europe. Pablo Picasso, a famous Spanish artist, invented a new style of painting after he saw African art for the first time. Asian music influenced Italian opera composers in the 1800s. In Spain, the beautiful Alhambra Palace is a remnant of Islamic culture in Europe.

Religious Heritage Throughout history, armies, traders, and missionaries have passed through Southern Europe. This activity resulted in religious and cultural exchanges. Historians continue to study these events, as they still have a great effect on modern society.

In Rome, Italy, the tiny country of Vatican City serves as the worldwide center of the Roman Catholic Church. Saint Peter's Basilica, one of the holiest sites for Roman Catholics, was built near the site of an ancient Roman racetrack. Athens, Greece, a center of the Greek Orthodox Church, is also home to the Parthenon, an ancient Greek temple of the goddess Athena. Granada, Spain, blends Christian, Jewish, and Muslim influences. This is an example of **cultural diffusion,** or the spread of culture, and it is visible in Granada's colorful neighborhoods and restaurants and in local customs.

Artistic Richness Many famous artists, musicians, novelists, poets, and architects have come from the nations of Southern Europe. Italian architect Renzo Piano has designed buildings in cities around the world. Maria Callas, a famous soprano from Greece, sang many memorable roles for the opera stage.

Mediterranean Culture Mix

Along the Mediterranean, the nations of Southern Europe blend cultural influences that come from centuries of immigration, trade, art, and tradition. *What different cultural influences do you see below?*

For generations, Italians have celebrated religious holidays with city-wide processions that include holy statues. ▶

The Barcelos cockerel is a symbol of Portugal. ▶

◀ Dancing the flamenco, Yasmin keeps alive art from Spanish, Roma, Arabic, Jewish, and African cultures.

495

Southern Europe is rich in both classical and modern music. Spain's many classical composers include the pianist Isaac Albéniz who first performed at age four. Rock is popular everywhere, but world music has become a new favorite. Some of this music retains ethnic or folk traditions. Fado (FAH doo), sad songs about fate or destiny, is popular in Portugal, as is the music from African nations that were once Portuguese colonies. Flamenco, a Spanish dance, incorporates Arab music and African rhythms. The largest world music festival in the world is in Ariano Irpino, Italy.

Reading Check How has cultural diffusion influenced life in Spain?

Cheese-making is one of Italy's oldest industries. ▼

Modern, Prosperous Cities

Economic growth has been strong in this region, especially from 1980 to the early 2000s. Along with this growth, there has been a rise in living standards.

Economic Changes Many of the countries of Southern Europe lived under dictatorships until relatively recently. With the end of these regimes, these nations entered a new period of freedom and prosperity. In Spain, for example, the death of Francisco Franco in 1975 allowed a peaceful transition to democracy after decades of dictatorship.

As governments became more democratic, leaders liberalized, or made less strict, the laws for running businesses. This encouraged entrepreneurs to open new businesses. Jobs increased at both large and small companies. In addition, increasing privatization made businesses stronger and lowered prices.

Modernization has also boosted economic growth in the region. In Spain, for example, factories bought new, improved machinery. Modern factories can produce better goods for less money. Modern shipping companies then make sure that these goods reach buyers more quickly.

One challenge to Southern Europe's economy has been an increase in Asian imports. These imports are often some of the same goods made in Southern Europe. Because Asian manufacturers can make these goods in larger quantities and their workers earn less, their prices are lower. As a result, many countries in this region have had to work hard to compete.

Focus on Portugal Since joining the European Union in 1986, Portugal has experienced impressive economic growth. Much of this growth is due to Portugal's efforts to **diversify,** or add variety to, its types of industries. Many service-based industries, such as telecommunications, are now centered in Portugal.

Portugal's industries had once been limited to traditional products such as textiles, footwear, cork and wood products, and porcelain. Increasingly, a large service sector has developed. This sector includes telecommunications, financial services, healthcare, and tourism. Tourism is also a major industry for Portugal, bringing in almost $10 billion per year.

Privatization has also helped Portugal's economy. Moving businesses from government control to private control has helped business owners gain <u>confidence</u> in their nation's economy. This leads to growth in trade and and more jobs.

Portugal has also benefited from joining the EU single market. Soon after Portugal adopted the euro in 2002, the nation enjoyed a spike in economic growth that has since leveled off.

Still, Portugal has not escaped economic trouble. During the years of growth, debt increased. Repaying this debt will probably slow economic growth.

Effects of EU Membership Membership in the EU made this region better off. With access to open markets and funding from richer members, EU nations generally gain stronger economies and higher living standards.

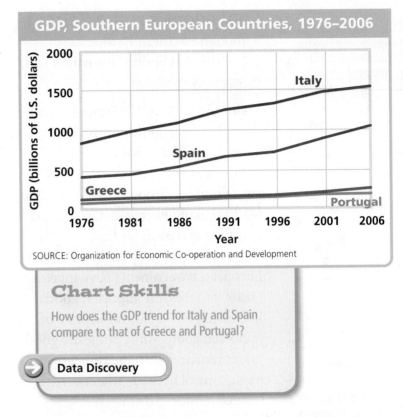

GDP, Southern European Countries, 1976–2006

GDP (billions of U.S. dollars)

SOURCE: Organization for Economic Co-operation and Development

Chart Skills

How does the GDP trend for Italy and Spain compare to that of Greece and Portugal?

➔ **Data Discovery**

Italy has long been an EU leader. Italy adopted the euro as its currency in 1999. Spain, Portugal, and Greece also experienced economic growth as EU members. This growth has slowed due to competition from Asia.

EU members sometimes find economic growth indirectly affected by the addition of new members. For example, Portugal has historically supplied Europe with low-cost labor. Recently, Portugal had its EU development funding cut by several billion euros. This happened with the entrance of new member nations such as Romania and Slovakia. Workers from these nations have begun to move to other EU countries like Portugal and are willing to work for lower wages.

Reading Check Describe one economic change in Southern Europe.

confidence, *n.,* the quality or state of being certain

my **worldgeography.com** Data Discovery

crisis, *n.,* an uncertain or difficult situation, possibly heading toward disaster

Challenges for the Region

Although Southern Europe has experienced economic growth, it still faces many challenges.

Maintaining Growth Europe is now part of a larger, global economy. This has benefits and drawbacks.

In recent years, products from China have flooded European markets. Chinese workers earn lower wages, so the products they make sell for less. To help domestic companies survive, Southern European governments have increased tariffs, or taxes, on imported goods. Increasing tariffs raises the price of imported goods while domestic goods' prices remain low. Increasing government control of the market may, however, hurt economic growth.

The worldwide financial <u>crisis</u> of 2008 also posed serious economic challenges.

The economies of Spain, Portugal, Italy, and Greece have all experienced slow-downs. Industrial production fell, leading to a decrease in GDP. Some experts think that Southern Europe's years of rapid economic growth may be at an end.

Regional Newcomers Badolato, a village in Italy, had almost disappeared when a group of Turkish Kurds arrived. The Italians welcomed these refugees, who gave new life to the village. Because Italians are no longer having large families, the population is decreasing. With fewer people to fill open jobs, many employers now rely on immigrants such as those that have come to Badolato and other cities in Southern Europe.

However, Southern Europeans don't want so much immigration that it threatens their jobs or culture. Their governments have tried to control immigration.

myWorld Activity
Southern Europe's Neighbors

Facing Regional Challenges

Muslim families in Rome (left) protest against anti-immigrant violence. At right, a woman enters an employment office in Spain, where unemployment has risen dramatically. *How does each photograph show challenges faced in Southern Europe?*

NO A VIOLENZA

NO AL DIALOGO

NO AL TERROR

NO ALLA VIOLENZA

NO AI MASSACRI

Comunidad de Mad

SERVICIO REGIONAL DE EMPLE

CONSEJERÍA DE EMPLEO Y MUJER

In Italy, the government uses fingerprinting to monitor immigrants. Some ethnic groups, such as the Roma (formerly known as Gypsies), believe these methods lead to discrimination.

The fear of **deportation,** or being sent back to one's home country, leads many immigrants to hide from officials in their new country. Any immigrant who does not follow a country's laws may be deported. As elsewhere in Europe, immigration shows the benefits and the challenges of living in an interconnected world.

Focus on Greece Since ancient times, Greek trading ships have brought back exotic goods from foreign lands. These same traders also introduced the world to Greek art and culture and important ideas such as democracy.

Shipping is still important in Greece, and China is a major trading partner. In 2007, Greek ships carried about 60 percent of China's imports of raw materials. These commodities included

▲ Colorful shipping containers fill the busy port at Piraeus in Greece. *How does the geography of Greece contribute to its shipping industry?*

coal, oil, and iron ore. In China, those products fueled the nation's explosive growth. This trade agreement benefited both Greece and China as well as other global trading partners. Yet, when global trade began to shrink in 2008, everyone involved in this trade experienced setbacks.

Reading Check What has caused Southern Europe's economic slowdown?

Section 4 Assessment

Key Terms

1. Use each of the following terms in a complete sentence: Iberian Peninsula, cultural diffusion, diversity, deportation.

Key Ideas

2. Describe three ways in which the past still affects Southern Europe.

3. What economic advantages did EU membership bring to Southern Europe?

4. What other cultures have spread ideas to Southern Europe through cultural diffusion?

Think Critically

5. **Identify Evidence** How has Southern Europe responded to immigration?

6. **Draw Inferences** Why are countries generally more open to immigrants during economic boom times?

? Essential Question

Is it better to be independent or interdependent?

7. Has the European Union helped Southern Europe? Explain why or why not. Go to your Student Journal to record your answers.

Skills for a Technological World

 Indiana

6.1.17 Discuss the benefits and challenges related to the development of a highly technological society.

6.4.7 Identify economic connections between the local community and the countries of Europe or the Americas and identify job skills needed to be successful in the workplace.

Living in a Technological Society

Today, we live in a highly technological society. Computers, machines, and other types of technology have changed many old ways of doing things. Innovation is constant, and a discovery in one field can lead to unintended changes in an unrelated field. The ways that people produce energy and communicate are two areas that have changed significantly because of technological changes.

Energy Sources

One way that technology has affected people's lives is through energy sources. As people worry about using up Earth's nonrenewable energy sources, technology is helping to find new sources of energy. Scientists have long been interested in harnessing solar power and wind power, for example, because their supplies are unlimited. However, for many years, storing these types of energy has not been practical or affordable. As technology has improved batteries and other ways of storing energy, these forms of energy are being used more often.

This wind farm provides electricity for people in Indiana. ▼

U.S. Electricity Generation (in million kilowatt hours)			
Year	Solar	Wind	Total
1990	367	2,789	3,037,827
1995	497	3,164	3,353,487
2000	493	5,593	3,802,105
2005	550	17,811	4,055,423
2010	1,212	94,652	4,125,060
2013	9,252	167,665	4,058,209

◄ As a result of improved technology for storing energy, the use of wind and solar power has increased greatly in recent years.

One source of energy, made available by twentieth-century technology, is atomic energy, also called nuclear energy. Atomic energy is created when the nucleus of an atom is either split into two parts or when two nuclei are combined into a single nucleus. Both of these actions release energy which humans can use. Producing atomic energy requires uranium, an element found in Earth's crust, so it is not considered a renewable energy source.

One benefit of atomic energy is efficiency. Small amounts of uranium can produce large amounts of energy, which can be stored and used whenever it is needed. In addition, atomic energy does not create the pollution that has been linked to climate change. A significant drawback, however, is that producing atomic energy creates radiation which can be dangerous, even deadly, to humans and other living things. Nuclear power plants take many safety precautions, but accidents have occurred in which radiation has leaked, killing and causing illness in large numbers of people. In 2011, an accident occurred at the Fukushima nuclear power plant in Japan, which forced people as far as 18 miles away from the plant to evacuate their homes.

Reading check How is atomic energy created?

◀ The possible dangers of atomic energy were revealed in March, 2011, when an earthquake caused an explosion at the Fukushima power plant in Japan.

Communications Technology

Another area of society that technology has greatly affected is communications. Computers and mobile devices allow people all over the world to immediately communicate via email, text messages, social networks, and other rapidly changing tools. These tools affect how companies conduct business, how schools educate students, how friends and families socialize, and how people change governments.

One benefit of increased communications technology is the ability of workers to telecommute, which means to work at home using technology to connect to a workplace. Between 2005 and 2012, the number of days that American workers telecommuted increased by almost 80 percent. Other benefits include the ability of students to take classes over the Internet and the ability of consumers to shop online.

One challenge communications technology creates is that it has made some jobs obsolete, and some people have lost their jobs. For example, when more people buy goods online, some traditional "brick and mortar" stores may go out of business. In addition, some people believe that the increase in high-tech communication means that people are more isolated because they have less face-to-face communication with others.

Reading Check How has increased technology made some jobs obsolete?

One benefit of improved communications technology is the ability to telecommute to work. ▼

▲ One downside is that as fewer people shop at traditional stores, the stores may close and workers may lose their jobs.

◄ Earning a college degree is more important than ever for getting a job in today's technological society.

Job Skills for Success

One result of living in a highly technological society is that job skills needed today are different from those needed in the past. For example, more people need a college education to get well-paying jobs. According to a 2013 study, about two thirds of the job openings between 2015 and 2020 will require some college credits, and about one third of those jobs will require a college degree.

Other skills for jobs in the future include understanding how to use technologies and tools for sharing information.

Those skills go beyond just operating the technology, however. Because the Internet provides so much information to learners and workers, people need to think critically to understand and evaluate that information. Technology connects people all over the world, so another important skill will be communicating across cultures. Lastly, because technology will continue to change, another important skill – maybe the most important – is the willingness and ability to learn new things.

Reading Check About what fraction of jobs in the next five years will require a college degree?

Assessment

1. What are one benefit and one challenge of using atomic energy?

2. What are some reasons why a person might want to telecommute?

3. Name two effects of high technology communications that have affected your life or your family's life.

4. What do you think is the most important skill for success in jobs in the future? Why?

Chapter Assessment

Key Terms and Ideas

1. **Discuss** Why does most of Western Europe have a mild climate?

2. **Describe** Where do most Western Europeans live, and why?

3. **Recall** What is a **constitutional monarchy,** and which nations have this form of government?

4. **Summarize** What does the **cradle-to-grave system** provide for citizens of Scandinavian countries?

5. **Explain** How does migration help cause **cultural borrowing** and **cultural diffusion**?

6. **Compare and Contrast** How are West Central Europe and Southern Europe similar? How are they different?

7. **Explain** What problems has Germany had to overcome since **reunification**?

8. **Recall** What cultures have influenced the artistic traditions of Southern Europe?

Think Critically

9. **Compare Viewpoints** How does the British viewpoint toward the EU compare to the viewpoint of France and Germany? Support your answer with details from the chapter.

10. **Draw Conclusions** How has immigration affected Western Europe? Explain.

11. **Predict** What long-term effect do you think EU membership will have on nationalism in Europe? Explain.

12. **Core Concepts: People's Impact on the Environment** What are some of the main causes of pollution? How has pollution affected Europe?

Places to Know

For each place, write the letter from the map that shows its location.

13. Scandinavian Peninsula

14. Italy

15. Iceland

16. France

17. Iberian Peninsula

18. Mediterranean Sea

19. Greece

20. **Estimate** Using the scale, estimate how far Iceland is from France.

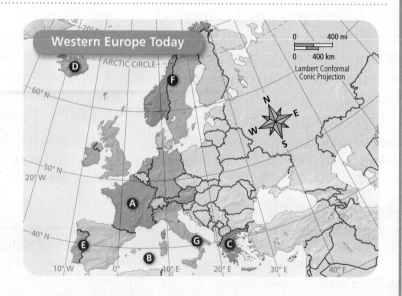

Western Europe Today

Essential Question

myWorld Chapter Activity

Norway and the European Union Follow your teacher's instructions to study data on whether or not Norway should join the European Union. Read and analyze graphs, photographs, and information about the advantages and disadvantages of EU membership for Norway. Take a stand based on your conclusions in support of your position on EU membership for Norway.

21st Century Learning

Develop Cultural Awareness

Western Europe's contact with other nations has added much to life on the continent. Make a small poster on each of the topics below to focus on cultural diffusion in Western Europe.
- Art and architecture
- Music
- Language
- Food

Document-Based Questions

Success Tracker™
Online at myworldgeography.com

Use your knowledge of Western Europe and Documents A and B to answer Questions 1–3.

Document A

Joining the Eurozone	
EU Member	**Year Euro Adopted**
Austria	1999
Belgium	1999
Finland	1999
France	1999
Germany	1999
Greece	2001
Ireland	1999
Netherlands	1999
Slovakia	2009
Spain	1999

1. Which Southern European country was last to adopt the euro?

A Greece

B Ireland

C Slovakia

D Spain

Document B

" The people of Denmark have voted to reject membership of the single European currency. . . . The leader of the far-right, anti-Euro Danish People's Party, Pia Kjaersgaard, described the outcome as a great victory. 'This victory is a victory for Danes' wish to defend democracy, self-determination and the country's sovereignty,' she said."

—"Danes Say No to Euro,"
BBC News Online, September 28, 2000

2. According to Kjaersgaard, why did the Danish people reject the euro?

A They don't trust other EU members.

B They are waiting to see if it succeeds.

C They want to control their economy.

D They have too much debt to switch.

3. **Writing Task** Explain why some Western European countries may want to have some independence from the EU.

myworldgeography.com Self-Test

Chapter 11

Eastern Europe

Essential Question

How can you measure success?

KEY
— National border
✪ Capital city
○ Other city

0   200 mi
0   200 km
Lambert Conformal Conic Projection

Tallinn ✪
ESTONIA
Baltic Sea
Riga ✪ **LATVIA**
LITHUANIA
Vilnius ✪
KALININGRAD
(Russia)
Minsk ✪
Vistula
BELARUS
Oder River
Warsaw ✪
POLAND
Prague ✪
CZECH REPUBLIC
Kiev ✪
Bezpalche ○
Dnister River
UKRAINE
SLOVAKIA
Bratislava ✪ ○ Budapest
MOLDOVA
Chişinău ✪
HUNGARY
SLOVENIA ✪ Ljubljana
✪ Zagreb
ROMANIA
CROATIA
BOSNIA AND HERZEGOVINA
○ Belgrade
Bucharest ○
Danube River
Black Sea
Sarajevo ✪
SERBIA
BULGARIA
Adriatic Sea
Priština ○
Sofia ○
Podgorica ✪
KOSOVO
MONTENEGRO
Skopje ○
Tirana ✪ **MACEDONIA**
ALBANIA

60° N
50° N
40° N
20° E

Where in the World Is Eastern Europe?

Washington, D.C., to Bezpalche: 4,930 miles

my Story

Serhiy's Leap

Explore the Essential Question
- at my worldgeography.com
- using the **myWorld Chapter Activity**
- with the Student Journal

In this section, you'll read about Serhiy, a young man who lives in the small town of Bezpalche in Ukraine. What does Serhiy's story tell you about life in Eastern Europe today?

Story by Mark Rachkevych for myWorld Geography Online

Serhiy lives in the historic farming hamlet of Bezpalche, located 80 miles (130 kilometers) east of the Ukrainian capital of Kiev. Its 640 people are proud of the village's roots. It was founded by Bezpalko, a famous Cossack. The Cossacks were free-roaming bands of warriors known for their expert horsemanship and fierce fighting tactics. They defended the Ukrainian frontiers from enemy attack.

Single-family brick homes with tile roofs line the village lanes. Wooden fences separate the yards. Behind the houses are small plots of land used for farming. A wooden Christian church is the tallest structure in the village. A school stands in the center of the village along an unpaved road. The village is small enough that it is easy to get around by walking.

This school is where 16-year-old Serhiy enjoys his favorite subjects of physical education, information technology, and the Ukrainian language. In his final year of study, Serhiy walks to school from home, where he lives with his parents, his older brother, and his elderly grandmother.

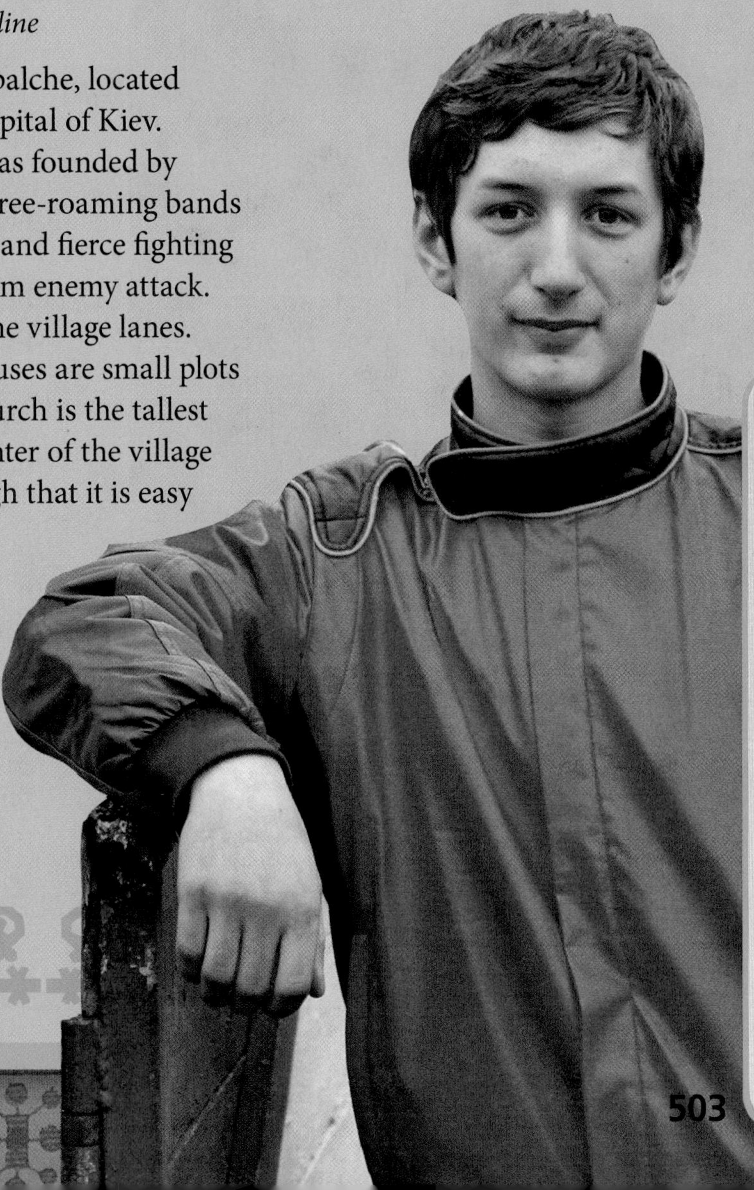

my worldgeography.com On Assignment

503

Serhiy buys bread at the only shop in Bezpalche.

Scattering corn for the chickens is one of Serhiy's regular afternoon chores. He also must feed the family's pigs (below).

His mother works a postal route three hours a day. On their small farm, his family grows beets, onions, cabbage, corn, and potatoes, and tends four pigs and three milking cows. Serhiy is personally responsible for caring for more than 40 rabbits. Small farms like this are common in Ukraine.

Ukraine used to be part of the Soviet Union. The Soviet government managed all the land in the country. Now Ukraine is an independent country. The new leadership broke up the large government farms, giving each family a small plot of land.

In villages like these, nature doesn't allow for breaks or long vacations. Serhiy rises at 6:00, feeds the livestock, and does other chores around the pens. Then he eats breakfast and heads to school for his first class, which begins at 8:30. He returns home at 2:30 and eats lunch. His favorite lunch is potatoes fried in lard and onions. His next chore is to take care of the rabbits. His grandmother pays him a small weekly allowance for this task. Then, at sunset, Serhiy starts his homework.

Short and broad-shouldered, Serhiy enjoys physical activity. He loves motorbikes and anything technical. "I even assembled a computer from scratch with a friend of mine," Serhiy says proudly, pointing at his PC, which he knows inside and out.

Serhiy plays games on a computer that he assembled himself, but he has no Internet connection.

The city of Kiev is about 80 miles from Serhiy's village.

But Serhiy can enjoy these hobbies only when time permits. On the weekends, his brother drives him 25 miles (40 kilometers) to the regional capital to take preparatory classes. Serhiy wants to go to the military academy in Kharkiv in eastern Ukraine. He hopes to become a pilot. But to do so, he will need to do well on the entrance exam. The prestigious and highly competitive academy accepts only one out of every four applicants.

Serhiy knows his small world and way of life will come to an end next summer when he graduates. Even if he is not accepted to the military academy, he will leave his village. The grocery store is the only real business in Bezpalche, so most young people must go elsewhere to make a living. Once his studies begin, he will not be able to take trips into the woods or drive his motorbike on country roads.

Still, Serhiy looks forward to military life. After all, could it be tougher than life in Bezpalche? Yet he worries, "Cities have wide boulevards, and I'll be a stranger among impersonal strangers."

He's willing to make the transition since he is drawn to the physical rigor of military exercises, the technical hardware and weaponry, and the challenges the regimen brings. "My family supports my decision, and my mother just worries like any other mother does," Serhiy says half-jokingly.

And if he doesn't get accepted when he applies in Kharkiv next summer, what is his backup plan? "Then I'll probably study computer programming in Cherkassy, the neighboring regional capital," Serhiy says.

How does he feel about leaving an environment where everything is familiar, where there are no surprises, and where everybody knows his name? "Well, I'm not just going to stay here," he says. "No one from my graduating class plans to remain in the village next summer, nobody."

Meet the Journalist

Name Mark Rachkevych
Favorite Moment Eating in a market and chatting with villagers in Bezpalche

→ **myStory Video**

Join Serhiy as he shows you more about his life in Ukraine.

my worldgeography.com | myStory Video

Chapter Atlas

IN Indiana

6.1.2 Describe and compare the beliefs, the spread and the influence of religions throughout Europe and Mesoamerica.

6.3.1 Understand the countries and capitals of Europe and the Americas.

6.3.2 Use latitude and longitude to locate the capital cities of Europe and the Americas and describe the uses of locational technology.

6.3.7 Locate and describe the climate regions of Europe and the

Americas and explain how and why they differ.

6.3.12 Compare the distribution and evaluate the importance of natural resources in Europe and the Americas.

Key Terms • ice age • mechanized farming • acid rain • emigrate

Reading Skill: Label an Outline Map Take notes using the outline map in your journal.

▲ The "Iron Gates" of the Danube River separate Romania from Serbia and the Carpathian Mountains from the Balkans.

◀ A young woman from Estonia

Physical Features

Eastern Europe is a region with both broad plains and high mountains. The most mountainous part of the region is the Balkan Peninsula, which juts into the Mediterranean Sea to the south. Two ranges, the Dinaric Alps and the Balkan Mountains, cover much of the peninsula.

Mountain ranges also stretch through the middle of Eastern Europe. The Carpathian Mountains begin close to the Danube River in Slovakia. They arch northeast and then bend back toward the Danube River, joining the Transylvanian Alps to the south.

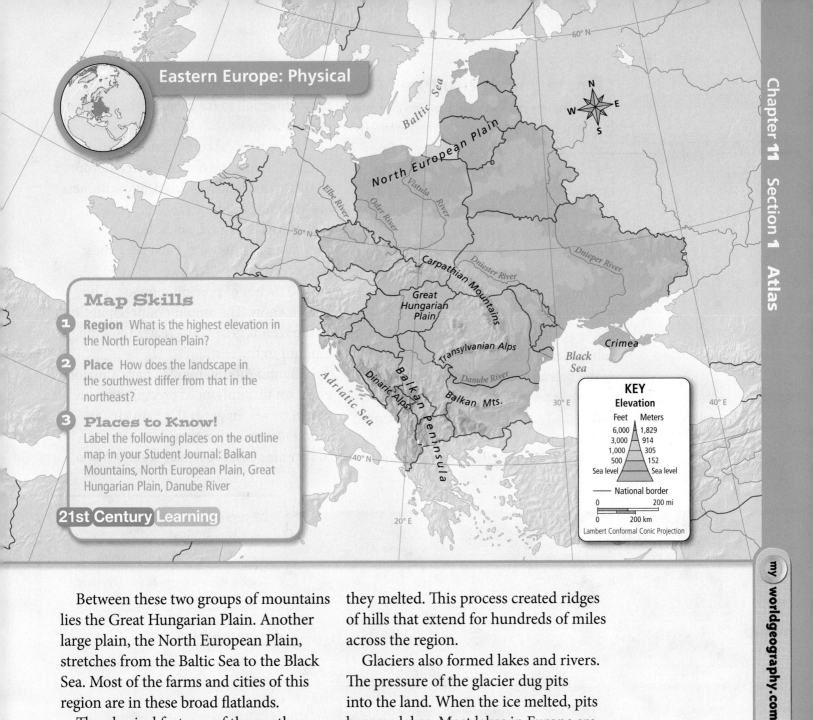

Eastern Europe: Physical

KEY
Elevation

Feet	Meters
6,000	1,829
3,000	914
1,000	305
500	152
Sea level	Sea level

— National border

0   200 mi
0   200 km

Lambert Conformal Conic Projection

Map Skills

1 **Region** What is the highest elevation in the North European Plain?

2 **Place** How does the landscape in the southwest differ from that in the northeast?

3 **Places to Know!**
Label the following places on the outline map in your Student Journal: Balkan Mountains, North European Plain, Great Hungarian Plain, Danube River

21st Century Learning

Between these two groups of mountains lies the Great Hungarian Plain. Another large plain, the North European Plain, stretches from the Baltic Sea to the Black Sea. Most of the farms and cities of this region are in these broad flatlands.

The physical features of the northern part of this region were shaped by an **ice age,** or time of lower temperatures when much of the land is covered in ice. Ice piled up as deep as two miles thick. Heavy sheets of ice, called glaciers, moved slowly across the land. Glaciers scraped up rocks and soil as they moved. They then dropped these materials when they melted. This process created ridges of hills that extend for hundreds of miles across the region.

Glaciers also formed lakes and rivers. The pressure of the glacier dug pits into the land. When the ice melted, pits became lakes. Most lakes in Europe are located in glaciated areas.

In the southern part of this region, deep valleys crisscross steep mountains. The Danube river flows through the Iron Gates, one of these deep valleys.

Reading Check What effects have glaciers had on the physical features of Eastern Europe?

Climate and Agriculture

The climate varies across Eastern Europe. In particular, the climate of the northern part of the region is very different from the climate of the southern part. As a result, farmers in the north face different challenges than farmers in the south. In the north, the winters can be very harsh. In the south, the mountains make cultivating the land difficult.

Latitude is the most important factor that influences climate in Eastern Europe. In the south, a band of Mediterranean and subtropical climate extends across much of the Balkan Peninsula. Summers here are dry, while winters are rainy. The rain and snow that <u>accumulate</u> in the mountains in wet winter months are very important for agriculture. During the hot, dry months of spring and summer, melting snow flows downhill to the crops in the parched valleys below.

The continental cool summer climate covers much of the rest of Eastern Europe. In this area, winters are cold, and summers are generally mild.

Patterns of rainfall across the region vary from east to west. Each year, most of Eastern Europe receives between 20 and 40 inches of precipitation, or falling rain or snow. The amount of precipitation in the west is generally greater than the amount in the east.

Hills and mountains also have a major effect on the amount of precipitation an area receives. In general, warm air can hold more moisture than cool air. The higher air goes, the cooler it gets. When

accumulate, *v.,* to build up over time

Eastern Europe: Climate

Continental, cool summer

Mediterranean

Map Skills

1 **Place** Identify one country in Eastern Europe with a mostly Mediterranean climate.

2 **Region** What is the relationship between climate and latitude?

Active Atlas

KEY
- Continental cool summer
- Continental warm summer
- Humid subtropical
- Mediterranean
- National border

0   300 mi
0   300 km
Lambert Conformal Conic Projection

508

air cannot hold as much water, the water falls back to the earth as rain or as snow.

It is easy to see, then, how mountains affect precipitation. When wind blows against a range of mountains, the air rises and cools. Then it drops its moisture and continues over the mountains. Therefore, the side of the mountains facing the wind receives much more rain than the other side. The result is big differences in climate over small distances. Areas along the Adriatic coast, for example, receive as much as 200 inches of rainfall a year. The dry valleys on the other side of the Dinaric Alps may receive only 30 inches of rainfall during the same period of time.

The growing season on the North European Plain is shorter than the growing season farther south in the region.

Still, many people farm in this region. **Mechanized farming,** or farming with machines, is easy on the large expanses of flat land. Wheat and rye are common crops in this region. They are well suited to the cooler climate and easy to harvest with machines.

Because machines are important for agriculture here, many farms in northeastern Europe are large. Large farms are not as common in the southern part of this region. Because of the mountains, mechanized farming is more difficult. Also, more people are available to work the land. Many crops such as citrus fruits, olives, and grapes grow well in the warm climate.

Reading Check How is agriculture in the north of Eastern Europe different from that in the south?

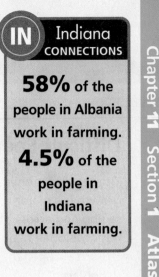

IN Indiana CONNECTIONS

58% of the people in Albania work in farming.

4.5% of the people in Indiana work in farming.

Harvesting Wheat in the North

Wheat grows best in areas without extremes of temperature. So wheat is a good crop for countries with cool summers and flat land.

Growing Olives in the South

Olive trees do well with warm, dry summers and cannot survive very cold winters. For that reason, olive growing is best suited to countries with a Mediterranean climate.

myworldgeography.com Active Atlas

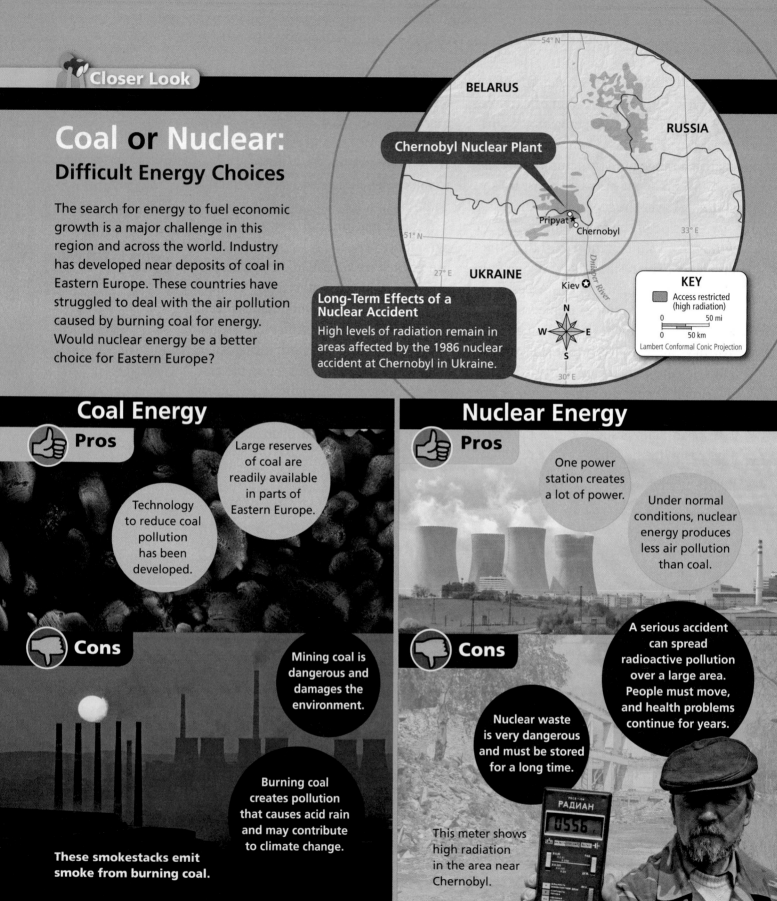

Coal or Nuclear:
Difficult Energy Choices

The search for energy to fuel economic growth is a major challenge in this region and across the world. Industry has developed near deposits of coal in Eastern Europe. These countries have struggled to deal with the air pollution caused by burning coal for energy. Would nuclear energy be a better choice for Eastern Europe?

BELARUS

RUSSIA

Chernobyl Nuclear Plant

54° N

51° N

33° E

27° E

UKRAINE

Pripyat ★

Chernobyl

Kiev ✪

Dnieper River

N
W   E
S

30° E

KEY

Access restricted (high radiation)

0   50 mi
0   50 km

Lambert Conformal Conic Projection

Long-Term Effects of a Nuclear Accident

High levels of radiation remain in areas affected by the 1986 nuclear accident at Chernobyl in Ukraine.

Coal Energy

👍 Pros

Large reserves of coal are readily available in parts of Eastern Europe.

Technology to reduce coal pollution has been developed.

👎 Cons

Mining coal is dangerous and damages the environment.

Burning coal creates pollution that causes acid rain and may contribute to climate change.

These smokestacks emit smoke from burning coal.

Nuclear Energy

👍 Pros

One power station creates a lot of power.

Under normal conditions, nuclear energy produces less air pollution than coal.

👎 Cons

A serious accident can spread radioactive pollution over a large area. People must move, and health problems continue for years.

Nuclear waste is very dangerous and must be stored for a long time.

This meter shows high radiation in the area near Chernobyl.

РАДИАН

0556

БЕЛВАР

Natural Resources and the Environment

Physical geography influences industry as well as agriculture. The location of Eastern Europe's factories depends on the location of natural resources. For example, industry has grown in areas of Poland where coal is available. Both iron ore and coal are found in one region of Ukraine. As a result, steel is an important industrial product there.

Oil and gas are in very short supply in Eastern Europe. Many countries must import the oil and gas they need to develop industry. For example, countries such as Ukraine, Moldova, and Belarus have become dependent on oil and gas imports from Russia.

The need for energy to fuel industry has created serious environmental problems. In 1986, an explosion occurred at one of the towers at the Chernobyl nuclear power plant in Ukraine. Winds spread radioactive pollution over a huge area in Europe. Many people became sick and died from the radiation. Farmland was contaminated, so that the food grown there was no longer safe to eat. More than

20 years later, the area around the power plant was still contaminated. A reporter described one city in Ukraine that had been evacuated shortly after the accident:

> 66 A dead city. Homes, schoolrooms, playgrounds, and other places are crumbling as wild nature reclaims the land. Pripyat once had some 50,000 residents. Now they are gone, perhaps forever. Only the artifacts of their lives remain behind, rotting to dust. 99
>
> —Jeffrey Young, Voice of America, June 10, 2009

Other Eastern European countries have drawn on their coal reserves. Burning coal and other fossil fuels sends chemicals into the air that cause **acid rain,** that is, precipitation that is acidic. Forests have been damaged by acid rain and other pollution. In parts of Poland and the Czech Republic, forests have been destroyed by acid rain, and soils are too contaminated for crops. Worse, polluted water and soil have caused higher rates of birth defects, cancer, and other diseases.

Today, many countries have begun to address environmental problems. To join the European Union, countries must install equipment to make power plants cleaner. Now the problem of acid rain is much less serious in Eastern Europe, and the forests are starting to recover.

Reading Check What has caused damage to the forests of Eastern Europe?

In 1994, nearly 55 percent of the forest land in Poland was damaged by acid rain. Since then, however, much of the damage has been reversed.

North
Sea

Baltic
Sea

ESTONIA

Riga ✡ LATVIA

LITHUANIA

Minsk ✡

BELARUS

POLAND

CZECH
REPUBLIC

SLOVAKIA

Kiev ✡

Kharkov ✡

UKRAINE

Dnepropetrovsk ✡

Budapest ✡

MOLDOVA

HUNGARY

Chișinău

Odesa ✡

SLOVENIA

CROATIA

ROMANIA

Black Sea

BOSNIA AND
HERZEGOVINA

SERBIA

MONTENEGRO

BULGARIA

KOSOVO

ALBANIA

MACEDONIA

KEY

Roman Catholicism
Eastern Orthodoxy
Islam
Protestant Christianity
✡ Large Jewish communities,
2008

0 ——— 300 mi
0 ——— 300 km
Lambert Conformal Conic Projection

Map Skills

1 **Regions** Identify one country that is mostly Catholic and one that is mostly Orthodox.

2 **Place** Where is Islam found? Why do you think Islam spread to those areas?

3 **Places to Know!**
Poland, Ukraine, Black Sea, Baltic Sea, Bosnia and Herzegovina

→ Active Atlas

Religious Diversity in Eastern Europe

Eastern Europe is a region with a diverse religious history. Christianity is the <u>dominant</u> religion. In addition, many Jewish people and Muslims call this region home.

The first major division in the Christian religion occurred with the split between the Catholic Church and the Eastern Orthodox Church in the year 1054. The pope in Rome led the Catholic Church, while the patriarch of Constantinople was the leading figure for Eastern Orthodoxy. Constantinople is now Istanbul, in Turkey. From these centers, both churches sent missionaries into Eastern Europe. Eastern Orthodoxy became dominant in much of the Balkan Peninsula, as well as in Ukraine and Belarus.

dominant, *adj.,* having the most power or influence

With the Reformation in the 1500s, Protestant groups broke off from the Catholic Church. The Reformation began in Germany, and Protestantism spread to countries in northeastern Europe, including Estonia and Latvia. The Roman Catholic Church remained stronger in most of Central Europe, including Poland, the Czech Republic, Slovakia, and Hungary.

Christianity is not the only religion in Europe. Today, Muslims are the largest group of non-Christians. Many Muslims live in Bosnia, Albania, Kosovo, and the Crimean Peninsula in Ukraine. In fact, the southern part of Eastern Europe has long been a borderland where the Christian and Muslim worlds meet. This boundary has shifted over time as control of the region passed between Christian and Islamic states.

A Catholic bishop from the Czech Republic

A Muslim imam from Bosnia

An Eastern Orthodox priest from Ukraine

A Jewish rabbi from Poland

Judaism also has a long history in Eastern Europe. Europe was once home to most of the world's Jewish people. But during the Holocaust of the 1940s, two thirds of the Jews in Europe were murdered. Many others later left the region. Since then, there has been a revival of Jewish communities in some areas. In others, Jewish people continue to **emigrate,** or leave one area to move to another. About 30,000 Jews leave Ukraine each year for the United States, Israel, and other places.

The laws of the Soviet Union restricted religion. For many years, Eastern European governments discouraged religion.

Today, many people in Eastern Europe do not belong to any religion. More than half of the people in the Czech Republic and 40 percent of those in Estonia claim no religious faith.

Still, religious life has become more active since the end of communism. Now people have more opportunities to start and join religious organizations. With the fall of communist governments, people in this region have had the chance not only to return to traditional religious practices, but also to live more freely in other areas of their lives.

Reading Check Where are many Muslims found in this region?

myWorld Activity
Hailstorm

my worldgeography.com Active Atlas

Section **1** Assessment

Key Terms

1. What causes acid rain?

2. Use the term *mechanized farming* to describe agriculture in Eastern Europe.

Key Ideas

3. Where are the major groups of mountains located in Eastern Europe?

4. How does the climate of Eastern Europe change from the north to the south?

5. What are some of the important resources of Eastern Europe?

Think Critically

6. Identify Cause and Effect Why are crops grown in the north different from those grown in the south of this region?

7. Draw Inferences What might influence whether people in a region practice one religion or another?

Essential Question

How can you measure success?

8. To join the European Union, countries must meet certain environmental standards. Do you think protecting the environment should be one measure of a country's success? Explain why or why not. Go to your Student Journal to record your answer.

Influence of Religion on Cultures of Eastern Europe

IN Indiana   **6.1.22** Form research questions and use resources to present data on people, cultures and developments in Europe and the Americas.

Key Terms • secular   • nationalism   • pilgrimage   • fasting   → **Visual Glossary**

Religion has shaped the traditions and cultures of the countries in Eastern Europe. Most of the region is Christian, but different forms of Christianity dominate in different countries. In other areas, Islam is the majority religion. And, while Judaism has never been the dominant religion in any country in Europe, Jewish communities have also influenced Eastern European culture. The examples below show some ways that religion has shaped the countries of this region.

St. Olaf's Church is located in Tallinn, the capital of Estonia. The first Protestant sermons in Estonia were delivered at this church.

Protestants in Estonia

Protestant Christianity is the main faith in Estonia. Roman Catholicism was long ago the chief religion. But after the Protestant Reformation, the country turned to Lutheranism, a form of Protestant Christianity.

Lutheranism brought many changes to Estonian culture. Previously, religious services had been held in Latin, the language of the Catholic Church. The Bible was in Latin, too. But Lutherans performed church services in the Estonian language. They translated the Bible into Estonian. As a result, many Estonians learned to read and write. Estonian literature began to develop. Pastors and teachers wrote children's stories based on traditional folk tales. These stories helped spread cultural and religious values.

The Estonian people today are mostly **secular,** that is, they are not very religious. But Lutheran beliefs still lie at the heart of Estonian culture.

Reading Check What is the main religion in Estonia?

Catholicism in Poland

The Roman Catholic Church plays a major role in a number of Eastern Europe countries. It is especially important in Poland. Most Poles belong to the Catholic Church. Catholicism is integral to Polish life. It is a key part of Poland's national identity.

For centuries Poland was occupied by its powerful neighbors, Russia and Germany. The Catholic Church in Poland opposed foreign rule. It helped unify Poles and promote Polish **nationalism**. Nationalism is a strong devotion to one's nation. The role of the Church as defender of Polish culture continued even under communist rule. The communists tried to stamp out religion. But they could not end Polish loyalty to the Catholic Church.

Today Catholicism continues to influence daily life in Poland. Most Poles go to church. They take part in religious holidays and parades. They also make **pilgrimages,** or religious journeys, to Catholic shrines. In many ways, Catholic values still guide Polish culture.

Reading Check How did the Catholic Church help unify Poland?

Pope John Paul II, below, was the first Polish pope. He supported Polish efforts to shake off communist rule. ▼

Map of the Jewish quarter of Kraków, Poland.

The Jewish Heritage of Eastern Europe

During the 1900s, the Jewish population of Eastern Europe endured great suffering. Millions were killed during the Holocaust. When the region was under communist control, many of the remaining Jews left the region because of prejudice and restrictions on practicing their religion. The Jewish population remains small, but many people now celebrate the contribution of Jews to the culture of Eastern Europe.

A band performing at the Jewish Culture Festival in Kraków

515

Orthodox Religion in Serbia

Eastern Orthodox Christianity is the main religion in Serbia and many other Balkan states. Orthodox Christianity shares ancient roots with Catholicism. In the Middle Ages, however, disagreements over beliefs and practices led Christians to split into separate Catholic and Orthodox churches.

Instead of a single authority, the Orthodox church has nine patriarchs, or high-ranking bishops. The Serbian Orthodox Church has its own partriach.

In Serbia, Christian holidays are celebrated according to the Orthodox calendar. For example, Christmas is celebrated on January 7 rather than December 25. The Christmas feast includes roast pork and special bread with a coin baked inside. Whoever gets the piece with the coin is said to have good luck for the coming year. Orthodox families in Serbia also have a patron saint whom they honor on a particular day.

Serbia is home to other religions, too, including Islam. But many Serbians believe that Orthodox Christianity is a key part of their national identity.

Reading Check What is the main religion in Serbia?

An Orthodox priest leads a religious procession in Serbia.

Muslim Culture in Bosnia

Islam is the chief religion in Bosnia. Muslim influence there dates to the Ottoman conquest of the Balkans in the late 1300s. The Ottoman Turks ruled the region for 500 years. Many Bosnians converted to Islam during this time.

Bosnian Muslims tend to be less strict in their religious practices than Muslims in Southwest Asia. Some consume alcohol, pork, and other foods seen as forbidden by Islam. More women work outside the home. In addition, Bosnian Muslim women do not generally cover their heads, as do many Muslim women in Southwest Asia.

Still, Islam is important in the lives of many Bosnians. They read the Quran, the Muslim holy book. They celebrate the key Muslim holidays, known as the Eids. They also observe Ramadan, a month of **fasting**, or limits on eating. During this period, Muslims avoid eating between sunrise and sunset every day.

Bosnia has a long history of religious tolerance. The Ottomans allowed non-Muslims to practice their own faiths. Bosnia has suffered ethnic conflict in recent years. But most Bosnians continue to maintain a tradition of tolerance.

Reading Check **How did Islam enter Bosnia?**

Like all Muslims, these Bosnian men are expected to pray five times each day.

Assessment

1. How did Lutheranism promote literacy in Estonia?

2. How are religion and national identity linked in Poland and Serbia?

3. How is Bosnia different from many Muslim countries?

4. Why do you think Eastern Europe became home to many religions?

5. How does religion in Eastern Europe reflect divisions within Christianity?

Eastern Europe Today

IN Indiana

6.2.1 Compare and contrast forms of governments in Europe and the Americas throughout history.

6.2.6 Describe the functions of international political organizations in the world today.

6.3.4 Describe and compare major cultural characteristics of regions in Europe and the Western Hemisphere.

6.4.4 Describe how different economic systems in Europe and the Americas answer the basic economic questions.

6.4.6 Analyze current economic issues in the countries of Europe or the Americas using a variety of resources.

Key Terms • entrepreneur • capital • cuisine • secede • ethnic cleansing

Visual Glossary

Reading Skill: Compare and Contrast Take notes using the graphic organizer in your journal.

This skyscraper was built in Warsaw while Poland was under communist rule. Today, it stands at the heart of Poland's financial district.

Each country in Eastern Europe has taken a different path since the end of communism. Some countries have built strong economies. Some countries are successful democracies. Other countries have broken apart, divided by ethnic conflict.

Poland and the Baltic Nations

Poland and the Baltic nations of Lithuania, Latvia, and Estonia have been among the most economically successful countries in Eastern Europe. They have also created democratic governments. Still, this change has not been easy. The people of these countries faced challenges and uncertainty after the fall of the Soviet Union.

Poland's Quick Reforms Poland was the first nation in Eastern Europe to make the transition to democracy at the end of the communist era. In the 1980s, a Polish labor union called Solidarity opposed the communist party, which controlled the government. After the fall of communism, the popular leader of Solidarity, Lech Walesa (lek vah WEH suh), was elected president.

Poland's leaders then took on the challenge of creating a market economy. In the communist system, the government controlled prices and planned production for the economy. In the early 1990s, the government stopped controlling prices, cut support for old state-owned factories, and encouraged new private businesses. After a slow start, the Polish economy recovered and grew throughout the 1990s.

Many citizens became **entrepreneurs**, people who organize and manage their own businesses. This Polish entrepreneur comments on starting a new business:

> 66 I truly never would have thought my idea of opening a high-end art supply store would work out when my country became independent from the Soviet Union. But because the arts are so important here in Poland, and the government helped me all along the way, it's been a very exciting time. 99
>
> —Entrepreneur from Bialystok, Poland

The Transition in the Baltic States The Baltic nations of Lithuania, Latvia, and Estonia were once republics of the Soviet Union. All three nations left behind the communist economic system and moved to a market economy during the 1990s. They now have democratic governments.

Estonia's economy has been especially successful. Industries in Estonia have **capital**, money or wealth used to invest in a business. Capital allows businesses to obtain more modern equipment to make high-quality goods. They can export these goods to other countries. Today, Estonia's main trading partners are Finland, Germany, and Sweden. Latvia and Lithuania have also experienced growth. Although Russia is still Lithuania's main trading partner, Lithuania now trades with Germany and Poland as well.

All of the Baltic nations as well as Poland have been accepted into the European Union. Membership in the EU has helped these nations to find new trading partners and improve their economies.

Cultural Life in Poland and the Baltic States Poland and the Baltic nations are well known for their rich cultural heritage. Poles have worked hard to preserve their history and culture. Many Polish cities have art and history museums. Poles also celebrate their cultural heritage at festivals. For example, music festivals highlighting the music of the famous Polish composer Frederic Chopin are popular.

In recent years, people in the Baltic States have revived traditions and religious practices that the Soviets banned. For example, Latvians now celebrate the summer festival of Jani (YAH nee) with traditional songs and dances.

Reading Check What is one reason Estonia has had economic success in recent years?

Each June, Latvians celebrate the Jani festival. Women and men—even cattle—wear wreaths of flowers or leaves.

519

Central Europe

The countries of Central Europe include the Czech Republic, Slovakia, Hungary, and Slovenia. Like other countries of Eastern Europe, these nations needed to build new governments and strengthen their economies.

Slovakia and the Czech Republic In 1989, communism gave way to democracy in Czechoslovakia. Soon, representatives of the Czechs and Slovaks disagreed about how to run the country. They divided peacefully in 1993 into two nations: the Czech Republic and Slovakia. Most people in the Czech Republic are of the Czech <u>ethnic</u> group. The majority of people in Slovakia are ethnic Slovaks.

Both nations have built democratic governments and experienced economic growth. The change to a market economy was easier for the Czech Republic. This nation had a strong economy with many different industries. It was able to modernize many of its factories fairly quickly.

Under Soviet control, Slovakia's economy was less diverse. Because building new industries takes time, economic growth was slow at first. However, Slovakia's government took action. In 1998, it lowered taxes for any foreign companies that created new businesses and jobs. Foreign investment increased rapidly, bringing more money to help improve Slovakia's economy. Both Slovakia and the Czech Republic have joined the European Union and expanded trade with the nations of Western Europe.

ethnic, *adj.,* defined by a shared nationality, identity, or heritage

Chart Skills

To figure out each nation's growth rate as a percentage, subtract the 1993 number from the 2008 number. Then, divide this number by the 1993 number. Which nation had a higher growth rate during this time period, Slovakia or the Czech Republic?

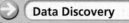

→ **Data Discovery**

Industrial Growth in the Former Czechoslovakia

Since they separated in 1993, both Slovakia and the Czech Republic have enjoyed economic growth. These figures represent economic output per person in each nation.

Czech Republic

| 1993 | $12,774 |
| 2008 | $26,000 |

Slovakia

| 1993 | $8,371 |
| 2008 | $21,900 |

SOURCE: *CIA World Factbook*

Workers in a Czech car factory ▼

Hungary Hungary has had some economic and political success since the fall of communism. It now has a stable, democratic government and a market economy. Debt has been a challenge, however. Hungary borrowed from other countries to modernize its economy. The resulting heavy debt has slowed economic growth. The government must deal with this problem for Hungary's economy to develop successfully.

Hungarians have also been returning to many traditions since the end of communism. Most Hungarians are Roman Catholic. Traditional Christian holidays are celebrated again as national holidays. The Hungarian language is different from other languages spoken in Europe. Hungarians also cook a unique **cuisine**, that is, style of food. Many Hungarian dishes use the spice paprika, which is made from bell or chili peppers. Hungarians take great pride in their distinct cultural heritage.

Slovenia In 1918, Slovenia became part of the new country of Yugoslavia. There was tension between the different republics of Yugoslavia. Many Slovenians came to believe that their homeland would be better off if they split from Yugoslavia. The leaders of Slovenia had managed their economy more successfully than some other republics in Yugoslavia.

In 1990, fully 90 percent of Slovenia's citizens voted for independence. Slovenia fought the short Ten-Day War to separate from the rest of Yugoslavia. Slovenia then began to build a democratic government and a free market economy. Despite many challenges, Slovenia has improved its economy. It became the first Balkan country to join the EU and the North Atlantic Treaty Organization (NATO) in 2004.

Reading Check How has Hungary changed since the end of communism?

The Danube River flows through Budapest, the capital of Hungary. Budapest is a major center of business, transportation, and culture. ▼

Culture Close-Up

The Balkan Nations

All the former communist nations of the Balkan Peninsula have gone through major political changes since 1990. At times, these changes involved warfare and the breakup of nations along ethnic or religious lines. Conflicts and political problems have disrupted the economies of the region.

Yugoslavia Splits After World War I, the country of Yugoslavia was created from six different territories—Serbia, Croatia, Slovenia, Macedonia, Montenegro, and Bosnia (formally known as Bosnia and Herzegovina). Each of these territories formed a republic within Yugoslavia. In each republic, a different ethnic group formed the majority.

After World War II, Yugoslavia's strong leader, Josip Broz Tito, kept the country united. But after Tito died in 1980, the union began to weaken.

Serbia was the largest republic and dominated the national government. Other republics resented Serbia's power. They began to **secede**, or break away, from the union. In 1991, Slovenia and Croatia declared independence. Macedonia broke away later that year, followed by Bosnia a year later.

The new countries combined different ethnic groups. For example, most people in Croatia are Croats, but many Serbs also live there. Conflicts broke out among the different ethnic groups. Some groups tried to gain complete control of an area by attacking and forcing out the other ethnic groups. This policy is called **ethnic cleansing**. Serbs in some areas of Bosnia, for example, killed Muslims or forced them from their homes. Serbs then took control of those areas. Ethnic cleansing is a violation of international law.

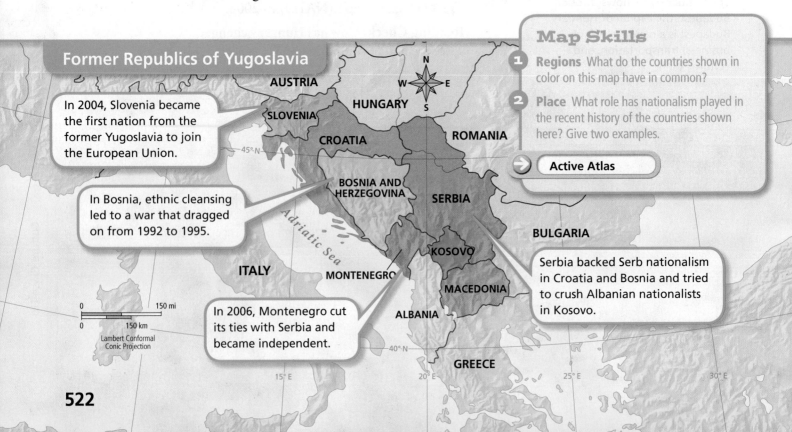

Former Republics of Yugoslavia

In 2004, Slovenia became the first nation from the former Yugoslavia to join the European Union.

In Bosnia, ethnic cleansing led to a war that dragged on from 1992 to 1995.

In 2006, Montenegro cut its ties with Serbia and became independent.

Serbia backed Serb nationalism in Croatia and Bosnia and tried to crush Albanian nationalists in Kosovo.

AUSTRIA
HUNGARY
SLOVENIA
CROATIA
ROMANIA
BOSNIA AND HERZEGOVINA
SERBIA
BULGARIA
KOSOVO
ITALY
MONTENEGRO
MACEDONIA
ALBANIA
GREECE
Adriatic Sea

45° N
40° N
15° E
20° E
25° E
30° E

0   150 mi
0   150 km
Lambert Conformal Conic Projection

Map Skills

1 **Regions** What do the countries shown in color on this map have in common?

2 **Place** What role has nationalism played in the recent history of the countries shown here? Give two examples.

→ Active Atlas

Ethnic Conflict Continues As conflicts arose in the 1990s, the United Nations, the United States, and other European countries worked to negotiate peace between warring groups. The United Nations and NATO sent troops to enforce peace treaties. These efforts have brought an end to large-scale warfare in the region. Still, ethnic violence continues in some areas.

These conflicts disrupted economies in the region. Unstable conditions made trade difficult. In addition, many people were forced from their homes and had to start new lives in different countries.

Some governments in this region are trying to make reforms in order to join the European Union. In general, the governments of the former Yugoslavia have been slow to shift from government control to private enterprise. The standard of living in these countries is low compared to that of many other nations of Eastern Europe.

Other Balkan Nations Yugoslavia was not the only communist nation on the Balkan Peninsula. Romania, Albania, and Bulgaria also became communist after World War II. Unlike Yugoslavia, Romania and Bulgaria were dominated by the Soviet Union. When communism ended in the late 1980s, these countries also shifted to market economies.

Political corruption was a problem in all three countries. Bulgaria and Romania have been accepted as members of the European Union after dealing with many political and economic problems. Albania, by contrast, has not been accepted into the European Union. This country remains poorer and less developed. Still, Albanians continue to work to improve their economy and control crime. Albania also hopes to be accepted into the European Union.

Reading Check **Why did some republics secede from Yugoslavia?**

Albania was the last country in Eastern Europe to give up communism. It is still one of the poorest nations in Europe.

Ukraine, Belarus, and Moldova

Ukraine, Moldova, and Belarus all gained independence from the Soviet Union in 1991. Since then, all have changed in different ways. Ukraine is a democracy. Belarus is the only example of a dictatorship in Europe today. Moldova is a small country with a very weak government that cannot control all of its territory or provide many basic services.

Ukraine has become a working democracy. Traveling ballot boxes allow people in remote villages, like this woman, to vote in their own homes.

potential, *n.,* ability, possibility

Ukraine Ukraine is the second-largest country in Europe in land area and the sixth largest in population. Since gaining independence, Ukraine has created a democratic system of government. Freedom of the press has increased since independence. Ukraine still faces serious political problems such as corruption. However, Ukraine's democracy has also survived some serious conflicts. For example, disputes over the results of the 2004 presidential elections led to widespread protests, but the different parties worked out a peaceful resolution.

Still, Ukraine's economy has not grown rapidly. Corruption and complicated business laws have discouraged foreign companies from investing. Russia is still the largest trading partner for Ukraine.

In addition, efforts to expand agriculture have been difficult. The Soviets had set up collective farms, where land and equipment were shared among many farmers. The Ukrainian government divided this land among the families who lived on each farm. However, small farms without advanced equipment are not profitable. Many people, like Serhiy, are leaving rural areas because they cannot make a living on their small family farm. Still, Ukraine has rich soil. Many believe that this country has the <u>potential</u> to improve its agriculture and achieve more economic success.

Belarus Since 1994, Belarus has been ruled by President Lukashenko. The country's constitution lists many freedoms. In reality, the government limits liberties such as freedom of the press and freedom of religion. People who have opposed Lukashenko have been punished.

Belarus must import many of the raw materials and energy resources that it needs from other countries. The country's main trading partner has been Russia. These close ties create another risk. When Russia's economy has difficulties, the economy of Belarus also suffers. Economic growth has been slow. Almost half of the population lives in poverty.

Moldova Moldova is a tiny country with ties to its neighbor Romania and also to Russia. Many of its people speak Romanian, but there are also large numbers of Ukrainians and Russians.

This protest sign compares President Alexander Lukashenko of Belarus to two notorious dictators of the past: Joseph Stalin of the Soviet Union and Adolf Hitler of Nazi Germany.

About 80 percent of the people of Moldova live below the poverty line. Many poor peasants in rural villages, like this boy, have barely enough to survive.

Moldova continues to face political turmoil, economic challenges, and corruption.

Most of the Russians and Ukrainians live in a region called Transdniestria. This region declared its independence in 1990. Moldova fought a war to keep the region from seceding. The leaders of Transdniestria and Moldova agreed to stop fighting, but they could not find a solution. Moldova still claims the territory, but it does not control the area. Transdniestria still claims independence. Other governments have accused Transdniestria of being a center for smuggling, or illegal trade.

Moldova has also had slow economic growth. Thousands of people have left the country to look for jobs in Romania. Many Moldovans must live on the money that their relatives abroad send back to them. Like Belarus, Moldova is one of the poorest countries in Europe. The government faces many serious political and economic challenges.

Reading Check What is one challenge faced by Moldova?

myWorld Activity
Press Conference

Section 2 Assessment

Essential Question

How can you measure success?

Key Terms

1. Use the terms *secede* and *ethnic cleansing* to describe the breakup of Yugoslavia.

2. What is capital?

Key Ideas

3. What political and economic changes have taken place in Poland and the Baltic nations since the end of communism?

4. What is one reason that conflict broke out in the Balkans in the 1990s?

5. Which country is more democratic, Ukraine or Belarus? Explain your answer.

Think Critically

6. **Identify Cause and Effect** How could joining the European Union improve a country's economy?

7. **Draw Inferences** Why were many Polish citizens able to become entrepreneurs in the 1990s?

8. Give an example of one country in Eastern Europe that has been successful in recent years. Why do you think this country has been successful? Go to your Student Journal to record your answer.

Ethnic Conflict in Bosnia

IN Indiana

6.1.21 Differentiate between fact and interpretation in historical accounts and explain historical passages.

6.1.23 Identify issues related to an event in Europe or the Americas and give arguments for and against that issue.

Bosnian Muslims, Serbs, and Croats had lived in peace for years. But when Bosnia declared independence in 1992, many Bosnian Serbs felt threatened. They did not want to live in a Muslim-led country. In fact, some Serbs had long resented their Muslim neighbors. This distrust went back to Muslim Turks' conquest of Serbia in the late 1300s. Determined to create a unified Serbian nation, Bosnian Serbs went to war. In the following sources, the former president of Serbia calls for ethnic unity, and a Bosnian Muslim soldier explains his views on Bosnia and why he chose to fight.

▲ This newspaper was found in the streets of war-torn Bosnia.

Slobodan Milosevic (mee LOH sheh vich), leader of Serbia, 1989–1997, and leader of Yugoslavia, 1997–2000 ▼

Stop at each circled letter on the right to think about the text. Then answer the question with the same letter on the left.

Ⓐ Identify Main Ideas What "greatest evil" is Milosevic talking about?

Ⓑ Draw Inferences Who might Milosevic be referring to here as "those who would take away our dignity"?

Ⓒ Draw Conclusions What do you think Milosevic wanted Serbs to do?

sap, *v.*, to drain, reduce

coalition, *n.*, alliance, groups working together

For a Unified Serbian People

❝ Serbia and the Serbian people are faced with one of the
Ⓐ greatest evils of their history: the challenge of disunity and internal conflict. This evil, which has more than once caused so much damage and claimed so many victims, more than once <u>sapped</u> our strength, has always come hand in hand with
Ⓑ those who would take away our dignity. . . . All who love Serbia
Ⓒ dare not ignore this fact, especially at a time when we are confronted by the . . . forces in the anti-Serbian <u>coalition</u> which threaten the people's rights and freedoms. ❞

Slobodan Milosevic, quoted in "The Fall of Yugoslavia"

Stop at each circled letter on the right to think about the text. Then answer the question with the same letter on the left.

D **Identify Evidence** Why did Tica (TEE tsuh) think there was a "terrible misunderstanding"?

E **Summarize** Why did Tica decide to fight?

F **Compare and Contrast** How does Tica compare Serbian plans for Bosnia with life in the United States?

shell, *v.,* to bomb, fire upon

canton, *n.,* small territory

For a Diverse Bosnia

66 Bosnia is a mixed country. There has always been some kind of tolerance, in this town anyway. In the first days of this war, I thought there was some

D terrible misunderstanding. When they started shelling my city, I understood only one thing: someone wants to destroy my life, take my job, kill my parents, wreck my apartment. When I started

E fighting, it was just to defend my family. . . . My country is Bosnia, with all three peoples in it. I call myself a Bosnian, and I know what that means. But the Serbs and Croats want ethnic cantons, racially pure. Who . . . wants to live in an ethnic canton?

F I don't. It would be like having California for the whites and Chicago for the blacks, instead of America. It's completely mad. 99

Emir Tica, quoted in *Seasons in Hell: Understanding Bosnia's War*

During the ethnic conflict in Bosnia, heavy shelling left many people homeless. ▼

Analyze the Documents

1. **Compare Viewpoints** How are the views of Milosevic and Tica in direct conflict?

2. **Writing Task** Nationalism can be a positive or negative force. Which role did it play in Bosnia? Write a paragraph explaining your thinking.

Chapter Assessment

Key Terms and Ideas

1. **Recall** Why is **mechanized farming** common on the North European Plain?

2. **Compare and Contrast** Why can the climate differ on different sides of a mountain range?

3. **Explain** How have resources influenced industry in Eastern Europe?

4. **Recall** What are the main traditional religions in Eastern Europe?

5. **Explain** How has Poland's economy been successful since the breakup of the Soviet Union?

6. **Compare and Contrast** Did the Czech Republic or Slovakia have faster economic growth after the breakup of the Soviet Union and the end of communism? Why?

7. **Explain** Why did many Balkan states **secede** from Yugoslavia?

Think Critically

8. **Make Inferences** Why might agriculture on the Hungarian Plain and the North European Plain be similar? Use the maps in this section to answer the question.

9. **Draw Conclusions** What long-term effect might the end of communist policies toward religion have on religious practices in Eastern Europe?

10. **Solve Problems** What action did the government of Slovakia take to improve its economy?

11. **Core Concepts: People's Impact on the Environment** What is one economic activity that has resulted in damage to the environment in this region?

Places to Know

For each place, write the letter from the map that shows its location.

12. **Bosnia and Herzegovina**

13. **Poland**

14. **Ukraine**

15. **Balkan Mountains**

16. **Baltic Sea**

17. **Black Sea**

18. **Estimate** Using the scale bar, estimate the distance from the Black Sea to the Baltic Sea.

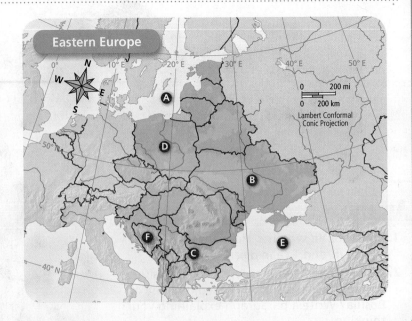

Eastern Europe

Self-Test
my worldgeography.com

Essential Question

myWorld Chapter Activity

Open for Business You work at a business that is hoping to open a new branch in Eastern Europe. Evaluate information about different countries, and choose the country that would offer the best location for your business.

21st Century Learning

Evaluating Web Sites

Search for three different Web sites that provide information on nuclear energy. What benefits and drawbacks does each site give for nuclear energy? Find the name of the organization that created each site. Can you find the goals of this organization? Do the goals of the organization influence the information that is presented on the site?

Document-Based Questions

Success Tracker™
Online at myworldgeography.com

Use your knowledge of Eastern Europe and Documents A and B to answer Questions 1–3 below.

Document A

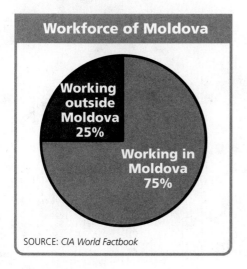

Workforce of Moldova

Working outside Moldova 25%

Working in Moldova 75%

SOURCE: *CIA World Factbook*

1. According to the graph, what percentage of Moldovan workers had jobs in other countries?

A 15 percent

B 20 percent

C 25 percent

D 30 percent

Document B

" Many specialists, doctors, go to work abroad. They go where they are paid better, but for the country, this is not a solution."

—Grigore,
a student in Moldova

2. According to Document B, why do some people go abroad to work?

A They do not like Moldova's government.

B They cannot find jobs in Moldova.

C They think the weather in Moldova is too cold.

D They earn more money if they work abroad.

3. **Writing Task** What do you think the speaker in Document B meant when he said "for the country, this is not a solution"? Write a paragraph explaining both the benefits and drawbacks to Moldova of so many people leaving the country to find jobs.

Chapter 12

Russia

Essential Question

What should governments do?

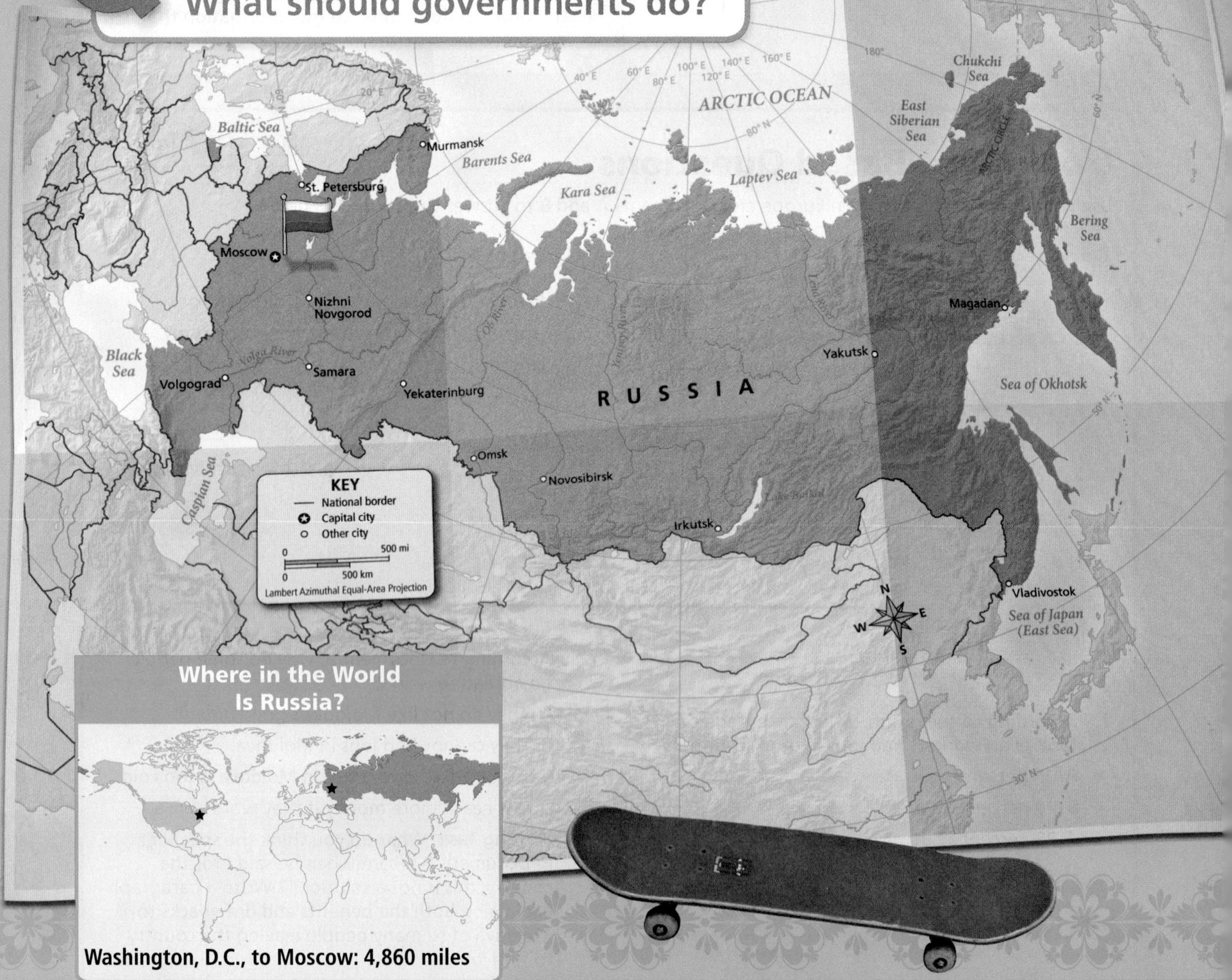

Baltic Sea
Murmansk
Barents Sea
St. Petersburg
Kara Sea
Laptev Sea
ARCTIC OCEAN
East Siberian Sea
Chukchi Sea
Bering Sea
ARCTIC CIRCLE
Moscow
Nizhni Novgorod
Black Sea
Volga River
Samara
Volgograd
Yekaterinburg
Ob River
Yenisey River
Lena River
RUSSIA
Yakutsk
Magadan
Sea of Okhotsk
Omsk
Novosibirsk
Caspian Sea
Lake Baikal
Irkutsk
Vladivostok
Sea of Japan (East Sea)
40° E
60° E
80° E
100° E
120° E
140° E
160° E
180°
20° E
80° N
60° N
50° N
30° N
N
E
S
W
KEY
National border
Capital city
Other city
0
500 mi
0
500 km
Lambert Azimuthal Equal-Area Projection

Where in the World Is Russia?

Washington, D.C., to Moscow: 4,860 miles

my Story

Boris's Bigspin

Explore the Essential Question
- at my **worldgeography.com**
- using the **myWorld Chapter Activity**
- with the **Student Journal**

In this section, you'll read about Boris, a young skateboarder living in Moscow. What does Boris's story tell you about life in Russia today?

Story by Dmitry Saltykovskiy for myWorld Online

It's a sunny day in Moscow, and people hurry past a huge monument to the German philosopher Karl Marx. The 200-ton block of stone bears the inscription "Workers of the world, unite," a quote from Marx that became famous among communist workers. When the statue was unveiled in 1961, Russia was a communist nation, and Marx was an honored figure. Today, Russia is a very different place, and the monument to Marx is better known as a fun place for skateboarders to try tricks like the ollie or the bigspin.

Boris, a 15-year-old Russian skateboarder, loves to try jumps off of the step at the base of the monument. When the Soviet Union collapsed in 1991, Boris had not yet been born. He has never lived under communism, but he still has clear memories of hard times in Russia.

"I was born in troubled times," Boris says. "After the Soviet Union fell, people were trying to make money. It was a dangerous period with lots of crime and fighting between businesses. My father disappeared around that time. I was just four years old. He owned his own business, and he was kidnapped. We never saw him again. I am sad that I can't really remember what he looked like now."

Boris talks with friends after school.

Boris on a Moscow city street

Boris in front of a monument to Karl Marx

Boris goes everywhere by skateboard, including the skate park. At the indoor skate park, skaters ride curved ramps, and the clatter of decks hitting the floor fills the air.

During the Soviet era, the sport of skateboarding did not exist. Boris is one of the first young Russians to take part in paid skateboard competitions. He even has a sponsorship by a major sports brand—something else that's new in Russia.

"There was no skateboarding during Soviet times—things have changed so much since then. In those days, people couldn't travel at all outside the Soviet Union. Today, I am able to travel all over the world to participate in competitions."

"My mom was really proud when I started winning competitions," Boris recalls. "She was amazed when I managed to get a sponsorship deal. It was a really nice moment for me when I could use some of my prize money to make her birthday special."

Boris says that his mother and stepfather are proud of his skateboarding, although they worry about him being injured. They also hope that he will consider a professional career someday. "Moscow is growing so quickly that I've become interested in real estate!" Boris laughs.

532

Boris at the skate park in Moscow

Boris shoots basketball at the park.

Working on the computer at home

Following the 2008 Russian invasion of Georgia, Boris decided to change his last name. Georgia had once been part of the Soviet Union, but it declared its independence in 1991. Since then, relations have been tense between Russia and Georgia.

"My father was half Georgian, and he had a very un-Russian sounding last name. With all the problems between our two countries, my mom decided that we should change our name. I was really sad because I felt like I was giving away a piece of my father, but really we had no choice. Russians have become quite anti-Georgian and my name marked me as different."

The tension between Russia and Georgia also means that Boris has been unable to visit family in Georgia. "I used to go there every summer. It was really nice to get out of Moscow when the weather was hot. Now there are no airplane flights."

The wheels of Boris's deck leave the ground, and then he rolls off to the park for a game of basketball. For Boris, his skateboard is not only the best way to get around Moscow, but also a ticket to a promising future in the new Russia.

Meet the Journalist

Name Dmitry Saltykovskiy
Favorite Moment Seeing Boris in action at the skate park

→ **myStory Online**

Skateboard along with Boris as he shows you life in his city.

IN Indiana

6.3.1 Understand the countries and capitals of Europe and the Americas.

6.3.3 Describe and compare major physical characteristics of regions in Europe and the Americas.

6.3.5 Give examples and describe the formation of river deltas, mountains

and bodies of water in Europe and the Americas.

6.3.8 Identify major biomes of Europe and the Americas and explain how these are influenced by climate.

6.3.12 Compare the distribution and evaluate the importance of natural resources in Europe and the Americas.

Key Terms • Siberia • Ural Mountains • Lake Baikal • steppes
• Kamchatka Peninsula • permafrost

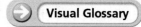
Visual Glossary

🌐 **Reading Skill: Label an Outline Map** Take notes using the outline map in your journal.

A teen in front of the Kremlin in Moscow, Russia's capital city

Physical Features

Today, a plane flight from one end of Russia to the other takes 11 hours. It took the early explorers more than a year to cross Russia's dense forests, wide plains, and high mountains as they made their way east to the Pacific Ocean. Most of the journey involved crossing **Siberia,** or the Asian part of Russia, including the vast West Siberian Plain.

Russia is the world's largest country in area. It has 11 time zones. Since there are a total of 24 one-hour time zones on Earth, this means that Russia stretches almost halfway around the world.

Russia: Physical

ARCTIC OCEAN

ARCTIC CIRCLE

Baltic Sea

Barents
Sea

Kola
Peninsula

Kara
Sea

Chukchi
Sea

Bering
Sea

East
Siberian
Sea

Laptev
Sea

RUSSIA

Russian
Plain

Cherskiy Range

Kamchatka
Peninsula

Central
Siberian
Plateau

Lena River

Sea of
Okhotsk

Sakhalin
Island

Kuril Islands

PACIFIC
OCEAN

West
Siberian
Plain

URAL MOUNTAINS

Yenisey River

Ob River

S I B E R I A

Volga River

Lake
Baikal

Black Sea

Mount Elbrus
18,510ft (5,642m)

CAUCASUS MTS.

Caspian Sea

Sea of
Japan
(East Sea)

50° E

60° E

70° E

80° E

90° E

100° E

110° E

120° E

130° E

80° N

70° N

60° N

50° N

40° N

30° N

KEY
Elevation

Feet	Meters
6,000	1,829
3,000	914
1,000	305
500	152
Sea level	Sea level

0   600 mi
0   600 km

Lambert Conformal Conic Projection

N
W   E
S

Map Skills

1   **Place**   In which mountain range is Mount Elbrus?

2   **Region**   Which ocean lies north of Russia?

3   **Places to Know!**
Label the following places on the outline map in your Student Journal: Siberia, Kamchatka Peninsula, Ural Mountains, Kuril Islands, Lake Baikal.

→ Active Atlas

Russia spreads across two continents, Europe and Asia. The dividing line runs along the low peaks of the **Ural Mountains,** a range that separates European Russia from Asian Russia. European Russia is located east of Latvia, Lithuania, Estonia, Belarus, and Ukraine. Asian Russia lies immediately north of China, Mongolia, and Kazakhstan.

A Vast Land

Russia has many different kinds of landforms and waterways. The Russian Plain covers much of European Russia.

It stretches east to the Ural Mountains. South of the Russian Plain are the Caucasus Mountains. These mountains run east-west between the Caspian Sea and the Black Sea. They form the southern border between European Russia and Asia.

East of the Urals is the broad West Siberian Plain. Farther east are central and eastern Siberia. This huge area consists of rugged plateaus framed by high mountains on the east and south.

myworldgeography.com | Active Atlas

spectacular, *adj.,* striking or excellent

Many of these <u>spectacular</u> mountains are volcanic in origin. Some are covered by glaciers year-round.

European Russia's longest river, the Volga, flows into the Caspian Sea. This river is famous in the songs and stories of the Russian people. Russia's European rivers also include the Don, which flows into the Black Sea, and the Dvina, which flows north to an arm of the Arctic Ocean.

In Siberia, there are many other large rivers that flow north to the Arctic Ocean. These include Russia's longest, the Yenisey, as well as the Ob and Lena. Another important Siberian river is called the Ankara. Far to the east is the mighty Amur River, which forms the border between Russia and China.

Despite its many rivers, canals, and long coastlines, Russia lacks many good harbors and ports. In European Russia, usable ports include St. Petersburg, Kaliningrad, Novorossiysk, and Sochi. In addition, there are ports in Murmansk in the far north on the Arctic Ocean and Vladivostok on the Pacific coast.

Russia: Climate

ARCTIC OCEAN

Bering Sea

East Siberian Sea

Barents Sea

KEY
- Tundra
- Subarctic
- Continental cool summer
- Continental warm summer
- Humid subtropical
- Semiarid

0   600 mi

0   600 km

Lambert Conformal Conic Projection

RUSSIA

Sea of Okhotsk

PACIFIC OCEAN

Caspian Sea

Sea of Japan (East Sea)

Semiarid

Continental, cool summer

Subarctic

Map Skills

1 **Location** Along which body of water does Russia's southernmost semiarid region lie?

2 **Region** How much of Russia's land is subarctic?

Active Atlas

Russia, however, does have many large lakes and seas. Perhaps the most famous is **Lake Baikal** in the heart of Siberia. More than one mile deep, Lake Baikal holds about 20 percent of Earth's fresh water—more than all of the North American Great Lakes combined. Baikal is also home to plants and animals found nowhere else. Due to the threat of pollution from factories located along its shores, Lake Baikal was the birthplace of Russia's environmental movement.

Reading Check Which landform separates European Russia from Asian Russia?

Climate and Vegetation

Vast stretches of Russian lands have a subarctic climate because they lie near the Arctic Circle. North of this area is the tundra climate region, a cold, dry, treeless area covered in snow for most of the year. European Russia in the southwest has a continental climate. In cities such as Moscow and St. Petersburg, people experience long, cold winters and warm summers. Parts of southern Russia have a semiarid, or moderately dry, climate.

Russia's natural vegetation is closely tied to its climate. In the cool continental climate north of Moscow, thick coniferous forests grow. South of Moscow are temperate forests. To the east, vast areas of grasslands called **steppes** cover the land. Here, mild, moist summers and rich soils make good farmland.

In Siberia, weather and climate are more extreme than in European Russia. Here, winters are long and cold. Cold, dry conditions in parts of Siberia account for a type of low-lying vegetation called tundra. Tundra covers about one tenth of Russia and stretches all the way from the Finnish border east to the **Kamchatka Peninsula.** This peninsula in the Russian Far East is famous for its 160 volcanoes, 29 of which are active.

Near Yakutsk, Siberia, a family hauls water that they took from a hole in the ice on a local lake.

South of the tundra is the Russian taiga, a land of dense coniferous forests. The Russian taiga covers more than four million square miles (10 million square kilometers). One of the many challenges for human settlement in northern Russia is **permafrost**. This is permanently frozen soil that often lies beneath the tundra and the taiga. It makes construction of roads, railroads, and housing difficult.

Vegetation in Russia's Far East region differs from that of the rest of the country. Because this area is close to the ocean and is located farther to the south, it is warmer and has vegetation similar to the nearby Koreas. Its animals include the Amur tiger, the world's largest cat. The eastern edge of Russia features the Kuril Islands and the Kamchatka Peninsula.

Reading Check Where in Russia are there active volcanoes?

myWorld Activity
Roam Across Russia

Russia's Resources

Russia has rich mineral and energy resources, especially in Siberia. Its resources include timber, fish, and hydroelectric power. About one third of all of Earth's coal is located in Siberia. In spite of extremes of climate and the country's massive size, vast reserves of oil and gas in West Siberia have made Russia wealthy in recent years.

Russia also has metal ores such as iron, gold, cobalt, nickel, and platinum ore. It sells these valuable minerals to many different buyers around the world for industrial use.

It can be difficult to mine Russia's rich natural resources because they are so hard to reach. Long distances and harsh climates separate resources from processing plants and markets.

Railroad Mileage	
Country	Total Mileage
Russia	
Germany	
France	
Poland	
Italy	
Spain	

SOURCE: *CIA World Factbook*

5,000 miles

Chart Skills

Why might there be more miles of railroad tracks in Russia than in other European nations?

➜ **Data Discovery**

The Trans-Siberian Railroad runs through a snowy Russian landscape.

538

This makes it important for Russia to build and <u>maintain</u> an extensive transportation system to move products to markets. The poor quality of roads can make transport difficult. Truck drivers often find it easier to drive on frozen rivers and lakes than on Russian roads.

Many of Russia's great rivers are navigable, or passable, for only a few months of the year because they are usually blocked by ice. Underground pipelines generally transport Russia's huge reserves of oil and natural gas. An extensive railroad network moves goods to consumers.

Large-scale economic development in Siberia began only after the Trans-Siberian Railroad was completed in 1905. This famous railroad connects the city of Moscow in the west with Vladivostok on the Pacific. It also connects with rail lines running to Mongolia and China. It was built to help Russians settle the open lands of Siberia, to develop industrial centers, and to transport troops to the Pacific to protect Russia against threats of invasion by Japan and China.

Reading Check Name two challenges Russia faces in developing its economy.

maintain, *v.,* to keep in good condition

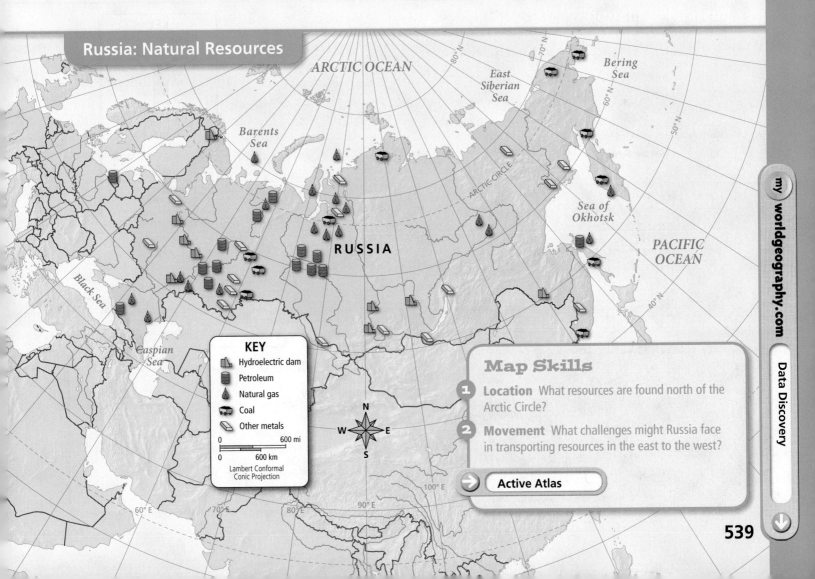

Russia: Natural Resources

ARCTIC OCEAN

Barents Sea

East Siberian Sea

Bering Sea

ARCTIC CIRCLE

Sea of Okhotsk

PACIFIC OCEAN

RUSSIA

Black Sea

Caspian Sea

KEY

Hydroelectric dam
Petroleum
Natural gas
Coal
Other metals

0   600 mi
0   600 km

Lambert Conformal
Conic Projection

N
W   E
S

Map Skills

1 **Location** What resources are found north of the Arctic Circle?

2 **Movement** What challenges might Russia face in transporting resources in the east to the west?

Active Atlas

my **worldgeography**.com

Data Discovery

539

The People of Russia

Russia has a population of about 140 million people. Most live in the European part of the country. Russia's most densely settled areas also have the best climates and soils for agriculture. In contrast, the huge landmass of Siberia is sparsely populated, with around 20 people per square mile.

The largest cities are also located in the west, in European Russia. Moscow, the capital, is the largest metropolitan area in Russia, with more than 10 million people.

St. Petersburg, Russia's second largest city, is located on the Baltic Sea. It was called Leningrad during the Soviet era. St. Petersburg was founded by Russia's tsar, or emperor, Peter the Great, to rival the capitals of Europe.

Russia's huge population consists of many diverse ethnic groups with many languages and customs. The first Russians were East Slavs, who migrated into the area from east-central Europe. Today, about 80 percent of the population are Russian-speaking Slavs.

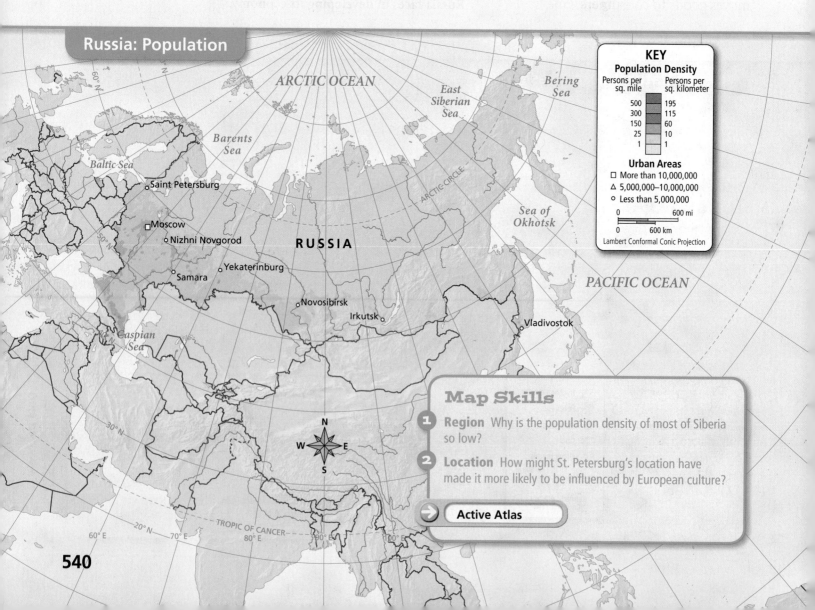

Russia: Population

KEY

Population Density

Persons per sq. mile	Persons per sq. kilometer
500	195
300	115
150	60
25	10
1	1

Urban Areas
□ More than 10,000,000
△ 5,000,000–10,000,000
○ Less than 5,000,000

0 — 600 mi
0 — 600 km
Lambert Conformal Conic Projection

Map Skills

1 Region Why is the population density of most of Siberia so low?

2 Location How might St. Petersburg's location have made it more likely to be influenced by European culture?

Active Atlas

540

In Moscow, Boris (right) joins his friends to talk about sports and school. Boris participates in skateboarding competitions all over the world.

Language Lesson

This family lives in a village near Siberia's Lake Baikal. They belong to the minority Buryat nationality but also speak Russian.

Traditionally, the Slavic people who form most of the population were Russian Orthodox Christians. However, the communist rulers of the Soviet Union <u>pursued</u> a policy of discouraging religion. Today, after the collapse of the Soviet Union, more and more Russians attend Orthodox churches. Religious observance has also increased for Russia's many Muslims, Protestants, Jews, and Buddhists.

Along with Slavic Russians, there are at least 100 other ethnic and nationality groups in Russia. Each has a distinctive culture, language, and religion. Since Russian-speaking Slavs have dominated the nation for such a long time, many of these minority groups struggle to maintain their unique identities.

pursue, *v.,* to follow

Reading Check Who were the first Russians?

Section **1** Assessment

? Essential Question

Key Terms

1. Use each of the following key terms in a complete sentence: Siberia, Ural Mountains, Lake Baikal, steppes, Kamchatka Peninsula, permafrost

Key Ideas

2. What challenges does climate present for human settlement in Russia?

3. Where are most of Russia's mineral resources found?

4. Why does the Far East region of Russia have a milder climate than most of the rest of the country?

Think Critically

5. **Identify Evidence** What facts could you use to explain why Siberia has a low population density?

6. **Solve Problems** What might minority groups do to preserve their identity in a country whose population is mostly ethnic Russian?

What should governments do?

7. Look at the railroad mileage chart in this section. The Russian government paid the cost of building the Trans-Siberian Railroad. Why might governments invest in transportation systems? Go to your Student Journal to record your answer.

my worldgeography.com Language Lesson

Section 2
History of Russia

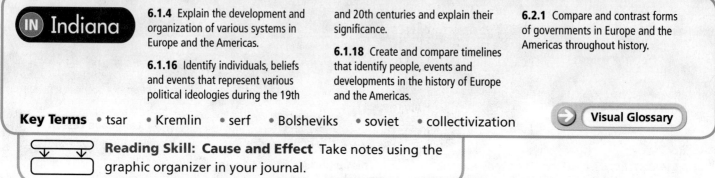

IN Indiana

6.1.4 Explain the development and organization of various systems in Europe and the Americas.

6.1.16 Identify individuals, beliefs and events that represent various political ideologies during the 19th

and 20th centuries and explain their significance.

6.1.18 Create and compare timelines that identify people, events and developments in the history of Europe and the Americas.

6.2.1 Compare and contrast forms of governments in Europe and the Americas throughout history.

Visual Glossary

Key Terms • tsar • Kremlin • serf • Bolsheviks • soviet • collectivization

Reading Skill: Cause and Effect Take notes using the graphic organizer in your journal.

Russia's history spans many centuries. It is a rich story of invaders, ruthless leaders, and dramatic change that continues today.

Russia Emerges

Modern Russians are descended from East Slavs who migrated from Poland and Ukraine into western Russia in the 400s and 500s. They encountered invading Goths from Germany, along with Huns, Avars, Magyars, and Khazars from Asia.

The East Slavs The East Slavs were energetic traders. They founded trading posts along rivers that became the cities of Kiev and Novgorod. By the 800s, Scandinavian raiders and merchants, called Vikings, dominated Novgorod, Kiev, and other trading centers. They soon merged with the Slavic population.

Early Russia The Scythians, who arrived on the steppes before the East Slavs, were skilled goldsmiths. ▼

Kievan Rus Period The Viking prince Rurik and his allies invade Kiev in this medieval Russian drawing. ▶

East Slav						
200	300	400	500	600	700	800

542

The role of Vikings in Russian history remains uncertain. Russia's *Primary Chronicle* claims that Slav and Finnish tribes invited a Viking of the Rus tribe to rule them. Some later scholars claimed that "Rus" refers to a Slav, not Viking, tribe. In any case, it was the Rus who gave their name to the first known East Slavic state: the Kievan Rus.

The Kievan Rus Forms Located in present-day Ukraine, Kiev became the region's economic and cultural center. Kiev's early rulers grew rich from trade and united the Slavic tribes. Under Vladimir, the Kievan Rus formed close ties with the Byzantine empire around the year 1000.

Vladimir adopted the Byzantines' Eastern Orthodox Christianity. He converted all of Kiev in a mass ceremony. Byzantine culture influenced Russian language, art, and music as well as the architectural style of Russian churches.

Gradually, many tribal leaders became princes. Princes were granted large areas of land, or appanages. They ruled these appanages and passed them on to family members. Competition between princes in the Kievan Rus was fierce. Some historians believe this rivalry weakened the state and invited a Mongol invasion.

In 1240, Mongol armies from Central Asia, known as the Golden Horde, took Kiev. The Kievan Rus collapsed. Russian princes now had to accept the authority of Mongol khans, or rulers.

As Kiev declined, the city of Moscow began to grow in importance. Its princes ruled an area known as Muscovy. It was a key trading center, and the Mongol khans favored its rulers. In 1328, the head of the Eastern Orthodox Church moved to Moscow, making the city even more important.

Reading Check What caused the fall of the Kievan Rus?

Mongol Period Tamerlane, a Turkic chief, challenged Mongol rule in Russia in the 1300s. ▼

Muscovy Period Ivan IV, or Ivan the Terrible, was the first Russian ruler to be crowned tsar. ▶

1156 Building begins at the Kremlin.

Kievan Rus		Mongol Rule		Muscovy
900 ● 1000	1100 ● ●	1200	1300	1400	1500

988 Prince Vladimir converts to Christianity.

1147 Moscow is founded.

Timeline

543

Imperial Russia

Prince Ivan III of Muscovy overthrew the Golden Horde by 1480. He set about establishing a Russian state to rival those of Europe. He began by calling himself **tsar,** or emperor, a term derived from *Caesar,* the title of the Roman emperors.

The Rise of the Tsars

Ivan III was eager to show Russia's greatness to the world. He invited European architects to design the **Kremlin,** a grand complex of palaces, state offices, and churches in Moscow.

The reign of tsar Boris Godunov was a time of political unrest and lawlessness. People left the farms for cities. Food shortages resulted. Godunov forced people to work the land by beginning the practice of serfdom. A **serf** is a peasant who is legally bound to live and work on land owned by his or her lord.

The Romanov Dynasty

In 1613, an assembly elected a new tsar, Michael Romanov, the 16-year-old son of an influential noble. The Romanovs ruled Russia for the next 300 years.

The first great Romanov tsar, Peter the Great, dreamed of a Russia to rival European nations. As an absolute monarch, he modernized and westernized Russia, importing western ideas and technologies.

Catherine II, known as Catherine the Great, took power in 1762. She ruled as an "enlightened despot," or wise ruler. Catherine transformed the new capital, St. Petersburg, into a cultural center. By the end of her rule in 1796, Catherine had greatly expanded Russia. She added some 200,000 square miles through wars, including much of Ukraine and parts of Poland.

Closer Look   *Westernization of Russia*

Peter the Great used force in his efforts to westernize Russia. His reforms called for changes to very old customs. Many Russians resented the tsar's autocratic, or unlimited, power. Still, his reforms improved life in Russia greatly. Peter set up academies of science, mathematics, and engineering. He also increased trade with Europe. This brought new technologies to Russia.

THINK CRITICALLY Why might Russians have resented westernization by force?

Peter the Great
(1682–1725)

Peter insisted that Russian nobles shave their beards to follow the European custom of being clean-shaven. ▶

544

In spite of their reforms, neither Peter the Great nor Catherine the Great helped the serfs, who made up most of the population. To maintain power, the tsars needed the support of nobles. Nobles lived off of the work of the serfs, so they preferred to keep them in <u>servitude.</u>

The Imperial Age Ends In spite of westernization, Russia lagged behind Western Europe in many ways. While many European nations moved toward democracy in the 1800s, Russia's tsars clung to absolute monarchy. Where much of Europe began to industrialize, Russia's economy remained dependent on agriculture and serf labor.

Russia lost the Crimean War to Britain, Turkey, and France in 1856. This loss shocked the nation. In addition to the loss of life and land, the war revealed the poor state of the Russian army. Soldiers used outdated equipment, and most marched in their own ragged clothing. Many were escaped serfs who had joined the army hoping for liberty.

Russia's leaders aimed to modernize. Support grew for emancipation, or freeing, of the serfs. Tsar Alexander II freed them in 1861, but made them pay nobles for land. Peasants did not gain economic freedom and remained desperately poor.

Some Russian reformers pushed for greater democracy. Meanwhile, in 1905, violent worker unrest scared Russia's leaders. Tsar Nicholas II responded with the October Manifesto. This charter granted civil rights and limited democracy. Russian troops crushed the worker revolts, but the peace was short-lived.

Reading Check **Why didn't early Russian tsars free the serfs?**

servitude, *n.,* a legal requirement to work for another

Peter hired Italian architects to design his new capital, St. Petersburg, in a European style. ▼

Catherine the Great (1762–1796)

Russian artists used European techniques to make fine decorative objects such as this china vase. ▼

myWorld Activity
Making a Living
Timeline

Communist Russia

Russia's monarchy collapsed during World War I. The war put a huge burden on Russia. Because peasants had to leave farms to fight in the army, food production fell dangerously. Inflation pushed prices out of reach of workers. Nicholas II increased his powers and tried to prevent unrest.

However, Russia's parliament forced Nicholas II to give up the throne in March, 1917. In October of 1917, Vladimir Lenin and the Bolsheviks took power. The **Bolsheviks** were a Russian political group that called for worker control. The Bolsheviks killed Nicholas and his family in 1918. After 300 years, the Romanov dynasty had come to an end.

The Bolshevik takeover is known as the Russian Revolution. The Bolksheviks put in place a new political and social system called communism.

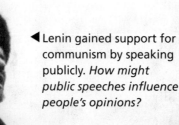

◄ Lenin gained support for communism by speaking publicly. *How might public speeches influence people's opinions?*

Culture Close-Up

What Is Communism? Lenin based the Bolshevik government on his understanding of the works of Karl Marx, a German philosopher from the 1800s. Marx wrote during the Industrial Revolution. He wanted to ease the widespread poverty that had developed among workers.

Marx thought that the people as a whole, not individuals, should own workplaces. In this way, everyone would share the goods and services produced. Marx believed that the working class, or people who work for a living, should control both the government and the economy as a group. The working class would in time no longer be a group separate from the owners. Instead, a classless, or communist, society would develop.

Lenin and the Bolsheviks used Marx's arguments before the revolution to try to gain support in **soviets,** or workers' councils. Lenin claimed that the Bolsheviks spoke for the working class.

After the revolution, the Bolsheviks renamed themselves the Communist Party. Lenin put the government and the economy under Communist Party control. The Communists fought a civil war in Russia. They crushed their opponents.

Repression and Domination In 1922, Russia united with other parts of the former Russian Empire to form the Soviet Union.

After Lenin died in 1924, Josef Stalin took control of the party and government. He issued Five-Year Plans pushing for the development of heavy industry and rapid collectivization of agriculture.

Collectivization is a shift of control from an individual or company to a group called a collective.

These policies forced many peasants to become tenants on their land, with the state acting as landlord. Stalin used brutal tactics to enforce his policies and maintain power. He crushed all opposition and sent millions into prisons and labor camps. Millions died there.

The horrible famine of 1932–1933 showed how disastrous collectivization could be. Collectives in Ukraine and the Caucasus region were forced to send all their grain to Russia. This left none for the Ukrainians. More than six million people died. Still, one of Stalin's officers called the famine a great success. He said it showed the peasants "who is the master. It cost millions of lives, but the collective farm system is here to stay."

Cold War Russia The Soviet Union worked with Western powers to defeat Germany during World War II. After the war, however, relations with the West, particularly the United States, chilled.

Soviet troops had occupied Eastern Europe. They opposed democracy and set up pro-Soviet communist governments. This brought tension with the United States and other Western nations.

The West aimed for containment, an effort to contain, or to stop the spread of, communism throughout the world. The United States and the Soviet Union vied for economic, political, and cultural power around the world. This rivalry, which stopped short of direct, armed conflict, was called the Cold War.

Reading Check How did Stalin deal with opposition?

Understanding Communism

The two basic elements of communism are a centralized, one-party government and government economic control. The government made all decisions about where people should live and work. People had to obey the government completely. *Does government control ensure the loyalty of the people? Explain why or why not.*

The figures in this Soviet monument carry a hammer and a sickle, the symbols of the Soviet Union. ▶

SOVIET GOVERNMENT

- Controlled by the Communist Party
- Centrally-planned economy
- The state owns all land, businesses, and housing.
- The state provides healthcare, childcare, and education.

COMMUNIST PARTY

Central Committee
Top members of the Communist Party who elect the Politburo and general secretary

Politburo
The "Political Bureau" of the Communist Party, it set government policies.

General Secretary
The leader of the Communist Party and Politburo and head of the government

Communism to Nationalism

Stalin's successor, Nikita Khrushchev, <u>denounced</u> Stalin's brutal tactics. Still, the Communist Party kept tight control.

denounce, *v.,* to reject publicly

The Communist System Weakens The communist system slowly weakened. To compete in the Cold War, the government focused on building weapons and military vehicles. The government failed to invest in new technologies.

Meanwhile, state ownership gave farmers little reason to grow more food. As a result, the Soviet Union went into debt to import food and high-technology goods. The Soviet economy could not meet its people's wish for better living standards.

During the 1980s, the Soviet Union fought a failed war to support a communist government in Afghanistan. As with the Crimean War, the lost war in Afghanistan brought calls for reform.

Openness and Restructuring Real reform in the Soviet Union began with Mikhail Gorbachev. After he came to power in 1985, he introduced two new policies, glasnost and perestroika. Glasnost, or "openness," meant greater freedom of speech and media freedom.

Glasnost destroyed the myth that people were living well under communism. It highlighted failures in the country's long war in Afghanistan. Glasnost also forced the government to reveal details about the 1986 Chernobyl nuclear accident. This accident caused serious health problems and environmental damage.

Perestroika, or "restructuring," reduced government control over the economy and created freer markets. Also, for the first time, the government allowed non-communist parties to form.

The Collapse Comes The Soviet Union eased its control over Eastern Europe. People in non-Russian parts of the Soviet Union began to seek independence.

Some top Communist Party officials resisted these changes. In August 1991, Soviet security officials seized power.

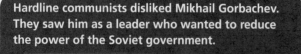

Hardline communists disliked Mikhail Gorbachev. They saw him as a leader who wanted to reduce the power of the Soviet government.

Boris Yeltsin raises his fist in triumph after the 1991 coup. Yeltsin's actions broke the power of the Communists and led to the fall of the Soviet Union.

Within three days, supporters of democracy forced the Soviet officials to back down. At the end of 1991, the Soviet Union officially broke apart, and the Cold War came to an end. All of the former Soviet republics gained independence. The largest of these was Russia.

The Russian Federation As the first president of a new Russia, Boris Yeltsin was head of a nation on the verge of economic collapse. The sudden shift to a free-market economy brought great hardship. Inflation and unemployment soared. A very few individuals gained control of state-owned property. These well-connected individuals, known as oligarchs, held great influence over the politics and economy of Russia.

The Russian Federation, as the country was now called, also had to deal with unrest in its non-Russian regions. From 1994 to 2005, Russia fought a war against rebels in Chechnya who wanted independence. Both sides brutally mistreated

The Soviet Union and Present-Day Russia

KEY
- Soviet Union, 1991
- Russia, 1992

people. The region was left in ruins by the time Russia regained control.

Yeltsin resigned in 1999, naming Vladimir Putin as acting president. Putin then won an election in 2000. Putin reduced the power of the oligarchy and increased the power of the government.

Reading Check What new policies did Gorbachev set?

Section 2 Assessment

Key Terms

1. Explain how the following key terms describe power relations in Russian history: tsar, serf, Bolshevik

Key Ideas

2. What changes did Peter the Great make to Russia?

3. What changes did Lenin make to the economy and government of Russia?

4. What were some results of collectivizing agriculture?

Think Critically

5. **Compare Viewpoints** How were Stalin's and Gorbachev's ideas about government different?

6. **Synthesize** What caused the Soviet Union to collapse?

Essential Question

What should governments do?

7. Think about the famines that have occurred throughout Russian history. What actions might a government take during disasters such as famines? Go to your Student Journal to record your answer.

The Russian Revolution

IN Indiana | **6.1.21** Differentiate between fact and interpretation in historical accounts and explain historical passages. | **6.1.23** Identify issues related to an event in Europe or the Americas and give arguments for and against that issue.

▲ A Russian serf weaves cloth on a loom, about 1910.

For centuries, tsars ruled Russia with absolute power. Under their rule, a huge gap existed between wealthy landowners and poor workers. In 1905, a revolution led to the creation of a parliament, but it was ineffective. The suffering caused by World War I caused even more discontent among Russians. In early 1917, starving people rioted in the capital, St. Petersburg. The tsar was forced to give up his throne. In October 1917, revolutionary Bolsheviks, led by Vladimir Lenin, overthrew the government. Civil war broke out, and the Bolsheviks used increasingly harsh measures to maintain control.

Lenin addresses a political meeting in 1917. ▼

Stop at each letter on the right to think about the text. Then answer the question with the same letter on the left.

A Analyze Cause and Effect What have the revolutionaries already done, and why does that make it important to act quickly?

B Identify Evidence How does Lenin try to cover up his intention to take power? Explain.

C Identify Main Ideas and Details For whom does Lenin claim the revolutionaries are acting?

disarm, *v.,* to force a person or country to give up a supply of weapons

cadet, *n.,* a person who is training to become a military officer

relinquish, *v.,* to give up or surrender

A Call to Power

❝ We must at all costs, this very evening, this very night, arrest the **A** government, having first <u>disarmed</u> the officer <u>cadets</u>, and so on. We must not wait! We may lose everything! Who must take power? **B** That is not important at present. Let the Revolutionary Military Committee do it, or "some other institution" which will declare that it will <u>relinquish</u> power only to the **C** true representatives of the interests of the people, the interests of the army, the interests of the peasants, the interests of the starving. ❞

—Vladimir Lenin, "A Call to Power," October 24, 1917

550

Stop at each letter on the right to think about the text. Then answer the question with the same letter on the left.

D Identify Bias What attitude toward Lenin is conveyed by the words "bloodthirsty beast"?

E Draw Conclusions In the beginning, how did ordinary people feel about the revolution?

F Compare and Contrast According to the Russian Red Army soldier, what did the revolution bring about? Is that similar to or different from what he expected?

intrude, *v.,* to force oneself into a situation where one isn't wanted

ranks, *n.,* a body of people grouped together as members of an organization

Constituent Assembly, *n.,* an elected legislature that the Bolsheviks disbanded

existence, *n.,* standard of living

Letter to Lenin

D " My words to you, you bloodthirsty beast. You <u>intruded</u> into the <u>ranks</u> of the revolution and did not allow the <u>Constituent Assembly</u> to meet. You said: 'Down with prisons, Down with shootings, Down with soldiering. Let wage workers be secure.' In a word you promised heaps of gold and a heavenly <u>existence</u>. The people

E felt the revolution, began to breathe easily. We were allowed to meet, to say what we liked, fearing nothing. And then you, Bloodsucker, appeared and took

F away freedom from the people. . . . You've organized a terror and thousands of the people are shot mercilessly every day; . . . workers are starving, the people are without shoes or clothes. "

—a Red Army soldier, "Letter to Lenin," December 25, 1918

▲ This military cap and the seal above it bear the hammer and sickle, symbols of the Soviet Union.

Red Army soldiers, 1932 ▼

Analyze the Documents

1. **Draw Inferences** What do you think happened to the soldier who wrote the letter to Lenin? Explain.
2. **Writing Task** Write your own letter to Lenin in which you tell him what, if anything, you think he should have done differently.

Russia Today

IN Indiana

6.2.1 Compare and contrast forms of governments in Europe and the Americas throughout history

6.2.5 Discuss the impact of major forms of government in Europe and the Americas on civil and human rights.

6.2.7 Define and compare citizenship and the citizen's role throughout history in Europe and the Americas.

6.4.4 Describe how different economic systems in Europe and the Americas answer the basic economic questions.

6.4.7 Identify economic connections between the community and the countries of Europe or the Americas and identify job skills needed to be successful in the workplace.

Visual Glossary

Key Terms • KGB • disposable income • censor • superpower

Reading Skill: Identify Main Ideas and Details Take notes using the graphic organizer in your journal.

Shoppers walk through a new public plaza in Moscow. ▼

Few nations have experienced as much upheaval as Russia did in the 1900s. Since 2000, the country has continued to change at a remarkable pace.

Russia Recovers

Gorbachev's policies of glasnost and perestroika opened a new era of social and political change in Russia. One of the biggest changes has been Russia's increasing self-confidence.

Finding a New Identity At the end of the Soviet period, Russians discovered that communism was more than a political system—it was also a cultural identity. If Russia was no longer a communist nation, then what should it be? In 1990, historian James Billington said:

> 66 It boils down to whether [Russians] can find an…identity for themselves as a way of feeling good about themselves without feeling hostile to others. 99

The hardships that occurred in the shift to a market economy brought a rise in depression and alcoholism. The country also faced violence, crime, and corruption. Although there had been corruption during the Soviet era, it increased greatly in the years that followed.

Restoring Confidence Elected president in 2000, Vladimir Putin acted quickly to rebuild the country. He did this through strong leadership and by increasing government control. Since then, some have charged that Putin's policies undermine human rights, democracy, and peaceful relations with Russia's neighbors and the United States.

Some scholars point to Putin's background as a member of the **KGB,** the Soviet secret police. His past may have led him to favor strong government control. Supporters argue that his policies reduced political corruption, crime, and terrorism. His reforms to banking, private property, and labor law helped Russia's economy grow. Under Putin, some Russians began to believe that state-controlled capitalism might work better than a free-market economy.

However, many Russians preferred the Soviet era, when the government was in charge of pensions, healthcare, and wages. Many feel that under communism they faced less uncertainty.

Putin strengthened the Russian military. He <u>demonstrated</u> Russia's renewed military might by crushing unrest in regions on Russia's borders, such as Chechnya, where rebels had fought Russian control since 1994.

Putin's three terms as president also brought real improvements in daily life. His economic reforms reduced poverty and led to the emergence of a new middle class. Many in this new middle class are professionals who work in fields related to the global economy. The middle class now makes up about one fifth to one third of the population. Since 1999, Russians on average have doubled their **disposable income,** or the amount of money left after taxes are paid. By the end of 2007, fewer than 15 percent of all Russians lived below the poverty level. Just ten years earlier, 38 percent lived in poverty.

Putin also oversaw dramatic growth in Russia's energy industry. This industry took advantage of Russia's vast oil and natural gas reserves. Russia became one of the world's leading producers of oil and gas.

Reading Check **How did Putin change the role of Russia's government?**

demonstrate, *v.,* to show the workings of

Contrasting Systems

Under the communist Soviet Union, Russians, such as the woman at the left, faced empty shelves in stores. American shoppers, such as the woman at the right, seldom encounter such shortages. *How might communism affect the supply of items such as food and clothing?*

Communism

- The Communist Party makes all political decisions.
- Command economy (The government makes most economic decisions and owns most property.)
- The political leadership values obedience, discipline, and economic security.

Democratic Capitalism

- The people and their elected representatives make decisions.
- Market economy (Private consumers and producers make most economic decisions and own most property.)
- The political leadership values freedom and prosperity.

Comparing Standards of Living

Life Expectancy

	United States	Russia
Overall	78.1 years	65.9 years
Male	75.3 years	59.1 years
Female	81.1 years	73.1 years

Infant Mortality (per 1,000 births)

	United States	Russia
Total	6.3 deaths	10.8 deaths
Male	7.0 deaths	12.3 deaths
Female	5.6 deaths	9.2 deaths

SOURCE: *CIA World Factbook*

Chart Skills

How does life expectancy for men in Russia compare with that for men in the United States? How does it compare for women in these two nations?

Data Discovery

◄ Two Russian women haul coal to heat their homes and to cook food.

Russia Faces Challenges

Russia's new wealth and stability brought newfound confidence. However, Russians have also been facing some serious challenges.

Social and Economic Woes With change came new health concerns. Russia's birth rates and life expectancy are low. Life expectancy is the number of years a person can expect to live. Male life expectancy is the lowest of all industrialized nations in the world. Alcoholism is a major problem in Russia. Half of working-age men die due to excessive drinking. Rates of infectious disease are also high. These include HIV/AIDS and tuberculosis, a lung disease.

Social and economic changes since the 1990s have led to an increase in migration. After the fall of the Soviet Union, civil unrest and unemployment forced thousands of people to leave their homes. Many left polluted cities with high unemployment. Some returned to former lives in the countryside. There, they could raise some of their own food. At the same time, others migrated from rural areas to more thriving cities to try to find work. Large numbers of Russians, many of them skilled workers, have left their homeland to seek better lives in North America, Israel, and Western Europe.

Putin Draws Criticism Putin's efforts to solve some of Russia's major problems have had mixed results. He remains popular among Russians, but criticism continues in spite of the government's efforts to silence it.

The Russian constitution calls for freedom of speech and of the press. However, the government continues to control the media. The government owns most of the large radio and television stations. This means that if the government doesn't want the general public to know about a news story, they can **censor** it, or keep it from being reported.

One of Putin's most controversial actions was to put Russia's energy industry under government control. Private energy companies suddenly lost all that they owned to the government. Putin argued Russia needed control of its energy industry to regain its status as a global superpower. A **superpower** is an extremely powerful nation.

Human Rights and the Law Russia's record on human rights remains uneven. Ethnic and religious tensions continue, especially with Muslims and others from the Caucasus region. A few Russian journalists who have criticized the government have died under suspicious circumstances. Some have accused the Russian government of killing them.

Corruption in business practices and politics is common in Russia. In 2008, Dmitry Medvedev won election to follow Putin as president. Medvedev promised to fight corruption, although critics questioned his commitment. Medvedev said,

66 [Corruption] must receive our sustained attention because this problem is a profound and important one. 99

Reading Check How does the Russian government control the media?

Russia and the World

Russia remains one of the world's leading powers. It has the world's largest stockpile of nuclear weapons. It is also one of the world's top energy producers.

A World Partner Russia is a member of the Group of 8 industrialized nations, or G-8. As a member of the G-8, Russia joined the United States in 2006 to announce shared anti-terror initiatives. Russia has worked with the G-8 on other issues. These include climate change, energy, and economic development.

Russia has also taken part in other international efforts. One of these was the North Korean Six-Party Talks, aimed at convincing North Korea to give up nuclear weapons.

Russia has strongly opposed efforts by the former Soviet republics of Ukraine and Georgia to join NATO. Both countries border on Russia.

◀ A protester holds a photograph of Russian journalist Anastasia Baburova, who was killed in 2009.

IN Indiana CONNECTIONS

In Russia, the GDP per person is

$18,000.

In Indiana, the GDP per person is

$39,000.

myworldgeography.com Data Discovery

myWorld Activity
Russia Trivia Game

Russia has supported independence movements in the Georgian regions of Abkhazia and South Ossetia. Georgian troops entered South Ossetia in 2008 to try to regain control of the region. Russian troops responded by driving Georgian troops out of South Ossetia. Russian forces also bombed and invaded other parts of Georgia. Russia's invasion of Georgia damaged its relations with the United States and other Western nations.

Russian Energy Russia has also flexed its muscles in global energy markets. Russia is the second largest oil-exporting nation in the world. Russia is also the world's largest exporter of natural gas. Oil and gas pipelines from Russia reach far into Europe and Asia. In the past, Russia has halted the flow of natural gas to Western Europe through Ukraine. It has done this in response to disagreements with the government of Ukraine. Russia has signed exclusive agreements to supply gas to Germany and other European nations to try to win their backing for Russian policies. Western Europeans have criticized Russia for using energy to increase its power.

Cooperation and Conflict Russia controls much of the energy supply for the European Union (EU). Russia has opposed the EU membership of former Soviet republics such as Estonia, Latvia, and Lithuania.

Transporting Russian Energy

Map Skills

1 **Region** According to the map, Russian oil pipelines extend to which European nations to the west?

2 **Movement** Through which nations must Russian gas travel to reach Italy?

Active Atlas

KEY
— Oil pipeline
— Gas pipeline

0   500 mi
0   500 km

Lambert Azimuthal
Equal-Area Projection

However, Russia has <u>cooperated</u> with the EU on matters such as energy and climate change. These agreements include other former Soviet republics such as Ukraine, Belarus, and Kazakhstan.

Russia is a trading partner with Iran, which has poor relations with the United States. Russia has also loaned money to Iran to build nuclear reactors.

The United States has objected to this project. It is concerned that Iran will use the reactors to develop nuclear weapons. Russia's relationship with the United States has remained calm but cool.

Another foreign policy issue is Russia's relationship with China, the world's largest country in population. The Soviet Union and China had been competitors and enemies. This changed when Russia and China formed the Shanghai Cooperation Organization with several Central Asian countries in 2001. This organization has become a loose alliance. Joint military practices between Russia and China have worried Western nations.

The Future of Russia Strong post-Soviet leadership has reshaped Russia's politics and economy. Rich natural resources and continued superpower status make Russia an important player on the global stage. Whether it works together with the United States and other Western powers or takes a more hostile attitude, Russia has the world's full attention.

Reading Check What is the Shanghai Cooperation Organization?

cooperate, *v.,* to work together toward an agreed goal

Georgian soldiers run past a building bombed by Russian warplanes during the 2008 conflict. ▼

Section 3 Assessment

Essential Question

Key Terms
1. Define each key term using a complete sentence: KGB, disposable income, censor, superpower.

Key Ideas
2. In what ways did the Russian government under Vladimir Putin halt democratic reform?

3. How did Russia's petroleum industry change under Putin?

4. What are some of the major health problems in Russia?

Think Critically
5. **Draw Conclusions** Why do you think Russia has opposed membership in the European Union for former Soviet republics?

6. **Draw Inferences** Why might Russia want closer relations with China?

What should governments do?
7. Think about the life expectancy and infant mortality graphs in this section. What do you think the government can do about the health problems in Russia? Go to your Student Journal to record your answer.

The Soviet Industrial Legacy

IN Indiana

6.1.15 Describe the impact of industrialization and urbanization on people's lives and on trade and cultural exchange between Europe and the Americas and the rest of the world.

6.1.17 Discuss the benefits and challenges related to the development of a highly technological society.

6.1.22 Form research questions and use resources to present data on people, cultures and developments in Europe and the Americas.

6.1.23 Identify issues related to an event in Europe or the Americas and give arguments for and against that issue.

6.4.6 Analyze current economic issues in the countries of Europe or the Americas using a variety of resources.

Key Terms
- Five-Year Plan
- command economy
- industrialization
- heavy industry
- gulag

These days, most adults in the village of Muslumovo on the Techa River have health problems. "What can we do?" says a local man. "We need water. Cows drink it, birds drink it, we drink it. And by the time we're forty, we're all ill." Recently, scientists discovered the cause of this widespread sickness. In 1957, there was an explosion at the nearby Mayak nuclear plant. The radiation that is making everyone ill dates back even further to the Soviet industrial push of the 1930s.

Both men and women worked on Soviet industrialization projects. ▼

Build for the Motherland

Following Lenin's unexpected death in 1924, a new Soviet leader emerged. Josef Stalin wanted to transform the Soviet Union with a series of **Five-Year Plans.** These were government plans for the economy that made basic decisions and set priorities for five years. Each Five-Year Plan pushed for the collectivization of farms and rapid **industrialization,** or development of industry. These government plans concentrated on building **heavy industry,** or the manufacture of steel, equipment, or weapons. Stalin's plans indeed transformed the Soviet Union, but at a terrible cost.

Stalin believed that for communism to survive, the Soviet Union would have to become a world industrial leader. He imposed a full-scale **command economy,** or one in which the government makes all basic economic decisions. He expected citizens to accept all economic hardships as honorable sacrifices for the Soviet motherland.

By the 1930s, millions of workers were working on the nation's construction projects as inmates of forced-labor camps. Later known as **gulags,** these camps housed political prisoners charged with crimes such as private ownership of land or criticism of the government.

Industrialization and the Gulags

Millions of gulag prisoners built Stalin's factories, dams, and canals. Perhaps as many as 20 million people passed through the gulags from 1928 to 1939. Conditions in the camps were horrible. Prisoners lived in fear and exhaustion. Food was poor and medical care almost nonexistent. Millions died as a result.

THINK CRITICALLY How did Stalin use the gulags for industrialization?

▲ Gulag laborers were treated like beasts of burden.

Soviet Industrial Growth

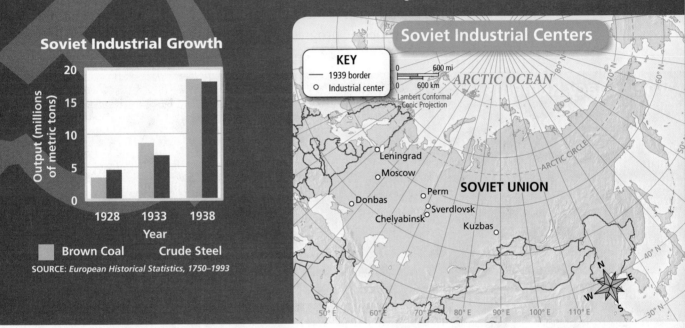

SOURCE: *European Historical Statistics, 1750–1993*

Soviet Industrial Centers

Stalin believed that the success of the Five-Year Plans depended on education. Before the Revolution, 65 percent of the population was illiterate. The government taught millions to read and write. Worker training programs also prepared men and women for Five-Year-Plan projects.

Stalin expanded universities so that students could learn math, science and engineering. Even there, Stalin attempted to dictate the behavior and thinking of professors and students.

At first, people were eager to work on Stalin's projects. They believed that if they worked hard, they would live well. However, workers soon discovered that they were expected to produce a great deal for low wages. In addition, they paid heavy fines if they were late or absent.

Many Soviets expected that the Five-Year Plans would raise standards of living, but Stalin pushed only heavy industry. This led to widespread shortages in clothing, housing, and food.

Reading Check Why did Stalin want to transform the Soviet economy?

Stalin's Industrial Legacy

Industrialization left its mark on all of modern Russia. Factories, mines and industrial cities cover what had been Siberian wilderness. Universities expanded by Stalin educate today's scientists and business people.

The rush to industrialize also meant that the Soviet government ignored pollution, health issues, and environmental concerns in favor of economic progress.

Acid rain has damaged thousands of acres of woodlands. Vast areas of what was once good farmland are now unusable due to soil contamination. Waterways and habitats remain damaged from dams built to generate hydroelectric power. Perhaps the most serious threat is radioactive pollution such as that found in Muslumovo.

Reading Check What have been some of the negative effects of industrialization?

The Legacy Remains

Muslumovo

In the 1930s, the region around Muslumovo supplied copper for industry and the military. People began to become ill in the 1950s, but they kept quiet. They feared the government's reaction if they complained. The modern Russian government has been more sympathetic, offering villagers new homes in another town.

▲ A sign in Muslumovo forbids villagers from fishing in the area due to high levels of radiation.

Kuzbass

Kuzbass, or the Kuznetsk Basin, holds some of the largest coal deposits in the world. This coal fueled new factories in the basin and elsewhere along the Trans-Siberian Railroad. The basin also supplied iron, steel, zinc, and aluminum. Today, the Kuznetsk Basin remains an important industrial center in Russia.

▲ A woman walks through snow covered with soot released by the factories in the Kuzbass region.

Norilsk

During the Soviet era, foreigners were not allowed to visit Norilsk. The Soviets did not want outsiders to know about the missiles kept there. This secrecy also hid the city's pollution. Norilsk processes nickel, copper, platinum, gold, and silver, and almost half of the world's supply of palladium, a metal used in automobile exhaust systems.

▲ A copper worker in Norilsk breathes through a filter to keep contaminants out of his lungs.

The New Russian Economy

After the fall of the Soviet Union, the Russian economy collapsed. The recovery and boom of the early 2000s came mainly from earnings from Russia's massive energy resources. Wages rose, and Russians could afford to purchase consumer goods they had never before owned.

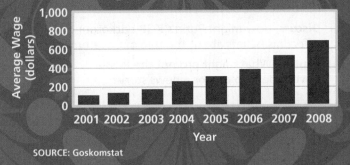

Russia: Average Monthly Wage, 2001–2008

SOURCE: Goskomstat

Chart Skills

In modern Russia, stores selling electronic goods (such as the one above in Moscow) are relatively new. Compare the average monthly wage in 2001 with the wage in 2008. How much did the average monthly wage change during these years?

The New Russian Economy

Industrialization left another kind of legacy in Russia. A recent survey showed that many Russians have a favorable view of Stalin's dictatorship. They believe that Stalin did much for Russia. They, too, see themselves working to make Russia great.

Many of the more successful Russians in today's economy are under age 35. One young company executive recently exclaimed, "Is there anything better that can be offered to me than creating the new Russian economy?"

This younger generation has grown up since the collapse of communism, and many accept the uncertainties of a market economy. They use computers, cellphones, and the Internet—all of which are fairly new to Russia. Many are optimistic about being able to earn good wages and about starting new businesses.

The push to industrialize had both positive and negative results for Russia. Stalin's vision for Russia continues to influence life today.

Reading Check Why might modern Russians have a positive view of Stalin?

Assessment

1. Summarize the main purpose of Stalin's Five-Year Plans.

2. How did Stalin use education to promote industrialization?

3. State one way in which each city on the previous page shows evidence of the Soviet push to industrialize.

4. How might more economic freedom change Russia?

5. What types of technology can modern Russians use that were not available during the Soviet period?

Chapter Assessment

Key Terms and Ideas

1. **Recall** In what ways does **Siberia** present Russia with great advantages and great challenges?

2. **Compare and Contrast** Describe the climate and vegetation on the tundra and the **steppes.**

3. **Explain** What sort of rulers were the Russian **tsars?**

4. **Recall** How did the buildings of the **Kremlin** demonstrate power in imperial Russia?

5. **Discuss** How did communism shape the Soviet government and economy?

6. **Summarize** What was **collectivization** and how did affect the Soviet Union?

7. **Discuss** How might Putin's **KGB** background affect his beliefs about the role of government?

8. **Explain** What might prompt the Russian government to **censor** a news story?

Think Critically

9. **Draw Conclusions** Why do you think Josef Stalin took actions such as collectivization and the jailing of opponents? Explain.

10. **Compare Viewpoints** One of Stalin's officers said the Great Famine would show the peasants "who is the master. It cost millions of lives, but the collective farm system is here to stay." Do you think Stalin agreed with him? Why?

11. **Identify Evidence** What historical evidence would support the statement "Russia has a long history of autocratic government"?

12. **Drawing Inferences** Why do you think many Russians want the government to be in control of wages, pensions, and healthcare?

Places to Know

For each place, write the letter from the map that shows its location.

13. **Kamchatka Peninsula**

14. **Yakutsk**

15. **Lake Baikal**

16. **Moscow**

17. **St. Petersburg**

18. **Ural Mountains**

19. **Estimate** Using the scale, estimate the distance from Moscow to Lake Baikal.

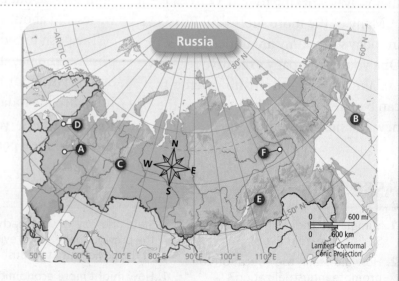

Essential Question

myWorld Chapter Activity

Memo to Russia Follow your teacher's instructions to examine information on some of the challenges facing Russia today. Consider environmental data, Russian health and crime figures, as well as the nation's international partnerships and other information as you set priorities. After your review, prepare an official government memo detailing which problem Russia should address first and why.

21st Century Learning

Search for Information on the Internet

Search for three different Web sites for additional information about the political, economic, and social challenges facing Russia. The following types of Web sites might prove helpful:
- encyclopedias or museums
- international organizations, such as the UN or World Trade Organization
- U.S. sites such as *CIA World Factbook*

Document-Based Questions

Success Tracker™
Online at myworldgeography.com

Use your knowledge of Russia and Documents A and B to answer questions 1–3.

Document A

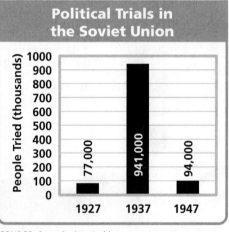

Political Trials in the Soviet Union

People Tried (thousands)

Year	Value
1927	77,000
1937	941,000
1947	94,000

SOURCE: Open Society Archives

Document B

" You might well ask why a prisoner worked so hard for ten years in a camp. . . . In the camps they had these gangs to make the prisoners keep each other on their toes. . . . It was like this—either you all got something extra or you all starved."

—Alexander Solzhenitsyn, *One Day in the Life of Ivan Denisovich* (a book about life in a Soviet prison camp)

1. How did the number of people brought to trial change from 1927 to 1937?

   A It decreased.

   B It increased by half.

   C It increased by more than 10 times.

   D It increased by 100 times.

2. What would be the punishment if a prisoner stopped working hard?

   A The guards would whip him in front of his gang.

   B The guards would take food away from his gang.

   C He would be put into a new labor camp.

   D He would have to give his food to his gang.

3. **Writing Task** What do you think the gang would say to a prisoner who stopped working hard? Write a dialogue.

my worldgeography.com Self-Test

Media Watchdog

Your Mission Use the Media Analysis Checklist to study the poster on the facing page. Examine how the poster conveys its message. Then go online and evaluate an article or opinion piece.

Media messages are everywhere in modern society. Can you believe everything you see, hear, and read on television, in print, or on the Internet? Who keeps track of the media's honesty and objectivity? When a member of the media is accused of bias, how can you know who is right?

By understanding how to analyze media content, you can spot bias and persuasive messages. Practicing this skill will help you to evaluate whether or not public officials and news sources are telling you the truth. You can also apply these techniques to advertising, which will help you decide how to spend your money more wisely.

Media Analysis Checklist

1. Author
2. Intended audience
3. Words or phrases
4. Images and other design elements
5. Overall message
6. Persuasive techniques
7. Examples of bias, if any

STEP 1

Determine the Message.

Copy the Media Analysis Checklist at the left onto your own paper. Use it to record your observations about the poster at the right. Who published the poster, and who is its intended audience? (Hint: Look at the flag at the bottom of the poster.) Read the poster and study its visual elements, such as the use of colors or photographs. Considering the words and visuals together, what is the poster's message?

STEP 2

Check for Bias.

Next, evaluate how the poster uses persuasive techniques such as bright colors or a photograph with children. Note how the poster uses words that are short, simple, and to the point. Do these words encourage you to feel a certain way? Consider whether or not your reaction is based on facts or on opinions and feelings. Record your observations on your Media Analysis Checklist.

STEP 3

Analyze Online Media.

Make a second, blank copy of the Media Analysis Checklist. Now go online to sources suggested by your teacher. Find a podcast, article, or opinion piece about Europe or Russia, and analyze it as you did the poster. Once you have completed your Media Analysis Checklist, use your findings in a class discussion.

It's not them and us,
it's you and me

2008 European Year of
Intercultural Dialogue

www.dialogue2008.eu

European Union

9 May – Europe Day

The World: Political

ARCTIC OCEAN

GREENLAND
(Denmark)

ALASKA
(U.S.)

ARCTIC CIRCLE

Reykjavik ✪
ICELAND

CANADA

NORTH

AMERICA

Ottawa ✪

UNITED STATES

Washington, D.C. ✪

ATLANTIC

OCEAN

Rabat ✪
MOROCCO

TROPIC OF CANCER

HAWAII
(U.S.)

20° N

MEXICO

Mexico
City ✪

CENTRAL AMERICA
AND THE CARIBBEAN
For detail, see map
North and South
America: Political.

WESTERN SAHARA
(Morocco)

WEST AFRICA
For detail, see map
Africa: Political

PACIFIC

OCEAN

Caracas ✪

VENEZUELA

Georgetown ✪
Paramaribo ✪

FRENCH GUIANA
(France)

Bogotá ✪
COLOMBIA

GUYANA

SURINAME

EQUATOR

Quito ✪
ECUADOR

GALÁPAGOS
ISLANDS
(Ecuador)

N

W   E

S

SAMOA

Apia ✪

COOK ISLANDS
(New Zealand)

PERU

Lima ✪

SOUTH

AMERICA

ATLANTIC

OCEAN

FRENCH POLYNESIA
(France)

La Paz ✪
BOLIVIA

Sucre ✪

Brasília ✪

BRAZIL

20° S
Nuku'alofa ✪
TONGA

PITCAIRN ISLAND
(U.K.)

TROPIC OF CAPRICORN

PARAGUAY

Asunción ✪

CHILE

KEY
- - - Disputed border
——— National border
✪ Capital city

Santiago ✪

Buenos
Aires ✪

URUGUAY

Montevideo ✪

40° S

ARGENTINA

FALKLAND ISLANDS
(U.K.)

SOUTH GEORGIA
(U.K.)

60° S

SOUTHERN OCEAN

80° S

ANTARCTICA

20° E 40° E 60° E 80° E 100° E 120° E 140° E 160° E

SVALBARD
(Norway)

RCTIC OCEAN

80° N

ROPE AND SOUTHWEST ASIA
detail, see maps Europe: Political
and Asia: Political.

ARCTIC CIRCLE

RUSSIA

60° N

Moscow

ASIA

EUROPE

KAZAKHSTAN

Astana

Ulaanbaatar

MONGOLIA

NORTH
KOREA

40° N

Tashkent Bishkek
UZBEKISTAN KYRGYZSTAN
TURKMENISTAN TAJIKISTAN
Ashgabat Dushanbe

Beijing

P'yongyang
Seoul
SOUTH
KOREA

JAPAN

Tokyo

TURKEY

Tunis
TUNISIA
Tripoli

IRAQ
Baghdad
Kuwait
KUWAIT

Tehran
IRAN

Kabul
AFGHANISTAN

CHINA

PACIFIC
OCEAN

Cairo

LIBYA

EGYPT

BAHRAIN Manama
QATAR Doha
Riyadh Abu Dhabi
Muscat

Islamabad
Kathmandu
PAKISTAN NEPAL
New Dhaka
Delhi

BHUTAN
Thimphu

Taipei

TAIWAN

TROPIC OF CANCER

20° N

SAUDI
ARABIA

OMAN

INDIA

MYANMAR

Hanoi

AFRICA

Khartoum ERITREA
Asmara
SUDAN
N'Djamena Sanaa
CHAD YEMEN
DJIBOUTI
Djibouti

UNITED
ARAB
EMIRATES

BANGLADESH

LAOS
Yangon Vientiane
THAILAND VIETNAM
Bangkok CAMBODIA
Phnom Penh

Manila

MARSHALL
ISLANDS

Majuro

GER

CENTRAL
AFRICAN
REPUBLIC
ERIA
Bangui SOUTH
SUDAN Juba
MEROON
Kampala Nairobi
REPUBLIC
OF THE
CONGO Kigali
zzaville Bujumbura RWANDA
NDA BURUNDI
gola) DEMOCRATIC
REPUBLIC OF
nasa THE CONGO
nda

SRI
LANKA

ETHIOPIA
Addis Ababa
SOMALIA
Colombo
Male
MALDIVES

Mogadishu

PHILIPPINES

BRUNEI

PALAU
Melekeok

Palikir

FEDERATED STATES
OF MICRONESIA

KIRIBATI

Tarawa

UGANDA
KENYA

Kuala Lumpur
MALAYSIA

Bandar Seri Begawan

Singapore SINGAPORE

EQUATOR

NAURU Yaren

0°

SEYCHELLES

Victoria

INDONESIA

Jakarta

Dili

ANGOLA

TANZANIA
Dodoma
Dar es Salaam
MALAWI
ZAMBIA Lilongwe
COMOROS
Moroni

EAST TIMOR

PAPUA NEW
GUINEA

SOLOMON
ISLANDS

TUVALU

Honiara

Funafuti

Port
Moresby

Lusaka MOZAMBIQUE
ZIMBABWE
Harare
Antananarivo

NAMIBIA BOTSWANA
Vindhoek Gaborone
Pretoria Maputo
Bloemfontein Mbabane
SOUTH SWAZILAND
AFRICA
Cape Town Maseru LESOTHO

MAURITIUS
Port Louis

RÉUNION
(France)

MADAGASCAR

INDIAN
OCEAN

VANUATU
Port-Vila

NEW
CALEDONIA
(France)

AUSTRALIA

FIJI
Suva

20° S

Canberra

NEW
ZEALAND

0   2,000 mi

0   2,000 km

Robinson Projection

40° S

Wellington

20° E 40° E 60° E 80° E 100° E 120° E 140° E 160° E

60° S

SOUTHERN OCEAN

ANTARCTIC CIRCLE

ANTARCTICA

80° S

The World: Physical

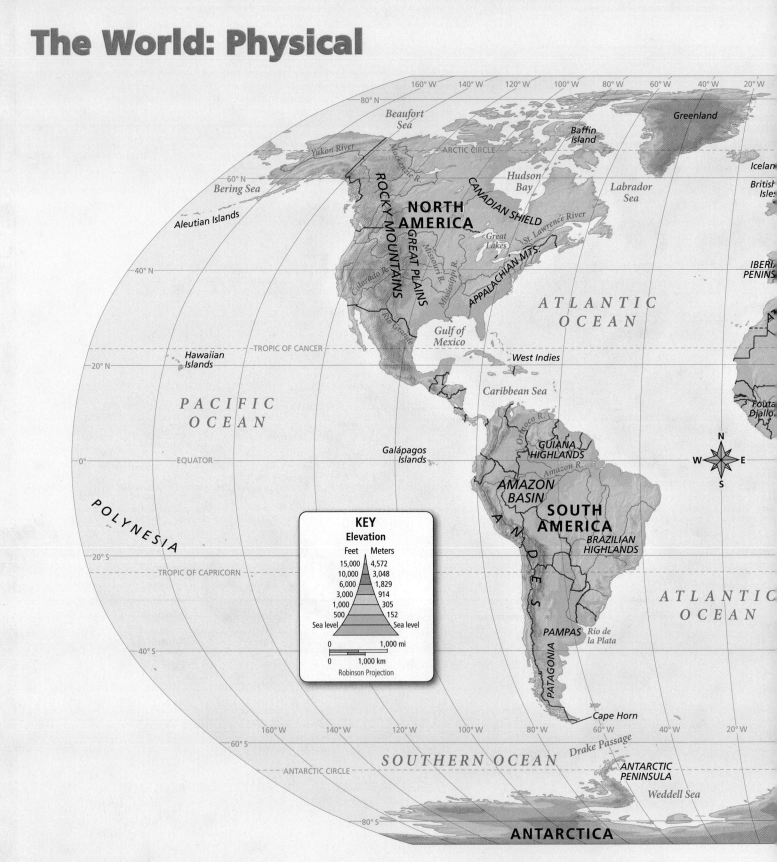

KEY
Elevation

Feet	Meters
15,000	4,572
10,000	3,048
6,000	1,829
3,000	914
1,000	305
500	152
Sea level	Sea level

0   1,000 mi

0   1,000 km

Robinson Projection

ARCTIC OCEAN

SCANDINAVIA
Kara
Sea
Baltic
Sea
URAL MOUNTAINS
Ob River
Yenisey River
SIBERIA
Lena River
CHERSKIY RANGE
ARCTIC CIRCLE
60° N
NORTH EUROPEAN PLAIN
Volga River
Aral
Sea
ASIA
ALTAY SHAN
Lake
Baikal
Amur River
Sea of
Okhotsk
EUROPE
CAUCASUS
MTS.
Caspian Sea
TIAN SHAN
GOBI
Hokkaido
40° N
Black Sea
HINDU
KUSH
KUNLUN SHAN
NORTH
CHINA
PLAIN
Sea of
Japan
(East
Sea)
Honshu
Mediterranean Sea
IRANIAN
PLATEAU
PLATEAU
OF TIBET
Huang R.
Yellow
Sea
HIMALAYAS
Chang R.
East
China
Sea
PACIFIC
OCEAN
SAHARA
Persian
Gulf
Red Sea
ARABIAN
PENINSULA
DECCAN
PLATEAU
Taiwan
TROPIC OF CANCER
20° N
SAHEL
Arabian
Sea
Bay of
Bengal
INDOCHINA
PENINSULA
South
China
Sea
Philippine
Sea
MICRONESIA
AFRICA
Nile R.
ETHIOPIAN
HIGHLANDS
Sri
Lanka
Philippine
Islands
CONGO
BASIN
Congo R.
Lake
Victoria
Serengeti
Plain
Malay
Peninsula
Borneo
Sulawesi
New
Guinea
MELANESIA
0°
Sumatra
Java Sea
Arafura Sea
INDIAN
OCEAN
Zambezi R.
Java
Lesser Sunda
Islands
Coral Sea
KALAHARI
DESERT
Madagascar
AUSTRALIA
TROPIC OF CAPRICORN
20° S
Great Sandy
Desert
Great Victoria
Desert
GREAT DIVIDING RANGE
Tasman
Sea
New
Zealand
Cape of
Good Hope
40° S
Tasmania

80° N

60° N

40° N

80° E
100° E
120° E
140° E
160° E
20° E
40° E
60° E
20° S
40° S
60° S

SOUTHERN OCEAN
ANTARCTIC CIRCLE
80° S

ANTARCTICA

North and South America: Political

ASIA

ARCTIC OCEAN

GREENLAND (Denmark)

EUROPE

Bering Strait

Beaufort Sea

Bering Sea

ALASKA (U.S.)

Baffin Bay

Great Bear Lake

Great Slave Lake

Hudson Bay

Labrador Sea

CANADA

Lake Winnipeg

Great Lakes

Ottawa

Toronto

Chicago

San Francisco

UNITED STATES

Ohio R.

New York City

Washington, D.C.

ATLANTIC OCEAN

Los Angeles

HAWAII (U.S.)

Dallas

Rio Grande

TROPIC OF CANCER

Gulf of Mexico

MEXICO

Nassau

BAHAMAS

DOMINICAN REPUBLIC

Mexico City

Havana

CUBA

Port-au-Prince

PUERTO RICO (U.S.)

VIRGIN ISLANDS (U.S.)

JAMAICA

ST. KITTS AND NEVIS

Kingston

Santo

ANTIGUA AND BARBUDA

Belmopán

BELIZE

HAITI

Domingo

GUADELOUPE (France)

GUATEMALA

HONDURAS

DOMINICA

Guatemala

Tegucigalpa

Caribbean Sea

MARTINIQUE (France)

San Salvador

ST. LUCIA

PACIFIC OCEAN

EL SALVADOR

NICARAGUA

Caracas

BARBADOS

Managua

Panamá

ST. VINCENT AND

San José

VENEZUELA

THE GRENADINES

COSTA RICA

Georgetown

GRENADA

Paramaribo

0° EQUATOR

PANAMA

COLOMBIA

Bogotá

TRINIDAD AND TOBAGO

Quito

SURINAME

FRENCH GUIANA (France)

GALÁPAGOS ISLANDS (Ecuador)

ECUADOR

GUYANA

Amazon R.

B R A Z I L

São Francisco R.

N

W   E

S

Lima

PERU

Brasília

La Paz

Lake Titicaca

BOLIVIA

Paraná R.

20° S

Sucre

Rio de Janeiro

TROPIC OF CAPRICORN

CHILE

PARAGUAY

São Paulo

Asunción

0   1,000 mi

0   1,000 km

Azimuthal Equal-Area Projection

Santiago

URUGUAY

ATLANTIC OCEAN

Buenos Aires

Montevideo

Rio de la Plata

KEY

— National border

✪ Capital city

○ Other city

ARGENTINA

40° S

FALKLAND ISLANDS (U.K.)

Cape Horn   Tierra del Fuego

180°   160° W   140° W   120° W   100° W   80° W   60° W   40° W   20° W

North and South America: Physical

ASIA

ARCTIC OCEAN

Greenland

EUROPE

ARCTIC CIRCLE

Bering Strait

Beaufort Sea

Bering Sea

Baffin Bay

Baffin Island

Davis Strait

Mt. McKinley
20,320 ft. (6,194 m)

Aleutian Islands

Alaska Range

Great Bear Lake

Mackenzie R.

Labrador Sea

Gulf of Alaska

ROCKY MOUNTAINS

Great Slave Lake

Hudson Bay

Canadian Shield

Lake Winnipeg

Newfoundland

40° N

Great Lakes

GREAT PLAINS

ATLANTIC OCEAN

Great Basin

Missouri R.

Colorado R.

Mississippi R.

Ohio R.

Appalachian Mts.

Coastal Plain

Hawaiian Islands

TROPIC OF CANCER

20° N

Baja California

Sierra Madre Occidental

Rio Grande

Sierra Madre Oriental

Yucatán Peninsula

Gulf of California

Gulf of Mexico

Cuba

Hispaniola

Lesser Antilles

Greater Antilles

Caribbean Sea

PACIFIC OCEAN

0°—EQUATOR

Isthmus of Panama

Orinoco R.

Guiana Highlands

Galápagos Islands

ANDES

AMAZON BASIN

Amazon R.

São Francisco R.

20° S

Lake Titicaca

ANDES

Paraguay R.

Paraná R.

Brazilian Highlands

TROPIC OF CAPRICORN

Gran Chaco

KEY

Elevation

Feet	Meters
15,000	4,572
10,000	3,048
6,000	1,829
3,000	914
1,000	305
500	152
Sea level	Sea level

—— National border

0   1,000 mi

0   1,000 km

Lambert Azimuthal
Equal-Area Projection

Aconcagua
22,834 ft. (6,960 m)

Pampas

Río de la Plata

ATLANTIC OCEAN

40° S

Patagonia

Falkland Islands

Cape Horn   Tierra del Fuego

N
W   E
S

180°   160° W   140° W   120° W   100° W   80° W   60° W   40° W   20° W   0°

60° N

80° N

United States: Political

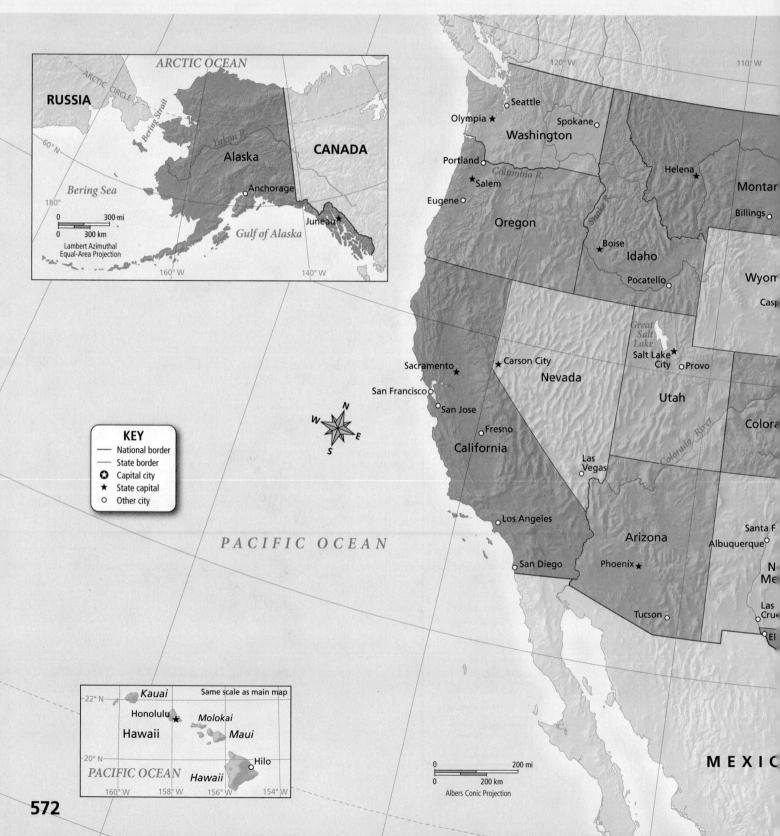

ARCTIC OCEAN

RUSSIA

ARCTIC CIRCLE

60° N

Alaska

CANADA

Bering Strait

Yukon R.

Bering Sea

180°

Anchorage

160° W

0   300 mi
0   300 km

Lambert Azimuthal
Equal-Area Projection

Juneau ★

Gulf of Alaska

140° W

120° W

110° W

Seattle

Olympia ★

Spokane

Washington

Portland

Columbia R.

Helena ★

Montar

Salem ★

Eugene

Oregon

Boise

Idaho

Snake R.

Billings

Wyom

Pocatello

Casp

PACIFIC OCEAN

KEY

National border
State border
⊗ Capital city
★ State capital
○ Other city

N
W ⊕ E
S

Great
Salt
Lake

Sacramento ★

San Francisco

San Jose

Fresno

California

Carson City ★

Nevada

Salt Lake ★
City

Provo

Utah

Colorado River

Colora

Las
Vegas

Los Angeles

San Diego

Arizona

Phoenix ★

Santa F

Albuquerque ○

N
Me

Tucson

Las
Cru

El

22° N

Kauai

Honolulu ★

Molokai

Same scale as main map

Hawaii

Maui

20° N

Hilo

PACIFIC OCEAN

Hawaii

160° W   158° W   156° W   154° W

0   200 mi
0   200 km

Albers Conic Projection

MEXIC

CANADA

Lake Superior

Lake Huron

Lake Michigan

Lake Ontario

Lake Erie

North Dakota
Bismarck ★
Fargo ○

Minnesota

South Dakota
Pierre ★
Sioux Falls ○

St. Paul ★
Minneapolis ○

Wisconsin
Green Bay ○
Madison ★ Milwaukee ○

Michigan
Grand Rapids ○
Lansing ★ Detroit ○

Maine
Augusta ★
Portland ○

Vermont
Montpelier ★

New Hampshire
Concord ★

Boston ★

New York
Albany ★

Massachusetts
Providence ★
Hartford ○

Rhode Island

Connecticut

Rochester ○
Buffalo ○

Nebraska
Omaha ○
Lincoln ★

Iowa
Cedar Rapids ○
Des Moines ★

Illinois
Chicago ○
Springfield ★

Indiana
Fort Wayne ○
Indianapolis ★

Ohio
Cleveland ○
Columbus ★
Dayton ○
Cincinnati ○

Pennsylvania
Harrisburg ★
Pittsburgh ○

New York City ○
Trenton ★

New Jersey
Philadelphia ○

Baltimore ○
Washington, D.C. ✪ Annapolis ○
Maryland

Dover ○
Delaware

West Virginia
Charleston ○

Richmond ★
Virginia
Norfolk ○

Kansas
Topeka ★
Kansas City ○
Wichita ○

Missouri
Jefferson City ★
St. Louis ○

Frankfort ★
Louisville ○
Kentucky

Raleigh ★
North Carolina
Charlotte ○

Oklahoma
Tulsa ○
Oklahoma City ★
Fort Smith ○

Arkansas
Little Rock ★

Memphis ○

Nashville ★
Knoxville ○
Tennessee

South Carolina
Columbia ★

Charleston ○

Texas
Fort Worth ○ ○ Dallas
Austin ★
Houston ○
San Antonio ○

Shreveport ○
Louisiana
Baton Rouge ★
New Orleans ○
Gulfport ○

Mississippi
Jackson ★

Alabama
Birmingham ○
Montgomery ★
Mobile ○

Georgia
Atlanta ★
Augusta ○
Columbus ○
Savannah ○

Charleston ○

ATLANTIC OCEAN

Jacksonville ○
Tallahassee ★

Orlando ○
Florida
Tampa ○

Miami ○

Gulf of Mexico

Missouri River
Platte River
Missouri R.
Arkansas River
Mississippi R.
Ohio River
Tennessee R.
Red River
Rio Grande

Cheyenne ★
Colorado Springs ○

100° W
90° W
80° W
70° W
50° N
40° N
30° N

Europe: Political

ARCTIC OCEAN

Barents Sea

ARCTIC CIRCLE

70° N

KEY
— National border
⊛ Capital city
○ Other city

0   200 mi
0   200 km

Lambert Conformal Conic Projection

ICELAND

Reykjavík

White Sea

Lapland

60° N

20° W

FAROE ISLANDS
(Denmark)

N
W   E
S

SWEDEN

FINLAND

Gulf of Bothnia

Tampere

RUSSIA

NORWAY

Bergen

Helsinki

St. Petersburg

Oslo

Göteborg

Stockholm

Gulf of Finland

Tallinn

ESTONIA

Nizhni Novgorod

Samara

North Sea

Glasgow

UNITED KINGDOM

DENMARK

Copenhagen

LATVIA

Riga

Moscow

Volga R.

IRELAND

Dublin

Manchester

Birmingham

London

Amsterdam

NETHERLANDS

The Hague

Brussels

BELGIUM

Paris

FRANCE

Hamburg

Berlin

GERMANY

Frankfurt

LUXEMBOURG

LIECHTENSTEIN

Prague

CZECH REPUBLIC

Munich

LITHUANIA

KALININGRAD
(Russia)

Vilnius

Minsk

BELARUS

Warsaw

POLAND

Kiev

UKRAINE

Donets'k

ATLANTIC OCEAN

10° W

50° N

English Channel

Bay of Biscay

SWITZERLAND

Bern

Lyon

Toulouse

Marseille

PORTUGAL

ANDORRA

Madrid

Barcelona

SPAIN

Lisbon

Seville

GIBRALTAR
(U.K.)

0°

Corsica

Balearic Islands

Sardinia

SAN MARINO

MONACO

Milano

ITALY

Rome

VATICAN CITY

Naples

Baltic Sea

SLOVAKIA

Bratislava

Budapest

Vienna

AUSTRIA

HUNGARY

SLOVENIA

Ljubljana

Zagreb

CROATIA

BOSNIA AND HERZEGOVINA

Sarajevo

Podgorica

MONTENEGRO

MOLDOVA

Chişinău

ROMANIA

Timişoara

Belgrade

SERBIA

Priština

KOSOVO

Skopje

Bucharest

Constanţa

Sea of Azov

Black Sea

Caspian Sea

BULGARIA

Sofia

MACEDONIA

Danube R.

Tirana

ALBANIA

TURKEY

Istanbul

Ankara

ASIA

GREECE

Athens

Mediterranean Sea

Tyrrhenian Sea

Sicily

Ionian Sea

Valletta

MALTA

AFRICA

30° N

10° E

20° E

30° E

40° E

574

Europe: Physical

ARCTIC OCEAN

Barents Sea

Kola Peninsula

Iceland

ARCTIC CIRCLE

White Sea

Norwegian Sea

URAL MOUNTAINS

Kjølen Mountains

SCANDINAVIAN PENINSULA

Northern Dvina R.

Faroe Islands

Lake Ladoga

Gulf of Bothnia

Shetland Islands

Lake Vänern

Gulf of Finland

Volga River

North Sea

Gotland

Jutland

Baltic Sea

Sjælland

NORTH EUROPEAN PLAIN

Central Russian Upland

Ireland

Great Britain

Elbe R.

Vistula R.

Thames R.

Oder R.

Dnieper River

Volga River

English Channel

Rhine R.

ATLANTIC OCEAN

Seine R.

Dniester R.

Don River

Danube R.

Carpathian Mountains

Loire R.

Bay of Biscay

A L P S

Sea of Azov

Crimea

CAUCASUS MTS.
Mount Elbrus
18,510 ft
(5,642 m)

Garonne R.

Mont Blanc
15,781 ft (4,810 m)

Massif Central

Po River

Rhône R.

Transylvanian Alps

Dinaric Alps

Danube River

Black Sea

Caspian Sea

Pyrenees

Douro R.

Apennines

Adriatic Sea

Balkan Mts.

Bosporus

Ebro R.

Meseta

Corsica

BALKAN PENINSULA

ASIA

Tagus R.

IBERIAN PENINSULA

ITALIAN PENINSULA

Pindus Mts.

Dardanelles

Guadalquivir R.

Sardinia

Tyrrhenian Sea

Aegean Sea

Balearic Islands

Sicily

Ionian Sea

Peloponnisos

KEY
Elevation

Feet	Meters
10,000	3,048
6,000	1,829
3,000	914
1,000	305
500	152
Sea level	Sea level

Maltese Islands

Crete

Mediterranean Sea

0   200 mi
0   200 km

AFRICA

Lambert Conformal Conic Projection

70° N

60° N

20° W

50° N

10° W

0°

10° E

20° E

30° E

40° E

30° N

N W E S

Africa: Political

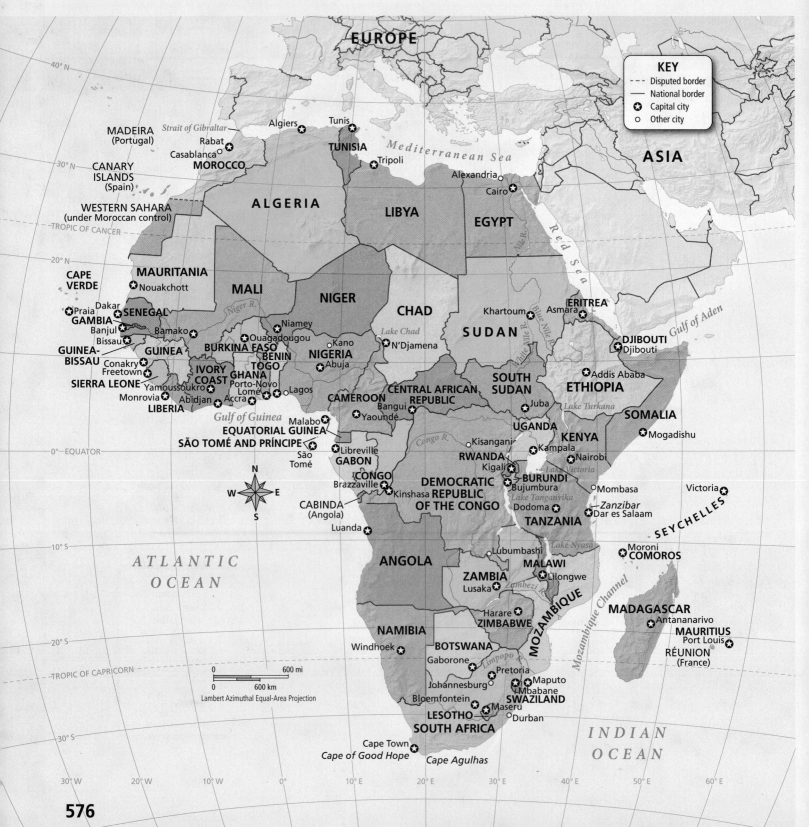

MADEIRA (Portugal)

Strait of Gibraltar

Algiers ⊛

Tunis ⊛

CANARY ISLANDS (Spain)

Rabat ⊛
Casablanca ○
MOROCCO

TUNISIA

Tripoli ⊛

Mediterranean Sea

Alexandria ○
Cairo ⊛

ASIA

EUROPE

KEY
- – – – Disputed border
- ——— National border
- ⊛ Capital city
- ○ Other city

WESTERN SAHARA (under Moroccan control)

ALGERIA

LIBYA

EGYPT

Red Sea

Nile R.

TROPIC OF CANCER

CAPE VERDE

MAURITANIA

Nouakchott ⊛

MALI

NIGER

CHAD

SUDAN

Khartoum ⊛

Asmara ⊛
ERITREA

Blue Nile R.

Gulf of Aden

Praia ○
Dakar ○
SENEGAL
GAMBIA
Banjul ⊛
Bissau ⊛
GUINEA-BISSAU

Niger R.

Bamako ⊛

Niamey ⊛

Ouagadougou ⊛
BURKINA FASO

Kano ○

N'Djamena ⊛

Lake Chad

White Nile R.

SOUTH SUDAN

Addis Ababa ○
ETHIOPIA

Djibouti ⊛
DJIBOUTI

GUINEA
Conakry ⊛
Freetown ⊛
SIERRA LEONE
Yamoussoukro ⊛
Monrovia ⊛
LIBERIA
Abidjan ○

IVORY COAST
GHANA
Porto-Novo ⊛
Lomé ⊛
Accra ⊛
BENIN
TOGO

NIGERIA
Abuja ⊛

Lagos ○

CAMEROON
Yaoundé ⊛

Bangui ⊛
CENTRAL AFRICAN REPUBLIC

Juba ⊛

Lake Turkana

SOMALIA

Mogadishu ⊛

Gulf of Guinea

Malabo ⊛
EQUATORIAL GUINEA
SÃO TOMÉ AND PRÍNCIPE

São Tomé ○

Libreville ⊛
GABON

UGANDA
Kampala ⊛

KENYA
Nairobi ⊛

Kisangani ○

Congo R.

RWANDA
Kigali ⊛
BURUNDI
Bujumbura ⊛

Lake Victoria

Mombasa ○

Victoria ⊛

Brazzaville ⊛
CONGO

Kinshasa ⊛
DEMOCRATIC REPUBLIC OF THE CONGO

Dodoma ⊛
Zanzibar ○
Dar es Salaam ○

SEYCHELLES

CABINDA (Angola)

Luanda ⊛

Lake Tanganyika

TANZANIA

N
W **E**
S

Lubumbashi ○

Moroni ⊛
COMOROS

ATLANTIC OCEAN

ANGOLA

ZAMBIA
Lusaka ⊛

Lake Nyasa

MALAWI
Lilongwe ⊛

Zambezi

MOZAMBIQUE

Mozambique Channel

MADAGASCAR
Antananarivo ⊛

Harare ⊛
ZIMBABWE

NAMIBIA

Windhoek ⊛

BOTSWANA
Gaborone ⊛

Limpopo

Pretoria ⊛

Maputo ⊛
Mbabane ⊛
SWAZILAND

MAURITIUS
Port Louis ⊛
RÉUNION (France)

TROPIC OF CAPRICORN

0 ——— 600 mi
0 ——— 600 km
Lambert Azimuthal Equal-Area Projection

Johannesburg ○
Bloemfontein ⊛

Maseru ⊛
Durban ○

LESOTHO
SOUTH AFRICA

Cape Town ○
Cape of Good Hope

Cape Agulhas

INDIAN OCEAN

30° W   20° W   10° W   0°   10° E   20° E   30° E   40° E   50° E   60° E

40° N   30° N   20° N   10° N   EQUATOR 0°   10° S   20° S   30° S

Africa: Physical

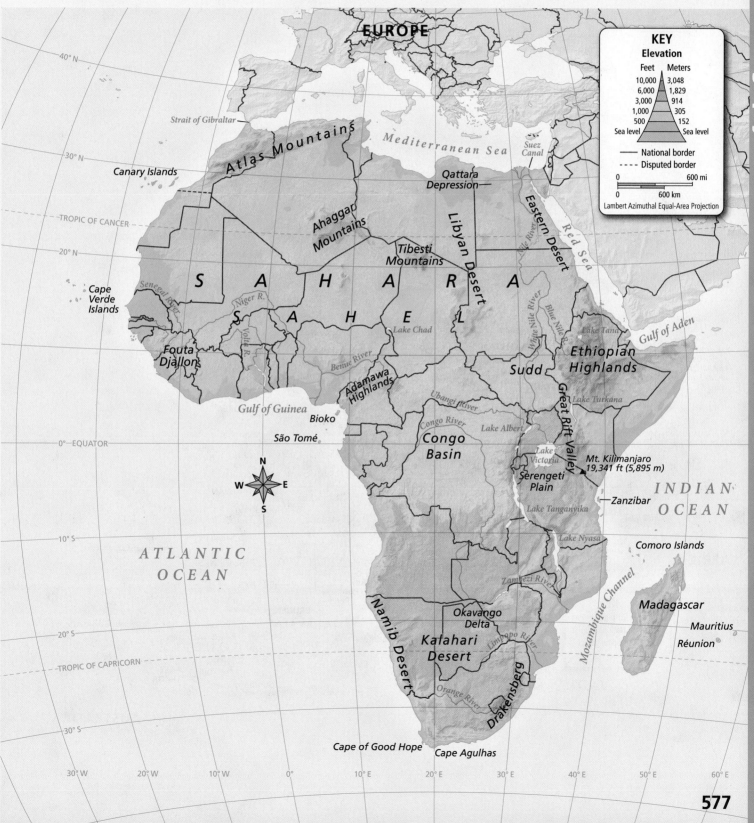

EUROPE

KEY

Elevation

Feet	Meters
10,000	3,048
6,000	1,829
3,000	914
1,000	305
500	152
Sea level	Sea level

—— National border

- - - Disputed border

0   600 mi

0   600 km

Lambert Azimuthal Equal-Area Projection

Strait of Gibraltar

Canary Islands

Atlas Mountains

Mediterranean Sea

Suez Canal

Qattara Depression

TROPIC OF CANCER

Ahaggar Mountains

Tibesti Mountains

Libyan Desert

Eastern Desert

Red Sea

Nile River

20° N

Cape Verde Islands

S A H A R A

S A H E L

Senegal River

Niger R.

Lake Chad

White Nile River

Blue Nile River

Lake Tana

Gulf of Aden

Fouta Djallon

Volta R.

Benue River

Adamawa Highlands

Sudd

Ethiopian Highlands

Gulf of Guinea

Bioko

São Tomé

Ubangi River

Congo River

Lake Albert

Great Rift Valley

Lake Turkana

0°—EQUATOR

Congo Basin

Lake Victoria

Mt. Kilimanjaro 19,341 ft (5,895 m)

Serengeti Plain

INDIAN OCEAN

Zanzibar

Lake Tanganyika

10° S

ATLANTIC OCEAN

Lake Nyasa

Comoro Islands

Zambezi River

Mozambique Channel

Madagascar

Namib Desert

Okavango Delta

Mauritius

Réunion

Kalahari Desert

Limpopo River

TROPIC OF CAPRICORN

Drakensberg

Orange River

Cape of Good Hope

Cape Agulhas

N W E S

30° W   20° W   10° W   0°   10° E   20° E   30° E   40° E   50° E   60° E

40° N

30° N

30° S

Asia: Political

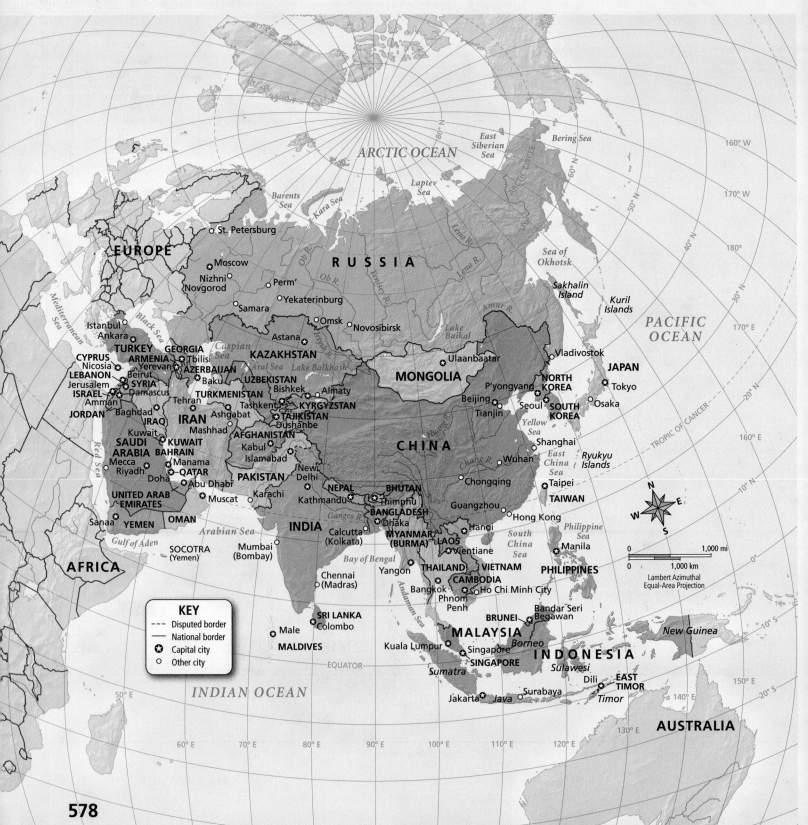

KEY
- - - Disputed border
- —— National border
- ⊛ Capital city
- ○ Other city

578

Asia: Physical

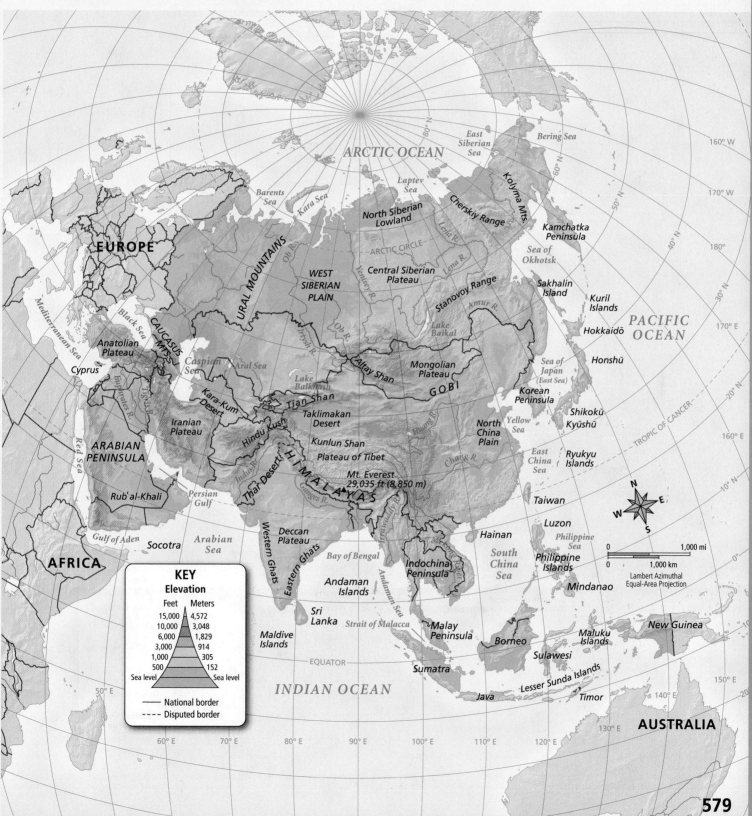

ARCTIC OCEAN

EUROPE

AFRICA

AUSTRALIA

PACIFIC OCEAN

INDIAN OCEAN

Bering Sea

East Siberian Sea

Laptev Sea

Barents Sea

Kara Sea

Sea of Okhotsk

Sea of Japan (East Sea)

Yellow Sea

East China Sea

Philippine Sea

South China Sea

Arabian Sea

Bay of Bengal

Andaman Sea

Black Sea

Caspian Sea

Aral Sea

Mediterranean Sea

Red Sea

Gulf of Aden

Persian Gulf

Gulf of Aden

Lake Baikal

Lake Balkhash

North Siberian Lowland

Cherskiy Range

Kolyma Mts.

Kamchatka Peninsula

Central Siberian Plateau

WEST SIBERIAN PLAIN

URAL MOUNTAINS

Stanovoy Range

Sakhalin Island

Kuril Islands

Hokkaidō

Honshū

Shikokū

Kyūshū

Ryukyu Islands

Taiwan

Luzon

Hainan

Philippine Islands

Mindanao

Mongolian Plateau

GOBI

Korean Peninsula

North China Plain

Plateau of Tibet

HIMALAYAS

Mt. Everest 29,035 ft (8,850 m)

Kunlun Shan

Taklimakan Desert

Altay Shan

Tian Shan

Hindu Kush

Kara-Kum Desert

Iranian Plateau

Thar Desert

Deccan Plateau

Western Ghats

Eastern Ghats

Sri Lanka

Maldive Islands

Andaman Islands

Indochina Peninsula

Malay Peninsula

Sumatra

Borneo

Java

Sulawesi

Lesser Sunda Islands

Timor

Maluku Islands

New Guinea

Anatolian Plateau

Cyprus

CAUCASUS MTS.

ARABIAN PENINSULA

Rub' al-Khali

Socotra

Strait of Malacca

EQUATOR

ARCTIC CIRCLE

TROPIC OF CANCER

Ob R.
Irtysh R.
Yenisey R.
Lena R.
Amur R.
Huang R.
Chang R.
Mekong R.
Ganges R.
Indus R.
Irrawaddy R.
Tigris R.
Euphrates R.

N of N

60° E 70° E 80° E 90° E 100° E 110° E 120° E 130° E 140° E 150° E 160° E 170° E 180° 170° W 160° W

50° N 40° N 30° N 20° N 10° N 0° 10° N 20° N 30° N 40° N 50° N

KEY
Elevation

Feet	Meters
15,000	4,572
10,000	3,048
6,000	1,829
3,000	914
1,000	305
500	152
Sea level	Sea level

—— National border
- - - Disputed border

0   1,000 mi
0   1,000 km
Lambert Azimuthal
Equal-Area Projection

N E S W

Australia and the Pacific

TROPIC OF CANCER

Philippine Sea

NORTHERN MARIANA ISLANDS (U.S.)

GUAM (U.S.)

MARSHALL ISLANDS

Majuro

Melekeok

Caroline Islands

Palikir

PALAU

FEDERATED STATES OF MICRONESIA

Tarawa

EQUATOR

NAURU

Yaren

K I R I B A T I

PAPUA NEW GUINEA

SOLOMON ISLANDS

Honiara

TUVALU

Funafuti

TOKELAU (New Zealand)

Port Moresby

Arafura Sea

Timor Sea

Cape York Peninsula

Great Barrier Reef

Coral Sea

VANUATU

Port-Vila

FIJI

Suva

SAMOA

Apia

AMERICAN SAMOA (U.S.)

NIUE (New Zealand)

Kimberley Plateau

Great Sandy Desert

AUSTRALIA

NEW CALEDONIA (France)

TROPIC OF CAPRICORN

Nuku'alofa

TONGA

COOK ISLANDS (New Zealand)

PACIFIC OCEAN

Gibson Desert

Simpson Desert

Great Artesian Basin

Great Dividing Range

Brisbane

Great Victoria Desert

Darling Range

Nullarbor Plain

Darling River

Perth

Great Australian Bight

Adelaide

Sydney

Canberra

Murray River

Melbourne

Tasman Sea

Auckland

North Island

INDIAN OCEAN

Bass Strait

Tasmania

Hobart

Cook Strait

NEW ZEALAND

South Island

Wellington

Christchurch

Dunedin

KEY
Elevation

Feet	Meters
6,000	1,829
3,000	914
1,000	305
500	152
Sea level	Sea level

— National border
⊛ Capital city
○ Other city

0 — 600 mi

0 — 600 km

Mercator Projection

580

The Arctic

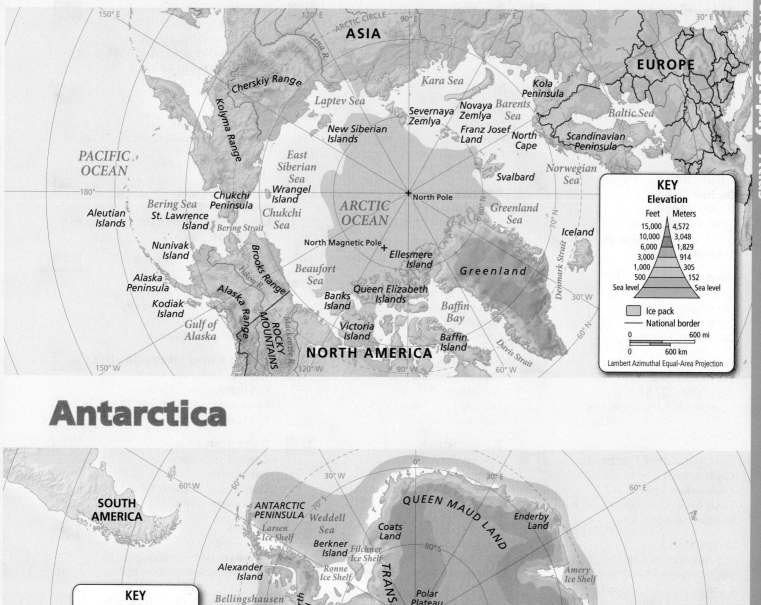

ASIA

EUROPE

150° E

120° E

ARCTIC CIRCLE

90° E

60° E

30° E

Cherskiy Range

Kara Sea

Kola Peninsula

Kolyma Range

Laptev Sea

Severnaya Zemlya

Novaya Zemlya

Barents Sea

Baltic Sea

New Siberian Islands

Franz Josef Land

North Cape

Scandinavian Peninsula

PACIFIC OCEAN

East Siberian Sea

Svalbard

Norwegian Sea

180°

Wrangel Island

Chukchi Peninsula

Chukchi Sea

ARCTIC OCEAN

North Pole

Greenland Sea

Bering Sea

Aleutian Islands

St. Lawrence Island

Bering Strait

70° N

Iceland

Nunivak Island

North Magnetic Pole

Ellesmere Island

Denmark Strait

Alaska Peninsula

Brooks Range

Beaufort Sea

Greenland

Yukon R.

Kodiak Island

Alaska Range

Banks Island

Queen Elizabeth Islands

Baffin Bay

30° W

Mackenzie R.

ROCKY MOUNTAINS

Gulf of Alaska

Victoria Island

Baffin Island

60° N

150° W

120° W

90° W

NORTH AMERICA

Davis Strait

KEY
Elevation

Feet	Meters
15,000	4,572
10,000	3,048
6,000	1,829
3,000	914
1,000	305
500	152
Sea level	Sea level

☐ Ice pack
— National border

0 — 600 mi
0 — 600 km

Lambert Azimuthal Equal-Area Projection

Antarctica

SOUTH AMERICA

60° W

30° W

0°

30° E

60° E

QUEEN MAUD LAND

ANTARCTIC PENINSULA

Weddell Sea

Coats Land

Enderby Land

Larsen Ice Shelf

70° S

Berkner Island

Filchner Ice Shelf

80° S

Amery Ice Shelf

Alexander Island

Ronne Ice Shelf

Bellingshausen Sea

TRANSANTARCTIC MOUNTAINS

Polar Plateau

ANTARCTICA

90° W

Ellsworth Land

▲ Vinson Massif
16,067 ft (4,897 m)

South Pole

90° E

KEY
Elevation

Feet	Meters
10,000	3,048
6,000	1,829
3,000	914
1,000	305
500	152
Sea level	Sea level

☐ Ice pack
☐ Ice shelf

0 — 400 mi
0 — 400 km

Lambert Azimuthal Equal-Area Projection

Amundsen Sea

Marie Byrd Land

Queen Maud Mts.

Ross Ice Shelf

WILKES LAND

ANTARCTIC CIRCLE

120° W

Roosevelt Island

Ross Sea

Victoria Land

South Magnetic Pole

150° W

180°

60° S

120° E

581

Country Databank

Afghanistan

Capital: Kabul
Population: 32.7 million
Land Area: 647,500 sq km; 250,000 sq mi
Continent: Asia

Albania
Capital: Tirana
Population: 3.6 million
Land Area: 27,398 sq km; 10,578 sq mi
Continent: Europe

Algeria
Capital: Algiers
Population: 33.8 million
Land Area: 2,381,740 sq km;
    919,590 sq mi
Continent: Africa

Andorra
Capital: Andorra la Vella
Population: 82,627
Land Area: 468 sq km; 181 sq mi
Continent: Europe

Angola
Capital: Luanda
Population: 12.5 million
Land Area: 1,246,700 sq km;
    481   551 sq mi
Continent: Africa

Antigua and Barbuda
Capital: Saint John's
Population: 84,522
Land Area: 442 sq km; 171 sq mi
Continent: North America

Argentina

Capital: Buenos Aires
Population: 40.5 million
Land Area: 2,736,690 sq km;
    1,056,636 sq mi
Continent: South America

Armenia
Capital: Yerevan
Population: 3 million
Land Area: 28,454 sq km; 10,986 sq mi
Continent: Asia

Australia

Capital: Canberra
Population: 21 million
Land Area: 7,617,930 sq km;
    2,941,283 sq mi
Continent: Australia and Oceania

Austria
Capital: Vienna
Population: 8.2 million
Land Area: 82,444 sq km; 31,832 sq mi
Continent: Europe

Azerbaijan

Capital: Baku
Population: 8.2 million
Land Area: 86,100 sq km; 33,243 sq mi
Continent: Asia

Bahamas
Capital: Nassau
Population: 307,541
Land Area: 10,070 sq km; 3,888 sq mi
Continent: North America

Bahrain
Capital: Manama
Population: 718,306
Land Area: 665 sq km; 257 sq mi
Continent: Asia

Bangladesh

Capital: Dhaka
Population: 153.5 million
Land Area: 133,910 sq km; 51,705 sq mi
Continent: Asia

Barbados

Capital: Bridgetown
Population: 281,968
Land Area: 431 sq km; 166 sq mi
Continent: North America

Belarus
Capital: Minsk
Population: 9.7 million
Land Area: 207,600 sq km; 80,154 sq mi
Continent: Europe

Belgium
Capital: Brussels
Population: 10.4 million
Land Area: 30,278 sq km; 11,690 sq mi
Continent: Europe

Belize
Capital: Belmopan
Population: 301,270
Land Area: 22,806 sq km; 8,805 sq mi
Continent: North America

Benin
Capital: Porto-Novo
Population: 8.5 million
Land Area: 110,620 sq km; 42,710 sq mi
Continent: Africa

Bhutan

Capital: Thimphu
Population: 682,321
Land Area: 47,000 sq km; 18,147 sq mi
Continent: Asia

Bolivia
Capitals: La Paz and Sucre
Population: 9.2 million
Land Area: 1,084,390 sq km;
    418,683 sq mi
Continent: South America

Bosnia and Herzegovina
Capital: Sarajevo
Population: 4.6 million
Land Area: 51,197 sq km; 19,767 sq mi
Continent: Europe

Botswana

Capital: Gaborone
Population: 1.8 million
Land Area: 585,370 sq km; 226,011 sq mi
Continent: Africa

Brazil

Capital: Brasília
Population: 196 million
Land Area: 8,456,510 sq km;
    3,265,059 sq mi
Continent: South America

Brunei

Capital: Bandar Seri Begawan
Population: 381,371
Land Area: 5,270 sq km; 2,035 sq mi
Continent: Asia

Bulgaria

Capital: Sofía
Population: 7.3 million
Land Area: 110,550 sq km; 42,683 sq mi
Continent: Europe

Burkina Faso

Capital: Ouagadougou
Population: 15.3 million
Land Area: 273,800 sq km; 105,714 sq mi
Continent: Africa

Burundi

Capital: Bujumbura
Population: 8.7 million
Land Area: 25,650 sq km; 9,903 sq mi
Continent: Africa

Cambodia

Capital: Phnom Penh
Population: 14.2 million
Land Area: 176,520 sq km; 68,154 sq mi
Continent: Asia

Cameroon

Capital: Yaoundé
Population: 18.5 million
Land Area: 469,440 sq km; 181,251 sq mi
Continent: Africa

Canada

Capital: Ottawa
Population: 33.2 million
Land Area: 9,093,507 sq km;
3,511,009 sq mi
Continent: North America

Cape Verde

Capital: Praia
Population: 426,998
Land Area: 4,033 sq km; 1,557 sq mi
Continent: Africa

Central African Republic

Capital: Bangui
Population: 4.4 million
Land Area: 622,984 sq km; 240,534 sq mi
Continent: Africa

Chad

Capital: N'Djamena
Population: 10.1 million
Land Area: 1,259,200 sq km;
486,177 sq mi
Continent: Africa

Chile

Capital: Santiago
Population: 16.5 million
Land Area: 748,800 sq km; 289,112 sq mi
Continent: South America

China

Capital: Beijing
Population: 1.33 billion
Land Area: 9,326,410 sq km;
3,600,927 sq mi
Continent: Asia

Colombia

Capital: Bogotá
Population: 45 million
Land Area: 1,038,700 sq km;
401,042 sq mi
Continent: South America

Comoros

Capital: Moroni
Population: 731,775
Land Area: 2,170 sq km; 838 sq mi
Continent: Africa

Congo, Democratic Republic of the

Capital: Kinshasa
Population: 66.5 million
Land Area: 2,267,600 sq km;
875,520 sq mi
Continent: Africa

Congo, Republic of the

Capital: Brazzaville
Population: 3.9 million
Land Area: 341,500 sq km; 131,853 sq mi
Continent: Africa

Costa Rica

Capital: San José
Population: 4.2 million
Land Area: 50,660 sq km; 19,560 sq mi
Continent: North America

Croatia

Capital: Zagreb
Population: 4.5 million
Land Area: 56,414 km; 21,781 sq mi
Continent: Europe

Cuba

Capital: Havana
Population: 11.4 million
Land Area: 110,860 sq km; 42,803 sq mi
Continent: North America

Cyprus

Capital: Nicosia
Population: 792,604
Land Area: 9,240 sq km; 3,568 sq mi
Continent: Europe

Czech Republic

Capital: Prague
Population: 10.2 million
Land Area: 77,276 sq km; 29,836 sq mi
Continent: Europe

Denmark

Capital: Copenhagen
Population: 5.5 million
Land Area: 42,394 sq km; 16,368 sq mi
Continent: Europe

Djibouti

Capital: Djibouti
Population: 506,221
Land Area: 22,980 sq km; 8,873 sq mi
Continent: Africa

Dominica

Capital: Roseau
Population: 72,514
Land Area: 754 sq km; 291 sq mi
Continent: North America

Dominican Republic

Capital: Santo Domingo
Population: 9.5 million
Land Area: 48,380 sq km; 18,679 sq mi
Continent: North America

Ecuador

Capital: Quito
Population: 13.9 million
Land Area: 276,840 sq km; 106,888 sq mi
Continent: South America

Country Databank (continued)

Egypt

Capital: Cairo
Population: 81.7 million
Land Area: 995,450 sq km; 384,343 sq mi
Continent: Africa

El Salvador

Capital: San Salvador
Population: 7.1 million
Land Area: 20,720 sq km; 8,000 sq mi
Continent: North America

Equatorial Guinea

Capital: Malabo
Population: 616,459
Land Area: 28,051 sq km; 10,831 sq mi
Continent: Africa

Eritrea

Capital: Asmara
Population: 5.5 million
Land Area: 121,320 sq km; 46,842 sq mi
Continent: Africa

Estonia

Capital: Tallinn
Population: 1.3 million
Land Area: 43,211 sq km; 16,684 sq mi
Continent: Europe

Ethiopia
Capital: Addis Ababa
Population: 82.5 million
Land Area: 1,119,683 sq km;
      432,310 sq mi
Continent: Africa

Fiji
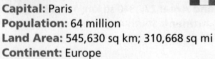
Capital: Suva
Population: 931,741
Land Area: 18,270 sq km; 7,054 sq mi
Continent: Australia and Oceania

Finland
Capital: Helsinki
Population: 5.2 million
Land Area: 304,473 sq km; 117,557 sq mi
Continent: Europe

France
Capital: Paris
Population: 64 million
Land Area: 545,630 sq km; 310,668 sq mi
Continent: Europe

Gabon

Capital: Libreville
Population: 1.5 million
Land Area: 257,667 sq km; 99,489 sq mi
Continent: Africa

The Gambia
Capital: Banjul
Population: 1.7 million
Land Area: 10,000 sq km; 3,861 sq mi
Continent: Africa

Georgia

Capital: T'bilisi
Population: 4.6 million
Land Area: 69,700 sq km; 26,911 sq mi
Continent: Asia

Germany
Capital: Berlin
Population: 82.4 million
Land Area: 349,223 sq km; 134,835 sq mi
Continent: Europe

Ghana

Capital: Accra
Population: 23.4 million
Land Area: 230,940 sq km; 89,166 sq mi
Continent: Africa

Greece
Capital: Athens
Population: 10.7 million
Land Area: 130,800 sq km; 50,502 sq mi
Continent: Europe

Grenada

Capital: Saint George's
Population: 90,343
Land Area: 344 sq km; 133 sq mi
Continent: North America

Guatemala

Capital: Guatemala City
Population: 13 million
Land Area: 108,430 sq km; 41,865 sq mi
Continent: North America

Guinea
Capital: Conakry
Population: 9.8 million
Land Area: 245,857 sq km; 94,925 sq mi
Continent: Africa

Guinea-Bissau

Capital: Bissau
Population: 1.5 million
Land Area: 28,000 sq km; 10,811 sq mi
Continent: Africa

Guyana
Capital: Georgetown
Population: 770,794
Land Area: 196,850 sq km; 76,004 sq mi
Continent: South America

Haiti
Capital: Port-au-Prince
Population: 8.9 million
Land Area: 27,560 sq km; 10,641 sq mi
Continent: North America

Holy See (Vatican City)

Capital: Vatican City
Population: 824
Land Area: 0.44 sq km; 0.17 sq mi
Continent: Europe

Honduras

Capital: Tegucigalpa
Population: 7.6 million
Land Area: 111,890 sq km; 43,201 sq mi
Continent: North America

Hungary

Capital: Budapest
Population: 9.9 million
Land Area: 92,340 sq km; 35,652 sq mi
Continent: Europe

Iceland
Capital: Reykjavík
Population: 304,367
Land Area: 100,250 sq km; 38,707 sq mi
Continent: Europe

India

Capital: New Delhi
Population: 1.15 billion
Land Area: 2,973,190 sq km;
      1,147,949 sq mi
Continent: Asia

Indonesia

Capital: Jakarta
Population: 237.5 million
Land Area: 1,826,440 sq km;
      705,188 sq mi
Continent: Asia

Iran

Capital: Tehran
Population: 65.9 million
Land Area: 1,636,000 sq km;
631,660 sq mi
Continent: Asia

Iraq

Capital: Baghdad
Population: 28.2 million
Land Area: 432,162 sq km; 166,858 sq mi
Continent: Asia

Ireland
Capital: Dublin
Population: 4.2 million
Land Area: 68,890 sq km; 26,598 sq mi
Continent: Europe

Israel
Capital: Jerusalem
Population: 7.1 million
Land Area: 20,330 sq km; 7,849 sq mi
Continent: Asia

Italy
Capital: Rome
Population: 58.2 million
Land Area: 294,020 sq km; 113,521 sq mi
Continent: Europe

Ivory Coast
Capital: Yamoussoukro
Population: 20.2 million
Land Area: 318,000 sq km; 122,780 sq mi
Continent: Africa

Jamaica
Capital: Kingston
Population: 2.8 million
Land Area: 10,831 sq km; 4,182 sq mi
Continent: North America

Japan
Capital: Tokyo
Population: 127.3 million
Land Area: 374,744 sq km; 144,689 sq mi
Continent: Asia

Jordan
Capital: Amman
Population: 6.2 million
Land Area: 91,971 sq km; 35,510 sq mi
Continent: Asia

Kazakhstan
Capital: Astana
Population: 15.3 million
Land Area: 2,669,800 sq km;
1,030,810 sq mi
Continent: Asia

Kenya

Capital: Nairobi
Population: 38 million
Land Area: 569,250 sq km; 219,787 sq mi
Continent: Africa

Kiribati

Capital: Bairiki (Tarawa Atoll)
Population: 110,356
Land Area: 811 sq km; 313 sq mi
Continent: Australia and Oceania

Korea, North

Capital: Pyongyang
Population: 23.5 million
Land Area: 120,410 sq km; 46,490 sq mi
Continent: Asia

Korea, South

Capital: Seoul
Population: 48.4 million
Land Area: 98,190 sq km; 37,911 sq mi
Continent: Asia

Kosovo

Capital: Pristina
Population: 2.1 million
Land Area: 10,887 sq km; 4,203 sq mi
Continent: Europe

Kuwait

Capital: Kuwait City
Population: 2.6 million
Land Area: 17,820 sq km; 6,880 sq mi
Continent: Asia

Kyrgyzstan

Capital: Bishkek
Population: 5.4 million
Land Area: 191,300 sq km; 73,861sq mi
Continent: Asia

Laos

Capital: Vientiane
Population: 6.7 million
Land Area: 230,800 sq km; 89,112 sq mi
Continent: Asia

Latvia
Capital: Riga
Population: 2.3 million
Land Area: 63,589 sq km; 24,552 sq mi
Continent: Europe

Lebanon
Capital: Beirut
Population: 4 million
Land Area: 10,230 sq km; 3,950 sq mi
Continent: Asia

Lesotho
Capital: Maseru
Population: 2.1 million
Land Area: 30,355 sq km; 11,720 sq mi
Continent: Africa

Liberia
Capital: Monrovia
Population: 3.3 million
Land Area: 96,320 sq km; 37,189 sq mi
Continent: Africa

Libya
Capital: Tripoli
Population: 6.2 million
Land Area: 1,759,540 sq km;
679,358 sq mi
Continent: Africa

Liechtenstein

Capital: Vaduz
Population: 34,498
Land Area: 160 sq km; 62 sq mi
Continent: Europe

Lithuania
Capital: Vilnius
Population: 3.6 million
Land Area: 65,300 sq km; 25,212 sq mi
Continent: Europe

Luxembourg
Capital: Luxembourg
Population: 486,006
Land Area: 2,586 sq km; 998 sq mi
Continent: Europe

Macedonia
Capital: Skopje
Population: 2.1 million
Land Area: 24,856 sq km; 9,597 sq mi
Continent: Europe

Country Databank (continued)

Madagascar

Capital: Antananarivo
Population: 20 million
Land Area: 581,540 sq km; 224,533 sq mi
Continent: Africa

Malawi
Capital: Lilongwe
Population: 13.9 million
Land Area: 94,080 sq km; 36,324 sq mi
Continent: Africa

Malaysia
Capital: Kuala Lumpur
Population: 25.3 million
Land Area: 328,550 sq km; 126,853 sq mi
Continent: Asia

Maldives
Capital: Malé
Population: 385,925
Land Area: 300 sq km; 116 sq mi
Continent: Asia

Mali
Capital: Bamako
Population: 12.3 million
Land Area: 1,220,000 sq km; 471,042 sq mi
Continent: Africa

Malta
Capital: Valletta
Population: 403,532
Land Area: 316 sq km; 122 sq mi
Continent: Europe

Marshall Islands
Capital: Majuro
Population: 63,174
Land Area: 181.3 sq km; 70 sq mi
Continent: Australia and Oceania

Mauritania
Capital: Nouakchott
Population: 3.4 million
Land Area: 1,030,400 sq km; 397,837 sq mi
Continent: Africa

Mauritius

Capital: Port Louis
Population: 1.3 million
Land Area: 2,030 sq km; 784 sq mi
Continent: Africa

Mexico

Capital: Mexico City
Population: 110 million
Land Area: 1,923,040 sq km; 742,486 sq mi
Continent: North America

Micronesia, Federated States of
Capital: Palikir (Pohnpei Island)
Population: 107,665
Land Area: 702 sq km; 271 sq mi
Continent: Australia and Oceania

Moldova
Capital: Chisinau
Population: 4.3 million
Land Area: 33,371 sq km; 12,885 sq mi
Continent: Europe

Monaco
Capital: Monaco
Population: 32,796
Land Area: 1.95 sq km; 0.75 sq mi
Continent: Europe

Mongolia
Capital: Ulaanbaatar
Population: 3.0 million
Land Area: 1,554,731 sq km; 600,283 sq mi
Continent: Asia

Montenegro
Capital: Podgorica
Population: 678,177
Land Area: 13,812 sq km; 5,333 sq mi
Continent: Europe

Morocco
Capital: Rabat
Population: 34.3 million
Land Area: 446,300 sq km; 172,316 sq mi
Continent: Africa

Mozambique
Capital: Maputo
Population: 21.3 million
Land Area: 784,090 sq km; 302,737 sq mi
Continent: Africa

Myanmar (Burma)
Capital: Yangon (Rangoon)
Population: 47.8 million
Land Area: 657,740 sq km; 253,953 sq mi
Continent: Asia

Namibia

Capital: Windhoek
Population: 2.1 million
Land Area: 825,418 sq km; 318,694 sq mi
Continent: Africa

Nauru
Capital: Yaren District
Population: 13,770
Land Area: 21 sq km; 8 sq mi
Continent: Australia and Oceania

Nepal

Capital: Kathmandu
Population: 29.5 million
Land Area: 143,181 sq km; 55,282 sq mi
Continent: Asia

Netherlands
Capital: Amsterdam
Population: 16.7 million
Land Area: 33,883 sq km; 13,082 sq mi
Continent: Europe

New Zealand
Capital: Wellington
Population: 4.2 million
Land Area: 268,021 sq km; 103,483 sq mi
Continent: Australia and Oceania

Nicaragua
Capital: Managua
Population: 5.8 million
Land Area: 120,254 sq km; 46,430 sq mi
Continent: North America

Niger
Capital: Niamey
Population: 13.3 million
Land Area: 1,226,700 sq km; 489,073 sq mi
Continent: Africa

Nigeria
Capital: Abuja
Population: 146.3 million
Land Area: 910,768 sq km; 351,648 sq mi
Continent: Africa

Norway

Capital: Oslo
Population: 4.6 million
Land Area: 307,442 sq km; 118,704 sq mi
Continent: Europe

Oman

Capital: Muscat
Population: 3.3 million
Land Area: 212,460 sq km; 82,030 sq mi
Continent: Asia

Pakistan

Capital: Islamabad
Population: 172.8 million
Land Area: 778,720 sq km; 300,664 sq mi
Continent: Asia

Palau

Capital: Koror
Population: 21,093
Land Area: 458 sq km; 177 sq mi
Continent: Australia and Oceania

Panama

Capital: Panama City
Population: 3.3 million
Land Area: 75,990 sq km; 29,340 sq mi
Continent: North America

Papua New Guinea

Capital: Port Moresby
Population: 5.9 million
Land Area: 452,860 sq km; 174,849 sq mi
Continent: Australia and Oceania

Paraguay
Capital: Asunción
Population: 6.8 million
Land Area: 397,300 sq km; 153,398 sq mi
Continent: South America

Peru
Capital: Lima
Population: 29.2 million
Land Area: 1,280,000 sq km;
 494,208 sq mi
Continent: South America

Philippines
Capital: Manila
Population: 96.1 million
Land Area: 298,170 sq km; 115,123 sq mi
Continent: Asia

Poland
Capital: Warsaw
Population: 38.5 million
Land Area: 304,459 sq km; 117,552 sq mi
Continent: Europe

Portugal

Capital: Lisbon
Population: 10.7 million
Land Area: 91,951 sq km; 35,502 sq mi
Continent: Europe

Qatar

Capital: Doha
Population: 824,789
Land Area: 11,437 sq km; 4,416 sq mi
Continent: Asia

Romania

Capital: Bucharest
Population: 22.3 million
Land Area: 230,340 sq km; 88,934 sq mi
Continent: Europe

Russia
Capital: Moscow
Population: 140.7 million
Land Area: 16,995,800 sq km;
 6,592,100 sq mi
Continent: Europe and Asia

Rwanda

Capital: Kigali
Population: 10.2 million
Land Area: 24,948 sq km; 9,632 sq mi
Continent: Africa

Saint Kitts and Nevis

Capital: Basseterre
Population: 39,817
Land Area: 261 sq km; 101 sq mi
Continent: North America

Saint Lucia

Capital: Castries
Population: 159,585
Land Area: 606 sq km; 234 sq mi
Continent: North America

Saint Vincent
 and the Grenadines

Capital: Kingstown
Population: 118,432
Land Area: 389 sq km; 150 sq mi
Continent: North America

Samoa

Capital: Apia
Population: 217,083
Land Area: 2,934 sq km; 1,133 sq mi
Continent: Australia and Oceania

San Marino

Capital: San Marino
Population: 29,973
Land Area: 61 sq km; 24 sq mi
Continent: Europe

São Tomé and Príncipe
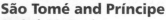
Capital: São Tomé
Population: 206,178
Land Area: 1,001 sq km; 386 sq mi
Continent: Africa

Saudi Arabia

Capital: Riyadh and Jiddah
Population: 28.2 million
Land Area: 2,149,690 sq km;
 829,997 sq mi
Continent: Asia

Senegal
Capital: Dakar
Population: 12.9 million
Land Area: 192,000 sq km; 74,131 sq mi
Continent: Africa

Serbia
Capital: Belgrade
Population: 10.2 million
Land Area: 77,474 sq km; 29,913 sq mi
Continent: Europe

Seychelles
Capital: Victoria
Population: 82,247
Land Area: 455 sq km; 176 sq mi
Continent: Africa

Sierra Leone
Capital: Freetown
Population: 6.3 million
Land Area: 71,620 sq km; 27,652 sq mi
Continent: Africa

Singapore
Capital: Singapore
Population: 4.6 million
Land Area: 683 sq km; 264 sq mi
Continent: Asia

Slovakia

Capital: Bratislava
Population: 5.5 million
Land Area: 48,800 sq km; 18,842 sq mi
Continent: Europe

Country Databank (continued)

Slovenia

Capital: Ljubljana
Population: 2 million
Land Area: 20,151 sq km; 7,780 sq mi
Continent: Europe

Solomon Islands
Capital: Honiara
Population: 581,318
Land Area: 27,540 sq km; 10,633 sq mi
Continent: Australia and Oceania

Somalia
Capital: Mogadishu
Population: 9.6 million
Land Area: 627,337 sq km; 242,215 sq mi
Continent: Africa

South Africa
Capitals: Cape Town, Pretoria, and Bloemfontein
Population: 48.8 million
Land Area: 1,219,912 sq km; 471,008 sq mi
Continent: Africa

Spain
Capital: Madrid
Population: 40.5 million
Land Area: 499,542 sq km; 192,873 sq mi
Continent: Europe

Sri Lanka
Capital: Colombo
Population: 21.1 million
Land Area: 64,740 sq km; 24,996 sq mi
Continent: Asia

Sudan, South
Capital: Juba
Population: 9,385,000
Land Area: 644,330 sq km; 248,777 sq mi
Continent: Africa

Sudan
Capital: Khartoum
Population: 36.7 million
Land Area: 1,844,797 sq km; 712,280 sq mi
Continent: Africa

Suriname
Capital: Paramaribo
Population: 475,996
Land Area: 161,470 sq km; 62,344 sq mi
Continent: South America

Swaziland
Capital: Mbabane
Population: 1.1 million
Land Area: 17,203 sq km; 6,642 sq mi
Continent: Africa

Sweden
Capital: Stockholm
Population: 9 million
Land Area: 410,934 sq km; 158,662 sq mi
Continent: Europe

Switzerland

Capital: Bern
Population: 7.6 million
Land Area: 39,770 sq km; 15,355 sq mi
Continent: Europe

Syria
Capital: Damascus
Population: 19.8 million
Land Area: 184,050 sq km; 71,062 sq mi
Continent: Asia

Taiwan
Capital: Taipei
Population: 22.9 million
Land Area: 32,260 sq km; 12,456 sq mi
Continent: Asia

Tajikistan
Capital: Dushanbe
Population: 7.2 million
Land Area: 142,700 sq km; 55,096 sq mi
Continent: Asia

Tanzania
Capitals: Dar es Salaam and Dodoma
Population: 40.2 million
Land Area: 886,037 sq km; 342,099
Continent: Africa

Thailand
Capital: Bangkok
Population: 65.5 million
Land Area: 511,770 sq km; 197,564 sq mi
Continent: Asia

Timor-Leste

Capital: Dili
Population: 1.1 million
Land Area: 15,007 sq km; 5,794 sq mi
Continent: Asia

Togo
Capital: Lomé
Population: 5.9 million
Land Area: 54,385 sq km; 20,998 sq mi
Continent: Africa

Tonga
Capital: Nuku'alofa
Population: 119,009
Land Area: 718 sq km; 277 sq mi
Continent: Australia and Oceania

Trinidad and Tobago
Capital: Port-of-Spain
Population: 1.2 million
Land Area: 5,128 sq km; 1,980 sq mi
Continent: North America

Tunisia

Capital: Tunis
Population: 10.4 million
Land Area: 155,360 sq km; 59,984 sq mi
Continent: Africa

Turkey

Capital: Ankara
Population: 71.9 million
Land Area: 770,760 sq km; 297,590 sq mi
Continent: Asia

Turkmenistan
Capital: Ashgabat
Population: 5.2 million
Land Area: 488,100 sq km; 188,455 sq mi
Continent: Asia

Tuvalu

Capital: Funafuti
Population: 12,177
Land Area: 26 sq km; 10 sq mi
Continent: Australia and Oceania

Uganda
Capital: Kampala
Population: 31.4 million
Land Area: 199,710 sq km; 77,108 sq mi
Continent: Africa

Ukraine
Capital: Kyiv (Kiev)
Population: 46 million
Land Area: 603,700 sq km; 233,090 sq mi
Continent: Europe

United Arab Emirates

Capital: Abu Dhabi
Population: 4.6 million
Land Area: 83,600 sq km; 32,278 sq mi
Continent: Asia

United Kingdom

Capital: London
Population: 60.9 million
Land Area: 241,590 sq km; 93,278 sq mi
Continent: Europe

United States

Capital: Washington, D.C.
Population: 303.8 million
Land Area: 9,161,923 sq km;
3,537,424 sq mi
Continent: North America

Uruguay

Capital: Montevideo
Population: 3.5 million
Land Area: 173,620 sq km; 67,100 sq mi
Continent: South America

Uzbekistan

Capital: Tashkent
Population: 27.3 million
Land Area: 425,400 sq km; 164,247 sq mi
Continent: Asia

Vanuatu

Capital: Port-Vila
Population: 215,446
Land Area: 12,200 sq km; 4,710 sq mi
Continent: Australia and Oceania

Venezuela

Capital: Caracas
Population: 26.4 million
Land Area: 882,050 sq km; 340,560 sq mi
Continent: South America

Vietnam

Capital: Hanoi
Population: 86.1 million
Land Area: 325,360 sq km; 125,622 sq mi
Continent: Asia

Yemen

Capital: Sanaa
Population: 23 million
Land Area: 527,970 sq km; 203,849 sq mi
Continent: Asia

Zambia

Capital: Lusaka
Population: 11.7 million
Land Area: 740,724 sq km; 285,994 sq mi
Continent: Africa

Zimbabwe

Capital: Harare
Population: 11.4 million
Land Area: 386,670 sq km; 149,293 sq mi
Continent: Africa

SOURCE: *CIA World Factbook Online, 2009*

Landforms and Water Features

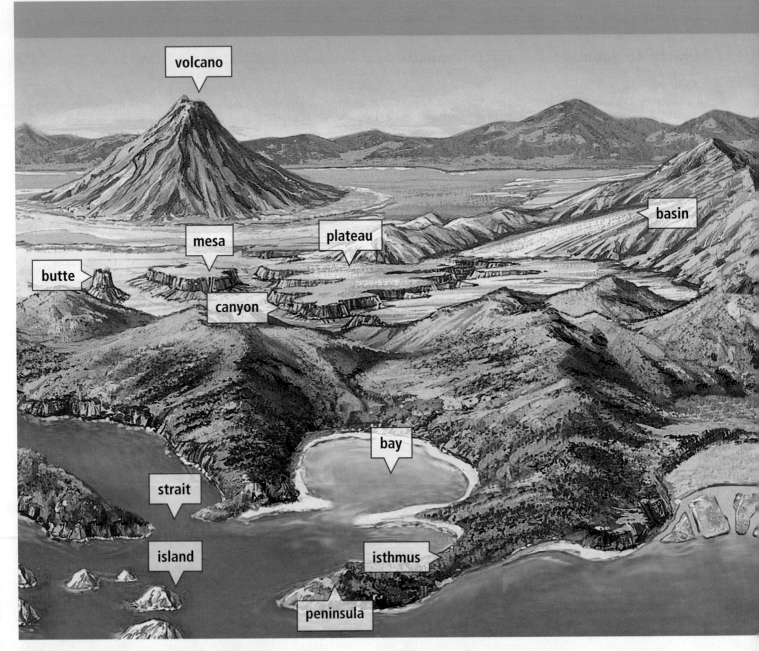

volcano

basin

mesa

plateau

butte

canyon

bay

strait

island

isthmus

peninsula

basin an area that is lower than surrounding land areas; some basins are filled with water

bay a part of a larger body of water that extends into the land

butte a small, high, flat-topped landform with cliff-like sides

canyon a deep, narrow valley with steep sides; often has a stream flowing through it

cataract a large waterfall or steep rapids

delta a plain at the mouth of a river, often triangular in shape, formed when material is deposited by flowing water

flood plain a broad plain on either side of a river, formed when sediment settles during floods

glacier a huge, slow-moving mass of snow and ice

hill an area that rises above surrounding land and has a rounded top; lower and usually less steep than a mountain

island an area of land completely surrounded by water

isthmus a narrow strip of land that connects two larger areas of land

mesa a high, flat-topped landform with cliff-like sides; larger than a butte

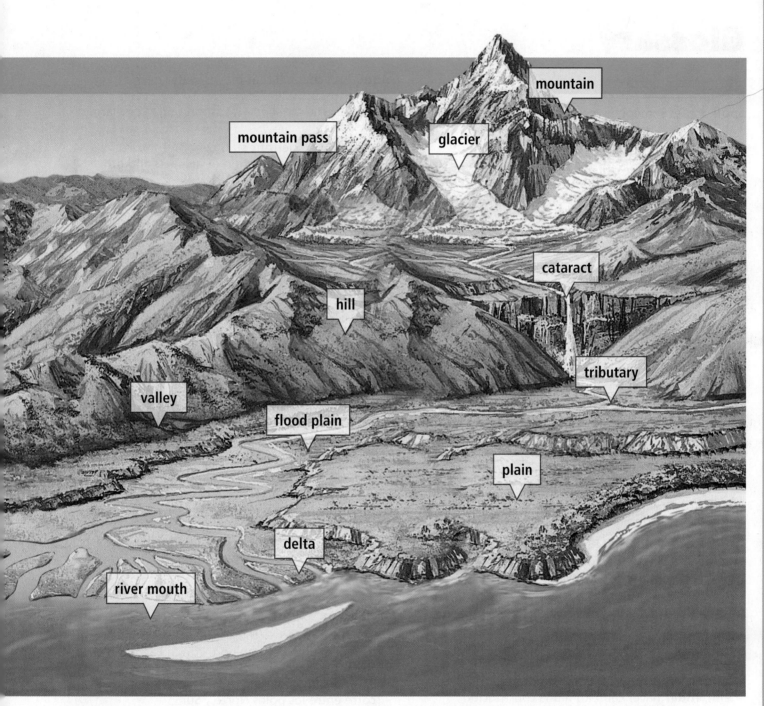

mountain

mountain pass

glacier

cataract

hill

tributary

valley

flood plain

plain

delta

river mouth

mountain a landform that rises steeply at least 2,000 feet (610 meters) above surrounding land; usually wide at the bottom and rising to a narrow peak or ridge

mountain pass a gap between mountains

peninsula an area of land almost completely surrounded by water and connected to the mainland by an isthmus

plain a large area of flat or gently rolling land

plateau a large, flat area that rises above the surrounding land; at least one side has a steep slope

river mouth the point where a river enters a lake or sea

strait a narrow stretch of water that connects two larger bodies of water

tributary a river or stream that flows into a larger river

valley a low stretch of land between mountains or hills; land that is drained by a river

volcano an opening in Earth's surface through which molten rock, ash, and gases from Earth's interior escape

591

Glossary

A

abolitionist someone who wanted to end slavery (p. 354)
abolicionista dícese de una persona que quiso acabar con la esclavitud

absolute location exact position on Earth in terms of longitude and latitude (p. 6)
ubicación absoluta posición exacta en la Tierra según la longitud y la latitud

absolutism centralized and unlimited government power (p. 436)
absolutismo poder ilimitado y centralizado del gobierno

acid rain rain, snow, or mist that is acidic (p. 511)
lluvia ácida lluvia, nieve o neblina con ácidos disueltos

adapt to change according to available resources or other existing conditions (p. 152)
adaptar cambiar según los recursos disponibles o las condiciones presentes

aerial photograph photographic image of Earth's surface taken from the air (p. 8)
fotografía aérea imagen fotográfica de la superficie de la Tierra que se tomó desde el aire

ally political or military partner (p. 265)
aliado asociado político o militar

Altiplano high plateau in Peru and Bolivia (p. 313)
altiplano meseta de gran altitud en Perú y Bolivia

altitude height above sea level (pp. 35, 213)
altitud altura sobre el nivel del mar

Amazon basin all the land drained by the Amazon River (p. 345)
cuenca amazónica área de drenaje del río Amazonas

amend make changes to a constitution (p. 333)
enmendar hacer cambios a una constitución

annex take control of (p. 153)
anexar hacer propio algo

anthropology study of humankind in all aspects, especially development and culture (p. 123)
antropología estudio de todos los aspectos de la humanidad, especialmente el desarrollo y la cultura

aqueduct channel that moves water over a long distance (pp. 223, 395)
acueducto canal que transporta agua por largas distancias

archaeology scientific study of ancient cultures through the examination of artifacts and other evidence (p. 123)
arqueología estudio científico de las culturas antiguas a través del análisis de artefactos y otros tipos de evidencia

architect person who designs buildings (p. 94)
arquitecto persona que diseña edificios

architecture the design and construction of buildings (p. 94)
arquitectura diseño y construcción de edificios

arid climate very dry desert climate (p. 41)
clima árido clima desértico muy seco

artifact object made by a human being (p. 120)
artefacto objeto hecho por un ser humano

astronomy the study of the stars and planets (p. 223)
astronomía estudio de las estrellas y los planetas

atmosphere thick layer of gases or air (p. 23)
atmósfera capa gruesa de gases o aire

austerity measure government policies meant to save money (p. 293)
medidas de austeridad políticas gubernamentales con fines de ahorro

authoritarian government in which all power is held by a single person or a small group (p. 107)
autoritario gobierno en el que todo el poder yace en un individuo o grupo pequeño

autonomy self-rule (p. 337)
autonomía gobernarse a sí mismo

axis imaginary line running through Earth between the North and South Poles (p. 18)
eje línea imaginaria que atraviesa la Tierra y que corre entre los polos Norte y Sur

B

Berlin Wall a wall built by the East German government in 1961 to divide East and West Berlin; this wall came to symbolize Cold War divisions (p. 453)

Muro de Berlín muralla construida por el gobierno de la antigua República Democrática Alemana (RDA) en 1961 para dividir las partes este y oeste de Berlín; se convirtió en un símbolo de la divisiva Guerra Fría

bias unfair preference for or dislike of something (p. 121)

prejuicio preferencia injusta o disgusto por algo

biodiversity variety of different kinds of living things in a region or ecosystem (p. 367)

biodiversidad variedad de clases diferentes de seres vivos de una región o un ecosistema

biofuel fuel from organic material (p. 477)

biocombustible combustible proveniente de material orgánico

birth rate number of live births per 1,000 people in a year (p. 74)

tasa de natalidad número de nacimientos por cada mil habitantes durante un año

Bolsheviks Russian political group that called for worker control (p. 546)

bolcheviques grupo político ruso que defiende el control por parte del proletariado

bond certificate issued by a company or government promising to pay back borrowed money with interest (p. 69)

bono certificado emitido por una compañía o un gobierno que promete pagar el dinero prestado con intereses

boom and bust cycle period of strong economic growth followed by a period of sharp decline (p. 354)

ciclo económico período de gran crecimiento económico seguido de un fuerte declive

brazilwood wood that produces a red dye (p. 353)

madera de brasil tipo de madera que produce un tinte rojo

budget plan that shows income and expenses over a period of time (p. 68)

presupuesto plan que muestra los ingresos y los costos para un período de tiempo

C

canopy the upper leaves of rain forest trees (p. 348)

dosel forestal hojas superiores de los árboles de la selva tropical

capital money or goods that are used to make products (p. 519)

capital dinero o bienes que se usan para crear productos

caravel a small, light ship developed by the Portuguese that performed well on long voyages (p. 432)

carabela nave pequeña y ligera diseñada por los portugueses, especialmente efectiva en viajes largos

cardinal directions north, east, south, and west (p. 4)

puntos cardinales norte, sur, este y oeste

carnival religious festival primarily observed by Roman Catholics (p. 258)

carnaval fiesta religiosa que observan principalmente los católicos romanos

cartography the science of making maps and globes (p. 432)

cartografía técnica de trazar mapas y globos terráqueos

cash crop crop grown mainly for export (p. 148)

cultivo comercial cultivo con fines de exportación

Catholic Reformation changes made by the Catholic Church to keep Catholicism strong; response to the Reformation (p. 428)

Reforma Católica cambios que la Iglesia Católica hizo para fortalecer al catolicismo; fue una respuesta a la Reforma Protestante

caudillo chief or dictator (p. 292)

caudillo jefe o dictador

censor to suppress or delete anything considered objectionable (p. 555)

censurar ocultar o borrar cualquier cosa que se considere ofensiva

chronology list of events arranged in the order in which they occurred (p. 118)

cronología lista de sucesos organizados en el orden en que ocurrieron

citizen legal member of a country (p. 112)

ciudadano miembro legal de un país

city-state independent state consisting of a city and its surrounding territory (pp. 106, 383)

ciudad-estado estado independiente que consiste en una ciudad y el territorio aledaño

Glossary (continued)

civic life activities having to do with one's society and community (p. 113)
vida cívica actividades relacionadas con nuestra sociedad o comunidad

civic participation taking part in government (p. 113)
participación cívica tomar parte en asuntos del gobierno

civil rights movement movement for African American equality (p. 151)
movimiento de los derechos civiles movimiento por la igualdad de derechos de los afroamericanos

climate average weather of a place over many years (p. 32)
clima tiempo promedio de un lugar a lo largo de muchos años

Cold War post-World War II period of hostility between the United States and its allies on one side and the Soviet Union and its allies on the other side (p. 452)
Guerra Fría período de hostilidad entre los Estados Unidos y la Unión Soviética, más los aliados de ambos, posterior a la Segunda Guerra Mundial

collaborating helping the enemy (p. 304)
colaborar con el enemigo ayudar al enemigo

collectivization shift of control to a group, or collective, from an individual or single entity (p. 546)
colectivizacion cambio del control a un grupo o colectivo de un individuo o entidad individual

colonization movement of new settlers and their culture to an area (p. 51)
colonización mudanza de pobladores nuevos y la cultura de éstos a un área

colony group of people living in a new territory with ties to a distant state (p. 253)
colonia grupo de personas que viven en un territorio nuevo que están ligados a un estado distante

command economy economy in which the central government makes all basic economic decisions (pp. 63, 558)
economía dirigida sistema económico en el que el gobierno central toma todas las decisiones económicas básicas

communism political and economic system in which government owns all property and makes all economic decisions (pp. 107, 447)
comunismo sistema político y económico en el que el Estado posee toda propiedad y toma todas las decisiones económicas

compass rose diagram of a compass showing direction (p. 10)
rosa de los vientos diagrama de una brújula que indica la dirección

competition struggle among producers for consumers' money (p. 60)
competencia rivalidad entre los productores por el dinero del consumidor

compromise establishing common ideas that people agree to follow (p. 182)
acordar establecer ideas en común que las personas se comprometen a seguir

coniferous tree tree that produces cones to carry seeds (p. 42)
árbol conífero árbol que produce frutos en forma de conos que contienen las semillas

conquistador Spanish soldier-explorer (p. 224)
conquistador soldado explorador de origen español

constitution system of basic rules and principles by which a government is organized (p. 105)
constitución sistema de reglas y principios básicos que establece la organización de un gobierno

constitutional monarchy system of government in which the laws in the constitution limit the monarch's or emperor's powers (pp. 191, 480)
monarquía constitucional sistema de gobierno en el que las leyes de la constitución limitan los poderes del monarca o emperador

consumer person or business that buys, or consumes, products (p. 59)
consumidor persona o negocio que compra o consume productos

cordillera chain of mountains (p. 282)
cordillera cadena de montañas

core sphere of very hot metal at the center of Earth (p. 22)
núcleo esfera de metal muy caliente en el centro de la Tierra

coup sudden violent overthrow of a government, often by the military (p. 354)
golpe de estado derrocamiento repentino y violento de un gobierno, generalmente por parte de las fuerzas armadas

cradle-to-grave system system of basic services provided to citizens at every stage of life by Scandinavian governments (p. 483)
sistema "desde la cuna hasta la tumba" sistema de servicios básicos que les ofrecen los gobiernos escandinavos de por vida a sus ciudadanos

credit arrangement in which a buyer can purchase something and pay for it over time (p. 69)
crédito arreglo que permite al consumidor comprar algo y pagarlo durante un plazo de tiempo

criollo person of spanish descent born in Spain's American colonies (pp. 220, 322)
criollo persona de origen español nacida en una colonia española de las Américas

Crusades religious wars in which Christian soldiers from Europe aimed to stop the spread of Islam and to retake control of Palestine, also called the Holy Land (p. 408)
Cruzadas guerras de índole religiosa en las que los soldados cristianos de Europa buscaban frenar la difusión del islam y retomar el control de Palestina, también conocida como la Tierra Santa

crust thin layer of rocks and minerals that surrounds Earth's mantle (p. 22)
corteza capa fina de rocas y minerales que rodea el manto de la Tierra

cuisine style of food (p. 521)
cocina estilo de comida

cultural borrowing absorbing ideas or customs from other cultures (p. 485)
préstamo cultural absorción de ideas y costumbres de otras culturas

cultural diffusion spread of cultural traits from one culture to another (pp. 96, 495)
difusión cultural diseminación de los rasgos culturales de una cultura a otra

cultural hearth place where cultural traits begin and from which they spread to surrounding cultures and regions (pp. 96, 384)
corazón cultural lugar donde nacen los rasgos culturales y desde donde se difunden hacia las culturas y regiones aledañas

cultural landscape geographic area that has been shaped by people (p. 86)
paisaje cultural área geográfica moldeada por la gente

cultural mosaic place where people from different areas retain their cultural identity (p. 190)
mosaico cultural lugar donde personas de distintos lugares mantienen su identidad cultural

cultural trait idea or way of doing things that is common in a certain culture (p. 86)
rasgo cultural idea o manera de hacer las cosas que es común en una cultura determinada

culture beliefs, customs, practices, and behavior of a particular nation or group of people (p. 86)
cultura creencias, costumbres, prácticas y comportamientos de una nación o un grupo de personas determinado

culture region area in which a single culture or cultural trait is dominant (p. 86)
región cultural área en la que predomina una sola cultura o rasgo cultural

D

death rate number of deaths per 1,000 people in a year (p. 74)
tasa de mortalidad número de muertes por cada mil habitantes durante un año

deciduous tree tree that loses its leaves in the fall (p. 42)
árbol de hoja caduca árbol que pierde sus hojas en el otoño

deforestation the loss of forest cover in a region that results from the trees in a forest being destroyed faster than they can grow back (pp. 52, 251)
deforestación destrucción acelerada de los árboles de un bosque que impide su regeneración y resulta en la pérdida de una región boscosa

degree unit that measures angles (p. 4)
grado unidad que se utiliza para medir ángulos

delta a flat plain formed on the seabed where a river deposits material over many years (p. 25)
delta llanura plana que se forma en el lecho marino donde un río deposita sedimento a través de los años

demand desire for a particular good or service (p. 59)
demanda interés en un bien o servicio determinado

democracy form of government in which citizens hold political power (p. 106)
democracia tipo de gobierno en el que los ciudadanos tienen el poder político

demographer scientist who studies human populations (p. 74)
demógrafo científico que estudia las poblaciones humanas

deportation being sent back to one's home country (p. 499)
deportación acción que consiste en devolver a alguien a su país de origen

deposition process of depositing material eroded and carried by water, ice, or wind (p. 25)
depósito proceso de depositer material que ha sido erosionado y transportado por el agua, hielo o viento

developed country country with a strong economy and a high quality of life (p. 64)
país desarrollado país con una economía fuerte y un alto nivel de vida

developing country country with a less productive economy and a lower quality of life (p. 64)
país en vías de desarrollo país con una economía menos productiva y un nivel de vida más bajo

development country's economic growth and quality of life (p. 64)
desarrollo el crecimiento económico y la calidad de vida de un país

diaspora spread of people from one place to many others (p. 260)
diáspora dispersión de personas de un lugar a muchos otros lugares

dictatorship government controlled by a single leader (p. 255)
dictadura gobierno bajo el control de un solo líder

diplomacy managing communication and relationships between countries (pp. 111, 160)
diplomacia manejo de las comunicaciones y relaciones entre países

direct democracy government in which citizens take part directly in the day-to-day affairs of government (p. 385)
democracia directa tipo de gobierno en el que los ciudadanos participan directamente en los asuntos diarios del gobierno

disposable income money left after taxes are paid (p. 553)
ingreso disponible dinero restante después de pagar los impuestos

dissenter person whose religious beliefs differed from the state's religion (p. 147)
disidente persona cuyas creencias religiosas son distintas a la religión del estado

distortion loss of accuracy (p. 9)
distorsión pérdida de exactitud

diversified economy economy that depends on a variety of exports or products (p. 331)
economía diversificada economía que depende de exportaciones o productos variados

diversify to add variety (p. 497)
diversificar agregar variedad

diversity cultural variety (p. 97)
diversidad variedad cultural

dominion territory that governs itself but is still tied to its colonizing country (p. 176)
dominio territorio sujeto al país colonizador pero que goza de autonomía plena

E

economic region place where people do particular kinds of work (p. 158)
región económica lugar donde las personas se dedican a ciertos tipos de trabajo

economics study of how people meet their wants and needs (p. 58)
economía estudio de cómo la gente satisface sus deseos y necesidades

ecosystem group of plants and animals that depend on each other and their environment for survival (pp. 43, 285)
ecosistema grupo de plantas y animales cuya sobrevivencia depende de la relación entre sí y con su medio ambiente

ecotourism tourism that focuses on the environment and seeks to minimize environmental impact (p. 263)
ecoturismo tipo de turismo que se enfoca en el medio ambiente y trata de minimizar el impacto ambiental

El Dorado legendary gold-rich region (p. 290)
El Dorado leyenda solore una región con grandes reservas de oro

El Niño warming of ocean water along the west coast of South America (p. 314)
El Niño calentamiento de las aguas oceánicas de la costa oeste de América del Sur

elevation height above sea level (p. 12)
elevación altura sobre el nivel del mar

embargo ban on trade (p. 267)
embargo prohibición de comerciar

emigrate to migrate out of a place (pp. 79, 513)
emigrar dejar un lugar

empire state containing several countries or territories (p. 106)
imperio estado que incluye a varios países o territorios

encomienda legal system to control Native Americans in Spain's American colonies (p. 253)
encomienda sistema legal que se creó para controlar a los indígenas americanos en las colonias españolas en América

English Bill of Rights an act passed in 1689 that limited the power of the English monarch and increased Parliament's power (p. 440)
Declaración de Derechos inglesa ley aprobada en 1689 que limitaba el poder del monarca inglés y aumentaba el poder del Parlamento

Enlightenment a period during the 1600s and 1700s when scholars studied culture and society by applying reason and natural laws (p. 439)
ilustración período del siglo XVII al siglo XVIII en que los eruditos estudiaron la cultura y la sociedad a partir de la razón y las leyes naturales

entrepreneur person who organizes and manages his or her own business (p. 518)
empresario dícese de la persona que organiza y maneja su propia empresa

equinox point at which, everywhere on Earth, days and nights are nearly equal in length (p. 18)
equinoccio momento en el que la duración de los días y las noches es casi la misma en todos los rincones de la Tierra

erosion process in which water, ice, or wind remove small pieces of rock (p. 24)
erosión proceso en el que el agua, hielo o viento desgasta la roca

ethics beliefs about what is right and wrong (p. 92)
ética creencias sobre el bien y el mal

ethnic cleansing attempt to create an area with only one ethnic group by removing or attacking other ethnic groups (p. 522)
limpieza étnica intento de crear un área donde sólo habite un grupo étnico por medio del ataque o el traslado de otros grupos étnicos

European Union economic and political partnership among member nations (p. 455)
Unión Europea asociación económica y política de países miembros

evaporation process in which a liquid changes to a gas (p. 37)
evaporación proceso en el que un líquido se convierte en gas

export good or service produced within a country and sold outside the country's borders (pp. 67, 156)
exportación bien o servicio que se produce en un país y se vende fuera de los confines del país

export economy economy based on exports (p. 353)
economía de exportación economía que se basa en exportaciones

extended family family that includes parents, children, and other family members such as grandparents, aunts, uncles, and cousins (p. 88)
familia extensa familia que incluye a los padres, los hijos y otros parientes como los abuelos, los tíos y los primos

F

family two or more people who are closely related by birth, marriage, or adoption (p. 88)
familia dos o más personas que están estrechamente vinculadas por los lazos de sangre, el matrimonio o la adopción

597

Glossary (continued)

fascism a political system that stresses national strength, military might, and the belief that the state is more important than individuals (p. 447)
fascismo sistema político que enfatiza la fuerza nacional, el poderío militar y la creencia de que el estado es más importante que el individuo

fasting limited eating (p. 517)
ayuno alimentación limitada

fault seam in Earth's crust (p. 26)
falla quiebra en la corteza terrestre

favela Brazilian slum (p. 351)
favela barrio marginal en Brasil

federal system system of government in which power is divided among central, regional, and local governments (p. 108)
sistema federal sistema de gobierno en el que el poder se divide entre los gobiernos centrales, regionales y locales

feudalism in medieval Europe, a system in which land was owned by lords but held by vassals in return for their loyalty (p. 404)
feudalismo sistema que se practicó en Europa durante la Edad Media en el que la tierra era propiedad de los señores nobles, quienes se la concedían a vasallos a cambio de su lealtad

First Nations native groups who lived south of the Arctic region in Canada (p. 182)
Primeras Naciones grupos indígenas que habitaron la región al sur del Ártico en Canadá

Five-Year Plan one of a series of plans introduced by Josef Stalin that was intended to transform the Soviet Union's economy (p. 558)
Plan Quinquenal uno de una serie de planes para la transformación económica de la Unión Soviética introducido por Josef Stalin

foreign policy set of goals outlining how a country plans to interact with other countries (p. 110)
política exterior conjunto de metas que describe cómo un país planea interactuar con otros

fossil fuel nonrenewable resource formed over millions of years from the remains of ancient plants and animals (pp. 49, 477)
combustible fósil recurso no renovable formado durante millones de años de los restos antiguos de plantas y animales

free market economic market in which businesses operate with few governmental restrictions (p. 234)
libre mercado mercado económico en el cual las empresas operan con restricciones mínimas del gobierno

free trade removal of trade barriers (p. 67)
libre comercio eliminación de las barreras comerciales

French Revolution a political movement that removed the French king from power and formed a republic (p. 441)
Revolución francesa movimiento político que derrocó al rey francés y estableció una república

G

geographic information system (GIS) computer-based system that stores and uses information linked to geographic locations (p. 8)
sistema de información geográfica (SIG) sistema computarizado que archiva y usa información relacionada con sitios geográficos

geography study of the human and nonhuman features of Earth (p. 4)
geografía estudio de las características humanas y no humanas de la Tierra

glacier slow-moving body of ice (p. 469)
glaciar gran masa de hielo que se desliza lentamente

government group of people who have the power to make and enforce laws for a country or area (p. 104)
gobierno grupo de personas de un país o área que tiene el poder de crear y hacer cumplir las leyes

Great Depression worldwide economic slump during the 1930s (p. 446)
Gran Depresión crisis económica mundial durante la década de 1930

gross domestic product (GDP) total value of all goods and services produced in a country in a year (pp. 64, 484)
producto interno bruto (PIB) valor total de todos los bienes y servicios que produce un país durante un año

gross national product (GNP) annual income of a country's companies and residents (p. 489)
producto nacional bruto (PNB) ingreso anual de las empresas y los residentes de un país

guerrilla soldier who makes surprise raids on enemies (p. 302)
guerrillero soldado que usa la táctica de los ataques sorpresa

guild association of people who have a common interest (p. 412)
gremio asociación de personas que comparten un interés común

gulag Soviet forced-labor camp (p. 558)
gulag antiguo campo de concentración de la Unión Soviética

H

habitat natural environment (p. 367)
hábitat entorno o ambiente natural

hacienda huge farm or ranch in Spain's American colonies (p. 254)
hacienda granja o rancho grande en las colonias españolas en las Américas

heavy industry the manufacture of steel, equipment, or weapons (p. 558)
industria pesada aquella que requiere procesar grandes cantidades de materias primas, por ejemplo la fabricación del acero, de máquinas o de armas

hemisphere one half of Earth (p. 5)
hemisferio una mitad de la Tierra

high latitudes areas north of the Arctic Circle and south of the Antarctic Circle; also known as polar zone (p. 34)
áreas de latitud alta áreas al norte del Círculo Polar Ártico y al sur del Círculo Polar Ántártico; también se conocen como zonas polares

historian person who studies the past (p. 118)
historiador persona que estudia el pasado

historical map special-purpose map that provides information about a place at a certain time in history (p. 125)
mapa histórico mapa con el propósito especial de dar información acerca de un lugar en un momento determinado de la historia

Holocaust the mass murder of Jews by the Nazis during World War II (p. 449)
Holocausto exterminio masivo de judíos por el régimen nazi durante la Segunda Guerra Mundial

human–environment interaction how people affect their environment and how their environment affects them (p. 7)
interacción humanos–medio ambiente manera en la que los seres humanos afectan su medio ambiente y viceversa

humanism the study of secular, or nonreligious, subjects such as history (p. 423)
humanismo estudio de temas laicos, o no religiosos, como la historia

humid subtropical climate climate with year-round precipitation, mild winters, and hot summers (p. 40)
clima subtropical húmedo clima de precipitación continua durante todo el año, inviernos templados y veranos cálidos

hurricane tropical cyclone that forms over the tropical Atlantic Ocean (pp. 39, 246)
huracán ciclón tropical que se forma sobre el Océano Atlántico tropical

hydroelectric power the power produced by water-driven turbines (p. 214)
energía hidroeléctrica poder que producen turbinas impulsadas por agua

hydropower power generated by flowing water (p. 478)
energía hidráulica energía que genera la corriente del agua

I

Iberian Peninsula Spain and Portugal (p. 494)
Península ibérica España y Portugal

ice age time of lower temperatures when much of the land was covered with snow and ice (p. 507)
edad de hielo período de temperaturas bajas donde gran parte de la tierra estaba cubierta de nieve y hielo

igloo Inuit home made from blocks of snow (p. 178)
iglú vivienda de los inuit construida con bloques de nieve

immigrate to migrate into a place (p. 79)
inmigrar llegar a un lugar

Glossary (continued)

immunity natural defense against disease (p. 322)
inmunidad defensa natural contra las enfermedades

import good or service sold within a country that is produced in another country (pp. 67, 156)
importación bien o servicio que se vende en un país pero es producido en otro

incentive factor that encourages people to behave in a certain way (p. 59)
incentivo factor que motiva a la gente a actuar de cierta manera

independence right to rule oneself (p. 254)
independencia derecho de gobernarse a sí mismo

industrialization growth of machine-powered production and manufacturing (pp. 51, 558)
industrialización aumento de la producción a máquina y la manufactura

Industrial Revolution a time in which new technologies transformed manufacturing and changed society forever (p. 442)
Revolución Industrial período en el que nuevas tecnologías transformaron la industria manufacturera en particular y la sociedad en general

infant mortality rate number of infant deaths per 1,000 births (p. 75)
tasa de mortalidad infantil número de muertes infantiles por cada mil nacimientos

inflation general increase in prices (p. 61)
inflación alza general de los precios

Institutional Revolutionary Party political party that dominated Mexico's government for much of the 1900s (p. 231)
Partido Revolucionario Institucional partido político que dominó el gobierno mexicano por gran parte del siglo XX

insurgent rebel (p. 300)
insurgente rebelde

interest price paid for borrowing money (p. 69)
interés precio que se paga por el dinero prestado

interest group group that seeks to influence public policy on certain issues (p. 113)
grupo de interés grupo que busca influir en la política pública en relación a cuestiones particulares

intertropical convergence zone belt of rising air near the Equator (p. 38)
zona de convergencia intertropical cinturón de aire ascendente cerca del ecuador

Inuit indigenous people in Canada's Far North (p. 178)
los inuit población indígena del extremo norte de Canadá

investing act of using money in the hopes of making a future profit (p. 69)
invertir usar el dinero con la esperanza de obtener ganancias futuras

irrigate to supply water to (pp. 99, 217)
irrigar aportar agua

isthmus strip of land with water on both sides, which connects two larger bodies of land (p. 244)
istmo franja de tierra con agua en ambos lados, que conecta dos territorios más grandes

K

Kamchatka Peninsula a peninsula in the Russian far east known for its volcanic activity (p. 537)
Península de Kamchatka península del lejano oriente ruso conocida por su estado volcánico

key section of a map that explains the map's symbols and shading (p. 10)
leyenda sección de un mapa que explica el significado de sus símbolos y áreas sombreadas

KGB the Soviet-era secret police (p. 553)
KGB policía secreta de la era soviética

Kremlin a great complex of Russian official buildings, including palaces, state offices, and churches (p. 544)
Kremlin gran recinto de edificios oficiales rusos que incluye palacios, oficinas del Estado e iglesias

L

Lake Baikal a huge lake in Siberia that is more than one mile deep and holds about 20 percent of Earth's fresh water (p. 537)
lago Baikal gran lago localizado en Siberia que tiene más de una milla de profundidad y contiene aproximadamente 20 por ciento del agua dulce de la Tierra

land distribution ownership of land (p. 302)
distribución de la tierra se relaciona con la propiedad de la tierra

landform shapes and types of land (p. 23)
accidente geográfico formas y tipos de terreno

land reform program to redistribute land to poor farmers (p. 335)
reforma agraria programa de redistribución de las tierras entre los agricultores más necesitados

language set of sounds or symbols that make it possible for people to communicate (p. 90); also, the language of a community or a nation
lenguaje conjunto de sonidos y símbolos que hacen posible la comunicación entre las personas; **idioma** lengua de una comunidad o una nación

Latin America areas of Middle and South America influenced by the cultures of Spain, France, or Portugal (p. 297)
América Latina regiones de México, América Central y el Caribe y América del Sur con influencia cultural de España, Francia o Portugal

latitude distance north or south of the Equator measured in degrees (p. 4)
latitud distancia en grados que se mide al norte o al sur desde el ecuador

limited government government structure in which government actions are limited by law (p. 105)
gobierno limitado estructura gubernamental cuyas acciones están limitadas por la ley

literacy ability to read and write (pp. 265, 332)
alfabetismo capacidad de leer y escribir

literature written work such as fiction, poetry, or drama (p. 95)
literatura obras escritas como la ficción, la poesía o el drama

Llanos lowland plains in Colombia and Venezuela (p. 283)
Llanos llanuras de tierra baja de Colombia y Venezuela

locator map section of a map that shows a larger area than the main map (p. 10)
mapa localizador sección de un mapa que amplía un área del mismo

loess a dustlike material that can form soil (p. 470)
loes material polvoroso que puede formar tierra

longitude distance east or west of the Prime Meridian measured in degrees (p. 5)
longitud distancia en grados que se mide al este o al oeste desde el Primer meridiano

lords in medieval Europe, noblemen who gave land to other noblemen in return for services (p. 404)
señores en la Europa medieval, señores nobles que cedían terrenos a otros señores nobles a cambio de sus servicios

low latitudes area between the Tropic of Cancer and the Tropic of Capricorn; also known as tropics (p. 34)
latitudes bajas área entre el Trópico de Cáncer y el Trópico de Capricornio; también se le llama trópico

M

magma stream of soft, nearly molten rock (p. 26)
magma flujo de roca blanda y casi fundida

Magna Carta document that limited the English king's power (p. 413)
Carta Magna documento que limitaba el poder del rey de Inglaterra

maize corn (p. 222)
maíz choclo

Manifest Destiny idea that the United States should expand across the North American continent (p. 149)
Destino manifiesto mentalidad que propone la expansión territorial de los Estados Unidos por todo el continente norteamericano

manorialism in medieval Europe, the economic relationship between a lord and the peasants who worked for him (p. 405)
señorío en la Europa medieval, relación económica entre un señor y sus trabajadores campesinos

mantle thick, rocky layer around Earth's core (p. 22)
manto capa rocosa gruesa alrededor del núcleo de la Tierra

maritime climate climate that is wet year-round, with mild winters and cool summers (p. 40)
clima marítimo clima que es húmedo todo el año, con inviernos templados y veranos frescos

market organized way for producers and consumers to trade goods and services (p. 60)
mercado intercambio organizado de bienes y servicios entre productores y consumidores

Glossary (continued)

market economy economy in which individual consumers and producers make all economic decisions (pp. 62, 156, 362)
economía de mercado economía en la que los consumidores y los productores toman todas las decisiones económicas

Marshall Plan an economic program initiated by the United States to help Europe recover from World War II (p. 452)
Plan Marshall programa económico iniciado por los Estados Unidos para la reconstrucción europea tras la Segunda Guerra Mundial

Maya Native American society living in Central America (p. 252)
Maya sociedad indígena americana que habita en Centroamérica

mechanized farming farming with machines (p. 509)
mecanización agrícola uso de maquinaria en la industria agrícola

mercantilism economic system in which colonies sent raw materials to the mother country; in return, colonists were expected to buy products from the country (p. 323)
mercantilismo sistema económico en el que las colonias enviaban materias primas a la madre patria; a cambio, se esperaba que los colonos compraran los productos del país

MERCOSUR trading bloc of the South American countries Brazil, Argentina, Uruguay, and Paraguay, formed in 1991 (p. 331)
MERCOSUR tratado de comercio elaborado en 1991 entre los países sudamericanos de Brasil, Argentina, Uruguay y Paraguay

mestizo person of mixed Spanish and Native American ancestry (pp. 220, 322)
mestizo persona con ascendencia española e indígena americana

metropolitan area a single city or several cities close together (p. 144)
área metropolitana una ciudad o varias ciudades aledañas

Mexican Revolution armed rebellion in which the Mexican people fought for political and social reform (p. 226)
Revolución mexicana rebelión armada en la que el pueblo mexicano luchó por establecer reformas políticas y sociales

microcredit small loan (p. 262)
microcrédito préstamo pequeño

middle latitudes areas between the high and low latitudes; also known as temperate zone (p. 34)
latitudes medias (zona templada) áreas entre las latitudes altas y bajas

migration movement of people from one place to another (pp. 78, 142)
migración desplazamiento de personas de un lugar a otro

mixed economy economy that combines elements of traditional, market, and command economic systems (p. 63)
economía mixta economía que combina elementos de los sistemas económicos tradicional, de mercado y dirigida

mixing zone an area where warm and cool water combine and stir nutrients from the ocean floor; fish feed on these nutrients (p. 175)
zona de mezcla área donde la combinación de agua cálida y agua fría revuelve los nutrientes del suelo marino; los peces se alimentan de estos nutrientes

monarchy form of government in which the state is ruled by a monarch (p. 107)
monarquía tipo de gobierno en el que el Estado está regido por un monarca

movement how people, goods, and ideas get from one place to another (p. 7)
movimiento manera en la que las personas, los bienes y las ideas van de un lugar a otro

music art form that uses sound, usually produced by instruments or voices (p. 95)
música arte que usa sonidos, normalmente producidos por instrumentos o voces

N

Nahuatl Aztec language that contributed many words to modern Spanish (p. 221)
náhuatl lengua azteca que contribuyó muchos vocablos al español moderno

National Action Party Mexican political party that took power in the 2000 presidential election (p. 231)

Partido Acción Nacional (PAN) partido político mexicano que tomó el poder en las elecciones presidenciales del 2000

nationalism strong devotion to one's nation (p. 515)

nacionalismo gran devoción de un individuo hacia su nación

nationalize government taking ownership of a company (p. 293)

nacionalizar situación en la cual el gobierno toma posesión de una empresa

nation-state state that is independent of other states (p. 107)

estado-nación Estado que es independiente de otros

natural resource useful material found in the environment (p. 48)

recurso natural material útil que se encuentra en el medio ambiente

New France French colony in what is now eastern Canada (p. 195)

Nueva Francia colonia francesa ubicada en lo que hoy se conoce como Canadá oriental

nonrenewable energy energy that cannot be replaced (p. 477)

energía no renovable energía que no se puede reemplazar

nonrenewable resource resource that cannot be replaced in a relatively short period of time (p. 49)

recurso no renovable recurso que no se puede reemplazar en un período de tiempo relativamente corto

norm behavior that is considered normal in a particular society (p. 86)

norma comportamiento que se considera normal en una sociedad determinada

northwest passage hypothetical North American passage between the Atlantic and Pacific Oceans (pp. 179, 434)

Paso del Noroeste ruta marítima hipotética en Norteamérica que conecta los océanos Atlántico y Pacífico

nuclear family family that consists of parents and their children (p. 88)

familia nuclear familia constituida por los padres y sus hijos

O

oligarchy government in which a small group of people rule (pp. 324, 383)

oligarquía tipo de gobierno en el que un grupo pequeño de personas tiene el poder

opportunity cost cost of what you have to give up when making a choice (p. 59)

costo de oportunidad costo de lo que se pierde al elegir una opción

oral tradition community's cultural and historical background, passed down in spoken stories and songs (p. 123)

tradición oral trasfondo cultural e histórico de una comunidad, trasmitido por cuentos hablados y canciones

orbit path one object makes as it circles around another (p. 18)

órbita trayectoria que traza un cuerpo al desplazarse alrededor de otro

P

paramilitary group private army (pp. 293, 304)

grupo paramilitar ejército particular

Parliament British legislature (p. 481)

parlamento asamblea legislativa británica

patricians wealthy aristocrats in ancient Rome (p. 393)

patricios aristócratas adinerados de la antigua Roma

Pax Romana period of stability in the Roman Empire under Augustus (p. 395)

Paz Romana período de estabilidad del Imperio Romano bajo el mandato de Augusto

peasant poor farmer who farms a small plot of land (p. 335)

peón trabajador agrícola humilde que cultiva un terreno pequeño

peninsula area of land almost completely surrounded by water but connected to a mainland (p. 468)

península área de tierra rodeada en su mayoría por agua pero conectada a un territorio más extenso

Glossary (continued)

peninsular colonial Mexican who came to Mexico from Spain (p. 220)
peninsular relativo a un colono español que emigró a México

period length of time singled out because of a specific event or development that happened during that time (p. 118)
período lapso de tiempo resaltado debido a un suceso o desarrollo específico que sucedió durante ese tiempo

permafrost permanently frozen soil (p. 538)
permafrost tierra permanentemente congelada

perspective a technique that allows artists to portray a three-dimensional space on a flat surface (p. 423)
perspectiva técnica que permite al artista crear un espacio tridimensional en una superficie plana

philosophy general study of knowledge and the world; Greek for "love of wisdom" (p. 387)
filosofía estudio general sobre el conocimiento y el mundo; en griego significa "amor por la sabiduría"

physical map map that shows physical, or natural, features (p. 12)
mapa físico mapa que muestra las características físicas o naturales

pilgrimage religious journey (p. 515)
peregrinación viaje por motivos religiosos

place mix of human and nonhuman features at a given location (p. 6)
lugar combinación de características humanas y no humanas en un sitio determinado

plain large area of flat or gently rolling land (p. 25)
llanura área extensa de terreno ondulado o llano

plantation large commercial farm (pp. 148, 434)
plantación granja grande con fines comerciales

plate block of rock and soil that makes up Earth's crust (p. 26)
placa bloque de piedra y tierra que forma la corteza de la Tierra

plate tectonics theory that explains how huge blocks of Earth's crust called "plates" move (p. 26)
tectónica de placas teoría que explica el movimiento de las placas de la corteza terrestre

plateau large, mostly flat area that rises above the surrounding land (p. 25)
meseta gran extensión de terreno, generalmente plano, que se eleva sobre la tierra circundante

plebeian nonpatrician citizen of ancient Rome (p. 393)
plebeyo ciudadano de la antigua Roma que no se consideraba patricio

plural society society in which distinctive cultural, ethnic, and racial groups are encouraged to maintain their own identities and cultures (p. 194)
sociedad plural sociedad en la que se fomenta la conservación de la identidad cultural de los distintos grupos culturales, étnicos y raciales

polar zone areas north of the Arctic Circle and south of the Antarctic Circle; also known as high latitudes (p. 34)
zona polar áreas al norte del Círculo Polar Ártico y al sur del Círculo Polar Antártico; también se conocen como áreas de latitud alta

polders areas of dry land reclaimed from lake bottoms or the seabed (p. 489)
pólderes áreas de tierra seca ganadas a los lechos laguneros o marinos

political map map that shows political units, such as countries or states (p. 13)
mapa político mapa que muestra las unidades políticas, como países o estados

political party group that supports candidates for public offices (p. 113)
partido político grupo que apoya a los candidatos que postulan a cargos públicos

pollution waste that makes the air, soil, or water less clean (pp. 53, 473)
contaminación desechos que alteran la pureza del aire, el suelo o el agua

population density measure of the number of people per unit of land (pp. 77, 144)
densidad de población medida del número de personas por unidad de territorio

population distribution spreading of people over an area of land (p. 76)
distribución de población dispersión de las personas a lo largo de un área geográfica

precipitation water that falls to the ground as rain, snow, sleet, or hail (pp. 32, 182)
precipitación agua que cae sobre la tierra en forma de lluvia, nieve, aguanieve o granizo

prehistory time before humans invented writing (p. 119)
prehistoria época anterior a la invención de la escritura

primary source information that comes directly from a person who experienced an event (p. 120)
fuente primaria información sobre un suceso que proviene directamente de una persona que experimentó el suceso

privatization individual and private group ownership of businesses (p. 488)
privatización situación en la que individuos o grupos privados son los dueños de las empresas

producer person or business that makes and sells products (p. 59)
productor persona o negocio que fabrica y vende productos

productivity amount of goods and services produced given the amount of resources used (p. 65)
productividad cantidad de bienes y servicios producidos en relación a la cantidad de recursos empleados

profit money a company has left over after subtracting the costs of doing business (p. 60)
ganancias dinero que sobra después que una compañía deduce los costos de operar el negocio

projection way to map Earth on a flat surface (p. 9)
proyección manera de trazar un mapa de la Tierra sobre una superficie plana

province territory that is under the control of a larger country (p. 185)
provincia territorio que se encuentra bajo la administración de un país más grande

pull factor cause of migration that pulls, or attracts, people to new countries (p. 79)
factor de arrastre causa de la migración que arrastra o atrae a la gente a países nuevos

push factor cause of migration that pushes people to leave their home country (p. 79)
factor de empuje causa de la migración que empuja a la gente a dejar su país de origen

R

rationing controlled distribution of scarce resources and goods, such as food (p. 267)
racionar controlar la distribución de recursos y bienes escasos, como la comida

recession zero or negative economic growth for six or more months in a row (p. 61)
recesión cero o crecimiento económico negativo por un período continuo de seis meses o más

Reconquista reconquering of Spain by Christians beginning in the 1000s (p. 410)
Reconquista la conquista cristiana de España que comenzó en el siglo XI

referendum vote held to reject or accept a law (p. 333)
referéndum someter una ley al voto para rechazarla o aceptarla

Reformation a religious movement in which calls for reform led to the emergence of non-Catholic, or Protestant, churches (p. 426)
Reforma Protestante movimiento religioso cuya convocación de la reforma de la Iglesia Católica conllevó a la creación de iglesias protestantes o no católicas

region area with at least one unifying physical or human feature such as climate, landforms, population, or history (p. 7)
región área con al menos una característica física o humana que es unificadora, como el clima, los accidentes geográficos, la población o la historia

relative location location of a place relative to another place (p. 6)
ubicación relativa ubicación de un lugar con respecto a otro

religion people's beliefs and practices about the existence, nature, and worship of a god or gods (p. 92)
religión creencias y prácticas de los seres humanos acerca de la existencia, la naturaleza y la adoración de un dios o dioses

remittance money sent to another place (p. 237)
remesa envío de dinero

Renaissance a time of a renewed interest in art and learning in Europe; "rebirth" (p. 422)
Renacimiento período de renovado interés en el arte y el aprendizaje en Europa; "un nuevo nacimiento"

605

renewable energy energy sources that can be replaced (p. 476)
energía renovable recursos de energía que se pueden reemplazar

renewable resource a resource that Earth or people can replace (p. 49)
recurso renovable recurso que la Tierra o las personas pueden reemplazar

representative democracy democracy in which people elect representatives to make the nation's laws (p. 393)
democracia representativa democracia en la que el pueblo elige representantes que redactan las leyes de la nación

reunification process of becoming unified again (p. 490)
reunificación proceso para volver a unificar

revenue money earned by selling goods and services and by taxes (p. 60)
ingresos dinero recaudado de la venta de bienes y servicios y impuestos

revolution circular journey around the sun (p. 18)
revolución vuelta alrededor del Sol

rotation complete turn (p. 20)
rotación vuelta completa

rural settlement in the country (p. 80)
rural poblado del campo

S

Santeria Cuban religion that combines Catholic and West African beliefs (p. 259)
santería religión cubana que combina el catolicismo y creencias de África occidental

satellite image picture of Earth's surface taken from a satellite in orbit (p. 8)
imagen de satélite fotografía de la superficie de la Tierra que tomó un satélite en órbita

savanna parklike landscape of grasslands with scattered trees that can survive dry spells, found in tropical areas with dry seasons (pp. 42, 345)
sabana pradera con árboles dispersos que pueden sobrevivir periodos de sequía; se encuentra en las áreas tropicales que tienen estaciones secas

saving setting aside money for future use (p. 68)
ahorrar reservar dinero para el uso futuro

scale relative size (p. 8)
escala tamaño relativo

scale bar section of a map that shows how much distance on the map represents a given distance on the land (p. 10)
barra de escala sección de un mapa que muestra la correspondencia entre las distancias del mapa y las distancias reales sobre la Tierra

scarcity having a limited quantity of resources to meet unlimited wants (p. 58)
escasez tener una cantidad limitada de recursos para satisfacer deseos ilimitados

schism split (p. 401)
cisma división

science knowledge of the natural world (p. 98)
ciencia conocimientos sobre el mundo natural

Scientific Revolution a series of major advances in science during the 1500s and 1600s (p. 438)
Revolución Científica serie de grandes avances científicos durante los siglos XVI y XVII

secede to break away (p. 522)
separarse desprenderse

secondary source information about an event that does not come directly from a person who experienced that event (p. 120)
fuente secundaria información sobre un suceso que no proviene directamente de una persona que experimentó el suceso

secular not religious (p. 514)
laico no religioso

semiarid climate dry climate (p. 41)
clima semiárido clima seco

serf a peasant who is legally bound to live and work on land owned by a lord (p. 544)
siervo persona que está legalmente forzada a vivir y trabajar en la tierra de su noble

Siberia Asiatic Russia (p. 534)
Siberia Rusia asiática

sinkhole depression on the surface of the land caused by the collapse of a cave roof (p. 211)
dolina depresión de la superficie de la tierra causada por el colapso del techo de una cueva

slash-and-burn method used to clear land for planting that involves cutting down all vegetation in an area and burning it (p. 365)
tala y quema método de deforestación que consiste en cortar al ras la vegetación de un área que luego se incinerará

slum poor, overcrowded urban neighborhood (p. 80)
barrio marginal vecindario urbano pobre y sobrepoblado

social class group of people living in similar economic conditions (p. 89)
clase social grupo de personas que tienen una condición económica similar

social services programs designed to help the poor (p. 363)
servicios sociales programas con el fin de ayudar a los pobres

social structure pattern of organized relationships among groups of people within a society (p. 89)
estructura social patrón de las relaciones organizadas entre los grupos de personas de una sociedad

society group of humans with a shared culture who have organized themselves to meet their basic needs (p. 88)
sociedad grupo de personas con una cultura compartida que se han organizado para satisfacer sus necesidades básicas

solstice point at which days are longest in one hemisphere and shortest in another (p. 18)
solsticio momento en el que la duración de los días es más larga en un hemisferio y más corta en el otro

sovereignty supreme authority (p. 110)
soberanía autoridad suprema

soviet a republic or unit of government under a central communist government (p. 546)
sóviet república o unidad gubernamental bajo un gobierno central comunista

specialization act of concentrating on a limited number of goods or activities (p. 60)
especialización concentrarse en una cantidad limitada de bienes o actividades

special-purpose map map that shows the location or distribution of human or physical features (p. 13)
mapa temático o de propósito particular mapa que muestra la ubicación o distribución de características humanas o físicas

sphere round-shaped body (p. 4)
esfera cuerpo geométrico de forma redonda

spillover an effect on someone or something not involved in an activity (p. 53)
externalidad efecto sobre alguien o algo que no participa en una actividad

standard of living level of comfort enjoyed by a person or society (p. 99)
nivel de vida nivel de comodidad que posee un individuo o una sociedad

state region that shares a common government (p. 106)
estado región que tiene un gobierno común

steppe vast area of grasslands (p. 537)
estepa territorio extenso de llanuras

stock share of ownership in a country (p. 69)
acción porción de la propiedad de una compañía

subarctic climate climate with limited precipitation, cool summers, and very cold winters (p. 41)
clima subártico clima de precipitación limitada, veranos frescos e inviernos muy fríos

subduct movement of one part of Earth's crust under another (p. 313)
subducción movimiento de una parte de la corteza terrestre por debajo de otra

subsidence sinking of the ground (p. 298)
hundimiento inmersión de la tierra

suburb residential area on the edge of a city or large town (p. 51)
suburbio área residencial ubicada en los límites de una ciudad o un pueblo

suburban sprawl spread of suburbs away from the core city (p. 81)
dispersión suburbana extensión de los suburbios lejos del centro de la ciudad

superpower an extremely powerful nation (p. 555)
superpotencia nación sumamente poderosa

supply amount of a good or service that is available for use (p. 59)
oferta cantidad disponible de un bien o servicio

T

taiga thick forest of coniferous trees (p. 471)
taiga denso bosque de árboles coníferos

Glossary (continued)

tariff tax on imports or exports (p. 67)
arancel impuesto a las importaciones o las exportaciones

technology practical application of knowledge to accomplish a task (p. 65)
tecnología aplicación práctica del saber para ejecutar una tarea

temperate moderate in terms of temperature (p. 140)
templado de temperatura moderada

temperate zone areas between the high and low latitudes; also known as middle latitudes (p. 34)
zona templada área entre las latitudes altas y bajas; también se le llama latitudes medias

temperature measure of how hot or cold the air is (p. 32)
temperatura medida de cuán caliente o fría se encuentra la atmósfera

terraced farming sculpting the hillsides into different levels for crops (p. 288)
cultivo en terrazas laderas que han sido esculpidas para crear superficies de cultivo niveladas o escalonadas

timeline line marked off with a series of events and their dates (p. 118)
línea cronológica línea marcada con una serie de sucesos y sus fechas

time zones areas sharing the same time (p. 20)
husos horarios áreas que comparten la misma hora

tornado swirling funnel of wind that can reach 200 miles (320 km) per hour (p. 39)
tornado túnel de aire giratorio que puede alcanzar una velocidad de 200 millas (320 km) por hora

tourism business of providing food, places to stay, and other services to visitors from other places (p. 249)
turismo industria que facilita comida, hospedaje y otros servicios a visitantes de otros lugares

trade exchange of goods and services in a market (p. 66)
comercio intercambio de bienes y servicios en un mercado

trade barrier something that keeps goods and services from entering a country (p. 67)
barrera comercial obstáculos para la entrada de bienes y servicios a un país

traditional economy economy in which people make economic decisions based on their customs and habits (p. 62)
economía tradicional economía en la que la gente toma decisiones económicas de acuerdo a sus costumbres y hábitos

treaty formal agreement between two or more countries (p. 111)
tratado acuerdo formal entre dos o más países

triangular trade three-stage trade pattern that carried goods and enslaved people among Europe, Africa, and the Americas (p. 436)
comercio triangular sistema comercial de tres partes que transportó bienes y personas esclavizadas entre Europa, África y las Américas

tribune representative of plebeians in ancient Rome (p. 393)
tribuno representante de los plebeyos de la antigua Roma

tropical cyclone intense rainstorm with strong winds that forms over oceans in the tropics (p. 39)
ciclón tropical aguacero intenso con vientos fuertes que se forma sobre el océano en los trópicos

tropical wet and dry climate climate with a wet season in summer and a dry season in winter (p. 40)
clima tropical húmedo y seco clima de temporada húmeda durante el verano y temporada seca en el invierno

tropical wet climate climate with hot temperatures and heavy rainfall year-round (p. 40)
clima tropical húmedo clima de temperaturas cálidas y lluvia abundante durante todo el año

tropics areas between the Tropic of Cancer and the Tropic of Capricorn; also known as low latitudes (p. 34)
trópico área comprendida entre el Trópico de Cáncer y el Trópico de Capricornio (latitudes bajas)

tsar ruler of imperial Russia; a term used by Byzantine rulers, derived from the Latin *caesar*, or king (p. 544)
zar gobernador del Imperio Ruso; término derivado del latín *césar*, o rey, que usaban los gobernadores del Imperio Bizantino

tundra area with limited vegetation, such as moss and shrubs (pp. 173, 470)
tundra área con vegetación limitada, como musgos y arbustos

tundra climate climate with cool summers and bitterly cold, dry winters (p. 41)
clima de tundra clima de veranos frescos e inviernos gélidos y secos

tyranny unjust use of power (p. 105)
tiranía uso injusto del poder

U

unitary system system of government in which a central government has the authority to make laws for the entire country (p. 108)
sistema unitario sistema de gobierno en el que un gobierno central tiene la autoridad de hacer leyes para todo el país

universal theme subject or theme that relates to the entire world (p. 94)
tema universal materia o tema que se relaciona con todo el mundo

unlimited government government structure in which there are no effective limits on government actions (p. 105)
gobierno ilimitado tipo de gobierno en el que no existen límites sobre las acciones del gobierno

Ural Mountains low-lying mountains that separate European Russia from Asiatic Russia (p. 535)
Montes Urales cadena montañosa de poca elevación que separa a Rusia europea de Rusia asiática

urban located in cities (p. 80)
urbano localizado en la ciudad

urbanization movement of people from rural to urban areas (p. 80)
urbanización desplazamiento de personas de las áreas rurales a las áreas urbanas

urban planning the planning of a city (p. 360)
planeación urbana planeación de una ciudad

V

valley stretch of low land between mountains or hills (p. 25)
valle extensión de terreno bajo ubicado entre montañas o colinas

vassals in medieval Europe, noblemen who received land from other noblemen in return for their services (p. 404)
vasallos en la Europa medieval, señores nobles que recibían terrenos de otros señores nobles a cambio de sus servicios

vertical climate zones climate zones in a region that change according to elevation (p. 315)
zonas climáticas verticales zonas climáticas de una región que cambian de acuerdo a la altura

visual arts art forms such as painting, sculpture, and photography (p. 94)
artes visuales expresiones artísticas como la pintura, la escultura y la fotografía

vital important (p. 155)
vital importante

W

water cycle the movement of water from Earth's surface into the atmosphere and back (p. 37)
ciclo del agua movimiento del agua desde la superficie de la Tierra hacia la atmósfera y viceversa

weather condition of the air and sky at a certain time (p. 32)
tiempo condiciones del aire y el cielo en un momento determinado

weathering process that breaks rocks down into tiny pieces (p. 24)
meteorización proceso que rompe la roca en pedazos muy pequeños

wind turbines giant windmills that use large blades to collect the wind's energy (p. 478)
turbinas eólicas grandes molinos que utilizan grandes palas para recoger la energía del viento

World War I 1914–1918, sometimes called the Great War, the first truly global conflict (p. 444)
Primera Guerra Mundial 1914 a 1918, a veces llamada La Gran Guerra, fue el primer verdadero conflicto global

World War II 1939–1945, the second major global conflict (p. 448)
Segunda Guerra Mundial 1939 a 1945, segundo gran conflicto global

Index

The letters after some page numbers refer to the following:
c = chart; g = graph; m = map; p = picture; q = quotation.

615

Index (continued)

Index (continued)

Index (continued)

Index (continued)

R

Race Day. *See* Día de la Raza
racial discrimination, 151
railroads, 142
rain forest, 2*p*, 364–367, 364*p*, 365*c*, 366*m*, 367*p*
  in Brazil, 348, 348*p*, 360, 360*p*
  mapping the, 3
  in Mexico, 213, 213*p*
Rastafarianism, 259
rationing, 267, 605
Rebellion in the Backlands (Da Cunha), 356, 356*p*, 356*q*
recession, 61, 605
Reconquista, 410, 605
Red Cross, 110*p*
reefs, 247
referendum, 333, 605
Reformation, 605. *See also* Protestant Reformation
region, theme of, 7, 605
regional government, 108, 108*p*
Reign of Terror, 441, 441*p*
relative location, 6, 605
religion, 605
  in ancient Greece, 387
  art and, 409
  in Balkan Nations, 512–513, 512*m*, 513*p*
  in Bosnia, 517, 517*p*
  in Brazil, 359
  in Canada, 184
  in Caribbean, 258–259
  Case Study, 514–517, 514*p*, 515*p*, 516*p*, 517*p*
  Catholic Reformation, 428–429
  in Central America, 259
  culture and, 87, 92–93, 92*m*–93*m*
  definition of, 92
  dissenters and, 147
  in Eastern Europe, 512–513, 512*m*, 513*p*, 514, 515, 515*p*
  in England, 428, 428*p*
  in Estonia, 514, 514*p*
  in Europe, 427*m*
  in France, 488
  in Germany, 428
  Greek Orthodox Church, 495
  in Hungary, 521
  in Italy, 495
  Maya, 253
  in Mexico, 224, 225*p*, 233
  monotheism, 396
  in Poland, 515, 515*p*
  Protestant Reformation, 426–428, 427*m*, 428*p*

Roman Catholic Church, 495
  in Roman empire, 396–397, 396*m*
  in Russia, 541
  separation of church and state, 148–149
  in Serbia, 516, 516*p*
  in Soviet Union, 513
  technology and, 99
  traditional, 92*m*–93*m*, 93
  in Western Europe, 472
  See also Buddhism; Christianity; Crusades; Islam; Judaism; Sikhism
religious tolerance, 440, 517
remittance, 237, 605
Renaissance, 422–425, 422*p*, 423*p*, 424*p*, 425*p*, 605
  Primary Source, 430–431, 430*p*, 430*q*, 431*p*, 431*q*
  trade in the, 422–423, 424
renewable energy, 476–479, 606
renewable resource, 49, 49*c*, 477, 479, 606
representative democracy, 106, 112, 393, 606
reservations, 149
reunification, 490, 606
revenues, 60, 606
revolution, Earth, 18, 606
Revolutionary War. *See* American Revolution
Rhine River, 469, 473, 474
Rhine-Ruhr region, 475, 475*m*
Rhode Island, 134*m*, 147*m*
Rhodes, 134*m*, 382, 383*m*
Ring of Fire, 27*m*
Rio de Janeiro, 350, 352
Rio de la Plata, 312, 313*m*
Rivera, Diego, 224*p*–227*p*, 232
rivers
  of Canada, 174, 174*p*, 175
  of Central America and Caribbean, 245, 245*m*
  of Russia, 535*m*, 536
  of the United States, 139, 139*m*
  of Western Europe, 469, 473, 478
road maps, 11, 11*m*
Robespierre, 441*p*
Robinson projection, 9, 9*m*
Rocky Mountains, 25, 130*m*, 130*p*, 139, 139*m*
Roma ethnic group, 499
Roman calendar, 119, 119*p*
Roman Catholic Church, 401, 495
  in Central America and Caribbean, 258–259

  in Eastern Europe, 515, 515*p*
  Inquisition, 410
  in Mexico, 220, 224, 225*p*, 233
  Protestant Reformation and, 420, 426–428, 427*m*, 428*p*
  women in, 404
Roman empire, 124*m*, 394–397, 394*m*, 395*p*, 396*m*, 398–399, 398*p*, 398*q*, 399*p*, 399*q*
Romania, 456, 502*m*, 523
Romanov Dynasty, 544–545, 544*p*, 546
Roman republic, 392–394, 392*p*, 393*c*
Rome, 392. *See also* Roman empire; Roman republic
Roosevelt, Franklin D., 120*q*, 151, 165*q*
Rosas, Juan Manuel de, 324
rotation, 20, 20*p*, 606
Rousseau, Jean-Jacques, 440
rule of law, 403
runoff, 250
rural areas, 80, 81*c*, 606
Russia, 457, 530*m*
  Alaska and, 155
  animal life in, 538
  atlas, 534–541, 535*m*, 536*m*, 537*p*, 538*g*, 539*m*, 540*m*, 541*p*
  climate of, 536*m*, 537–538
  Communist Party in, 546–547, 547*c*
  Crimean War, 545
  economy of, 561, 561*g*, 561*p*
  energy resources in, 479
  environmental concerns in, 537
  ethnic groups in, 540–541
  European Union and, 556–557
  Five-Year Plans, 546–547
  government of, 545–549, 546*p*, 547*c*, 548*p*
  history of, 542–549, 542*p*, 543*p*, 544*p*, 545*p*, 546*p*, 547*c*, 548*p*, 549*m*
  human geography, 376–377
  language in, 540
  myStory, 531–533, 531*p*, 532*p*, 533*p*
  natural resources of, 538–539, 539*m*
  physical features of, 534–537, 535*m*
  physical geography, 374–375
  population density of, 540–541, 540*m*
  regional flyover, 375

  regional overview, 372–377
  religion in, 541
  rivers of, 535*m*, 536
  Russian Revolution, 445, 447, 546, 550–551, 550*p*, 550*q*, 551*p*, 551*q*
  timeline of, 542–543
  transportation in, 538*g*, 538*p*, 539
  tsars in, 544–546, 544*p*
  vegetation in, 537, 538
  volcanoes in, 537
  westernization of, 544–545
  World War I and, 445, 445*m*, 546
  See also Russian Federation; Soviet Union
Russian empire, 418*m*
Russian Federation
  alliances of, 555–556
  China and, 557
  disease in, 554
  economy of, 549, 553
  energy in, 555, 556, 556*m*
  government of, 549, 552, 554–555
  human rights in, 555
  Iran and, 557
  migration from, 554
  NATO and, 555
  Putin and, 553, 554–555
  standard of living in, 554, 554*c*
  See also Russia; Soviet Union
Russian Orthodox Christians, 541
Russian Plain, 535, 535*m*
Russian Revolution, 445, 447, 546, 550*p*, 550*q*, 551
Rus tribe, 542*p*, 543
Rwanda, 110*p*

S

Sabato, Ernesto, 333*q*
Saint-Domingue, 254
Saint Lawrence River, 171, 171*m*, 174, 174*p*, 175
Saint Petersburg, 536, 537, 540, 540*m*, 544, 545*p*
Saladin, 409
Salamis, Battle of, 389
San Francisco, 26
San Martín, José de, 323, 324*q*
San Salvador, 246
Santander, Francisco de Paula, 292
Santeria, 259, 606
São Paulo, 347*m*, 350
Sarkozy, Nicolas, 299, 299*p*
Saskatchewan, 166*m*

Index (continued)

Acknowledgments

The people who made up the **myWorld Geography** team—representing composition services; core design, digital, and multimedia production services; digital product development; editorial; editorial services; materials management; and production management—are listed below.

Leann Davis Alspaugh, Sarah Aubry, Deanna Babikian, Paul Blankman, Alyssa Boehm, Peter Brooks, Susan Brorein, Megan Burnett, Todd Christy, Neville Cole, Bob Craton, Michael Di Maria, Glenn Diedrich, Frederick Fellows, Jorgensen Fernandez, Thomas Ferreira, Patricia Fromkin, Andrea Golden, Mary Ann Gundersen, Christopher Harris, Susan Hersch, Paul Hughes, Judie Jozokos, Lynne Kalkanajian, John Kingston, Kate Koch, Stephanie Krol, Karen Lepri, Ann-Michelle Levangie, Salena LiBritz, Courtney Markham, Constance J. McCarty, Anne McLaughlin, Rich McMahon, Mark O'Malley, Alison Muff, Jen Paley, Gabriela Perez Fiato, Judith Pinkham, Paul Ramos, Charlene Rimsa, Marcy Rose, Rashid Ross, Alexandra Sherman, Owen Shows, Melissa Shustyk, Jewel Simmons, Ted Smykal, Emily Soltanoff, Frank Tangredi, Simon Tuchman, Elizabeth Tustian, Merle Uuesoo, Alwyn Velásquez, Andrew White, Heather Wright

Maps
XNR Productions, Inc.

Illustration
Kerry Cashman, Marcos Chin, Dave Cockburn, Jeremy Mohler

Photography
FRONT MATTER: Pages vi–xxix, Bkgrnd sky, Image Source/Getty Images; viii, T, ZZ/Alamy; LB, Jim Sugar/Corbis; RB, GoGo Images Corporation/Alamy; ix, SuperStock/age Fotostock; x–xi, B, Peter Bush/Dorling Kindersley; xii–xv, All, Pearson Education, Inc.; xvi, LB, Pearson Education, Inc.; xvi–xvii, B, Vidler Vidler/Photolibrary; xviii–xxiii, All, Pearson Education, Inc.; xxvi, LB, Pearson Education, Inc.; Bkgrnd, Shutterstock; M, Perrush/Shutterstock; xxviii, LB, Laurence Gough/Shutterstock; xxviii–xxix, B, Gordon Wiltsie/Getty Images; xxix, RB, Randy Faris/Corbis; xxx, Bkgrnd, Michele Falzone/JAI/Corbis; LT, Pearson Education, Inc.; TM, Pearson Education, Inc.; RT, Pearson Education, Inc.; xxxi, RM, iStockphoto.com.

CORE CONCEPTS: Pages xxxii–1, Bkgrnd sky, Image Source/Getty Images; xxxii, L, Shutterstock; LM, Jim Sugar/Corbis; M, Fabian Gonzales/Alamy; RM, All Canada Photos/Alamy; R, Gavin Hellier/Getty Images; 1, L, Reed Kaestner/Corbis/JupiterImages; LM, Gavin Hellier/Getty Images; RM, Todd Gipstein/Corbis; R, Digital Vision/Getty Images; 2, LT, Shutterstock; RT, Photo courtesy of Jason Young; B, Beth Wald/Aurora/Getty Images; LB, Harley Couper/Alamy; 3, LT, Photo courtesy of Jason Young; RT, Photo courtesy of Jason Young; 4, LM, Mike Agliolo/Corbis; 6, Saul Loeb/AFP/Getty Images; 8, RT, Silver Burdett Ginn; LM, Bill Curtsinger/National Geographic Stock; 16, RT, Jim Sugar/Corbis; LT, Shutterstock; M, Jerry Driendl/Getty Images; 17, RT, Stephen Alvarez/Getty Images; Inset, Courtesy of Tamsen Buriak; LT, Hyogo Prefectural Government/epa/Corbis; 24, Goodshoot/Corbis; 25, RT, Shutterstock, Inc.; RM, Digital Vision/Alamy; 26, L, Jim Sugar/Corbis; 27, RM, Hyogo Prefectural Government/epa/Corbis; RB, AP Photo/Ric Francis; 30, RT, NOAA; M, David J. Phillip/AP Images; LT, NASA/Corbis; 31, RT, Photo courtesy of Airin McGhee; LT, Alex Brandon/Newhouse News Service/Landov; TM, Smiley N. Pool/Dallas Morning News/Corbis; 32, LB, Paul Zahl/National Geographic/Getty Images; 33, LT, AP Photo/M. Spencer Green; RB, Indranil Mukherjee/AFP/Getty Images; 39, B, Wave RF/Photolibrary; 40, Francisco González/age Fotostock; 41, RT, B. & C. Alexander/Photo Researchers, Inc.; RB, James L. Stanfield/National Geographic Stock; 42, T, Fabian Gonzales/Alamy; LM, Joseph Sohm-Visions of America/Getty Images; TM, John Glover/Getty Images; LB, Jake Rajs/Getty Images; M, David Ball/Getty Images; 42–43, B, Macduff Everton/Corbis; 43, TM, Radius Images/Photolibrary; M, Mike Tittel/Getty Images; T, Ruth Tomlinson/Getty Images; LM, Ron Sanford/Photo Researchers, Inc.; RB, Bill Curtsinger/National Geographic Stock; 46, LT, Jon Holloway/Stock Connection; RT, Marilyn Humphries/The Image Works; M, Ashley Cooper/Picimpact/Corbis; 47, RT, Photo courtesy of Lauren Hexilon; TM, Frank Perry/AFP/Getty Images; LT, Atlantide Phototravel/Corbis; 48, LM, Melanie Stetson Freeman/The Christian Science Monitor/Getty Images; B, vario images GmbH & Co./KG/Alamy; 50–51, All, Pearson Education, Inc.; 52, B, Paul Hanna/Reuters/Corbis; 53, RT, All Canada Photos/Alamy; 56, RT, San Rostro/age Fotostock; LT, Alexey U/Shutterstock; B, Jim Russi/age Fotostock; 57, RT, Photo courtesy of Chris Krestner; TM, Imagebroker/Alamy; LT, J. R. Bale/Alamy; MT, James A.Isbell/Shutterstock; 58, LB, LWA/Getty Images; BM, Ariel Skelley/Blend Images/Corbis; BM, fotog/Getty Images; RB, Getty Images; 59, RT, Brigitte Sporrer/zefa/Corbis; 62, B, Dennis MacDonald/PhotoEdit; M, Bruno Morandi/age Fotostock; 63, T, Reuters/KNS Korean News Agency; 64, LB, Gavin Hellier/Getty Images; RB, Mike Cohen/Shutterstock; 66, B, SuperStock/age Fotostock; 67, LB, The Seattle Times/Newscom; RB, Photo by Wang Kai/ChinaFotoPress/Newscom; 68, LB, Ed Kashi/Corbis; 69, RT, Hou Jun/Newscom; 72, M, Reed Kaestner/Corbis/JupiterImages; LT, DDCoral/Shutterstock; RT, Mark Gabrenya/Shutterstock; 73, RT, Photo courtesy of Ludwig Barragan; TM, Pearson Education, Inc.; LT, Steven Senne/AP Images; 74–75, B, Shutterstock; 75, RT, ©2008 by Ira Lippke/Newscom; LB, Thony Belizaire/AFP/Getty Images; 76, B, Travelpix Ltd/Getty Images; 77, B, PCL/Alamy; 78, LT, Private Collection/The Bridgeman Art Library; B, Bettmann/Corbis; 79, RT, Jack Kurtz/Newscom; 80, LT, Paul Almasy/Corbis; LB, iStockphoto.com; 81, RT, Bettmann/Corbis; RB, Fly Fernandez/zefa/Corbis; 84, B, Interfoto/Alamy; RT, Sylvain Grandadam/age Fotostock; LT, Sergei Bachlakov/Shutterstock, Inc.; 85, TM, Photo courtesy of Joanna Baca; RT, David Muench/Corbis; RT, Photo courtesy of Joanna Baca; 86, LT, Gavin Hellier/Getty Images; LB, Pearson Education, Inc.; BM, Pearson Education, Inc.; RB, Pearson Education, Inc.; 87, All, Pearson Education, Inc.; 88, LM, Glenda M. Powers/Shutterstock; B, GoGo Images Corporation/Alamy; 89, RB, Rubberball/Getty Images; RM, Kuzma/Shutterstock; RT, Silver Burdett Ginn; TM, Kokhanchikov/Shutterstock; TM, Lebedinski Vladislav/Shutterstock; M, George Doyle & Ciaran Griffin/Getty Images; M, Pearson Education, Inc.; TM, Cecile Treal and Jean-Michel Ruiz/Dorling Kindersley; 90, LT, Pearson Education, Inc.; LT, Pearson Education, Inc.; LM, Pearson Education, Inc.; LM, Pearson Education, Inc.; LB, Pearson Education, Inc.; LB, dbimages/Alamy; 91, RT, Pearson Education, Inc.; RT, Pearson Education, Inc.; RM, Rubberball/age Fotostock; RM, Jaime Mota/age Fotostock; RB, Pearson Education, Inc.; RB, Pearson Education, Inc.; 94, LT, Carp (1848), Taito. Woodcut/The Granger Collection, New York; B, Jarno Gonzalez Zarraonandia/Shutterstock; 95, BM, Hellestad Rune/Corbis Sygma; T, Bob Krist/eStock Photo; 96, Stephane De Sakutin/AFP/Getty Images; 97, TM, Dmitry Kosterev/Shutterstock; RT, Dave King/Dorling Kindersley; RM, Luchschen/Shutterstock; RB, Dorling Kindersley; BM, Owen Franken/Corbis; RB, James Marshall/Corbis; 98, L, Alistair Duncan/Dorling Kindersley; LB, Michael Holford/Dorling Kindersley; RB, Bruce Forster/Dorling Kindersley/Courtesy of the National Historic Oregon Trail Interpretive Center; 99, LB, Swim Ink 2, LLC/Corbis; RB, Matthew Ward/Dorling Kindersley; 102, RT, Kim Sayer/Dorling Kindersley; B, Tom Sliter/The Stennis Center for Public Service Leadership; RT, Phil Sandlin/AP Images; 103, LT, Reuters/Hans Deryk; RT, Photo courtesy of Anne Marie Sutherland; 104, LB, Art Resource/Musée du Louvre; RB, Spc Katherine M. Roth/HO/epa/Corbis. All Rights Reserved; 105, L, Todd Gipstein/Corbis; R, Imaginechina via AP Images; 106, R, Pool/Anwar Hussein Collection/Getty Images; L, Karel Prinsloo/AP Images; 107, John Leicester/AP Images; 108, T, Kim Sayer/Dorling Kindersley; M, L. Clarke/Corbis; B, AP Photo/Douglas Healey; 109, M, White House Photo Office; T, Wally McNamee/Corbis; B, The Collection of the Supreme Court of the United States; 110, Alan Gignoux/age fotostock; 111, B, Kote Rodrigo/EFE/Corbis; T, Karel Prinsloo/AP Images; 112, B, Jeff Greenberg/PhotoEdit; T, William Whitehurst/Corbis; 113, RB, Wally McNamee/Corbis; 116, RT, Jim Zuckerman/Corbis; LT, Digital Vision/Getty Images; B, El Comercio Newspaper, Dante Piaggio/AP Images; 117, RT, Photo courtesy of Brian McCray; LT, Ira Block/National Geographic/Getty Images; TM, University of Oregon/AP Images; 118, LB, The British Museum/Dorling Kindersley; LB, O. Louis Mazzatenta/National Geographic Stock; RB, Ivonne Wierink/Shutterstock; M, Giles Stokoe/Felix deWeldon/Dorling Kindersley; 119, RT, Dagli Orti/Picture Desk, Inc./Kobal Collection; M, Andy Crawford/Dorling Kindersley, Courtesy of the University Museum of Archaeology and Anthropology, Cambridge; RB, Getty Images/De Agostini Editore Picture Library; 120, LB, Bettmann/Corbis; LM, Bettmann/Corbis; 121, RB, Hulton Archive/Getty Images; L, The Granger Collection, New York; 122, LT, Sean Hunter/Dorling Kindersley; B, Martin Gray/National Geographic Stock; R, Robert F. Sisson/National Geographic Society; 123, LB, O. Louis Mazzatenta/National Geographic Stock; LB, Anders Ryman/Corbis.

Acknowledgments (continued)

UNIT 1: Pages 128–133, T, Bkgrnd sky, Image Source/Getty Images; **129, L,** Pearson Education, Inc.; **R,** Pearson Education, Inc.; **Bkgrnd,** Ray Juno/Corbis; **130, LB,** Jupiter Unlimited; **131, LT,** Life in Frames Photography/Shutterstock; **LB,** iStockphoto.com; **M,** gary718/Shutterstock; **132, L,** Archive Holdings Inc./Getty Images; **R,** Dragan Trifunovic/Shutterstock; **133, T,** Pearson Education, Inc.; **T,** Pearson Education, Inc.

CHAPTER 1: Pages 135–137, All, Pearson Education, Inc.; **138, LB,** Karl Weatherly/Getty Images; **LB,** John Shaw/Photo Researchers, Inc.; **140, RB,** Pearson Education, Inc.; **RM,** Mark Karrass/Corbis; **RM,** LeCajun/Shutterstock; **RM,** Gavin Hellier/JAI/Corbis; **LB,** Shutterstock; **142, LB,** Robert Llewellyn/age Fotostock; **RB,** PCL/Alamy; **143, LB,** Gregory Wrona/Alamy; **RB,** Rudi Von Briel/PhotoEdit; **145,** Spencer Grant/Photo Researchers, Inc.; **146, LB,** Dynamic Graphics/age Fotostock; **147, RT,** Bettmann/Corbis; **RM,** Corbis; **RB,** Corbis; **150, LT,** Corbis; **LM,** Corbis; **LB,** AP/Wide World Photo; **152, LT,** KRCrowley/Alamy; **LB,** Dorling Kindersley; **R,** Philip Scalia/Alamy Images; **153,** The Granger Collection, New York; **154, T,** The Granger Collection, New York; **C,** Library of Congress; **B,** The Granger Collection, New York; **156, LB,** Pearson Education, Inc.; **157, B,** Shutterstock; **RT,** Michael Rosa/Shutterstock; **RM,** Laurence Gough/Shutterstock; **RB,** Gai Mooney/Corbis; **RB,** Flashon Studio/Shutterstock; **159, LB,** moodboard/Corbis; **BM,** Wally McNamee/Corbis; **RB,** Robert Galbraith/Reuters; **161,** Stefan Rousseau/PA Wire URN:5867212 (Press Association via AP Images); **162, T,** Joseph Sohm/Visions of America/Corbis; **B,** Hisham Ibrahim/Alamy; **163, T,** Library of Congress; **B,** Corbis.

CHAPTER 2: Pages166–169, All, Pearson Education, Inc.; **170, LB,** Randy Faris/Corbis; **Bkgrnd,** Rudy Sulgan/age Fotostock; **172, LB,** Kurt Werby/Photolibrary; **LM,** Alaska Stock/age Fotostock; **RM,** John E Marriott/Getty Images; **RM,** Oleksiy Maksymenko/Alamy; **174, LT,** Alaska Stock/age Fotostock; **RT,** Michael Klinec/Alamy; **176, LT,** Volkmar K. Wentzel/National Geographic Stock; **177, RT,** Ulga/Shutterstock; **178,** Picture Contact BV/Alamy Images; **179, L,** The Granger Collection, New York; **R,** The Granger Collection, New York; **B,** Shutterstock; **180, Bkgrnd,** Shutterstock; **T,** Goddard Space Flight Center Scientific Visualization Studio/NASA. The Blue Marble data are courtesy of Reto Stockli (GSFC/NASA); **B,** Shutterstock; **181, T,** Maarten Udema/age Fotostock; **182,** Nathan Benn/Alamy; **183, RB,** Stock Montage/Getty Images; **184, LB,** Colored gravure reproduction (1894) of a painting by Augustus Tholey. The Granger Collection, New York; **185, RB,** Austin Andrews/Zuma Press/Newscom; **LB,** Library and Archives Canada/Charles Walter Simpson collection/C-013945; **186, B,** Illustrated London News Ltd/Mary Evans/Everett Collection; **187, RT,** Library and Archives Canada/C. J. Patterson,Lawson and Jones Limited/C-029568; **188, T,** Earl & Nazima Kowall/CORBIS; **B,** AP Photo/CP, Ian Barrett; **B,** inset, Earl & Nazima Kowall/Corbis; **189, T,** AP Images/CP, Paul Chiasson; **B,** Maridav/Shutterstock; **190, LB,** Reuters/Andy Clark AC/SV/Corbis; **192, LB,** Corbis/Bettmann; **193,** UN Photo; **194, LM,** Chris Cheadle/Photolibrary; **LB,** Peter Mintz/age Fotostock; **LB,** Gunter Marx Photography/Corbis; **LT,** Pete Ryan/National Geographic Stock; **195,** Pearson Education, Inc.

UNIT 1 CLOSER: Page 198, Bkgrnd, Stacey Lynn Payne/Shutterstock; **199, B,** Péter Gudella/Shutterstock

UNIT 2: Pages 200–205, Bkgrnd sky, Image Source/Getty Images; **201, LM,** Pearson Education, Inc.; **RM,** Pearson Education, Inc.; **Bkgrnd,** Gary718/Shutterstock; **202, LB,** Michael Boyny/age Fotostock; **LT,** Robert Francis/Photolibrary; **RB,** Dreamtours/Photolibrary; **203, LT,** Sébastien Boisse/Photononstop/Photolibrary; **204, LM,** Susana Gonzalez/Newsmakers/Getty Images; **LB,** Brian Bailey/Getty Images; **RM,** Richard Bickel/Corbis; **RB,** Andoni Canela/Photolibrary; **205, L,** Pearson Education, Inc.; **R,** Pearson Education, Inc.

CHAPTER 3: Pages 206–209, All, Pearson Education, Inc.; **210, Bkgrnd,** Travel Ink/Alamy; **B,** Robert Fried/Alamy; **212, LT,** Scott S. Warren/National Geographic Stock; **LB,** Ales Liska/Shutterstock; **RB,** LOOK Die Bildagentur der Fotografen GmbH/Alamy; **RT,** Radius Images/Alamy; **213, RT,** Didier Dorval/Radius Images/Jupiter Images; **RB,** urosr/Shutterstock; **LB,** Geoff Dann/Dorling Kindersley; **RM,** Rusty Dodson/Shutterstock; **215, RM,** Richard Melloul/Sygma/Corbis; **217, R,** AFP Photo/Jorge Uzon/Newscom; **218,** Peter Wilson/Conaculta-Inah-Mex. Authorized reproduction by the Instituto Nacional de Antropología e Historia/Dorling Kindersley; **219, B,** Ken Welsh/age Fotostock; **220, T,** The Art Archive/Museo Ciudad Mexico/Gianni Dagli Orti; **B,** Agencia el Universal/Newscom; **221, T,** Glowimages RF/age Fotostock; **B,** Holger Mette/Shutterstock; **222, LB,** The Trustees of The British Museum/Art Resource, NY; **223, T,** Demetrio Carrasco/Conaculta-Inah-Mex. Authorized reproduction by the Instituto Nacional de Antropología e Historia/Dorling Kindersley; **M,** The Granger Collection, New York; **B,** The Granger Collection, New York; **224,** The Art Archive/National Palace Mexico City/Gianni Dagli Orti; **R,** The Art Archive/National Palace Mexico City/Gianni Dagli Ort; **225, L,** The Art Archive/National Palace Mexico City/Alfredo Dagli Orti; **226,** Schalkwijk/Art Resource, NY; **227, L,** The Art Archive/National Palace Mexico City/Gianni Dagli Orti; **R,** Schalkwijk/Art Resource, NY; **228, RB,** Bettmann/Corbis; **RT,** David Crossland/Alamy; **229, B,** Adam Woolfitt/Corbis; **230,** Jeff Topping/Reuters; **231, LB,** Library of Congress; **BM,** AFP/Getty Images; **RB,** Jorge Silva/Reuters; **RM,** Holger Mette/Shutterstock; **232, LB,** L. Zacharie/Alamy; **RB,** Danny Lehman/Corbis; **232–233,** Peregrina/iStockphoto.com; **233, LB,** Robert Harding Picture Library/age Fotostock; **RB,** Andy Mead/Icon SMI/Newscom; **234, L,** Linda Whitwam/Dorling Kindersley; **235,** AP Photo/Carlos Osorio; **236, LB,** Paul E. Rodriguez/Newscom; **BM,** Keith Dannemiller/Alamy; **LT,** Ivan Vdovin/age Fotostock; **RT,** Ivan Vdovin/age Fotostock.

CHAPTER 4: Pages 240–243, All, Pearson Education, Inc.; **244, RB,** Frans Lemmens/zefa/Corbis; **Bkgrnd,** P. Narayan/age Fotostock; **246, LT,** Jeff Grabert/Shutterstock, Inc.; **RT,** Demetrio Carrasco/JAI/Corbis; **RM,** Stephen Frink/Corbis; **RB,** Radius Images/Alamy; **247,** Jeff Greenberg/PhotoEdit; **249,** John Miller/Robert Harding World Imagery/Corbis; **250, B,** Enrique de la Osa/Reuters; **251,** Lynn M. Stone/Nature Picture Library; **252, L,** Jim Clare/Nature Picture Library; **LB,** The Art Archive/Archaeological Museum Tikal Guatemala/Gianni Dagli Orti; **253, RT,** The Granger Collection, New York; **RB,** The Art Archive; **254,** Time & Life Pictures/Getty Images; **255,** AP/Wide World Photo; **256, T,** The Art Archive/National Anthropological Museum Mexico/Gianni Dagli Orti; **B,** John Elk III/Alamy; **257, T,** I. Kolesnik/Shutterstock; **B,** The Print Collector/Alamy; **258,** Laurent Grandadam/age Fotostock; **259, L,** Owen Franken/Corbis; **LM,** www.imagesource.com/Newscom; **R,** Pearson Education, Inc.; **RM,** Holly Wilmeth/Aurora Photos/Corbis; **RT,** AP Images; **T,** Sharon Hudson/Corbis; **260,** Mark Edwards/Still Pictures/Peter Arnold, Inc.; **261,** Didi/Alamy; **262, T,** Pearson Education, Inc.; **263, RB,** Pearson Education, Inc.; **264, L,** Corbis; **264, R,** Alvaro Leiva/age Fotostock; **267,** Reinhard Rohner/age Fotostock.

UNIT 2 CLOSER: Page 270, iStockphoto; **271,** Pearson Education, Inc.

UNIT 3: Pages 272–277, Bkgrnd sky, Image Source/Getty Images; **273, LT,** Pearson Education, Inc.; **RT,** Pearson Education, Inc.; **TM,** Pearson Education, Inc.; **Bkgrnd,** Wildlife/Peter Arnold Inc.; **274, T,** Martin Harvey/Corbis; **B,** Blickwinkel/Alamy; **275, LT,** Paul Harris/Photolibrary; **277, T,** Pearson Education, Inc.; **RT,** Pearson Education, Inc.; **TM,** Pearson Education, Inc.

CHAPTER 5: Pages 278–281, All, Pearson Education, Inc.; **282, Bkgrnd,** James Sparshatt/Corbis; **B,** Reuters/Jorge Silva; **284, M,** Patricio Robles Gil/naturepl.com; **RB,** Demetrio Carrasco/JAI/Corbis; **BM,** Ann Johansson/Corbis; **LB,** Neil Beer/Corbis; **285, LB,** blickwinkel/Alamy Images; **B,** Frank Greenaway/Dorling Kindersley; **RB,** Imagebroker/Alamy; **286,** Danita Delimont/Alamy; **287, L,** Charles Bowman/age Fotostock; **R,** Jody Amiet/AFP/Getty Images; **288, All,** Pearson Education, Inc.; **290,** The Art Archive/Museo del Oro Bogotá/Dagli Orti/Picture Desk; **291, R,** Illustration from *Book of Pirates*, Howard Pyle/National Maritime Museum, Greenwich, London; **M,** Tina Chambers/British Museum/Dorling Kindersley; **292,** Photoshot Holdings Ltd/Bruce Coleman; **294,** *Simón Bolívar* (1783–1830), (pre-20th century), Artist unknown, Chromolitho. Private Collection/Archives Charmet/Bridgeman Art Library; **296,** Pearson Education, Inc.; **297, RM,** Doug Benc/Getty Images; **RB,** Suraj N. Sharma/Dinodia Picture Agency; **L,** Philippe Giraud/Goodlook/Corbis; **272,** Neil Beer/Getty Images; **299, LT,** Fernando Ruiz/AFP/Getty Images/Newscom; **LT,** Martin Bernetti/Agence France Presse/Getty Images; **TM,** Roslan RahmanAFP/Getty Images; **RT,** Timothy A. Clary/AFP/Getty Images/Newscom; **RT,** Pascal Le Segretain/Getty Images; **300, LM,** Juan Barreto/AFP/Getty Images/Newscom; **LB,** Juan Barreto/AFP/Getty Images/Newscom; **301,** ESA/AP Images; **302, L,** Daniel Munoz/Reuters; **303, L,** Carlos Linares /Reuters; **R,** Jamie Marshall/Dorling Kindersley; **305, R,** Mauricio Duenas/Newscom.

CHAPTER 6: Pages 308–311, All, Pearson Education, Inc.; **312, Bkgrnd,** Gordon Wiltsie/Getty Images; **314, RM,** Andoni Canela/age Fotostock; **BM,** Javier Etcheverry/Alamy; **LB,** Cephas Picture Library/Alamy; **LB,** Tui De Roy/Minden Pictures; **316, RM,** Paul Harrison/Photolibrary; **RB,** Diego Giudice/Corbis; **317,** Frans Lanting/Corbis; **319,** Jeremy Hoare/Alamy; **320,** Travel Ink/Getty Images; **321, B,** Pete Oxford/naturepl.com; **RB,** Stephanie Colasanti/The Art

Archive; **322,** Museo Municipal, Quito, Ecuador/The Bridgeman Art Library; **324, B,** AP Images; **325,** Private Collection/Archives Charmet/The Bridgeman Art Library; **326, T,** The British Museum/Dorling Kindersley; **B,** The Granger Collection, New York; **327, T,** The Art Archive/Biblioteca d'Ajuda Lisbon/Gianni Dagli Orti; **B,** Shirley Vanderbilt/age Fotostock; **328,** Pearson Education, Inc.; **329, BM,** WIN-Initiative/Getty Images; **RB,** SuperStock/age Fotostock; **330, BM,** Claudio Frias Beyer/Newscom; **RB,** MIXA Co., Ltd./Alamy; **331, LB,** Steve Allen/Getty Images; **LB,** AFP/Getty Images; **333,** Ricardo Mazalan/AP Images; **334,** Scala/Art Resource, NY; **335,** Pearson Education, Inc.; **337,** AP Photo/Juan Karita.

CHAPTER 7: Pages 340–343, All, Pearson Education, Inc.; **344, Bkgrnd,** Michael David/age Fotostock; **LB,** Reuters/Christian Veron; **346, RM,** Jacques Jangoux/Alamy; **RM,** Digital Vision/Alamy; **RB,** Ricardo Junqueira/Alamy; **RB,** Berndt Fischer/age Fotostock; **348, B,** Shutterstock; **349, RB,** Pearson Education, Inc. Education; **LM,** Dorling Kindersley; **BM,** iStockphoto.com; **LB,** Todd Pusser/naturepl.com; **M,** iStockphoto.com; **350, LT,** NASA; **L,** David R. Frazier/Photolibrary, Inc./Alamy; **351, B,** Paulo Fridman/Corbis; **352, LB,** Michel Renaudeau/age Fotostock; **354, LB,** The Art Archive/Bibliothèque des Arts Décoratifs Paris/Gianni Dagli Orti; **LB,** Guilherme Gaensly; **355,** Reuters/Jamil Bittar; **356, T,** public domain; **B,** Stephanie Maze/Corbis; **357, T,** Art Resource, NY; **B,** Underwood & Underwood/Corbis; **358,** Pearson Education, Inc.; **359, RM,** Sergio Moraes/Reuters; **RB,** Sergio Moraes/Reuters; **360,** M-Sat Ltd/Photo Researchers; **RB,** Paulo Fridman/Corbis; **361, B,** Marcelo Rudini/Alamy; **M,** Carlos Cazalis/Corbis; **LM,** Collart Herve/Corbis Sygma; **RM,** Marcelo Rudini/Alamy; **364,** Paulo Fridman/Getty Images; **365,** Reuters/Ricky Rogers RR/CCK; **366, T,** Victor Englebert/Photo Researchers; **B,** Michael & Patricia Fogden/Corbis; **367,** Tom Brakefield/Corbis.

UNIT 3 CLOSER: Page 370, LB, Shutterstock; **Bkgrnd,** iStockphoto.com; **BM,** Barnabas Kindersley/Dorling Kindersley; **RB,** PeterK/Shutterstock; **329, L,** GlowImages/Alamy; **R,** Insadco Photography/Alamy.

UNIT 4: Pages 372–377, Bkgrnd sky, Image Source/Getty Images; **373, All,** Pearson Education, Inc.; **Bkgrnd,** Vidler Vidler/Photolibrary; **374, TM,** Robert Zywucki/Shutterstock; **LT,** Roy Rainford/Robert Harding World Imagery; **375, M,** Pichugin Dmitry/Shutterstock; **376, T,** Hulton Archive/Getty Images; **B,** Jose Fuste Raga/Photolibrary; **377, All,** Pearson Education, Inc.

CHAPTER 8: Pages 378–381, All, Pearson Education, Inc.; **382, LB,** HO/AFP/Getty Images/Newscom; **384–385, RB,** Jonathan Potter/Dorling Kindersley; **385, RB,** Peter Hayman/The British Museum/Dorling Kindersley; **RB,** Paul Harris/Dorling Kindersley; **386, M,** The Art Archive/Agora Museum Athens/Gianni Dagli Orti; **RT,** The Art Archive/Agora Museum Athens/Gianni Dagli Orti; **387, RT,** Nick Nicholls/The British Museum/Dorling Kindersley; **388, LM,** Hoberman Collection/Corbis; **390, T,** Art Resource, NY; **B,** Picture Desk, Inc./Kobal Collection; **391, T,** The Trustees of The British Museum/Art Resource, NY; **B,** Alessandro Saffo/Grand Tour/Corbis; **392, L,** Réunion des Musées Nationaux/Art Resource, NY; **394, LT,** John Heseltine/Dorling Kindersley; **395, B,** Franck Guiziou/Hemis/Corbis; **397, RT,** PoodlesRock/Corbis; **398, T,** Bildarchiv Preussischer Kulturbesitz/Art Resource, NY; **B,** The Art Archive/Musée du Louvre Paris/Gianni Dagli Orti; **399,** Erich Lessing/Art Resource, NY; **400, LB,** Cameraphoto Arte, Venice/Art Resource, NY; **401, RB,** Museum of History of Sofia, Sofia, Bulgaria/Archives Charmet/Bridgeman Art Library. All Rights Reserved; **405, RT,** Réunion des Musées Nationaux/Art Resource, NY; **406, T,** Art Resource, NY; **B,** Erich Lessing/Art Resource, NY; **407,** HIP/Art Resource, NY; **408, LB,** Geoff Dann/Dorling Kindersley; **409, RT,** Werner Forman/Art Resource, NY; **411, RB,** SIME s.a.s/eStock Photo; **412, L,** Bridgeman Art Library; **LB,** Bettmann/Corbis; **413, RB,** Snark/Art Resource, NY; **414, M,** Bettmann/Corbis; **LB,** *The Dance Macabre* (detail, 1485), Artist unknown, Fresco. L'Oratorio dei Disciplini/SuperStock; **LT,** Frank Greenaway/Dorling Kindersley; **L,** maxstockphoto/Shutterstock.

CHAPTER 9: Pages 418–421, All, Pearson Education, Inc.; **422,** Philip Gatward/Dorling Kindersley; **423, RM,** *The Last Supper* (1495–1498), Leonardo da Vinci. Fresco. Santa Maria della Grazie, Milan/A.K.G., Berlin/SuperStock; **RB,** Dorling Kindersley; **424, LT,** Ellen Howdon/Dorling Kindersley, Courtesy of Glasgow Museum; **T,** FPG/Getty Images; **RT,** Pearson Education, Inc.; **425, M,** Dorling Kindersley; **RB,** Adrea Pistolesi/Getty Images; **428, BM,** *Portrait of Henry VIII* (16th century), Hans Holbein the Younger, Oil on canvas. Belvoir Castle, Leicestershire. The Bridgeman Art Library Ltd.; **LB,** Portrait of Catherine of Aragon (1485–1536), 1st Queen of Henry VIII (1825), from "Memoirs of the Court of Queen Elizabeth," watercolor and gouache on paper. Private

Collection/The Bridgeman Art Library; **430, RB,** Scala/Art Resource, NY; **430, RT,** The Granger Collection, New York; **431, RT,** Scala/Art Resource, NY; **431, RB,** Alinari Archives/Corbis; **432, Bkgrnd,** Joel W. Rogers/Corbis; **433, RT,** Reuters New Media Inc./Corbis; **BM,** James Stevenson/Dorling Kindersley, Courtesy of the National Maritime Museum, London; **RB,** Clive Streeter/Dorling Kindersley, Courtesy of The Science Museum, London; **LT,** Dorling Kindersley; **434, LB,** *Padshahnama: Europeans Bring Gifts to the Shah Jahan.* The Royal Collection, Her Majesty Queen Elizabeth II; **435, RT,** Chas Howson/The British Museum/Dorling Kindersley; **436, LB,** Erich Lessing/Art Resource, NY; **437, RM,** *Louis XIV, King of France* (1701), Hyacinthe Rigaud. Oil on canvas, 277 x 194 cm. Louvre, Paris, France. Photo: Herve Lewandowski. Louvre, Paris, France. Réunion des Musées Nationaux/Art Resource, NY; **IN437a** ©North Wind Picture Archives/Alamy; **IN437c T** Album/Art Resource, NY, **B** bpk, Berlin/Art Resource, NY; **IN437d** ©North Wind Picture Archives/Alamy; **438, LB,** Martin Jones/Corbis; **439, LT,** The Granger Collection, New York; **T,** Shutterstock; **441, RB,** Reduced model of a guillotine (18th century), French School, wood and metal. Musée de la Ville de Paris, Musée Carnavalet, Paris, France, Giraudon/Bridgeman Art Library; **RT,** Getty Images/De Agostini Editore Picture Library; **BM,** Musée de la Révolution Française, Vizille, France/The Bridgeman Art Library; **442, TM,** Lebrecht Music & Arts Photo Library; **RT,** The Francis Frith Collection/Corbis; **443, RT,** Underwood & Underwood/Corbis; **LT,** Musée National de l'Education, Rouen, France/The Bridgeman Art Library; **IN443a T** ©Heritage Image Partnership Ltd/Alamy, **B** ©Beryl Peters Collection/Alamy; **IN443b** ©Mary Evans Picture Library/Alamy; **IN443c** ©Everett Collection Historical/Alamy; **IN443d** UniversalImagesGroup/Contributor/Getty Images; **444, B,** Bettmann/Corbis; **446, LB,** Hulton-Deutsch Collection/Corbis; **447, RB,** Dorling Kindersley; **448, LT,** Andy Crawford/Dorling Kindersley/Imperial War Museum, London; **449,** PhotoDisc/Getty Images; **450, RT,** PhotoDisc/Getty Images; **450, RB,** Hulton Deutsch Collection/Corbis; **451, B,** Bernard Bisson/Sygma/Corbis; **452, B,** Bettmann/Corbis; **453, RT,** U.S. Navy/Photo Researchers; **454, RB,** AP Images; **B,** Bettmann/Corbis; **456, BM,** Bettmann/Corbis; **LB,** Bettmann/Corbis; **457, L,** The Punch Cartoon Library; **R,** Str Old/Reuters; **458, T,** Peter Dejong/AP Images; **LT,** Peter Dench/Corbis; **459, T,** Dorling Kindersley; **460, RT,** Popperfoto/Getty Images; **RB,** Portrait of Lajos Kossuth (1802–1894) at the Chain Bridge in Budapest, 1849 (19th century), Hungarian School, Coloured engraving. Hadtörténeti Muzeum, Budapest, Hungary, Archives Charmet/The Bridgeman Art Library; **461, RT,** Liba Taylor/Corbis; **461, B,** Peter Turnley/Corbis.

CHAPTER 10: Pages 464–467, All, Pearson Education, Inc.; **468, Bkgrnd,** Sylvain Grandadam/age Fotostock; **B,** J. D. Heaton/age Fotostock; **470, RM,** iStockphoto.com; **M,** Dhoxax/Shutterstock; **T,** Pierre Jacques/Hemis/Corbis; **M,** Bo Zaunders/Corbis; **RB,** Rick Price/Corbis; **RB,** Gavin Hellier/Robert Harding World; **473, B,** Lawson Wood/Corbis; **RM,** Simon Fraser/Photo Researchers; **476,** Davide Erbetta/Grand Tour/Corbis; **477, T,** British Touring Car, Eleanor Bentall/Corbis; **478, T,** Aneese/Dreamstime.com; **LB,** Ethanol Fuel, Car Culture/Corbis; **RB,** Chen Haitong/XinHua; **480,** Dallas and John Heaton/Stock Connection; **483, M,** Pearson Education, Inc.; **RB,** Erik Svensson and Jeppe Wikstrom/Dorling Kindersley; **R,** David Lomax/Robert Harding/Getty Images; **484,** Annie Griffiths Belt/Corbis; **485,** Ken Straiton/Corbis; **486,** Patrick Müller © Centre des monuments nationaux, Paris; **487, T,** Britta Jaschinski/Dorling Kindersley; **B,** Prentice Hall School; **RB,** Le Segretain Pascal/Corbis Sygma; **RM,** Perrush/Shutterstock; **488,** Cristophe Ena/AP Photo; **489,** Bjorn Svensson/Photolibrary; **490,** George Hammerstein/Solus-Veer/Corbis; **491,** Fancy/Veer/Corbis; **492, T,** Pearson Education, Inc.; **B,** LWA-Dann Tardif/Corbis; **493, T,** Ean Christophe Verhaegan/AFI images; **B,** Ullstein-CARO/Peter Arnold Inc.; **494,** Dorling Kindersley; **495,** Pearson Education, Inc.; **RM,** Bob Sacha/Corbis; **RB,** iStockphoto.com; **496,** Massimo Borchi/Corbis; **498, RB,** Reuters/Susana Vera (SPAIN); **499,** George Christakis/epa/Corbis; **IN499a** Stephen B. Goodwin/Shutterstock; **IN499b** DigitalGlobe/Contributor/Getty Images; **IN499c L** ©AZP Worldwide/Flotila, **R** Bloomberg/Contributor Getty Images; **IN499d** michaeljung/Shutterstock.

CHAPTER 11: Pages 502–505, All, Pearson Education, Inc.; **506, Bkgrnd,** Erich Lessing/Magnum Photos, Inc.; **LB,** Stefano Pensotti/age Fotostock; **508, LB,** Per Karlsson-BKWine.com/Alamy; **LB,** Jaroslaw Grudzinski/Shutterstock; **509, M,** Dean Conger/Corbis; **B,** AFP/Getty Images; **510, RB,** Zaichiki/Alamy; **RB,** Reuters/Vasily Fedosenko; **RM,** David Veis/AP Photo/CTK; **LM,** iStockphoto.com; **LB,** Photoshot Holdings Ltd./Alamy; **511,** Stan Kujawa/Alamy; **513, TM,** Idealink Photography/Alamy; **RT,** ziontek/Dabrowski-KPA/Zuma Press, © 2004 by Wziontek/Dabrowski-KPA (Newscom TagID: zumaphotos661194)

Acknowledgments (continued)

[Photo via Newscom]; **LT,** Hidajet Delic/AP Photo; **LT,** Martin Bureau/AFP/Getty Images; **514,** Bernie Epstein/Alamy; **515, RT,** Wojtek Buss/age Fotostock; **RB,** Pegaz/Alamy; **L,** James L. Stanfield/National Geographic/Getty Images; **516,** Reuters Photographer/Reuters; **517,** AFP photo/Milan/Radulovic; **518, LB,** Steven May/Alamy; **519, RB,** imagebroker/Alamy; **520, B,** Petr Josek Snr/Reuters; **521, B,** Carlos Nieto/age Fotostock; **523, B,** Getty Images/De Agostini Editore Picture Library; **524, RT,** Viktor Drachev/AFP/Getty Images; **525, LT,** East News/ Getty Images; **RT,** AFP Photo/Daniel Mihailescu/Newscom; **526, RB,** Frederic Hugon/AFP/Getty Images/Newscom; **RT,** Antoine Gyori/Corbis Sygma; **527, B,** Brauchli David/Corbis Sygma.

CHAPTER 12: Pages 530–533, All, Pearson Education, Inc.; **534, Bkgrnd,** Sergey Yakovlev/Shutterstock; **LB,** David Turnley/Corbis; **536, R,** isoft/iStockphoto.com; **M,** Dean Conger/Corbis; **L,** SuperStock; **537,** Gerd Ludwig/Corbis; **538,** Sovfoto/ Eastfoto; **541, R,** Gideon Mendel/Corbis; **L,** Pearson Education, Inc.; **542, L,** Werner Forman/Art Resource, NY; **R,** Erich Lessing/Art Resource, NY; **543, L,** Jeremy Horner/Corbis; **R,** *Ivan the Terrible* (20th century), English School, Gouache on paper. Private Collection/© Look and Learn/The Bridgeman Art Library; **544, L,** The Art Archive/Russian Historical Museum Moscow/Alfredo Dagli Orti; **R,** The Granger Collection, New York; **545, LB,** David South/ Alamy; **LT,** The Gallery Collection/Corbis; **RB,** Réunion des Musées Nationaux/ Art Resource, NY; **546,** Photos 12/Alamy; **547,** Charles & Josette Lenars/ Corbis; **548, L,** Gianni Giansanti/Sygma/Corbis; **R,** Peter Turnley/Corbis; **550 RB,** Hulton-Deutsch Collection/Corbis; **RT,** Scheufler Collection/Corbis; **551, RB,** Fabian Cevallos/Corbis Sygma; **RM,** Darryl Sleath/Shutterstock; **RT,** Krasowit/ Shutterstock; **552,** Iain Masterton/Alamy Images; **553, L,** Peter Turnley/Corbis; **R,** David Young-Wolff/PhotoEdit; **554,** Vasily Fedosenko/Reuters/Corbis; **555,** Lystseva Marina/ITAR-TASS Photo/Corbis; **557,** Gleb Garanich/Reuters/Corbis; **558, RB,** Bettmann/Corbis; **559, RT,** The Art Archive/Private Collection/Marc Charmet; **560, LB,** Sergei Karpukhin/Reuters; **ML,** Gerd Ludwig/Reuters; **RB,** David Tunley/Corbis; **561,** Sysoyev Grigory/ITAR-TASS/Corbis.

UNIT 4 CLOSER: Page 564, B, Shutterstock; **LB,** Shutterstock; **RT,** Shutterstock; **RT,** Shutterstock; **564–565, Bkgrnd,** Shutterstock; **565, R,** European Communities, 1995–2009; **R,** Shutterstock.

Text Acknowledgments

Grateful acknowledgment is made to the following for copyrighted material:

Page 300 Excerpts from "Rift in Venezuelan Society," by Nick Miles, from *bbc. com, May 7, 2002.* Copyright © BBC.

Page 327 Excerpt from "Letter to a King," by Huamán Poma, arranged and edited by Christopher Dilke. First published copyright © 1978 by George Allen & Unwin, Great Britain. This translation copyright © 1978 by Christopher Dilke, ed. Unwin Hyman Limited. Used by permission.

Page 406 Excerpt from "Hildegard to Odo Soissons," from *Hildegard of Bingen: Selected Writings,* translated by Mark Atherton. Translation copyright © Mark Atherton 2001. Penguin Group. All rights reserved. Used by permission.

Page 456 Address at the Institute of Contemporary Arts, London; quoted in *The Independent, March 22, 1990.*

Page 558 Excerpt from "Russia Close-Up: Overcoming Soviet Industrial Legacy," from *Russia Today, July 29, 2007.*

Page 561 Excerpt from "Russia Rising," by Fen Montaigne, from *National Geographic, November 2001.* Copyright © National Geographic Society.

Note: Every effort has been made to locate the copyright owner of material reproduced in this publication. Omissions brought to our attention will be corrected in subsequent editions.